THE BEST OF

Selections and Stories from the Fanzine That Grew Up, 1977-86

EDITED BY
TONY FLETCHER

FOREWORD BY
BILLY BRAGG

OMNIBUS PRESS
London / New York / Paris / Sydney / Copenhagen / Berlin / Madrid / Tokyo

THE BEST OF

EDITOR'S NOTE: It's likely that many (if not most) people bought *Jamming!* for interviews with and updates on their fave acts who, as the covers illustrate all too readily, were predominantly British, male, white and working together as bands. But from the off, *Jamming!* had a wide remit, and once readers got beyond those traditional front cover heroes, they could read about reggae, hip-hop, electro, world music, folk and no shortage of eclectic emerging artists; there was a regular poetry section, and articles and reviews covering films, books, television and what was then the ever-so-exciting world of VHS tapes. *Jamming!* profiled sports icons, visual artists, authors and directors; and it never, ever shied away from the world of politics. Rather than a Greatest Hits of its most popular acts, *The Best of Jamming!* aims to reflect the magazine's editorial variety, and in doing so, offer a wider insight into those times. **Tony Fletcher, May 2021**

CONTENTS

With additional new contributions from Brett 'Buddy' Ascott, Mark Bedford, Anthony Blampied, Janine Booth, James Brown, Jeff Carrigan, Gary Crowley, Bruce Dessau, Tiny Fennimore, Ross Fortune, Chris Heath, Lee Hirons, Peter 'Jaf' Jervis, Tim Kelly, Alan McGee, Jack McIlroy, Alan McLaughlin, Mick Middles, Mike Peters, Guy Pratt, Pedro Romhanyi, Mike Scott, JG Thirlwell, Brian Young, Russell Young.

FOREWORD

I t was a different time. Before the invention of social media, music played a vanguard role in youth culture. For an adolescent desperate to create their own identity after a childhood dominated by their parents' taste, music offered the most accessible means of self-expression. When the expectations of adults began to chafe, music provided an alternative set of values that pushed back against the conformity of curriculum and careers advice.

In the confusing years of your early teens, music offered unambiguous messages about what was cool; it told you how to feel about the world and your place in it, how to express yourself; music told you who to hang out with and who to shun. It gave you a bond with like-minded fans, a community with its own language and symbolism.

And it created an obsessive thirst for information.

In the 1970s, pop music culture played a central role in the lives of under 25s in the UK. Five weekly newspapers dedicated to rock music were able to flourish, with as many again catering to the pop market. They were a crucial source of information for fans living outside the major cities – especially if they happened to be not yet old enough to get into gigs.

For young teens, the best chance to see your favourite band play live was on TV. While the pop programmes of the day were largely made by light entertainment departments, whose booking policies had one eye on the mums and dads, there were places where new and challenging styles could surface.

The Old Grey Whistle Test featured live performances, but went out too late in the schedule, long after parents had taken control of the TV. *Top of the Pops*, on the other hand, was broadcast at 7pm and as it was based around the singles chart, music fans had some input into who appeared each week.

That notion of record buyers challenging the pop hegemony was never more powerful than during the rise of punk rock. This new wave of music had little respect for the long-haired rock of the mid-70s and none whatsoever for the niceties of light entertainment. Punk was a provocation, a visual and aural rejection of the mainstream melodies that were a constant reminder that pop music had lost its edge since the glory days of the 1960s.

First of the punk bands to invade the nation's living rooms was The Jam, who appeared on *Top of the Pops* in May 1977, performing their debut single, 'In The City'. Furiously thrashing away at their Rickenbacker guitars, their bodies were taut and their moves staccato, as if struggling to contain the energy of their youth. For teenagers all over Britain who also felt they had a thousand things to say, this was a galvanising experience.

Among them was a 13-year-old Tony Fletcher. Over the summer of 1977, he was drawn to The Jam and when he returned to school in September, he was struck by the idea of creating a fanzine. Entitled *In The City* it was written with a classmate and printed on the school's mimeograph duplicating machine. By the end of the year, they had sold fifty copies to school friends.

The fanzine wasn't a product of punk rock – music fans had been creating their own low-fi publications since the skiffle craze of the

1950s. But punk's central ethos of do-it-yourself creativity empowered its adherents to make their own culture, whether it be music, fashion or journalism. The most influential fanzine, *Sniffin' Glue*, had appeared in July 1976. Its creator, south Londoner Mark Perry, refused contributions from would-be writers, telling them to go and start their own fanzines.

While the older journalists of the mainstream music press struggled to understand and articulate the excitement of punk rock, the fanzine writers were there in the crowd at the gigs, selling their creation to peers who were equally fired up about the bands they were hearing. For a brief moment, fanzines were the cutting edge of pop culture, which explains how a young teenager like Tony Fletcher could write to his favourite band and secure a reply from the lead singer and an exclusive in-person interview.

But fanzines are by their nature a hobbyist venture, done for love rather than money. While their image is very much of the moment, their deadlines are elastic. It may take a year to get one together, which is a long time in pop music. By 1980, fashions had moved on and the egalitarianism of punk was being replaced by the cliquery (cliquishness?) of the new romantics.

After several years of being relegated to an afterthought, style was reasserting its dominance over content, a sea-change underscored by the fact that The Jam metamorphosed into The Style Council. *Jamming* underwent its own metamorphosis, becoming a full colour bi-monthly magazine, proclaiming 'A New Optimism for the 80s' above the title.

The turn of the decade also heralded a new professionalism. A mix-up with the printing might be acceptable in a fanzine – accidentally half-toning pages so that they become unreadable only adds to the DIY feel of the thing. But a magazine needs to look good to stand out on a newsstand among other publications covering the same topics. Choosing the right cover star can be make-or-break. If a fanzine doesn't sell, you just end up with piles of copies stacked on your bedroom floor. If a *magazine* doesn't sell, you have an overdraft to contend with.

Jamming followed the cultural flow as the 70s turned to the 80s, mixing pop and politics with a publication pitched somewhere between the inky radicalism of the weekly music papers and the shiny-paged pop mags like *Smash Hits*, becoming one of the few DIY fanzines to successfully make the transition to the racks of the nation's newsagents.

The magazine came of age at a time when pop was suffused with ideas, and did its damnedest to give a platform to those challenging the mainstream. It did so with that youthful optimism as proclaimed on its front cover, a refreshing counter to the cynicism that was the default setting for its rock press rivals. Ultimately, it was edged out by the corporate culture that was taking over everything in the 1980s, but not before it had built a solid bond in the hearts of its readers up and down the country.

This then is Tony Fletcher's testimony to the challenges of holding on to your ideals in the face of commercial pressure, and to the lessons learned while guiding his labour of love through the surging waves and countercurrents of late 20th century youth culture.

Billy Bragg, March 2021

THE VIEW FROM THE CLASSROOM

I was into music and pop culture from an early age (I bought my first record, 'Metal Guru' by T. Rex, when I was 8 years old), so when I started secondary school at Archbishop Tenison's I gravitated naturally towards kids with similar interests. Lawrence Weaver was the first of them. We bonded despite the fact that he was into heavy metal and prog rock; it was his *love* of music that was important to me. Also, his parents were super cool: I would visit their flat in Brixton on Saturdays where Lawrence and I would play his dad's records – Led Zeppelin, Rush and Thin Lizzy especially, although I never loved the first two bands. It transpired that Lawrence's dad, Alf, was friends with Robert Plant and ran a company that provided security at gigs, and at age 13 I found myself backstage at Hammersmith Odeon at a Thin Lizzy gig! When *The Song Remains the Same* film was released, Lawrence handed out promo Led Zeppelin t-shirts that all thirty pupils in our class wore to the next gym session, much to the surprise of our PE teacher.

Tony – Anthony, back then – was another of the music mad kids I met at Tenison's, and our friendship flourished as the punk movement gained popularity. We formed part of a gang of kids in our class who obsessed over new punk records, TV appearances and gigs. We scrutinised the *NME* and *Melody Maker* every week and started visiting the Rough Trade and Virgin Records shops where we'd buy some of the many fanzines that were cropping up. Tony suggested we start our own fanzine but for some strange reason I declined and pointed him in the direction of Lawrence Weaver: I obviously thought a punk/prog rock/heavy metal crossover magazine was just what the world needed! Heavily influenced by our love of The Jam, Tony named the fanzine *In The City* (despite the fact that one of the better known fanzines at the time had the same title). His drive to persuade the school secretary to let him use the school printer to produce it was impressive; unfortunately the same can't be said of his decision to appoint himself head of the *In The City* art department as his illustration for the first front cover was pretty awful.

Tony's enthusiasm, coupled with Lawrence's reputation as a tough nut, meant that most of the pupils in my year were persuaded to part with 10p for a copy of the fanzine, which led to a sell-out success and preparation for a second issue. Already regretting my decision not to be involved in the first issue, I wrote a review of Elvis Costello & The Attractions' album *This Year's Model*, which Tony published in *In The City* Issue 2, now renamed *Jamming*.

After that, *Jamming* quickly gained momentum. On several occasions I skipped school with Tony to go to Rough Trade and Virgin Records, this time to *sell* copies of the fanzine. We went to numerous gigs where Tony also sold copies of *Jamming*; we saw shows by The Jam, Delta 5 and Echo & The Bunnymen (with U2 as support). Tony's focus and opportunism gained *Jamming* interviews with many of our idols, Paul Weller and Pete Townshend amongst them, which was unbelievable to a bunch of 14-year-old schoolkids. Tony developed a great friendship with Weller, which led me to a visit to the pub with the leader of the biggest band in Britain at the time. Paul bought the beers for us as we were still four years below the legal drinking age.

When I left Tenison's I lost contact with Tony for several years but remember buying a copy of *Jamming!* in a W H Smith's and thinking how far it had progressed since it was run off the school copy machine. As I grew older the memories I have of the early days of *Jamming!* and Apocalypse (the band Tony formed with fellow classmates) became more and more surreal, with numerous 'did that actually happen?' moments. Fortunately, Tony's memoir *Boy About Town* came along and provided much needed clarity and perspective on a very special time in my life. I suspect this book will do the same.

John Matthews

Far left: Jeni de Haart. Centre of back row: Jeff Carrigan (partly obscured), Tony Fletcher (eating). Front row centre: Richard Heard (Jam t-shirt), John Matthews (black Fred Perry). Photo courtesy of Jeni De Haart.

JAMMING AND US

Jamming was born in 1977 at a time when the world of music was changing for ever. That music was everything for us 13-year-olds, and at that stage (for a little while anyway), it even transcended relationships with the opposite sex! For me and I think Tony at that time, it was mainly about The Jam. Tony had introduced me to the 'Best fucking band in the world' around the time he started *Jamming,* and right away they were both a key part of the same landscape.

In those early days, creating *Jamming* was a very manual process, from hand printing the early copies in the school office, to getting together in Tony's bedroom in Dulwich to spray paint 1,000 copies of the title banner for Issue 5. Perhaps it was all part of Tony's career plan; we were just glad to be part of it.

As for distribution, if you took a tube with Tony in 1978, he knew precisely which carriage to sit on to get you the quickest route through the interchanges so you could get to Rough Trade and back to school in your lunchbreak. It was all pretty hands-on stuff.

Probably the biggest thing for me that would not have happened without *Jamming* was our 'personal' relationship with The Jam. In the summer of '79, Tony had lined up an interview with the band at the Town House Studios in Shepherd's Bush and Tony, Jeff Carrigan and I headed west by bus and tube: Tony to do the interview, Jeff to take photos and me to just do my best to look like Weller! One of the most vivid memories from that day was sitting in the studio control room whilst the band finished some takes for *Setting Sons* and producer Vic Coppersmith-Heaven asking to see Tony's tape recorder to make sure he wasn't recording the session, 'in case you get the album out before we do...' We were 15 years old!

That day at the Town House, The Jam were recording *Thick As Thieves* and looking back, to when *Jamming* was part of our lives, the title perfectly described the relationship between Tony and me. Unlike the characters in the song, we have pretty much stayed that way, 'for all time'. Without realising it, *Jamming* was the vehicle to our dreams. It led to some life affirming moments, which I am sure will live with us forever.

Richard Heard

I came to know *Jamming* at Issue 5. There had been rumours of this home-made music 'fanzine' in circulation at the boys' grammar school (Archbishop Tenison's), at the other end of the Camberwell New Road from our own girls' grammar school (Charles Edward Brooke). We were in rehearsal for the annual joint musical production, this one being held at Tenison's. We had the libretti in hand, Gilbert & Sullivan being sung in full harmony, whilst a copy of this *Jamming* passed between some of us, secreted in front of the 'Pirates of Penzance' sheet music in the time-honoured, global tradition of appearing to concentrate on schoolwork whilst being completely distracted by something way more exciting. This stapled bunch of A4 pages, typed out with some handwritten notations... I was fascinated. Enthralled. Who were all these bands? Would I ever get to see any? Would my mum EVER let me?

Jeni de Haart

Photos from the Archbishop Tenison's/Charles Edward Brooke exchange trip to Nantes, May 1979. Back row. Far left: Tony Fletcher. Centre: Richard Heard, with arms around Shona Groves (left) and Jeni de Haart (right). Front row: Far left: Jeff Carrigan. Photo courtesy of Jeni De Haart

IN THE CITY No.1

January 1977

Price: 10p

MODERN

NEWS OF THE ^ WORLD

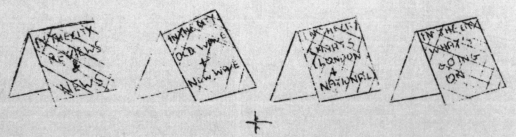

+

THE STORY OF LED ZEPPELIN

This is rarer than any 12" single, and cheaper, so BUY IT!

We had just returned to classes after a summer in which punk rock had swept into the mainstream and challenged our 13-year-old male musical (and fashion) values with it. To be clear, I was not an overnight convert. I came from a musical family, I played cello, I was in the school choir, and my most recent concert had been Pink Floyd at Wembley Empire Pool; all this back-to-basics three-chord simplicity went against my thoroughly ingrained instincts. But over a summer of listening, watching and reading about the new wave, I couldn't help but find myself influenced; specifically, after seeing The Jam perform it on *Top of the Pops*, I bought their second single, 'All Around The World', and it was an epiphany. Something exciting was happening on my generation's watch and being at school near Central London put me, in theory at least, a little closer to the action. A fanzine? Why not?

On the way out of that maths lesson, I asked my friend John Matthews if he wanted to work on the project with me; somewhat to my surprise, he said no, and instead suggested I ask Lawrence Weaver, the class resident expert in all things hard rock. Lawrence, equally to my surprise, promptly said yes, and the two of us set about producing that elusive 'something', which I decided to call *In The City* after The Jam's debut single and LP, not that I owned either as yet. For some reason, it took us three months to write and 'design' all of six pages, though memory serves that much of that time was spent waiting for the decidedly unhurried (and equally unimpressed) school secretaries to print fifty copies on an ancient Roneo machine, just in time for the Christmas holidays. The Roneo couldn't handle photographs, so for the front cover I took it upon myself to draw the summer's riot in neighbouring Lewisham, where the National Front had been stopped in their tracks by assorted anti-racists. Unfortunately for those who ended up owning a copy, I could not actually draw; it was all stick figures. I handwrote the date 'January 1978', knowing that magazines

---

SPILLS SPILLS SPILLS
The gossip and the news

...SPILLS-To give you the thrills.

To start off with, for those of you who like the Boomtown Rats, do you know what Joey's On The Street Again is about? Well, although the words are given with the LP, Bob Geldoff made a mistake when writing them. He informs us Joey is dead, but he is in fact, only stabbed. And being stabbed, he's rarely been out, and so some people, like Geldoff, think he's dead. Now as for Mary Of The 4th Form, we all know what that's about!

Whose Rod Dept: Radio and The Hot Rods released Do Anything You Wanna Do as the Rods, to simplify matters. Apparently though, it caused too much confusion (it certainly confused me), and they have now reverted to Eddie And The Hot Rods. Didn't stop the single selling though....

New Singles Dept: Sex Pistols are planning to release Belsen Is A Gas (geddit?) as their next single - count the seconds before it's banned - and The Stranglers will release 5 Minutes in early January. Meanwhile, you can get Grip/Sometimes/Something Better Change/No More Heroes by The Stranglers, white vinyl with red streaks, as an import at £1.50. Or for the more extravagant, you can get All Around The World (live)/The Modern World (L.F. version) by The Jam, in 12", white vinyl, with The Jam printed in black on the actual vinyl; 1 side of the cover is the All Around The World cover and the other The Modern World cover. This Japanese import, with 7½ mins music, is available for a mere £2.50! Or if you know where to look, Spunk, the Sex Pistols bootleg, is on sale at an imminent London market for £6.

Sounds' centre pages for 29/10,were taken up by a COLOUR double-page advert for R.L.O.'s new double, Out Of The Blue. It was very attractive, depicting a space scene, but just think of the cost-1)For using 2pages 2)For using the centre pages, and 3) for having it in colour. They deserve to sell a million, just for their confidence in the album.

Tours for the new year: Sex Pistols (hopefully); Be-Bop Deluxe, who finish at Hammersmith on Feb 28; The Stranglers, who are to play unannounced club dates; Rush, who are to play 2 London dates; and Blue Oyster Cult.

It's been interesting watching Top Of The Pops recently-6 months

ago we were lucky to have a group playing live in the studio; but then everyone started playing live, until some bright spark came up with the idea of plugging in amplifiers and everything, except not switching on the amplifier. Recent examples of this have been Nazareth & Stranglers So on 7/12, it was good to see The Boomtown Rats not even pretending to mime, as the drummer played away with magazines, and the keyboard player pogoed, tickling his ivories with either a single finger, or a mass of all 10. Elvis Costello was another one who didn't mind showing that he was miming, while prats like The Dooleys still try and pretend they really are singing. At the other end of the spectrum, John Otway and 'Wild' Willy Barrett were playing as live as I've seen anyone on TOTP; Otway forgot to pick up his guitar, and we had a thrilling few moments while everyone waited as he fumbled on his axe to the sound of silence/giggles. Great stuff.

On the subject of the BBC, whatever we think of them, they still have an (unfortunately) great influence on the charts, so it's a pity they've completely ignored the Kursaal Flyers' Television Generation and The Adverts' "Safety In Numbers".

Full marks to The Clash for taking care of the Regard, Swedish gang who had already attacked the Damned Jam and Stranglers. When they took on the Clash, they were suprised to find The Clash take them on. In the end, the Regard lost, and settled down to listen, & even talked peacefully with our English heroes afterwards. Shows which of the British PR groups has most guts....

Who can tell us the correct Tom Robinson Band address. We are told that badges are free from ITB, 4 Tilney Street, W1; but what happened to 25 Montpelier Grove, London NW5. And NM gave a 3rd, new address on 10/12/77. Which one is right?

IN THE CITYIN THECITYINCITYTHRCITY
Editor: Anthony Fletcher (& typing)
Assistant editor:Lawrence Weaver
Printing:Archbishop Tenison's
     School (thanks both of you)
In the future, we'd love to hear your thoughts on the mag, or the music biz. The address:
In The City; 5 Little Bornes;
Alleyn Park; LONDON SE21 8SD.

- 6 -

NEVER MIND IN THE CITY

HERE'S Jamming

Number 2.   10p
April 1978

RUSH   THE JAM
BOOK REVIEWS
NEW HEARTS
RICH KIDS

WIN AN LP WIN AN LP WIN AN LP

POWERPOP

FRIEND OR FOE?

Most likely you've all heard about Powerpop. But what is it? Well, apparently, a few high-up people thought 'Punk Rock' was not the thing, so they invented a succesor. That's why I really felt sick when someone wrote to NME (18/2/) asking what Powerpop is, & recieved this reply: "Well we got bored being punks, didn't we?" For the past 6 months all I've read has been the decline of Punk, yet all the time the audiences have been growing, more people have become punks, and more records have been selling. What's the rule then, kids with more than 50p pocket money can't cut their hair and buy a pair of straights? You enjoy yourself right through 1977, and then get told it was a dry year. And now, Powerpop. The first mention of it that I can remember is a couple of weeks before Christmas, when it was used to describe New Hearts. As yet they're the only group I've noticed who really fit into this pouch-they're colourful, energetic, witty and play heavy pop(!) which doesn't attack you with swearwords and uncomprehensible backing, but isn't exactly teenybop fodder. Hopefully, they're the start of a new generation.

The point is, the following groups have all been brought together in Powerpop:- The Pleasers, Rich Kids, XTC, Tonight, Magazine, Yellow Dog, Buzzcocks, Nick Lowe and plenty others. All great groups, but in there you've got Thamesbeat, Space Rock, ex-Sex Pistols, early punk groups, New Wave Producers and plenty wierdos. It may be fun making classifications, but how can you class that lot together?

I'm looking for a free society where you can dig what you want, where Radio 1 play all new records, and where the charts are better compiled, so that our Top 50 is a fair representation of current music (Rich Kids is about the only song I know that beat the system) where everything is simply called rock and roll, and you can go to a concert dressed as you like.

— AF

ELECTRIC CHAIRS: Eddie And Sheena. Ed is a ted, Sheena's a punk, so the first ¾ are a sort of rockabilly ballad, with an obvious tune that makes it all the more likeable. Then the last ¼ is for less rebelling the story. listen to it and buy it

-6-

SINGLES

STEEL PULSE: Klu Klux Clan. Powerful reggae song which for 4 minutes bounds along forcefully, then has another 3 minutes jamming. The lyrics give a proper message, sung in a tuneful way, with soul. The 7 min. version is available as a 12" - £1.50 -otherwise it's 4 mins & 7". As far as reggae songs go, this is a classic.

EDDIE AND THE HOT RODS: [...] Line.The 3rd single from [...] the same name, and alt o[...] is memorable and enjoyabl[...] can buy the album, why b[...]

RUBINOOS: Rock And Roll [...] with records like this a[...] A heavy rocker, in a cla[...] own.

GENESIS: Follow You, Fol[...] is playing 3 minute love [...] it's in the charts, but [...] the reason. It grows on [...] a few times, lifts you o[...] drums, with it's melodic [...]

SURBURBAN STUDS: I Hate [...] than wot the Pistols use[...] plenty energy, but this [...] late. That's the trouble [...] dates.

SQUEEZE: Take Me, I'm YO[...] Don't kid. The new gener[...] hesized pop songs. The v[...] backed by a rubber beat [...] synthesizer, then we hea[...] tar solo. Certainly orig[...]

GENERATION X: Ready Stea[...] nly their best, pity they[...] it up on TOTP. Should ge[...] around your bathroom, wi[...] sant beat. Great fun.

JACKSON BROWNE: Running [...] good song for people who [...] sort of rock. Has a good [...] words, good backing, but [...] me sit up and wonder

DEVO: (I Can't Get No) S[...] Mongoloid. They've now g[...] attention for their '80'[...] Rock'n'Roll'. Satisfacti[...] it's nothing like the St[...] but bounces along in an [...] I've only heard Mongoloi[...] the tune is catchy it wo[...] head. Their method is st[...] to bare essentials, then [...] them. These 2 singles de[...]

The Kids Are Alright — JAM CONCERT/SINGLE REVIEW AND GENERAL PRAISE

Sat. Feb 25th at the Marquee, and it's the second date of The Jam's London Blitz. The Jolt weren't very good-although they played very competently, they failed to reach me, or by the looks of it, anyone else. The disco played New Wave Classics up to The Jam,getting the crowd very excited. Mr. Weller introduced The Jam with a plea for things to calm down, and on trooped the lads.

The Modern World kicked off the set which is a more sensible starter than Changed My Address, and the crowd went crazy. After that song, and almost every other song, Paul Weller asked everyone to move back, because "there's some people really getting crushed down the front"-very true. The Jam were very keen on playing the new stuff, in fact they played all 9 tracks off the new LP they could- the other three are pretty impossible live - as well as 2 tracks off their new EP-News Of The World and Aunties And Uncles. But it wasn't just a case of listening to the LP- there was an incredible atmosphere about the gig that put the crowd in ecstacy.

Sounds From The Street, Bricks And Mortar and In The City were the only tracks played from their debut set, and the latter closed the set triumphantly. The sweat was running down the walls, but nobody went home, and The Jam didn't take long to get back on stage. "I've learned tonight that Jam fans are the biggest load of ponces in the world - along with all the rest," says Paul Weller, and into In The Midnight Hour. Carnaby St. follows, and the Jam finish with All Around The World.

If you think 45 minutes is a bit short for a set, then I challenge anyone to try and play in those conditions:- it was a sell-out, there were people smoking and pogoing all the time, and there was very loud music blaring away for three hours. But that's not the point - if you compare this gig to Hammersmith, the sound was much better (it was the worst I'd heard last time), the playing was better, the pacing was better, and there was freedom; at Hammersmith you couldn't move away from your seat - here you could do as you wanted. There was a kind of

contact - at Hammersmith, you could be about 70th from the lads, this time it ranged from 0-20 yds, and there was just an amazing atmosphere. There were no special effects, nothing but 3 young people playing, and yet, I dare anyone to go to a concert like this, and not enjoy it.

It seemed to me during the set that Paul Weller plays the tough man, taunting the crowd, even insulting them,while Bruce Foxton plays the nice man, handing round his towel after drying himself, & together they make an irresistable pair. The other ingredient in this Jam is Rick Buckler, who never says or sings anything, and rather than attacking the drums, leans back on them. Yet he is 1 of the best drummers around- listen to any Jam song and you'll see what I mean.

Their recent LP, This Is The Modern World, is a real masterpiece of pop/ rock/punk. Unlike In The City, it is extremely varied - we get stereo effects, guitar tricks, feedback & even accoustic guitars. Life From A Window, Standards and I Need You are the best examples - they put me in ecstacy. Put it this way, everyone I know who's heard or got the album (a lot) thinks it's a classic. Why not but the LP and join them?

The Jam are undoubtably getting better with every step, so we can look forward, and accept the new EP with glee:-

News Of The World is Bruce Foxton's first A-side effort, and he handles it very well. This song has the best guitar by The Jam yet- Paul Weller ripping out your guts all the way through. The whole song delivers the message "Don't believe the papers" very competently, but somehow it doesn't pack everything into it's 3½ mins like The Jam usually do in two, but maybe it just doesn't compare with the flip....

Aunties And Uncles and Innocent Man must be the best B-sides ever. For the first time with The Jam, I don't want to turn the volume up, but just sit back & listen to Aunties And Uncles, which is magic pop, like the good old Beatles and Who used to do. It is....cute.

Innocent Man is a 4-min story by Foxton - accoustic guitar and piano (by Paul Weller) back his excellent voice, as the song reaches a climax in the middle.

And you thought that Jamming was a thing of the past...

AF

-7-

WE'RE JAMMING…

ISSUE #2 03/78

I'd taken the idea of a 'fanzine' just seriously enough to write to Tom Robinson, every 13-year-old would-be lefty's idea of a politically correct new wave hero, for an interview. Too late for the first issue, and without committing to the interview itself, he wrote back to tell me there was already a 'very good mag called *In The City* run from somewhere outrageous in Neasden'.

Oh well. I quickly decided on *Jamming,* instead. Genuinely, I was thinking of the Bob Marley & The Wailers hit of the previous summer, but I can't deny a connection to my 'new wave' band of choice. Since *my In The City* had been 'published', I'd seen The Jam twice, bought both their LPs, and was now besotted: my piece on the band in this first *Jamming* (confusingly numbered as the second issue) indicated as much. Several of my school friends shared my obsession, and a couple chimed in with enthusiastic articles on other

new wave heroes. John Matthews atoned for his absence from the first issue and reviewed the new Elvis Costello & The Attractions LP, *This Year's Model*. And a kid I'd met outside the school gates on our very first day as pupils, a kid who'd been something of a swot until now, a kid who I'd end up forming a band with that would dominate the next seven years of our lives even more so than *Jamming*…

Jeff Carrigan wrote about meeting The Rich Kids at soundcheck the night they played the college at the top of his road (we claimed an 'exclusive' interview), and also took the time out to design something approximating a proper front cover. That cover benefited from being switched to a better school printer – called a Gestetner, I believe – which churned out 100 copies in total. To our incredible shock and disappointment, given what we thought was an obvious improvement on its predecessor, most remained unsold.

JAMMING

No.3

JUNE / JULY

10p

RAIN-ALBUM-BOW HISTORY

CARNIVAL AGAINST THE NAZIS

FULL REPORT

TRB ALBUM

LASERIUM AND

RATTUS

STORY OF THE WHO.
WIN AN LP OF YOUR CHOICE

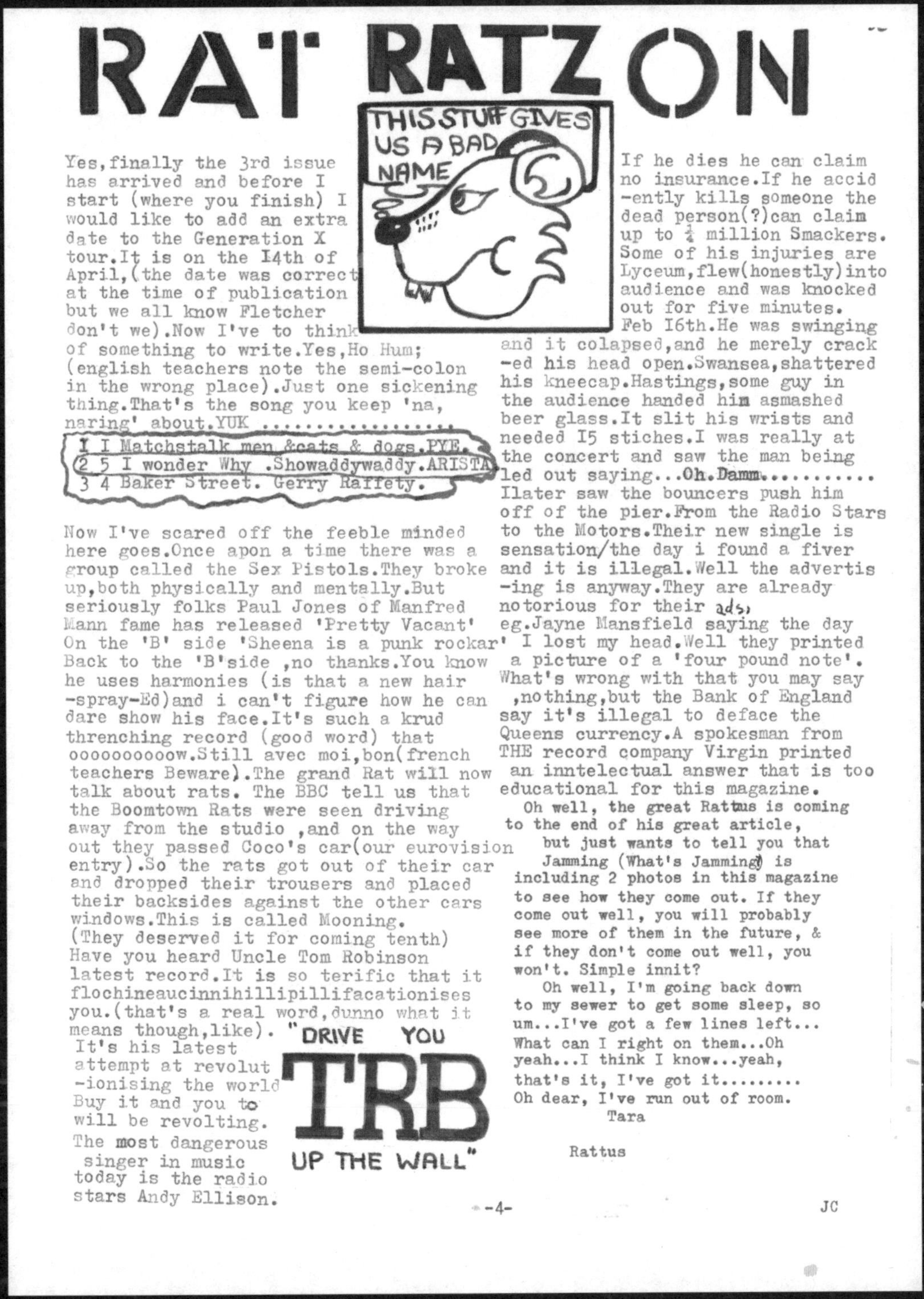

RAT RATZ ON

THIS STUFF GIVES US A BAD NAME

Yes, finally the 3rd issue has arrived and before I start (where you finish) I would like to add an extra date to the Generation X tour. It is on the 14th of April, (the date was correct at the time of publication but we all know Fletcher don't we). Now I've to think of something to write. Yes, Ho Hum; (english teachers note the semi-colon in the wrong place). Just one sickening thing. That's the song you keep 'na, naring' about. YUK..................

I I Matchstalk men &cats & dogs. PYE.
2 5 I wonder Why .Showaddywaddy. ARISTA
3 4 Baker Street. Gerry Raffety.

Now I've scared off the feeble minded here goes. Once apon a time there was a group called the Sex Pistols. They broke up, both physically and mentally. But seriously folks Paul Jones of Manfred Mann fame has released 'Pretty Vacant' On the 'B' side 'Sheena is a punk rockar' Back to the 'B'side, no thanks. You know he uses harmonies (is that a new hair -spray-Ed) and i can't figure how he can dare show his face. It's such a krud threnching record (good word) that oooooooooow. Still avec moi, bon(french teachers Beware). The grand Rat will now talk about rats. The BBC tell us that the Boomtown Rats were seen driving away from the studio, and on the way out they passed Coco's car(our eurovision entry). So the rats got out of their car and dropped their trousers and placed their backsides against the other cars windows. This is called Mooning. (They deserved it for coming tenth) Have you heard Uncle Tom Robinson latest record. It is so terific that it flochineaucinnihillipillifacationises you.(that's a real word, dunno what it means though, like). It's his latest attempt at revolut -ionising the world Buy it and you to will be revolting. The most dangerous singer in music today is the radio stars Andy Ellison.

"DRIVE YOU TRB UP THE WALL"

If he dies he can claim no insurance. If he accid -ently kills someone the dead person(?)can claim up to ¼ million Smackers. Some of his injuries are Lyceum, flew(honestly)into audience and was knocked out for five minutes. Feb 16th. He was swinging and it colapsed, and he merely crack -ed his head open. Swansea, shattered his kneecap. Hastings, some guy in the audience handed him asmashed beer glass. It slit his wrists and needed 15 stiches. I was really at the concert and saw the man being led out saying...Oh. Damm.......... Ilater saw the bouncers push him off of the pier. From the Radio Stars to the Motors. Their new single is sensation/the day i found a fiver and it is illegal. Well the advertis -ing is anyway. They are already notorious for their ads, eg. Jayne Mansfield saying the day I lost my head. Well they printed a picture of a 'four pound note'. What's wrong with that you may say, nothing, but the Bank of England say it's illegal to deface the Queens currency. A spokesman from THE record company Virgin printed an inntelectual answer that is too educational for this magazine.

Oh well, the great Rattus is coming to the end of his great article, but just wants to tell you that Jamming (What's Jamming) is including 2 photos in this magazine to see how they come out. If they come out well, you will probably see more of them in the future, & if they don't come out well, you won't. Simple innit?
Oh well, I'm going back down to my sewer to get some sleep, so um...I've got a few lines left... What can I right on them...Oh yeah...I think I know...yeah, that's it, I've got it......... Oh dear, I've run out of room.
Tara

Rattus

-4-   JC

Considering we were still a bunch of 'third years', according to the parlance of the times, *Jamming* 3 was not bad. Certainly, there was plenty by way of content. But that content remained hopelessly conflicted. My gushing review of the Tom Robinson Band's LP sat opposite Lawrence's similarly unrestrained rave of a Rainbow concert. Queen shared a spread with The Stranglers. I wrote a two-page 'History of The Who' so riddled with errors I am now glad Keith Moon did *not* accept the lone copy I had on me when we met at the ICA that summer. (He autographed the article instead, then handed me his home address to deliver an additional zine in person. Shortly after that, he was dead.) Fortunately, Jeff Carrigan designed the cover again and, less fortunately for our readers, was rewarded with a page to let loose an alter ego 'Rat Ratz On'.

The centrepiece, however, was my four-page account of the Anti-Nazi League/Rock Against Racism Carnival Against the Nazis, a generation-defining event that started with a rally in Trafalgar Square and continued, after a lengthy march through the East End, with a concert in Tower Hamlets' Victoria Park featuring TRB, Steel Pulse, The Clash, X-Ray Spex and Patrick Fitzgerald. As many as 80,000 people attended, and peacefully so. The April 1978 event coalesced the new wave's battle against racism; affording it so much space in the fanzine helped define *Jamming*'s own stance in turn. Memory serves that this issue shifted about 200 copies, some of which may have been a rare (possibly the only) 'reprint'.

ISSUE #3 05/78

CARNIVAL AGAINST

Sunday April 30th was a day to remember: it was the day 80,000 people showed that blacks, whites, yellows, browns and polka-dots CAN all get on together. And this is a full account of a day countless people will never forget.

The rally at Trafalger Square was due to start at 11.00, but the crowds had been growing since 9.00. By 11.00 there were about 40,000people present and it was practically impossible to find someone who didn't have a badge, banner, magazine or flag supporting the cause. The rally got under way with a steel band playing on the platform of Nelson's Column, who were greeted very enthusiastically. A double line of stewards linked arms across the front of the crowd, but they were unnecessary - the crowd was very good-natured and nobody wanted to push. The half-hour of speeches seemed to drag on a bit, but all were interesting, and a quote from a German U-Boat Commander can stand as a guidance to us all: "When the Nazis came to power, they first went for The Jews, and because I wasn't a Jew, I didn't help. Then they went for the Communists, and because I wasn't a Jew, I didn't help. Then they went for the Trade Unionists, and because I wasn't a Trade Unionist, I didn't help. Then they went for me, and there was noone left to help." The MP for Coventry gave a very short message, and Tom Robinson had a short, but good message "Hands off our people. Black, white, together, forever", but too often the speeches hinted at 'Vote Socialist' rather than 'Smash NF'. All the time, magnificent effigies of Nazi Hitler, Nazi Webster & Nazi Tyndall stared fearfully at the angry masses.

At nearly 12.00, the first of 40,000 peoppeople set off down The Strand towards Victoria Park. On the way we were entertained by steel bands playing from trucks, stiltmen and an arts exhibition, while EMI had distributed a few thousand whistles, and there were chants for all of the 1½-2 hour march. The march must have been about 90% under 30's, which is a very reassuring sign. A large number of these were punks, who have proved they know what they're doing more than the people who criticize them - I even saw one girl with 'Smash NF' written in her hair. And before you say they were only there to see The Clash and others then why did they go to an hour-long rally and on a long, tiresome 5-mile walk?

The whole affair was organized jointly by Rock Against Racism and The Anti-Nazi League, with a load of other small groups helping out. Rock Against Racism has been running since the autumn of '76, and now regularly holds concerts, which have previously featured TRB, Sham 69, Steel Pulse, Fabulous Poodles and many others. They have a magazine called TempoRARy Hoarding, and you can get badges and info from:- RAR, Box 'M', 27 Clerkenwell Close, EC1. The ANL was started less than a year ago, and has since become almost a household name. It ranges from having placed adverts in The Guardian to distributing leaflets on the terraces. It can supply worthy information (with badges etc) from 12 Little Newport St. WC2.

Of course the main worry of violence was on the march, which explained the large amount of police, but the only NF to turn up were at Petticoat Lane, and luckily for them were surrounded by a cordon of police.

I was at the front of the march, and just as we reached the park, the police recieved the message that the march had just left Trafalgar Square! As soon as we reached the park, everyone ran towards the area of interest with a look of wild glee on their faces. Somewhere in the distance one could pick out a small make-shift stage, It obviously wasn't going to suffice, but even The

14 | ISSUE 3 | 05/78

THE NAZIS

Socialist Worker only expected 20,000. Pink Floyd had offered to lend their huge PA, but as they didn't have a permanent crew to set up the equipment a very expensive PA had to be hired. A line of trees marked a kind of boundary to the arena, and kids were scrambling up these at every opportunity. From there, people onstage were a mere speck, and it seemed rather pointless climbing them, yet at 6.00 the back of the crowd was behind these trees! Over to one side were stalls selling squash (which ran out almost instantly) information and first-aid tents. There were also stalls selling food, but the queues for this literally meant an hour long wait. Note: nowhere were cans or bottles sold.

Anyway, the first live act were X-Ray Spex, at about 1.45, fronted by Poly Styrene, wearing a day-glo green scarf made into a turban on her head. The set was played well, held steady by the confident band. Only for the first time, being close to the front, do I notice that Poly is coloured, which just goes to show how stupid this race-hate thing is - some people want to exterminate certain other people, while the rest of us can't see they're different... Trying to get a good view, I climbed a couple of inches of the front fence (I was right over on one side) and glancing round me, was amazed to see a sea of about 25,000 heads, stretching all around me - strangely haunting. Those at the front, just 2-300 were pogoing in unison, and those at the very front were being crushed like flies:- the fence had dipped in at the middle, & people were passing out all the time. Poly seemed rather scared by it all, begging with the crowd to move back

Oh Bondage!Up Yours closed the set triumphantly, but encores were out for the day, with the tight time schedule. Even so I didn't notice X-Ray Spex play Dayglow, their great new single. As for a review of the group, if you like Poly's voice, they might be the saviours of rock. If you don't.....

The compere pointed out that we're all in it together, and told us Jimmey Pursey was backstage. The skinheads went crazy, and proceeded to sing the more well-known Sham songs, interspersed with huge shouts of "We want Sham! The full relevance of this comes later.

Next on was Patrick Fitzgerald, whose only accompaniment was an accoustic guitar. Having already won a lot of attention for his Safety Pin Stuck In My Heart EP, he proceeded to delight the crowd with his unusual act. But some of the assorted punks and skinheads at the very front thought it 'in' to throw cans etc at him. Patrik had performed some very honest and entertaining songs - Sounds Of My Street, Banging And Shouting, and a short, abrupt Lewisham - and was about a minute through a bitter When I Get Famous when a can hit his guitar. His reaction - to start again. Next was the well known Safety Pin, but this time he was interrupted for good, when a can hit him in the face. Many (75%) of the crowd tried to get Fitzgerald back on, and his return to the stage was met with a huge cheer. But he just said- "If you hated the NF as much as you hated my set, you'd be well away. His only reward was the number of fans he made.

Anyway, The Clash were on very soon after, and there was something magic about them as soon as they hit the stage. But although the sound had been bad up to now, The Clash destroyed what was left by turning up their guitars from the start, and thumping into Complete Control. They only played 3 songs from their debut album, and their set included at least half-a-dozen (as yet) unrecorded songs. The sheer power of The Clash is undeniable, as demonstrated by London's Burning, Clash City Rockers etc. Mick Jones sung on Jail Guitar Doors, and for the rest of the time acted the perfect guitar

CONTINUED OVER

-10-

The Clash in Victoria Park

hero; Joe Strummer (suprisingly) also had a guitar for the whole set, although he'd partly lost his voice; Paul Simonon strutted the stage in an almost illuminous blue shirt, and Nicky Headdon I couldn't see. Tommy Gun, Last Gan In Town and When Johnny (Janie) Comes Marching Home were the most promising of the new songs, but for me the high point came with Police And Thieves, which they played really well. In fact, the sound was pretty unimportant - it's not hard to get off on The Clash.

It was pretty obvious there was only one song left, but apparently they'd run out of time. That hurdle was overcome, and Jimmy Pursey took lead vocals on White Riot, which turned into a fantastic closing song.

The crowd now announced at 60,000, with people still arriving from the march, an indication of it's size is the fact that it took me almost half-an-hour to walk right round the crowd. That was about the gap between The

Clash and Steel Pulse, the only reggae group of the day. They were over-conscious of the poor sound and there was a 3 or 4 minute gap between each song while they tried to correct the sound, and the compere gave out messages. They even cut their set short because of it. That aside, Steel Pulse must be one of the best, if not the best reggae band Britain has produced. People were dancing everywhere, and the music was a refresher: even the sun came out to beam it's approval. Ku Klux Klan was, of course, the best known, and they had a special song written for the event-Rock Against Racism. It was still a bad mistake to worry so much about the sound, though.

It was now that the crowd really came together. Where the trees were there was a van with groups blasting out various rock and reggae, as it had been doing all afternoon; there were stilt-men and clowns entertaining the crowds on one side, and trampolines elsewhere. Add to this that there were people from

-11-

This is the original artwork for page 11: look closely and you can see the Tippex marks.

We knew we couldn't reproduce photos properly on the school machine, but it was time to try it anyway, so we 'borrowed' a picture of The Clash at Victoria Park from the *NME*. (The word 'Clash' fell off the original art somewhere over the ensuing forty-plus years.) The result was harsh black and white, ensuring restraint with any future use of (borrowed) photos in this printing format.

right round the country mixing in together - a huge group from Glasgow (worst housing, employment, violence, least immigrants), people from Cardiff Liverpool, Birmingham, Wolverhampton, Oxford University, and of course Leyton, Croydon and Dagenham. There were banners from Gays Against Facism, Women Against Fascism, Schools Against The Nazis, and countless other groups. The fact that The Tom Robinson Band had hit the stage was almost second-place to the party atmosphere.

With the attendance now quoted at 80,000, TRB came on at 5.30 and started off with their great single Up AgainstThe Wall. It's pretty incredible to think there was as as many people seeing (and enjoying) a year-old band as saw The Who at Charlton 2 years ago, and probably nearly as many as will see Genesis at Knebworth this year. Mark Ambler left the group just after recording the debut album, and someone -I don't know who- made an excellent live debut on the organ, although apparently he's not permanent. Martin was sung along to by most people, like Glad To Be Gay ("You don't have to be black to like Bob Marley, you don't have to be a woman to like Joni Mitchell, and you don't have to be gay to sing along to this song... but it helps"). A new song, 'almost' written for this occasion, was let loose in Let My People Be, and the set continued with Winter Of '79, & We Ain't Gonna Take It, both vicious fighting songs from the album. The whole crowd was singing along, loving every minute-NONE of the other acts had this effect. It's hard to know what it is about TRB that has made them such a live attraction - their music is played with real power, at a very good standard, it has a real meaning, and is sung with such conviction you can't fail to be moved by it. Another important factor is Tom's character. Although all the group are characters, it's Tom who does the speaking, and there was a marvellous monologue in the middle of Power In The Darkness, where he put on a party nose, and pretended to be from the GLC's Parks Council, speaking in a very posh voice. I wish I had a tape recorder, but suffice to say, although

it had serious connections, it was hilarious. If you've heard this bit from the recorded version, this was about 10 minutes long.

The GLC Parks Council had actually said that the music should be over by 6:15 and so TRB finished around then with 2-4-6-8 Motorway. Again, to see 50,000 people punching the air during the chorus line was a great sight. I made to leave, but...

The festivities were not yet over, for there was still to be the final jam session. This saw Danny Kustow and Mick Jones on lead guitar (what was that about The Clash playing early to get to Birmingham that evening?) Dolphin on drums, the TRB bloke on keyboards, and Tom Robinson, Jimmey Pursey and a handful each out of 90 Degrees Inclusive & Steel Pulse. I guess it was one of the latter 2 groups who supplied bass, and there may have been other players, but I had a very limited view. The song was We Have Got To Get It Together, written by Tom for the event, with the only other words "Black, white, together, tonight" - the rest was ad-lib. However the 10-15 minute jam allowed time for guitar solos, keyboard solos, and for each singer to add his bit, change it around and swap it around. It was a great moment, and at the end there was talk of another Carnival next year. I hope so.

Of course, the most remarkable thing was the absolute lack of violence. There were NO police in the park, which was only right because they weren't needed-where were the pick-pockets, the muggers and the NF? If you weren't at the very front of the crowd, you found yourself surrounded by thousands and thousands of people with nobody pushing, but instead all sharing drinks and cigarrettes. The £10,000 the Carnival cost was collected almost entirely from 10p donations Nobody there could ever forget it - I know I won't.

Despite th e fact that this was the biggest Anti-Fascist Demonstration since before the war, none of The Sun, Mirror, Express or Mail could raise themselves enough to even give it an inch of newsprint. We all know the coverage it would have got with just 1 violent outburst, but to quote from Ain't Gonna Take It: "Better get it together/Big trouble to come/And the odds are against us/'Bout 20to 1."

-12-   But at least we've begun...

AF

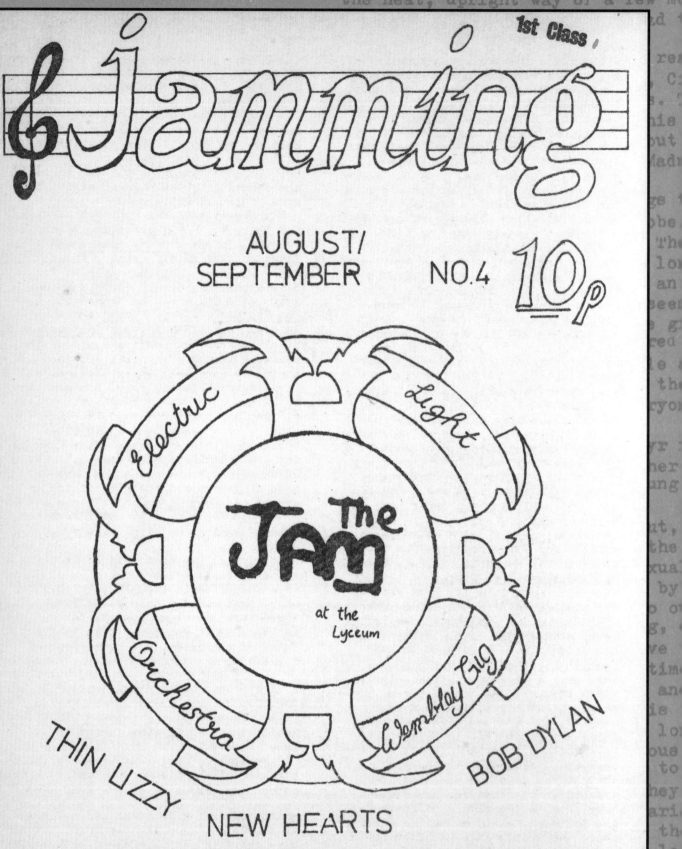

jamming

AUGUST/
SEPTEMBER   NO.4   10p

1st Class

Electric   Light

The JAM

at the
Lyceum

Orchestra   Wembley Gig

THIN LIZZY   BOB DYLAN

NEW HEARTS

WIN AN L.P. OF YOUR CHOICE

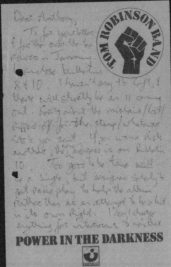

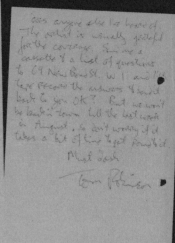

& BEST & LIVE & BRILLIANT AND THUNDEROUS & DANGEROUS & TRIUM

Here's one of the competition entries that almost won, but not quite. It is a review of

THIN LIZZY: Wembley Empire Pool

The night of June 23rd started off with a burst of applause as the lights went down on the Wembley Arena. There were a few noises coming from the stage, and on came Horslips, an Irish folk-rock group. They started out with a few folk songs, and then sung some more heavy, rockier numbers. The reception was mixed.

Horslips left and the lights came back on. We waited for Lizzy.

The crowd was getting impatient. People were standing on the chairs trying to get a good view - the front of the arena was packed. The lights went down and on came Thin Lizzy. The noise was unbelievable as they burst into Jailbreak. Lasers spelt out Thin Lizzy at the back of the arena. As the music got louder, so did the applause - the music was ringing in my ears. Chairs were breaking as people tried to get a glimpse of Lizzy playing their fantastic music.

Rosalie, the current single, was really fantastic, and then the crowd called out for Whiskey In The Jar, their first hit single, & one of the most popular songs. Baby Drives Me Crazy (which, like nearly all the set is on the album Live And Dangerous) was one of the best songs played at the concert, in my opinion. Phil Lynott sung and played bass

as well as ever, while Brian Robertson and Scott Gorham thrashed out guitar lick after guitar lick, to the solid backing of Brian Downey.

The set continued with Lizzy classics like The Boys Are Back In Town, Johnny The Fox, Dancin' In The Moonlight, Don't Believe A Word, Southbound and Emerald, and the crowd was thrust into ecstacy.

Of course Thin Lizzy came back to do an encore, and they played a great song called Me And The Boys Were Wondering How You And The Girls Were Getting Home From Here Tonight. The group then left for a second time and the crowd was going wild in it's efforts to get more. There was a great cheer as Phil Lynott led the band back on and commenced to play The Rocker - one of their best and most famous songs. The group went again, but not for long, as they came back for a third encore. Phil Lynott,

although I couldn't see him, was moving towards the microphone. The fans were still cheering as he said, "Now a lot of you have been asking us to play Whiskey In The Jar, but if we did that it would be suicide." As he said this, he burst into a song called Suicide. The concert came to an amasing finish, and Phil Lynott gave a great warning: "We'll be back again."

David Webb.

AND GREAT

"Gotta try and impress Jamming." Phil Lynott in concert.

- 11 -

POWER IN THE DARKNESS

Dear Anthony

Thanks for letter, I'm really sorry, but I've lost the cassette... so, if you could write a list of questions and send them to 69 New Bond Street (not the box No), I'll answer them onto a (new) cassette and send it back OK?

Sorry mate love Tom

In my eagerness to get another issue out before the summer holidays, I accepted just about any contribution from anyone, and ended up with the names of Electric Light Orchestra, Bob Dylan and Thin Lizzy on the cover, all of whom were reviewed in concert, and none by myself. (Thin Lizzy marked the thin line that separated the new wave kids at school from the hard rock fans, while appealing to both; the page shown is the original artwork.) At age 14, I was only just starting to attend gigs, and when I did, it was usually to see The Jam (whose show at The Lyceum I duly raved about), or their favoured support band, the New Hearts (whose own gig at the Marquee, ditto). The Marquee was the only club venue that let *any* of us schoolkids through the doors, so our options remained limited even as we spent our pocket money on the newest of the new wave singles – and occasionally sought to shoplift them from HMV, as detailed, embarrassingly, in *Boy About Town*.

Jamming's relative frequency was evidently becoming a burden on the school's Media Resources department and, as with the first issue, printing was not completed until almost the final day of school. As a result, I struggled to sell many copies at Tenison's, but I had somehow convinced Virgin Marble Arch to stock Issue 3 and now dared ask some local newsagents to stock Issue 4 as well; they did not all say no. I concluded that *Jamming!* had come as far as it could in its current format, and determined that if I was serious about this fanzine business – and by now, I was – I needed to do it properly. I had the summer holidays in front of me to set about the sea change.

ISSUE #4 7/78

Back in 1978 I worked at Charles Edward Brooke Girls' School in Camberwell. I was 18 and training as an AV Technician in the Media Resources Department. One day I was asked to print this 'magazine' a boy at Archbishop Tenison's had put together; the two schools shared various resources. I remember it needed to be done that afternoon and I was somewhat peeved that I had to stay late to finish it. But then I flicked through the copy of *Jamming*… I was a massive music fan, and just starting to move beyond Dylan and The Beatles into Elvis Costello, Graham Parker, Dr Feelgood, and then Buzzcocks, The Jam, The Clash etc. So if I had to stay late and print *something*, it might as well be *Jamming*. We used an old Roneo Vickers ink duplicator and a Gestetner, and I think this one was printed on the latter.

I saw the cover online about twenty years ago and said to my kids, 'I printed that!' **Jack McIlroy**

JAMMING

25P

EXCLUSIVE INTERVIEW WITH
THE JAM

No.5

In the studio with Paul Weller. New LP!!!

AND MORE EXCLUSIVE INTERVIEWS WITH
ADAM-&-THE-ANTS· JOHN PEEL
READING FESTIVAL· CARNIVAL 2
ULTRAVOX·BE-BOP DELUXE+LOTS MORE

JAMMING

JAMMING

When you could only afford black ink for printing, a can of spray paint and a stencil was cutting edge technology... **JC**

The spray was so corrosive, I made at least two stencils, as can be seen with the differences in type between the different colours. **TF**

Jamming needed interviews if it was to be taken seriously. So, over the summer, I wrote to several different bands, using whatever addresses I could find. For The Jam, I honed in on the fan club in Woking, which I figured to be frontman Paul Weller's family home. I was right. Paul replied, promptly and alone among the names on my short list, inviting me to RAK Studios in North London, where The Jam were recording their third album, *All Mod Cons*. Nervous though I surely must have been given that this was my very first interview and that it was with my punk/new wave hero, everyone at the studio sought to put me at ease, and I did not blow the opportunity; I did, though, write up the piece in such a blatant approximation of conventional music press templates that it reads like a job application to the *NME*.

Meantime, neighbourhood friend Chris Modica, also just 14, was following a band called Adam & The Ants around London, and arranged an interview with the frontman. For reasons I can't excuse, I relegated Chris to photographer and interviewed Adam, in a Notting Hill Gate management office, on my own. This was all the more inexcusable given that I hadn't heard a note of the Ants' music! Still, I bluffed my way through the exchange, and Chris supplied superb photos from the Marquee all the same. (Chris was later immortalised in the song 'Hello' by The Beloved.)

An older Tenisonian, Ray Hoyle, had by now angled to come on board, turning me on to Ultravox! in the process. (We saw them, as fronted by John Foxx, at the Marquee two days before seeing them again at Reading, alongside The Jam, The Pirates, Penetration, Sham 69 and the New Hearts on a day marred by Sham's violent following.) Ray also took it upon himself to corner the great Radio 1 DJ John Peel at Broadcasting House, secure

ISSUE #5
10/78

an interview, conduct it himself and present it as a *fait accompli*.

Three solid interviews meant the makings of a proper magazine. Lawrence Weaver disagreed, citing the name of Adam & The Ants as reason to quit. I breathed a sigh of relief; I was long done with the hard rock content but Lawrence was not a person to dismiss lightly.

Jeff Carrigan, however, remained fully on board, and when his dad secured the services of an offset litho printer in Hastings, the two of us seized on the opportunity to use Letraset for headlines, turn our gig photographs into half-tones, and lay out the pages with painstaking precision – so painstaking that by the time the deadline rolled around we had barely finished half the magazine. We duly stayed up almost all weekend in Hastings, giggling uncontrollably on lack of sleep and an abundance of cow gum, running completed pages down to the printer every few hours.

Several days later, Jeff's dad dropped 1,000 uncollated copies at my house, some pages printed on yellow paper given we had run other supplies dry. I now had the fun of not only collating and stapling, but spray painting the logo through home-made stencils, an idea lifted from the TRB LP and a mild stroke of marketing genius: the visual effect served as a distinguishing 'fanzine' *and* 'pop art' factor to offset the otherwise conventional layout. With a proper magazine in hand, I took to hawking *Jamming* around London's independent record and book shops, after – and occasionally during – school hours. Though almost every key outlet agreed to sell it, the print run still proved optimistic in the extreme, with at least half the copies remaining obstinately piled up on my floor – even as we ploughed straight on to the next issue.

Welcome to ....

ANT MUSIC

Adam And The Ants are an unknown quantity. Only a few facts are known:-

They were at the start of the 2nd wave of punk.

They have an incredibly loyal following.

They were led by glamour punk girl Jordan, but are now led by Adam Ant.

They are hated by the press.

So now to find out some more. Adam And The Ants are:-

ADAMANT (which must be a clue to his name):- vocals

MATTHEW:- guitars
DAVID BARBE:- Drums
ANDY WARREN:- Bass

They have just signed a 1-year deal with Decca, and their first single is out on October 20th. It's:- YOUNG PARISIANS/LADY, and is a double-A side complete with picture cover and lyrics. Young Parisisians is the commercial track, and Lady is for the kids. After one listen, it's certainly not as good as some of their others (almost 30 in all) but is certainly different. Their numbers include stuff like Catholic Day, Friends, Deutsche Girls, and pretty great stuff in Whip In My Valise

and Never Trust A Man With Egg On His Face. They are based on starkly heavy guitar riffs (more like Deep Purple than the Sex Pistols) with Adam's distinctive voice stating his own personal feelings, as in Rubber People:-

Rubber people are lovely people,
They long for latex beside their skin,
The feel they get from a sheet of rubber
The strengh you get from a support chin
Those rubber people are charming people
Their tastes produce quite a bizarre
Not a steak or a private table   dish
But a rubber mack with it's rubber swish

Adamant himself is a very intelligent person. It's no suprise to learn that he's been to art school. He has very firm views that noone will shake, and goes intothem in great detail - there's hardly any need for my questions to be printed they're so few. I don't necessarily agree with everything he says, but then again, there's been enough worthless criticism of the group, so let AdamAnt have his say, and then decide if you want to join their growing legions of very loyal fans..

Dave, Matthew, Andy, Adam at The Marquee.
Pic: Chris Modica.

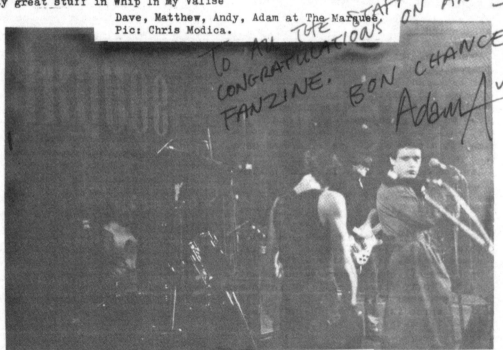

TO ALL THE STAFF AT [TAMMING] CONGRATULATIONS ON AN EXCELLENT FANZINE. BON CHANCE ! AdamAnt

⊲ 5 ⊳

AA: The world premier of Adam And The
Ants was in a bedroom in Muzzell Hill,
and in the audience was Polystyrene of
X-Ray Spex who liked us, and got us
gigs at The Man In The Moon; but the
official debut of the band was at the
ICA Restaurant. I told them we were a
country & western band to get the gig,
and we got kicked out after one song!
We went on and finished the evening at
The Theatre, which was a great success,
and since then it's sort of steamrolled.
We've had a few line-up changes, but now
we're 100%

I have many, many influences. Basically, I like things like Shirley Bassey
and Perry Como (this is serious, folks!)
I like a guy called Dave Berry, but my
favourite group is The Doors. We modell-
ed our presentation on Roxy Music, and
then, for fun, I listen to people like
The Residents.

As for new wave bands, the only new
wave band I can stomach at the moment
is a little band called The Nobodies,
who play in The Moonlight Club. I like
support bands, but there's no good band
in London, say, over the age of 16. All
the kids of 16 and under, they're really
terrific, but there's not many of them
about - they're just starting.

I SUPPOSE YOU FEEL PRETTY RELATED TO
THE PUNK MOVEMENT?

Oh yeah, well, I have to make clear to
you what my defenition of punk is. Punk
is not anarchy, it's not chaos, it's
destruction of 1 thing:- the supergroup
situation, the hippy movement, the whole
drug thing, and the complacency that
one was up against in the '70's - you
couldn't get a gig for love or money.
I've been in bands before this one, and
it was impossible to get a gig at The
Marquee, because there was a whole wall
there....if you didn't play guitar like
Eric Clapton, and if you didn't stand
there with your legs open and long hair,
you've 'ad it mate, you've 'ad it. The
Sex Pistols did one thing in my opinion
and that is...they smashed that all
down, and I'll love 'em for it until
the day I die. From that point of view,
I believe that the music for the future
will come from the streets. And therefore I'm still a punk, but I've never
worn safetypins, I'm not interested in
the fashion side of it, I'm not interested in the 'Blank Generation'.

HOW WOULD YOU DESCRIBE THE BAND'S MUSIC?

Er...Antmusic; sexmusic -it's very
sexual music - it's just beginning to
go from one phase to another, taking
the best from the early phase - the raw
ness, and putting it into more adventurous frameworks. I think the music's
becoming more thoughtful, and a bit more
mellow, but I like to get the audience
into a frame of mind where they're just
dreaming away, when suddenly we hit
them in the head with 10,000 Watts of
pure energy. I think basically it's
dangerous to discuss music, it's very
dangerous to discuss art, because it's a
gut feeling.

The people that come to our gigs are
all very young, and that's what I like
about it, because that means they're
very energetic, and they seem to come to
us because we come up with the energy. I
think The Jam are very energetic...I
just admire people who don't forget
their roots. You know what I mean?

YEAH, BUT IN 10 YEARS YOUR AUDIENCE WILL
ALL BE 26-28.

Yeah, but by then there'll be another
movement, and we'll all be boring old
farts.

SO YOU RECKON YOU'LL TURN OUT JUST LIKE
WHAT YOU'RE CRITICISING?

Backstage at The Marquee. Pic: Chris M.

No, I hope to...time overtakes you, and makes you seem like that, but I think certain artists have dealt with it... I wouldn't describe Lou Reed, Johnathan Richman or David Bowie asboring old farts. There are survivors, but very few, because all the survivors have to work really, really hard to stay where they are, and the reason is they have to change all the time.

YOU'VE GOT AN EXTREMELY LOYAL FOLLOWING. HOW COME?

I don't know where they come from, but I just love them. As far as I'm concerned, The Ants fans are the best; they're like a breath of fresh air; they're pure optimism; they're very thoughtful kids; and they're very honest about their feelings. If they wanna bang their head on the floor, they'll do it, but they don't affect anybody else. I mean, 5 of them came to Belgium to see 1 gig!! With people like that, you can't go wrong. They also say they like the band because we change all the time, they say they like the band because we're the only band the press hate. We are, and always will be, an underground group.

DO YOU WANT TO BE FAMOUS AND SUCCESFUL?

I want to be in the position where I can perform to vast numbers of people; I want to be able to produce very, very, very, very high quality music, the way we want it as a band, with production,

presentation, and graphics. I believe graphics are very important - if you get a recordyou look at a nice piece of cardboard that's cost you £4.50, but why not have a black and white picture with a whole lot of stuff inside. Basically, though, fame's a very abstract word - I think everybody will be famous for 15 minutes as Warhol said, but great fame can only be achieved by very, very hard work.

CAN YOU TRY AND EXPLAIN THE WHOLE SEX/ BONDAGE/NAZI THING?

I believe that people have the right to do whatever they want, whenever they want, in the privacy of theor own home, as long as it's mutual between 2 consenting people. Homosexuality, lesbianism, transvestism, rubber fetishism, leather fetishism, fur fetishism - there's 20 kinds of fetishism. When I was at art school, I did a thesis on these taboos, and did a lot of reading, which was very interesting, and I discovered that there was a lot of material left to write.

As for the Nazi thing....The Press & everybody believe I'm a Nazi. I state quite categorically obviously I'm not. I hate the National Front, I detest everything they stand for. I would have to be verystupid to be a Nazi, because I am a roaming gypsy, and my drummer is black, and my manager is Jewish. But as an artist, when one goes on stage and projects a sort of personage as I do - the person sitting here is not the person you see

Matthew, Andy, Adam. Pic: C. Modica.
◁7▷

on stage - one is open to every criticism. I believe any writer, any artist, anybody has the right to choose to draw upon any subject matter, however offensive and use it in his material, as long as he has the guts - and I reiterate this - as long as he has the guts to stick by it 100%; and take the crap the National Press throws at him, and keep going. 'Cos if you don't that shows that you're guilty. What annoys me is people call me a Nazi, and they don't know what Naziism is. My father was involved in the war, and he saw Belsen and told me about it, and I think anybody who gets off on that, or who can promote it, must be very, very ill in the head, and virtually inhuman. To me it's very hurtful, but if people wanna say that about me they can, but I will remember them - I will remember their names.

BUT DIDN'T YOU USED TO HAVE SWASTIKAS OVER THE PLACE?

I have never had a swastika at all, ever, in my entire life. Never (AF blushes all over)

IT WAS THAT PAGE IN RIPPED AND TORN YOU DID WHICH GAVE THAT IMPRESSION.

That page was quite the reverse situation. At the top I put what they've written about me, and then I've tried to give them what they want, to show how ridiculous it is, and then there's a poem at the bottom which is very important. They say I'm into Naziism/decadance/bondage, so I drew a picture to show how stupid that would look. It was just to show how stupid it all is.

WHY DID JORDAN LEAVE?

Jordan left because her career took her to pastures new. After Jubilee, a big director from 20th Century Fox thought she was amazing, and wants to put her in a film with Charles Bronson. So she's

waiting for the script for that, and has had to change her whole image again.

Jubilee was a very enjoyable experience - I think it's the sort of film that's ahead of it's time, and it will take 5 years for people to realise how good it is.

WHAT ARE YOUR RECORDING PLANS FOR THE MOMENT?

The single has to get into the Top 75 for us to do an album. So if this doesn't make it, Friends will probably be the next single, but it's a case of....you have to take it very steadily. There's no point bringing out an album if nobody buys it; and I don't want the singles to be on the album. I want the album to contain 13/14 fun songs, like when you go to a concert; the album's going to be very self-indulgent...it will be very much what we want to do; it will be very unorthodox; it will be very crude; it will be very raw; and very unslick - or slick depending which way you look at it.

If the situation arises where none of our singles make the Top 75, we'll release a bootleg album. You see, it's very trendy to say "Oh yeah, go with a small company", but all they wanna do is make themselves fat and rich and then in a few months they sign to a big company, so in the end they're copping out like everybody else. The thing to do is sign to a big company who've got a lot of dough, and who can promote you, and who can get you albums and concerts and give you the fairest means of communicating your music and your ideas to the people that wanna see you. And that's what us and The Banshees have done - but I don't think they'll manipulate Polydor as well as we'll manipulate Decca. But you have to manipulate them. Why destroy something when you can destroy it from the inside? The way to kill something is to get inside and cause an awful lot of havoc.

HOW LONG DO YOU RECKON THE GROUP WILL KEEP GOING?

Oh I envisage lots of albums...we've already got three albums kind of recorded - 26 tracks. I think the band will go on as long as we can keep it fresh and interesting.

All the Ants fans are very young - I've never met one older than 17, and they all design their own clothes. We like doing the small clubs, because we know the kids can see. You're my bread & butter, all your mates, and the kids in your class...

They're the people I'm thinking about when I write a song.

Anthony Fletcher

Backstage again: Pic: C.M.

setting the standards with The JAM

Anyone chancing accross the summer issue of New York's premier fanzine - NY Rocker - would find a small story in the centre pages to the effect of:-

PETER FRAMPTON WANTS TO JOIN THE JAM. He has said "I think my music is totally boring - it's all pretty boy stuff that I've been doing for years. I mean - 7 million LP's. I can't see how the public falls for it. I want to join a new wave band, and The Jam are where it's at. Paul Weller replied "He's just a rich old fart. At the audition he just couldn't keep up with us - even if he cut his hair we wouldn't let him join."

Unfortunately, the story's not true. At least, Paul Weller knows nothing about it. But it shows where The Jam's strength really lies - heavy, strong, fast rock and roll, in the age-old tradition; words that have meanings, with personal feelings included; and always delivered with incredible venom; always in contact -never sitting on the money; and probably most important of all - never lazy. By this Christmas The Jam will have completed 7 sets of dates (6 at the least) in 12 months - from sets

of 4 & 5 to 2 major British tours and one in America.

"We just don't like being lazy really" muses Paul Weller. "A lot of bands don't do much, just a couple of major tours a year, and that's their lot...I just think it's nice to put in a few gigs here and there."

He's speaking from the RAK Studios in North London, where The Jam have been recording their third LP (in 18 months), set for October 20th release. All the backing tracks have been done, and Paul's been in on his own, adding overdubs on guitar and piano. The Jam have moved studios yet again for this LP, and are pretty content with this one - more space, better accoustics and...a 24-track studio! The production is the same - Vic Smith and Chris Parry - and the studio has a kind of family atmosphere, with rarely more than 5 people there. Paul asks me what I thought of Reading, and my answer is I thought there was too much aggro, Sham were pretty poor, and The Jam were great, but...uneasy. Why?

"Oh, it's nothing to do with the crowds or anything. It's just like the sound problems on stage - it was such a bad sound we couldn't hear each other. It's just like trying to guess what the other 2 are playing."

Well, it was rather odd - The Jam were headlining and yet were the only group with sound problems. It meant a couple of mis-placed verses (Standards), an absent solo (News Of The World) and even-

Paul Weller in the studio.
Pic: Anthony Fletcher

▶▶ POSITIVE ◀◀

—10—

tually (Here Comes The Weekend) a
smashed guitar - £400 broken right
down the middle. What about the
claim he was encouraging violence?

"Well, I didn't mean it to encourage violence, I just got annoyed with
it. Everyone gets frustrated and
aggressive, and I'd sooner take my
aggression out on a guitar or something, than on a person."

And so, from Reading, THE JAM's most
important date so far, to the found-
ings. You all went to the same school
in Woking, didn't you?

"Yeah, we did, but it sort of started after school. I vaguely knew Rick
at school, but it mainly happened
after we all left. There used to be 4
of us - I played bass, and we had a
keyboard player for a couple of months.
I suppose The Jam in all different
forms has been going since I was 14,
but as the three of us we've been going
about 3½ years."

What type of gigs did you used to
play?

"Anything and everything. Anything
we could get hold of. Mainly it was
just around Woking - like little social
clubs and youth clubs."

When did you start doing London gigs?

"I dunno really. I suppose it was
about 2 years ago. But when I say we
were doing London gigs, we were getting
a gig every 3 months or so."

What sort of places were they?

"Just boozers, like The Greyhound in
Fulham, Hope And Anchor, those sort of
places. There was no real movement or
anything then - it was just people either liked the band or they didn't."

What sort of songs were you playing?

"Sort of r'n'b really, and Motown."
Did you have anyoriginals?

"A couple, stuff like Nonstop Dancing."

Did you have any reasons for starting
a group?

"I dunno, it was just an alternative
for not working at the time.

I wasn't very academic at school."

The Jam have always been distinguished by their mod clothes, Rickenbacker
guitars and Vox Amps. So, obvious
question, why do you wear all the mod
gear?

"Well, it's difficult for me to explain without sounding pretencious, but
I've been wearing this sort of stuff

for years."

What, since a school kid?

"Well, no, I suppose in the last 3
years. It's just something I've picked
up on, and I can't really explain it.
There's just some reason I'm really
related to it. I bought a scooter and
done the whole works. It was just like
my own private fantasy. Everybody thought I was fucking mad in Woking, but
it was just something for me to do. I
mean, at the time, I really wanted
something like the punk movement to
come along, with, like, everyone playing to kids your own age. Up until then
we were just playing to, like, 40-year
old hippies, which I've got nothing
against, but I needed something to relate to."

So with that cue from Paul - The Punk
Movement. What's your thoughts on it?
Do you think The Jam are relevant?

"Well I'm a little adverse to using
the actual word 'punk', but as regards
the movement, we was in at the foundat-
ions of it, we was in at the beginning,
I don't care what anyone says. We were
the first, if you want to call it 'punk'
band, to get on Top Of The Pops anyway,
with In The City. And that opened up the
door for other bands with airplay.

"People have always tended to put us
outside of that, and maybe we have ourselves in a way, but we mainly did that
sort of thing because we didn't want

Bruce Foxton, Rick Buckler, Paul Weller

⏵⏵ Direction ⏴⏴

⏵ 11 ⏴

to become known as a punk band. We were jus The Jam -it's not rock'n'roll, it's not punk rock, it's The Jam, it's Jam music."

Do you see yourself as a punk?

"I dunno, I suppose I identify with the attitude I mean that's what I really latched onto. Like when I was down the 100 Club for the first time, it was a really great atmosphere.

"Of course, it's changed a lot now", he adds.

That tac is taken up again when we are discussing the In The City LP, which turns out to be the most interesting part of our conversation. I put forward the argument that how could a kid from a Woking estate get up and sing 'In The City'?

"Well, if you read the lyrics properly it doesn't say that I'm from the city, and I'm singing about London."

OK then - 'In The City there's a thousand things I wanna say to you'.

"Well the song was more about imagery really. It was just a case of wgen I did go to London, and I saw these things happening, like the punk thing was just starting to happen, it just sort of inspired me a lot, and I knew there was going to be a real change in music, which in a way there was and in a way there wasn't. It's come to a sort of paradox really - it started off OK, but I don't know, it just sort of got fucked up somewhere along the line."

But you don't reckon that's going to affect The Jam?

"No, I don't think it's going to affect any of the real good bands now, because...The Jam are The Jam and they play Jam music. And The Clash etc."

So you don t want to be compared with any other groups?

"I don't think you can compare the bands really, they're their own thing. I'm talking about only the good bands - all the second and third-rate bands you could probably lump together."

Another argument was how could you sing 'All Around the world I've been looking for new' and 'This is the modern World' when you're so into the '60's stuff?

Paul Weller

"Well, I'm not looking back to the '60's or nothing-there's just things I dig out of the '60's, and I'm only updating them for me own uses. Like these clothes I wear, they're really totally irrelevant-you could say that Teds have become irrelevant, but they dig it - it's culture. I don't care what anyone says about The Jam, and especially me - I'm into what's happening now, and the '60's doesn't really mean a lot to me. I just like the clothes and some of the music."

Last of the common criticisms is your reputation for being arrogant. Would you agree to that?

"No, I don't think so at all. I mean, what they call arrogant is when some reporter says to me "'oo's the greatest band in the world?" and I say "We are" - I don't call that arrogant...if I didn't think we were the greatest band in the world, I wouldn't be in the group..."

in performance, I reckon The Jam match up to any of the '60s greats. Foxton and Buckler are a faultless rhythm section; Weller and Foxton are possibly the greatest vocal partnership since Lennon/McCartney and the Davies brothers; and as for Paul Weller's guitar playing, his rhythm arsenal is so complete I can even forgive him for calling Hendrix "shit".

In The City (LP) was released on May 13 1977; less than 6 months later The Modern World came out. Not suprisingly, it was criticised for being 'too soon' 'not enough good songs' 'bad production' 'nothing new' etc etc. The real fact is, it demolished In The City and, in my opinion, is the best LP from the last 5 years. And that's not just me - 90% of the people I know who've heard or got the LP reckon it's an all-time classic. From the raucous Standards, Combine & In The Street Today, through the ultimate 3-minute wonders of London Girl, Modern World & Here Comes The Weekend to the vividly emotional Life From A Window, Tonight At Noon and I Need You, the LP is a joy to behold. And yet, it was a failure chartwise-something I'll never understand. Obviously, Paul Weller was disappointed: "Oh yeah, I thought we were going to have a Top 5 LP"

So what do you think happened?

"A lot of things really...Bad marketing-it was released at the wrong time - you had all the Christmas records like The Smurfs and The Wombles

ↇ reaction ↄ

◁12▷

Greatest Hits". Slightly wrong facts, but the LP was reviewed with all the Christmas records, from ELO, Eric Clapton & Queen to the Sex Pistols - although I can't see that this LP will be any better off in this respect. There was a vague concept - "the forces in society today and all that mad intellectual stuff" - but it was never properly arranged. No matter, one day you'll have to admit 'Modern World' was a hidden classic - why not get it now so you don't feel an idiot later?

Bruce Foxton

The talk moves onto concerts. Paul explains how on the technical side of things he's never happy. Does he prefer the small clubs?

"I don't know - as long as there's an atmosphere at a gig it doesn't matter, I think."

Well, would you play Hammersmith again?

"I wouldn't like to, no - after the last Hammersmith I said I never want to play that place again. But it's okay making a statement like that, and I'd like to stick to it, but there's nowhere else to fucking play in London - at least not that capacity. It's really difficult, unless you do what The Clash did, & play 4 nights at The Music Machine, which I don't really like. It's a bit like a museum-people come and see you night after night."

What about the Marquee, do you like that place?

"Yeah, but it only holds like 500 (700) at the most, and you'd have to do like 3 months there!"

Do you get nervous before you go on stage?

"Yeah, very - once I'm on I'm okay, it's just before - there's times I've spewed up before I've gone on. Usually I keep really straight before I go on stage, but just lately, I've been starting to have a few drinks before I go on stage, and I get into it a bit more - don't get so nervous."

Would you ever play anything like Life From A Window on stage?

"No, I don't think we've got the capabilities of doing it, because you've got, like, accoustic and electric guitar."

But you do Tonight At Noon?

"Yeah, that's easier to get away with. Maybe in time, you know?"

How comes you don't do Modern World live any more. I mean, when you've only done 5 singles....

"Well, really, we're just cheesed off playing it, you know, we've played it so many times. We don't want to get too stale. Like when this new lp comes out, we hope to have a completely new set. I know that it's a danger of all groups to turn into Greatest Hits bands, which I don't wanna do; it's not creative at all-it doesn't get you anywhere."

One thing I've noticed is that on stage or in photos you never smile.

At this he laughs: "I do smile sometimes."

Yeah, you do round here in the studios. But on stage it's always a sort of grimace.

"Er, it's just a tension thing. In one of your reviews you said I act out the tough guy, but I don't mean to, 'cos I'm not a tough guy at all. I suppose I just concentrate a lot, on what's happening and what I'm doing."

The Jam seem to be moving about less and less on stage; has the music got more difficult?

"I don't think more difficult-possibly we're just trying to play it a bit tighter and a bit better. I suppose we do move around less than we used to, and I don't want to lose it, but it's just subconcious - we haven't been planning it at all. Maybe we're getting old!"

In Sounds dated August 12, there was a very 'revealing' article on The Jam, which displayed the group as nervous wrecks, who are failures, and have no good songs left. The bloke I was interviewing was shown to be an un-talkative introvert, who was just worried about being slagged off. Obviously, Paul had quite a bit to say about Mr. Pete Silverton, who wrote the article:-

"I think that geezer got the totally wrong impression-he was a right prat for a start. They do these so-called 'On The Road' things, but their On The Road consists of 1 day travelling with the band, and seeing 1 gig. And like, he spent the whole night trying to score some speed, which I know for a fact, so he didn't see any of the gig anyway. He's just full of shit.

"That's why I didn't give him an interview, because he was a cunt. Like you've come here for a purpose, but all he'd come for was to give us a slating, so that's not very positive. At least you're doing something."

creation

Have you got a message to give?
"Not really - I'm not trying to force anything down anybody's throat - but if people pick up on what I write, and understand what I'm saying, that's a bonus."

Do you reckon you've achieved anything?
"Yeah. Put it this way - if you can get 4000 people into the same place and they're all digging the same thing, then I reckon you've achieved something."

And so onto the new LP. It's title is
ALL MOD CONS   and the tracks are

1.1. All Mod Cons
1.2. To Be Someone (Didn't We Have A Nice Time?)   1.3. Mr. Clean
1.4. David Watts
1.5. The Night
1.6. English Rose
1.7. In The Crowd
2.1. Billy Hunt
2.2. It's Too Bad
2.3. The Place I Love
2.4. Fly
2.5. 'A' Bomb In Wardour Street.
2.6. Down In The Tube Station At Midnight

After an aborted live EP and an unsuccessful attempt at recording the new LP, The Jam have made a definite progression on this LP, into a very interesting position: "I agree that it's got a softer approach than the other two LP's, with stuff like Mr. Clean, but if you'd heard it as we recorded it, there was quite a lot of tension on it. I think it's still there, but the songs are maybe a bit more subtle" And subtle is the only real way of describing it. The album is much more contained and drawn out, but still has the fire and charisma that _is_ The Jam.

All the songs are by Weller, except of course David Watts (old Ray Davies/Kinks song) and The Night (Bruce Foxton) The single David Watts/A-Bomb I won't tell you about - you should all have it. And so to the best tracks - they're the final ones from each side - In The Crowd and Down In The Tube Station.

In The Crowd is very hard to describe-it has a magical flow to it, that is rather like a brush, sweeping all before it. There is a long, strong, fade-out similar to Bricks & Mortar, and the tune just won't leave my head.

Tube Station also has a great tune, and is sung with incredible venom.It tells a really great story alongside a consistent

bass/guitar trick riff, and Foxton chants uniquely during the chorus, which keeps coming back and back, until you don't want it to go. And now it's the new single. What more can I say?

Most Jam fans should know Billy Hunt from the OGWT/In Concert. It's the most trypical Jam song on the LP - pop-orientated, fast, hard and great chord changes. However, it does seem rather influenced by David Watts (although the characters are complete opposites - Watts is the flash man who has everything, and Hunt is the loser-your drinking partner) so why they're doing David Watts as soon as having written Billy Hunt I don't know.

Admittedly, I haven't yet heard the All Mod Cons track, but the title isn't just a 'comment on society'(a mod con is a new and up-to-date fad) but also getting at the new cons of today, very subltlely (that word again). The very vague concept is just of pros + cons of the Modern World, which explains why both the singles are on it. And the LP's also 40 mins long - the last 2 were both only 31.

The Night is very short (1:40) & sharp with Foxton's voice taking on a distinctive tone, until there's a sudden 'Goodnight' and it's over ...And then comes English Rose, the only dissappointment. It's just Weller and acoustic guitar, & although no way is it bad, it just isn't The Jam. Maybe later on, but not when you're only 20.

To Be Someone and Place I Love I keep grouping together - the songs have the same set-up, lacking the normal ferocity & speed of Jam songs, but replacing them in their own special way. Like the lyrics of To Be Someone:-
To Be Someone must be a wonderful thing,
A famous footballer or rock singer
Or a big film star-ye I think I'd like that
...Getting drugged up with my trendy friends
    They really dig me man and I dig them
And the bread I spend -
    -like my fame - is quickly
                diminished
So there's no more swimming
    in a guitar-shaped pool,
No more reporters at my beck
    and call/ No more cocaine,
now it's only ground chalk,
No more taxis now I'll have
    to walk........
            It's Too Bad is
very much a pop song, whereas
Mr. Clean is very like Away
From The Numbers in approach-
it snarls, bounces & attacks.
    Which leaves Fly-very odd.
Again it runs smoothly, with

⋙ negaтive ⋘
⊲14⊳

Continued on Page 23

JAM CONTINUED FROM PAGE 14

nice harmonies, but the piece never set-
tles into 1 mood/mould. I would suspect
it's the first of Weller's attempts at
writing many tunes into one song, as he
said he wanted to do.

I need more listening to the record to
say how it really compares with the othe
two, but certainly, The Jam are not heading up a musical cul-de-sac, they're already exploring new, unused areas. The LP
really is unlike anything I've heard before (it could just be ahead of it's time
- which leaves it up to you whether you
like it or not.

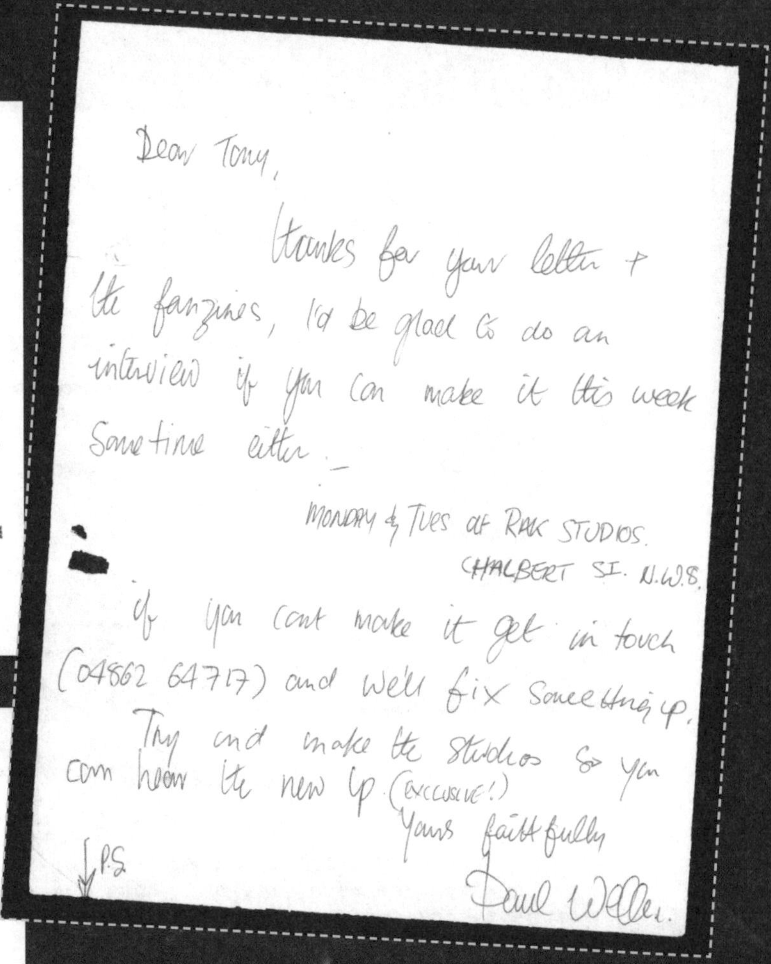

JAM

I only disagree with Paul Weller in one
part of our conversation - the connection
with The Who. Paul reckons they're not his
favourite group, and that the papers started it. But The Jam have a lot in common
with The Who, and it stretches further
than the songs and the fact they used to
do Who oldies, but in the whole set-up -
Weller plays his guitar like Pete Townshend used to (the back of the In The City
shows him identical to the famous Who poster); the chord progressions are similar;
the Union Jacks on the amps (like the
tapes on the jumpers) is an old WHo trick
and most important of all, The Jam are developing just like The Who did. They've
already got piano and softer, more detailed tracks,and much as Weller hates The
way The Who have turned out, I reckon
they're going to turn out similar to
that. And I don't think that's a badpoint.
I don't know what Paul Weller will be
doing in 14 years, but it may well be, a
Jam By Numbers. And sorry Paul, but the
comparisons are there.

And to end:-
Do you want to be really succesful?
"I don't know; it depends what you mean
by really succesful. I don't want to sell
my soul."

Well, a no. 1 hit?
"I don't think I'd like a no. 1 single;
I wouldn't mind a no. 1 LP. I think a no.
1 single would be a bit scary, 'cos you've
always got to follow it up. I want to keep
my freedom, like releasing what we want,
when we want; whereas if you do get a no.1
you really are stuck, you've got to follow
it."

But would you want to be remembered in
the future?
"Yeah, of course.
I think everyone wants to be remembered
in the future."

Anthony Fletcher

Dear Tony,

Thanks for your letter +
the fanzines, I'd be glad to do an
interview if you can make it this week
Sometime either.

MONDAY & TUES at RAK STUDIOS.
CHALBERT ST. N.W.8.

If you can't make it get in touch
(04862 64717) and we'll fix something up.

Try and make the studios so you
can hear the new LP (EXCLUSIVE!)

Yours faithfully
Paul Weller.

P.S

THE JOHN PEEL INTERVIEW

(What else can we say ?)

From 10:00 until 12:00 every evening Monday to Friday, JOHN PEEL is on Radio 1. He plays new-wave, reggae, punk, rock and folk; he does not play pop, disco or jazz. Why not give him a listen? Or will you go on listening to Blackburn and Capital Radio because you think it's 'in'? Well, just listen once, and then make up your mind.

I think that's clear enough.

Q: What did you think of our magazines?
A: Well, I haven't read 'em yet because I only got them last night, but I think that just the idea of them is very good - the more magazines and record labels the better really. Anything which is an alternative to the big newspapers and so on I think is a good thing.
Q: How long has your show been going out?
A: I've been doing programmes for Radio 1 for 11 years now, it's been it's current time and length for 18 months or so, before that it was just an hour a night for about a year.
Q: Does it go out live all five nights a week?
A: No, wednesday is always pre-recorded so I can have a bit of time at home.
Q: Whereabouts do you live?
A: I live in Suffolk, out near Ipswich
Q: Isn't it inconvenient travelling all this way and back?
A: It's very inconvenient, but I'd sooner live in the country, I don't like London much , I'm not a Londoner.
Q: What would happen if you got caught in a traffic jam and couldn't make it in time?
A: I always make sure I'm not. Actually, I admit I was nearly caught on Monday in the Bank Holiday traffic, but I'm the kind of bloke who arrives

very early for everything.
Q: Have you ever considered retiring?
A: Not really, no. Obviously, if the time came when I wasn't enjoying it, I'd have to really, I couldn't fake it - I couldn't go on the air and be a kind of 'groovy DJ', I do it, just because I like doing it - obviously they pay me well!
Q: If - and I hope it won't be for a long time yet - you do consider retiring, who do you think could take over as succesfully?
A: I don't know really, 'cause obviously I'm a DJ for a different reason than the rest of 'em - the majority aren't really interested in the music. Some of them are - Kid Jensen listens to records quite a but - but I think generally speaking there wouldn't be anyone who'd take such a wide interest in it. I collect records, that's my main interest - that and football are the things that I'm most interested in in the world really.
Q: How do you get your sessions?
A: Well, they come about in a lot of different ways - sometimes we go out and see a band playing in a club, and we ask them if they'll do one for the show. More often than not, we hear a demo tape or first single and we think "Oh, that's great", get in touch with

them and say "Will you do a session for us?" I'm the one who chooses what sessions to have.

Q: Who are your favourite group or groups?

A: I don't actually have favourites very much, they tend to change with my mood - I could come up with a list of about 25 that were me favourites, but I haven't got an altogether favourite.

Q: Have there ever been records you weren't allowed to play because of their lyrics - not including swearing?

A: Well the BBC doesn't often ban records outright, you just know that there are certain records that, if you played 'em, it would get complaints, and there are certain things like this er, 'Dave Goodman And Friends' single, and a song by The Angelic Upstarts, which are both about Liddle Towers, and as the case is

LIDDLE TOWERS was a man arrested for being 'drunk and disorderly' - he later died from injuries given to him while in custody. The amazing bit is - the inquest jury came up with a verdict of Justifiable Homicide!!!! But how come Capitol played the record?!

'subjudice' at the moment, they're illegal to broadcast for the time being.

Q: A couple of nights ago you played Anarchy by The Pistols - I though it'd been banned in the UK, I've certainly never heard it on the Radio before.

A: Well, I've played it quite a few times actually - I've played God Save The Queen quite a few times as well. As I say, the BBC rarely bans records outright, but the thing is, you know that if you get a record with a very loud 'fuck' in it, or something like that, it's not going to offend me, it's not going to offend you, it's not going to offend most of the people listening, but there are people who listen to the radio in order to be offended so that they can phone or write in to complain, but the BBC is answerable to the public, so you just have to play records at your own discretion really.

Q: Have you ever been threatened not to play a certain type of music, eg reggae by the NF?

A: No - well, you get the balmy letter; playing Irish music is seen by some as being a political statement -

I play a bit of Irish traditional music which I like. I just go ahead and play whatever records I wanna really.

Q: Have you ever had a session from The Sex Pistols?

A: No, we never did, by the time we did get around to asking them, they were too big to do one.

Q: ...The Clash?

A: We tried to get one from The Clash - we actually got them into the studios, but they were a bit out of it (drunk?) and they couldn't record at all.

Q: ...X-Ray Spex?

A: Oh yeah, we've had X-Ray Spex.

Q: ...Ultravox!?

A: Er, no we haven't had Ultravox yet actually - I haven't been extremely convinced by them, I must admit.

Q: What did you think of Jimmy Pursey's behaviour at Reading? - his so-called 'fans' ruined The Automatic's set, concussed the New Hearts' guitarist and invaded the stage. He's always going on about how he's against violence, and what does he say when he comes on stage? - "Thankyou to the worlds' greatest fans", - I think he's a lying hypocrite.

A: Yeah, well, I must admit I was a bit dissapointed with it, it's a bit like Tommy Docherty when he was at Manchester United, he was always saying "Oh, we've got the best fand in the world" and this is just after they've eaten the referee or something like this. It seems to me that he can only control his fans if he does what they want him to do - so really, the fans are controlling him rather than the other way around, and I think that's a pity - I like Jim, I think he's a nice bloke, but he's very confused at the moment - I don't think he knows what's going on.

And that's it.

Ray Hoyle

sorry about the mess, **ULTRAVOX** continued but......
alight - Frozen Ones & Fear In The Western World from Ha!Ha!Ha, and Wide Boys, Wild Beautiful And Damned, and especially Sat'day Night from >>>Ultravox! It seemed they'd do the latter for an encore, but no, it was another new one, Someone Else's Clothes.

We're not just writing about some boring or plain silly group, we're writing about a group who sing every kind of song there is. So please take interest, because the group are defenitely worth seeing, but if they could just revise their set, they will become the group to see.

Anthony Fletcher
& Ray Hoyle

DON'T FORGET - 10-12 pm Monday - Friday.

OVERSPILLS

Every group in the country must have envied THE REZILLOS around the start of August. They came from being just another band to almost the hottest name around, via Can't Stand The Rezillos LP and Top Of The Pops single. It seemed like every magzine you picked up had interviews - Zigzag, NME, In The City, Virgin's Blank Space (all in August) and loads more, as well as interviews on loads of local radios. Every DJ seemed to be playing their stuff, from Radio 1's John Peel through Mike Allen, Peter Young and Nicky Horne on Capital. The result of course - a Top 20 LP and...yes, the single got the vital push and was actually on Top Of The Pops. It was great seeing Peter 'I'm-A-Prat' Powell introducing it as

"named after the great TV show", when if he'd looked at the lyrics:-

We're not going to write a tribute to KEITH MOON, because it wouldn't do him justice. He was always in the handful of the world's best drummers, and was maybe rocks most extravagant character. All we can do is relay a quote from Roger Daltrey in Sounds a couple of weeks before he died. It could so easily have been said by Keith Moon:- what a great life. I'm a shit from Shepherds Bush, love a street kid, a gang member probably would have been in the nick. All my other mates have been in and out of nick like yo-yos. I've got three other musicians who are probably the best rock and roll band there ever will be — what a great life. Shit, if I go tomorrow I'll have had a wonderful time."

Does it matter
What is shown
Just as long as everyone knows,
What is selling - what to buy
The stock market for your Hi-Fi.

Alright
Hold tight   - so you make the grade
Just wait - to the buck you made
        - you've been rated for
        constipated peak viewing time

Just like to pass on word of a group called BACK NUMBERS. They were a 5-piece, but are now reduced to 4 in the shape of drums, bass, guitar and vocals/occasional guitar. A London New-Wavish group, they are now moving into their own identity, with hand-written stuff like Walk, and pretty great cover versions of The Clash's 'Capital Radio' and the standard 'Slow Down'. Check 'em out - they're worth a chance.

Rezillo Fay Fife:
"I like it, I like it!"

Whereas the Sex Pistols and Damned got huge obituaries in the music press when they split up, noone seemed to notice the end of BE-BOP DELUXE, so here's to make amends:-

Be-Bop Deluxe were led by guitar hero Bill Nelson, and had a very unique sound in the 'medium wave' (aren't these titles ridiculous?) spectrum. Nelson wrote very poetic lyrics, as well as singing and playing various instruments, and highlighted each song by guitar works, which soon got him recognised. All 7 of their LP's were connected with music/guitars/ their songs, and all had the lyrics. The first of these was Axe Victim in 1974. The group of 3 only lasted one LP, and with Futurama, album 2, the group's firm line-up and sound began to take shape. Unfortunately, critical acclaim didn't help sales.

'76 was their biggest year. They released Sunburst Finish, a Top album, yielding their only hit single Ships In The Night. The LP is regarded as their best, with epic tracks like Fair Exchange and Sleep That Burns. With a fixed line-up of Bill Nelson - vocals, guitars; Simon Fox - percussion; Andrew Clark - keyboards; and Charlie Tumahai - bass, they stormed into a sell-out British tour. '76 also saw Modern Music, not quite as great A live LP - Live! In The Air-Age was released in '77, but it didn't turn out to the Be-Bop sampler it should have been. Early '78 saw a completely new approach with Drastic Plastic and Nelson announced the split in August The last, final album is The Best And The Rest Of Be-Bop Deluxe, out now, a double album unfortunately with a Greatest Hits LP compelling Be-Bop fans to buy it for the other LP which the band finished just before splitting.

If you missed out on Be-Bop Deluxe, you missed out on a lot of good music.

FROM THE NOTEBOOKS

COPIES STAPLED

Date	No.				
11/10/18	177	177	7/10	46	735
14/10	63	240	4/1/80	20	755
15/10	18	258	by 6/4	17	772
19/10	70	328	28/5	10	782
20/10	10	338	30/8	15	797
23/10	51	389	10/11	10	807
2/11	27	416	22/11	15	822
3/11	12	428	9/1/81	25	847
4/11	22	450	10/1/81	10	857
5/11	15	465	10/1/81	20	877
13/11	7	472	11/1	10	887
16/11	5	477	12/1	10	897
17/11	38	515	13/1	17	914
20/11	23	538	THAT'S IT		
25/11	17	555			
27/11	25	580			
2/12	40	620			
4/12	21	641			
30/5/79	18	659			
	30	669			

JAMMING SHOPS

Date	No.	Shop	Price	Paid/sor
9/10	10	ROUGH TRADE	20p	P
9/10	11	VIRGIN (Marble Arch)	20p	P
9/10	10	SHILLINGS	18p	SOR/
10/10	10	STREATHAM NEWSAGENT	18p	SOR/
10/10	16	STREATHAM NEWSAGENT	20p	SOR/
11/10	10	PHOENIX	25%	P
11/10	5	ROCK ON STALL	18p	SOR/
11/10	3	HONEST JON'S (Monmouth St.)	19p	P
12/10	15	COMPENDIUM	20p	SOR/
12/10	15	VIRGIN WAREHOUSE	20p	SOR/
12/10	10	SMALL WONDER	20p	P
15/10	7	PAGE 43	20p	SOR/
19/10	10	COUNTERPOINT	25p	SOR/
20/10	50	PHOENIX	12½p	SOR/
24/10	18	VIRGIN WAREHOUSE	20p	P
21/10	10	VIRGIN MARBLE ARCH	20p	P
22/10	10	JEFF'S LOCAL		SOR/
24/10	10	NEWSAGENT OPP BELAIR	17p	SOR/
24/10	3	HONEST JON'S (Monmouth St.)	19p	P
24/10	10	ROUGH TRADE	20p	P
1/11	10	VIRGIN Oxford Walk	20p	SOR/

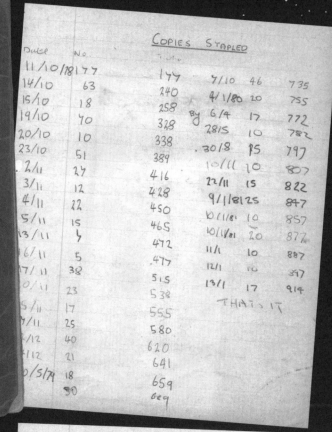

Date	No.	Shop	Price	Paid/sor
1/11	10	VIRGIN Marble Arch	20p	P
1/11	15	VIRGIN Warehouse	20p	P
4/11	5	HONEST JON'S Golborne Road	20p	P
9/11	10	COUNTERPOINT	25p	SOR/
14/11	25	PHOENIX	15p	SOR/
18/11	11	DISC JOCKEY	20p	SOP
20/11	10	WEBSTERS		SOR/
21/11	10	VIRGIN Warehouse	20p	P
22/11	12	SMALL WONDER	20p	P
23/11	10	VIRGIN Oxford Walk	20p	SOR/
24/11	4	COMPENDIUM	20p	SOR/
25/11	5	HONEST JON'S (Golborne Road)	20p	P
18/1	10	BEGGARS BANQUET (Richmond)	20p	P
14/1	3	HONEST JON'S (Golborne Road)	20p	P
16/3	10	ROUGH TRADE	20p	P
14/4	5	5TH COLUMN	25p	SOR/
5/5	10	ROUGH TRADE	20p	SOR/
24/5	2	HONEST JON'S (Golborne Road)	20p	P
24/5	9	ROUGH TRADE	20p	P
17/6	3	5TH COLUMN	25p	SOR/
27/7	5	5TH COLUMN	25p	SOR/
25/7	4	ROUGH TRADE	20p	P

From Issue 5 through Issue 12, I used a liberated school exercise book to track the number of magazines collated and stapled, distributed and sold, along with the printer's bills. It would evidently be January 1981 before the last copies of Issue 5 were gathered off my floor – and then only because we were moving house.

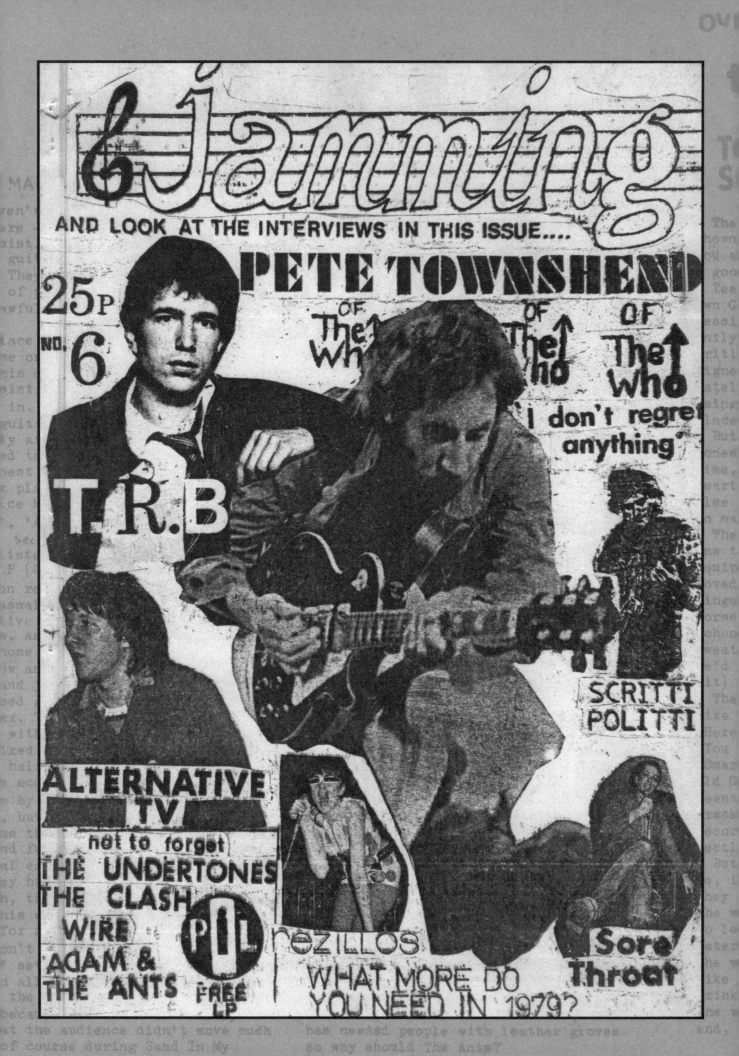

jamming

AND LOOK AT THE INTERVIEWS IN THIS ISSUE....

PETE TOWNSHEND

25P NO. 6

OF The Who   OF The Who   OF The Who

"I don't regret anything"

T.R.B

SCRITTI POLITTI

ALTERNATIVE TV

not to forget
THE UNDERTONES
THE CLASH
WIRE
ADAM &
THE ANTS

PIL FREE LP

rezillos

WHAT MORE DO YOU NEED IN 1979?

Sore Throat

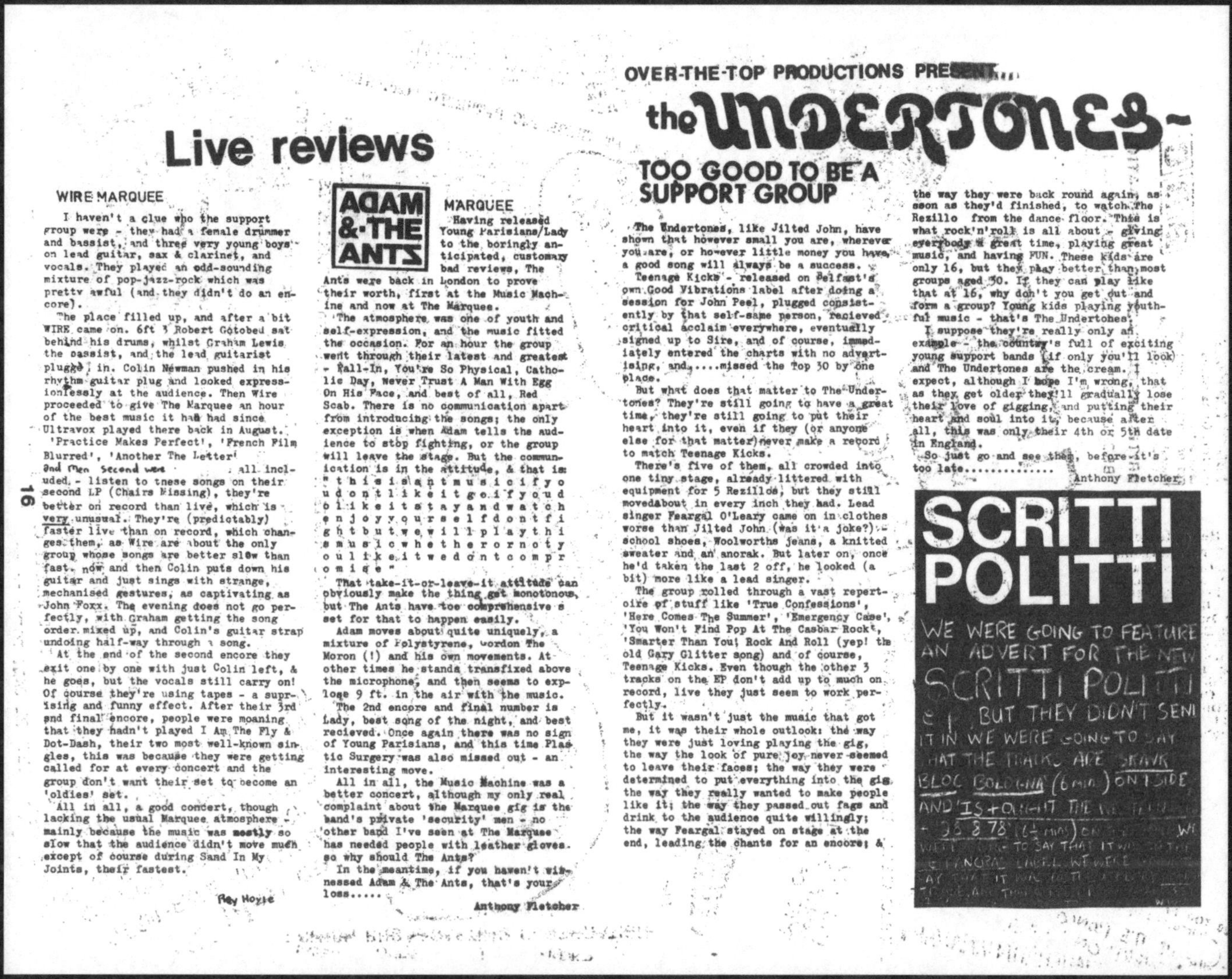

Live reviews

WIRE MARQUEE

I haven't a clue who the support group were - they had a female drummer and bassist, and three very young boys on lead guitar, sax & clarinet, and vocals. They played an odd-sounding mixture of pop-jazz-rock which was pretty awful (and they didn't do an encore).

The place filled up, and after a bit WIRE came on. 6ft 3 Robert Gotobed sat behind his drums, whilst Graham Lewis the bassist, and the lead guitarist plugged in. Colin Newman pushed in his rhythm guitar plug and looked expressionlessly at the audience. Then Wire proceeded to give The Marquee an hour of the best music it has had since Ultravox played there back in August.

'Practice Makes Perfect', 'French Film Blurred', 'Another The Letter' and then Second Wire ... all included - listen to these songs on their second LP (Chairs Missing), they're better on record than live, which is very unusual. They're (predictably) faster live than on record, which changes them, as Wire are about the only group whose songs are better live than fast, now and then Colin puts down his guitar and just sings with strange, mechanised gestures, as captivating as John Foxx. The evening does not go perfectly, with Graham getting the song order mixed up, and Colin's guitar strap undoing half-way through a song.

At the end of the second encore they exit one by one with just Colin left, & he goes, but the vocals still carry on! Of course they're using tapes - a suprising and funny effect. After their 3rd and final encore, people were moaning that they hadn't played I Am The Fly & Dot-Dash, their two most well-known singles, this was because they were getting called for at every concert and the group don't want their set to become an 'oldies' set.

All in all, a good concert, though lacking the usual Marquee atmosphere - mainly because the music was mostly so slow that the audience didn't move much except of course during Sand In My Joints, their fastest.

Ray Hoyle

ADAM & THE ANTS — MARQUEE

Having released Young Parisians/Lady to the boringly anticipated, customary bad reviews, The Ants were back in London to prove their worth, first at the Music Machine and now at The Marquee.

The atmosphere was one of youth and self-expression, and the music fitted the occasion. For an hour the group went through their latest and greatest - Fall-In, You're So Physical, Catholic Day, Never Trust A Man With Egg On His Face, and best of all, Red Scab. There is no communication apart from introducing the songs; the only exception is when Adam tells the audience to stop fighting, or the group will leave the stage. But the communication is in the attitude, & that is:

"thisisn'tmusicifyoudontlikeitgoifyoudlikeitstayandwatchenjoyyourselfdontfightbutwewillplaythismusicwhetherornotyoulikeitwedontcompromise"

That take-it-or-leave-it attitude can obviously make the thing get monotonous, but The Ants have too comprehensive a set for that to happen easily.

Adam moves about quite uniquely, a mixture of Polystyrene, Gordon The Moron (!) and his own movements. At other times he stands transfixed above the microphone, and then seems to explode 9 ft. in the air with the music.

The 2nd encore and final number is Lady, best song of the night, and best recieved. Once again there was no sign of Young Parisians, and this time Plastic Surgery was also missed out - an interesting move.

All in all, the Music Machine was a better concert, although my only real complaint about the Marquee gig is the band's private 'security' men - no other band I've seen at The Marquee has needed people with leather gloves, so why should The Ants?

In the meantime, if you haven't witnessed Adam & The Ants, that's your loss.....

Anthony Fletcher

OVER-THE-TOP PRODUCTIONS PRESENT...

the UNDERTONES –
TOO GOOD TO BE A SUPPORT GROUP

The Undertones, like Jilted John, have shown that however small you are, wherever you are, or however little money you have, a good song will always be a success.

Teenage Kicks - released on Belfast's own Good Vibrations label after doing a session for John Peel, plugged consistently by that self-same person, recieved critical acclaim everywhere, eventually signed up to Sire, and of course, immediately entered the charts with no advertising, and....missed the Top 30 by one place.

But what does that matter to The Undertones? They're still going to have a great time, they're still going to put their heart into it, even if they (or anyone else for that matter) never make a record to match Teenage Kicks.

There's five of them, all crowded into one tiny stage, already littered with equipment for 5 Rezillos, but they still movedabout in every inch they had. Lead singer Feargal O'Leary came on in clothes worse than Jilted John (was it a joke?) - school shoes, Woolworths jeans, a knitted sweater and an anorak. But later on, once he'd taken the last 2 off, he looked (a bit) more like a lead singer.

The group rolled through a vast repertoire of stuff like 'True Confessions', 'Here Comes The Summer', 'Emergency Case', 'You Won't Find Pop At The Casbah Rock', 'Smarter Than You; Rock And Roll (yep! the old Gary Glitter song) and of course, Teenage Kicks. Even though the other 3 tracks on the EP don't add up to much on record live they just seem to work perfectly.

But it wasn't just the music that got me, it was their whole outlook: the way they were just loving playing the gig, the way the look of pure joy never seemed to leave their faces; the way they were determined to put everything into the gig, the way they really wanted to make people like it; the way they passed out fags and drink to the audience quite willingly; the way Feargal stayed on stage at the end, leading the chants for an encore; &

the way they were back round again, as soon as they'd finished, to watch The Rezillos from the dance-floor. This is what rock'n'roll is all about - giving everybody a great time, playing great music, and having FUN. These kids are only 16, but they play better than most groups aged 30. If they can play like that at 16, why don't you get out and form a group? Young kids playing youthful music - that's The Undertones!

I suppose they're really only an example - the country's full of exciting young support bands (if only you'll look) and The Undertones are the cream. I expect, although I hope I'm wrong, that as they get older they'll gradually lose their love of gigging, and putting their heart and soul into it, because after all, this was only their 4th or 5th date in England.

So just go and see them, before it's too late.............
Anthony Fletcher

SCRITTI POLITTI

WE WERE GOING TO FEATURE AN ADVERT FOR THE NEW SCRITTI POLITTI E.P. BUT THEY DIDN'T SEND IT IN. WE WERE GOING TO SAY THAT THE TRACKS ARE SKANK BLOC BOLOGNA (6 min.) ON 1 SIDE AND 'IS+ONIGHT' THE ... [illegible handwritten text]

Issue 5 had come in for considerable, and arguably deserved, criticism from the 'real' fanzines for its conventional approach. Ray Hoyle chose to wage a very public war on our sudden rivals, while contrarily insisting on imitating their cut-and-paste designs. Our attempts at visual street cred might have worked had we too been using Xerox machines, but proved disastrous when the printers, secured through a distant friend from the football terraces, half-toned entire pages without consultation, rendering them grey, depressing and largely unreadable. Those pages included the front cover, which I had haphazardly slapped together due to Jeff Carrigan's ill-timed unavailabilty; to save face, we photocopied the original cover artwork and stapled it over what was meant to have been a professional print job. To this day, I can't look at that cover without feeling sick.

…Nor, apparently, could most of the fanzine buying public. The majority of the insanely optimistic print run of 1,500 copies took up permanent residence on my bedroom floor.

Nonetheless, the content appears to have endured. Ray Hoyle finagled an interview with my original idol Pete Townshend, but knew better than to present it after the fact; four of us descended on Eel Pie in all, where I did most of the talking on *Jamming*'s behalf. Tom Robinson finally responded to the questions I had mailed him about a year earlier, while Mark Perry of Alternative TV (and *Sniffin' Glue* fanzine prior to that) agreed to an in-face meeting at first request. And Scritti Politti welcomed a group of us into their dressing room prior to their debut gig, on a legendary Rough Trade bill at the Acklam Hall; for me, it was the start of a beautiful friendship.

Over Christmas, I came to conclude that *Jamming* was very much my own creation, and I told Ray as much. An unpleasant period of neighbourhood harassment followed, which was doubly difficult as I was also enduring some severe bullying at school, including from my original partner in the venture. I was, I'm sure, a horribly precocious little prick at times, but it was a tough period.

According to my obsessively kept notebooks, the final copies were not stapled until May…. of 1982, at which point it transpired that we had been shorted 10 per cent of the promised 1,500 copies. Ah well.

ISSUE #6 12/78

Letraset typesetting was so 1978. **Jeff C.**

Who's there!
AN INTERVIEW WITH PETE TOWNSHEND

We're not going to do a run-down of the history of The Who - most of it is well-known (and if it isn't, we did it in Jamming No.3). The following is a reflection on the 14 years The Who have been going, from the start of the mod revolution to their future plans. There's no need for any inbetween comments, because Pete's answers were very full, and should explain it all. And if, at the end, you still don't understand what makes The Who what they are, then that's your lods.

Drawings: John Gilhooly.
Photos: Ray Hoyle

WHEN DID YOU START PLAYING GUITAR?

When I was about 12 - I got a guitar for Christmas from my terrible grandmother.

AND WHEN DID YOU START WRITING SONGS?

When I was about 16.

WHAT WAS THE FIRST ONE YOU WROTE THAT HAS BEEN RECORDED?

The first song that I ever wrote was actually recorded. It was called 'It Was You' and it was recorded 2 years after I wrote it. by a group called The Naturals. Our first record was with Phillips/Fontana, and I didn't even write the music for that. Our manager wrote the songs for that - that's I Am The Face/Zoot Suit.
  And the first song I wrote after that was I Can't Explain, which I think was about the 3rd song I'd ever written.

WHO CAME UP WITH THE NAME OF THE WHO?

When I was at art school, I shared a flat with a bloke called Peter Barnes, who helped me write a book called The Story Of Tommy, and he came up with the idea - we were sitting about, swapping names around, and he came up with it. We thought it was completely daft at the time, but

he said that sub-editors would like it, you know, the people who write the titles. And they did. And they still do - Who's Who In The Who and Guess Who & all that rubbish. (or Who's there!)

DID YOU HAVE ANY IDEALS ABOUT THE START OF THE GROUP? ANY BIG AMBITIONS?

My original ambition was to be rhythm guitarist - all the bands of that time had a rhythm guitarist and a lead guitarist - and my fascination was rhythm guitar. So when I got the job of lead guitarist - because Roger Daltrey decided he didn't want to be the lead guitarist anymore; he wanted to be singer, I didn't adapt my style at all - I just carried on playing rhythm.

WHAT WERE THOSE EARLY GIGS LIKE THAT WERE SUCH A SUCCESS, LIKE AT THE MARQUEE AND IN THE SUMMER OF '65 AT PLACES LIKE BRIGHTON?

It was amazingly exciting - I can't really explain how exciting it was, it was very glamorous in a way. I used to actually go up to the Marquee on the tube from Ealing Common; and go home on the tube, with my guitar, and it was just a very wierd feeling. After about the second or third week (we had a residency there, on a Tuesday) we managed to pack it out, and we actually managed to build up our own connection of hard core

fans.

The Brighton dates were slightly different, because that was around the time of the Mod-Rocker fights, and The Who wasn't quite so important; it could have been any band. That particular period of our career was very, very exciting - we're talking about possibly the first 3 or 4 months The Who got a record out, and at that particular time we really thought that we were only going to last for about a month. So the excitement was like "We're 'ere now, we're 'ere now, and 'oo knows what might happen in a yearor two", and we really lapped it up.

HOW DID THE SMASHING YOUR GUITAR BIT COME ABOUT?

It's ever so simple. At the time we were very arty, and I was saying things like "We've got to change the face of music, we've got to change the face of society" and all this kind of thing so what I was trying to do was pull off things that would just totally amaze people. I used to bang the guitar on the amplifier, and at this club in Harrow, I used to bang it on the ceiling as well. And one day, I was banging it on the ceiling, and the bloody machine-head fell off. And the people that had been coming week after started to laugh, you know - "ahhha, that'll show him, the flash cunt, jumping all over the satge and pretending he's mad. Now look what's happened to him - he's broken his guitar." So I decided to carry onaand do it - it made me slightly angry and I thought "I'll show 'em", and just completely smashed the guitar up. Then I picked up another guitar taht I had (because I used to have a Rickenbacker 12-string and a Rickenbacker 6-string), and the 6-string got smashed, so I just picked up the 12-string and carried on as if it didn't matter.

Then the next week we arrived, the place was packed, PACKED with people all come to see this lunatic smash his guitar. And not to be out done, of course, Keith Moon smashed his drumkit, Roger started throwing his mike around and that's how it started.

In the end, it turned out to be the most important thing about the band; it really got us through a lot of difficult spots. I can't really say that as musicians we're particularly proud of it,

because I've wrecked a lot of really good guitars - I've wrecked a lot of really shitty guitars as well that've really deserved to be smashed up - but I have wrecked a lot of good guitars. What it's really helped us through is when we've gone abroad to places like France and Germany, people haven't understood the music, they haven't understood what we've been singing about - in the early days - but what they have understood is when we've smashed the gea r up - they go fucking barmy

Also, it's always been a great finale, it was a great way to get loose - if you had a show that you thought wasn't going well, instead of running off the stage and screaming at the sound manager, or going out and getting drunk or in a fight or smashing a car, you completely wreck the stage, and you end up feeling quite happy at the end of it.

HOW DID YOUR CONNECTION WITH POP ART COME ABOUT? YOU WERE SUPPOSED TO HAVE 'CREATED' POP ART....

That was a bit of a scam... the mod fashions of the time were very grey - they were great but they weren't particularly exciting. And one of the problems was, when you took it on stage, it was always a bit shady to look at. And there were bands like The Kinks going on in brocaid jackets and long, flowing hair, and Mick Jagger with silk shirts and that, and we just wanted to fight back, but keep the images fairly mod. The idea of pop art was that you made your own art - you didn't go down Carnaby Street and buy some piece of shit that Lord John's were trying to sell you, you made your own clothes. And we used to do things like dye white jeans green and wear rows of medals. It was getting close to some of the things that have happened in punk, like jewellery & stuff like that. I once went on Top Of The Pops with a lamp shade on me head! Again it was all that thing about shocking people; the way we always imagined it was - Supposing we're on TOTP tonight, and there's a kid sitting there next to his dad, what we want to do is start a fight between the dad and the son. We want the son to say "They're great", and we want the dad to say "They're bloody terrible, give me Frank Sinatra anytime" - that's the kind of thing that we wanted to do. And - obviously just on a musical level -

11

show that we were doing something different; and to annoy people.

WERE YOU SUPRISED AT THE INSTANT SUCCESS OF I CAN'T EXPLAIN?

It wasn't automatic - you know we had bloody good managers. It was really to do with that programme on the telly at the time called Ready Steady Go, and we got on that. We used to have this group of 100 fans, called the 100 faces, and we used to take them around everywhere. And what happened on this occasion was that Ready Steady Go couldn't get an audience for some reason, so my manager said to the producer of the show "Look, I can get you 100 great kids, great dancers, great dressers, just like that" and she was really pleased, because it saved her giving away tickets in the street. So what our manager did was to get our fans to go on as the audience for that week. So they sat there, and Donovan came on, and they all sat there miserably, and Doris Droy came on and they all sat there miserably, and somebody else came on and they all sat there miserably, and The Rolling Stones came on, and they all fell asleep! and then we came on and they all got up and went "Whaaay" and were waving these coloured scarves. And that had a really big effect on the single.

MOST OF THE MOD GROUPS, INCLUDING THE WHO GENERALLY SEEMED TO KEEP OFF POLITICAL LYRICS. DID YOU EVER FEEL THE NEED TO

People try to put us down
Just because we get around
The things they do look awful k
Hope I die before I get old
Why don't you all fade away
And don't try an dic what
'm not trying to cause a b
s talkin' bout my Generation

Talkin' bout My Generation

PETE TOWNSEND

WRITE POLITICAL LYRICS?

Well, as soon as I realised a lot of people were listening to the lyrics I was writing, I started to be concious of "Well, maybe I should be very careful of what I write." For example, Substitute was just a string of words - it wasn't meant to mean anything. And yet people took that song and said "This means so-and-so" and "What Townshend is trying to say is this..." and so I thought I had to be very careful about what I wrote. And I would say that you're right - I would say that I delibarately steered away from politics - it had nothing to do with the music of the day.

But rock has now got to the point where one of the walls you're knocking at is a political wall - it's powerful enough to do that; wheras when we started, people were saying "Well, rock'n'roll's only going to last another year"; the thought that a group like The Who would still be going in another 15 years was prepostuous, because rock'n'roll itself was only going to last another 6 months. So the fact that today a band can be rehearsing in a basement in Brixton next week, and then quoted in a national newspaper the week after just goes to show the power of it.

DO YOU REGRET HAVING WRITTEN THE 'MY GENERATION LYRICS?

No, I don't regret anything.

DO YOU RECKON YOU'VE GOT OLD YET, IN THAT SENSE?

Yeah...I'm one of the few rock'n' roll grown-ups! I think one thing that being in the rock business has taught me is you've got to be honest, otherwise you can't survive. My Generation was written while I was in a flat in Belgravia... Belgravia's where all the Embassy's are, and where all the Lords and Ladies live. And as soon as we made it, our manager bought me a flat, and I moved out of my mums house - which wasn't a bad house - and got a flash American car and a flat in Belgravia. And I was sitting up there in this flat in Belgravia, surrounded by recording equipment and we'd had a couple of hit records, and those were the circumstance I was in when I wrote My Generation. And what I was saying was 'rather than be like those lords and ladies and ambassadors I'd rather die. And I feel very much the same now - if somebosy put me on a rack and said "Listen, either you're gonna become the person that you feel is a right cunt, or we'll kill you", I'd say "Kill me." I mean I don't want to become a member of the National Front, I don't want to become a Lord, I don't want to become any of those things.

12

HOW DID TOMMY COME ABOUT?

What had actually happened was we'd had a string of single hits up until, I think, a record called Dogs. And they'd all been very successful - we were a singles band, that's what we did, that's what I was good at, that's what The Who were good at. It was 'stick-a-single-out-go-on-the-road-into-the-studio-stick a single-out-go-on-the-road- and suddenly it stopped working. And it wasn't because they were bad records, because Magic Bus and I Can See For Miles are two of our best songs, really fucking great singles, and they FLOPPED. And I got scared, I thought we were gonna starve, because we didn't have any money - any money that we'd made we'd smashed up in equipment; we were about £40-50,000 in debt, which was unbelievable And I thought,"Well, the only thing I really know how to do is write singles, but I'm determined to push the band and British rock music a little bit further. I think rock is capable of more than just a string of singles." So I was determined to pull something off, and I used a technique of singles. In other words, everything on Tommy, originally, was a single, and I just strung them togrther. And it worked - it did exactly what I wanted it to; I used the technique that I was good at, and made rock'n'roll do a little bit more.

HAVE ANY OF THE STORIES ABOUT SMASHING HOTEL ROOMS BEEN EXAGGERATED?

No they haven't. Although I think what might have happened is - people used to regard us as completely notorious, and one day in 1967 we smashed a television set - because it didn't work basically - we threw it in the swimming pool, and that was blown out of all proportion until....and, if you're well known for smashing hotel rooms you might as well enjoy doing them. So we used to make an art out of it - Keith in particular was an artist - it was all very calculated. You end up hating the ro.e, and you love it as well. You love it because it leads you to the audience, but you hate it because while you're getting to the audience, you have to go through aeroplanes, hotels, airports, cars, trips, roads, all those things. It's very hard to explain - you spend 6 or 7 weeks never really having anything of your own except what's in a suitcase, and you start to go slightly barmy - there's no question about it. In America, they have these Holiday Inns, which all look completely the same, and you go into the lobby of one and you think "Hold on a minute, we've just travelled 600 miles and IT'S EXACTLY THE SAME. The hotel

13

desk is over there, the furniture's exactly the same, the foods the same, the person behind the bar looks the same, same uniforms; you go into the room and it's exactly the same, and you end up h ting it. So when you actually get off stage, & your energy's up and you have a couple of drinks, it gives you the greatest possible pleasure just to smash that thing up. And you pay dearly - we knew it was going to cost about 1000 dollars every time we did it, but we did it anyway.

DID JOHN & ROGER JOIN IN DOING IT?

John used to sit and laugh; Roger was never really there much; Keith used to do it fairly regularly, and when Keith did i it, I used to feel bound to do it. I'll probably never smash another hotel room in my life now, because half of it was the fact that Keith and I used to do it for one another.

WHY DID YOU START USING SYNTHESIZERS IN YOUR MUSIC?

Mainly frustration - The Who have always had this unwritten rule that we'd never use orchestras (up until the last LP when we broke that) and I wanted to use noises other than just guitars, so I got meself a synthesizer & started mucking about on it.

WHAT WOULD YOU SAY IS THE WHO'S BEST ALBUM?

I don't know - it's very difficult because we haven't actually made that many. I like Quadrophenia a lot because I feel it was quite a successful concept; the best sounding album is Who's Next, but I don't think it's a definitive Who album; I think the most definitive Who album is Who Sell Out - it's got my adverts on it, and stuff like that, a very good album.

WHY DID THINGS START GOING WRONG WITH THE WHO IN THE MID-70'S?

Well we were working too hard on the road, especially in America, and the Tommy film took up a year's time; and I think that's basically it. We've never made enough albums - they've always taken far too long to make. That's not to say that we sit in the studio for hours and hours going "No, a little bit more treble on the drums..." What we do is walk in, say, "Right, let's do this, right, done it, OK....let's play darts," or alternatively "Go home", and

not go back into the studio for months on end.

WOULD YOU AGREE THAT TOMMY YOU CAPTURES THE SPIRIT OF THE WHO AGAIN?

Well, I like it. I'm very pleased we got it done. But that's really for you to say. What do you think?

I THINK IT CAPTURES THE SPIRIT AGAIN. IT'S VERY MUCH A TWO LP TO PAS I DIDN'T QUITE WHO BY THMBERS WAS. I THOUGHT THAT WAS MORE LIKE A LETR TO TOMMY SOLO LP.

Well I think to some extent the definitive Pete Townshend solo LP could also be Quadrophenia. What happened with The Who By Numbers was I got the fucking blame, but it wasn't all my fault. I came up with a lot of material for that LP; and the material that was picked, all seemed to have this fairly bitter quality to it. The whole band seems to be in a mess at that particular time - Roger was very unhapy with the managers and everything. I was unhappy because Roger was unhappy. And I was unhappy because the Tommy film seemed to be turning the band into a bloody machine. We di n't seem to be a rock group anymore. Then I just got overworked, and started to go a bit crackers.

WHAT WERE YOUR REASONS FOR DOING THIS INTERVIEW WITH US?

I've always had, as it were, a totally open-door policy when I'm dealing with anybody that isn't actually through the basic commercial press. I've done every fansine interview that I've been asked to do - I've only been asked to do 3 and I've done them all.

YOU SAY THAT YOU NEVER GO ON STAGE AND ACT. WHO GENERALLY, WHEN YOU SMASH GUITARS ON STAGE IT'S QUITE A TOUGH IMAGE, BUT PEOPLE ARE ALWAYS SUPRISED WHEN THEY SEE YOU ON TV OR HEAR YOU ON THE RADIO BECAUSE YOU'RE A VERY QUIET PERSON.

I think what you've got to realise is you get in a very different frame of mind when you go on stage. I know one thing - it's not showmanship; I can't act aggressive, but i do get aggressive. Then I smash the guitar, i haven't got anything against the guitar, or the floor, I just do it because folks want to see it, it's a part of the act - I do it because it's part of our past as much as anything else.

WHAT ABOUT THE TIMES PEOPLE REALLY WANT SEE YOU SMASH YOUR GUITAR AND YOU DON'T. ANY REASON OR DON'T YOU WANT TO SMASH IT

14

I think that's it. I wouldn't do it if I thought my heart wasn't in it. There have been times when the audience have forced me to do it, by going "smash your guitar, smash your guitar" and I've done it and that's often been when I really have got angry. Particularly when I've got a guitar that I've really liked I've thought "Ah, this is fucking great, if I can get this guitar off the stage in one piece it'll be really useful for the next album. You know, the frets are in the right place, and it's got pick-ups that go on & off.

IS KENNY JONES DRUMMING WITH THE WHO AT THE MOMENT?

He's drumming on the Quadrophenia tracks that we're doing at the moment, yeah. And he's working quite well - he did play some drums on the Tommy soundtrack.

WILL THERE BE ANY CHANCE OF THE WHO PLAYING LIVE AGAIN?

I don't think we'll tour, but we'll probably do some live gigs. We're going to try and do a Who album in March/April next year; I'm getting some material together, but I'm confused as to what's happening. I mean Kenny's obviously there - he's not a Keith Moon by any stretch of the imagination but he's a more formal, good drummer. But I must admit I've lost the urge to play live; I've never gone on the stage and acted, that's one thing I've always been very, very serious about. If I've ever gone on the stage it's because I've wanted to be there. And I haven't got this mad drive to get up and...other people are doing it for me.

WHAT ABOUT THE NUMBER OF PEOPLE WHO WANT TO SEE YOU PLAYING LIVE?

Well....you can't please everybody.

DID JOHNNY ROTTEN OR JIMMY FURSEY END UP STARRING IN QUADROPHENIA?

What happened with them was they both said exactly th same thing. They both said "If you've auditioned that cunt for the same role you're asking me to play I am NOT fucking doing it." So neither of them did it.

WHAT'S HAPPENING AT THE MOMENT WITH NEW LP'S, AND THE FILMS - QUADROPHENIA, THE KIDS ARE ALRIGHT?

The Kids Are Alright has got an LP ial which will come out with the film in Febuary/March.
The Quadrophenia film has got a new album coming out, but that's just a soundtrack album - we've redone Can You See The Real Me, and that's come out pretty good, but I don't think there'll be any new material. And that should come out in the mid summer.
I'm hoping to work on a solo album; an album of demos which'll be about lo albums (!) dating right back to the beginning.
Roger's doing a solo album which we're all working on, which I'm working on and writing for, and which John's going to produce, in the spring. Our priority is obviously at the moment - get the films done, and then hopefully do a Who album to come out next winter.

That doesn't sound much like a group that's been written off for dead in 1979, and two films, and that, after Keith Moon has died.
If The Who are dead, what is life?

Anthony Fletcher

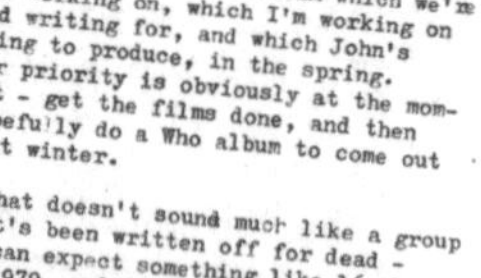

15

2-4-6-8 it's never too late FOR TOM ROBINSON....

JAMMING: Why the Tom Robinson Band?

TOM ROBINSON: Apart from anything else, when I just had the pick-up band with friends helping me out, I was the only member that I knew would be there every night. Also, if I put my name on the front of the band, I could be sure of getting maybe half-a-dozen Cafe Society fans along to the gigs, which, when a group is starting up, is very important to have a nucleus - it's much easier to start with a small nucleus and build it up than start from scratch. Once we'd got a little bit successful in our own right there didn't seem any point in changing our name and confusing shit out of people.

(text within the fist graphic) This has got to be the most dif-ficult inter-view Jamming ever attempt over a writing (when we Issue 1 last pre-After question-arrange a after naires, meeting, letter having nother for ing a-waiting their tape back just NO. 5 CAME OUT. will Well year after first for an interview thought it mike make or 2) we sent it. sending trying to having letter lost, sending a with questions on, that lost, send-questionnaire, TRB to finish tour, recieving a TWO DAYS AFTER the result is considering then All we can do is ions and answers fully, not it is date. So... of the 'never-fanzine' style and lets get on with it......

TOM ROBINSON

J:What are your influences, past and present?

TR:Well, anybody who gets to the age of 29, which I am, and tells you that they haven't been influenced by The Beatles & The Stones & The Kinks & The Who & Bob Dylan are either lying through their teeth or are too naive to realise it. I mean, you can't avoid the mass music of a generation, so all those are influences.

J:From mid-77 you've been providing free badges, stickers and regular bulletins. What were the reasons for this?

TR:When EMI made the stickers we thought we might as well give 'em to everybody else. Same with the badges at first - they gave us 4-5,000 so we gave them away. After them we got another lot so we gave them away as well and after that we had to start paying for them ourselves, so they've suddenly started shrinking in size. The bulletins are very important just to keep people in contact when the band's not touring. I have a private theory that the only things that matter are the group itself & the audience - a band is only as good as it's following, and a band without a following is a useless band.

You should all know TRB were formed in 1977 (January) when Tom left Cafe Society and formed a band, recruiting Anton Mauve (Roy Butterfield) on guitar, followed by Danny Kustow when he left, Dolphin (Brian Taylor) on drums, and Mark Ambler on keyboards, who is now replaced by Ian Parker. Instant live success prevailed, resulting in an EMI contract and a Top 5 single with 2-4-6-8 Motorway. The rest is common knowledge, so here's the interview........

22

So maintaining contact with the following is very important. Now adays it's also very useful, because the distorts media generally write what one says or ur lies or are inaccurate. But if you can actually write something down on paper - like the bulletin - you can be sure of communicating directly to the public with-out any shit getting in the way. For instance, in Bulletin 11, we were able to put the record straight about Cuba, after all this nonsence that the had been going on in Melody Maker.

Bulletin No.8 January 16th 1978 — fax/info/propaganda from the TRB

J:How indebted do you think you are to Capital Radio, considering the ammount of attention they've given you, right from the start?

TR:Well certainly, they have been very much behind us, particularly with the Glad To Be Gay EP, because they were practically the only radio station in the country that played us, & they gave us absolutely fearless support on that. It was around that time that the Capital Radio Awards were made, and we won 2 of the sections. So, all in all, we're very indebted to Capital Radio for helping us with the London following, and at times when a lot of people set on us. But what really counts in terms of a national following is Radio I, which is heard right around the country. So one is also veey indebted to people like Kid Jensen, who plugged Motorway in the very early days, and John Peel, who had us on a session very early on, and generally to the fact that we got Motorway on to the Radio 1 playlist in it's first week of release.

J:You stated that Rising Free was a cop-out yet 16 minutes for 75p seemed very good value. Were you being serious?

TR:Well it was only a cop-out in so much as Glad To Be Gay should maybe have been an A-side, or maybe Martin should have on an ordinary single rather than a live recording. But definitely, 16 minutes for the price of a single was the idea; the idea was to provide real value for money and make a whole sort of little package, a mini-album, for fans. It was the

You can write to the group and get bulletins, badges & stickers by writing to....

TRB
Box 4XT
LONDON W1A, 4XT

You MUST include a medium-large sized envelope - the band just can't afford to pay for them all.

est way of giving people a good idea of what they'd get if they came to a TRB concert - there's a little bit of fun, a bit of politics, a bit of anger, and a couple of tracks with some fairly hard rock'n'roll on it - I hope.

J:What have EMI been like as a record company? Have you been given the freedom to choose when to release what records, and when to go on tour for how long?

TR:Yes, we have that freedom, basically due to our management. EMI have been a great record company, for instance, they've coughed up 50,000 free badges for this tour for no good reason; those 50,000 free badges aren't going to sell a lot more records, so it was a sheer favour that they did that for us.
As for the freedom to choose when to tour, what records to release, that's entirely our decision - between the management and us. We figure that out for ourselves, talk to EMI about it, and EMI are 100% co-operative about it. They did consult us before releasing Too Good To Be True as a single, and explained it in terms of just trying to get more airplay, so we said go ahead. No complaints.

J:Why did Mark Ambler leave TRB? Is Ian Parker a definite member?

TR:Mark left TRB 'decommitted'. He was getting bored with us. Towards the end of the time he was in the band, he was playing with one hand, and drinking beer or lighting fags with the other, and playing well below his proper standard. So we said 'Look, do you wanna do it? Because if you don't

23

---

really like it, we'd rather have someone that enjoyed it,' so he went.
Nick Plytas stood in, and marked time on his solo career for a bit, and after him we found Ian. Ian is definitely a member. I'm knocked out with Ian - he's completely transformed the band; it's a new group.

J:You previously claimed you were in this first and foremost for an ego trip. Does this mean you include politics just to help you get famous, or even, as some people claim, that you're insincere. Can you tell us what you are in the business for, and how important politics are to TRB?

TR:Ha... you see, if they don't get you one one, they get you on the other. The two questions that people ask, quite often within the same interview, are firstly...
"Well you're just using music to sell your politics, and the two don't mix, & you're wrong to try and mix politics with music." Then quite often within the same breath they say...
"Well, you're just using your cheap & nasty politics as a gimmick so that you'll be successful in the group." So you see, you can't have it both ways - I mean, you're either using your politics to sell the music, or using the music to sell your politics - according to them. Rock'n'roll comes first and foremost - I mean, I formed a group to play rock'n'-roll, and the guys joined the group to play rock'n'roll. Given that the rock'n'roll group existed, & that it had an audience, the lyrics had to be about something, I did pretty much the same as

any songwrit which is write about the things I felt at the time. At that time, I had to be feeling very bitter, very angry, very much part of what was going on - and I still do to a certain extent - and I write about the things that move me. And if the things that wind me up happen to be on touchy subjects like homosexuality or the National Front, too bad.
'Claimed that you were in it for an ego trip'...Well, in interviews, around a year ago, while people were building us up, before they started knocking us down, we were starting to get painted a bit like a sort of Florence Nightingale figure, a do-gooder coming in to save the world by means of music, bringing it's message of how everyone can save the world and make everything better. So in other words they were implying that I formed the group to put over a sincere message and open people's eyes, and spread awareness all over the place; so to deflate that kind of martyr image I said 'No, look, I do it 'cos I enjoy it, because I enjoy playing to audiences - it gives me a great ego trip to do it, like any performer.' So, because I didn't want to seem like a martyr, I ended up like a bighead, so you can't win.
As to including politics to help me get famous, I mean that's just totally ludicrous - the first record we made had nothing to do with politics, and was by far and away our most successful record. 2-4-6-8 Motorway was a straight forward rock'n'roll song, and the reason it's sold over 250,000 copies, and the reason it's by far our most famous song to date, and by far and away our biggest success compared to any of the other

records - including the LP - is because it was a good rock'n'roll record. So the idea that politics is helping make us successful is ludicrous - we could have gone on doing 2-4-6-8 Motorway and tried to follow on in that veni perfectly easily, and probably a lot more successfully Up Against The Wall/I'm Alright Jack which is probably our most political package of the lot, flopped. So if someone says it's only politics that's made me successful - RIDICULOUS.
As for sincerity - I can tell you I'm sincere; I know I'm sincere, but whether people believe it or not is up to them. If they don't believe I'm sincere, that's their problem.

J:What's your favourite TRB song and why?

TR:I think I'm Alright Jack, because it's fast, it's punchy, it's recorded live in the studio - there's no real overdubs. It was done pretty spontaneously as it happened - we just did the vocal afterwards, and a couple of little bits of guitar that you can hardly hear in the verses. The solo was done completely live as it happened, at the same time as the drums and everything, and there's no extra guitar underneath the solo, and I think it's the best guitar solo Danny Kustow's ever recorded - fantastic. And also, I like the words a lot, they're one of the best lyrics I've written....

J:Don't you feel your pushing your Communist views is just like someone pushing their right-wing views, except you're on opposite sides of a table?

TR:Yeah, except I hope not to be pushing Communist views. I am not a practising Communist - I have certain sympathies with the left, and I do agree that something like Better Decide Which Side You're On is probably a bit strong and absolute, and yeah, like someone pushing their right-wing views.
...As to album No. 2, we've been trying out a few of the new songs on the current tour, and changed them about to see how they'd go with the audience. We're fully aware of the possibilities of the tracks not being as good as previous ones if they have been written & shoved straight onto an LP. That won't be the case - I think this is going to be miles better than the first one, as you will see. All this means that it won't be out before Feb. '79 at the earliest - we certainly wont release anything substandard.
Now that TRB are being slammed left, right and centre, we can't be sure they won't. Remember, TRB are not finished, they are still a great group and I'm sure the next LP will prove that.

Anthony Fletcher

24

25

ALTERNATIVE TELLY - a chat with MARK PERRY (and DENNIS BURNS)

Most of you should know that without Mark Perry you probably wouldn't be reading this magazine. Mark Perry - then Mark P. - started up the first punk fanzine - Sniffin' Glue - in mid-'76, and since then has had a very adventurous time im music, both with SG and his band - Alternative TV - who are very unique, and well worth probing into. He's been labelled all sorts of things, because of his rapidly changing views, and because these views are so interesting, he was an obvious choice for an interview.

Mark started Sniffin' Glue, "just 'cos I was into rock'n'roll, and The Ramones came along, so I started my own fanzine to be able to write about the Ramones. The Pistols didn't come into it until about the third issue, and that was a bad review. I think we said that we didn't like the posing and make-up in the audience."

By the time it go to the end, it had a circulation of 15,000!! because, being the first, it was helped by everybody. But by then, Mark P's opinions of punk had changed - "It's a bit going back on old things I've said before, but when The Clash signed to CBS I still think that was a let-down. I feel that there's no way that you can handle yourself properly in a big record company like CBS. I think it's still going on - bands are bringing out albums, and they're dissappointing, they're just rubbish; big record companies don't do anything for the music really, they just sort of dampen it."

Around the time Mark started putting these opinions to paper (March '77) he formed Alternative t'TV (the t' was later dropped) with Alex Ferguson, and things started moving. "We went for a session in the EMI studios, and done Love Lies Limp. And Mickie Most said something about our being too political 'Cos we were swearing and something like that - really stupid. So we weren't offered the deal."

I was going to point out that if The Clash were criticised for signing with CBS, why were they going to sign with EML But Mark saw the question coming - "No, I wasn't thinking of signing with them. The reason I did that thing with them was they were giving us free studio time."

Then if they had offered you a deal, would you have turned it down?

Interview by Anthony & Ray

"I don't know. I didn't know much about record companies then; from what I know now I would have turned them down. But then I was very sort of "Oh great, we're going into EMI studios, wow, wh m bam, thankyou man" and perhaps I'd have signed on and been just like any other smut. We went in there because you don't turn down free studio time."

As it was, the single 'Love Lies Limp' was given away in SG 12 as a flexidisc, which saw the end of the magazine's £400 profits. Mark chucked in the editorship of The Glue to concentrate on ATV, NOT solely because he was dissillusioned, & it carried on for a bit afterwards, before packing in. So what's his present opinion of fanzines?

"I think anybody doing anything on their own is good, whether the product is good or not. I think anyone who changes his life and actually starts writing is incredible. You're still at school yeah? When I was at school, I did nothing but write in school, but you're actually writing outside school as well; I think it's great you're doing something apart from your ordinary life - a way of escapism, you should all try and escape."

...as he was then...
Drawing: John Gilhooly

6

or would have collapsed. The group
k the stage to a rapturous welcome

At first ATV did a lot of gigs, and were building up, and being treated as 'hot' property. But then the group completely changed - it's now changed line-ups and style so much that it takes time to realise there's only 2 people now - Mark Perry and Dennis Burns, using other musicians when necessary. So what's been happening?

Mark: "We started out as a normal rock combo, and we've changed into 2 musicians working together, rather than the 'we're all in a band, lets have fun' attitude."

So why all the line-up changes?

Mark: "I would say that I don't get on with people very well. I don't really take people's feelings for granted - I'm abit selfish sometimes."

Dennis: "I would have thought it's because we've picked the wrong people - I think we've felt we had to have a drummer, and that we had to have another guitarist..."

The first big change was Alex Ferguson, who was considered the main working force of the band. "He left because I didn't want to work with him anymore. At the time I didn't really chuck him out - I spoke to the other people in the group, Chris Bennett and Tyrone Thomas, - Dennis wasn't in the band at the time - and said to them 'Listen, I think Alex should leave, but if you don't want him to leave, I'll leave'. But Chris & Tyrone didn't want to play with Alex, they wanted to play with me. So we chucked Alex out instead.

"Those were mostly musical, and because of those musical differences, it was getting very tense...."

Then Chris Bennett left as well....

Mark: "Yeah (laughs) - but Tyrone went before him! Chris went because, well, he just doesn't like the music I like really, I don't think he feels musically the way the way me and Dennis do."

Dennis: "There wasn't really the space for a rock drummer either."

Most of these changes were caught on **their debut album** 'The Image Has Cracked', released, like all ATV's records, on their own Deptford Fun City Records, part of Faulty Products, also started by Mark. The LP came out last summer, & was extremely interesting, whatever you thought of the music.

Mark: "The first side's mostly songs that I feel we had to do because we'd been playing them for a year - which could have been the wrong attitude. The first side's like the stuff with Alex, and the second side's like new stuff."

The LP defenitely DOES have a chronological feel, and captures the band between two moods - their earlier, shorter stuff, and later, more poetic things. The most interesting track without doubt is Alternatives, where Mark Perry invites the audience to get up on stage and talk about something. But predictably, most of them waste the

...and is now..
Pic: Chris Modica

"Wow, heavy, man."

opportunity, and the result is a fight. "It always ends up a bit of a riot that number anyway. There's always b en a bit of argument and a lot of heckling, but we never had a soapbox except when we recorded it.

"I usually do a really good Alternatives; I usually talk a bit about the TV and make up a story, and on that night, because it was being recorded, I was so nervous that I just thought up the idea of having people on stage."

The LP follows through fast, new-wave stuff like Action Time Vision and Why Don't You Do Me Right, developing into a very musical, rock style, with things like Viva Le Rock'n'Roll and Nasi Little Lonely. The latter songs were a pointer to their present direction, and a couple of the new songs - Going Round In Circles & Fellow Sufferer - can be found on the Here And Now/Alternative TV live LP (What You See Is What You Are), available for £1.50 from Faulty Products - not bad for 50 minutes music. The tour was a very successful free one, which is why Mark feels so suspicious of groups 'keeping prices down' to £2.00.

But since then, Alternative TV haven't been back on the road; and the reason is NOT because they're 'resting', 'writing', or have nobody else in the group....

Mark: "I don't think it's very relevant if a band goes and plays 40 dates in clubs that cost £1.50 to get in, with drinks that are too high prices. If ATV were to go out and play, we'd have to play clubs, baecause we're not quite big enough for halls. But I don't want people to come &

7

ALTERNATIVE TV....

see us in clubs - I don't like them The reasons I don't like clubs & halls is they're all run by bullshit promoters. I won't work for anybody that's a bullshitter ar a crook.

"I'd like to find alternative places to play.... On the Here & Now free tour we played out in a field and we played in a London playpark. I'm interested in finding other places for music. I'd like there to be more places to play without the restrictions of clubs, you know - any age-group can come in, and you don't hit your head on the ceiling.

"I don't want to play live again until we can find a place for a 2-hour show."

Mark Perry has said how much he hates Action Time Vision, yet it was very recently released as a single. Why?

"Because people like it. If other people like it, and they want to buy it, I'll let them buy it."

' Then if somebody comes to a concert and wants to hear the old stuff...

"They won't hear it."

Yeah, but they like it.

Dennis: "We didn't record Action Time Vision because people liked it, we recorded it because we wanted to record it. But it was released because people want to hear it."

Mark: "People have come to our gigs and asked for it, but they won't hear it. That's ehy I say in interviews I don't like it, because then people won't ask for it. I don't really feel the need to play a song live, when they've got it as a single, because if we did play it live, we'd play it exactly as it is on the single."

Mark's also voiced his strange theory that a band is not necessary, and that people are only needed to play the mus

Dennis Burns sizes up the situation
Pic: Chris Modica

8

ic. Wouldn't it be better if they had a band, who knew each other, and knew how to fit in?

Dennis: "We don't actually employ people...."

Mark: "What I meant was, well - I use Dennis to perform my songs, and he uses me to play what he wants to play. And so it's a mutual thing. The bit about the band is true - I don't feel that keeping a band together for ever is necessarily a good way to make music, because the truth is usually that a number of the band will go faulty, because you just can't trust them."

But if you could find a group of people who you trusted in, would you play live as a group again?

Mark: "I play with people I want to play with, I don't know if I'd say they're a good group or not. We're gonna play live again, and we're gonna use other people, but we're not going to call them part of ATV.

The future of ATV is that their new album is out any minute now, called 'Vibing Up The Senile Man', and to describe it...."There's a lot of poetry on it, with atmospheric music - there's lots of words with music accompanying it. There's tons of lyrics on it, but they'r e changing as well, although they're still really serious.

"We play all different things really - there's no 2 tracks with the same line-up of instruments, and there's only 3 track with drums on them. There's a bit of tapes, a bit of piano, Dennis plays some recorder, and there's a little bit of this and that."

Dennis: "The album tells everybody where we're going; I think what we're doing is finding our own way."

Alternative TV will never be a great success, because they constantly change, and won't let anyone mould them. Even if Action Time Vision had been a no. 1 hit, there would have been no proper follow-up, because that was their music of 18 months ago, and now they are something completely different.

And still, they are changing...

Mark: "I haven't got any aims at the moment with the band, because I want to make it not a band. I just want to make music I think is interesting.

"The name ATV may go completely, and we wouldn't get another. We'd just go out with our names - Mark Perry and Dennis Burns, anyone else who plays.

"After all, jazz musicians do."

Anthony Fletcher

....or are they?

FROM THE NOTEBOOKS

20p P
15p ✗

17/12/78 229

COPIES STAPLED

20p P	18/12	253	24/12 - 860	23/3/80 — 1174	
20p ✗	19/12	373	3/1 - 872	3/7/80 - 1184	
20p ✗	20/12	402	5/1 - 891	30/12/80 - 1200	
20p ✗	20/12	416	5/1 - 894	16/1/81 - 1211	
20p P	22/12	437	12/2 = 909	20/1 - 1221	
18p ✗	22/12	456	14/2 = 922	25/1 - 1241	
20p ✗	28/12	480	17/2 = 947	27/1 - 1306	
15p ✗	30/12	499	17/2 = 953	13/5/82 - 1340	
20p P	5/12/19	542	20/2 = 995		
20p P	8/12	562	20/2 = 1002		
20p ✗	10/12	587	22/2 = 1016		
18p ✗	13/12	608	25/2 = 1023		
20p ✗	14/12	664	23/3 = 1035		
20p P	16/12	683	16/3 = 1045		
20p P	19/12	711	23/3 = 1063		
20p P	22/11	725	14/4 = 1072		
20p P	22/11	743	21/4 = 1093		
25p ✗	13/11	753	21/4 = 1108		
20p P	16/11	766	10/9 = 1130		
20p P	26/11	845	7/10 = 1159		
20p					

SHOPS

30/12

16/12/78	5 ROCK ON	18p ✗		
16/12	10 SHOP OPPOSITE BELAIR (THE NOOK)	20p	24/1	5/1
		18p		5/1
18/12	10 SHILLINGS	25p	P	6/1
18/12	20 VIRGIN WAREHOUSE	20p	P	6/1
18/12	5 HONEST JON'S (Monmouth Road)	15p	✗	8/1
18/12	50 PHOENIX	20p	P	
18/12	20 ROUGH TRADE	20p	P	10/1
18/12	25 SMALL WONDER	20p	✗	11/1
18/12	10 VIRGIN OXFORD WALK	20p	P	13/1
19/12	10 VIRGIN MARBLE ARCH	20p	✗	13/1
20/12	10 H.G. WELLS	20p	P	15/1
20/12	10 HONEST JON'S (Golborne Road)	20p	✗	19/1
21/12	5 HONEST JON'S (Camden Town)	20p	P	22
21/12	25 COMPENDIUM	18p	✗	22/1
22/12	15 WEBSTER'S	20p	✗	22/1
22/12	5 VIRGIN (Croydon)	20p	✗	24/1
23/12	15 COUNTERPOINT	20p	P	25
29/12	5 VINYL SOLUTION	20p	P	25/1
30/12	12 SUPERDISC	20p	P	25/1
30/12	10 BEGGARS BANQUET (Ealing)	20p	P	

JAMMING

NO.7 25p

ASSORTED
FREAKS IN
THIS ISSUE...

(in alphabetical order.....)

TOMMY

RAINCOATS

SHRINK

POLL RESULTS

CURE

FLOWERS of ROMANCE

LURKERS

pragVEC

RED NOISE

FANZINE ROUNDUP

This important transition issue was almost entirely conditional on the kindness of strangers. I went the conventional route to secure an interview with Bill Nelson, whose Be Bop Deluxe served as serious pre-punk inspiration, and when the publicist cancelled at a day's notice, I dared to show at the assigned venue, the Brixton Astoria (now the Academy) regardless. Bill took me in, granting a long interview even though he was on dress rehearsal with his new group Red Noise. Similarly, Jeff and I went to see The Undertones at the Marquee, and when it transpired that they'd cancelled due to illness, The Lurkers stepping in at short notice, we asked for and were granted an interview with Fulham's finest. Jeff and I by now had a busy dual life with our band Apocalypse, and during a brief period in which an older and much wiser ex-punk called Mark fronted our rehearsals, he gave us a copy of the debut issue of his 1976 fanzine *Skum* and permission to use its interview (possibly the first) with the recently deceased Sid Vicious. Additionally, a reader called Dave Jennings got in touch from Birmingham, and offered to start writing for us (for free, of course), sending in a timely review of The Cure.

But the crucial act of generosity came from Joly MacFie. When I visited Better Badges in Notting Hill Gate in hope of securing an ad to help cover the exorbitant print costs I was being quoted everywhere, Joly, the genial hippie proprietor, went one better: he'd just taken delivery of a litho press for his badge manufacturing and volunteered to print *Jamming!* at cost as a guinea pig.

So began a bountiful creative relationship and a lifelong acquaintance… though at the time, neither Joly nor I knew much about the actual printing process, and after dozens of hours in the dark room (on the Portobello Road, above the Westway, where he had just moved his business), and even after scrapping hundreds if not thousands of test pages, the resulting issue was full of ink where ink shouldn't have been and a lack of ink where it should. It was no less unreadable in places than Issue 6, partly because I immediately went over the top with the printing possibilities. But still… It was a fanzine! It had variety, attitude, a couple of decent interviews, it offered value for money – and given that I reduced the print run by about 50 per cent, which I could afford to do now that print was at cost, I was not stuck with a bedroom floor's worth of paper. *Jamming* was finally in business.

ISSUE #7 04/79

Becoming *friends* with the No.3 Bus stop at Gypsy Hill Roundabout, because I spent so much time waiting there. **Jeff C.**

SID VICIOUS

SKUM

FLOWERS

ROMANCE

We all know the image of Sid — Vicious - violent, sick, degraded, worthless, conned punk puppet. And most of us believe and accept that. But rather than write an obit- uary saying that, how about finding out what he was like right at the start. This inter view took place in December '76, when vicious was in the Flowers Of Romance, and is probably the first ever inter view with the man. It appea- red in 'Skum' no. 1, and port rays a completely different Vicious from the one we all know and hate....

The Flowers Of Romance were....
Sid vicious - vocals
Steve Walsh - guitar (now in
Manicured Noise)
Viv Albertine - bass (now in
The Slits)
Steve ? - guitar

If you gained a big following and the critics acclaimed you, would you play big places like The Rainbow?
SID: I'm not into that superstar trip or anything like that. I'll never go to secret places or have body-guards, I'll just be the yob that I am now.

How would you describe yourselves musically?
SID: Energetic. Our lyrics are more like sounds to the music. I'm not into politics, that's just a load of drivel. I don't understand it anyway.

Do you genuinely want to bring back music by kids for kids?
SID: Yes, and I just want to have fun; to me music is all about fun, and if it isn't fun, it's just dull, tedious nonsense.

Do you want to be established as a band?
SID: I just wanna have fun, play gigs. Just so I don't have to compromise for any cunt, I'll be totally happy.

Do you hate hippies or teds?
SID: Only if I feel like it... If I feel like killing a hippie I will - I don't have to be angry to do that. That's what I mean about being numb - I'm more of a robot than a person.

If you ever became established, have you any ambitions to go onto anything more complicated?
SID: No, I don't think anyone can get above their own station in life.
(Viv): Just keep it down to basics.
SID: Yeah, if I ever got the urge to do something like that, I'd consider myself a total cunt, and I'd blow my brains out.

Thanks to Mark for the interview.

Revolt into style with BILL NELSON'S RED NOISE

A brave new band for young moderns

Bill Nelson - ex-leader of Be-Bop Deluxe, guitarist extraordinaire, poetic lyricist, self-styled songwriter, and a very interesting person. Now he's got a new group - RED NOISE - and Britain has just been exposed to LP, singles, and tour, more of which later.

The following interview took place in an old cinema at Brixton where Red Noise were rehearsing for their tour. It proved to be one of the best Jamming's ever done, so here goes for the definitive (ha!ha!) Bill Nelson interview:-

JAMMING: How did you go about doing your solo LP?
BILL NELSON: That, Lord Of The Dream? Well, it was the first batch of songs I'd ever written that I wasn't too ashamed about, and some friends who owned a record store in Wakefield (Yorkshire, his birth place) had the money to make it. It was just done locally in a small studio, and we had it printed off by the local newspaper - I drew the front cover, a friend took the photographs, and we just had 250 done. It was totally home-made from start to finish, and we used to sell it around Wakefield.

J:How did Be-Bop Deluxe come about?
BN:It was formed really out of frustration at the bands that had been playing around Wakefield, and were doing just covers and things. And by the time I first cottoned onto The Lord Of The Dream album, I'd got Be-Bop Deluxe in it's initial form together, and we were gigging locally, so that when I asked me to go down with a view to signing as a solo artist, I took a turn to play, and some photographs, a eventually persuaded the to come and see us play, and do auditions and things.

J:Why were there so many line-up changes at first?
BN:Basically, because the people who were in the first band were the re mainly because they were friends, rather than good musicians or anything. And as it became necessary to get better as a songwriter, it needed more competent musicians to be able to play it, so I just had to stop and start again.

J:Why did all your album titles concern music or guitars?
BN:The first 3 were conceived that way - they were a trilogy; those 3 titles all had a feature of modern guitar playing, so you've got Axe Victim, Futurama and Sunburst Finish - those 3 formed a guitarist's trilogy.
J:How do you see yourself, because you've been called poet, visionary, ...all sorts of things?
BN:Before I was a musician, I was at art college, and I was going to be a tutor of modern art at the end of it. So the only thing I remember doing in any creative sense was drawing & painting - taking a visual idea. So the imagery in the songs is very visual...
J:...A sort of aural painting?
BN:Yeah, but I don't know whether that rule's true all the time - I constantly revise all my ideas. I think obviously, art's a dirty word in music: the idea of a rock musician

<19>

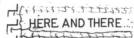

LIVE HERE AND THERE...

...INTRODUCING OUR FAB NEW WRITER DAVE JENNINGS, WHO'S GOING TO BRING US ALL THE NEWS OF WHAT'S GOING ON AROUND BRUM THESE DAYS, STARTING WITH THE BIG REVIEW... THE CURE: Birmingham Barbarellas

RAINCOATS/SCRITTI POLITTI: Chippenham/ Aklam Hall:

Two seperate gigs where two of our best hopes for the '80's played two great concerts at two very contrasting venues:

The Chippenham was Scritti Politti' second gig & it provided a perfect paradox to their first (Aklam Hall, November). That time it was note-perfect, with 5 songs, this time it was very informal, very spontaneous, rather chaotic and 40 minutes long. They played a host of new songs, 2 off the EP, and 3 made up on the spot. In the middle of the set, good ol' Jeff Carrigan somehow connected 2 live wires & blew half the lights! Result: a made-up song called 'Please Turn The Lights On'. At the Aklam Hall, I had to go the moment they came on, but can tell you they appeared worn out from the effects of a long tour, but more direct and confident.

The Scrit's music is very trebly, & filled with reggae drumming, loud bass parts and impossible guitar chords. Together they make a mixture of reggae & Pere Ubu-style rock, with stop-start beats. Easy to dance to as well.

The Raincoats combine a line-up of guitar, bass, drums and violin, played by Anna, Tina, Palmolive & Vicky respectively. Their music's not unlike The Slits, but more refined and more classy, with the violin taking the part of a lead guitar. They often play slow verses and fast choruses, while Palmolive relies heavily on the drums, rather than the cymbals, which makes a welcome change. As they started their first song at the Aklam, with the beat gradually getting faster, it had a real magical feel to it, and a beat that compelled me to dance. They come over very professionally, and the only chaos is when Anna & Tina start singing (?) together. As for titles to songs; tough luck, they don't introduce them. Although they play outside basic musical structures, both sets ended with pure white noise, followed at The Aklam by an encore where they all changed instruments. They have a single out soon, and while you go out and buy that, here's promising an interview for no. 8.

Both Scritti Politti and The Raincoats are worth going out of your way to see: if you don't mind finding something different, you won't be disappointed.

Anthony Fletcher

been to some sleazy local dive to see a bunch of your mates making their first attempts at playing in a band? If you have, then you'll know the customary behaviour patterns of bands appearing at such events - nervous smiles at the audience and each other; furtive, frantic adjustments to the amps between numbers; & an all round air of self-consciousness and tension. Well that's what The Cure are like live, with one big difference: The Cure play great music. They can't be out of their teens yet, but in terms of originality and inventiveness, they've achieved more already than Status Quo have managed in 15 years. The Cure play atmospheric, powerful, emotional music, simultaneously reminiscent of the Jam, with whom they share the guitar/bass/drums format and a strong sense of melody, and Wire, with whom they share economy, austerity and experimental leanings. Their best known song, 'Killing An Arab' was taken at a faster pace than on record and worked better in this context because of it.

I can't tell you the names of the band members, or any other song titles, because the band didn't make one intelligible introduction all night. It's a pity, because the fluent bass player deserves particular praise for his melodic but punchy style. It's an even bigger pity because the atmosphere at this gig was continually deflated by the long, tedious pauses between songs as drinks were taken, running orders read, hurried conferences held. But there was no mistaking the potential of this band, even though it's a potential which seems far more likely to be realised on record than on stage. The Cure are a fine band; it's about time that they themselves realised it.

Dave Jennings

FROM THE NOTEBOOKS

In 1979, I worked behind the singles counter at Virgin Records Oxford Walk, on Oxford Street in London. We sold several fanzine titles at the store, but *Jamming* was the most popular. We even kept back issues in stock, which Tony would bring by himself. He was always very enthusiastic and personable, and a real music nerd, like myself, so we would chat a lot. He was much younger than me – I was 19, so he would have been 14 or 15. But he was already self-assured, positive and excited for the world. His passion bled into his fanzine. I met him again several years later when we had both moved to NYC and Tony had moved on to another phase in his life. I read his autobiography and it vividly brought back those whirlwind days in late 70s/early 80s London, and the hurricane of creativity it was. *Jamming* was there to capture it on its bristling, smudgy pages. **JG Thirlwell**

		SHOPS	
14/4	50	ROUGH TRADE	20p P
14/4	6	5TH COLUMN, Westway Market	25p
14/4	20	HONEST JON'S Golborne Road	20p P
14/4	10	VINYL SOLUTION	20p P
14/4	75	VIRGIN Marble Arch	20p P
14/4	37	VIRGIN Warehouse	20p
19/4	25	COMPENDIUM	20p
14/4	15	HONEST JON'S Golborne Road Camden	20p P
14/4	5	ROCK ON stall	18p SOR
15/4	10	SHILLINGS	19p SOR
17/4	100	PHOENIX	15p
17/4	50	SMALL WONDER	20p P
17/4	20	F.A. BELLAMY	18p
17/4	10	VIRGIN Oxford Walk	20p
18/4	10	VIRGIN Croydon	20p P
18/4	15	WEBSTERS Croydon	18p
18/4	10	COUNTERPOINT	20p
19/4	5	BEGGAR'S BANQUET North End Road	20p P
19/4	10	BEGGAR'S BANQUET Ealing	20p P
19/4	10	GOODNESS RECORDS	20p

JAMMING

NO.8 — 25p

YES, IT'S BACK-TO-ROOTS TIME IN JAMMING 8, WITH A....

NEW GROUP SPECIAL

THE BIG GROUPS HAVE HAD THEIR SAY. THIS IS THE REAL SOUND OF THE EIGHTIES.....

▶ The CHORDS ◀

PUNILUX HUMAN LEAGUE

HOMO SEXUALS

SPEEDBALL

SPIZZ

ENERGI

36 pages!

TEEN BEATS

turn to back cover for even more details

lods Mods Mods M

swell maps
A TRIP TO MARINEVILLE

Suddenly, everything came together. I turned 15 and celebrated with five gigs in five nights. One of these was The Who at the Rainbow, their first show since Keith Moon's death, and three others were part of the mod revival that The Who had inspired. Me and my schoolfriends – because as rapidly as it had started, the bullying stopped – proved perfect targets for this mod movement, and though I firmly resisted the parkas and suits, I did profile those bands I thought (and still think) had something special, The Chords and Speedball, while Jeff, in the midst of growing an impressive punk mohawk, interviewed Hastings' own mod icons, Teenbeats.

The fifth gig of those five nights was by a group called The Homosexuals, who were 'managed' out of the basement of the record shop close to school. That manager took me to what may have been their debut show, the night Margaret Thatcher was elected Prime Minister, and I duly wrote about the band despite the fact that they refused to be interviewed.

Spizzenergi rounded out this 'New Group Special', a theme accentuated by features on Getting Gigs and DIY Records (the latter including a rare outside contribution, from Johnny Waller),

reviews of Swell Maps, The Human League, Red Lights and The Raincoats, 'scene' articles sent in from Glasgow and Birmingham, and a decidedly independent and international page of singles reviews. (The Zips EP alone is now valued at £400.)

Joly had by now sorted out the teething issues with his printing press, and informed me we could use colour ink whenever he ran off badges that needed it. He also continued printing at cost, with the understanding that I bring him other fanzine business in turn. The combination of the vibrant cover, the vitality of the layout (even the errors looked deliberate, as with the 5th Column ad), the 25p cover price and the hip quota of the featured artists made it an easy sell to record and book shops – and at gigs – all over London. In fact, for the first time since I had set off on this unexpected adventure, *Jamming* sold like proverbial hotcakes; the last of the 1,200 copies was stapled and sold just seven weeks after the first ones came off the press. (I paid off Joly's print bill two weeks before that.) Unexpectedly, though in hindsight not without justification, *Jamming* had become a flagship fanzine; a series of national music press reviews, which included a reprint of our DIY Records piece in *Record Mirror* as well as a profile in *The Young Observer*, paradoxically served as confirmation.

Waiting for Tony for three and a half hours outside Westbourne Park tube station to go to Joly's in Portobello Road. In the days before mobile phones, you just waited. **Jeff C.**

The HOMO SEXUALS

This group are ... the wierdest you are ever likely to come across in Jamming. They take the diy/ 'people can come to us' ideas of other groups to a total extreme - they play music, they record music, you can take it or leave it, it doesn't bother them. And nothing gets in the way of that. It makes writing constructively about them virtually impossible.

At the moment, The Homosexuals are three men whose names I don't know. The line-up is guitar, bass, drums, vocals, recorder, toy trumpets, and nobody specifically plays any one instrument... starting to get the picture? They'd like to be four, with a permanent drummer, but meanwhile they overdubbed drums on their single, and have taped drums for their vital songs live, only to find it not loud enough.

Some examples of The Homosexuals actions -

1/ They released a single - Hearts in Exile/Soft South Africans (reviewed last issue except it's grown on me a lot more since then), making 2000. They had <u>no</u> press handouts, <u>no</u> advertising, <u>no</u> review copies, and yet sold 1500 copies in 2 days. Although 'selling out' (ha ha) by printing colour photos of them on the cover, they recommended shops to sell it for 65p, and gave no addressfor the record label. They have now brought out a second record - a 12" EP, with 6 tracks and evn less publicity. There are no credits, it's a 'Les Incroyables' Production (like the first) with 'Labjabs' also mentioned, and the emblem appears to be a heart.

2/ When they play concerts, they offer no advertising, no selling themselves. If the place publicises heavily, then that's part of the success.

3/ The Homosexuals do not do interviews. They do not feel them as either necessary or relevant. If someone wants to write about the music, let them, and that's as far as it goes.

4/ On stage they play about 25 fast, thin songs, none lasting much more than 2 minutes. They invite (aural) audience participation, and disclose nothing. When I saw them, on election night (and just think what's happened since then), they provided 3 televisionsfor election coverage. Their songs do not contain so much lyrics, as images, words and phrases joined together by trebly guitar, stop-start rhythms, danceable and wierd. One member talks more than others, introducing songs with different accents each time, enjoying himself. The guitarist comes from a hard rock/heavy metal background (listen to the solo on Soft South Africans). He now totally rejects this image, and joins the other 2 in their aims. These aims are to <u>completely</u> avoid orthodox channels of rock music; to sell many records and get good receptions at concerts by doing it their way; to play music and let people listen as they want. They dearly want to be the first group to succeed without bowing to the music papers, without having to advertise, without going to people. They want to provide a perfect alternative.

A good example is the new record - 6 tracks (5 short, 1 long), in plain pink 12" cover, with sticker over the top listing tracks. No proper credits anywhere - it's the music that counts. And here there's no mistake. Astral Glamour is a great all-round song, spanish guitar adding a lot. Collected Of You is typically wierd (and not so good) for the 1st $\frac{3}{4}$, and just before the end goes es

A deliberately boring layout for a group who

said "When you get glossy, it's finished."

(28)

into a lovely accoustic guitar bit that finishes all too soon. The Birds Have Risen is a typical Homosexuals song - stopping/starting/stopping - it has about 8 differnt themes - some great, some disgraceful. Divorce Proceeding(s) From Reality I remember distinctly from the gig because their followers go on stage to join singing, it has a good title, and it goes into the chorus after about 10 seconds, and stays there until finishing. The nearest The Homosexuals will ever get to a pop song. Mecho Madness is the long one, no set rhythm or tune, the conga keeps returning, a few scattered vocals. The last 5 seconds are perfect, it's as annoying as Collected Of You. Vociferous Slam is apparently light-hearted, cockney, resembles Small Faces/Barrett-Pink Floyd. Magic.

I've given this record a long review because it deserves it - it's an important release, original and proving the Homosexuals musically. A very highly reccomended purchase.

OK. All that is a description of The Homosexuals. There are obviously MANY good points in all that; you shouldn't need me to spell them out for you. But as it's my article, I want to give my personal views:-
1/ Offering complete anonymity may sound good, but why no contact, why no interviews? Lyrics are never totally clear on stage with any group, and people may want to find out more about the songs. It's true they can do so at concerts, but what if they have to get home? Interviews offer a chance for groups to explain their motives, songs and feelings, and even if a group doesn't want to do that

(as it's obvious The Homosexuals don't), interviews still give a chance for people to ask about things they want clearing up. There's a lot that mystifies me about this group, a lot I would like to ask (eg why are they called The Homosexuals? and it's not as obvious as you think), why do they not give me answers?
2/ On stage, though I hate to say it, the group are slightly bigoted - they have their own 3 or 4 special followers on stage at certain times, but they don't seem keen for other people to get up. Why not?
3/ I have slightly exaggerated their unwillingness for attention. They do want people to buy their records, and they do want people to listen to them, but it's your choice.
4/ I wish The Homosexuals luck; I think what they're doing is not just unique, it's commendable. Also, they've produced two of the best records this year. Musically, you should see them if it's not too much bother, but for their attitude, it's worth travelling. I personally am desperate to see them again, but are they ever going to publicise their gigs well enough for me to know about it in advance? However, they must know, as well as me, that the road is long and difficult, and that they have a very small chance of achieving their aims (though it would be fantastic if they do). Perfect example, when playing at a college, the front-man announced "Any requests?"

A long-haired, conformist student replied "Louie Louie".
Will they ever learn?

AF

SINGLES reviews
A couple of late

CABERET VOLTAIRE: Nag Nag Nag

At last, some first-rate material from a generally very bad group. Great fuzzy guitar and drum rolls on a drum machine along with just the right voice. Hawkwind-ish. The b-side shows the group up for what they too often are though - boring, pretentious etc etc, stick to the Nag Nag Nagging and you won't go wrong.

GLORIA MUNDI: YY?

A pleasant enough record, but not what we've come to expect from Gloria Mundi. Basically, a pop tune, it's something I'd listen to quite happily, but I wouldn't miss it otherwise. Do You Believe? starts off really well, but gets lost at the end in a repetitive chorus. Or as the headmaster would say-"Could do better."

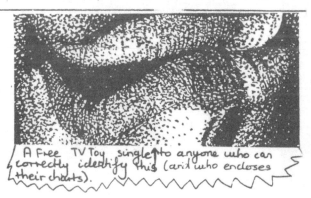
A Free TV Toy single to anyone who can correctly identify this (and who encloses their cheats).

THIS IS THE FUTURE
OF??? no. 394

Billy Hassett –
vocals, guitar

Chris Pope –
guitar, vocals

Martin Mason –
bass, vocals

Brett Ascott –
Drums

The Chords are the most well-known of the new 'mod' bands, and one of the hottest bits of property going. If you're hoping for a first-ever slag-off of The Chords, then look elsewhere, 'cos this lot are superb. Through classic pop songs (God! that phrase again) like Now It's Gone, Something's Missing and It's No Use, alongside a youth anthem-to-be Maybe Tomorrow, and their other songs are no part-time affairs either – I Don't Wanna Know, Don't Go Back, and (just) Dream Dolls. They also do pretty great versions of Circles, She Said, Hey Girl and Hold On, I'm Coming. We're not just talking about good songs, 'cos they're one of the best live bands going. The group put <u>everything</u> into gigs and they'll get their rewards.

One thing we found at the interview (Marquee, 3rd night of mod fest.) was a sort of split down the middle of the group; within minutes of starting, Billy & Brett were well away, enjoying it immensely, but Martin didn't contribute a word to the interview, although Chris was better – one word!

We're hoping you already know a bit about The Chords, and just to balance out the mag, here's a no-frills straight-forward interview; it's got our opinions put over as questions anyway...

PICS: JEFF CARRIGAN

Why are you particularly a mod band?

Billy: Well we never labelled ourselves a mod band. We were doing this sort of music anyway. It's just the mods really took to it... well it is sort of moddish.

Are you saying you're not the ones who call yourselves mods?

Billy: Well look at Chris, does he look like a mod to you?

That's what I've been thinking.

Billy: Yeah, Pope's Pope.
Brett: If they dig the music they're welcome to come along (not sure if that's him or an already-said quote).

Do you agree that a lot of the fans and groups who call themselves mods are so because it's an excuse to have a small, friendly movement?

Billy: Well, it's like I'm supposed to be talking now for a whole set of people I don't even know about really. I

Type 'The Chords Now It's Gone' into YouTube – go on, try it now. Find the footage posted by TheBelieversUK: it's a recorded version of the song playing over some repetitive clips of The Chords at The Wellington in Waterloo, London, England, May 1979. Ignore the gurning of the scrawny half-naked drummer and freeze-frame it at 47 seconds. Who is that screen right, standing behind the belligerent manager of the pub, blond hair bobbing up and down and singing along?

Why, it's none other than Tony Fletcher. He looks the very picture of an angelic little cherub but at this juncture the barely-15-year-old already had over a year's experience of writing and producing his own music and culture magazine – because 'fanzine' seems just too small a word for what *Jamming* quickly became. Arriving at a time when these fan-driven only know about my mates and this lot here, and they believe in the movement.

What do you think, so far, are the good and bad things to come out of this new mod movement?

Billy: A lot of good new groups - like us.
Brett: You can go and see 4 bands for a quid...

...Or 3 for £1.75 (as at this gig)!

Brett: Um...yes...we had no control over the prices.
Billy: Like the punk movement had something to identify with, the mod movement is very friendly.
Brett: Half the audience are friends & know each other.

What about any bad things?

Brett: Violence, between punks and mods and teds and skinheads and grannies ...

Everybody's tipping The Chords as the mod group to succeed. Do you think that's something you can cope with?

Brett: 'If we don't we deserve to die' (courtesy Chris Pope in NME Mod Special)
Brett bursts out laughing and has a go at Chris, content to read an old Jamming.

How long do you reckon the movement will last at this level? You've already come out of The Wellington to selling out The Marquee. What's to stop you doing tours finishing at Hammersmith?

Brett & Billy groan no's and no's...
Brett: Not this week anyway!
Billy: It's mostly the press that's given it all this.
Brett: If the press hadn't got hold of it, it would have lasted for years. It already has lasted for years though.
Billy: Here, it's the same bands, the same people, it's just a bit more decent place.

So how long do you reckon it will continue like this?

Brett: It could be a matter of months or years. People will carry it on for the rest of their lives.

What are your influences?

Brett: It's like there's two different dates - '65 & '76.

(To Billy) We can guess your reaction but on stage it does seem as if you're imitating Paul Weller...

Billy: Well, it's not meant for a start. Every time you hold a guitar, you want to bust it. And it's just energy released - when we come off stage we're fucked. Like you witnessed that on Friday, we'd knack-

ered ourselves after the first 3 numbers. And it's not an imitation, I'm not trying to rip any one off, it's just the way I feel. I _wanna_ fuckin' jump in the air, like the people down the front - they wanna jump about, why can't I?

You've only been gigging 6 months, and you've got to this stage already; do you reckon it might overtake you at all?

Brett: Maybe it already has to a certain extent, because when it comes to writing and rehearsing we haven't got any time at the moment.
Billy: A couple of months ago we were playing for nothing, tonight it's £1.75. Even though it's nothing to do with us.
Brett: We'll make it clear we're not into the money side of it at all, 'cos we've just blown our advance away on new equipment (£1100 drum kit!).
Billy: ...To get a better sound - we hope anyway, we still go up and talk to people - we'll never become superstars (even Popey?). But we hate signing autographs.

What's happening about the single?

Billy: Now It's Gone, coming out on Polydor. JP's fallen through.

What did you think of Jimmy Pursey?

Brett: I used to think he was sincere & nice, I don't now. He's just interested in himself, which is fair enough, but why he goes around pretending to be interested in kids I don't know.

In the middle of a discussion about the songs and their meanings, Chris (songwriter) walks up.
Brett: What are the songs about Chris?
Chris: Life.   And walks off!

Do you get other A&R men turning up?

Billy: No, everyone thinks we're with Polydor.

So would you mind?

Billy: We wouldn't mind anyone...Brett's willing to bend over forwards for a friend...!!!

And you must admit that sounds like a pretty interesting group. And if you've heard their John Peel session or seen them live you'll know what we mean. No way could we fit all we wanted onto two pages, but one last interesting point we do want to mention is that Chris is not a mod, Martin is not a mod, Brett is not a mod, and Billy is the only member who is. All by their own admissions. So could we all agree it's the music that counts first and foremost. And if that's so, The Chords will be with us for a long time.

AF with photos by JC.

P.25.

journals were springing up on virtually every street corner, Tony's contribution stood head-and-shoulders above the crowd, and The Chords were proud to be included in it.

Jamming had style, substance and a professional feel but was never bland or boring. Esoteric but not elitist, knowing but not cynical. And perhaps most importantly for a magazine written by – and for – fans, it was enthusiastic but never fawning.

Tony would continue to champion The Chords, even within the hallowed pages of _The Face_ magazine. While being aware of the changing styles and fashions of those heady New Romantic times, Tony still fought for those whose music and ideals he identified with. **Brett 'Buddy' Ascott**

SPEEDBALL

Speedball first came to my attention when Roger Allen, editor of the Surrey Vomet, became manager of the only group ever to have been interviewed in his mag, and hassled me into seeing their first ever London gig at the Moonlight Club. Not expecting anything spectacular, especially after no soundcheck and the nerves of a first London gig, all I can remember now is this amazing group who started with a killer of a song called Don't You Know Love. Despite all they felt about it, the gig immediately showed Speedball to be an extremely promising group; having seen and heard them a hell of a lot more, I can now confidently call them one of the best bands around (talk about hypes!). They've changed their line-up (for the better) since the Moonlight Club, and are now:-

Robin Beulo - vocals, guitar, singing with eyes shut and (ahem!) into strange sexual relationships!!!
Dave Dyke - drums,'stud', over 6ft. with peroxide hair and a rock star to be (or so he says).
Guy Pratt (now don't laugh) - Bass, backing vocals, bopping on stage, & thinking he's Pete Townshend on bass.

All are incredible cigarette poncers (irrelevant but true) and, cue the history, Robin...

"We used to be a 4-piece (Barry Godwyn - lead guitar, Paul Dunne - bass, Robin & Dave), called Idiot..."
Dave: "Then we split up. Me and Rob were in a group called Deeno's Marvel-'s; we were supposed to do a farewell concert, but it went so well we decided to get back together; called it Speedball, but then Barry & Paul got this court case for nicking musical instruments, so they left by mutual agreement. We auditioned Guy, and since then it's just been the 3 of us."

Having read that, you might realise Speedball aren't as new or inexperienced as their recent arrival on the scene might have you believe. This is a problem a lot of out-of-London (mod?) bands are having at the moment - a reason for interviewing The Teenbeats as well in this issue. And like The Teenbeats, Speedball haven't always been mods, so... How long have you been mods?
Robin: "We were down the Zero-6 (Southend mod club) about 9 months ago."
Dave: "Another reason why Barry & Paul were pulled out was because they weren't mods."

Yeah, but is that important?
Dave:- "No, but you've got to have the same basic things that you're after. The group split into 2 halves, me & Rob, and Barry & Paul."

But if someone wasn't a mod, yet you had the same sort of agreement...
Robin: "Yeah, it's inside here" (not sure if he's pointing to his brain or his ridiculous haircut!) "And anyway, they couldn't do backing vocals, which was a bit off, 'cos I need backing vocals for my songs."

What about when the mod thing falls through?
Robin: "Well it won't make any difference, because the way we want to play is the way we'll do it."
Dave: "Anyway, whenever there's been a movement, all the good bands have pulled through."

Which shows that Speedball have the confidence as well as the talent. When I first saw them, Dave was going on about how good he thought the mod movement was, so imagine the suprise at the interview hen he announced "It's really bad - 99% of the mods are creeps."

Er hang on Dave, you've changed your view a bit, haven't you...?
"Well, I've since been to Bishops Stortford Mod Festival."
Robin: "There was a group there who wanted to be mods so they phoned up Maximum Speed and asked what to wear!"
Guy: "Some of the bands weren't bands, they were an insult to all the people who'd travelled to get there."

6

Jamming was the first publication I appeared in and will therefore always have a special place in my heart, even though the interviews themselves – including this one with my first band, Speedball, back in the spring of mod-revival 1979 – show up all the cringeworthy earnestness of youth. Tony, who I'd first met at a Boxing Day party through long-forgotten family connections, was unbelievably tenacious, and him getting interviews with Townshend and Weller and the like alongside the up and coming bands he knew was gobsmacking. The literal embodiment of the punk DIY aesthetic, *Jamming* stands as a proud testament and witness to its time. **Guy Pratt**

OVERSPILLS

Most of this page is just non-libellous (we hope) gossip about the usual elite bunch we feature. So off we go...

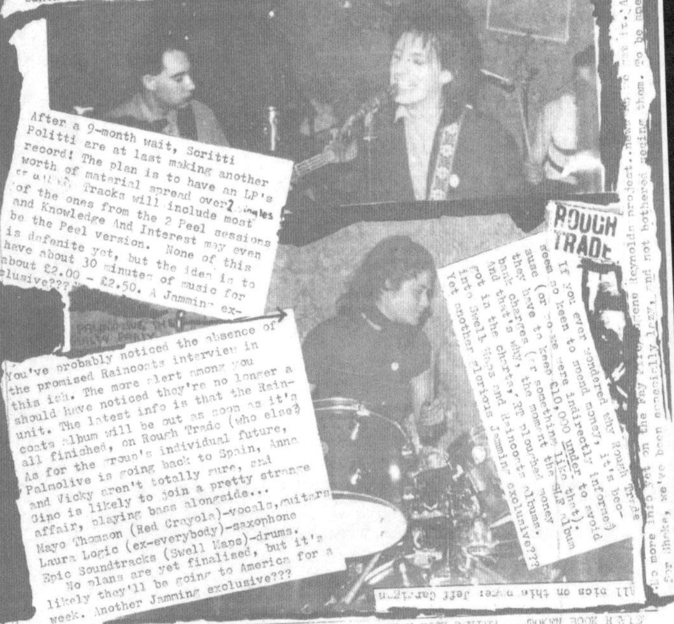

After a 9-month wait, Scritti Politti are at last making another record! The plan is to have an LP's worth of material spread over 2 singles [illegible]. Tracks will include most of the ones from the 2 Peel sessions and Knowledge And Interest may even be the Peel version. None of this is defenite yet, but the idea is to have about 30 minutes of music for about £2.00 - £2.50. A Jamming exclusive???

You've probably noticed the absence of the promised Raincoats interview in this ish. The more alert among you should have noticed they're no longer a unit. The latest info is that the Raincoats album will be out as soon as it's all finished, on Rough Trade (who else?) As for the group's individual future, Palmolive is going back to Spain, Anna and Vicky aren't totally sure, and Gino is likely to join a pretty strange affair, playing bass alongside...
Mayo Thomson (Red Crayola)-vocals, guitars
Laura Logic (ex-everybody)-saxophone
Epic Soundtracks (Swell Maps)-drums.
No plans are yet finalised, but it's likely they'll be going to America for a week. Another Jamming exclusive???

ROUGH TRADE

If you ever wondered why Rough Trade seem so keen to spend money, it's because (or so we were indirectly informed) they have to keep £10,000 under to avoid bank charges (or something like that). And that's why, the moment the SLF album got in the charts, RT ploughed money into Swell Maps and Raincoats albums. Yet another glorious Jamming exclusive???

[illegible] Reynolds project..news [illegible] not bothered seeing them. To be amended. [illegible] more info yet on the way [illegible] we've been especially lazy [illegible]

All pics on this page: Jeff Carrigan

....TOKEN BOOK REVIEW....TOKEN BOOK REVIEW....TOKEN BOOK REVIEW....TOKEN BOOK REVIEW

PATRIK FITZGERALD: Poems

The first book of poems I know of that's come from a new wave artist. Put out by Tower Hamlets Art Project (THAP) 75p may seem a lot for 30 small pages, but it's better than paying £3.00 for 10 Buzzcocks songs, isn't it?

It's hard to review a book. Basically, this is a collection of Patrik's well-known and not so well-known (to me) poems, with a few pictures here and there. Well-known stuff like Make It Safe ('Come and get your punk in Woolworths/Bondage trousers twelve pounds/Mohair jumpers sold next to cardigans'), The Paranoid Ward and I Wandered Lonely, but practically all lesser-known, though just as impressive, stuff like The Alien In Tottenham Ct. Rd, Do Something Constructive, Robotic and especially The Pigs At Gigs (Bouncers).

All in all, 17 poems and 3 bits of prose makes a very worthwhile book. Patrik Fitzgerald may now be on Polydor, but he's always been witty, honest, and accusing when he need be. For anyone who's ever liked him (or for anyone who wants to), go out and get this now. And let's hope more books like this come out, and soon...

31

SINGLES

A grass-roots column this week, all in alphabetical order. 7 groups from Scotland 4 from Bristol, 3 from America, 2 from London, 1 from France, 1 from Scandinavia and 1 from Yorkshire. Local scenes erupting at last...

FOUR ALTERNATIVE'S EP:- THE NUMBERS - Alternative Suicide; X-CERTS-Blue Movies; J E PUBLIC-Hotel Rooms; 48 HOURS-Back To Ireland.

Four young groups all from Bristol (and I thought there was nothing down there). Best tracks are the X-Certs 'Blue Movies', which is very Boysish, and especially 48 Hours 'Back To Ireland', this sounding a lot like the late Clash, except better. The politics I only hope are from personal experience, or else it's another Ulster Boy. Joe Public's is a pretty good pop/rockabilly song, and The Numbers are also (just) worth a listen. A very worthwhile EP; it's time more local labels did this sort of thing (there's another coming up later)....

ALTERNATIVE PAISLEY: MOD CONS - Buildings Of The '70's/ XS DISCHARGE - Machette Shuffle/SNEEX - Radio Mania/POETS - Posters On The Wall/MENTOL ERRORS - Irrelevance

Another local EP (see interview with Tommy Kayes) and this aims to be a lot more informal. The result is a possibly good EP, completely ruined by pathetic recording quality. Example: Mentol Errors did their track seperately - it immediately sticks out as best track. Mod Cons may be promising, but as I XS Discharge is very forgettable, straightforward punk, The Sneex again have a good song, again ruined by poor quality. The Poems are pretty weak anyway, just words over a normal riff, and as I said, the Mentol Errors succeed through best sound, despite an average song.

The other fault is the unoriginality among the groups. I really admire Tommy Kayes for getting something like thistogether, but next time how about making it just a bit more professional? Out-of-Paisley listeners feel alienated..

CURE: Boys Don't Cry

After all their wierdness, a simple, perfect pop song. Matching the Buzzcocks best stuff, it's real magic. My only worry is tiring of it quickly. Plastic Passion is also well-worth a second listen. Great single.

DESTROY ALL MONSTERS: November 22nd 1963

Still not over-impressed with this USA group of all-stars. It has a certain undeniable quality, concerning Kennedy's assasination - "Jackie Kennedy, hold on to his brains" sounds pretty eery. As for the press slip calling it best rock'n'roll song ever written about the Kennedy assasination, it's just as well the Ants haven't yet released Catholic Day. 'Meet The Creeper' isn't so good - it's mainly the girl's voice that bothers me. Approach with caution.

PATRIK FITZGERALD: Improve Myself

The limit. PF with electrical instruments is one thing, PF trying to make a pop song is too much. There's only 70 seconds of actual song here, and however much it gets the feet tapping, Patrik should stick to what he's good at. My New Family is average Fitzgerald, but Bingo Crowd is matchless. His best track, with power, feeling and sense, this should have been the a-side of his first single, not the b-side of his worst. Iwon't say pay £1 for 1 minutes good music, but get thistrack.

HOLLYWOOD BRATS: Then He Kissed Me

This lot ripped off the New York Dolls three years ago and released one album in Scandinavia before splitting. Then He Kissed Me sounds like it would if the Mekons did it; a great version, I love it, but is it really necessary? The b-side, 'Sick On You', is pure '77 punk; first time round it gave me a headache, but now it's not too bad. They'd have gone a-bomb on this lot at The Roxy.

pragVEC: Expert

An example of how long diy singles take to do. When the last issue came out they'd just begun recording it, and it's taken 3 months to get into the shops. Anyway, after that irrelevancy, Expert is a great single, certainly the best track pragVEC have committed to vinyl. The single has everything a good, wierd single should have, and if you want to know what that everything is, then get it. Follower's a disappointment though - it showed a lot of promise on the Peel session, but has lost a lot on the way. If pragVEC can only get away from their 3-month sposmadic periods, they'll soon make a firm impression.

TELEPHONE: La Bombe Humaine

France's (almost) only punk-rockers on, believe it or not, telephone-shaped vinyl! And available in about 12 different colours! And somehow it's produced by Martin Rushent. The a-side is very watered-down rock (all this for a hit eh lads?), but the b-side is aok - J'Suis Parti de Chez Mes Parents. Once again, '77 punk (or is that heavy metal?) and great with it. I was going to invent an excuse for reviewing this when you can't get it in England, but as I just heard Peel play from the album, maybe you can. If so, get it.

TV TOY: For What It's Worth/Instant This, Instant That

There should have been an article on this lot, but as we never got the info in time, here's a single review. A New Jersey arty type, it seems a bit stupid to do a non-original for a debut a-side (concession to American FM?), 'cos the other side bodes a lot better for the future, especially the lyrics. Is this new wave? Is this too professional? Completely unavailable here, except from US! If you want a copy (worth it for b-side), then 50p, inc. p&p, from us. A bargain.

VISITORS: Electric Heat EP

The first fanzine to have a record company, though Johnny Waller seems keen to disconnect the two (see his bit elsewhere for all the gory details). Apparently, they find it curious to be compared to The Stranglers, yet that is a blatently obvious influence. Electric Heat is a good song, but Moth is a great one, best bit being the simple but effective backing vocals. One Line is sombre, occasionally exploding. The main fault is the lack of tunes - too many lines are spoken. Whatever, well worth getting.

ZIPS: EP

Leaving the best 'till last, another Scottish group pave the way. Four great pop songs, recorded in a 4-track studio (mind you, it shows), in the mould of Teenage Kicks. So what if people will say "Who?" in 10 years (I hope they don't), the best has always been basic, emphasized by Take Me Down, Don't Be Pushed Around, I'm In Love and Over And Over. They start on the weakest track, & then Don't Be Pushed Around is a sort of main, if not classic, song. I'm In Love is perfect pop, and Over And Over is the same. It may have been recorded 8 months ago, but chances are you haven't heard it. In which case, send £1 to It Ticked & Exploded (only place I know) NOW.

FROM THE NOTEBOOKS

Assistant Jeff Carrigan, left, and editor Anthony Fletcher

Meet a fanzine editor

MEET Anthony Fletcher, 14, editor of *Jamming* – an independent music magazine or fanzine. 'I've produced about six issues so far. I get about 1,000 copies printed, which costs about £150, and then I sell them for 25p a copy. The money for the printing comes from profits from the previous issue. I'm trying to get an issue out every two months.' Anthony lives in Dulwich in south London and has had interviews with stars like Pete Townshend, John Peel and Tom Robinson. 'There are lots of other fanzines around the country and we should have a good communications network going soon.'

Lizzie Lemon

NO. 8

	STAPLED		
		20/9	1082
9/8	337	21/9	1111
10/8	401	23/9	1136
	461	28/9	1169
	507	29/9	1199
11/8	547		
	602		
12/8	695		
	700		
14/8	725		
15/8	743		
15/8	840		
22/8	900		
28/8	924		
	934		
30/8	976		
7/9	1003		
17/9	1042		
18/9	1042		

28/8	£98.25 July		8/10 £15
	£34.50		20/10 £10
	£15		

Paid

25p JAMMING no. 9

BACK TO OUR OLD SELL-OUT WAYS WITH 40 PAGES OF......

THE JAM

The Fall

Shrink

THE SELECTER

THE PACK

RUDI

& ACK~ACK

Plus Stuff On The Radio Tribalism Poems

Reviews of Speedball Essential Logic Clash PIL Cabaret Voltaire SLF

Local Scenes. Sheffield New Jersey

ISSUE #9
11/79

Much of the summer and autumn of '79 was spent hanging out at the Town House studio in West London with school friends while The Jam recorded the *Setting Sons* LP, so it only made sense for myself, Jeff Carrigan and our school year's resident 'Ace Face' Richard Heard to pause from playing Space Invaders in the studio lounge long enough to interview Paul Weller, Bruce Foxton and Rick Buckler – together, for what turned out to be a brutally hilarious and politically incorrect conversation. On my own, I had an equally enjoyable conversation with Mark E. Smith and Marc Riley from The Fall, whose popularity among *Jamming* readers was surpassed only by The Jam themselves. (Smith subsequently wrote a letter in praise of the finished issue.) Jeff conducted unabashedly enthusiastic interviews with his new South London glam hero Shrink, and a Rough Trade band called The Pack that featured a young Kirk Brandon. I raved with zeal about Belfast's punk-pop pioneers RUDI, having no idea what our collective future would hold, and interviewed Coventry's second-finest 2-Tone band, The Selecter, after soundcheck at their London debut, opening for The Beat.

Elsewhere in its forty pages, *Jamming* found space for scene reports from Sheffield (by Tony Perrin) and New Jersey (from Red Noise/TV Toy drummer Steve Peer), printed poems for the first time, and seemingly set out to review just about every independent single released that year – and most of the fanzines too! But perhaps the most important and certainly the most discussed piece in the entire zine was my rant about 'tribalism'. (The summer of '79 saw a horrific increase in violence at gigs, bus stops, tube stations and just about anywhere else that any combination of mods, skinheads, punks, and some form of 'rockers' gathered in numbers greater than two.) Almost immediately, it generated written responses from Crass, Garry Bushell and others at the receiving end of my complaints, further evidence that *Jamming* was now influential. The ludicrously low 25p cover price, the fact that The Jam scored a breakthrough Top 3 hit with 'The Eton Rifles' as soon as Issue 9 was published, and *Jamming's* word-of-mouth reputation served to ensure that all 2,000 copies would be sold by the spring.

Meeting so many bands, taking so many photos, and not remembering a quarter of it. **Jeff C.**

The Jam

ULTIMATE INTERVIEW

Alright, so it's only a year since the last one, but a lot's happened to The Jam since then - they've 'risen from the dead' (as the weeklies would have you know), had four hit singles, a silver album, toured round the world, been held responsible for a mod revival, and alongside The Clash, have established themselves as the most popular of the vanguard of new-wave groups still going. Obviously, attitudes have changed, and there are new things to ask. Also, there's rarely, if ever, been an interview with the three together, something we've 'sort of' remedied. Add to that the fact that we've deliberately kept The Jam out of Jamming as much as we could in nos 6,7 & 8 (it was your votes that won them the poll in issue 7), and that only a quarter, at the most, of the people reading this read the last one, we felt it was time to go back and discuss the changes. Also, to try and get an exclusive on the album, but that's something it's never easy for fanzines to get, by the time they've gone to print.

The interview was done during a late-summer of madness in Virgin's plush, new Town House studios (used by both The Ruts & XTC for their new records). Certain things about the recording we'll never forget, eg Paul & Rick's addiction to Space Invaders (can I be the first to say I reckon it's ripped off the last episode of Blakes 7?), Bruce and Paul's addiction to **pool**, Rick's addiction to Mayfair (sorry about that Rick!), football matches against the NME, endless cups of coffee, constant one-liners from Rick & Bruce, neither ever willing to let the other have the last line, and lots more memories besides.

The interview is, in fact, 2 interviews, done over a gap of 4 days:- the first was with all 3, Bruce being in a terrible mood, and the interview getting nowhere fast, before we got some decent answers, and then the jokes started coming, ending up with Bruce being in a great mood all day; the 2nd was a (slightly) more serious affair, with just Rick & Paul, giving a good balance.

Doubtless you think we've said enough, so here goes with the first interview, joining it with the group just starting to talk...

WHAT DO YOU THINK OF THE WAY IT'S TURNED OUT - THE SITUATION NOW WHERE YOU REGULARLY HAVE 3 NEW-WAVE INFLUENCED BANDS IN THE TOP 10?

Rick: I think it's good, it's great.
Paul: It depends who you're talking about really...

...WELL ARE THEY JUST PUTTING OUT STUFF 'COS THEY KNOW PEOPLE WILL BUY IT? SMASH HITS & THAT LOT... THE BANDS WHO GET IN ARE THE TYPE THAT APPEAL TO LITTLE KIDS....

Paul: But you've got The Clash in there, and I wouldn't think The Clash come under that.
Rick: I don't think The Buzzcocks do either.
Paul: But you've got to think like... how many real bands get in the Top 10? The Boomtown Rats don't count, or Costello, or Dury- it's good when bands like The UK Subs and The Ruts get in there.... Punk has taken off on a real nationwide level now. And in a sense, it's 2 years too late. But it's still good - at least something's going on.

BUT I (JC) RECKON IT'S BEING WATERED DOWN FOR THE SMASH HITS MARKET - THE STUFF THAT GETS IN THE CHART THAT IS.

Rick: I know what you mean. You mean the word 'punk' has got a broader meaning on it now...
Paul: Well it's acceptable innit?

YEAH IT IS. BUT YOU WOULDN'T GET BANDS LIKE THE PACK IN THERE, WHO ARE LIKE IT SHOULD HAVE BEEN.

Paul: I don't know if you can say that really - there's lots of obscure bands that suddenly leap out of nowhere. Like The Upstarts - 3 years ago, there was no way a band like The Upstarts could have got in the Top 20. And I wouldn't say their music's been watered down. But as I said, I

At the interview.

-14- All photos by Jeff Carrigan

think people like The Rats, Sham and Costello have that acceptable meaning.
Rick: I think there are bands though that
have been influenced by saying "We've got
to get radio airplay" and then bringing
out a single that would appeal to those
sort of people...
Paul: It's like I Fought The Law, you know
- what the fuck are the Clash doing with a
pop ditty like that? I thought they were
against all that.

THEN WOULD YOU SAY THE NEW-WAVE HAS ACHIEVED
ANYTHING WHEN YOU'VE STILL GOT HITS BEING
MADE ON THE BASIS OF THE BBC PLAYLIST?

Paul: Well I think, as I said, the main
thing it's achieved is that bands like The
Upstarts and The Subs - regardless of
whether you like them or not - there's no
way they would ever have got in the charts
3 years ago. And it's not imperative to go
on TOTP, or be on the playlist, anymore.
The Pistols smashed all that down.

BUT WERE THEY THE ONLY ONES WHO COULD?

Paul: I dunno, yeah. Well, like with The
Ruts, I didn't hear Babylon's Burning on
the radio hardly at all, and that still
got in the Top 10.

WHAT BANDS DO YOU LIKE AT THE MOMENT?

Paul: Ruts, Skids, Members and The Undertones.

YOU LIKE THE CHORDS DON'T YOU?

Paul: Yeah, they're pretty good. And the
Purple Hearts. I ain't hardly seen any of
these bands - I've only heard the records.

WELL THAT BRINGS US MORE OR LESS STRAIGHT
ONTO THE MOD MOVEMENT (crafty lik-up between
punk and mod eh?), WHICH YOU'RE QUOTE,
'RESPONSIBLE FOR'. HOW DO YOU FEEL ABOUT IT?

Paul: I think it's got nothing to do with
us really.
Rick: I think we've been through all this
before.
IT SEEMS THAT THE ONLY TIME YOU'VE SPOKEN
OUT STRONGLY AGAINST BEING RESPONSIBLE FOR
IT WAS ZIGZAG, IN JANUARY. WE GET A LOT OF
LETTERS SAYING THE JAM HAVE SOLD OUT TO A
MOD REVIVAL.

Paul: Well most people who say that are
fuckin' idiots. Every time anyone's asked
me, I've said it's nothing to do with us.
Rick: It was the same situation in the punk
thing really.

YEAH, BUT GROUPS LIKE THE PISTOLS WERE
GLAD THEY HAD PUNKS FOLLOWING THEM. WHERE-
AS YOU'VE GOT YOUR OWN INDIVIDUAL MOD
STAND, AND NOW THERE'S A WHOLE LOAD OF
GROUPS AND PEOPLE PICKING UP ON SOMETHING
THAT'S 15 YEARS OLD.

Rick: Well, we're not prejudiced against
anyone who comes to see us; if they want
to wear mod gear or anything else.

Paul: If people feel the need to be stig-
matised to one thing, then it's their
fault, not ours. All our songs are about
individuals, like, I don't see why people
have to be punks or mods or anything. Well
I do - on a superficial level it's good to
have a bit of culture, but ultimately it's
fucking boring, when it comes down to
fighting or anything. I mean, when you
won't got to see a band 'cos they ain't
punks or they ain't mods - that's just
fucking rubbish.
DO YOU RECKON PEOPLE CAN CHANGE FROM PUNK
TO MOD SUCCESSFULLY?

All: Secret Affair!!!
Paul: Well what is a real mod? Is it going
out and trying to buy ome blues, just to
live out the part - that's just a joke man.
That thing happened 15 years ago. It's just
as stupid as punks going out and buying
stuff from Seditionaries; punk wasn't
really about getting your clothes from a
certain shop.

SO WHAT ABOUT ALL THE PEOPLE WHO GET RICK-
ENBACKERS AND TRY AND PLAY GUITAR LIKE
YOU?

Paul: What can I say? It's up to them
innit? But then again, I bought a Rickenbacker 'cos I saw photos of Pete Townshend
with one and thought he looked great. So
I can't really knock it, but I can't con-
done it either.

SO DO YOU ALL CALL YOURSELVES MODS?

Paul: I call him (Rick) Pube!*

Pube himself.

Rick: I think if people want fads, they
ought to create their own.
Paul: I'm into 'foppism'. I'm trying to
revive fops and dandies.

TELL US MORE, WE MIGHT GET A WHOLE GENERAT-
ION GOING!

*= An old member of the group used to be
called 'Pube' 'cos he looked like one. When
he left, the name was given to Rick, who
hasn't been able to shake it off.

(To keep tongue-in-cheek) the quotes in R&R, Paul weller said that if you gigs both against racism we don't need to play under a big red banner to prove it.

Paul: Basically, all you need is just a white laced hankie, which you tuck under your cuff; and you get it out now and again and dab your forehead!!!
(Interview collapses into laughter)
Paul: That's about it - that's all you need. It's quite an inexpensive fad really.

CAN WE JUST HAVE THAT BIT ABOUT SQUIRE AGAIN - YOU SAID THEY USED TO BE A HEAVY METAL GROUP.

Paul: They used to wear kaftans and that, & they used to rehearse every Sunday in this little church, and I used to go and smoke their dope for them...
Rick: ...Smash up their guitars.
Paul: The thing is, when you've been playing for 4 or 5 years, and suddenly everyone around you is taking off, you start to have bum-trouble about it. So therefore you have to latch onto something and get in there, which is fair enough in a sense. It depends if you're gonna be honest and say that's the reason you're doing it. There's so many bands saying "We was a mod before they were". What the fuck does it matter? Punk bands did that - there was only one original punk band and that was The Pistols. That's it.

SO WITHOUT TRYING TO STAY ON THE SUBJECT TOO LONG. WOULD YOU SAY MODS ARE RELEVANT?

Paul: yeah, I think they are - I think any new movement is good. I'm talking more about music...

THAT'S ALL IT SHOULD BE...

Paul: Exactly. That about sums it up doesn't it? All the rest - the beachfights, and trying to renact 1964 is just fuckin' pointless. It would be better if all those kids whothink clthes are so much, flogged their parkas and scooters and went out and bought guitars and drums.

YOU MENTIONED SECRET AFFAIR, 'COS YOU USED TO KNOW THEM REALLY WELL WHEN THEY WERE THE NEW HEARTS. WHAT DO YOU THINK OF THEM?

Bruce: (What's this? Bruce woken up?) They-'re just a classic changing their colours aren't they, to cash in? You know 'Punk is dead shock horror. Mods tell all.'
Rick: They weren't really into the punk thing very heavily.
Paul: They've got a grudge against the punks 'cos the punks never took to them.

DO YOU THINK IAN PAGE IS PUTTING ON ANY SORT OF FRONT, BECAUSE HE SEEMS TO BE LIKE THE JIMMY PURSEY OF THE MODS?

Rick: Does he?
Paul: All of a sudden you see him with these big thick eyebrows - "Kids....like you... and me...". I think it funny though - you know that song 'Just Another Teenage Anthem' which takes the piss out of teen anthems? Well, Time For Action smacks a bit of teen anthem to me...

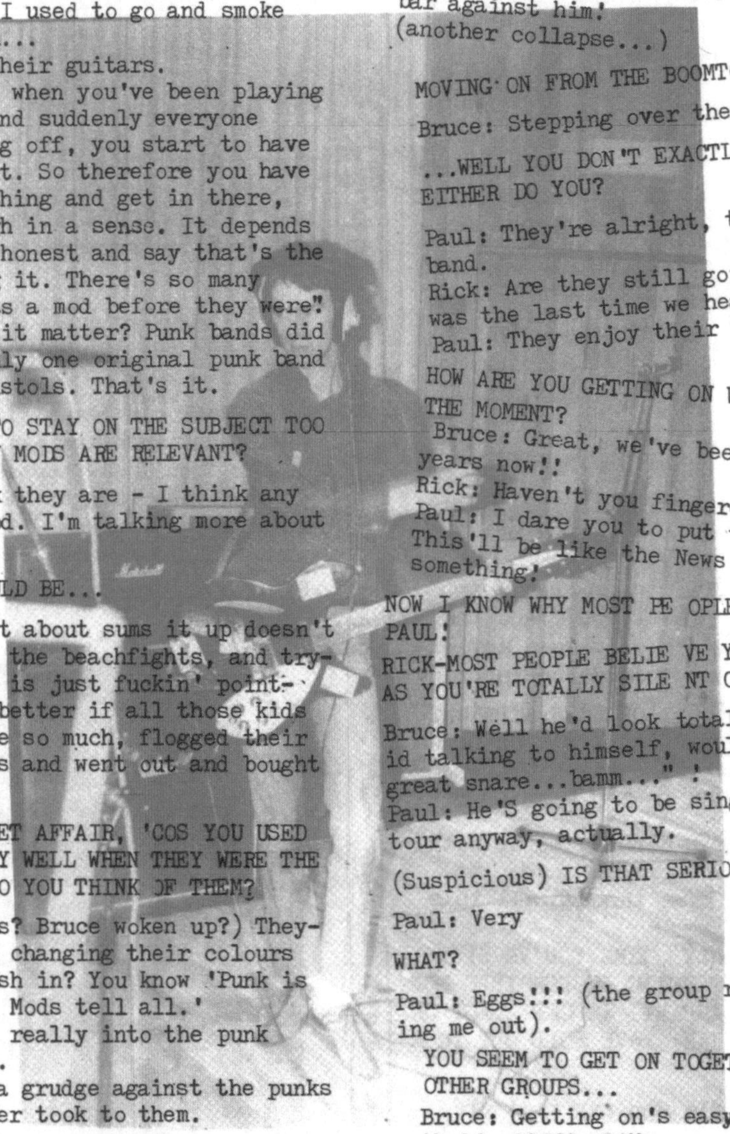

From now on, there are no serious answers to this interview......

WHY IS IT YOU LOVE BOB GELDOF SO MUCH?

Paul: 'Cos he's a wonderfully fab person.
Rick: He's 'hip'isn't he?
Bruce: He's 'in?'
Paul: He's 'no. 1'.

JC: IS THAT SARCASTIC OR WHAT?

Interview collapses as everyone hurls abuses at Jeff.)

WHAT IS IT YOU ACTUALLY HOLD AGAINST HIM?

Bruce: (quietly) I'd love to hold an iron bar against him!
(another collapse...)

MOVING ON FROM THE BOOMTOWN RATS...

Bruce: Stepping over them you mean!!

...WELL YOU DON'T EXACTLY LIKE THE CLASH EITHER DO YOU?

Paul: They're alright, they're a good live band.
Rick: Are they still going? Fuck me, when was the last time we heard from them?
Paul: They enjoy their work anyway...

HOW ARE YOU GETTING ON WITH POLYDOR AT THE MOMENT?
Bruce: Great, we've been going out for 3 years now!!
Rick: Haven't you fingered it yet??!!
Paul: I dare you to put that down... This'll be like the News Of The World or something.

NOW I KNOW WHY MOST PE OPLE ONLY INTERVIEW PAUL!
RICK-MOST PEOPLE BELIE VE YOU CAN'T SPEAK, AS YOU'RE TOTALLY SILE NT ON STAGE...

Bruce: Well he'd look totally fucking stupid talking to himself, wouldn't he? "Oh great snare...bamm...".
Paul: He'S going to be singing on the next tour anyway, actually.

(Suspicious) IS THAT SERIOUS?

Paul: Very

WHAT?

Paul: Eggs!!! (the group rejoice in catching me out).

YOU SEEM TO GET ON TOGETHER BETTER THAN OTHER GROUPS...
Bruce: Getting on's easy, it's getting off that's difficult!
Interview collapses...
Rick: We're not cracking up are we??

DO YOU 2 GET AT ALL JEALOUS OF PAUL GETTING ALL THE ATTENTION AND INTERVIEWS?

Bruce: Not if they're like this all the time...
Rick: You're fucking alright mate...

And that's as good a place as any to leave Interview 1.
Part 2 starts now,without Bruce.....

YOU ALL WENT TO SEE THE WHO AT THE RAINBOW DIDN'T YOU? WHAT DID YOU THINK OF IT?

Rick: I was a bit disappointed really - partly because you expect to see something, and then because Keith Moon wasn't there. I don't think it's the same now as people rave about or remember.
Paul: It's just like going to see Christ rising from the dead, 'cos they're such a monument. Obviously, you go expecting too much. All said and done, they're just a rock'n'roll group - it's only drums and guitars.

DO YOU THINK THAT COULD HAPPEN TO THE JAM?

Paul: I dunno... It's really hard to say... I don't think we wanna become one - you get trapped.
Rick: That sort of thing's not really in your hands though.

BUT THE WHO COULD HAVE AVOIDED IT IF THEY'D BEEN MORE ACCESIBLE, AND DONE MORE GIGS.
Paul: Yeah, that might be true.
Rick: I dunno. I think you'd only probably just delay it. People think so much of a band they tend to idolise them - they do the putting up, rather than the band.
Paul: It's like The Pistols though - there's so many Pistols fans who haven't even seen the group. That's the same as The Who though - it was the first time I'd ever seen them, at The Rainbow, yet I was always like a no. 1 Who fan.

LAST YEAR, I WAS SAYING HOW PLEASED I WAS THAT THE JAM HAD NO SET FORMAT OR ANYTHING - THEY WERE PLAYING GIGS AND DOING ALBUMS WHEN THEY FELT LIKE IT. AND IN THE LAST YEAR, IT SEEMS AS IF YOU MIGHT BE SETTLING DOWN INTO THE TYPICAL ROCK THING OF 1 LP, 2 MAJOR TOURS, AND 3 SINGLES A YEAR, WHICH I'D HATE TO SEE HAPPEN.

Paul: Yeah, it's a question of getting caught up in it - you're in a rut. I mean you've got to plan out like a year ahead of you, and this album's coming out in November, exactly the same as last year.

Welcome to another new Jamming slot - Photos Request. You tell us something in rock'n'roll you want to see a phot of, and we will try and oblige.

This issue: Cherry scarlet of Nottingham has her foot fetish satisfied, as we publish a picture of Paul Weller's leg!

All requests to the usual address.

And then supposedly there's going to be an American tour in February, which will mean another British tour in May, which is going to put us back in the same boat next year as well, which we don't want to do. We wanna do like a summer album or something, 'cos otherwise it's going to be like "Ah, it's October 20th, time for a Jam album"thing. It's like an Annual Meeting or something. It's not always your fault though - if you've got commitments you've got to do them.

WELL, LIKE I STARTED OFF LAST TIME, SAYING THAT YOU'D PLAYED 6 LOTS OF BRITISH DATES, PLUS 2 AMERICAN TOURS, AND THIS YEAR YOU'VE ONLY PLAYED 2, AND THE ONLY PLACE IN LONDON TO SEE YOU HAS BEEN THE RAINBOW.

Paul: Yeah, it gets hard. I quite agree with you though, but it's fuckin' 'ard. Like we wanted to those those one-offs, that were scheduled for the end of August, but we had to pull out 'cos we were doing the LP. But it just gets boring, it's all mapped out - you know next year you've got two major British tours, an American 6-week tour, a European tour, and an LP and 2 singles, and the usual quota... I'd sooner not do that at all than do it every year. Hopefully it's going to change next year.

HAVE YOU GOT ANY IDEA HOW?

Paul: Well we're just going to have to miss out something, or shuffle things about a bit more. Hopefully, we're going to concentrate more on recording now. It's all down to a question of material. Again it's down to not having enough time to write.
Rick: You can't just keep going out with the same material- we got fucked up with that earlier this year.
Paul: We just had no time at all - it was straight off the All Mod Cons tour, a month's rest, then a European tour, then to the States, then straight back here for a tour.
Rick: We didn't want to do that, because of material. We'd have done somethig else-Europe, or not done anything at all.
Paul: Then again, that would have been a year 'till anyone had seen us again in Britain.

YOU'RE SAYING YOU WANT TO SPEND MORE TIME RECORDING, BUT TO MY OPINION OVER, I'D MUCH SOONER THERE WERE MORE GIGS. I THINK THE MAJORITY OF PEOPLE PREFER GIGS 'COS THEY'VE GOT THE RECORD ANYTIME.

Paul: Yeah, but the trouble is, if you're touring all the time, like this year, then you've got 3 weeks to write an LP in, which is ridiculous. I'd sooner do like 2 weeks here and there, or like a week's gigs and have 2 weeks off.

I WOULDN'T MIND A WEEK'S GIGS, AND 2 WEEKS OFF...

Paul Weller, August '78.

"I didn't think we were the greatest band in the world, I wouldn't be in the group..."

-17-

Paul (in posh voice): Well, we'll see what we can do for you
Rick: Where'smy secretary. Ah, make a note of that will you.
Paul: No, I agree with you. That's one thing I have noticed about fanzines- there's a lot of babbling that comes out about what a group should do and shouldn't do; it's not always that easy you know?

BARBED WIRE FANZINE POSED THE QUESTION ABOUT YOU HAVING THE SOUND OF '65 IN '77, '66 IN '78, AND WHAT ABOUT YOUR GETTING INTO '67, WHICH YOU STRONGLY DENIED. BUT APPARENTLY, YOU'REALL INTO EARLY PINK FLOYD NOW AREN'T YOU?

Paul: Yeah right. Yeah, it's definitely coming back - psychedelia next year. We just wanna make sure we're the forerunners of it. On the next tour we're wearing gaily colour-ed kafghans, and beads...
Rick: Flowers in our hair...
Paul: And we're gonna start taking acid,man.
Rick: Floating on stage.
Paul: Dry ice man.   There's all that bullshit - to me it's just a laugh. I think we've always sounded contemporary.

I DON'T MEAN ANYTHING AS SUDDEN, BUT SUPPOSE YOU STARTED - SERIOUSLY - MAKING PSYCHEDELIC MUSIC?

Paul: We always have really. I mean, In The City's psychedelic innit? And When You're Young breached psychedelia really. Syd Barrett all over.   Nah, I dunno abo ut that. We never try and make confusing music 'cos it's not worthwhile.   We'll have to stick to '66 for a while or we're liable to run out of years. Get to '69 and start all over agian - go back to '64....
(Ever felt you're being made a fool of?)

HOW LONG DID IN THE CITY TAKE TO DO?

Rick: Recordd in 11 days.

WHAT ABOUT THE MODERN WORLD?

Paul: 2 weeks.

ALL MOD CONS?

Both: 3-4 weeks.

THIS ALBUM?

Rick (Burst out laughing, spotting question) Well we've been on it 1 month, with another month planned.
Paul: That's going back to the old thing about touring - I never have time to write or anything. We don't have any time to re-hearse. At the moment I'm going away, writing a song, coming back over a weekend, we're rehearsing it, putting it down, I'm going away...

SO IS THERE ANY WAY THE ALBUMS ARE GOING TO START TAKING LONGER AND LONGER?

Rick: It is possible, because as you carry on, you feel you get more specialist.
Paul: Yeah, but even so, with any of the tracks, like Burning Sky - we've rehearsed them for like 2 days, and put them down in a day, so one track's taken 3 days. What it boils down to is the writing. Say we had 12 or 14 songs when we came into the studio - they'd all have been down by now. It's only 'cos of a lack of material - not even lack of material - I've got loads of ideas, but not enough time. I don't want to rush them, and them turn out like shit. I'd soon-er not make an LP this year than do that - I'd wait 'till next year.

JOHN (MANAGER) WAS SAYING, I THINK, THAT THERE'S 24 STANDING VENUES OUT OF 27 ON THIS TOUR, WHICH SEEMS PRETTY GOOD...

Paul: Yeah, well London's a real problem, 'cos there's nowhere that's unseated that we can actually play, apart from The Lyceum, they all seem to shut down. Notre Dame shuts down, and The Hammersmith Palais won't let us play there for some reason.
Rick: If you look into London gigs, there isn't a big choice is there.
Paul: There's a competition for you - if anybody in London knows of any 2,000 stand-up places, let us know.

YOU WERE SAYING IT'S ONLY THE FIRST 4 ROWS COMING OUT AT THE RAINBOW, BUT SOME GROUPS GET IT ALL STANDING...

Rick: You've got to put down £3000 just to have the seats taken out for one night.
Paul: They say there's manpower, and stor-age - it's all bullshit obviously.
Rick: They've got to put them in again for the next day which is totally daft. If you're lucky enough to get the situation where there's 4 bands on night after night, and they all want the seats out, then you can spread the costs between them.

WHAT ABOUT THE FACT YOU'RE PLAYING 3 NIGHTS IN A ROW?

Rick: He's got a point there hasn't he? (Ever thought I should be their manager?)
Paul: Yeah I know, but it would still cost us 3 grand.
Rick (quick on the uptake): Yeah it would still cost us 3 grand.
Paul: We'can't afford 3 grand - and the sup-port bands can't afford to chip in. We don't even know if we're gonna have enough money to go on tour.   It's a viscious circle.

And that's the last suitably relevant quote we got. And now, the time-old question - how do you close thearticle? We'll try by saying that anyone who knows of a decent-sized, 2000 stand-up venue in London, or one that might open, get in contact with The Jam, 'cos they're as fed up with you with seated venues like The Rainbow. I'm not going to finish with any sort of catchy quote, but merely say the LP review is on the opposite page, and so continues the saga of the best band in the world.......

'Thick as Thieves' 2 mins 14 seconds into the track. Standing next to John Weller watching Paul on his own through the Shepherds Bush studio's control room glass window. The most powerful guitar I've ever heard. **Jeff C.**

Punk, ted, skinhead, rude boy, rock-a-billy, mod... we've had it so much over the last few years we ought to be used to it by now. But all the time, these little tribes keep to themselves, don't bother mixing. Punk fights mod just 'cos one dresses differently from the other, but what's the point? There are men high up there who want to see all the kids fighting each other, because if they do they don't have time to fight the system, challenge the power. But still it carries on...

Like the punk at a Nashville Spizz Energi gig, who had a brief flick through Jamming 8, and then threw it viciously back at me, saying "It's all fuckin' niggers and mods" (even though there were no 'niggers' in it). Also at that gig, police were called to prevent skins from kicking their way in, and on the way back, two 16-year-old punks got stabbed by teds at the Elephant & Castle tube station. On the same night, Quadrophenia opened in London, and saw the start of a new wave of tribalism - mods vs rockers (though most mods don't know whether they're fighting rock-a-billies, teds or Hells Angels).... Good news all this, ain't it?

Then to cap it all, Sounds let Garry Bushell print that pathetic piece on the Southend Bank Holiday 'riots'. Apart from the fact that it was completely ripped off Can't Explain fanzine's Easter account (which was basically anti-aggro), the article just glorified violence and encouraged aggression. I was going to write a letter to Sounds, but thought at least I could get all my views down here. The article was based around The Jam's "When You're Young" lyrics.... "I hope he's taking the piss, 'cos that song is"- Paul Weller. Unfortunately, it didn't seem that he was.

Then the NME calls Jamming a mod fanzine, when we're actually trying to bridge the gap, so that mods can see the UK Subs safely, and punks can see Secret Affair, except what chance is there of that when the latter sing "We hate the punk elite" in Time For Action, and continually droan "Punk is dead"....

...As it is, 'punk' is getting stronger, not dying - the effects of '77 and the deserved shake-up the music biz got are growing all the time. No longer is there that mysterious shroud over the making of records, and more and more punks are keeping to punk ideals, living against the state. The prime example is Crass, but then their music is so harsh it just encourages violence, and gets it.

Where's it going to end? We all know, the way things are going, it's just going to get worse, and some rich fat businessman is going to laugh even louder.

This article seems to have got lost somewhere down the line, and may come over as a pile of shit. It hasn't really got a purpose, just asking questions - if you've got an answer write to me and I'll print some replies next time. Better still, start your own 'zine - the fact there's over 100 going now is another far-reaching effect of the explosion.

The latest thing is rude boys/girls - the thin line between skin and mod. As said elsewhere in this issue, ska has a better chance than anything else of being a unifying force, but for how long can 3 groups hold together mods, skins, rude boys, punks and even rockabillies? The answer is it doesn't have to be 3 groups, and the rest is in your hands.......

Tony Fletcher

"WE ARE The Fall

NO SUBTITLES FOR US" SAYS MARK E. SMITH (BELOW)
PIC:AF

THE FALL:-
Mark E. Smith - vocals
Marc Riley - electric guitars, vocals
Mike Leigh - Drums
Craig Scanlan - electric guitar
Steve Hanley - Bass guitar, vocals

It seems from your chart votes that most of you already know about The Fall, but to recap, they have been going since the start of the new wave, based in Manchester, and have undergone many and frequent line-up changes, Smith being the only survivor. They have released 3 singles and 2 albums on Step Forward Records, these being:-
Bingo Master's Break-Out/Psycho Mafia/Repetition (SF7)
It's The New Thing /Various Times (SF9)
Rowche Rumble/In My Area (SF11)
Live At The Witch Trials LP (SFLP2)
Dragnet LP (SFLP4) (reviewed elsewhere)

The Fall are well-known for unordinary ideas, and being 'white crap', but there are two points I would like to say:-
1/ The Fall are rock'n'roll. Those who think they aren't misunderstand.
2/ The Fall do have a sense of humour, and are not the serious pseuds people imagine.

OK. The interview was done with Mark E. Smith and Marc Riley at the Faulty Products office. To avoid confusion with names, we will, this once, call them by their surnames.
And now, take it away...

DO YOU HAVE ANY IDEALS, AND IF SO WHAT?

Smith: Do you mean for the band, or personally?

WELL, FOR THE BAND, WHAT ARE YOUR AIMS? MOST GROUPS WANT TO GO TOP OF THE CHARTS, GO ON TOTP, WHERAS IT SEEMS THE FALL DON'T.

Smith: Yeah, we do shut it off a lot. But that's alot my fault, 'cos I like privacy. There's alot of times when we could have done things like that.
Riley: We want to expand on what we've got already.
Smith: It's just to keep The Fall going - that's my fuckin' thing in life, to keep it going as long as I can. It's like an institution really, 'cos no matter what we sound like, we're unique. There's got to be a demand though, 'cos a lot of the new wave bands are predictable, they do things like you said, you know. They do things even the old bands thought twice about doing - they do them like no questions asked.

I EXPECT YOU'VE BEEN ASKED THIS ONE MANY TIMES, BUT WHY IS THERE SUCH A PLAIN IMAGE?

Riley: Well it's not pretence is it?
Smith: We're 'Simpletons' (bursts out laughing). I don't get into it, you know - I think it's cheap. I'm just not into clothes - I don't get off on wearing clothes. Some people do, so that's alright. People get really personal about it - they say "Come on, you don't really dress like that", but it's just how I want.

DID YOU ORIGINALLY CONSIDER THE FALL AS ANYTHING TO DO WITH THE PUNK SCENE?

Smith: Er, yeah, no, (???) - I'd written songs for about a year before the new wave thing, but I didn't take myself seriously, you know. I think that's what the Pistols did for everybody - you saw bands and you could do better, you could do it. Before the new wave I used to like singing to myself, I used to write songs, I used to be into certain stuff that people were doing, but the barrier was broken down by The Pistols. Before the Pistols, I thought 'If I get up on stage and strt singing' - I can't sing right - 'people will just bottle me, or ignore me'. It was a waste of time, you know.

DO YOU CONSIDER THE OLD FALL MATERIAL AS STILL RELEVANT, OR AS SOMETHING THAT'S BEEN SAID - A STATEMENT?

Smith: I think most of our stuff's pretty timeless - maybe the style's slightly irrelevant nowadays.
Riley: After an album's been out for a year, if it doesn't age, it means you can still relate to it, which is alright. It's not like stuff like the Chelsea

-24-

Nightclub, which noone can relate to, not even The Members.

Smith: That is a common policy of the band - we wanna make music that will stay on for 10 years. I'm damned sure there'll be a lot more people listening to our stuff in 10 years than a lot of famous bands.

Smith: What songs are you talking about?

WELL, IT'S JUST THAT SOME GROUPS DON'T LIKE PLAYING THEIR EARLY MUSIC-THEY FEEL THEY'VE POSSIBLY CHANGED SINCE THEN, OR THAT IT'S A STATEMENT THAT'S BEEN SAID...

Smith: Well, we've dropped Repetition, and Bingo Master; partly because we feel the message is irrelevant, but also because the band's bored with it.

Riley: If we pooled in all the songs we have we'd have about 60. We've got too many songs now, and there's only about 3 old songs in the set.

Smith: And it's wrong to suppress that creativity. It's like bands that have hit singles, you know, - by the time the single hits the charts, they've been playing it for a year, and they're going to have to play it for another year.

Riley: That's why we like getting things down while they're fresh. Like we have with the new album - all the stuff on it, except for 2, was written after Martin left, so all the album is fresh.

Smith: If there's a fault with Witch Trials, it's that we were over-familiar with the songs.

Riley: I was, and I'd only been in the band 6 months at the time.

WHY HAVE THERE BEEN SO MANY LINE-UP CHANGES? IS IT SOMETHING YOU'VE WANTED?

Smith: It's not something you want at the time, but it's worked out good when you look back at it.

Riley: It's all very personal - if you don't like it you leave, and that's that. It's strange with something like Martin to break it off, and just say "I'm leaving", and see what happens when he's been there for like 2 years.

DO YOU STILL CONSIDER IT THE FALL?

Smith: Yeah. Defeinitely. A band is what it's got to say, and I've always spoken for the band through the lyrics; so I think it would be different if the lyric-writer had left, but he hasn't, ie I haven't. I was throughly bored with the Witch Trials sound, I needed a fuckin' change, it was horrible - well it seems horrible to me now. It works really good - the energy a line-up change injects into a band is incredible.

A LOT OF PEOPLE GO ON STAGE THINKING OF THE AUDIENCE, AND WHAT THE AUDIENCE WANTS TO HEAR; DO YOU PLAY WHAT THE AUDIENCE WANTS, OR WHAT YOU WANT?

Smith: Well we don't pander to audiences, but then audiences can make a difference. I find our audiences totally unpredictable- I don't know what's going to happen with

them next time, and I think that's good. The YMCA was wierd - that wasn't what I expected at all (details of the YMCA gig are on Page 39)...

Riley: It's like when we played Warrington, yonks ago, with Karl, and it was just like hundreds of kids there, with a mass of po-going. Then we played there 6 months later with Mike, and it was suddenly different - a load of people just stood there watching.

Smith: London is always different as well. So is Manchester. The Fall haven't got a fixed audience. The YMCA gig was really wierd, because there was like, all the intellectuals there, and then a core of dancers at the front going wild, and all these guys with moustaches behind them, going "Ummm...yes...".

DO YOU THINK YOU 'WCN' AT THE LYCEUM?

Smith: Er... yeah. People made a big fuss about that thing, wheras we thought it was just another gig. We just thought we'd made a mistkae playing the Lyceum again, 'cos we knew it was going to be like that.

Riley: ...After the Gen X thing. We played with Gen X there and it was pretty horrible, but we decided to play there again...

Smith: 'Cos we thought it would be a lot better. We were playing with what we thought then were 'kindred spirits', ie Gang Of 4, Mekons, Stiff Little Fingers...but they turned out to be a oack of shit. It was good to play it though - The Fall thrive on that. Me & Marc were talking about it just the other day, it's really good - it brings the best out of us insituations like that.

Riley: It's like if something goes wrong before we go on, we're all wound up. Like at The Marquee, Yvonne (P awlett) was

L-t - Mark smith (may scanley, marc kiley, Steve Hanley, Mike leigh

PIC: Brendan Jackson

-25-

supposed to turn up, and she didn't. So
we said "Alright, fuck you". It's like
spite, I suppose.
Smith: Something like The Lyceum brings out
The Fall's attitude. Like the YMCA was a bit
too easy really.

WAS LATWT CAREFULLY PLANNED OUT IN ADVANCE,
LIKE IT WAS A RUN-DOWN OF '78 FOR YOU?

Smith: Yeah it was rather 'In Retrospect'.
Riley: It was getting rid of old songs.
Smith: Well it wasn't so much that- we had
about 4 other songs to go on it; we just
had too many songs for it. That was the
drag. The only bit of real spontaneity was
the title track- it was made up there.

WAS IT DELIBERATE TO RECORD IT IN ONE DAY
AND MIX IT IN ONE DAY?

Smith: It was and it wasn't. We had 5 days,
but I got sick for the first 3. There was a
lot of fuss made about that as well - I
mean, why bands have to take more than 3-4
days to do an album is beyond me personally.
Especially bands that do the, like, guitar,
bass,drums line-up like we do. Why they
have to go in for months is beyond me.
Riley: Some people go in, and they do dubs
on this, and dubs on that. Ours is a very
straightforward sound.
Smith: The best sound The Fall get is live-
it always has been.
Riley: ... Which is why Rumble got more of
a live sound.

IS THE "I STILL BELIEVE IN THE R'N'R DREAM"
LINE SARCASTIC OR SERIOUS?

Smith: It's half and half- it's ambiguous.
But I do ina lot of ways. People say The
Fall aren't rock'n'roll you know; my attitude is that we are rock'n'roll and no
other fucker is.
Riley: It's just what they consider to be
rock'n'roll, like screwing and...
Smith: Like if you get down to the basics
of rock'n'roll, if you go back to the mid-
'50's - those bands had the right attitude.

I WAS GOING TO ASK WHETHER YOU DID CONSIDER
YOURSELF ROCK'N'ROLL...

Smith: I do. I consider other bands not
rock'n'roll. The term rock'n'roll is over-
used and it stinks, which is why I said
"R'n'R" - an abbreviation.

WHY DO YOU CONSIDER OTHER BANDS NOT ROCK'
N'ROLL?
Smith: Because a lot of them don't keep to
the spirit - they get into technique, they
get into effects in the studio,and they
get into playing their instruments. Or
they get into bringing singles out, bringing albums out, doing tours - that's not
rock'n'roll. Like people used to say "Oh,
you've got a really good drummer" or "Oh,
you've got a really good guitarist"-
that's a fucking stupid thing to say.
Nobody knows - who cares? Audiences don't
know who's a good musician, but they know
what's good - they feel it and they know

it's good. It's like me - I can't sing
but I knwo what I'm doing is good. And I
know that rock'n'roll is not the plying
of instruments - you don't play instruments
in rock'n'roll, and bands that do are
copping out in my estimation. Bands that,
like, go in the studio, do a guitar solo,
then go back and put loads of effects on
it, so it's not actually a guitar solo
you're listening to, but a control board.
Do you get me? And I think that's not
rock'n'roll.

marc Riley Pic AF

HAVE YOU EVER THOUGHT OF PUTTING IN THE
LYRICS?

Smith: No. I don't believe in it. I think
that's another thing that's wrong with
rock'n'roll at the moment - the consumer
is getting everything on a plate. You
notice these new wave bands, they took
the bad angle of it, like the accessibility
- it's so fuckin' accessible that there's
no work required by the band or the listener. And, like, - why should people
have lyric sheets - it's a wasye of fuckin time. The greatest thing I ever saw
was the first Ramones album where they
put the lyrics in. It was so fucking
funny. That was a really good bit of piss-
taking of the American rock market. Like
"You're a loudmouth baby, you're a loudmouth"...   No, I'm dead against it.
We've got a lot of letters asking for
lyrics, and if I've got them handy, I
send them.
    I don't like lyrics for people to read.
I like lyrics to go with music. I'd be a
fuckin' poet wouldn't I? I wouldn't
write like I write if they were meant to
be read. It's like some of the new stuff
that the band's going to do soon - there's
no lyrics actually in it. Most of them
are like sounds, sort of sub-words.

HOW IMPORTANT IS SUCCESS TO YOU?

Smith: We don't go after it, because, as I
said before I like privacy, and things have
been offered us we've turned down. All I
want success for is money to keep the band
going. What we've attained now is great,
because there's no pressure - it's a good
tension between us and these buggers here

-26-

(faulty Products). And it's like afight to survive - but we're surviving now. Whereas, about a year ago, we were just so fucking broke.But then again, if we started getting big, it takes off, and I donₒt want that either.

DO YOU THINK, THAT, IN REJECTING FAME, AS YOU ADMITTED YOU ARE, THERE'S A DANGER OF YOUR BECOMING A CULT BAND?

Smith: Yeah, I understand that, that's bad. What's been going wrong is the kids can't get the recors. We did gigs in Lancaster & places like that, and kids came up to us & said "We can't get your records". So you say "Oh, well, we're an underground band", but that's not the fucking kids fault - they should be able to get therecords. Step Forward is ideal, 'cos their distribution's getting it's shit together at last. And once we've done that, we've cracked it -

as long as people have the option to buy our records, itₐs good. I don't want to force it down people'sthroats.

WHAT HAVE YOU GOT TO DO WITH RAR?

Smith: We used to do gigs with them, until it looked as if theywere using us - they'd have Max Bygravessif he could sell more RAR stuff. I thought in those days - if you're going to have a revolution it's going to take place in musicaas well,but that isn't RAR's attitude. They were asking us to do benefit gigs, and the money was going to go so big bands could do free gigs.

HAVE YOU THOUGHT THAT THIS ALBUM IS COMING OUT WITH ALL THE CHRISTMAS MARKET?

Smith: Oh fuck, yeah! I don'ⅰ think it affects us that much though - we just want it out. If people want to buy the Clash album instead of ours, that's their loss

The Fall- draGnet

1: Psykick Dancehall/A Figure Walks Behind You/Printhead/Diceman/Before The Moon Falls/
Your Heart Out
2: Muzorewi's Daughter/Flat Of Angles/Choc-Stock/Spectre vs Rector/Put Away

Before starting the review, I must point out my copy is a test pressing that was refused for a couple of jumps and unbearable quality. The review is therefore not easy to write - I just assume the finished version will therefore be better than my review makes out.

With this record The Fall really come out and prove that they have a songwriting team,that, if it gave the rigt songs to the right groups, would have a series of hits on it's hands. There are 3 songs on the album that this specifically refers to- Psykick Dancehall, Your Heart Out, and Choc-Stock. These were all written with Craig Scanlan, new member from 'Staff 9'. The reason I mention this is it seems this might well be anew direction for The Fall (sort of), if Scanlan carries on by writing a lot of music for them. These 3 songs are pretty amazing, in that they have unforgettable tunes/riffs and yet are just so ordinarily played. As usual, I'm confused. But The Fall evidently consider this to be the right way, and I admire them for that. These 3 tracks take the album by storm.

A Figure Walks is full of tribal drums and a tale of being followed home late at night. The album is going extremely well at the moment, Printhead following, being a more rocky, riotous piece with a lot of shouting. As Smith says on the sleeve note "This song could be very BIG nowadays". Not as big as Your Heart Out, though.

Dice Man is a short piece about all Fall members, short and to the point. Before The Moon Falls has a lot of talking, and again is effective.

So that's side 1. At this point, the album looks like being an all-time Top 10 runner as long as the final version gets rid of the way itsounds like it's been recorded in a bathroom. If not, The Fall are defeinitely taking teir straightforward attitude too far.

Unfortunately, side 2 is weaker. Not enough to stop this being a classic album, but still enough to lower it a bit. Firstly though, Muzorewi's Daughter features those tribal drums again, & a uite nice tune. Flat Of Angles has a C/W feel, and is a fairl y good song (sorry this review's so insubstantial). Seems like a title track to the album. After Choc-Stock somes the longest and wierdest track, Spectre vs Rector. Something about it annoys me, possibly it drags on, or jsut the feel of it. Anyway, the LP ends rather weakly w ith Put Away.

I realise I seem to have got a bit down-cast there, so I must point out that this is [...] worth every one of [...] ruins [...] beats [...] side 2 [...] thing [...] Divisi[...] liste[...]

stru[...] music[...] but o[...] (very[...] ary [...]

Appalling layout on this page

Just felt an unexplicable urge to drop a few words....
Thought Jamming 9 stuff on us was excellent and well edited, but that's not what I wrote to tell you, really. Just that I think your attitude is fucking great and I wish it was more prevalent. For instance your stuff on us gave a unique angle to The Fall that I've never read before, and also you've made me seriously rethink my attitude to mod and a few other things. Thanks. I think you-'ve got The Fall pretty sussed and I don't think many people have - we're about HEART really and people either over-praise us or underrate us.
Re 'Dragnet' - we're into bad tribal sounds but most of side 2 sounds better without the original Pye window-polish-ridden pressing, whatever stick to your views.
Mark E. Smith, The Fall, Manchester

RUDI

The layout on these 2 pages is terrible, but was done at printers in rush, we only got the info the day we were going to print.

Rudi - Good Vibrations first signings, and 2 years later, still in the same place. Although I remember a lot of fuss being made about their first record 'Big Time', the first I really heard of them was when Peel played I-Spy, off their new EP, which really is one of the best singles ever released. It starts off with the James Bond riff before going into it's own riff that remindsme of every happy moment I've ever had - it's that good. The rest of the EP is good-time music with in credibky banal lyrics, but doesn't detract from the greatness of I-Spy itself. The EP was recorded as a 4-

piece, but the group are now 3 in the shape of:-
Brian YOUNG - guitar and vocals
Graham MARSHALL - drums & backing vocals
Ronnie MARSHALL - bass and vocals

I wrote to the group for some more info. I got so much that I think it would be better to quote Brian's letter directly:-

"RUDI - named after the Jook's record 'Oh, Oh Rudi'. Formed in late 75 when we were all still at school to 'play' our fave songs. Found a like-minded, influenced and sounding music with the explosion in the UK in mid '76. Gradually established ourselves as the first of the Ulster bands, and got very popular. In late '77 were approached by local fanzine Alternative Ulster to record a flexi-disc of 'Cops' to give away with it. We found it would be as cheap to do a real single, so for financial aid approached Terri Hooley of the new Good Vibrations record shop. Thus was born Good Vibrations label (sounds like an epic eh?). BIGTIME/NO. 1 sold so well that T erri decided to continue Good Vibes as a label.

"We moved to London in August '78 and lived in Clapham 'till November whem we had to come home after falling foul of thecops and SPG and Graham and Ron had both been in jail fro a while. This was just as we were finding our feet in England, getting at last a few gigs and press interset after broken promises by McClaren and Rhodes (seperately). We came back after Belfast became fashionable, but don't want to be linked with Belfast as such. Any categorisations like that ie Akron/Sheffield/Glasgow even skin/punk/mod etc does everybody harm.

"Meanwhile 'Overcome By Fumes' recoredd even before we went to England surfaced on the Battle Of The Bands EP and was so badly produced. Production also ruined I-SPY EP which we did last FEB, but only came out in August. It makes us sound too nice and not raw enough. In the last few months we've cut the band to a 3-piecc based around the 3 original members and it works better in every way now Ron has switched to bass, as we are far tighter and better both musically and visually. Also we play and practice a lot more instead of resting on our laurels. We're still a bit jealous that someof the bands who copied/followed us have made it, but we aren't too worried because we are now better than any of them (If you don't believe in yourself, whoelse will?) and we hope to be negotiating a big contract around Christmas."

Brian Young

graham marshall

-30-

As you can see, the group have had a lot of bad luck, including falling into the life-long trap of going to find the gold-paved streets of London. Anyway, let's just hope things go well now.
The group also sent a tape of a session they recorded for Belfast's Downtown Radio which had a hell of a lot more power than the EP, and it's obvious they've got other classics lined up in Claws And Clutches, and Radio On. Also promising are The Pressure's On and Who??You. Live, I can't imagine this band being anything but a killer.
I only got all this info the morning before going to press, so all this is scrappy, but hopefully, the picture's been got across.
If you don't go out now and buy I-Spy, then you'r. simply missing out on something you can't afford to miss out on.

AP

Ronnie marshall

FANZINES (PUNK, OK?)

Ah, fanzines - the great mouth of the music, truespress, etc - all with their own little Fanzine Writer's Co-Op - isn't it wonderful? Well it ing of the co-op, which went well, but didn't get enough fixed, and after that -sweet fa. Keith has packed in impulse, and the actual fanzine co-op seems to be getting nowhere fast. The idea of a catalogue was popular, but still hasn't gone ahead, because nothing is ORGANISED. I really can't imagine the Co-Op achieving anything worthwhile in the future at all. Sorry, but it's true.
Well, having made that downcast statement, all I can do is the usual thing of reccommending some zines to you - with a brief description, not a slagging off or 'Big Brother' attitude as one person (see letters page) claims......

AFTER HOURS - 9 Roden Street, London N7 (no. 2, 20p). The most independant fanzine yet; tends to go over the limit.
CAN'T EXPLAIN - Not quite all the paper's make it out to be, but a very good guide to mod-staie '79. From Rough Trade, no. 1 20p
CHAINSAW - Box 757, 1 North End Road, LONDON W14. Getting better all the time - very rough, fanzinistic attitude.
DAMAGED GOODS - Cockstone Hill Farm, Goldsborough, Nr. Knaresborough, Yorks HG5 8NT. One of the best, tends to concentrate on local bands. No. 4 soon. 25p?
GET UP AND GO - c/o Rough Trade. No. 2 20p. What would you do if I said I liked it lads? A good mod-zine, but no. 2 was a step back.
HEATWAVE - The first ever Jamming copy! Features Speedball, Teenbeats, Chords, our quotes and our photos. What more do you want? 6 Bellevue Road, Barnes, London.
IT TICKED AND EXPLODED - Greystones, Linwood Road, Paisley, Scotland. Not a fanzine ha! Concentartes on local bands. No. 8.
POSER - A good collection of photos. c/o Better Badges. No. 2 20p
SAFE AS MILK-45 Greenvale Road, London SE9. Still one of the best, but no. 3 didn't improve where it could have. 20p.

And that's it. More communication is needed between fanzines - I know there's about 150 going. Half-hearted Fanzine Co-Ops is not the answer.

-31-

The first issue I saw of *Jamming* was in November 1979 when Tony raved about our current Good Vibrations 45, 'I-Spy'. Seizing on the DIY punk ethic, RUDI had kickstarted the Belfast scene from scratch – finding venues and staging our own gigs when no one wanted to have anything to do with us, refusing to take no for an answer. *Jamming* embodied the same no-nonsense attitude, evolving swiftly from a scrappy schoolboy project into a serious and respected periodical – no mean feat. Though it certainly reflected the tastes of its editor, unlike most zines at the time *Jamming* wasn't tied to any one particular musical genre and punched well above its weight – thanks largely to Tony's single-minded vision, passion and boundless optimism, a remarkable achievement for a spiky-topped teenager. And that was important too: unlike all the big names in UK punk back then, RUDI were actual teenagers and Tony was even younger than us. (To put it in perspective he was over a decade younger than Joe Strummer!) Recognising each other as kindred spirits, Tony and I hit it off immediately and became active pen-pals, though I never dreamt that barely a year or so later RUDI would end up as the first band on a record label he was running... **Brian Young**

Second of the local scenes featured this time is...

SHEFFIELD~ home of muzik

There's been so much written and said about the Sheffield 'scene' over the last year or so by people with little insight into what's really going on that I thought you might like to hear about Sheffield from someone who's seen the scene from the inside........

Unquestionably the single most important factor in Sheffield's rise must be Cabaret Voltaire. Though that may seem a bit of a sweeping statement when you consider that The Cabs (as we in the know call them) aren't exactly household names yet, they acted as the initial spark that inapired so many people to get off their arses and do something - maybe even something CREATIVE?
The Cabs music is nothing if not moving. Brooken, fragmented, often unsettling noises. I don't proffer to understand the music, as I'm not quite sure if there's anything to be understood at all - The Cabs anything to be faced with 'critics' trying to analyse their music. Me, I suspect the Cabs do what interests them and if you want to read something deep into it, then so be it. On stage they open up whole new dimension, but their gigs tend to be precarious affairs often ending prematurely (It has been known for the unsuspecting to stray upon the Cabs during one of their more 'experimental' sets and mistake it for a soundcheck!) Anyway, Cabaret Voltaire have been around for 5 years or so and their first LP is out now on Rough Trade, entitled 'Mix Up'. One thing for sure is that it won't go unnoticed.

If there's one band whose name you won't forget after hearing it once is the brilliantly monikered They Must Be Russians. The name is so good it has been ripped off by at least one, possibly two, other bands, but I can assure you the Sheffield Russians are the originals. The Russians started off as a piss-take of The Cabs, and have ended up a piss-take of themselves. It has been rumoured they're going to change their name to The Human Leg and turn to electronic pop musik!?

The Russians are in a way like the Marx Brothers, possessing the remarkable abiliity to spread chaos wherever they go. One of the best songs in their set is their version of 'Nellie The Elephant' which also appears on their debut EP. I'm quite sure the Russians appalling sense of time, poor taste and their ability to fail will see them as superstars in the '80's.

Artery are for me Sheffield's pride, & though you may have come across their debut single, it doesn't do them justice. However, their follow-up -The Slide- should see them established as one of the hottest acts going. Their sound has a hypnotic quality that's hard ti describe - I've seen them time and time again and everytime I enjoy them more. Vocalist Royce Ashley has developed a brilliant rapport with his audience, but how they will cope with larger, impersonal venues is yet to be seen.

Which brings us to Mr. Marcus Featherby, manager of Artery, Limited Edition Records boss, entrepenaur and ex-mod - among other things. He is, to say the least, something of a contraversial figure in Sheffield at the moment - a much maligned character who's stirred up a lot of mixed feelings. His arrival had the effect of livening up a scene that was beginning to show signs of tiring, and though the end result of his involvement in Sheffield is yet to be seen, it is clear some things have changed for the better.

The Stunt Kites (??) aren't exactly what people expect from Sheffield, no avante garded drum machines and synthesizers with this lot. They unashamedly say "76 was the best year and we're gonna stay there". The Stunt Kites play anywhere, anytime for anything - an attitude that has won them a lot of friends. Though I can't imagine their changing the face of rock music, their affairs are currently in the hands of the very capable Martin X Russian!

42

Great Portland Street W1 was only a number 3 bus ride away from home in West Dulwich. The gig was in a basement venue filled with mainly teenage mods easily flouting the drinking-age laws. A small batch of *Jamming* fanzines held in the crooks of our arms, Shona Groves and I edged through the crowd offering the latest copy for sale at 25p. Dark, sweaty, loud, smoky and bustling; 'D'ya wanna buy a copy of *Jamming*? It's got an interview with Weller in it!' shouted into the ears of Weller clones and wanna-be Ace Faces who at times offered pills in barter exchange. It was the first time I'd ever been offered drugs! But no: clammy coins to the value of the cover price were the only accepted currency. Some wanted to browse before they bought. 'It's not a fucking library, the front cover tells you what's inside!' Trying to keep the copies pristine was hazardous enough given the constant threat of beer-spillage, dog-eared corners and fag burns: boys' grubby hands we could do without if they weren't going to buy! Nevertheless, selling fanzines at gigs was a regular occurrence. Schoolwork and band distractions (oh and girls too) meant that a new issue only surfaced when it was ready and not by any recognised schedule; we would be trying to sell an issue that was months old if Tony still had copies on the floor of his room vying for space with everything else. He wasn't tidy. Just a teenage boy for whom, as our mate Richard Heard put it, 'school was an occupational hazard of being young'.

Jeni de Haart

ever wondered what goes on behind a commercial radio station? Dave Jennings blows it open, and it's not as pleasant as you'd like...

AND THE RADIO IS IN THE HANDS OF...

I joined Pennine Radio, the commercial radio station covering the Bradford and Leeds area, for the month of June this year, hoping to gain practical experience to supplement the course I'm taking in media and communications. The experiences I had there explained quite a lot about the deficiencies of both the British radio and the rock business in general....

I started my service in the newsroom, & it was immediately obvious that the people there were the youngest on the staff, the DJs being mainly middle-aged. The place was littered with teleprinter news-bulletins from the IBA in London, and the occasional record; I noticed a disco 12", as well as Anita Ward's new album. I said what a pity it was that so many fine soul artists felt the need to go disco, and got a response I might have expected had I expressed admiration for the Yorkshire Ripper. Disco, I was ternely informed, was a very happy music (this justified everything), and I'd better get used to it because it would be the dominant trend for the next few years. Viv Mackeson, one of the news staff, kindly suggested that I visit a club in Leeds which I was told would get me out of my 'Bob Dylan Syndrome'. This, I believe, was a reference to my suggestion that music was usually better when the lyrics had some meaning, either socio-political, or emotional.

The true depth of the Pennine presenters interest in contemporary music was revealed by their remarks on the air. One Top 10 single was introduced as 'yellow' by 'Rox-anne'; the b-side of the Buzzcocks's Harmony In My Head was played on the chart show without the DJ apparently realising his mistake; and the Banshees' 'Playground Twist' was followed by the disappointed comment "That's nothing like a twist" and the jocks' reminiscences on dancing in the sixties. The mistakes were frequent and ranged from the offensive to the amusing; the inadvertently-played Buzzcocks' track was entitled "Something Goes Wrong Again"! Midway through my stay I politely suggested to the programme controller, one Jeff Winston, that his staff's knowledge of the latest sounds lacked something. He agreed, but said "They're not DJs, they're presenters", and went on to explain that a knowledge of local events and affairs was at least as important as a knowledge in what he persisted in calling 'pop music'. Fair enough! I changed my tact and asked why new-wave, despite it's ever-increasing popularity, was largely ignored outside the chart rundowns. At this Winston became faintly embarrassed - "No offence", he ans-

wered, "but we're not really interested in your age group". The station's output, he told me, was aimed at 25-45 year-olds, because they were the ones who spent most money, and were therefore the ones the advertisers were interested in. End of argument.

From then on, it all became predictable. I was moved to the presenter's room, where the DJ shows are prepared, and heard one of the compilers play PIL's 'Death Disco' for all of 20 seconds before deciding it was totally unfit for airplay. The Ruts 'Baby-lon's Burning' was brought in as a new release, and the same man told me that it was "...terrible. It sounds ugly."I met one of the presenters, and was hardly surprised to find that none of them even remotely lived up to their on-the-air images. Brian McSharry is the morning housewive's DJ; on the air he's almost indistinguishable from Terry Wogan; off the air his favourite words are short and Anglo-Saxon. Julius K. Scragg is probably Pennine's star presenter-his broadcasting manner is the epitome of happy mindlessness, all jollity for the kiddies. When he's being himself, he's an oddly neurotic character with a disturbing psychotic stare. When I suggested he didn't take music seriously enough, he snapped angrily "I take music very seriously - probably more seriously than you. There 'n a lot of money involved in it". Pennine had one 2-hour rock show a week, concentrating on heavy metal and basic punk - more subtle is music was 'difficult to programme'. Scragg felt that two hours was too much; he informed me that rock was dying - "Rock talks to itself".

You may be wondering what all this has to do with you; after all, Pennine Radio only covers a relatively small area. But even if you're lucky enough never to have heard Pennine, the chances are that there's a commercial station near you with the same philosophy; another bunch of business people selling music, any music that isn't at all disturbing or thought-provoking. Or as Viv Mackeson said - "A pleasant beat in the background". In America, all radio is commercial, and a quick glance at their charts will give you an idea of the long-term effects of that. The safe, clean muzak supplied by Pennine, Capital, and the rest is, as they would say "happy music". To be more precise, it's happy, consumer music; music to keep buying and stop thinking by, which isn't unexpected when you realise that, in the end, it's the advertisers who decide what gets broadcast.

And they have all the time to play, to keep you in your place all day.

-20-

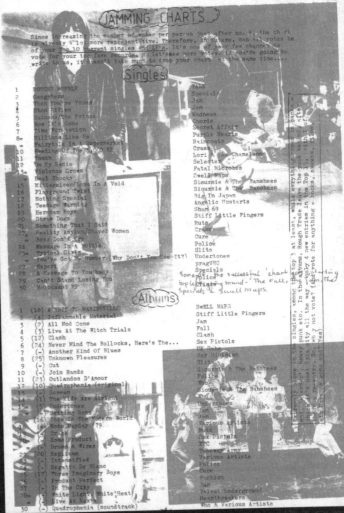

JAMMING!

N° 10

30p

DAMNED DELTA 5 "DIRECTIONS" CRASS
AU-PAIRS GIRLS AT OUR BEST
SECURITY RISK APOCALYPSE
DIY-RECORDS DISCUSSION
BRUM/S.LONDON SCENES
BREATHERS ZEITGEIST
CHORDS POP GROUP
MERTON PARK 4S
GLAXO BABIES
DER PLAN
FALL
I.C.U

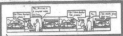

Jamming 9's success was followed by ten months' near silence as a combination of school exams, Apocalypse gigs and teenage kicks delayed completion of a new issue. When it did finally roll off the printing presses, *Jamming!* 10 came with an exclamation mark appended to its name as part of an amazing Roy Lichtenstein-influenced pop art cover, designed by Robin Richards of Fifth Column t-shirt design and The Jam's *Setting Sons* album cover fame. Knowing little the value of true art, I promptly devalued it by letrasetting the contents on the bottom left corner. Miraculously, Robin continued to speak to me.

Jamming! 10 also came with some enduring articles. The interview with The Damned, for which four of us ventured to a ramshackle Thornton Heath studio where the recently reformed and re-energised punk pioneers were demoing the decidedly hippyesque 'White Rabbit', remains a comedy classic. For all Captain Sensible and Dave Vanian's mockery of the term, it was the most joyfully anarchic few hours I have ever experienced, let alone captured on tape. Large parts of that interview were subsequently rendered unreadable due to the typically enthusiastic layout – black ink on blue photographs never being a good idea – and the reproduction here has been heavily doctored to enable overdue legibility.

The same four of us as per The Damned (Jeff, Stevo, 'Little' Paul and myself) then traipsed beyond the Essex end of the Central Line to spend an afternoon with the truly anarchic (and ardently pacifist) Crass at their countryside HQ, the group's Penny Rimbaud having written to counter my criticisms of the punk collective in the previous issue's Tribalism piece. That Tribalism piece ultimately merited a full page of printed responses, including one from a Jon Eaton who would soon be writing for *Jamming!* under a more poetic last name.

We weren't consciously making up for past male dominance by featuring The Au Pairs (interviewed in Birmingham by Dave Jennings), Delta 5 and Girls At Our Best! in the same issue, as much as that these mixed-gender bands were making some of the most interesting, insightful and delightful independent music of the era. The definition of 'independence' was further parsed in a round table discussion about DIY records, while the dying embers of the mod revival were poked with a feature on The Directions, who had themselves stirred the pot by releasing a single that named and shamed other mod bands.

As part of *Jamming!*'s at-cost deal with Better Badges, I had been sending other fanzines Joly's way so that he might benefit financially from his print endeavours. This backfired when I finally delivered Issue 10 to his Portobello Road HQ, and it was placed at the rear of a month-long backlog. Instead of hustling copies round London's independent shops during the holidays, I found myself doing so about two days into my sixth form, which led me to jump ship on my school education almost immediately.

A new business arrangement imposed on Joly from somewhere above now had fanzine producers purchasing copies at a 1/3 discount, while Better Badges distributed from its own stock to its own network. This eliminated the burden of an overwhelming print bill, but as most shops demanded a 1/3 discount anyway, it also did away with any prospect of profit. Additionally, *Jamming!*'s usual propensity for optimism meant that while 2,000 copies cleared through the distribution chain at relative speed, an additional 2,000 remained piled up in the Better Badges basement and on my own bedroom floor. Many remained unsold for decades, until I dumped the last few hundred during a major clear-out of my life. Individual copies now make but a rare appearance on eBay. You are welcome.

Realising that I should leave design to the big boys... Robin's masterful cover for *Jamming!* 10. **Jeff C.**

THE DAMNED

TAKE THE PISS

We decided straight after Jamming 9 that The Damned were going to be the main interview in Jamming 10. Getting the interview wasn't quite as easy though - record companies and publicity agents got nowhere, and it wasn't until we met Captain Sensible at a Security Risk gig that we got it fixed up. What follows is an all-time classic Jamming interview. It was done in the 8-track studios opposite Crystal Palace FC (cue rapturous applause), and featured the Captain and Dave Vanian. Rat Scabies wasn't about, which was probably as well, because I had rather a new tape-recorder with me! It was the reverse of last issue's Jam interview, starting off with as serious a talk as you can have with the Captain (not very), while Dave Vanian was trying to record 'White Rabbits'; and then a chaotic chat with the two of them. It hasn't really dated in the 3 months since it was done, either. Some of the comments might not read in the way they were meant, so take it all with a pinch of salt.....

FIRSTLY, CAN YOU TELL US WHAT'S BEEN HAPPENING SINCE CHRISTMAS?

CS: Well, we chucked Algy out.

WHY?

CS: Well, he's a fat ignorant cunt! He started growing tits!

WELL, HE MUST HAVE DONE SOMETHING WRONG...

CS: It wasn't my decision - I didn't mind him really, but he didn't get on with Rat very well. I did actually witness bottle fights between them - that might have had something to do with it!

SO THE CURRENT BASS PLAYER IS THE ONE FROM EDDIE AND THE HOT RODS?

CS: Yeah, Paul Grey - it's not 100% defenite though

WHAT BENEFITS DO YOU SEE IN YOUR SPLITTING UP AND REFORMING?

CS: It got rid of Brian (James), and Lou, and John Moss, who shouldn't have been there in the first place. I think people like that are better off in their arty-farty little jazz groups, you know?

DID YOU EXPECT WHEN YOU GOT BACK TOGETHER THAT YOU WERE GOING TO BE BIGGER THAN YOU WERE ORIGINALLY?

CS: I didn't think about it - I just thought about where my next wages were going to come from. One reason we got back together was 'cos I was absolutely broke. From all that time between when the group split up and when we got back together again I never got nothing. I never got a penny from noone.

WEREN'T YOU ON THE DOLE?

CS: I went down to the dole and they sent me a 5p cheque.

HOW COULD THEY DO THAT?

Paul Grey, Captain Sensible, Rat Scabies, Dave Vanian

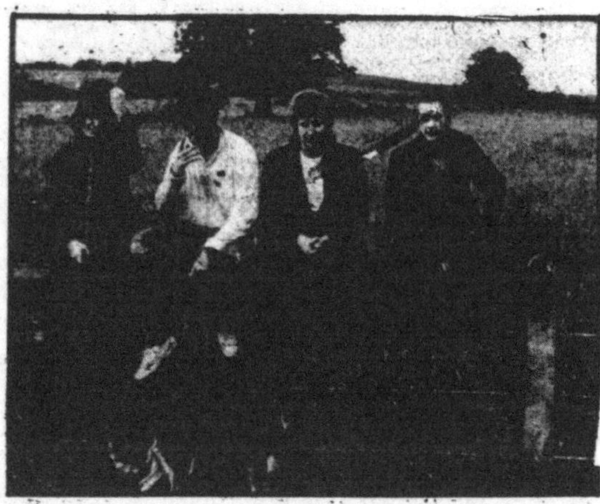

CS: 'Cos they know I'm amusician, and think that I'm working, like a lot of people do, and that was the lowest they could give me. I was skint, and Enry was a tosser - I was in a group called King, and this bloke Enry was a wanker, and I'd rather play with Rat.

ARE YOU THE SAME OFFSTAGE AS ONSTAGE?

CS: No, 'cos when you're on stage it's like that whole thing of the microphone, right? If I shouted that you four are a bunch of wankers and tossers and you ought to have your fucking kneecaps blown off and your heads chopped off and the head of a skunk stuck on instead and you'd still look the same (!), you'd probably say 'Fuck off' or something and I'd hear you. And I'd think 'Oh - they're answering me back.' But when you're onstage you can't hear them all answering you back - all you can hear is your voice booming out. And you can see them all going ...(shakes fists), but if you can't hear them, it's great.

DO YOU GET A FEELING OF POWER?

CS: Yeah, it's marvellous. And I abuse it as much as possible!

DO YOU FIND YOU HAVE TO LIVE UP TO YOUR IMAGE?

No, I couldn't care. It's total rubbish isn't it - image, music, pop stars; it's all crap.

SO WHAT'S YOUR VIEW ON THE WHOLE ROCK BUSINESS, AND THE PRESS AND ALL THAT?

CS: It's a total utter joke - the whole music business is a total joke. People get this inflated opinion of themselves, and punters might get an inflated opinion of these people. Putting them on a pedestal - it's a joke, total rubbish.

DO YOU EVER FEEL YOU GET TO BE A PART OF IT?

CS: No - this group's got nothing to do with that whatsoever. That's probably one of the reasons the music press don't like us - we won't play their little games, we won't go to their little ligs and things. I've been to a couple of ligs, but it's only been to drink some bastard record company's booze. Have some of their smoked salmon and that stuff.

WHO COMES UP WITH IDEAS FOR SONGS?

CS: All three of us. What we do - and I think this is a good little idea - we come down here and demo our stuff individually. Dave'll come down and do his couple of songs, I'll come down and do mine, same with Rat. Then we'll play them to each other and say "This bit and that bit change, and the lyrics, blah blah."

DO YOU MIX DIFFERENT SONGS IN TOGETHER?

CS: Yeah - that sort of thing. Each group has their different methods, that's ours.

WHAT WOULD YOU SAY IF I SAID SOME OF YOUR SOLOS ARE HEAVY METAL?

CS: Well, Mick Jones isn't heavy metal, but I am heavy metal.

MICK JONES IS HEAVY METAL...

-20-

Dave Vanian really is a vampire. Not proud of getting chased around the kitchen table by the real Nosferatu in leafy Selhurst Park. **Jeff C.**

It should be noted that the Captain's opinions do change consistently - in other words this interview is his opinions on this certain day - 2 weeks later they'd changed again.

The Captain kindly agreed to draw a picture of an average Jamming reader. Here it is:-

YOU
BY
Uncle
Cappers.

CS: Ah, umm.... if you said that, I'd say I couldn't give a shit. I'm not into heavy metal music; in fact I don't like any music at all. You just do what you want.

DO YOU EVER FEEL YOUR SOLOS GET TOO LONG?

CS: No. I think they could go on much longer.

DO YOU WORK THE SOLOS OUT BEFOREHAND?

Oh no - I never practise; I've never ever practised. But I do enjoy playing the guitar arrangements. If people don't like it they can fuck off - and buy someone else's records.

THE CLASH'S?

CS: Yeah, right. The Clash for example.

I DO THINK MICK JONES IS HEAVY METAL.

CS: Yeah, but he ain't very good at it. Look, let's face it - he can't play the guitar! The Clash are just the same as all the groups they tried to replace. They're exactly the same as the Stones, & all the others. And they smoke more dope than anyone I've ever seen. They're just rock stars.

HOW OFTEN DO YOU SEE THEM?

CS: Well, we made our album in the same studio as them. We were listening to what they were doing, & they were so stoned all the time that they couldn't play their instruments - only Topper could play. And they were just sitting there going 'Der-der', Strummer at the piano and Mick Jones, fucking all joints hanging out of their mouths. The stench was appalling and the sound was appalling. Absolutely disgraceful. Then the tapes went away, and next time we heard them, they were really proffessionally mixed, and there was an air of professionalism about them. And I think some cunt like the Buggles geezer, or someone like that, put all the synthesizers and keyboards and lots of effects on it, and they came back sounding really good.

WHAT DO YOU THINK OF HM IN GENERAL?

CS: I don't really like music; I try to avoid it as much as possible.

SO WHAT DO YOU DO IN YOUR SPARE TIME?

CS: Go out in the garden, and stroke the rabbit. I go down the pub, and I listen to Radio 4 a lot. Plays and things like that.

WHAT WAS IT THAT WAS SO WRONG WITH STIFF?

CS: They didn't pay us. The worst job in the world is the one you don't get paid for. Nobody works for nothing these days, but we did for two years with Stiff.

AND YOU CAME OUT OF IT TOTALLY SKINT?

CS: Absolutely. I didn't even have a guitar at the end of it. I had no guitar, no amplifier, no money - I was just dumped.

THE DAMNED SAY THEY'VE GOT NOTHING TO DO WITH POLITICS.

CS: Yeah.

DO YOU THINK IT'S POSSIBLE TO LIVE TODAY BY IGNORING POLITICS?

CS: No.   The thing is we can't speak with one voice on politics. I think we're all decided on the Queen - that she should have her head chopped off.

DO YOU BELEIVE IN DOING THINGS VIOLENTLY?

CS: Well, no, alright then - don't chop their heads off - give them 50 years hard labour.

THE QUEEN WOULD LAST A LONG TIME, WOULDN'T SHE?

CS: Right. She's never done a day's work in her life, has she? I mean, it's a lot of hard work going round on cruises, and fucking tours of the Caribbean and things like that - that's a lot of hard work. I reckon my mother ought to be Queen. She'd probably do it on £30 a week, rather than £2,000. The Queen's probably getting 20 times that - I don't know; it's all out of proportion, it's all rubbish. Off with their heads, right? I hope if they drop that bomb, it goes straight on Buckingham Palace.

DO YOU THINK THE QUEEN BRINGS IN ANY MONEY TO THE COUNTRY?

CS (Getting heated up): I think she ought to go, right? 'Cos it's inequality, and it's rubbish, in this modern day and age. England's the greatest, right, and we don't need that old slut leading us.

WHAT DO YOU RECKON THE PURPOSE OF THE DAMNED IS?

CS: To make me extremely rich! I just want to be so stinking rich, that my manager comes up to me & says 'You've got to spend £200,000 today or else we're going to get taxed to fuck.'I'm going to buy lots of rabbits and rabbit hutches - I'd buy the Young's brewery! No, that's what I hate about the

The Captain teaches Dave Vanian how to put your fingers on a guitar!

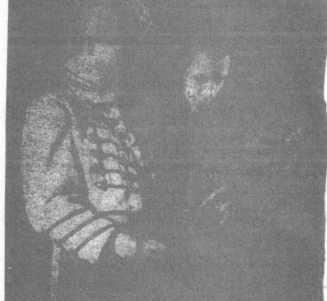

Clash - they say they don't want to get stinking rich, but of course they do. I mean, when your group get's going, what are you going to do with the money? Say 'No, sorry... don't want it'? I've never had any money and I want some now. I demand money. I just want to try it, and see what it's like. I want to have a few thousand quid just to see. And if I don't like it, I'll give the money back. I'll give it away at gigs if I don't like it - I might not like having loads of money. Then again I might enjoy it - but I just want to find out what it's like.

BUT DO GROUPS MAKE MONEY? THE ROCK BUSINESS IS OUT TO MAKE MONEY FOR THE BUSINESSMEN....

CS: Yeah, well that's disgusting.

HAVE YOU GOT ANY IDEAS FOR YOUR LONG-TERM FUTURE? IS THERE ANYTHING YOU COULD DO IN TEN YEARS?

CS: Well, in ten years time I still want to be playing on stage. I don't know what the rest of the hroup think, but in 20 years time, if the world's still going and I'm still alive, I still want to be going on stage, 'cos it's good fun. I think it would be really great to be about 60 years old, & jumping on stage and going 'You fuckers... you bastards'.... Come on in a wheelchair and say 'You ought to cut your fucking tits off and stick them up your bum! ' I think it would be great.

WHAT SORT OF KICKS DO YOU GET OUT OF INSULTING YOUR FANS THEN?

CS: I don't do it all the time.- it's just a laugh I think the whole gig situation is so ludicrous - all these people standing there, and there's a group up there, and they're all going.... (now stands up and starts imitating stupid but pleasant punters)... 'Oooh, that's good, I must run out and buy their records...' (realises he's doing well so he carries on)... 'Oooh, here's £2.50, I'm going to see my favourite group... hurray' (starts pogoing) 'Oooh, here they come...' (claps) 'Look, there's Rat.. "Hello Rat" - hurray, aah, spit-spit ....' - it's all rubbish, right?

WHAT DO YOU THINK THEY SHOULD DO THEN?

CS: I think they should get their own stinking groups together, so there's no more playing records and this rubbish. It's all crap. That's why I think it's so crazy - that's what I'm trying to say.

YEAH, BUT IT HASN'T STOPPED YOU GOING AND PLAYING THE ELECTRIC BALLROOM FOR £3.50, HAS IT?

CS: As long as there's mugs there who are going to come and see us.

WE'RE THE MUGS?

CS: Yeah, sure. If people really wanna see us we'll always be there. But I think the whole situation is absolutely ludicrous - do you know what I mean?

WHAT'S YOUR REAL NAME?

CS: Ray Burns - I don't care what people call me.

DO GROUPS PLAY LIVE ON TOTP?

CS: You've got to go down and re-record the song for TOTP, so you can do a completely different version if you want. All the groups have to go down to a little studio, and a BBC bloke comes down and watches that they record it - it's all supposed to be something to do with the union. It takes about 4 or5 hours.

WHAT STUFF BY THE DAMNED ARE YOU BEST PLEASED WITH

CS: The last album. The last album is superb.

DOES THAT INCLUDE THE SINGLES LEADING UP TO IT?

CS: Yeah, that's when I started liking this group. And I quite liked the first album.

SO YOU AGREE THAT MUSIC FOR PLEASURE IS AS BAD AS PEOPLE SAY...

CS: If I had loads of money, I'd go round and buy them all up, and destroy them all. I'd burn them with Brian James on the top in place of a guy. And Lou, and John Moss.

WHAT DO YOU THINK OF ANARCHY?

CS: What? Explain yourself.

WELL, WHEN PUNK STARTED, IT WAS ALL VERY MUCH TO DO WITH ANARCHY WASN'T IT?

CS: Was it? I never saw much anarchy. Well, what

do you mean 'anarchy'? What groups have done anarchy in the past? Apart from us?

IT DEPENDS HOW YOU DEFINE ANARCHY.

CS: Right. I mean, have the Clash and the Pistols done any anarchy?

THE PISTOLS APPEARED TO.

CS: They done fuck all anarchy. All they did was get themselves extremely rich by getting signed up to record companies and getting sucked, and coppin all the money.

THEY STIRRED THINGS UP...

CS: How? How did they do more than we did? What did they do that we didn't do? Apart from getting extremely rich?

THEY MADE MORE PUBLICITY OF THEMSELVES.

CS: Anarchy? Hang on... publicity and anarchy are completely different things. Anarchy is like breaking things up and going completely beserk isn't it? I'll tell you what - their music sounds like old Deep Purple, with some cunt screaming over the top of it. Their music is so boring, and it's been done for the last 10 years... the most boring music in the world. (Imitates it)... Really slow, turgid old heavy metal, with the only difference at all being Rotten's singing. But the rest of it was shit. There's no anarchy there old chap.

WERE THERE ANY PUNK GROUPS AT THE START THAT YOU LIKED?

CS: (Thinks for a long time) ... No, not really. I don't like any of them. I think they're all wankers. The Lurkers have got the right attitude, and the UK Subs are very very wonderful people.

WELL I TAKE IT YOU ACCEPT THAT PEOPLE WHO LIKE THE DAMNED LIKE OTHER GROUPS AS WELL?

CS: No, I don't think about it really. This bloke with a beard came up once and said he really liked the last album. And I didn't know how to take it! 'What's your favorite cricket trophy? The Gilette Cup? Her-her-her. What's your favorite T. Rex album? Beard Of Stars? Her-her-her.' When he walked away, he probably went home and smashed the record up!

Dave Vanian walks in to join the interview, and within 20 seconds him and the Captain have removed the tape and stuck a fag end in it!! Interview resumes....

WHY DID ALGY GET THE BOOT?

DV: I don't know really. The fact that he was an ugly fat tosser might have had something to do with it!
CS: There you go, see - the same answer as I gave you
DV: Next question.

ALRIGHT, I'LL ASK ABOUT YOUR CHARACTER...

DV: Which one do you want?!

ARE YOU...

DV: No I'm not. Do I look like one?
Vanian now snatches the question sheet and reads the whole lot out (a bit embarassing 'cos it contains the Captain's thoughts on him as well as ours). Complains he can't read my writing....

WELL, WHY DON'T YOU LET ME ASK THE QUESTIONS AND YOU ANSWER THEM?

DV: Why don't you shut up?
He reads the bit asking why Smash It Up was banned.
CS: They got the wrong impression about Smash It Up, you see - they thought it was about going round smashing things. Whereas in actual fact the song is all about... going round and shaking people's hands, and being generally nice to each other.
DV: And helping old ladies across the road.
CS: Yeah, that's what Smash It Up's all about.
DV: Just like Adolf Hitler did.
CS: Yeah he used to go round kissing little babies - he was a really nice bloke. His heart was full of love for mankind.
DV: Who's that - the bloke who works in the chip shop, Adolf?
CS: Oh - you were talking about that German bloke. We meant the bloke who works in the chip shop.

I DIDN'T MENTION ADOLF.

CS/DV: Yes you did, 'course you did!
DV: He's trying to make us sound like a fascist group, brandishing his politics all over the place

CS: 'Why do the Damned like Adolf Hitler?' I heard him mention that. And I was talking about the geezer down the chip shop.
DV: What - Adolf's Chip Shop?
CS: Yeah - Adolf's Chip Shop; a little bit greasy and that, but he's a really nice bloke.

DV: Now this looks quite good - 'Anarchy? Violence? Do you vote?' What's 'do you vote' got to do with 'anarchy' and 'violence'?
CS: Do you like anarchy?... Anarchy is like wanton destruction and chaos..;

IS IT THOUGH? CAN'T YOU SAY ANARCHY'S LIKE GETTING RID OF POWER AND POLITICS?

DV: Not really, but it is, obviously (!) because if everybody felt like that there wouldn't be any politics.

ALRIGHT, HE'S AN ANARCHIST (Points to one of two Jamming liggers).

DV: Kick him!
CS: Let's throw him out and see how bloody anarchistic he is then!
DV: Kick him a bit - 'doesn't look like an anarchist does he?' 'He doesn't feel like an anarchist' (They all pretend to be jumping on and kicking an imaginary body). 'Anarchists are meant to be tough; he's quite mushy'!...

ARE YOU LOT ACTUALLY GOING TO ANSWER ANY QUESTIONS?

CS: Alright, I will (snatches questions and starts reading them aloud like Vanian did. They all take the piss out of my writing).
  Five minutes mucking about later...
DV: Right, is that it?

YOU HAVEN'T ANSWERED ANY QUESTIONS YET!

DV: You haven't asked any!

ALRIGHT, ARE YOU A POSER?

DV: That's up to you to decide. What is a poser? Give me a defeinition of a poser?
(I wasn't particularly obsessed with this question - it was just the principle of getting him to answer something) SOMEONE WHO ACTS DIFFERENTLY IN ONE SITUATION TO GET ATTENTION, AND WILL ACT TOTALLY DIFFERENT WHEN THERE'S NO PEOPLE WATCHING.

DV: Ah well in that case - that's a totally different subject. No, I wouldn't say I'd act any differently when I'm hin another situation. If I was going to turn round and kick someone I'd do it whether or not people were watching.
CS: Like Gary Numan, for instance?
DV: What do you mean 'like for instance?'?
CS: Well, if Gary Numan was there on the floor, I'd tread on him.
Andy (engineer and wise guy): Ah, but would Gary Numan being on the floor constitute 'someone' else being in the room?!!

HOW HAVE YOUR ATTITUDES CHANGED SINCE THE START OF PUNK?

DV: What do you mean by attitudes?

WHY DO YOU ASK ME TO EXPLAIN EVERY WORD?

DV: Because you ask very general questions. You could be talking about musical attitudes, or things in general.

WELL BASICALLY CONCERNED WITH MUSIC? HOW HAVE YOUR FEELINGS CHANGED SINCE PUNK STARTED OFF?

DV: (in a rare moment of being serious) Well, punk was never about staying in one place, so obviously your attitudes change slightly - obviously we'd never stay exactly the same.

WHAT DO YOU THINK ABOUT ALL THE GROUPS FROM THE START OF PUNK GETTING THE CHART SUCCESS, LIKE...

DV: When you say 'all the groups'...
Even the Captain laughs at DV's questioning now.
DV: No, but when you say all the groups, I only see the Clash, and (Voice: Gary Numan) The Clash, and (Voice: Gary Numan)...

THE JAM?

DV: Yeah, well...(Voice: Gary Numan) The Jam weren't exactly right at the beginning, so when you say that, it doesn't bother me (Voice: And Gary Numan) that they get chart success, because there aren't as many from the beginning as you'd like to think. Things like the UK Subs, they came one year later..
CS: Gary Numan came much later...

YEAH, WELL I'M NOT TALKING ABOUT THE UK SUBS...

CS: You're not adverse to violence are you?
WHAT???

CS: Well stop fucking mentioning Gary Numan then!!
DV: I'll try and answer your question.

A LOT OF OTHER GROUPS HAVE HAD CHART SUCCESS AND YOU HAVEN'T. ARE YOU JEALOUS OF THEM? ARE YOU JEALOUS OF GARY NUMAN HAVING BEEN AT NO. 1?

CS: (stares at me, points at my particulars): There - kick him there!!!
DV gets up and starts fidgeting with the tape recorder.

THAT'S NEW, THAT IS!

DV: Is it? It won't be for long!
Andy: Oh it's new man - Numan!
DV: (through clenched teeth): No, of course I'm not jealous of certain persons. Why should I be jealous of him?
CS: He always wanted to be a machine didn't he? Just one day he became a tape recorder.

DO YOU THINK THAT PUNK ACHEIVED ANYTHING?

CS (mimicking DV): Well, what do you mean by...
DV: It acheived everything it set out to do.

WHAT DO YOU MEAN 'EVERYTHING IT SET OUT TO DO'?

DV: What it set out to do was just... there were groups playing music there, same as there's always been.

YEAH, BUT THEY DID IT IN A DIFFERENT WAY...

CS: The only difference between like punk groups and the groups that went before is that when the groups started out, like the Pistols, instead of singing nicely they just went 'Ahhhm on the doodle and sang really horrible. But the music is exactly the same, only slightly worse played.

THERE'S A DIFFERENCE IN ATTITUDE.

CS: Is there a difference in attitude between, say, The Clash and, say for example, Jethro Tull? And I'll tell you here and now there is no difference - none whatsoever.
DV: Yes there is - The Clash can't play flute!

AT LEAST THE CLASH PLAY GIGS NOW AND AGAIN.

DV: So do Jethro Tull.
CS: How many gigs do the Clash play nowadays?

THEY PLAY IN AMERICA ALL THE TIME.

CS: So do Jethro Tull - right, exactly the same. You can't pop down the road and see the Clash?

CAN YOU POP DOWN THE ROAD AND SEE THE DAMNED?

CS: Well you did.

IT TOOK US TWO MONTHS OF WORKING TO GET THIS INTERVIEW. WE'VE BEEN ON TO YOUR PUBLICITY AGENTS FOR ONE MONTH.

CS: Right then - we're only going to play Wembley once every five years; fuck you all! And it's going to be £50 a ticket, so bollocks!!...
...Basically, we're the best band in the world at being street credibility; we embody street credibility; we are street credibility all rolled into one nice little bundle, so go out and buy our stinking records.
DV: And make us stinking rich.
CS: There's more street credibility in this group than 10,000 other groups - is that what you want to hear?
DV: I can see him (me) getting extremely worked up - he keeps fidgety around that chair getting really uncomfortable.

IS THERE ANYTHING ELSE YOU WANT TO SAY?

CS: Yeah - buy us a drink. Please.

COME? GARY NUMAN LIKES COKE.

DV (Gets rather annoyed): I'm severely going off this shop. Do you like my new digital tape? I wanna know why these two characters are so noisy (the two Jamming liggers).
CS: The amount of anarchy I've seen out of these 2 is ridiculous. Bloody anarchy all the time...

WHERE'S ALL YOUR CHAOS AND DESTRUCTION THEN?

CS: You want to see some chaos? Quite easily arranged, old chap!
DV: I've always wanted to stick someone's head in a washing machine!!!

THE END. Interview by AF.
Large photos by JC.

Jeff Carrigan as supposed to be writing this up, but unfortunate circumstances mean I'm doing it in quite a hurry...

As you probably know, almost all fanzines have had Crass interviews. We didnt particularly want to do one to join them, but we felt there were certain things about the group that needed explaining. So, to sort out these problems, we went up to their farmhouse in Essex. What follows is, as I say, very very rushed and not as good as it could have been with more care.

At the time Penny, the main talker, seemed to be answering our questions satisfactorily, but at the end of each paragraph we were lost, and not always sure we were talking about the right thing! Probably we'll find this interview wll raise as many problems for other people as other ones have to us. What we did find though, is that whatever you may say about Crass, their ideals and their music, as people they are totally wonderful, and their way of living seems to have everyone else sussed. It seems strange for such heavy music and images to go with such peaceful people, but Crass are indoubtedly the ones that know what they're doing...

HOW DO YOU DEFINE ANARCHY, REMEMBERING PEOPLE HAVE SET IDEAS?

I think we're dealing on two levels. We're dealing with ourselves as individual people, and at the same time attempting to find ways of socially disrupting and subverting power through our activities. We try to state as individuals that it's a rejection of social control, refusing to accept the validity of the government and being under state control. Through refusing to recognise something, it effectively ceases to exist.

WOULD ANARCHY WORK?

If everyone was like us it would work. If everyone respected each other obviously it would work. We see anarchy as basically just respecting each other as individuals. Obviously, the word needs refining.

We try and deal with the conditions one objects too in a way that can try and create a mutual understanding - not just blindly going and hitting a policeman because you don't agree with him. The important thing is to try and reach him in some way or another, find some sort of contact. From that, something could develop - there's no point in animosity.

Just because you respect someone doesn't mean they're going to respect you...

No, of course not, but that's the place to start from. Rather than a situation where the SWP have already determined that they are going to have an aggressive attitude towards certain people, and the BM are determined that they are going to have an aggressive attitude. There's no chance of those 2 meeting of anything constructive occurring. Theres every chance that If I met up with the BM or SWP something could occur because I'm not taking a polarised position against them. I set myself up against them as a political identity. There is some potential of some sort of dialogue being created, and that's important.

THAT'S ON AN INDIVIDUAL LEVEL - WILL IT DEVELOP INTO A NATIONWIDE THING?

Well I don't think one should put it down on an idealistic levl; realistically one knows that one can develop a bigger network with people who basically under-

-38-

stand this and respect you.

The problem is that one shouldn't be destroyed by another person's lack of dignity, and I think it's very important not to be tricked and trapped brutally by t the society we live in.

DO YOU GET MUCH HASSLE FROM COPPERS?

We have had a lot of it, but very little is actually directed at us. It's at the shops and things like that

WHAT DO YOU DO WHEN IT ACTUALLY HAPPENS TO YOU, AND THEY'RE NOT RESPECTING YOU?

Well for example, the Vice Squad came down here to investigate Reality Asylum. We invited them in, had a cup of tea, chatted about how the kids were doing at school and attempted to somhow make contact beyond the job they had to do. They didn't really understand why they were here. Most of the time they go round shops in Soho looking for hard stuff, but they really didn't comprehend why they were in a quiet country house in the middle of Essex ananlysing a record that they didn't even understand. There's no point us getting done unnecessarily; at the same time there's no point from backing down on what we believe in, and we didn't.

Policemen have turned up to our gigs which is very frequent; we always go and meet them at the door and try and persuade them not to come in. And we've had some strange relationships, where they actually confide to some extent. And that's not a nice situation because they then go and screw some guy who's just sitting there with a glue or something.

DO YOU THINK POLICE FORCES ARE NECESSARY?

No, obviously they're not neccessary.

WHAT DO YOU DO WHEN SOMEBODY'S MURDERED?

You do whatever you feel you should do. I don't think the police force do a good job with people who murder others - they respond unint lligently with a lack of sympathy & lack of understanding. There's the whole question of who are murderers - one group of people can be legitimate terrorists, wheras a nother can be a soldier. Baader-Meinhof and Charles Manson did exactly the same thing - they set out ti destro what they're opposed to. On the one hand, one's a psychopath and on the other hand the same people regard Barder-Meinhof as some kind of a God.

WHAT I'M TRYING TO SAY IS IF ONE OF YOU WAS BADLY HURT OR MURDERED HOW WOULD YOU REACT TO THE PEOPLE WHO COMMITTED IT?

Well, it's so difficult to say isn't it? I've seen people hurt at gigs and I've got so angry I've wanted to take revenge - it's almost blind anger. Fortunately I've never been able to work out who it was who did the whacking, and by the time it's become clear I've calmed down enough to deal with it in a more gentle way.

The police force don't actually do anything - they don't catch most of the wild psychopaths. There's very very few loonies and they don't catch them. On the one hand, society is training people to kill as an everyday event, like soldiers, and on the other hand it's so unbeleivably malicious to anyone who actually kills someone else. I'm sure the Yorkshire ripper has given the police hundreds of opportunities to get into people's homes of people they wanted to, and they're no nearer getting him - I shouldn't think they care 2 fucks about him.

-39-

MOST PEOPLE CARE THAT PEOPLE LIKE THAT SHOULDN'T BE FREE TO GO AROUND KILLING.

No they shouldn't-that's what we're trying to say. The police force aren't doing any more than you or I,but I'm not advocating that the so-called psychopaths, loonies and murderers should be released to come and sit here in the garden.

CAN YOU EXPLAIN A BIT MORE ABOUT YOUR STAND ON RELIGION?

Religion is the absolute basis and foundation of our culture. It is the cause of the moral attitudes, everything our society's built on.

IT SEEMS TO ME THAT THE WAY YOU LIVE IS A VERY CHRISTIAN WAY OF LIFE...

That's giving Christianity too much credit. But I see what you mean - there are some attitudes of Christianity that we use, but when those ideals are put into practice they have been responsible for causing wars nd things. I was looking through the Bible the other day, and I sa 'Love your neighbour' and I thought that's really good, but then I went through the rest o f it, and it's .... the ultimate parody. When you look at Christ, when he was doing sensible things, like just strolling around talking to people, doing gigs, like The Sermon On The Mount, 'cos that's all he was - a performer, who did a bum deal at the end. Like Jimi Hendrix was really good, but I don't think it's good to smack out. I mean, Christ had the same sort o of choices - he could have rushed off, he shouldn't have humbly sat there in the g gardn waiting for them to come - he should have buggered off and done a gig some-where else. He was just a thoroughly bad performer. If you look at the grizzly bearded figure hanging on the cross with this tortur d idea...

WHAT DO YOU FIND SO REPULSIVE ABOUT IT?

Just bad theatre. It's a tasteless, over-the-top production. Look at a figure of Buddha, who represents joy, life and rligion, a beautiful happy little soul, sitting there, grinning away, and it make s you feel happy. But if I look at this tor-mented soul, who said all the same sort of things, but ended up doing that - it's depressing. it's desperate.

WOULD YOU RECKON PUNK WAS, TO AN EXTENT, ABOUT INDIVIDUALITY?

Yeah.

WELL, HOW CAN YOU BE INDIVIDUALS ALL WEARING BLACK?

It's a different situation when you choose to be in a band and go on stage. Most bands go on stage wanting to stand out - our wearing black stops us standing out.

BUT IS THERE ANYTHING WRONG WITH WEARING DIFFERENT CLOTHES?

No there isn't at all. But for the band - I remember when we didn't u ed to wear the same clothes, and I'd think "Wha am I gonna wear tonight", but now weall wear the same clothes, it saves bother and consideration. It's good though other people wearing different stuff½

THE SWEARING AND SCREAMING SOMETIMES SEEMS A BIT VIOLENT...
It's angry. I think there's times when we have gone over the top. I think that song about Garru Bushell, which was a result of feeling really angry and very upset at all the unfairness... that was the only time, in all our songs, we've gone over the top.

YOUR FLAG DOES LOOK VERY VIOLENT....

We attract violence more because we threaten. Our stuff threatens the STP, and I think they know it's right, which is why they're reacting like this, and it thr-eatens the BM a lot more. The reason is that a large number of BM aren't BM any-morethey come along and really enjoy a gig. They've lost membership because of it. We attract violence because we're having an effect.

The price of this issue has had to be raised to 30p. Sorry about this, but it was necessary to avoid financial suicide and 44 pages for 30p is hardly unreasonable. Anyway, no..11 should be back down in price, hopefully right down to 20p. Also, I want to add that Jamming may be picking up some kind of a good reputation; what-ever, we/I never promise to keep up to any standard or bring this out for the sake of it - it's done for fun, and if we release a bum issue now and again, well - sorry.

AU PAIRS

"Though I've got this special feeling I'd be wrong to call it love
For the word entails a few things I'd be well rid of"

Buzzcocks,'You Say You Don't Love Me'

Lesley - vocals, guitar
Paul - guitar, vocals
Jane - Bass
Pete - Drums

The following interview with the Au-Pairs was done with bassist Jane and guitarist Paul by DAVE JENNINGS, in Jane's flat in Harborne, Birmingham.

DAVE: I suppose the logical place to start is to ask what exactly you've been doing lately... I know you've been gigging quite a lot...

JANE: Yeah... all the gigs that we've done have been odd one-offs, you know... RAR gigs, supports, things like the Ally Pally gig.

PAUL: You see, we don't work through an agency, so people just phone up the office, say "Can you do this, can you do that?"

DAVE: What office do you mean?

PAUL: Oh, we've just got a room in a flat with a phone, and that's where our manager works from.

DAVE: How much have you got to do with O21 Records? Is it your organisation?

JANE: Yes and no - Martin (their manager) runs it really, Martin & Andy Burchill.

PAUL: Our record's keeping it running, & now the Iganda single's come out and that's selling really well. The idea of O21 Records is just to stay as a small label and give local bands a chance.

DAVE: Why has it taken you so long to follow up the 'Kerb Crawler' EP?

PAUL: No money! Simple as that.. I suppose about three months ago we could have done it, possibly going for another 1000 or 2,000 first pressing, but there was quite a bit of talk of us signing a publications deal - I don't know what's happening about that. I think Chrysalis offered us a one-off single, but a one-off single with a major label is not really worth doing. Bands like the Scars have done that, and they just get written off as tax losses. They don't bother pushing it or anything like that. Whereas if you put one out on your own label you get more money, and you've also got more control over it.

DAVE: What's the next record likely to be then?

PAUL: It'll probably be a cut-down version of 'Obvious'.

DAVE: That's a great song...

PAUL: Yeah... we will have to cut it down, 'cause I don't really think you can have a six-minute A-side and hope to get any airplay with it! That'll probably be one side, and I really don't know

about the other; we've got about 3 or 4 songs we'd really like to do.

DAVE: I think an awful lot of people would like to see 'Come Again' on record.

PAUL: Yeah.. a lot of people have said this, but speaking from a musician's point of view within the band, when you're recording, you always get a lot more of a buzz recording something new, or some thing recent; we've been playing that for six or seven months now, and we'd be much more enthusiastic to do one of the newer numbers. I dunno.. I mean the first, second number we ever wrote was 'Monogamy' which is basically just a three-chord bash with a catchy chorus, and a lot of people really, really want us to put that out. That won't be on a single, because we've changed completely since then. We want to get airplay, that's what we want to sort of think towards.

DAVE: This is going to sound rude, but do you think you're likely to get airplay whatever you do, apart from Peel & maybe the occasional adventurous BRMB person?

PAUL: We probably wouldn't, but I mean that's what the band are after. We want a number one single! We want to sign up to a big label that can push our music, 'cause we want to get across to as many people as possible.

Lesley   Paul   Jane

DAVE: I think lyrically your band is absolutely unique, in that your entire reportoire has been concerned with sexism in one way or another...
PAUL: Concerned with...?
DAVE: Concerned with sexual stereotyping
PAUL: The next song, which Les has written the lyrics for, is about the 32 women political prisoners in Armagh Jail. But really it's just about seeing things from a different angle.

DAVE: I'm sorry that Lesley can't be here for this next question, because there's one thing I'd make as my only real negative criticism of your songs; & that's that every male character who crops up in your songs is invariably a villain: the husband in 'Domestic Departure' and 'Repetition', the kerb crawler, the policeman doing over the prostitute in 'You'; and even in 'Come Again'... I think that was an excellent choice of material for a song, but you could have written a song about the way that sexual relationships...
PAUL (interrupting): Well 'Come Again' is for both sexes! It's defenitely written as much for men as for women; and against women as against men, if you like, although I don't like to use the word 'against'. It's pointing out what's been happening to both sexes, through different magazines and what you're told to think. I think though, that men have got more to answer to with regard to the position of women in soci ty, and Lesley just writes it from that angle, which is fair enough. As a man, I can see that's quite valid. Wouldn't you agree?
DAVE: I'm dubious... I've often felt personally oppressed, although that's rather a heavy word to use - I've often felt very restricted by the roles that you're expected to play as a man, in

that you're always supposed to be strong and essentially.. insensitive, I think. You're never supposed to be hurt, nevr supposed to show your feelings. I remember being around the gae of 13, 14, and feeling totally inadequate because I knew there was no way I could live up to the James Bond image - there was no way I could be strong or athletic - I just thought I was going to be totally unattractive for the whole of my life.
PAUL: Oh yeah - that's the problem of stereotyping; the imagery that's put across in adverts, films, in books and magazines. That defenitely affects both sexes, but at the same time, if you went up to Leeds you couldn't walk around late at night without fear of being cut up or anything like that, and that's the kind of oppression that's so much more heavy.
JANE: We're not prepared to keep going roun in circles to try to prove that we're not anti-men.
DAVE: It is interesting, I think, that a lot of women go to some pains to disassociate themselves from.. the phrase that's usually used is 'women's libbers'
JANE: Yes, but... this has been said by someone else, but it's still true... the more women that would admit that they were feminists, the less of a heavy tag it would become. You don't have to be some kind of separatist to be a femenist.
DAVE: I think it's interesting that the issue of sexism has been discussed a lot more in the music press over the last 3 years or so. It seems to have become polarised in a sense; there's been this big Heavy Metal revival, and Heavy Metal has always been the most macho music.
PAUL: But even there, now there are bands like Girlschool who are being accepted on their musical standing. Whereas they've told us stories like, apparently they went up to Sunderland to do a gig and the guy offered them £500 if they'd go on

Paul, Pete and Lesley
-18-

and play topless! But I think that women
are being accepted as the norm now, even
coming through into Heavy Metal.
DAVE: Do you think that women musicians
are now accepted without any kind of
prejudice?
JANE: Well.. we've certainly been more
accepted. It tends to be silly things
like, when we supported the Clash, we
turned up to the gig, myself, Lesley,
and Jane who's our roadie, and the tour
manager automatically assumed that we
were the band's girlfriends! And you
tend to get guys standing at the front
of the stage trying to see whether you
can play your instruments or whether
you're just going to make a prat of
yourself. And that tends to be thoroughly irritating...

Jane and Pete

DAVE: What are the latest lyrics about,
apart from the ones you've already
mentioned? What's 'Dear John' about?
PAUL: That's set in the war years. It's
about this woman who writes her husband
a 'Dear John' letter because she's been
fed up with the way he's been treating
her. Actually, these are some of the
most obscure lyrics; they were co-written by a friend of the band. There's
another new song written by a friend of
the band called 'Unfinished Business',
which is about people who get into
relationships on a one-night stand basis
and then expect... more than perhaps was
intended.
DAVE: What exactly is 'Monogamy' about?
PAUL: That's just saying that there is
an alternative to monogamy.
JANE: You're led to believe that you
should be monogamous, aren't you, and
it's just saying that you can fuck as
much as you... you know, there isn't
really any need to worry!
PAUL: There isn't! I think that's one
of the worst things to come out of Western society, and on a broader concept -
the whole idea of thinking about sexism,
before I joined the band, was very new;
I grew up for 20 years as a 'normal'
bloke, ie stereotyped into being sexist.
I'm not saying that I'm any different
now, although I do try; but it's very
difficult. I don't think I will ever be
The Non-Sexist male. That's another
thing; we've actually had people coming
up to Lesley after hearing 'Come Again',
and talking about their problems in bed!
We're just presenting our angle on it;
we're not pretending that we know any
more, that we're experts or anything.

'Love is... a word that a lot of people
are afraid of. So when Paul Morley and
Adrian Thrills concluded their heartfelt, beautiful tribute to Ian Curtis
with the words 'the value of Joy Division is the value of love', it was

tempting to dismiss that sentiment as
foolish pretention, falsely precious.
But... recently, this writer has been
through one of the worst periods of depression of his life, the immediate cause
of which was an evening spent with a
certain highly intelligent, highly articulate, but savagely cynical, former
'Sounds' writer, whose name it would be
vindictive and destructive of me to mention. He almost succeeded in convincing
me that none of the attention our generation pays to electronic music was in
any way significant. And now...the reason
I'm writing this for you is that if I
didn't believe my thoughts and feelings
could have some degree of significance,
then I could not live. What's more for me,
is that I feel that artists like Paul
Weller, Mark Smith, Kevin Coyne, Lesley
Woods and crowds of others are my friends,
although I've never met any of them. I
believe that because, through their music,
they confide in us, offering us their most
'private' thoughts in the hope that we
might find them helpful. For that, they
deserve our faith and our respect; and
the Au Pairs deserev the last word.
They're on our side, after all...

DAVE: How much of a role do you think
that men can play in fighting against
sexism, generally?
PAUL: Fifty per cent!
DAVE: I'm glad to hear you say that, because there is a school of thought among
feminists that it really must be a wom-
en's struggle entirely...
JANE: If that were the case, it would
never get any here, would it? No, men
have got to do their fair share, to try
to understand. Otherwise, we're just banging our heads against a brick wall.

DELTA 5 ~ A BAND FOR ALL REASONS

Delta 5 shouldn't need any introduction to Jammings readers. Certainly, from the chart votes they amassed for their debut single 'Mind Your Own Business', most of you have heard/seen them, especially the many people who've been writing to ask why we haven't featured them yet. Well, we've caught up with you lot at last, and here is an interview done with them backstage at the London School of Economics shortly before going on to do a benefit for something about Ireland (he says, deliberately vaguely).

The line-up is -

ROS - Bass, vocals
JULZ - Vocals, occasional bass
BETHANN - Bass, vocals
ALAN - Guitar
KELVIN - Drums

The interview ignores basic historical facts which make boring questions and boring reading, and is followed by a sort of review and some comments.

Why have you got the two basses?

Bethann: It's more possibilities for rhythm, because we really like the rhythm section, so why not have two, exploring the different tones? Like Ros's is a really bassy sound, and mine is more trebly.

One of them's fretless isn't it?

Ros: Yeah that's mine - I just prefer it. The two basses are an idea for getting out of the normal rock format of rhythm guitar, lead guitar, bass and drums. The idea is of having two basses, maybe both following a conventional bass line or doing something completely different.

1
2
3
4
5
1 - Bethann
2 - Alan
3 - Ros
4 - Kelvin
5 - Julz

How did you get the thing going with Rough Trade?
Kelvin: The Gang of Four let us use the studios they were doing their album in, & we went in and did a demo in two nights; we took it to Rough Trade and they liked it straight away.

Is the single the actual demo then?
Beth: Yeah, it's just remixed.

How many has 'Business' sold so far?
Ros: At least 14,000.

Has that suprised you?
Kelv: It's the way it's continued selling that's suprised me. It's really good.
Beth: That's what independant singles tend to do.
How many has Anticipation sold so far?
Beth: I think about 10,000.

Do you think it was as good as the first single?
Ros: I reckon in terms of what we wanted to getout of it as a finished product we weren't as pleased with it as we were with the finished product and final mix of 'Business'.
Alan: I prefer the second single to 'Business'. (Obviously the group disagree)

Are the cartoons on the covers a permanent feature?
Kelv: It's a friend of ours, Jon Langford - we asked him to do the first cover, and then let him do the second as well 'cos it came out good.
Julz: It would be quite nice to keep it

A lot of people go round making really serious music these days, but your songs seem reasonably light-hearted...

Ros: Yeah, some of them are pretty light.
Kelv: 'You' was written before I was in the band; it was done with everyone sitting round and saying a line.
Ros: Some lyrics have a more serious intent than others.

About the Leeds scene - do you think you're part of a clique up there?

Beth: We're a clique in as far as we've all been friends before the bands were formed. And in as much as we've carried on being friends then yes, we are a clique. But...
Kelv: People tend to play on this Leeds thing quite a bit.
Bethann: It's friends before the band - still friends now.
Julz: A lot of it's got to do with all coming from the same town. I mean, there aren't that many bands from Leeds.

10

Julz on stage at the LSE

(By now there was a lot more background noise, meaning things might not be 100% accurate).
You were saying you haven't done many gigs recently. Why's that?

Ros: Because I've been doing my finals at University - they've finished now.

Are you all working now, then?
Bethann: Sometimes we work, part-time. We can't really sign on, you see. We manage to pay ourselves, just when we're playing. It makes it better if you can go and do some other work; it gives you a bit of money, and keeps you going.

Was it always deliberate for the singers to be female?
Ros: No, we're trying to get out of it. We want Kelvin to sing. When Jon Langford used to play guitar for us, he sang as well. It's not a conscious policy to have a female ffont line - that's just the way it's worked.
Kelvin: Alan's going to be singing on a new song we've just written.

(Even more background noise now)
That leads onto asking how you stand in the femenist thing, 'cos a lot of people take that really seriously.
Bethann: Well we could never be a mutually exclusive group, like excluding men or that. I think the very fact that there's men and women in the band shows that you can have a relationship and you don't have to have the stereotyped band. I think that in the way groups like The Specials have mixed black and white without making a fuss, but showing that they can play together - that's how we treat Delta 5. I mean, I think some of the femenist bands are really good, but that's just another way of doing it.

A lot of the new wave groups with females in them tend to say 'We sing about what happens to females, and we don't sing love songs', but I notice you do, and the songs could be sung by men or women....

Ros: I think that they could be - there's a lot of things that could be alternated. We did a Rock Against Sexism gig, and they said in their leaflet 'Delta 5 claim their lyrics can be sung by a man or a woman; we don't agree.' And I think that's bad.
Julz: Everything's written in the third person; we say 'you' instead of 'he' or 'she'.

Alan, this is just a comment: when I saw you before, everyone was playing pretty much as I expected, but you were standing there playing power-chords like Pete Townshend....
Everyone laughs.
Kelvin: He gets a bit upset with being compared to Andy Gill of the Gang Of 4.
Alan: I dunno; I haven't got an overall set style really. I haven't really thought about Pete Townshend, but I'd rip anything off anyone! I'm changing all the time - it depends. I always say - I can't make a mistake 'cos I haven't anything set to do.

Who writes thesongs - everybody?
Kelvin: One person will have a basic idea and we'll all do things round it. It usually starts with a bass line or something like that.

Do you want to sign to a major record company?
Kelvin: We have no intentions... we are not looking for a deal as such.

Have you been approached at all?
Bethann: Yeah, 3 times. Well, we've heard rumours about people saying we could if we wanted to, but we don't.
Do you think you can acheive anything on Rough Trade?

Ros & Kelvin in the dressing room

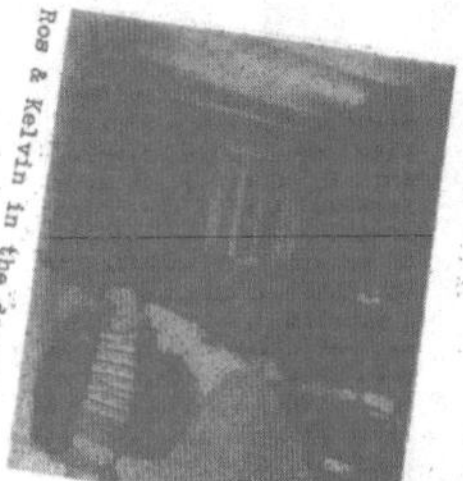

11

YEAH!
Kelvin: They're getting bigger, so we'll be able to get bigger with them.
Julz: We're acheiving what we want to. If it became impossible to acheive the things we wanted to, we'd think again. But so far, it's working fine.
Kelvin: We've had no restrictions.
Bethann: We never sign anything - we just do one-off things. We just do what we want to at the time.
Alan: It's a 50-50 split as well, which you wouldn't get on a major.
Kelvin: People said to me a year ago - 'You're never going to be able to turn professional and get a wage unless you sign to a major, but that's not true. We've found we can do it 2 just.
Julz: It seems to be a bit trendy to slag off Rough Trade after you've signed to a major now. I think that8s really pathetic.
Kelvin: At the time they don't say a word about it.
Bethann: SLF, Spizz, Mo-dettes...
KKelvin: If they've got complaints, they should say them at the time, 'cos Rough Trade are willing to learn from the band!

Bethann, the back of John, & your wondrous editor's nose & hairline!

Don't forget Jim, the invisible 6th member

Delta 5 on record have been an admirable success. But the groups real forte is playing live. Their singles can get a foot tapping ok, but it's at gigs they really take off, their music a non-stop invite to dance. The two basses usually start a song, the drums are often disco-like, vocals are normally doubled as well and the guitar jumps in more as a solo instrument than what is normally the basis of music nowadays. Admittedly, the formula is so well put together that songs tend to sound embarrasingly similar. This isn't a problem live, but on record new singles may not always be taken as new. The group seem to realise this to an extent, which is why they want Alan or Kelvin to sing - maybe I'm being unfair, but it's something that has struck me noticeably about them.

The set comprises over a dozen songs, 'Business', 'Anticipation' and 'You' always being the best received. Other highlights are 'Slow One', with its one riff that doesn't bore as the song gets quicker and louder, and Julz changes from singing to screaming. 'Colour' is a nice jaunty piece, and I'm particularly fond of the closing number, 'Leaving', which has a memorable chorus, and alwys leaves people shouting for more. 'Delta 5', 'Train', 'Make-Up', 'Innocenti', 'Triangle' and 'Journey' make up the rest of the set, while the encores tend to be less studious affairs - maybe a repeat of a single, and then a Gang Of 4 or Mekons song.

Another reason for Delta 5 being so much better live is the visual appeal. Julz tends to be most apparent with non-stop dancing (when she's not playing bass) that she never seems to tire of, while her, Ros and Bethann are continuously smiling on stage, showing a love of playing that many groups lack. Kelvin plays on in earnest hidden at the back, while Alan I find the funniest. At the LSE, he wore a hefty raincoat, looking like a dirty old man (with an innocent face) who would pace the stage and flash with his guitar (!) bringing out those strange chords and improvised solos that are as vital a part of Delta 5 as the 2 basses. An all-round treat.

But whereas all that gives the impression of a fun night out, and the lyrics are good but generally harmless, most gigs the group play are benefits, which almost inevitably means a political gig. On a recent week-long trip to London, two of the three gigs were that - one a very heavy thing about Ireland, and the other a benefit for the Leveller magazine. I can't help but think that in the end this will harm Delta 5 more than help them. Giving concrete reasons is difficult but it just creates a less easy atmosphere, and makes what is basically a very enjoyable band into something that will be looked upon as serious, and with a deep message.

But for now it doesn't stop their onslaught. Delta 5 are already popular, have released a couple of great singles, are totally captivating live, and will see even better things yet.

Interview & write-up by Tony Fletcher; photos by Jeff Carrigan

12

JAMMING CHARTS

Well, you can't exactly say these charts are up to the date. A pity about our 9 months wait, 'cos we got a good 100 votes for this. Keep the votes coming in - remember it's your Top 10 current singles and LPs. These charts are representative - we'll try and keep them up to date if you'll keep voting....

Just because these are old don't mean they're not interesting - Joy Division were at the top well before Ian Curtis' death, all that did was to raise the LP by one place; The Jam had all their singles in the charts before they were re-released, that only slightly helped them. In the LPs, The top few were very close until March, when the Jam ran off to win with 80 points more than Joy Div. It's good to see the amount of independant stuff, especially in the singles.

Singles

1	THE ETON RIFLES	JAM
2	Transmission	Joy Division
3	Going Underground/Dreams Of Children + EP	Jam
4	London Calling/Armagideon Time	Clash
5	We Are All Prostitutes	Pop Group
6	Mind Your Own Business	Delta 5
7	Where's Captain Kirk?	Spizz Energi
8	Rankking Full Stop/Tears Of A Clown	Beat
9	Rowche Rumble	Fall
10	Gangsters	Specials
11	Too Much Too Young EP	Specials
12	Strange Town	Jam
13	4 'A' Sides	Scritti Politti
14	Down In The Tube Station At Midnight	Jam
15	California Uber Alles	Dead Kennedys
16=	Jumping Someone Else's Train	Cure
=	You	Au Pairs
18	A Song From Under The Floorboards	Magazine
19	Treason	Teardrop Explodes
20=	Silent Command	Cabaret Voltaire
=	Blood & Lipstick	Pink Military
22=	Real Shocks	Swell Maps
=	At The Edge	Stiff Little Fingers
=	1980 - The First 15 Minutes	Vice Versa, ClockDVA, I'M So Hollow & Stunt Kites
25	Death Disco/And No Birds Do Sing	Public Image Ltd
26	Christine	Siouxsie And The Banshees
27	Hunted/Oh No It's You	Passions
28	Nag Nag Nag	Cabaret Voltaire
29	Love Will Tear Us Apart	Joy Division
30=	Electricity	Orchestral Maneuvres
=	When You're Young	The Jam
=	Turning Japanese	Vapors

Albums

1	SETTING SONS	THE JAM	(-)
2	Unknown Pleasures	Joy Division	(8)
3	Metal Box/2nd Edition	Public Image Ltd	(-)
4=	London Calling	Clash	(-)
=	Dragnet	Fall	(-)
6	All Mod Cons	Jam	(3)
7	Entertainment!	Gang Of Four	(-)
8	Specials	Specials	(-)
9	Stations Of The...	Crass	(-)
10	One Step Beyond	Madness	(-)
11	Raincoats	Raincoats	(5)
12	Clash	Clash	(9)
13	Cut	Slits	(1)
14	A Trip To Marineville	Swell Maps	(2)
15	Inflammable Material	Stiff Little Fingers	(6)
16	Never Mind The Bollocks, Here's The...	Sex Pistols	(-)
17	Mix Up	Cabaret Voltaire	(-)
18	Get Happy	Elvis Costello	(-)
19	Reproduction	Human League	(13)
20=	The Scream	Siouxsie & The Banshees	(-)
=	Dirk Wears White Sox	Adam And The Ants	(-)
22	17 Seconds	Cure	(-)
23	Nobodies Heroes	Stiff Little Fingers	(-)
24	154	Wire	(-)
25=	Y?	Pop Group	(-)
=	Beat Rhythm News	Essential Logic	(-)
27=	Three Imaginary Boys	Cure	(25)
=	Undertones	Undertones	(15)
=	Outlandos D'Amour	Police	(11)
30	Pretenders	Pretenders	(-)

3 BANDS TONITE

I was waiting for the show to go on
But the pa ain't arrived
And now the show's in jeopardy

It's alright, be here tonight
It's already 12.30
And nothing has arrived yet

CHORUS: The Teenbeats and the Sta-Prest
They wanna take their money and go
We were the only band in the show
Prepared to go on with the show

Oh yeah the kids are waiting
It's alright coat two quid signs are up
And the'no refund' signs are up

It's alright 1.30
It's already 1.30
And now the bands are pulling out

CHORUS

In the dressing room things were not as
happy themes, one is the rejection of
they should have been
they couldn't risk no following

Wanted extra money
Wouldn't play with a rough now
These things follow you around
They wouldn't let you know

CHORUS

Oh yeah it's alright
The pa has arrived before
So now stage clothes on
We're gonna show them
That we really mean it now

CHORUS

I've been speaking to The Teen-beats and from what they've said about the record, but they do insist it wasn't their fault. They say they cut their set by 3 or 4 songs so the Directions could play. Jeff (for the Teenbeats)

Tony: 'We were going to go on last; the Global Village shuts at 2.00, so the last group is the shittiest so everyone can go home. We had enough time to do a half-hour set each, but Sta-Prest went on & did 45 minutes, then took another 15 minutes to get their gear offstage — they wouldn't even use each other's equipment. The Teenbeats went on & did a 40-minute set, and they finished at 10 past 2.
Was it obviously totally deliberate?
John: 'It was more the way they said to the audience "Oh we hung around especially for you, we didn't want to let you down" and all that bollocks.... When 5 minutes before the pa actually came, the Sta-Prest were actually out in the van ready to go.'
Tony: 'I said to Huggy 'You go in the

paper and talk about mod unity, and you do things like that - people don't know what's going on behind the scenes." People like Huggy come out and they think everything's alright.'
Don't you think it might have been making a bit of an issue out of it to make a single out of it?
Tony: 'At the stage I wrote that song, we were still doing our residency down at The Trafalgar. The Global village was for us like fucking Empire Pool.'
John: 'The actual song is not being vindictive - it's not digging them out.'
Have you spoken to them since?
John: 'We've played with them.'
So what do they think about your doing a single where you slag them off?
Tony: 'They say to us they don't mind, & it's good to have their name on another record, but apparently they're not too happy about it. It wasn't just a 'get-them-back' thing - I was disillusioned with their attitude.'

GENERAL INFO & SONGS:- The Directions, it has to be said, is a pretty moddy name. When we went to see them, we were expecting a really moddy group. But they don't put over that feeling at all

⑦

TRIBALISM PART 2.

We had a lot of reaction to last issue's Tribalism piece, so have devoted a whole page of letters to it. Note, two opposite sides criticised leaping to their defence....

I read your article on tribalism, that mostly I agreed with, but I was both hurt and insulted by your reference to me; you almost seem to be saying that we "ART" trouble at gigs.
I don't know if you've ever been to one of our gigs, but of the 50 that we did last year (nearly all of them benefits), there was a trouble at only 3; all of them at London gigs, all of them for so-called'political reasons'. 2 of the gigs were broken up by people claiming to be NF/BM, and one of the gigs by people claiming to be RAR/SWP, so the present score is 2 to the right, 1 to the left, and 47 to us.
Our stance as a band have always had 2 major themes, one is the rejection of left/right politics, and the other is the promotion of peace. I find it sad that you choose to criticise us for effectively promoting violence, when of all the bands currently working we have made as much effort to oppose it - our latest album has a lot to say about gang violence and the whole male mythology that goes toward creating it (see Big Man). We have most consistently appealed to people to get together and realise that it is stupid fighting amongst ourselves; there are, after all, much more threatening enemies if one really wants a fight even then, we believe violence only creates violence, there is NOTHING to be gained from it.

'Nice though the mention was, Paul Weller was more on the ball than you. Not only was Sounds' Southend article NOTHING to do with Can't Explain's previous article (!) - I didn't even read that - but also the whole point was to show what a waste of time it was.
Obviously like Paul was lecturing kids on 'Don't do that' lines gets you nowhere fast and I thought a lot of letting them think for themselves might help, via the comic ending -

'Bleedin' work again tomorrow'
'Let you think you're a king but you're really a pawn.'
In other words you ain't changed nothing.
Obviously the 'hole thing was too subtle for most 'informed commentators' though a few mods got the point.
Garry Bushell, SOUNDS.

'PS Sounds is v. alert to the problems of violence and though we think that superficial put-downs achieve nothing I do think that it is not enough to just try and understand the way these kids think without trying to shut out the violence problem. Watch for more in issue soon....'

'...Tribalism don't be so dismissive about what we are trying to do; we want to offer more than just 'pop music' and inevitably that presents problems. Maybe it's just a dream, but for the while...
Love, anarchy and peace'
Penny Rimbaud, CRASS

Tribalism.... I fully sympathise and agree with your sentiments concern ing violence, and think I have tried searching for an answer, but perhaps I have become cynical in my old age for every one or creates. Further problem every mind seems or is searching for an identity, something to conform to, seemingly because of an insecurity during teenage years due to pressure from such things as society and the ever increasing pressure for them to conform to a pattern that parents see fit. Instead of kids getting together and fighting for what they believe on common grounds, it is thought to be absolutely great to kick shit out of each other. The only answer for the kids - that means ALL of us - to accept how other people look, ie. clothes, whether it is a skins' uniform, punk or hippie etc. After accepting that then we are free to rise up and shout about what is wrong & unjust in today's society instead of keeping an eye quite rightly said the people in influential positions & hippy people in influential positions happy if we are divided amongst ourselves have no chance of achieving anything. Like you did in your article, I mean to like you did in your article, I mean to get just and quite definitely have not said what I wanted to, but the basic structure is there.'
Alison, Brave New Soldiers fanzine.

In your piece on tribalism you say you don't like the segregation between the different factions in music - then in your review of Speedball's Brighton concert, you say you were disappointed that only a small percentage belonged to any movement. Surely there's more to it than wearing clothes?....
Martin Grimshaw, Northampton

'A lot of people raised this point of my hypocrisy over the Speedball review and tribalism piece. The point I tried to make (very badly, I admit) was that too many people at the concert were totally normal, with not a hint of individuality in them. A lot were students, a lot posers, and it seems Brighton's scene, which, would have to involve individuality, was non-existent. I wasn't trying to encourage gangs of punks, mods a skins torturn up and beat shit out of each other, just to wonder if they were all happily going back to their jobs in society on monday morning.

The article on tribalism was well meant, no doubt, but said nothing that wasn't already become a cliché among the majority of reasonably minded music lovers (is your readers). As a result it comes across as naive at best (my opinion) and bloody stupid at worst (the general opinion of my friends). I don't think it would have done any good anyway, even if it had inspired us all to write fanzines and form groups - and because you're preaching to the converted, and
tribalism, they've just another excuse for it. When there was little happening musically in the early '70s, the kids fought on the football terraces (well perhaps the situation isn't as hopeless as that.)
Vivian Kelly, Leeds

-16-

JAMMING

JAMMING FANZINE regrets to announce that issue no. 10, which has been due to appear since early March, will not now be available until late July. This is due to the fact of our having O-Levels from the start of June onwards. Although no. 10 was, in fact, mostly written and half laid-out, we realised there was no way it could be finished, printed and distributed before they commenced. Whether or not our O-Levels turn out to be of any use to us, there is no point going through 11 years of schooling only to fail them all.

Jamming no. 10 was to feature The Damned, Directions, Security Risk, Apocalypse and a discussion on DIY Records. It will most likely still feature these, along with possible things like SLF, Madness, Delta 5 and Crass. To make up for this being the first issue in 9 months, we will try and put as much as possible in it while still hoping to hold the price to 25p.

Our apologies to all the people who've sent us stuff that will now be out of date, but we believe we're doing the right thing. Jamming no. 10 WILL emerge.

Tony Fletcher
Tony Fletcher

Jeff Carrigan
Jeff Carrigan

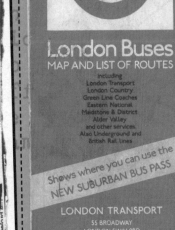

FROM THE NOTEBOOKS

LONDON SHOPS I KNOW ABOUT

1/ SMALL WONDER
2/ BEGGARS BANQUET Ealing
3/ 5TH COLUMN SHOP
4/ BETTER BADGES
5/ 5TH COLUMN STALL
6/ ROUGH TRADE
7/ VIRGIN NOTTING HILL
8/ VIRGIN Kensington
9/ VIRGIN Marble Arch
10/ COMPENDIUM
11/ VIRGIN Oxford Walk
12/ VIRGIN Megastore
13/ ROCK ART Cur Price
14/ FANS In Control
15/ ROCK ART Old Compton Street
16/ SHADES
17/ STREATHAM newsagent
18/ SHILLINGS
19/ 22- COUNTEADOWN
20/ WEBSTERS
21/ VIRGIN Croydon
22/ PAPERBACK Centre
23/ RE-ACTION
24/ CLOAKS
25/ HONEST Jon's Portobello Road
26/ DEEVIDES Dempsey
27/ BEGGARS BANQUET Hogarth Row

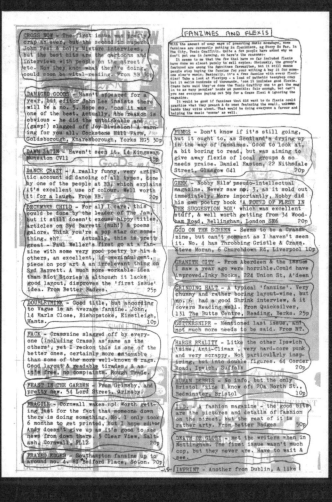

THE BEAT

Introductions should hardly be necessary for this. It was after Best Friend/ Stand Down Margaret was released, Jamming decided the Beat defenitely were on our side, and so the interview was fixed up. The Beat's full line-up, for those who don't know, is... Dave Wakeling - vocals, rhythm guitar
                                Ranking Roger - Toasting and backing vocals
                                David Steele - Bass
                                Saxa - saxaphone
                                Andy Cox - Lead guitar
                                Everett Moreton - Drums
    This interview was done mainly with David Steele, but Ranking Roger was also there for the first half an hour. David had a nasty habit of talking in a dead-pan voice while saying some very interesting things. But for the actual interview...

IS IT TRUE THAT THE RECENT MATERIAL YOU-'VE JUST DONE IS THE FIRST NEW STUFF SINCE YOU STARTED?

David: Probably, yeah. We've only had about 4 days rehearsal in the last year. It happened so quickly we never really got the time. We don't write songs individually, we write them as a group. Normally they start off with me and Andy, and when we've got something we play it to Everett; then Dave comes along. Then we've got Roger and Saxa to come along, so by the time we've got the 6th person fitting in, it's quite a long time.

DID YOU CALL DAVID 'SHUFFLE'?

Roger: Yeah, Shuffle. 'Cos he shuffles when he dances. Out of time!

WERE YOU EVER WORRIED AT ONE POINT THAT YOU'D DONE TOO MUCH TOO SOON?

L-r: Everett Moreton, Ranking Roger, David Steele, Andy Cox, Dave Wakeling and Saxa.

David: No, we don't really worry that much.
Roger: Why should ya? If you worry, you've got more problems.
David: I mean, there's so many things to worry about - God! The whole state of the country, the whole state of the music industry. It's enough to go mad. I mean, who knows what's going to happen tomorrow? Roger might walk out of here and get knocked over and die!
Roger: You (Dave) might get crushed by a steamroller!

THERE'S A LOT OF RUMOURS ABOUT SAXA, ABOUT HOW PERMANENT A MEMBER OF THE BAND HE IS. NOBODY EVER SEEMS TO KNOW.

David: No we don't really - no, we don't either, I'm afraid. If you met him, you'd realise that he's not at all part of the music scene as you know it: He's never read a music paper in his life, he never listens to Radio 1, he doesn't listen to any music you listen to. He doesn't worry about that sort of thing.
Roger: He's got sense.
David: He is a full member contract-wise. He gets as much money as anyone else.

WHY WERE THERE SO MANY SINGLES OFF THE LP?

David: I prefer singles; I don't really like LPs that much.
Roger (to David): I think you should get into that, you know.
David: I can't really understand this rip-off thing. I mean, people don't have to buy them if they don't want to. I really like singles - I wouldn't mind releasing every track off the LP as a single!

WELL I RECKON BEST FRIEND WAS PROBABLY BEST SINGLE OF THE YEAR, BUT NOT THAT

-8-

MANY PEOPLE BOUGHT IT, BECAUSE BOTH TRACKS WERE ON THE LP.

Roger: I don't think it was that, because Blondie can release nearly every track on their LP, and they all go to no. 1.

David: It didn't get played on the radio because of Stand Down Margaret.

Roger: I think it was 'cos of that - 'cos the other side was political. It was a double A side, remember.

David: Every other single we've brought out has gone straight on the playlist, but that didn't go on the playlist at all for the first 2 or 3 weeks. With Mirror In The Bathroom we got Top Of The Pops at about no. 58, but when Best Friend was no. 24 they still wouldn't give us it.

(Memories come back of Top Of The Pops playing it for all of one minute on one occasion!) DO YOU KNOW HOW MUCH WENT TO CND?

David: £15,000. If it had sold as much as the other singles it would have been £25,000.

Roger: Give us a doughnut, I'm starving!

David: Alright, you can have one. You can see what a racially mixed & integrated band we are - we even give each other doughnuts! That's the sort of quote you should get in, though - doughnuts. So many groups go on and on about - Dave for instance can sit and tell really patronising idiots for hours on end about how we got together and things like that. I just get really pissed off with it.

DO YOU RECKON STAND DOWN MARGARET GOT THROUGH TO A LOT OF PEOPLE THAT BOUGHT THE RECORD, LIKE THE LITTLE KIDS?

David: Oh yeah, I think so. 'Cos with things like Smash Hits it was stressed quite a lot - they gave it a whole half-page. It didn't get played on the radio of course.

DID ANYONE PLAY IT, APART FROM JOHN PEEL?

David: I think Anne Nightingale played it. Actually Peter Powell wanted to make it his record of the week, but the BBC got so wierd about that. They got really frightened, and said 'No, no - we can't have that', and so they made Best Friend the a-side and just played it a couple of times.

ARE YOU EVER WORRIED ABOUT GETTING THE IMAGE OF BEING A POP GROUP?

Dave: I dunno, I like pop groups.

Roger: We're not a pop group through. 'Cos when you say 'pop music' I don't think of it as dancing 'cos it's too commercial.

I WOULDN'T CALL YOU A POP GROUP, BUT I THINK A LOT OF OTHER PEOPLE DO. YOU'RE REALLY INTO THE SMASH HITS MARKET, WITH ALL THE LITTLE KIDS...

Dave: Well I like that sort of thing. It sounds really corny, but when we play matinees it's the most fun. It's good seeing little kids in the street. I think older people take it too seriously and the more little kids' magazines we can get into, the happier I'll be. I wouldn't mind if they were all little kids - by little, I mean we've got a lot of fans from 12 to 16.

A LOT OF PEOPLE SEEM TO CONSIDER DAVE WAKELING AS THE LEADER OF THE GROUP. WHY DO YOU THINK THAT IS?

David: He does loads of interviews - he likes talking to idiots. You do get so many prats coming along, and he'll quite happily chat to them for a couple of hours. He's the only one who's willing to do lots of interviews. I don't mind doing ones like this - it's just the real idiots.

DO YOU THINK ANY OF THE 2TONE GROUPS DID TOO MUCH TOO SOON, LIKE THE SELECTOR OR BODYSNATCHERS?

David: I think maybe they worked too hard.

Roger: I think you shouldn't tour too much. Like the Specials were touring continually. I used to see some of them in a night club and they'd look half dead.

David: I'd be quite happy if we never toured again. I hate touring.

Roger: I think it's great actually.

David: You don't mind doing the gigs, it's just the whole touring thing.

Roger: Oh Christ, yeah.

David: I like to play in England - I'm not bothered about Europe any more.

A COUPLE OF MONTHS AFTER TEARS OF A CLOWN CAME OUT, 2TONE WAS THE REALLY BIG THING - EVERY SINGLE HAD BEEN A HIT AND IT WAS GOING TO HAVE TO STOP AT SOME POINT.

David: Yeah I think that's cos there was 4 - well maybe the Selecter have gone down a bit - there was the Specials Madness, and us. All the 2Tone fans had already become fans of those three - there's only so many bands you can become fans of.

DO YOU THINK IT'S GOT ANYTHING TO DO WITH ONCE THE BBC STOPPED PLUGGING THE 2TONE RECORDS, IT COLLAPSED?

Roger: No, it's just that no movement can go on for so long. Once something makes it to the top - after a while it seems to sound all the same. I think some of the 2Tone bands, or bands playing that, are all going the same and you can hear them all going 'Chink-chink', & you think "Oh no, not another ska record." 'Cos I really got into ska for a

—9—

time, and then I went off it for a bit, 'cos it started to sound really the same - it got really boring.

THERE NEVER SEEMED TO BE THAT MANY SKA BANDS THOUGH.

Roger: No, but a lot of bands may do the odd ska number, or something that sounds very similar to ska. It's like when the Pistols came out, and got big, and every-body wanted to get in, you know. And 'cos everybody wanted to be a punk band, it killed punk off. And it was the same with ska.

YOU AS A GROUP HAVE ALWAYS DESCRIBED YOURSELVES AS A 'PUNK-REGGAE' GROUP; BUT YOU NEVER SEEMED TO ME TO BE VERY PUNKY.

Roger: Well I think we're going more to-wards reggae than anything else. We used to have a lot of punk numbers that we used to do really fast, even as fast as Click Click. And we changed our music to the way it suited us, and to the way we were all settling into one another. I think we've gone more reggae.
David: Yeah, we are more into reggae now. But then other members of the band might not be into reggae so it's a comp-romise.
(Ranking Roger now departs for the den-tist. The rest of the interview is with David on his own)

WHAT DO YOU THINK OF THE SPECIALS DOING MAGGIE'S FARM, AFTER YOUR STAND DOWN MARGARET. DO YOU RECKON THEY'LL GET SLAGGED OF FOR IT?

David (laughing): Yeah, they could do. But it's quite a good fashion, if it is a fashion anyway! It's like nuclear pow-er and arms. I don't think getting rid of that would solve anything whatsoever. They'd just find something else like germ warfare that would wipe us all out. Getting rid of nuclear weapons is becom-ing an easy topic - you can be against nuclear arms and you don't really have to worry about it: You don't have to think about old people dying or unemploy-ment. You can just think "Oh, I'll be anti-nuclear," and a lot of people have started doing that. It IS a bad thing, but the only way to change anything is to change the system. You're not going to change anything indivudually.

DO YOU RECKON ANYBODY WILL BE ABLE TO DO THAT?

David: What, change the whole system? No - I used to be really into that, I used to read a lot. But I suddenly realised although the world is in an absolutely vile state, there is nothing I think we can do about it. It's just fucked, bas-ically.

APPARENTLY WITH GO-FEET YOU'RE ALLOWED TO DO FIVE OTHER GROUPS SINGLES A YEAR. WHAT'S HAPPENED?

David: We haven't found anyone we like. We'll be releasing a single by the Mood Elevators in the new year, called 'Driv-ing By Night'. And we're going to release a reggae LP called Heart Of The Congos - it's a Jamaican group. It's not available in England, but it's really really good - one of the best reggae LPs ever. We were thinking of doing a 12" of four or five Birmingham groups, but the last couple of weeks is the first time we've been in Birmingham for some time. So now we've got the chance to go and see some groups.

WHAT SAY DO ARISTA HAVE IN GO-FEET?

David: None really - they have to put out what we tell them to put out. But they can bungle lots of things; for in-atance you can give them some artwork & they can lose it.

DO THEY DO THAT DELIBERATELY?

David: Oh yeah. Like when we released Hands Off, She's Mine & Twist'n'Crawl; that was supposed to be a double 'A' side. But the first pressings accidentally appeared with 'B-side' for Twist'n'Crawl.

ARE YOU HAPPY WITH THEM?

David: No I'm not. But compared to al-most every other record company we've got a really good deal.
IT SEEMS TO ME THAT THE BEAT ARE ABOUT THE MOST WIDELY-INFLUENCED BAND THERE IS.
David: Yeah, probably 'cos we don't

10- "What does he mean, 'quite good harmonies'?!"

really agree in music tastes. 'Cos I play bass I really like reggae bass & soul bass. Whereas as Andy & Dave play guitar, they're much more into guitar music. But then Roger's a toaster, & he likes toasting, although he can sing - he does do some quite good harmonies. Saxa's a saxaphone player, so he plays jazz. Everything's like a compromise. I don't like the guitar sound on the LP - they're too raunchy.

SO DO YOU EVER GET PROBLEMS WITH YOUR DIFFERENT STYLES, WITH EVERYONE TRYING TO WIN THEIR STYLE OVER?

David: Not really, because we usually compromise. Like on the LP there were things done that I agreed to, and it meant I could have things taken off Mirror In The Bathroom & Big Shot that I didn't like. We always compromise.

DO YOU GET MANY PUNKS AT YOUR GIGS?

David: We used to get loads, before we became a two-tone/mod group (he didn't say it in inverted commas, but probably meant it that way). And then for 2Tone mania we were just getting loads of mods and skinheads. Then when the LP came out we started getting lots of other people: hippies 'cos they're into reggae; punks 'cos they're into things like Two Swords and Click Click. Also - in places like London, everybody's a punk or a 'some-thing', whereas if you play somewhere like Wales, where they haven't got strong fashion bands, it's not like that. I mean, what is a punk anyway? I think its a bit wanky. I was really into punk at first - 1976, 77 - it was one of the most exciting things that had ever happ-ened. I was on the dole as well. So I got a bit pissed off with all these pat-hetic punk groups and all these idiots thinking they're punks. Instead of Stairway To Heavan, it's Anarchy In The UK - it's the same old 'Classic' crap.

WHAT DID YOU THINK OF THE MOD THING?

David: It's really wierd - down south it's all skinheads, but up north there's loads of mods. They seem to be more into into it, and there's some really good clubs. It was like when us & The Selecter did our first ever tours, together, & we'd play places like Blackpool and the Specials would come and see us.So there'd be like The Beat, The Selecter, The Spec-ials and maybe a couple of Madness all in the same club, and nobody had ever heard of us. And it was a really exciting atmos -phere - we thought something was happen-ing again, but it didn't last for long.

DO YOU THINK THAT'S FINISHED NOW?

David: Not up north. It seems that every-body's become a rude boy - the little kids anyway. A lot of mods I know have had their hair cut and started wearing

harringtons, just to stop themselves get-ting beaten up. But they still like the same music. It's skinheads <u>and</u> mods vs. punks, but it doesn't happen much up here. We get a lot more girls than the other 2Tone groups.

DO YOU THINK IT'S 'COS OF THE DANCING GIRL EMBLEM?

David: Yeah maybe, & maybe because of Roger and Dave being sex symbols! We get a lot of posters in Jackie & Oh Boy - I didn't realise how strong it had become until I went to see The Specials & The Selecter quite recently, and almost all the audience were male skinheads. Our audiences are in some places almost 50% female.It's just great, because I think it's really vile when you get a macho audience.

WELL I DON'T KNOW IF I MISSED THE POINT, BUT I THOUGHT HANDS OFF, SHE'S MINE WAS A REALLY SEXIST SONG.

Dave: NO! We never thought of that, ever. We never thought of it as sexist. But - if you've got a girlfriend or a wife or something, you certainly don't want to lose her. Maybe you do want to hold her, but it doesn't mean you want to dominate her. It was just like a pop song.I think maybe you - or rather, one - is taking things a bit too seriously.

WHAT WAS AMERICA LIKE?

David: Horrible. It was vile - a really stinking, degenerate place that's got no hope at all. It was really depressing, but each state's like a different count-ry. Saxa & Roger both enjoyed it anyway. We're going to do like 2 week tours in future, taking in a different area at a time. I really like playing in England anyway, especially on the last tour when we weren't getting any violence at all. You wouldn't know how wonderful Radio 1 is compared to American radio - there it would be an avant-garde radio. We think we're badly off, but compared to every-where else we're amazing.

AF

Dead Kennedys
Fresh Fruit for Rotting Vegetables?

We all know the story: Towards the end of 1979, out of San Francisco of all places, came a record called California Uber Alles by the Dead Kennedys. It was the first evidence of punk from the laid-back West Coast, and was such a good single nobody could ignore it. And nobody who was anybody did. The record, on Fast, sold thousands of copies, and was followed up in the middle of 1980 by Holiday In Cambodia, an equally disturbing and equally successful single. The band had now been officially signed to Cherry Red, and in the early Autumn, the Dead Kennedys were unleashed on a hungry public with an album, titled Fresh Fruit For Rotting Vegetables, and a tour of Britain, followed by one of Europe. In this country at least, the group became the new Messiahs of punk, and the album, despite terrible reviews, entered the BRMB Top 30, while a version of Kill The Poor was released as their third single, and made the BBC Top 50. All 3 singles are now permanently lodged in the Alternative charts Top 20.

The Dead Kennedys caused such an impact through being the American equivalent of the Sex Pistols: Lead singer Jello Biafra stood as mayor of San Francisco and came 4th out of 10, polling 6,500 votes. Reports filtered through of all their gigs bringing strong reactions - usually havoc and subsequent banning. Their songs were loud, fast, threatening and given a unique dimension by Jello's voice. Three-four years after the Ramones and Patti Smith 'invented' punk in America, the Dead Kennedys were acting it. They were America's most vital band for a decade.

My own high regard was seriously damaged by the album. The main fault seemed to be that they just didn't have enough songs to match the singles, but as the version of California on it demonstrated, this may have been because it was all taken so fast. Songs were recorded at breakneck speed, and the above mentioned track was an example of a song so fast it lost the character it had when first released. A few tracks - Kill The Poor, Let's Lynch The Landlord, Your Emotions, Holiday In Cambodia & Viva Las Vegas - were magnificent, but only added up to 12 minutes good music on what was already a short LP. I didn't hold this too much against the group, and lived in hope of the tour.

Dead Kennedys coming to Europe and England is the silliest, most wretchedly useless conceit I've heard all year. Why aren't they pushing 'Fresh Fruit' in America where it's urgently needed instead of peddling it second-hand in England where it's the very last thing we need?

— Dave McCollough, Sounds

And basically, I wasn't disappointed. Their Music Machine appearance was an excellent gig, even if it did end in the NME's idea of a full-scale riot. The songs were all well-played, all exciting and a couple of new songs promised a lot. Jello was an excellent front man, showing that if you look hard enough, you can find a decent Yank. But there lies the deep worry - and I'm not the only person to be plagued by this fear - are the Dead Kennedys acheiving anything by concentrating on Britain? Surely a band as exciting as them should be forcing America to wake up in the way the Pistols & others did to England - and if the DK's succeeded they'd be worth more than all the English bands of '76-'77 put together, when you consider America's backwardness. Their songs are about American attitudes, so why do the easy thing and become England's heroes? This isn't an inditement, just a nagging fear.

This introduction has been written, for the first time evr, before doing the interview. I've put down all the above before meeting Jello (having returned from their European tour), so that the encounter will be able to establish exactly what the Dead Kennedys are, and so that, for once, you can read the interview from the interviewer's viewpoint. Enough of this and on to the interview (done the day after the Carter-Reagan debate was shown on TV, and with Ray, guitarist, also present)....

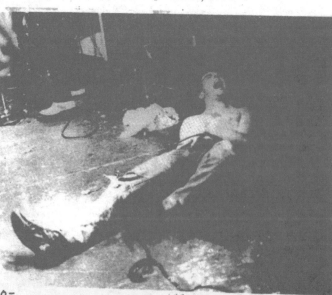

-20-

or: BRINGING COALS TO NEWCASTLE?

WERE YOU PLEASED WITH THE LP?

T: Overall, though ours was the problem in that the tapes sounded fine, but the mastering was done wrong, so there's very little bottom end - the bass guitar might as well not have been recorded, So the day we got here we got George Peckham to remix it, so that newer copies will sound right. They'll also sound slightly slower because we discovered the tape machine at the studio we recorded at was something like 15/100ths of a second too fast, so on the album my voice comes out a bit too chipmunk-like. So we slowed it down a teeny bit.

I WAS A BIT DISAPPOINTED WITH THE LP. I THOUGHT IT WAS INCREDIBLY FAST, LIKE ON CALIFORNIA UBER ALLES...

J: Yeah, that was a faster version simply because we play it faster now. One of the reasons we chose the particular songs we did is we took a calculated gamble that we'd be allowed to make another album, figuring that we'd record the best of our earlier material for the first album, rather than dropping it so that nobody would evr get to hear it.

ARE YOU GOING TO DO ANOTHER ALBUM WITH CHERRY RED THEN?

J: Er... I dunno if it'll be on Cherry Red or not. We like to do one-offs so as not to get stuck with anybody for too long, and not recognise ourselves.

I'D HAVE THOUGHT AFTER 'CALIFORNIA' HAD SOLD SO WELL, YOU'D HAVE HAD SOME OF THE BIG LABELS AFTER YOU.

J: You've got to remember that even in this country, although America is much worse, the big time record companies don't want anybody unless they think they can manipulate them and control them - they don't want anybody who hints of being too dangerous. I think that's one of the reasons they kept trying to shout us down with 'punk is dead' tirades in the major music weeklies, because they wanted something more sedative and less threatening. To emphasise this what did they try & replace it with? A Heavy Metal revival.

...If and when we do another album it's going to be pretty different from the first - there'll be a little more group-written material - more in the Holiday In Cambodia vein. Our newer songs... we played 'Halloween' on the tour,& 'Too Drunk Too Fuck' and 'Government Flu' we played sometimes, and also 'Bleed For Me' which is about torture. Oh yeah, 'Dreadlocks Of The Suburbs' - that's a really old song that didn't quite fit on the LP.

I say that my favourite trackson FFPRV were the group-written ones, and ask hopefully IS THE NEW STUFF LIKE THE GROUP-WRITTEN MATERIAL ON THE LP?

J: It's a bit more intricate, but still maintaining the punk guts - no matter what directions we may take, we will hang on to that... Actually, most of the guitars on the LP were overdubbed, and we got the guy from Van Halen to play under an assumed name - we hired him as a session musician!

WERE YOU SURPRISED AT YOUR SUCCESS OVER HERE?

J: We never really expected that - by American standards we cut a very, very dangerous album - there hasn't been anything like that by an American band released for God-knows-how-many-years. But then we come over here and find that we're labelled a 'commercial band'. That was quite a shock! We generally drew larger crowds than we do in the States - much larger on average.

YEAH - IT WASN'T REALLY THE LP THAT WAS THE SUPRISE, IT WAS CALIFORNIA UBER ALLES THAT SOLD SO WELL....

J: Yeah, it sold triple the number of copies over here as it did there and I was very suprised. We thought it was a good song or else we wouldn't have recorded it, but so few of the bands of our type on the West Coast have made any kind of breakthrough at all over here. We were a fluke over here - it was a complete stroke of luck that Bob Last was able to hear California, and was interested in it, and called us up and said he wanted to put it out in England. It could have been anybody, although we had more motivation than others to keep going; but on the other hand, what else is there to do in California?

THERE DOESN'T SEEM TO BE MANY BANDS ON THE WEST COAST ANYTHING AS GOOD AS THE DEAD KENNEDYS....

J: On the other hand, have you heard of - The Flippers, The Germs - who made a whole album before splitting - The Deadbeats, The Screamers - who never made an album - DOA and Subhumans from Vancouver?

THE MAIN ARGUMENT AGAINST THE DKs IS ABOUT 'BRINGING COALS TO NEWCASTLES'. DO YOU KNOW WHAT THAT MEANS?

J: No.

IT MEANS YOUR BEING A REBELLIOUS PUNK IN ENGLAND IS...

J: Well, punk is where you find it; there's punk bands in Germany, punk bands in Switzerland, punk bands in Japan & even punk bands in Poland. And basically anyone who cries 'punk is dead' or 'punk is an English-only phenomenon' can kiss my ass.

I'D BETTER TRY AND MAKE THIS CLEARER: PEOPLE ARE SAYING THAT WHAT YOU'RE DOING FOR AMERICA IS GREAT, BUT WHY AREN'T YOU CONCENTRATING ON AMERICA INSTEAD OF BRITAIN, WHERE YOU'RE ALREADY POPULAR.

Ray: The words don't just apply to the USA. Stupidity and apathy happen in every single country. California Uber Alles is not just about Jerry Brown, although he's the man mentioned; it's about fascists, and they're everywhere.
J: We've drawn in intelligent sector of the punk audience over here, and that means they know enough to read between the lines of our lyrics and see that a lot of it applies to them in England as well as our own situation. Plus I think it's the first time they've really been exposed to another point of view besides what we show on our TV, as far as what goes on in the States.

WELL, HAS THE LP BEEN RELEASED IN THE STATES?

J: No.

THAT'S ONE OF THE ARGUMENTS AGAINST YOU, THAT YOU'RE HAVING ALL THIS DONE IN ENGLAND, WHEN...

J: What they've got to realise is that most of the American bands that have been able to make LPs at all, have made them for European record companies because people are just more hip over here

Who would lead you Europeans if Russia hit us Americans first?

Sir,—In the United States, we are told, Europeans cry out for strong American leadership. Is this true?

In what arena do you need my country's guidance? Perhaps in economics? It's a civilised system of economics that allows the majority shareholder to lead the parade. True, the chair of leadership is purchased with dollars, not wisdom, but it's a system of order.

In the United States, we are told that our NATO friends in Europe live in absolute fear of the day your Russian neighbour swoops down and carts your children off to forced labour camps. We in America share that fear ourselves. Our best scholars have made it empirically clear that the present Russian Czars are just using "communism" as a cloak for world conquest and domination.

Just look at Afghanistan! And Brzezinski says that Western Europe is next. You do believe that, don't you? We Americans do. Even though there is no historical precedent for such a Russian move, one should not let history muddy up the waters of clear thought.

The Russians are cowards. I think that's well known. They won't confront us Americans straight on. They will attack you folks in Europe first, just to test our commitment. So I think it's best we stop the Russians on your homeland, lest they get bold and try to attack us directly.

This is why it's so important for you to up your defence spending, cut back on social services and accept our tactical nuclear weapons. If you Europeans don't provide a viable nuclear deterrent, the Russians are not going to bother to blow you up first. They will come straight after us. Then who will lead you?

As leader, we've decided the whole "order" rests on our mutual ability to contain the Russians. We thought you understood this; but in recent months you have made us very unhappy by doubting our conventional wisdom. Perhaps those rumours about our global weakness have led to your confusion.

But I assure you those are just rumours. I have just come from our major ally in Asia, South Korea. Now, you should remember that we have asked a great deal more of the Koreans than we have asked of you Europeans in the containment of communism.

The Koreans, like you, in recent months became confused. They got selfish and tried to go it alone. They tried to upset the order, and we simply did not permit it. Some distasteful measures had to be taken, but I think we have proven our willingness to spare no moral or financial expense in the maintenance of our commitment to those of you on the front line against communism.

Rest assured. We would do no less for you than we have for our South Korean friends.

Steven Clark,
(US Peace Corps: South Korea from April, 1978 to June, 1980).
Wisconsin, U.S.

This would be hilarious if it wasn't so sadly true. But what can we do about it? (From the Guardian a few months back)

for that kind of thing. As a result
there's a huge American cult audience
that buy nothing but imported records.
And that market is growing to the point
where if you put imports alongside domestic releases in the charts, there'd be
a substantial number in the Top 100. The
Clash sold close to 100,000 copies of
their first album outthere on import.(1)

...We're punk, but we're totally
different from the bands over here, simply because we live so far away, plus
there's a little more sense of humour in
our words. Despite the serious ideas behind our songs, we aren't afraid to use
humour as a weapon.

YOUR HUMOUR'S VERY CYNICAL THOUGH.

J: Yeah, well living in America has made
us very cynical, and also very distrust-
ing of those around us.

YOU TAKE THE TITLES, LIKE KILL THE POOR
AND CALIFORNIA UBER ALLES, AND IT TAKES
A FOOL NOT TO REALISE WHERE YOU STAND.

J: Then I'm suprised how many fools
there are in England. You only saw us at
the MM, but at the earlier gigs we were
greeted with an alarming number of seig-
heiling Hitler salutes, because of Uber
Alles. I don't think many of them were
hard-core Nazis or National Front or
anything, they just thought that that's
what you were supposed to do to the song.
And so, carefully I told them during the
part before 'now it is 1984' that basically
it's an anti-fascist song, all about fascists in disguise, and that the real
Nazis are the Global corporations, oil
companies and what-not who screw you up
the ass and try and stick you with a boring job, so that you're just another cog
in their machine. And that got through
to an awful lot of people.

I explain a bit about skins in England
being manipulated into Nazis...

J: Yeah, which of course is playing right
into the hands of the people who made
them so bitter in the first place. The
American equivalent, mentality-wise, of
the skinheads are Jocks. The jocks don't
come from working-class families or anything; they're usually middle- or upper-
middle-class suburban whites, who are
basically anti everyone who isn't a jock!
Beat up black people, beat up punks,
beat up lots of things. There was a case
in Cheeko (or however you spell it),
California, where a group of jocks had
been out hunting, and didn't find any
deer that day, so they drove around the
city until they found a black and shot
him instead!

DID THEY EAT HIM?

J: No, they just drove off and were caught
a while later. They were brought to trial
and pleaded guilty to 'un-premediatated
murder and crime of passion'; they were
guilty of first-degree murder but they
got done for (a bit blurred here...) the
American equivalent of manslaughter, and
only got 7 years in jail. And about 95%
of American kids are jocks! So you don't
have punks vs skins vs mods vs rude boys
vs whatever - you have everybody else
versus the jocks, because there's so many
of them, and they're in all parts of the
population. Jocks, after they stop being
jocks full-time, get jobs as businessmen,
cops, politicians - basically the cut-
throat jobs, And so the jock mentality
continues that way. The mentality is 'If
I don't understand it, I beat it up'!

HAVE YOU NOTICED HOW IN ENGLAND THE PEOPLE
AT THE TOP HAVE GOT IT SO THAT ALL THE
KIDS ARE FIGHTING EACH OTHER?

J: Yeah, that's really crafty of them
isn't it? And maybe they try and pass
themselves off as fans of the music, but
the music weeklies are very much to
blame. There were no punk-ted fights until - I think it was the MM - had 'Punk-
Ted Riot' plastered across the front; I
was in England when they did that. And

then a while later, instead of 'punks and
skinheads on the same side', it's 'punks
vs. skinheads!,deliberately trying to
defuse certain bands that they'd decided
to pick on for one reason or another.

THE NME RECENTLY HAD A BIG 'SHOCK-HORROR'
ON VARIOUS 'STARS' BEING ARRESTED...

J: Was that when they wrote about me being arrested, because I never was actually arrested? There were some early delays over my passport, so I was getting
it fixed at the passport office, but
instead of them taking the usual 1 hr or
1 day, they decided to fuck around for
a bit, and took 5 days! 'Oh, we're sorry
- we'll have it tomorrow. Oh, we're sorry
and guess what - lucky you! We're closed
all over the weekend.' So I had to back
on Monday and the result was no Dingwalls
gig.

The worst gig in England was Brady's
in Liverpool, which not only was 170°,
but the guitar amp went out during every
song, just great for the continuity of
the set! The fans responded by cheerfully
clapping 'You're gonna get your fucking
heads kicked in'! Afterwards they seemed
to have really liked it. Brady's is so
hot that your jeans drip.

Talk moves on to all the clubs forced to
close...(eg The Clarendon)...

J: The same sort of thing happens in San
Francisco. Basically, if you have a venue and the law wants to get you, they
will. Be it they can make up some fire
code regulation that they can pull out
of a hat, or they'll say "We saw somebody under age drinking a beer, therefore your days are numbered", or they-
'll say "There's too much noise", or
they'll say "There's too many fights
outside, that our plain clothes people
happened to start, but we won't talk
about that". Things like that. There's
a constant battle with the police as
far as halls go in San Francisco - it's
worse than Los Angeles.

WHAT DID YOU RECKON (interruption)...
OF THE EARLY AMERICAN PUNK BANDS FROM
NEW YORK?

J: New York is a very different scene
from anywhere in England or the West
Coast. On the West coast, the people
who go to gigs are fans; the NY scene is
dominated by people 30 years old on up,
who've been kicking around since the
days of the New York Dolls, and have put
together one copy band after another,
each even worse than the last. That's NY
currently - there were some good bands
in the beginning; CBGB's helped kick the
door open a little in America, though it
got slammed shut again. And you don't
see any spiked cuts in NY, because they
consider that too British.The standard
NY punk is about 30 years old, with
short black curly hair, a red and white
stripy t-shirt, Ramones jeans & tennis
shoes - there's so many of them it's
ridiculous. Then there's the disco punks
which are starting to spread like the
plague, both to Paris & the West Coast-
basically it's people who were disco
trendies yesterday who get Vidal Sassoon
or somebody to get them a perfectly
spiked hair cut. They pay like 30 or 40
dollars to look like they cut their hair
themselves; and they die their hair and
wear spandex pants. You don't see much
Spandex in England...
Ray: You see it on ToTP...
J: Right - if the giggle girls who do
the clapping and things on TOTP - if
they cut their hair and began wearing
Spandex pants, they'd be disco punks.
Both the NY scene & the Paris scenes are
among the worst to play to because they
all just stand there and judge you.
They're not into listening to you -
they're into picking out your faults.

I got used to the English clubs that
get really hot, & so if I wasn't dripp-
ing with sweat by the first few numbers
I figured something was wrong. In Amer-

ica there tends to be air conditioning-
or in NY they're not giving off any body
heat - they're just standing there. We
connected with some in NY but basically
we had to attack them before they reacted. In Max's Kansas City there's tables
& chairs all the way down to the front,
and they didn't start to dance until we
jumped out in to the crowd, and knocked
the tables over, poured their drinks
over them, pushed them out of their
chairs...! And then they started turning
round and doing it to the people behind
them, and then it began to be a fun gig!

DO YOU WANT TO TELL US SOMETHING ABOUT
THE AMERICAN WAY OF LIFE?

J: As far as exposing the horrors of American life, we despite it as much as
you do, therefore we figure it should be
exposed and ripped to shreds from the inside. Again, even though we're an American band I don't think it's bringing coals
to Newcastle. We zero in on American
problems rather than English ones. If we
began singing about 'this in the UK' and
'this elsewhere', then we'd really be
hopping on the bandwagon with no real
thought.

Generally, there is a kind of plastic
aura which you find in America; partly
because the standard of living is a little higher, therefore people figure they
should spend more, or at least are TAUGHT
TO THINK, that they should spend more
money on fancy technological gimmicks,
that they don't really need, and that
makes it very very plastic, and very,
very cold and hollow in a way. American's
have no soul - you'll find Canadians
have a little more spunk.

BUT THEY HATE BEING CALLED AMERICANS,

J: Well I couldn't blame them! I don't
like being called an American either,
but it's something I'm going to have to
put up with.

WHAT I FIND SICKENING, ESPECIALLY NOW
WITH THE ELECTION ON, IS THE IDEA AMERICA
HAS OF BEING 'LEADERS OF THE FREE WORLD,
AND OVER HERE WE HARDLY NEED AMERICA AS
OUR 'LEADERS'.

J: Define a free world anyway:- free to
be told by Global Corporations what to
buy, and get shut in mental instit-
ions if you don't buy it!

There was an amazing article in an
issue of Newsweek. They say 'Why America
isn't ready enough for war', building on
the war fever thing. 'The navy says "We
don't have enough ships"', and at the end
of the article - 'Well, we may not have
that big a navy, but it's still 3 times
bigger than the Russian navy', and 'Hey,
well see, the army may be short of so
many thousands of machine guns, but hey
the Air Force has that many sitting in
their warehouses, but they won't give
them to the army, because then the munit-
ions manufacturers don't get the profit
for making more machine guns'!! It's a
total con. The world is a total con designed to line the pockets of the people
who build the military hardware, and
everybody else on both sides loses.

I think a big factor in America's
economic decline is that though Germany &
Japan were the main losers of World War
II, they were still technological societies. They learnt to build things that did
more than just one little function, and
things that didn't break down in a couple
of years, meaning that if they needed to
change the model of a car, they could just
switch a few parts and change it, rather
than building a whole new factory, which
is what America is having to do. A friend
of mine went to art school in Los Angeles
- it was where they taught the bigshot
media men, a very important place - and
the people in the autodesign school were
submitting designs for a very few efficient
cars, safe cars, and good-looking cars at
the same time. But the people from the car
companies were saying "No, no, no, they're
nice cars, and we'd love to be able to
build them, we realise it would rescue us,

but we don't have the money to change over
all the machinery to do it. So you're going to have to keep buying your shitty
Chevettes and your shitty Ford Kidoos and
your shitty Granadas instead."! By contrast, the German automobile industry for
example, invented a computerised drill
press that can be programmed to drill literally hundreds of different kinds of
wholes, whereas in America they'd build a
hundred giant drills, each to do just one!
And that's what slowly dragged America
under, that and the 'Me Generation'. Americans are much more German than they are
British, in the way they think & behave.
You see Germany is a very plastic country
too, and the Americans are very rigid and
obediant in a way.
Ray: They think they rule.

THAT'S I™...

J: Of course. Reagan's main campaign feature is he's going to make Americans conceited again - he's going to make them
wildly proud to be American, and the way
he'll do it is push the button for World
War III. He's going to abolish the 55mph
speed limit and put it back up to 70-75 -
they've used it to coserve fuel, but Reagan says 'People should be able to drive
their cars as much as they want - we don't
have to cut down on oil. We don't have to
cut down on anything. We must drain all
the world of it's natural resources - who
cares if we cave in in 10 years because
I'm so fucking old I'll be dead by then.'!!

CARTER AND REAGAN BOTH USE THIS THING OF
AMERICA'S RESPONSIBILITY AS 'LEADERS OF
THE FREE WORLD'....

J: On the other hand, look at it this way:
would you like the responsibility of having
to lead the so-called 'free world'?! Would
you like to have to explain why you send
all this money and guns to dictators in
Chile, and claiming it's to protect the
free world? Being leaders of the 'free
world' is a pain in the ass!
Ray: But the alternative is Russia.
J: Right - there's no punk rock in Russia. Keep in mind that if Crass were to
release Stations Of The Cross in Russia
they'd be rounded up and shot within an
hour.

IT'S THE BEST OF A BAD DEAL REALLY, ISN'T
IT?

J: Yeah, I can see how you think that in
a way, but keep in mind, especially with
Carter in office, America's too stupid to
be anyone's big brother! It's the kind of
big brother where you learned from their
mistakes as you moved along behind them!
America's set such a horrible example to
the world that if the American empire
does get completely buried, Americans are
going to be the most trod upon people on
earth - everyone's going to hate them
for the next several hundred years.

DID YOU SEE THE CARTER-REAGAN DEBATE ON
TV LAST NIGHT?

J: That was last night? Oh shit, I wanted
to see that. Who won. Reagan? Yeah, well
he's got acting for the camera training.
I figure if you have, to pick between one
or the other, pick Carter, because he's
so stupid he can't get his job done. If
you've got the choice of two evil men
out to fuck up your lives, pick the one
who can't get his job done.

I HOPE REAGAN DOESN'T GET IN (some hope
it turned out), 'COS HE LOOKS MORE LIKELY
TO PRESS THE BUTTON.

J: Oh yeah! Make money for the people who
put him in power! War for profit! Russia
Incorporated versus the Western World's
Global Corporations. Like, I figure that

the reason the Russians invaded Afghanistan, was not because they wanted to take
it over, or because it was such an important country, but because in Vietnam
America had a whole test ground for their
fancy new weapons, and Russia never had
that. So, like dropping germ bombs on
little villages in Afghanistan, and all
kinds of wierd mines in the hills, including ones that look like flashlights &
pens - they've got pens that if you pick
them up, they blow up. Russia are just
experimenting on the Afghan people in
preparation for bigger things.

HOW DO YOU VIEW THE MIAMI RACE RIOT AND
THE NEW MEXICO PRISON RIOT?

J: It was two entirely seperate entities
because prison mentality & ghetto mentality are both intense, but in very very
different ways. The race riots are just
another backlash, because there's a gig-
antic, but unreported, rise in active racism by whites in America. People are starting to fight back in the same way as they
did in the '60's against it. The Ku Klux
Klan has more than doubled it's membership
by a long shot, in the last 3 years, & it
gets regular media coverage evry time it
has a rally. Just like the punks vs skins
or whatever, it's token encouragement for
the people to go out and join the KKK.
And... the Miami race riots were handled
by the National Guard the same as in the
'60's; that is - surround the rioters in
their own neighbourhood before they get to
the rich people's neighbourhood, so that
while they're still in a rioting mood,
they burn their own houses down! That way
they're oppressed by their own means for
the next 15 years, so the Nat. Guard
doesn't even have to bother sticking around. And I think that a lot more tension
like that's brewing... Atlanta's going to
brew up real soon.

WHO DO YOU THINK WILL BE PRESIDENT?

J: Still hard to say - either way the joke
is on the American people, and the people
who have to deal with America on a daily
basis.

Ray: There's a lot of stupid people who
help them out.
J: Yeah, Nixon had the 'stupid majority
aced in the hole. He called them the
'silent majority' because they were too
dumb to say anything, although that's not
why he called them that! Americans are
trained from day 1 to be stupid - 'Be stupid or be punished'.

IT'S HARD TO BELIEVE THAT OUT OF 240,000,
000 PEOPLE AMERICA PICKS CARTER & REAGAN
TO RUN THE COUNTRY.

J: Well look who runs Russia - they pick
a total stooge like Brezhnev. I wonder if
he died a few years ago, and they just
have a lookalike to stand there and utter
a few words every now and then.

THEN AGAIN, HE DOESN'T REALLY RUN RUSSIA,
DOES HE?

J: No, not anymore than Carter or Reagan
run America.

IS IT LIKE THAT THEN?

J: Well.... corporations, large corporations - they have a very gentleman's agreement.

At this point the tape infuriatingly ran
out, but I noted down about the Trilateral
Commission, which keeps a low profile, but
has on it's payroll Kissinger, Bush AND
Carter! Also the Bohemian Grove is a vital
organisation. Pity I couldn't learn more.

Four or five days later, an ex B-movie
actor, senile and decaying, was elected
President of the USA. Fresh fruit for
rotting vegetables indeed - America needs
the Dead Kennedys.

AF

ZEITGEIST

Given a brief mention in Jamming 10, Zeitgeist have lived a pretty busy life in the last third of 1980. My first encounter was earlier in the year, when they brought round a demo tape which was great, although the band appeared rather doomy and moderne. While no. 10 was at the printers, I got the chance to start witnessing the opposite - their first single was released on their own Enchainé label, called Shake/Rake & Sniper, & despite the poxy artwork, was a great single. I also saw them live, where they again appeared a much more straightforward and enjoyable group. And danceable. Over the next 6 weeks, gigs came regularly, & the band got a residency at the Bridge House, toured (well, did 2 gigs) in their native Cornwall, and even played Islington's legendary Pied Bull, supporting the Angelic Upstarts & Infa-Riot!

I did an interview with them soon after that, which was not the best ever conducted, but adequate enough to do an article on an 'up'n'coming band' who are 'doing something different' and 'are ready for the '80's'. The next news was that Zeitgeist had got a 3-single deal with Human Records. The first will be a reissue of the first single, with an extra track, Gimmick, and new artwork.

Looks like life is going just great for the crazy Cornwall combo. But next thing that happens is 'manager' Alan phones to say that guitarist Corin is moving back to Cornwall for a while, but will still be in the band! Eh? Yes, we're not limiting ourselves whatsoever, Alan says. This sounds interesting, & so off I trudge again to the Holloway Road, home of 8 people from Cornwall, including 'vocalist' Jaf, 'guitarist' Corin, 'bassist' Gary, 'drummer' Harry, & the member-who-doesn't-play-an-instrument, Alan. Other vocalist Zaz (the only female member) doesn't live there, so isn't in the photos.

Corin: "I think over the last 3 months we've gradually been dragged into the rock machine, and we realised just in time what was happening."

Alan: "If you start hankering after success it makes you narrow-minded, so we're not going to bother."

Corin: "It's the same as anything; if you've got blinkers on, you can only see in front of you."

And so, just over a year after initially moving to London as a band, spending 10 months playing toilets every few weeks and the other 3 months doing gigs regularly whenever they were asked to, Zeitgeist have got themselves sussed out.

Zeitgeist did their first gig in Cornwall in April '79, and played 7 down there before moving to London. Many people are currently against the idea of London as a nucleus, but as Zeitgeist explain they tried hard enough in Cornwall.

Jaf: "We used to play in this pub that had a pool room next door, and I used to say to everyone, 'Why don't you fucking come and watch us, we're great', and they'd say, 'Nah, I'd sooner play bloody pool, mate.'"

Corin: "We used to put on 2 bands and a disco for 50p, and everybody in the bar said 'I'd rather buy a pint'! That's the sort of attitude you're up against - we had to come up here to get anywhere."

The nucleus of the band moved up together, but Harry's arriving a few months later necessitated the use of a drum machine until then. It had the effect of most drum-machine bands:-

Jaf: "We used to be all doomy & serious on stage."

Alan: "We did take gigs seriously, but we don't anymore."

Jaf: "When you've got drums, you can speed things up. We enjoy gigs a lot more now."

Not suprisingly, these quotes came from the first interview, where I did mention that they seemed to be turning into a much more straight-forward band...

Corin: "It's more accessible now."

Gary: "It's more acceptable dance-wise."

But Zeitgeist also made it clear where

Jaf, Gary and Harry of Zeitgeist, a 'doomy, serious' band.

-4-

they stand with regard to other bands and the business...

Jaf: "I think the big labels are fucked."

Corin: "There's going to be some drastic changes in the set-up of the industry."

Jaf: "Also, we've found that the venues they seem to think they're the A&R guys. I think that they're worse than the press and the record companies. They choose what bands play, yet I don't really think there's anything worth going to see."

If there's nothing good on, is it worth your being in this industry?

Jaf: "Well, we're trying to do something different, and I think we are worth seeing."

One of the last bands worth seeing?

Jaf: "Hopefully, we're one of the first of a new lot worth seeing."

Alan mistakes Gary's guitar case for something else!

Although as you'll find out if you read on, Zeitgeist now consider themselves a lot more than a rock'n'roll band, they are a group playing music. This music is their own, and very soon, everybody will know it is. Zeitgeist sound like Joy Division meet disco meet the Ants meet Zeitgeist. Their music has a permanent beat, and it's normally loud but thoughtful. The themes are generally short and repetitive, bringing the tribal element into it - a captivating noise.

Shake/Rake is a slightly strange song, the disco influence being the heaviest, while Sniper is loud & heavy, building up to a noisy climax. On each number, vocals swap between Jaf & Zaz for maximum effect. The single, self-financed & recorded in an 8-track studio, sounds as professional as a lot more-organised ones do. The rest of their set is quite similar - the best number is Untitled, beginning with a very psychedelic and bloody excellent guitar intro. Other songs include Step 1-2-3, Puppeteer, Fact, In This Town & 1st Mistake among others. Zeitgeist are not the best band going by any account, but they're defenitely building towards it.

So now back to their plans (or lack of them) for the future. First off, there's the deal with Human. Shake/Rake, Sniper & Gimmick should be realised as you read this, and will be followed by Touch and another song as the second single. There's also an option on a single after that.

Meantime, back to the questions....If Corin's going back to Cornwall, what are you going to do about gigs? You were saying how much you enjoyed them.

Harry: "When we want to do one, Corin'll do it with us."

Corin: "WE'll do it when the time seems right."

Alan: "That might sound pompous, but it's not meant to be. All it is is we're just taking all the limitations away."

Jaf: "We're still going to carry on while Corin is in Cornwall. We're going to do things up here, and he's going to do things down there."

Corin: "It's a very fluid thing."

Harry: "What's 300 miles?"

Corin: "You can have a band with 5 people in, and all you can see is the next gig. You're blurred, and by doing that you're cutting off 340° of your vision."

So what would happen if you had a gig while Corin's in Cornwall that you wanted to play?

Corin: "It's down to the thing that no individual is indispensable, and if a gig came up next Friday that Zeitgeist wanted to do, the band would do it. It would just be a different version of the group."

Harry: "Zeitgeist is 5 people or 4 people or ? people or..."

Alan: "Or the whole world."

Corin: "I might get a disagreement of opinion here (he didn't), but I think it's worth saying - when we moved up from Cornwall to find somewhere to live, get jobs etc, the group couldn't take priority; it must never take priority, because any band should always be a hobby; it should never become an obsession. It should become 1 thing out of 100 things you're involved in, and if the band becomes 100% of your life, it's the same as working 9 to 5 in a factory."

We mention PiLs attitude, and agree on a few similarities....

Alan: "PiL say they're not a band- that's the same way as Zeitgeist think.

Corin: "Put it like this- you find something interesting, & you become totally involved in it to the extent that you don't acknowledge the existance of anything else. That's got to be what will be the downfall of the human race."

Jaf: "We want to do other things as well, apart from music. We're doing a fanzine, but it won't be about music or anything."

Corin: "You can't put 4 walls round something and expect it to last. The moment you put 4 walls round it it stops moving, & anything that stops moving decays. You've got to keep it moving, & that is the 'spirit of the age'." CONTINUED PAGE 16

-5-

most regular fanzines, is eratic. Suffers from large type makes quick reading but no. 11 has very good Dexy's & Sector 27 interviews. 41 Silchester Park, Glenageary, Co. Dublin Suddenly 30p

IMPOSSIBLE DREAM - Poison Girls 'zine, all graphical, heavy going. From BB. 25p

INTENSIVE CARE - A case of the first issue rule. A good 6 Minute War interview, but little else. Better Badges 25p

IN THE CITY - The one Jamming's always slagged with or praised with. This is because we're both 'established' (a deadly sin), but otherwise it's strange, because I don't feel any affinity to them at all. In The City is undoubtedly the poshest of them all - glossy cover, very neat layout etc. But they've got themselves in a terrible rut of groups (moving on from Ultravox-Tubeway Army-Gloria Mundi to Gary Numan-Crass-Adam & The Ants-Poison Girls - the first 3 were all interviewed in consecutive issues, while the Poison Girls were? apart) & it's not particularly invigorating reading either. No. 15 has a Poison Girls flexi which seems to have decreased sales (listen to it & find out why), but contrary to popular belief, they're a good couple of people & their hearts are in the right place. Pete & Frank, c/o Compendium, 234 Camden High St, London NW1 30p

IT'S DIFFERENT FOR GRILS - A new Sheffield fanzine split between being a photo mag & ordinary fanzine. The first issue is very good. From Gary Cartwright, Flat 3, 15 Roverdale Road, Sheffield 10 20p

KILLING TIME - A bit of a 'BB' fanzine. Looks attractive though doesn't always read so, & in it's attempts to help all local groups, writes about sexist HM bands called Mick Muff & The Divers. Mike Bowman, 192 Dane Valley Rd, Margate. 30p

KILL YOUR PET PUPPY - the 'Personal Anarchy' fanzine. If nothing else, great to look at, but only about 6 pages of reading. The embarrasing thing is, it's better than all the other mags. I saw no. 3 at the printers about 6 months ago & it had an interview with a band, so something's gone wrong! From RT. 25p

LET'S BE ADULT ABOUT THIS - Probably the definitive Rough Tradezine. First issue was excellent with Atoms, Scritz, Monochrome Set, Door & Window, Maps & a good layout. Get it while Rough Trade's still hip. From Better Badges. 25p

MAKING TIME - Not to be confused with Killing Time, this is from Herne Bay, & has a healthy modish attitude. No. 5 had some great groups while still finding it's feet; no. 6 had 52 pages including Weller, Perry, Chords, Hearts as well as the trap of when you've got easy printing, there's no quality control; & no. 7 has front & back covers by Weller, & a distinct lack of good interviews, but plenty of news on new bands (as important). It prints a lot of good poetry as well. Room for improvement, but defenitely one of the best. 34 Cobblers Bridge Road, Herne Bay, Kent 20p

MAXIMUM SPEED - 'Confidently expects to reach no. 20 some time next year' (1980) -Quote Heatwave fanzine. Well, they who laugh last laugh longest, eh? This thing did as much harm to the mod revival as any other aspect of the media - it's a pity a decent movement had to have this as it's mouthpiece. ps- there's still a couple of thousand left at BB. 30p

zeitgeist

continued from page 5

So what sort of things are you planning to do?

Corin: "A fanzine's one. There's someone here who does drawings, so it's quite possible that the second release on the Enchainé label will be a poster."

(As for record releases, Gimmick, Touch & No More Yellow Fridges have all been recorded for imminent release, & are quite brilliant. A very accessible sound - nobody ignore the second single.)

Corin continues his philosophy of life... "You shouldn't define anything - you should just do it. You have the ability in yourself to do anything & everything. You've also got the ability to do nothing - it's up to you. We could spend the next year, living round here, hassling people to try and get into the established venues, getting the right breaks etc. But it's a trap everyone falls into. They follow like sheep. It's time everybody started being a lot more individual, and as aresult, they'd become a lot more united. If every individual followed their own instincts completely, I think they'd end up at the same place anyway."

So were the 3 months as a 'new wave band on the London gig circuit' worth it?

Harry: "I think we enjoyed playing and did what we wanted to, and now is a different stage."

Corin: "You're not valid to comment on something unless you've actually been involved in it."

Obviously you'll need money & a chance to be full-time to fulfill your ideals...

Corin: "I think by nature of what we're trying to do we've got more chance of packing in our jobs than if we spent the next 10 years trying to be successful. I think the fact that it's going to be a very fluid arrangement will be more conjusive to people becoming involved. Rather than saying to someone "You've got to be there on Thursday for the practice"; it's in the human nature to resent being told what to do. It's not natural to be dictated to by anything."

And that's Zeitgeist. As you can see, a band with a lot to offer. It would seem a ridiculous idea for any other band to develop these policies, but with Zeitgeist, it's fitting. They were a different band from the start, but gradually became part of the rock'n'roll machine, and now want to be themselves again. What's so important is that they're a great band, and vital.

After the interview, Corin came up & said, with Jaf & Alan's agreement - "If the group became so fluid that it did fall apart then I think that would be the right thing to happen - it would be natural."

Catch Zeitgeist while you can. Literally

Article and photos by AP

We were newly arrived from Cornwall, an eager blue-eyed bunch of funk-soul brothers (and sister!) called Zeitgeist, looking to make a name in the Big City of London. We started gigging in a small way and sought to expand our reach by seeking out willing fanzine editors. We recorded a demo tape, pressed up 250 copies of it to sell at gigs, and took a bus to the farthest depths of South London, where we rang on the door bell of the address printed in *Jamming!* Not only was Tony in at the time, not only did he take a tape, but he also took a liking to it.

A few weeks later, Tony came to see us play at a deconsecrated church in Shoreditch, back when Shoreditch was an utter toilet of an area. He then interviewed us at our flat in Holloway, where we got him horrendously stoned afterwards; he was only 16 at the time and clearly not as familiar with the old 'erb as us. (Don't worry, he slept over.) It did the trick. At the start of 1981, a positive feature on Zeitgeist duly showed up in *Jamming!* 11. By the end of that year, we had become the second act signed to his Jamming! Records. We didn't quite crack the big time but we had lots of fun, our cover of 'Ball Of Confusion' got reviewed by the Bee Gees on Radio 1 ('a number one smash!' – Barry Gibb) and we released two further singles together. Most importantly, the friendships formed were never broken and we look back on those do-it-yourself days with bleary-eyed fondness. **Peter 'Jaf' Jervis**

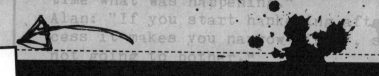

SWISS WAVE

The following account of Switzerland's 4 years of new wave is by Felix Fischer, who runs a Swiss fanzine called, coincidentally & very annoyingly for us, JAMMING.

"In the beginning there was rythm"... that's a true statement as concerns our small and creative Swiss new wave scene. There were two different types of rhythm in our beginning (around June '76): first a real hard and fast rhythm from shockingly bad punk bands, with names like 101 - Sick Of The One Day Kick, Nasal Boys, Sperma and Boghogys. All these bands had been heavily influenced by English punk groups. But there was a need for this new scene had a long look at London and every hard-core punk had to have been there at least once. There they bought all their punk accessories including fanzines, badges, clothes etc.

The fanzines are very important. The first was No Fun from Zurich but dozens of fanzines followed after - some were long living, while others died after one or two issues. But every fanzine is important because other mediums didn't like the new scene at the time. Today the Swiss wave is a solid part of the 'serious' music magazines here and you can hear the latest sounds from the 'new' on public radio.

Below: Silvia Holenstein of Mother's Ruin. Pic: Andi Erni

GROWTH OF THE SWISS CONFEDERATION

Scale 1:2,000,000 (32 miles = 1 inch)

The Original Cantons 1513
The Everlasting League in 1291
The Confederation in 1513

Allied States to 1798
Subject

On the other hand there were a number of artists or electric musicians who liked this new wave. So arose groups like Yello, Troppo and Herts. These groups found new technical sounds, but most of them have split and groups like Yello (the backing band of Dieter Meier, an all-round artist) or Troppo have give gigs anyway. An album from Yello, though, will be out soon on Ralph Records, while Troppo's singer Kurt Maloo has his own band now called Maloo Le La (!).

First the whole scene had a long look at London and every hard-core punk had to have been there at least once.

These two first Swiss labels were pretty rich and not so interested in other new wave bands. But more and more groups wished to make their own records, and in early 1979 the two most important labels sprung up: 'Another Swiss Label' and 'Off Course'. The owners of these companies are unprofessional but creative people.

Left: Liliput

Swiss Wave rules OK!

Felix Fischer

SINGLES

WAH! HEAT: Seven Minutes To Midnight/Don't Step On The Cracks (Inevitable)
This single hardly needs reviewing, as it's been given unanimous vocals and sold well in return. This is just to confirm that Seven Minutes/Cracks is the most powerfully emotional single I've heard all year. It is loud, fierce, frightening and terrifyingly lethal.

ART OBJECTS: Showing Off To Impress The Girls (Heartbeat)
A nice poppy backing with the lyrics, an enjoyable song, with a very live feel about it.

SOFT TOUCH: It's My Life (TJM)
Reams verses and nasty pop chorus - sounds like a white one.

LOCATE ANIMAL GROUP: (Warm-Pop)

CABARET VOLTAIRE: Seconds Too Late (Rough Trade)
Pretty much what you'd expect from a Cabaret Voltaire single.

THE NAUGHTIEST GIRL WAS A MONITOR: All The Naked Heroes (Aardvark)
from Sheffield, with a vocalist who sounds like Phil Collins.

FURNITURE: Shaking Story (The Guy From Paraguay)

SOY + SPERMA (Note)

THE GIFT: This Is Love/Yanks (Rough Trade)
Otherwise known as 'Whatever Happened To The Young Marble Giants'.

-26-

FROM THE NOTEBOOKS

PEOPLE WITH COPIES / COPIES SENT FOR SELLING

- Mark Ashton for 101 CLUB
- Martin for WEDGE in COVENTRY
- 10 Jeni for school.
- 50 Paul Blackwell
- 10 Linda for school
- 20 Mark for shop (3 paid)
- Simon
- 10 Richard
- 20 Eamon Dev Delaney, DUBLIN
- 6 Pete Mazzanti, ITALY
- 50 Tony Perri, SHEFFIELD
- 60 Alan - 40 for CORNWALL
  - 10 for CAMBRIDGE
  - 10 for friends
- John Lee, YORK LEEDS
- 40 Dave Jennings, BRADFORD/BRUM
- 60 Chris Maris, HUDDERSFIELD
- 4-7 Sue, friend
- 40 Kate, NORWICH
- 19 Martin for WEDGE in COVENTRY
- 35 Deanna SHINDE, Canada (see other ... 50 in all)
- 10 Chris MARIS
- 5 BEET MUGHONS

SHOPS

Date	Qty	Shop	Price
24/1	100	ROUGH TRADE	18p
26/1	12	HONEST JON's Portobello Road	20p
26/1	50	VIRGIN Marble Arch	22p
26/1	50	SHADES	19p
26/1	30	VIRGIN Oxford Walk	18p
26/1	50	VIRGIN Megastore	18p
27/1	10	PAPERBACK CENTRE	18p
27/1	40	SMALL WONDER	20p
27/1	50	COMPENDIUM	20p
27/1	10	HONKY TONK	20p
27/1	20	5th COLUMN	20p
27/1	10	DEGVILLE's	18p
27/1	24	HIP-KI-DO	20p
27/1	10	DINOSAUR	20p
27/1	10	BEGGARS BANQUET Highgate	20p
28/1	50	WEBSTERS	18p
28/1	100	BONAPARTE	
28/1	10	BEGGARS' BANQUET Ealing	20p
29/1	10	BALHAM FOOD & BOOKS	20p
29/1	10	TETRIC Clapham	20p
31/1	10	FANS	18p
31/1	10	BEGGARS BANQUET Richmond	20p

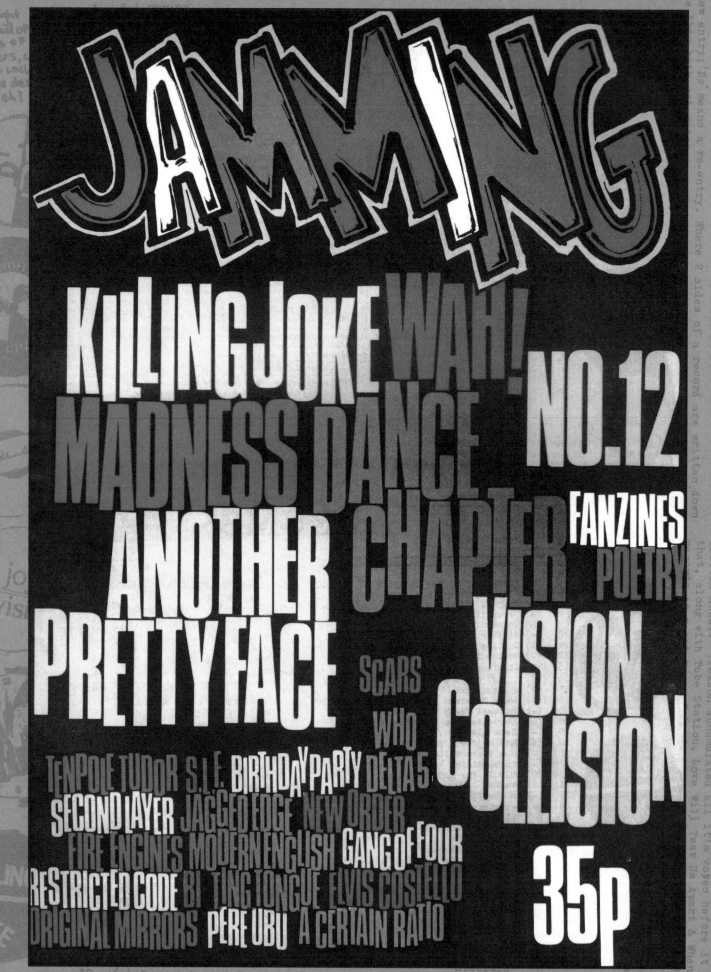

SINGLES

#	(last)	Title	Artist
1	(-)	REWARD	TEARDROP EXPLODES
2	(-)	Ceremony	New Order
3	(-)	Is Vic There?	Department S.
4	(-)	That's Entertainment/Tube Station (live)	Au Pairs
5	(7)	It's Obvious/Diet	Wah! Heat
6	(9)	Seven Minutes To Midnight	Crass
7	(-)	Nagasaki Nightmare/Big A, Little A	Teardrop Explodes
8	(6)	Treason	Fall
9	(22)	Fiery Jack	Altered Images
10	(-)	Dead Pop Stars/Sentimental	Talking Heads
11	(-)	Once In A Lifetime	Killing Joke
12	(-)	Requiem/Change	Adam & The Ants
13	(-)	Kings Of The Wild Frontier	Fall
14	(1)	Totally Wired	Jam
15	(Re)	Going Underground	Joy Division
16=	(-)	Love Will Tear Us Apart	U2
=	(4)	I Will Follow	Beat
18	(15)	Too Nice To Talk To	Jam
19	(3)	When You're Young	'Girls At Our Best!'
20	(5)	Getting Nowhere Fast/Warm Girls	Jam
21	(5)	Down In The Tube Station At Midnight	Joy Division
22	(9)	Atmosphere/She's Lost Control	Theatre Of Hate
23	(-)	Legion	T.V. Smith's Explorers
24=	(-)	Tomahawk Cruise	Teardrop Explodes
=	(10)	When I Dream	Dead Kennedys
26	(-)	Holiday In Cambodia	New Age Steppers
=	(-)	Fade Away	Orange Juice
28	(-)	Simply Thrilled Honey	Crass/Poison Girls
29	(97)	Bloody Revolutions/Persons Unknown	Josef K
30	(-)	It's Kinda Funny	Jam
31	(-)	Start!	Damned
32	(-)	New Rose	UK Decay
33	(17)	For My Country	Jam
34=	(11)	Strange Town/Butterfly Collector	Wah! Heat
=	(-)	Better Scream	Various Artists
=	(-)	Bullshit Detector	Fall
37=	(96)	How I Wrote 'Elastic Man'	A Certain Ratio
=	(-)	Shack-Up	B-Movie
39	(-)	Remembrance Day	Stiff Little Fingers
40	(26)	At The Edge	

ALBUMS

#	(last)	Title	Artist
1	(3)	SOUND AFFECTS	JAM
2	(2)	Closer	Joy Division
3	(8)	Grotesque (After The Gramme)	Fall
4	(-)	Boy	U2
5	(95)	Kings Of The Wild Frontier	Adam & The Ants
6	(15)	Kilimanjaro	Teardrop Explodes
7	(14)	Signing Off	UB40
8	(-)	Crocodiles	Echo & The Bunnymen
9	(-)	Unknown Pleasures	Joy Division
10	(-)	Killing Joke	Killing Joke
11	(-)	Setting Sons	Jam
12	(-)	Remain In Light	Talking Heads
13	(19)	Stations Of The Crass	Crass
14	(97)	I Just Can't Stop It	Beat
15	(7)	All Mod Cons	Jam
16=	(1)	Scary Monsters And Super Beasts	David Bowie
=	(-)	Colossal Youth	Young Marble Giants
18	(-)	Lubricate Your Living Room	Fire Engines
19	(-)	Black Album	Damned
20	(4)	Waiting For A Miracle	Combat Angels
21	(-)	Dirk Wears White Sox	Adam & The Ants
22	(-)	Chappaquidick Bridge	Poison Girls
23	(30)	This In The Modern World	Jam
24	(21)	Dragnet	Fall
25	(-)	In The Flatfield	Bauhaus
26	(Re)	Never Mind The Bollocks, Here's The...	Sex Pistols
27=	(-)	Oi! The Album	Various Artists
=	(10)	The Affectionate Punch	Associates
29	(9)	More Specials	Specials
30	(-)	Damned Damned Damned	Damned
31	(18)	Fresh Fruit For Rotting Vegetables	Dead Kennedys
32	(16)	So Far Away	Chords
33	(-)	He Who Dares Wins	Theatre Of Hate
34	(-)	Machine Gun Etiquette	Damned
35	(-)	Play.	Magazine
36	(24)	New Clear Days	Vapors
37	(12)	Metal Box	Public Image Ltd.
38	(-)	Dance Craze	Various Artists
39=	(-)	The Absolute Game	Skids
=	(Re)	17 Seconds	Cure

Thought that instead of photos of the winners, we could include badge designs - silly, eh!

2

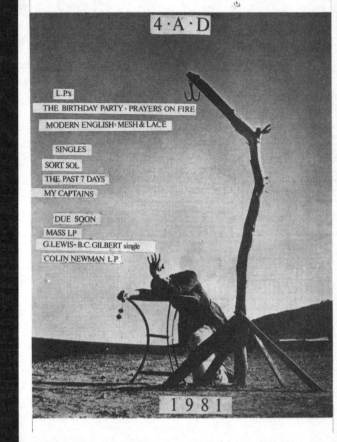

Continuing to offer his first main fanzine client preferential treatment, Joly provided *Jamming!* access to the A3 printer he otherwise reserved for full-colour badge printing, and we returned to a fold-out format, with staples down the middle, as first attempted so disastrously back with Issue 6. Better Badges was now farming out the litho-work to ease the printing bottleneck, but otherwise, this issue featured much the same creative team, with Robin Richards designing a cover that contained the band names and only the band names, presumably an artistic response to my graffitied ruination of Issue 10's originally immaculate design. Robin also laid out the Madness interview: the inclusion of Britain's top pop band in an 'indie' fanzine was a direct result of friendships formed with the Nutty Boys the previous summer over two nights in Nottingham, for a feature in *The Face*, itself my first official freelance writing gig.

An interview with Killing Joke was conducted over two distinctly memorable, spliff-filled encounters at the group's Notting Hill flat (see Anthony Blampied's sidebar), and those with Another Pretty Face's Mike Scott, and Wah! Heat's Pete Wylie, at the house I had recently relocated to with my mother in Crystal Palace. (I gave both acts permission to sleep at my mum's place when it transpired they had made no other plans for their long-distance, overnight trips to

ISSUE #12 6/81

'the smoke'. Such were the positive vibes on which the scene existed in those days – and such was the good will extended by my mother, who took remarkably in stride the sight of unwashed musicians cluttering her living space while she set about breakfast.)

Largely because Paul Weller was championing the form, there was a sudden surge of poetry doing the rounds, much of which was sent to *Jamming!*'s new South London address and, being something of a soft touch, I allowed the solicitations to fill three interior pages; the two-issue fanzine round-up was concluded with another three-page spread. There were those who would have said that *Jamming!* no longer qualified as a fanzine, and if I might have challenged that argument in the moment, that moment would pass… but not before Jamming! Records, financed by Paul Weller, launched with singles by RUDI (featured in *Jamming!* 9) and Zeitgeist (in issues 10 and 11), inevitably putting the magazine back on hiatus. The long wait for a future issue did at least provide opportunity to shift most of Issue 12's 5,000 copies. My notebook (I appear to have started a fresh one) suggests that Better Badges went back to charging me for the printing rather than for the magazines I took home with me, a debt that was only eventually paid off when *Jamming!* made a fortuitous leap into the truly big time a calendar year down the line.

KILLING JOKE

Killing Joke haven't got a reputation as the easiest group in the world to interview. In fact, following the abscence of any decent article in them, in big paper or small (mainly due to the group's unco-operative answers) we were wondering whether it would be worth it or not. But a chance meeting with Jaz at Better Badges showed the opposite of the paper's slag-offs of him, as he proved himself very keen, very talkative and very interesting. We arranged to simply 'call round' some time, to do a proper interview. This we did the Sunday of the Brixton riots (when as well as having to take a completely different route in London, I found Notting Hill - the group's home - crawling with an extra 400 police - just in case.), only to find Jaz wasn't in, and Youth was not keen on unknown people coming round. We didn't even get past the buzzer at the front door of the flats. But a phone call from round the corner got it sorted out, and we returned to do a half-hour interview with Youth. The room looked exactly as I'd guessed, and reggae music was blazing from the speakers. We asked Youth if he could turn it down for the tape-recorders sake; he replied 'No, I like it like this.' But all fair dues, Youth was a lot friendlier than is made out to be, and part 1 of the 'interview' got under way.

Youth: Come on then, give me a question.

WHAT'S THE ATTITUDE WITH DOING INTERVIEWS, BECAUSE EVERYONE SAYS...

Youth: A specific question

YEAH - A SPECIFIC QUESTION:- KILLING JOKE'S SUPPOSED TO BE REALLY AWKWARD TO INTERVIEW.

Youth: We are.

YEAH...

Youth: Yeah?

UM - WHY IS THAT?

Youth: 'cos we don't have a lot to say about ourselves. We're four individuals:- the drummer and guitarist get very manic when they're asked questions; Jaz really likes talking about the group, which is good, but there's a difference in that I really know what I'm talking about.

PEOPLE ALWAYS SAY EITHER YOU'RE VERY AWKARD TO TALK TO..

Youth: Well we are awkward people. We don't compromise; we only compromise in as much as what we feel is good. And in as much as leisure time is concerned, and leisure time as far as I'm concerned is 24 hours a day.

Even at this early stage, talk drifts off to vague mentions of magic and astrology, related to America's being a nation of pirates, the riots in Brixton, and the space shuttle. Well it was never going to be easy....

WHAT WOULD YOU CALL SUCCESS FOR KILLING JOKE?

Youth: Success? Tons of groupies, a pound of grass a week... I want lots of money - I want millions and millions of pound notes.

JAZ WAS GOING ON ABOUT THAT, ABOUT YOUR WANTING LOADS OF MONEY, BUT IF YOU JUST CARRY ON AS YOU ARE NOW...

Youth: We've all got different ideas- I mean I forgot how to play the bass last week, that's how responsible I am. But that's the way I am - when I play it, I play it the way I want, which is not technically perfect, but it's my way, which varies.

SO HOW ARE YOU GOING TO GET LOTS AND LOTS OF MONEY THEN?

Youth: Oh, I've got lots of schemes lined up.

WHAT - OUTSIDE THE GROUP OR INSIDE?

Youth: Oh both. I'm not just a musician, I'm a blatant businessman.

SO HOW ARE YOU GOING TO GET MONEY INSIDE THE GROUP?

Youth: by selling a lot of records.

SO YOU RECKON YOU CAN SELL A LOT?

Youth: Yeah, we've got a hit single on our hands. Requiem

got to no. 65, so this next single (Follow The Leaders) should be straight up there.

BUT YOU NEED AIRPLAY AND THINGS FOR THAT, DON'T YOU?

Youth: Yeah, well that's down to subtle persuasion. I don't mean anything blatant, like altering the sales figures just to get in the charts - I'm against all that. A lot of people get their kicks out of it, but once you've had your one hit, what do you do then?

IS THE GROUP LIKE A REALLY LOOSE THING?

Youth: Well we all hate each other, but we manage to compromise to the extent of making music. I'm the most difficult one of the lot to get on with because I'm so unconventionally cuntish.

SO COULD THE LINE-UP SPLIT AT ANY TIME?

Youth: No we ain't going to split for about 2 or 3 years.

IS THAT PLANNED?

Interview + write-up by Tony Fletcher
Transcript + photos of Youth by Lawrence Blampied

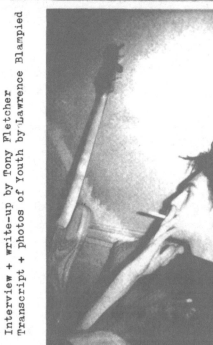

YOUTH SURVEYING HIS QUOTES.

~8~

Half a lifetime ago, I'm awoken by a knock at the door of my North London bedsit... 'Telephone!' Shivering on the landing, I find that it's Tony calling with concern over our planned rendezvous later that day with Killing Joke. Sleepy and bewildered, I ask what the problem is. 'You must be the only person in the country not to know!' he exclaims. 'The whole of Brixton went up last night.'

Youth: Well when we first formed, we said we'd just make it last for 5 years, to see what happens. And we've been going 2 years, so we've got another three to go, and not one of us is going to leave before then.

Youth sits down by the tape recorder, picks up his bass, and starts playing along to the reggae music. Yet at no point does he try and ignore us.

WHEN I WAS UP AT BETTER BADGES, JAZ WAS FLOGGING THE MASTER COPY OF A KILLING JOKE RECORD...

Youth (stops playing): That would happen.

HE SAID ALL THE BAND'S ALWAYS DOING IT.

Youth (starts playing again): I was doing it before Jaz.

IS THAT GOING TO FUCK UP THE GROUP AT ALL?

Youth: Nah, we love it. Paul gets a bit manic, Jaz gets a bit paranoid, & Geordie couldn't give a shit 'cos he comes from Newcastle.

SO WHAT DO YOU RECKON ABOUT MONEY THEN? BECAUSE A LOT OF GROUPS THAT PEOPLE THINK OF IN THE SAME TERMS AS KILLING JOKE...

Youth: Listen. Now the Killing Joke syndrome according to other bands is pathetic, 'cos they just don't like the way we do things, which is their own problem, 'cos it's nothing to do with us. But when it comes down to money:- we get what we can have, which is everything and any-thing, as long as it's a coin or paper.

IN THE LONG RUN, WOULD YOU LIKE TO SEE MONEY BECOME IRR-ELEVANT?

Youth: Well once I've got a lot of money I won't need it will I?

YOU'LL STILL NEED MONEY TO LIVE.

Youth: But if I've got it, I won't need to worry about making any more. That's what I'm saying.

IS THAT LIKE SAYING YOU DON'T GIVE A SHIT ABOUT OTHER PEOPLE?

Youth: Well I don't really. I'm an individual. Like if I'm screwing a bird, I'll make sure she has a good time: I'll give her some real in-depth inspiration! But if she asks if I love her or not, I'll tell her the truth. (Starts playing bass again).

WELL DO YOU RECKON KILLING JOKE HAVE BEEN SUCCESSFUL?

Youth: Successful? We're fucking here aren't we? We're alright - we've got a new album coming out soon, an ex-cellent single, we've got a good future ahead of us. The past has been great, 'cos we've gone through squatt-ing, we've gone through gigging, we've gone through HEAVY violence; we've gone through all that and we've learnt from our mistakes, and we're still laughing. But we're serious.

HOW MANY RECORDS DO YOU SELL?

Youth: We sold 40,000 of the last album at least, but I don't know the exact figures. And Wardance is continual-ly in the Alternative charts.

YOU SAY YOU'VE ALL GOT DIFFERENT ATTITUDES, BUT THERE'S SUPPOSED TO BE...

Youth: Well at one time Jaz had the idea of us smoking at the same time, eating at the same time, and regulating our life as a band totally. But I said that was a bit like communism, and I wasn't into that either.

YEAH, BUT WHAT I WAS ASKING IS YOU SAY KILLING JOKE ARE ALL VERY DIFFERENT PEOPLE...

Youth: Four different people, not including the manage-ment. 'Cos the management are very important - not as important as finance, but they're very important. We got a management contract that we specifically made, as that's what fucks most groups up. (He goes on to explain the difference between a 20% gross deal & 20% net deal for management, and how their management - the EG comp-any that handles Bryan Ferry & Eno - hardly make a penny out of them....)

WHAT I WAS TRYING TO ASK (3rd time lucky) IS THAT KILLING JOKE ARE FOUR DIFFERENT PEOPLE, BUT ISN'T THERE ALSO THE KILLING JOKE ATTITUDE? I'D HAVE THOUGHT IT WOULD HAVE MEANT THAT YOU'RE ALL INTO THE SAME THING.

Youth: No no, not all of us have the same interests in life. You've got to have a certain direction in which you want to go, and you can't regard that as like two directions, 'cos it can be 6 or 7.

YOU KNOW THAT PICTURE YOU USED FOR THE TOUR WITH THE

POPE WALKING THROUGH THE NAZIS? SOUNDS SAID IT WAS TWO PHOTOS....

Youth: No, they're lying (Bad one Valec). It's genuine. It's from a book about the third Reich. It's just to teach people a lesson.

Soon after, Youth kept to his promise and told us the interview was over as he was going out. He said we could call back the next day, when Jaz would be about, and was very suprised when we did. Unfortunately, Jaz WASN'T about, and I was told to go downstairs, where Geordie & Paul were, & Youth would follow us down. Only Geordie was there, and we agrreed this sounded like a fob-off, particularly as Geordie hates doing interviews. Luckily, Jaz appeared and we went back up to reccom-ence the interview. Geordie, despite making it clear that he didn't see any point in interviews, was very friendly, and in fact hung about, making occasional comments. Jaz showed great interest in the whole thing; and again proved that despite the image of uncooperation, he is as talkative as any band leader. He failed to remember me, until looking at Jamming & said 'I hope the review of the Ants is a slagging', and then 'I take it the review of The Jam is as well'. He then remembered our argument about the 2 at Better Badges...... It seems Killing Joke have fixed ideals about big papers being all bad, and fanzines being all good; they certainly treated us with a lot more respect than the other papers have made out.

SOME PEOPLE WERE COMPLAINING ABOUT THE LENGTH OF THE 1ST LP: THAT IT WAS A BIT SHORT, CONSIDERING IT HAD TWO PREVIOUSLY-RELEASED TRACKS ON IT.

Jaz: Yeah, I agree with that actually. But there again, the price was a lot cheaper, so there's no shitt-ing out or anything. It was only £3.99, though we could have put it out legally for £5.99 if we'd wanted. The latest album is a lot longer - there's eight tracks, but it's 43-44 minutes. And hopefully it should be a bit under the normal LP price.

DO YOU BELIEVE IN LEADERS?

Youth: Leaders?
Jaz: You're talking about 'Follow The Leaders', aren't you?

POSSIBLY - I HAVEN'T HEARD THE TRACK YET.

Jaz: Well I mean following leaders is a bit fucking... I mean, people have always followed leaders haven't they?

~9~

MORE JOKING...

It doesn't matter what stage civilisation gets to, they always fucking follow leaders. 'Follow The Leaders' is like the biggest most bland statement that's evr come out yet - wonderful, you know.

DO YOU RECKON SOME PEOPLE LOOK ON YOU AS LEADERS?

(Laughter).
Youth: I don't think so.
Jaz: I dunno, I like to think that people get a little peace of mind knowing that there's others in the same situation.

I JUST THINK THAT SOME PEOPLE OUTSIDE LONDON LOOK TO KILLING JOKE FOR THEIR ANSWERS...

Youth: You've got to find your own fucking answers.
Jaz: It's not hard to find the answer. It all comes down to your personal point of view again - everyone's got different points of view, and they're probably all as relevant as each other. I believe that before you start mouthing off about your fucking manifestoes and ideals and all that; I believe in establishing them first.
Youth: Doing what you're saying.
Jaz: Before you fucking start talking about what you're going to do to change the world, change it, and then fucking talk about it. Seems logical to me.
  We wanna be comfortable right? You know, naturally people want to fucking enjoy their lives and have a good time - we fucking do, anyway. But at the moment, it's on a very small scale. My faith is that I believe there's a lot of other people that realise the situation we're all in, and my faith lies with them, and their emotions and their feelings. Because I believe there's loads of people in this position, from Russia to Poland to East Germany to West Germany, and it's all the Killing Joke. There's people in Russia and everywhere, just like you and me, who are young, and have no control over their destiny, just like you and me haven't. You see what I mean, do you? That's the Killing Joke.

WHEN YOU SAY THERE'S A LOT OF PEOPLE WHO FEEL LIKE YOU, DO YOU MEAN JUST EVERYDAY PEOPLE WHO MIGHT NOT HAVE HEARD OF THE KILLING JOKE?

Jaz: Well I mean, Killing Joke is not just fucking music.

THAT'S WHY I'M ASKING...

Jaz: It's a gateway to put up loads of idaes, apart from music. Ideas, philosophies, films, music - anything you want, but it's just a frame of mind. You know what Killing Joke is. We don't want no manifestoes right, until we've done what we wanna do. When we've got somewhere, then we'll fucking talk about what it's been like getting to that point.

SO YOU ARE AIMING TO DO SOMETHING?

Jaz: Fucking right we are gonna do something! I'll tell you another thing I wanna talk about, and that's the 1st album. When we recorded that we were going through a heavy nuclear thing... I believe you live as long as you want to live, you see. Now if you've got a lot of people thinking 'God, there's gonna be a nuclear war', you're getting people who are invoking it; they're making other people feel fucking paranoid. Like when we play Wardance, that is just coming to terms, having a laugh at the situation, you know what I mean?
Youth: The music isn't exactly jolly music; it's an expression...
Jaz: I tell you though - every time we play it we have a laugh with that one. From Germany to France, you get all the fucking headbangers - they know what you're talking about when you play that one. And it's like a laugh, you get it off your chest.

WHEN YOU WERE DOING THAT THING AT TRAFALGAR SQUARE, YOU WERE TAKING THE PISS, SAYING 'YOU CAN'T CHANGE ANYTHING'

Jaz: Well they can't! What have they changed since that?
Geordie: It was forgotten - two inches in the fucking next day's press.

ARE YOU SAYING THEY CAN'T CHANGE ANYTHING, OR THAT NOBODY COULD?

Jaz: I'm not saying nobody could; I'm saying they couldn't. The odds are too much against them.

I THINK THE TRAFALGAR SQUARE THING WAS TO MAKE PEOPLE NOTICE IT...

Jaz: Yeah, but what does that do? People have known about it since that Cuba scare.

HOW DO YOU SEE THE GROUP GETTING BIGGER?

Jaz: We might get a new flat!! Fuck all changes - you hardly notice it. Money starts coming in, but we've got to pay back so much before we make any money anyway...
Youth: We're in debt.

HOW LONG WILL IT TAKE YOU TO PAY THAT BACK?

Jaz: About a century!

DO YOU RECKON YOU WILL?

Jaz: Yeah! I mean, the point is, we're still in a position to be able to do what we want. We can do it, pull a few strings.
  Go on, ask us another question then.

WHEN YOU WERE AT BETTER BADGES, YOU WERE GOING ON ABOUT GOING TO AMERICA AND GOING FOR THE HIGHEST BIDDER.

Jaz: Well naturally. I hate America though, it stinks. Noone gives a fuck about establishing any ideas or views in America - they just wanna get their money. Over here, people don't mind establishing their points of view or their fucking interests or whatever. There are some decent people over there.

WHEN YOU GO OVER THERE, DO YOU SAY 'AMERICA'S SUCH A SHITTY COUNTRY WE'LL PLAY ANYWHERE WE CAN GET THE MOST MONEY', WHEN YOU MIGHT NOT THINK LIKE THAT IN ENGLAND?

Jaz: We take anything we can get our hands on mostly. We did that one on New Years Eve, and it was the most memorable one for me. There was all these dumb, disco-type Americans standing in front of us with their mouths open. They were out looking for a nice boogie to celebrate New Year's Eve. And we were pretty extreme for them. But it was really funny - one minute they were all just like standing there, and the next minute they were all dancing like puppets. It was really pathetic. And there was that spastic Johnny Thunders. He asked to jam on stage with us. Spastic!

WHAT DID YOU SAY?

Youth & Jaz: FUCK OFF!
Youth: He jacked up on smack in our dressing room.
Jaz: He comes up and he goes (American accent) - 'Are you guys into Jamming?'

HOW ARE YOU SELLING IN AMERICA?

Geordie: We got to no. 4 in the Billboard disco charts.

YOU'RE IN THEM AS WELL?

Youth: We're quite popular over there. But there's only about 0.2% of the population who can think for themselves.

WOULD YOU GO DOWN TO PLAY PLACES LIKE CORNWALL WHERE YOU'D LOSE MONEY ON THE JOURNEY?

Jaz: We lose money on the fucking journey anyway. I mean we sell out the Lyceum, and we get a fiver each - you work that one out!
Youth: They made seven grand on the door.
Jaz: We got paid a lot, but we never saw the rest. After you've paid for your van and your PA and that... we always want the best sound possible.

WHO PUTS UP THE MONEY?

Jaz: Financers. Because legally, we're a management company, not a record company.

SO ARE THE MANAGEMENT OR FINANCE ACTUALLY CONNECTED WITH POLYDOR?

Jaz: Yeah, I mean - it's Bryan Ferry's lot. We've got the distribution to reach a lot more people than the indepndents. As well as the fact that we're not signed to a major label, legally.

SO CAN YOU GET MESSED ABOUT?

Jaz: No. We'd do them for breach of contract, because we spent about eight months getting the contract together with the best lawyers in town. If they make one fucking slip we can sue 'em.

DO YOU BELIEVE IN EQUALITY?

Jaz: I do. I mean, we've all got two arms, two legs, - unless you're a thalidomide.
Geordie: People should have the opportunity to be equal.
Jaz: Mr. Brezhnev has still got more than the fucking worker, hasn't he?

IS THAT YOUR DEFNITION OF EQUALITY THEN?

Jaz: No, it's a defenition.

YOU GO ON ABOUT WANTING TO MAKE MONEY, SO IF YOU BECAME REALLY RICH...

Jaz: If we became really rich and had £700 in our pockets, we'd have blown it in a week. (laughs).

ON DOPE, I EXPECT.

Jaz: No, not on dope, but dope does come into it!

DO YOU GET RAIDED A LOT FOR THAT UP HERE?

Jaz: No... I'd hear about it before it happened - my uncle's a councillor; he'd tell me before it happened.

WHAT ABOUT WHEN THE SPG CAME ROUND HERE?

Jaz: No, that was when we were living over in Elgin Crescent. I went out in the dark with a gun. And this was around the time of the Iranian thing; some reporter said he'd seen a 'dark person with a gun'... No listen right. Anyone with any sense will have as little to do with the police as possible. We live outside the police.

WHAT SORT OF DEAL DID YOU DO WITH REDBEAT?

Jaz: We just put out their single. They can use our label, because Malicious Damage is getting quite a big name. But they started demanding things we couldn't afford, like they demanded three grand, and we haven't got it. With Killing Joke, we take the 'We paid our dues man, we did our bit of grafting to get to this position' attitude, and they're not prepared to do all the gigs we did. We did all the shitty little gigs. And they want a deal like we've got with EG when they won't even do gigs. And 'cos of that they haven't even got a following. If you haven't got a following, how do you expect to draw money? Or fucking stay alive?

DID YOU GET A BIG FOLLOWING BEFORE YOU BROUGHT THE FIRST RECORD OUT?

Jaz: No, we'd only done one gig before bringing the record out! But then we gigged like fuck. In one year we did a European tour, three or four English tours, gigs here, gigs there. We had no record company behind us then.

DO YOU RECKON GROUPS SHOULD BRING OUT RECORDS FIRST, GETTING A NAME FOR THEMSELVES, OR SHOULD THEY...

Jaz: They can do it any way they fucking want, mate. It's up to them. But it is fucking work - there's no easy way from the Marquee stage to the.... Hammersmith Odeon stage. There's no shortcut around that.

Later on.....
Jaz: A lot of people in the Beatle's days were just accepting the first thing they were offered. If you've got that much faith in your music, then you know you're worth quite a bit of money. A lot of bands will just take anything because really they haven't got much faith in their own music.

HOW FAR AHEAD ARE YOU PLANNING AT THE MOMENT?

Jaz: To the summer... and then we've got a good idae of what we'd like to do after that. But like I say - we don't want to actually mouth off about things we haven't actually done yet.

SO WHAT DO YOU THINK OF GROUPS THAT DO?

Jaz: It's interesting - I was reading a Sex Pistols thing the other day, and compared it to the first Public Image, and then compared that with Public Image now, and it's just very very interesting. He was going to open his own studio, called Public Image studio, and all these things which never materialise

In the usual Killing Joke way, conversation turns to in-group matters, and an argument breaks out about giving a management/finance person a credit on the new album sleeve...

Jaz: We're not interested in that sort of shit. If he gets his name on it, I want my name on it. If you're going to have anyone's name on it, you might as well have everyone's name on it... Look, he's getting paid for it, isn't he? I just don't see why anyone should get

a fucking credit.
Youth: Well if you want to encourage him...
Jaz: Okay - in that case we'll put our fucking names on it.
Youth: We don't need to - everyone knows who we are anyway.
Jaz: He gets enough work. No.
Youth: I reckon he desrves something, even if it's just like a subtitle on the lyric sheet I don't see why it should affect us on the album that much. We've mentioned names before.
Jaz: Yeah, I didn't agree with that either.

SO YOU'VE GOT A LYRIC SHEET ON THE NEXT LP?

Jaz: Yeah.

WHY WASN'T THERE ONE ON THE FIRST LP?

Geordie: We knew them!
Jaz: Yeah (laughs). That's the whole fucking total attitude.

A friend of the group, who'd come in about 10 minutes before, looks at me suspiciously and asks, "Are you from a music paper?"

Jaz: No, he's alright. It's a fanzine. He'd be insulted if you say a music paper.

(Very simple defenition they've got there). **I WAS GOING TO ASK THAT - DO YOU HATE ALL INTERVIEWERS?**

Jaz: No - it's allright sitting here, asking questions & answering questions. It's just that you get some real tossers around here at times.

DO THEY TEND TO BE FROM THE BIG PAPERS?

Jaz: Yeah. I tell you, the worst journalist ever is Deanne Pearson. She shouldn't even be in it! The most pathetic...

SHE'S HATED BY EVERYBODY (I've never met a band who's liked her).

Jaz: Dreadful jouralism. It's all like what the music should be like. If you don't like it, don't fucking write about it. I'll tell you what happened with her. She turned up when we were living down the road, and she starts with 'What kind of background do you come from?' (Groans). And anyway, it was like now - somebody walked in, and we started talking to them, and we forgot she was there!
Youth: And she was gone!
Jaz: We were just talking, and about an hour & a half later it's 'Where's that bird gone?' She asked about two questions, and then we didn't even notice her go. A couple of fanzines have been good - 'Allied Propaganda' and Anti-Climax. I like fanzines 'cos they don't take such a pig-headed view of it. They don't really go in to rip a band to pieces - they just don't write about a band if they're not interested. I like fanzines, I think they're great.

DO YOU GET A LOT OF PEOPLE COMING UP TO THIS PLACE?

Jaz: We quite enjoy some people. If people really want to find us, they will. It was in Sounds - 'I went to their Arundel Gardens flat'. If they want to come and talk to us, have a smoke and have a bit of a laugh, it's alright. But if you've got the nutters who've got wierd ideas or want you to do favours for them - some we get all types of nutters in here.

I THINK THAT'S ABOUT IT...

Jaz: It is? Just keep going. See if you get any more ideas... that's how I prefer doing them.

THAT'S ANOTHER THING ABOUT BIG PAPERS - TO EARN THEIR MONEY, THEY ONLY SPEND HALF AN HOUR WITH A GROUP, SO'S THEY CAN DO A LOT OF GROUPS & GET A LOT OF MONEY. IF YOU DO A FANZINE AND YOU'VE GOT THE TIME, YOU CAN SPEND THE WHOLE DAY WITH A GROUP, AND WRITE A BETTER ARTICLE AT THE END.

Youth: That's the best way to do it, isn't it?
Jaz: ..... I'll tell you what - they're trying to rehouse all the black people in this area outside London.
Youth: They did that in the '50's...
Jaz: They're trying to do that now. I know, 'cos my uncle's in the fucking council and he knows.

DO YOU RECKON THE PEOPLE DOWN IN BRIXTON THIS WEEKEND HAVE GOT SOME SORT OF SUSS OF THE KILLING JOKE?

Jaz: Yeah, I think so. All types of people understand what we're getting to.

I MEAN THE ATTITUDE, WITHOUT KNOWING ABOUT THE MUSIC.

Jaz: they've got different words for it. They talk about pressure, we talk about the Killing Joke. It's all the same, isn't it?

'YOU WAH?!'

'WAH!'S GOT TO BE MY FAVORITE GROUP. IF I WASN'T IN WAH!, I'VE GOT TO MAKE IT SO THAT I'D WANT TO BE.'

Pete Wylie is accepted as one of the real characters in modern music, & following our chats on long-distance phone-calls, I was particularly looking forward to meeting him. The chance came when he was down in London on his own to mix their last Peel session. I turned up at about 3.00 to find Pete mentally wrecking the day of producer Tony Wilson plus his engineer. We made our introductions, and Pete picked up the phone to call Washington, the bassist, back in Liverpool, too broke to come down. Surely without prior thinking, Pete's opening words, in that unmistakable Scouse accent, were:-

"Across the miles, the mighty Wah!"

As the call continued, Pete explained to Washington that he was homeless for the night, and being the gent that I am, I offered to put him up. Suddenly it no longer seemed necessary to do the interview there and then - there was bound to be plenty of chances later. (In fact, the quotes used were recorded the next morning while Pete was consuming toast & worrying about catching his train -which he didn't! But then, that's life...)

I showed Pete a copy of Vox magazine with a feature on them, and he went crazy with joy at the photos (also recognising a girl he 'copped off with' in Dublin). We discussed Ian Cranna's article in the Face, where Pete was put over as the great white hope ('a hero in the making'). Wasn't it a bit over-the-top?'

"Yeah, it was a bit, but then I don't see anything wrong with having heroes. I've always had them, and I'd like to be one myself."

Is it a case of distinguishing between a hero, someone you admire, and an idol, somebody you think is immensely superior, infallible, and untouchable?

"Yeah, that's it EXACTLY!" Pete reached for an imaginary pen and scribbled it on an imaginary sheet of paper: "I'll remember that one."

> ❛Wah! must have 3 things that all my favourite groups in the past have had - The initial thing is just a massive thrill. It's not an intellectual thing, it's something you can't think about, something you can't plan, it's just there - that's what makes a great group special. Another thing was inspiration - it would make me want to go out and do things, or maybe even just want to talk about things. There are obviously a lot of people with some kind of talent, and they just need to hear or see something - a film or a book - that will bring it out in them & make them want to do something.
> The third thing is entertainment - you can't get away from it. It's a very stupid thing to deny, as it doesn't have to be a big showbiz thing:- I don't want to go to gigs and be bored to death. You don't want to have to kneel for people. You want to entertain them, but not pander to them.❜

The session being recorded consisted of Sleep, The Checkmate Syndrome, Cutout and the new single, Forget The Downs. All, like the first 2 singles, are atmos-pheric, and with that Hitchcock fear feel to them - Pete's own defenition. Looks like the album's going to pretty excellent - when's it out?

"DON'T call it an album. It's an LP"
Why's that?
"I'll tell you later." I never did get an answer.

It transpires that the Wah! line-up has been pretty unsettled recently, explaining the lack of gigs in 1981. Aside from Pete & Washington, they've been using a stand-in drummer Joey Musker from Dead Or Alive, and synth-player King Bluff is on his way out:-

> When we were playing in Ireland, he was rubbish, playing what he thought was musical, which is the wrong attitude. So after one song, I asked the p.a. people to turn him down. He said 'What did you do that for?', I said ''Cos you're playing rubbish', and so he walked offstage - in the middle of a gig! The keyboard player from Pink Military was there, and he just got up and played, even though he didn't know the songs. He just put handclaps on one of them, and it was so much better.❜

26

After Pete had finished convincing Tony Wilson that Wah! Heat was now just Wah! (the 'Heat' being unimportant), we left for Pete to do an interview with Studio B15, Radio 1's Sunday magazine show. This one was based on 'Liverpool's Unemployment and Music', a label Pete wasn't keen on, though he himself had spent 2½ years on the dole. In the interview, we heard the first of the day's many mentions of the 'Crucial Three', Pete vainly explaining it was a big-headed joke by him, Ian McCollough & Julian Cope that's been blown out of all proportion. Although hed earlier made it obvious him & Mac don't see eye to eye, he refrained quite noticably from saying so on the radio, pointing out the futility of bitching.

The radio people went home well pleased, and we went for a meal with Ian Wilson of Wasted Talent Agency....

❛When we were in Ireland, I knew from talking to people before we played that a lot of the groups that come over were condescending, because although the groups are doing the audience a favour, the audience are doing the group's a favour just by going. And this guy at one gig was shouting 'Patronizing!' at me, whereas I was just sending up that attitude, but the subtlety of it was lost. So I put my guitar down and went out to speak to him, as he couldn't understand me from onstage. But he thought there was going to be a fight, and people generally did, which was crazy you know. I wanted to try and get the audience into it, but they threatened to pull the plugs on the gig.❜

The dinner (paid for by Ian on expenses) was quite revealing. Wasted Talent wanted Wah! on their agency, & Pete wanted someone to line up a tour. For most of the meal, Pete & me merely talked about music, rather ruining the business chat; yet when that side of it was discussed, I was rather worried by Pete's willingness to become part of the rock' n'roll machine. This seemed rockist! But I should have known - Pete later explained he was spending the whole meal on an act, pretending to be just another hungry musician so as he could get Ian Wilson into the open, & thereby understand what Wasted Talent would do for Wah!...

EAT TO THE PETE! ALL PHOTOS BY LAWRENCE BLAMPIED..

❛I hate to use that word rockist, because it's a real symptom of the thing that people just pick up on a new word. We haven't used the word since the NME interview.

The crazy thing is we mentioned it as a joke, & then because it was in the NME it's the big thing, you know? It's just people's lack of imagination. It was a joke - rockisms a really corny word. But rockism, or anti-rockism, like involves getting rid of bad habits, ignoring the mythology and doing things that suit ya. Take U2 and Genesis... well I say Genesis -everyone slags them- but there's new bands whose attitudes are as bad, if not worse, than all the old crap because they should have learned from the past few years.❜

Our next stop was the Comsat Angels gig at the Sundown. We got in free - we had to because we were broke. Wah! were at this period of time negotiating a deal with Warner Brothers for their own 'Eternal' label (a complete control situation) & Pete's friend there, Dave Walters, was at the gig. Being keen to keep in with Wah!, he started splashing out on the drinks - I dearly hope for his sake they were on expenses. Another person from Warners said to me about signing Wah! - "I'm really looking forward to it because then we've got one of the Crucial Three" !?! Somebody tell me, why does this business have to have these attitudes? Pete himself was penniless, unlike the other 2/3 of the Excruciating Tree, as he had to come off the dole, yet hadn't seen a penny from the group for months - he'd been living on borrowed money....

❛We've got massive principles, but the bad thing is that people always think high ideals go hand in hand with no desire for money. I've never made any thing about money - I want to be able to do things without cutting corners. The press, & the people who read the press without even questioning it, make it difficult - when you read that by signing to a big label you're selling out, you start to believe it, and it's preying on your mind so much that you can't concentrate on throwing yourself into the music. Like Bowie! My favourite artist of the early '70's - well if having money is a dangerous thing, I'm into it, if I can make records like Aladdin Sane & Ziggy Stardust. I mean The Clash have got less money now than they ever had, so why isn't their stuff as good as it was? I think the danger of money is that if you've got faults in ya, then money just magnifies it❜

From the Sundown it was over to the Embassy for the Fire Engines gig (see live pages). We got in using Peter Powell's guest list (this is true!), & Dave Walters made the same trip over, now borrowing £20 notes to buy the drinks! Pete Wylie met up with Julian Cope and spent the time either talking to him or sussing out the Warner Bros. situation. I watched the gig....

> ❝ I wouldn't label Wah! anything - I'd rather say 'Wah!' than talk about it. Before people like Bob Dylan came along, the authentic rock'n'roll records didn't even have people singing half the time. They just shouted 'WAH!' with like a W, 93 A's, and an H! And that was it - it was just that buzz you know; the thrill. When Julian (Cope) sees me, he just goes 'Wah!' and I say 'Wah!' to him - it's just a word we used to greet each other with for years before the groups.
>
> I bring Wah! into as many things as I can. Like instead of saying'Excuse Me', I say 'Excuse mWAH!', and 'When we're famous we're going to write our memWAH!s' Things like that. (Laughs). I love it - having us enjoy it as much as it being a group. ❞

So ended an interesting little day in the rock'n'roll business. The outcome of the various things is that Wah! have signed to Warner Bros, getting an own-label deal described by the 2-Tone/Go Feet lawyer as one of the best he'd seen. But due to delays, Forget The Downs will be out independently, on Eternal through the Erics/Inevitable operation. The album will be out on July 3rd, and although the line-up STILL isn't settled, there will be a June/July tour, not being organised by Wasted Talent. The final grooves one each side of the single contain references to the Fall's slagging of them on Slates, Slags etc. But to leave the final quote to Pete, discussing the deal...

> ❝This deal is something we've thought about for a long time, and we've considered all the pros and cons. If it comes off, it'll be like an independent, but with the money to do things. Phoney martyrdom bullshit... I had a heated discussion with Geoff Travis of Rough Trade about betrayal and all this. He doesn't see that if we have money, we can give money to Inevitable, we can still help people, and be active. We can do an interview in the Sun and advertise the independent scene. If you've got a weak man who is getting stronger like the independent thing is, what's the use of getting another weak man to help you? If you can get somebody strong, it does things better. Geoff Travis propogated some idea that as soon as we signed we'd turn our backs on all that which is ridiculous you know.... just no way. ❞
>
> A.F.

TONY!
So there I was in Ian Broudie's underpants and the phone goes after 2 hours sleep and he says he's Paul Weller - 'Paul Weller?' who is this joker? And its him and he doesn't like our LP and he likes 3 minute pop hits — and so here it is Young Fletcher, you have here a copy of the new hit - 'Remember' - its out April 16 (Mummy's birthday) but don't let people who'll go tell the world how wonderful we are hear it yet — and you keep the secret close to your target t-shirt covered heart for now till contact re-establishes itself — maybe we could do an interview over toast in your mother's bed or something — and whatabout poor ol' Gary Crowley — hasn't heard from Wah! in centuries so give him of my best etc knowaramean?
Speak to you soon
⋔ Pete
⋔ Shambeko! Say Wah!

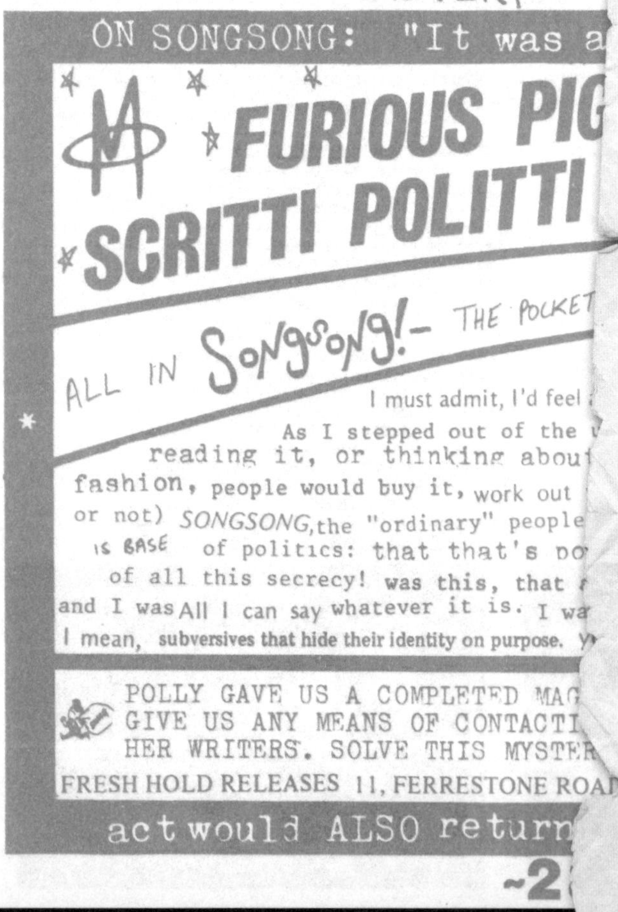

act would ALSO return a secret it didn't mak

MADNESS

Madness are probably accepted by the bulk of our readers as nothing more than a pop band.
Well in the last year, they've started making some astonishingly good records, and this interview
with them might help people realise Madness are as honest a band as they come, as well as giving
a bit of an insight into the way the music biz works. It was done on an'interview day' at Stiff,
with different members of the band doing dozens of interviews, and with me constantly being asked
to conclude our discussion by a Stiff press girl. Nevertheless I cornered Suggs and Mark Bedford
for an hour, and despite expecting a typical Madness piss-take event, found Suggs extremely talkative (& very fond of swearing), and came away with what seems like a pretty defenitive chat. Modest
bugger, aren't I?

DO YOU MIND ALL THE SINGLES COMING OFF THE LPS?

Suggs: Yeah we do, but the trouble is they have a
funny way of talking round things. It's the old story of 'If you don't want to buy it, then don't buy
it', although I know that's not wholly true. We
hardly make any money at all off a single - they're
just to promote albums really. (Goes in to see Stiff
supremo Dave Robinson & sorts out how much they <u>do</u>
earn)... Yeah, that (Los Palmos) 12" - we were losing
2p on each copy. And there was 20,000 of them. Singles off albums can go too far, but we won't release
any more off this album. It's just a line you've got
to work out yourself.

SO YOU STILL HAVE TOTAL CONTROL ON WHAT GOES OUT?

Suggs: Yeah. But if you spend an hour talking to Dave
Robinson when he wants you to put a track out, it's
really hard to come out convinced you were right when
you went in. But it's in our contracts, and we do get
on really well with Dave Robinson. But things like
Night Boat To Cairo - we wanted to remix it or put
another track on it, but we were away on tour. By the
time we came back it was all done and packaged, and
it was "Well, you can send it back if you want, but
it's on the presses".
Chris Foreman: We went to America, came back, and
that was done. It was a heavy argument.
Mark: It was our one big row with Stiff.
Suggs: And it was an EP, which never got advertised
at all.

**THE OTHER TRACKS WERE AS GOOD - IF NOT BETTER - THAN
NIGHT BOAT TO CAIRO ANYWAY.**

Suggs: That was the thing. He sent out all copies to
DJ's and people with just Night Boat and Don't Quote
Me on it.

**SO DO YOU PLAN ALL YOUR RECORDS WELL IN ADVANCE, BE-
CAUSE IT SEEMS LIKE YOU KNOW WHAT'S COMING OUT SIX
MONTHS BEFOREHAND?**

Mark: No, not that much. But we do know roughly
what we're going to do.
Suggs: But if you've got songs recorded it only
takes a minute to decide what your single's going
to be. We don't plan "Well, we'll record a single
in January"; we record a load of songs, and then
work out which will be a single and when.

DO YOU FEEL LIKE POP STARS?

Suggs: Yeah.   But I don't wanna be a pop star
though. I always talk about this - I was talking
about it to my girlfriend last night. I really
hate it. When we went to the BBC Rock & Pop Awards,
I hated it; I felt like being ill.
Mark: It was all the 'Hello darling' set. 'Oh David'
- all that sort.
Suggs: 'Wasn't it great?'
Mark: 'Fabulous'. It was all shit - a real load of
rubbish.

**THE THING IS THAT THOUGH YOU FEEL LIKE THAT, IT
COMES OVER ON TV AS THOUGH YOU REALLY ENJOY DOING
IT...**

Suggs: That's the hard thing:- are you going to be
forced into being in a really bad mood by a load of
old cunts, or are you going to be the best band in
the world? When you do your 'thing' or whatever -
maaan - you can't think about things like that or
you'd just sit there going...

**WHAT DID SUE LAWLEY THINK ABOUT THE CUSTARD PIE
IN HER FACE?**

Suggs: Well, we'll probably get a very annoyed
letter. We're not allowed on Tiswas anymore.
Mark: He removed one of Sally Jame's eyelashes.
Suggs: Yeah, I had a pair of gloves on, and I
squirted this stuff in her face. Then I did it
again by accident and thought 'Oh shit!'. SO I
tried to get it out of her eyes, and I pulled one
of her false eyelashes out!
Mark (laughing): That was great! So never again
will we appear on Tiswas. Or any other Stiff artists.
Suggs: But yeah - it's really hard being a pop
star and trying to remain normal. But you can't
have the best of both worlds I suppose.

**WHEN YOU WERE AT THE 101 CLUB A COUPLE OF WEEKS
AGO, IT WAS LIKE YOU WEREN'T BOTHERED ABOUT BEING
FAMOUS. YOU FELT YOU COULD GO TO A GIG AND NOT
WORRY ABOUT IT.**

Suggs: Well I'm determined to do that. Like concerts - I'll just go and have a drink in the bar,
and if I get fucking mobbed... well, I'm just go-

ing to fucking do it. Every night I'm going to go out, and if I can't have a drink at the bar and be normal - if I have to hide in the dressing room every fucking night; you know, get limos to go out and get a packet of fucking chips... You know, I wanna live a normal life. And though I am a pop star, I'm not going to be one in my own mind. I'm not going to do the rounds. I hate it, I really fucking hate it. I suppose I can't look at it objectively, but I just never ask for anybody else's autographs. Maybe 'cos I know what a bore it is. You just feel 'Why?'. Don't   look to me for fuck's sakes. If you're looking at me for inspiration or whatever, I'm just - I can't write any fucking lyrics, I can just about sing....

DO YOU GET STOPPED A LOT IN THE STREET?

Suggs: Yeah, all the fucking time.

DO YOU FEEL YOU HAVE TO PUT ON A SMILE, OR DO YOU SPEAK TO THEM ACCORDING TO HOW YOU FEEL?

Suggs: Sometimes I do, but sometimes I just walk off. Like I was having a drink in a pub once, and this bloke started grabbing my shoulder, and going 'Oi! It is! It is!' So I just walked out.

HAVE YOU HAD PEOPLE HASSLING YOU MUCH, 'COS THEY'-RE JEALOUS OR SOMETHING?

Mark:I've had a lot of trouble with someone ringing me up all the time, & that's really horrible. Suggs: Carl (Chas's real name) had two girls round his house at 1.00 in the morning, pissed, going "Let us in, we've got a right, we're your fans", and he was going "Fuck off, I wanna go to bed"; and they were there for an hour ringing the bell. But I think 'cos of what we're like, we haven't made many enemies in the public eye. I think a lot of people reckon 'Oh Madness - fucking pop band', they're indifferent to us, and won't listen to us, but nobody really hates us. We haven't made any really strong statements about anything, so there's nothing people can hate really - except that we're pop stars.

AT THE MOMENT HAVE YOU ACHEIVED WHAT YOU WANTED TO ACHEIVE?

Suggs: Well I think we've reached the stage where we're one-step-beyonding still, and we've just gone as far as we can with all that. We've defnitely reached where we wanted to reach with all that jumping up and down in porkpie hats and stuff. Mark: Shit, yeah. Suggs: So I think at the moment it's a new era for everyone. Noone in the music business knows what's going to happen next.

HAVE YOU GOT ANY IDEAS WHAT WILL?

Suggs: Not really. I think it's going to go back to glam stuff - Adam Ant will be the new Gary Glitter or David Bowie and it'll be like that, going back to superstars.

WHAT DO YOU THINK OF ADAM & THE ANTS?

Suggs: I like 'em. When we were coming back from the airport recently, we all got in this taxi, & we were going down the Westway, when this dirty great limo came past with Adam sitting in it on his own. Mark: I think he was as embarassed as we were.

(I SAY A BIT ABOUT ADAM'S LOSING ALL HIS EARLIER FOLLOWERS...)

Suggs: That's why I think that making statements - like all this 'Oi!Oi!' stuff - well, when you're in the music business you realsie you're just a part of it. You're just a fucking cog. The best **32**

that you can do is stay the same as you were and not make any great ideals about anything. Anything you do, you're only selling more records, which helps the record company, which helps the businessman, which helps... you know what I mean? Mark: Music won't really change anything.

DON'T YOU THINK THAT'S A BIT NEGATIVE?

Mark: No, I just think it's realistic. Suggs: I just think the best you can do is stay the same as you started out as. But you can't stay being a punk while earning £6,000,000 a year. You just can't. And I think The Jam have stayed pretty much the same, I think we have, the Specials have, and a couple of other people. And I think it's good that a lot of 'pop stars' now are just anti-pop stars.

BUT PEOPLE LIKE ADAM ANT ARE POP STARS.

Suggs: Yeah that's true. I can see them making it in America actually. But while it happened pretty quickly for us, after he worked two years in a punk band, I bet he loves every minute of it. Well he must be - releasing a single every day. He just wants to get as much out of it as he can.

(I mention the farce of all the reissues...)

Suggs: That's what I mean - it's all a fucking joke. And whatever reasons you make for things, it's really because you want to be more succesful and more popular and more rich or whatever. I mean that is the reason for everything you do. And to have more of a laugh. I mean all this 'Re-released to public demand' is just a load of arse.

DO YOU EVER GET BORED BY TOURING?

Suggs: Yeah, I think we did on the last tour. Mark: Two shows a night, and by the end of it, everyone was really tired. Suggs: We just weren't getting any fucking time. We wanted to think of something interesting to do on that tour. It's just really hard to make it more interesting but not to have things like smoke bombs and lasers. A change would be really good - that's why the film thing's being banded about.

IN ENGLAND, HAVE YOU THOUGHT ABOUT JUST DOING AN AREA OF THE COUNTRY AT A TIME?

Suggs: I think it would be really good just to do four dates in a row, then to have a weekend or 4 days off. We've got to have a think about it. Mark: We had a talk before the 2nd album came out, about what we were going to do now, and nothing really happened, except... Suggs: Suddenly we were on tour again! Writing the set list on the bus and all that bollocks. I enjoy doing just 5 dates though.

DO YOU FEEL EMBARASSED ABOUT THINGS LIKE TOTP WHEN YOU'RE ON IT? OR DO YOU TRY & GET INTO IT AND MAKE THE BEST OF IT?

Suggs: Sometimes it's embarassing. We like to make it interesting to watch, for ourselves as much as anybody. When we did Night Boat To Cairo once we wore all this stupid gear, and I felt really embarassed, 'cos UB40 & Dexy's were there as well, and we had all this ridiculous gear on.

I THINK IT'S MUCH SILLIER THE OTHER GROUPS THAT GO ON AND PRETEND THEY ARE SINGING.

Mark: That's the thing - trying to pretend you're playing live on TOTP is fucking incredible.

HOW DO YOU FEEL ABOUT GIVING OUT MESSAGES? YOU WERE SAYING EARLIER THAT THERE WEREN'T ANY, BUT

DOESN'T IT COME OVER AS JUST A BIT TOO MUCH ENTERTAINMENT AT TIMES?

Suggs: I dunno. Yeah well, I mean..... I dunno
(pauses).... I feel the same as everyone else
really, everyone else who's alright. I feel that I
hate Nazis; and I hate extremists of any description; and I hate Maggie Thatcher...
Mark: ...Violence...
Suggs: ...I drink my pints of beer with the lads—
yeah I hate violence at concerts; and I hate people
being charged too much for things; and I hate fucking businessmen; I hate everything that everyone
else hates - we all hate the same things! (Pauses
again).... I think you either... I dunno what I
fucking think really. (Sighs).... I wouldn't not
write a song about that, you know?

IT SEEMS LIKE EMBARASSMENT & NOT HOME TODAY - I KNOW
WHAT THE SONGS ARE ABOUT, BUT ONLY 'COS HE (MARK)'S
TOLD ME. I DON'T THINK PEOPLE BUYING THEM WOULD
UNDERSTAND WHAT THEY'RE ABOUT.

Suggs: I dunno, well yeah. What difference does it
fucking make?
Mark: I think it should be up to the individual
what they read into a song.
Suggs: If you're sitting at home and you put on a
record like 'Burn Down The System'; you take it
off and put Baggy Trousers on. It doesn't make you
think 'Maybe I should go and burn down the system'-
it makes you think 'Well I feel like that anyway'.
Mark: That's what I mean by saying that I don't
think that music can really change that much.
Suggs: And half the time you find that the cunts
who write songs like that aren't bothered anyway.
Johnny Rotten never gave a fuck about anything -
except himself really.

IN THE DAILY STAR IT HAD CHAS SAYING THAT BAGGY
TROUSERS WAS ABOUT HOW SCHOOL WAS GOOD.

Suggs: Yeah it was a bit - I said that actually.
But it was like that fucking Pink Floyd thing -
'Teachers leave the kids alone'. It's just a load
of bollocks. It's just about how it's boring for
the teachers, it's boring for the kids, but what
else is there? What do you do - just hang around on
street corners smoking fags and playing snooker all
day. Life isn't like that. Obviously, education
does have some importance.

(A debate follows for the next 5 minutes, with
Mark & Suggs saying school isn't great, but it
can't be changed, me disagreeing).

Suggs: What's funny though, is I can remember being at school & hating it, and everyone saying
'You'll look back on it, and like it'. I don't look
back on it and like it, but you look back at the
innocence of your youth. Same as when the band
started:- playing in a sweaty pub with £5 between
the 7 of us, and everyone saying 'You'll look back
on it and love this', and we thought 'Bollocks' -
we were having to shift our own gear - but I really
like looking back on it now.

I HAVEN'T SEEN DANCE CRAZE YET, BUT EVERYONE SAYS
IT SHOULD HAVE GONE MORE INTO TALKING TO THE FANS
AND THAT...

Suggs: We just didn't have any say in that film.
Jerry Dammers did.

I'D HAVE THOUGHT HE'D HAVE DONE IT WELL.

Suggs: I know - that's what made us all a bit sick.
When we were watching the premiere he walked out &
said he wouldn't have anything to do with it! And
he'd been up to the editing every day. What I thought
is that they should have taken one number from each
band and given it to the group's to do something
with. We'd have gone out and talked to a few people
& had a bit about the history of the band. I think
our videos are always pretty interesting, so we
could have done something a bit more varied than a
live show.
Mark: I think it's time though again. We didn't
have any, and Jerry didn't.

DO YOU GET A LOT OF PRESSURES ABOUT THAT? YOU HAVEN'T GOT THE TIME TO DO WHAT YOU WANT TO?

Suggs: Oh yeah - I mean we started off with the intention of designing our own bags & everything, 'cos
we're all quite artistic. Suddenly though, you're
on tour in Glasgow, and the single's out in London,
and it seems that we never have time to do anything.
Mark: It's like The Clash made all those statements
about what they were going to do, but they found
exactly the same. CBS say 'Whop, off you go on tour
boys', and it goes down the drain.
Suggs: Honestly thinking about it, we're like a lot
of bands would like to be. You know, we're in a pos
-ition where we're still enjoying it; we don't have
any leaders in the group telling us what to do;
we're all really free men in our band; we can go in
any musical direction we want to; we're popular; we
haven't made any statements that we have to regret
or get embarassed about - there's nothing we've
done we're embarassed about.

THAT BIT ABOUT NO LEADERS... WHEN I DID THE ARTICLE
FOR THE FACE, YOU (SUGGS) SEEMED TO DISAPPEAR DELIBERATELY THE MOMENT THE INTERVIEW GOT UNDER WAY,
AS THOUGH YOU WANTED THE OTHERS TO GET ATTENTION...

Suggs: Yeah that was it entirely:- I may be the
face of the group because I'm the singer, but I
don't have anything more to say than anyone else
does.
Mark: Yeah, I think the rest of the group - speaking as the rest of the group here! - I think we
pretty much accept it; truthfully it does sometimes
nark you, and you do want your say, but it's the
thing. I accept that Suggs definitely is the face
of the band, and they want him interviewed 'cos
it's good copy. That's the way the media works.

WHAT SORT OF MUSIC ARE YOU GOING TOWARDS NOW?

Suggs: I dunno really, like Grey Day is really
fucking meaningful man, because we've got something to say. Like I don't know what the fuck goes
on in Lee's mind, and he writes a lot of the lyrics; I don't know what Mike thinks - he writes
tunes; and noone knows what I think half the time.
So you can't really tell what's going to happen
next - it depends who the next song's by-

DO YOU GET ARGUMENTS ABOUT THAT A LOT? LIKE SOMEBODY
SAYING 'AH IT'S ABOUT TIME YOU DID ONE OF MY SONGS'?

Suggs: No, it's more like - 'You know that song you
wrote, well I've got these lyrics': 'Well Suggs has
written some already I'm afraid'; 'No, well fuck
them, give these a try, they're better'! I mean
noone gets really annoyed about it. Everybody's
had a bash at writing.

IS THE LINE-UP ALWAYS PRETTY STABLE
PEOPLE-WISE?

Suggs: Yeah it is, 'cos we all
realise our own abilities - we're
able to talk to one another. We
all look at ourselves pretty
objectively, and we all know we've
got our own failings.

Tony Fletcher.   "That's all, folks"

33

nother Pretty Face - single review in Jamming 10, gig review in no. 11, neither leaving totally impressed. But come December 1980, and APF release an amazing single, while nger Mike Scott produced possibly the most essential fanzine I've ever seen. We lined a proper meeting.... Which turned out 48 hours long, as Jamming's bed & breakfast ub-section put 3 of the band + 2 more up for 2 nights! (see Wah! feature for continuation). The following feature will be a complete, ultimate history of the band, because 1) It's bloody interesting. 2) It makes a pleasant change from straightforward interviews. 3) ¾ of our 2-hour conversation is lying in a tangle of unrepairable tape. Apologies for lack of quotes, but there's nothing like good journalism. And this is nothing like good journalism....

The Remodelling Of...
ANOTHER PRETTY FACE

Mike Scott & John Caldwell went to school in Ayr together, playing in a band called Karma (ugh!) at the age of 15/16. They drifted apart, until in '77-'78, they'd discovered punk, John in a band called The Argh, and Mike in a 3-chord thrash band called White Heat, at the same time doing 8 issues of Jungleland, apparently the first ever Scottish fanzine. Then, in early '79, APF were born, featuring:-

Mike Scott - Vocals, rhythm guitar, piano
John Caldwell - Lead guitar, vocals.
Jim Geddes - Bass.
Crigg - Drums.

The band played 10 gigs, and recorded a single:-

'All The Boys Love Carrie'/'That's Not Enough' for local label New Pleasures (Z1)

The record, out in May '79, featured Ally Donaldson, better known as William Mysterious, on sax, and generated a lot of interest in the band. Carrie was a loud rocker, which now sounds great live (Mike: 'We recognise it as one of our beat songs - it always works, always goes down well, & it always feels good to play'); That's Not Enough bore resemblances to a commercial Clash of that period. A brief line-up change in June saw Jim leave & Ray Taylor enter the arena. Then in October things started happening:

Crigg & Ray left, replacements were found, and the new line-up was:-

Mike Scott - Vocals, rhythm guitar, piano.
John Caldwell - Lead guitar, vocals.
Steve McLaughlin (Chic) - Drums.
Willy Kirkwood - Bass.
(Ally Donaldson - sax (ish).)

Suddenly Another Pretty Face were hot property. Virgin signed them up, Gary Bushell picked Scotland (the band now in Edinburgh) as the hip place and put them on the cover of Sounds in Jan. 1980, & Johnny Waller became their manager. The second single was released on February 15th 1980:-

'Whatever Happened To The West?'/Goodbye 1970's' (VS320).

APF did a series of London gigs in February, then found themselves supporting Stiff Little Fingers on a 24-date tour in March, finishing at the Hammersmith Odeon. They recorded an album produced by Alan Mair of the Only Ones.

Then the bubble burst, largely due to APF wanting it to, and they left Virgin by 'mutual agreement'. The album was never released, and the single deleted (though it's still in some shops)

Mike: 'Virgin signed us deliberately for the American market, based on stuff like 'That's Not Enough'. We were changing to our present style, & it was just a total clash. They've got things like an Artist's Delevopment Office, and they were trying to mould us into an ideal band to break America.' When Virgin refused to release the album, calling it rubbish, APF got to leave the label through the 'Release the record or release the band' clause. The situation now is undying hatred from APF towards Virgin. Reasons go deep & get involved, but APF have to take some of the blame for signing to a major when they had such hard attitudes. The hatred can be easily found in Jungleland, and also in a newer song called 'This Could Be Hell':-

'The crooked apostles of Vernon Yard,
Who play funny games of rebellion by proxy,
And send royalty statements to the heroin ward' (remember Sid?)

As stated, APF developed harder attitudes after signing:- Mike -70% of the group- and John - the other 30%- started writing to fanzines, and the band blew out a gig at the Fulham Golden Lion when punks weren't allowed in, getting paid & taking all the punters to the pub opposite for a chat. On tour with SLF, they watched the rock system:-

Mike: 'We've never played the same set twice, but Stiff Little Fingers played the same set every single night. Even their dub bits were absolutely identical, so it wasn't dub at all. They even had the same introductions!'

Not only Virgin & the gig situation leave APF bitter from that period, but also the Sounds coverage... 'I don't feel at all flattered about being on the cover of Sounds; in fact, I feel embarassed - especially as it was Gary Bushell who wrote the article. That paper's such a load of shit that we haven't sent them review copies of the last two singles. We respect Steve Keaton as a person, but apart from that, we don't want anything to do with the paper.'

PHOTO BY CHRIS WEBB. FROM LEFT: STUART, CYRUS, STEVE.

14

With APF no longer on a major, and no longer a hip band, people started giving them up for dead. But for 6 months the group continued, maybe a bit confused, but trying to work out their own alternative ideas. From April-October 1980 they gigged with Gordon McEwan now on sax. On their October tour, they took fanzines & records to sell. It was at the end of those gigs that I saw them at the Fulham Greyhound (see review no. 11). Meanwhile, another old APF was crumbling; another new one taking shape:-

November 1980 saw Chic leave to join The Scars, & Willie Kirkwood & Johnny Waller also sever connections. Temporarily without a band, Mike & John formed their own Chicken Jazz label, & released the 3rd single (recorded for the Virgin album) after a 10-month vinyl gap:-

'Heavan Gets Closer Everyday'/'Only Heroes Live Forever' (Jazz 1)

It was an astounding record. Heavan was a slow, moody, 5-minute track, with atmosphere, feeling and an element of fear in it. Heroes again showed Clash influences, and was a fast, storming song. The record was limited to 2,000 copies (almost all sold) for financial reasons, but according to Mike 'It did what we wanted, which was to get our name about again.'

At almost the same time, I received a copy of Mike Scott's 'Jungleland' no. 9. The energy in it was amazing - it's hard to imagine a singer doing fanzines anyway, let alone one that attacks Virgin and Sounds mercilessly (would you say what you thought about Sounds when you knew that by pandering to them they could generate interest in the band?). It also contained info on bands, fanzines, rock'n'roll & lyrics. It cost Mike, on the dole for nearly a year, 60p a copy to produce, and he sold it for 25p. There's integrity for you.

It seemed like John & Mike had found a sudden renewal of constructive enthusiasm - Mike produced an as-yet unreleased 2nd EP by Edinburgh band the One Takes; the two of them recorded 5 songs with Nikki Mattress of the Swell Maps, and they started releasing free info sheets on their current happenings. APF were building up that vital thing - a contact with their following.

As well as all this, Feb '81 saw the release of their first cassette:-

'I'm Sorry That I Beat You, I'm Sorry That I Screamed, But For A Moment There I Really Lost Control' (Jazz 2).

It's a living monument to what cassettes can be, as opposed to the scruffy idiocy they tend to be. It features Virgin studio versions of Heroes as well as Another Kind Of Circus (not their best) & Out Of Control (the opposite), a heavily emotional apocalyptic lyrical song:-

'I got about 8 minutes to get myself and my family, into some underground hole; where we can sit and play 20 Questions, while our leaders invent answers'.

The other 5 songs were live from late '80, including Hell, My Darkest Hour, Lightning That Strikes Twice, their 9-minute epic Graduation Day, & Carrie. The tape comes complete with a minizine containing lyrics & info - a vital buy.

Also in February 1980, a new line-up came to London to record a Peel session:-

Mike Scott -Vocals, guitar, piano, violin.
John Caldwell - Lead guitar, vocals.
Adrian Johnston - Drums.
Alan Mair - bass.

As well as Lightning & Out Of Control, they recorded a wonderful gospel-folkish 'I'll Give You Fire', & a more typically APF-like 'This Time It's Real'.

In March, Another Pretty Face played Liverpool Brady's, Chelsea Art College & the Fulham Greyhound, with Gordon back on sax & Steven Fraser on bass. This was when I met them and put them up. At the two London gigs, they were most impressive, with a set that included half-a-dozen of the mentioned songs (ending with the awesome ad-libbed Graduation Day); covers of Patti Smith's 'Mafia' & her 'Dogdream' poem put to music, 'A Boy Called Johnny' and others. John Caldwell spent the whole 45 minutes looking like Mick Jones (sorry!). At the same time, they released single no. 4:-

'Soul To Soul'/'A Woman's Place'/'God On The Screen' (Jazz 3).

Soul To Soul is the Virgin line-up once more, a tinny, echoey song that doesn't hit straight away; the other 2 are slower, more thoughtful & generally better, featuring Mike (on violin as well), John, & Adrian - with no bass. Once again it's well-packaged, but seems to have been released more as proof of their continued existence than current ambitions.

So what now? Well Mike & John are 99% towards signing with Ensign & moving down to London, due to the bass/drums problems (Alan, Adrian & Steve having just helped out). So are they going to fall for the biz all over again? I severely doubt it - APF, having been accepted as one of the most honest & active bands going, are now planning to record The Last Chant from Liverpool for Chicken Jazz release no. 4. Mike & John have been very careful with their Ensign deal, making sure they get their deserved recognition (though I've never seen a band so contented just reaching a small public) while maintaining their undoubted integrity.

Despite praising APF here, they're far from faultless. Sometimes the attitudes are just too hard-line (in my book, you don't AVOID interest in your band, you encourage it); and at the Greyhound, calls for an encore got Mike back to explain that they'd like to carry on but for GLC regulations, but for not wanting to jeapordise the Greyhound's license... Mike, we all know the laws of pub gigs- you could have just gone back on & admitted you'd done a good long set but overshot your time.

So.... a band with a fascinating history & some great music behind them. Now a duo of life-long pals, they're amongst the most active musicians in the country. You can write to APF (with sae) to the above address, where you can also buy their singles for £1, the cassette for a mere £1.70 & Jungleland for 35p (all inc. p&p), as well as get free info sheets. You'll find people who care that you take an interest.... and that's rare.

AF

APF, 1st Flat, 16 Cadiow Place, Edinburgh. Below: Mike

.... meeting another's. Pics: Daryll Collins.

OVERSPILLS

First up this time, we have news of Jamming's spreading world-wide empire's money-grabbing activities...

JAMMING! gigs are now happening every few Sundays at the Africa Centre, 38 King St., Covent Garden, about a hundred yards from the Rock Garden. The aim is to try and get gigs for the bands we write about, with a bit of atmosphere, similarity between groups, and to treat both audience and bands with a bit of respect. Also, to try and brighten up London's rapidly-dying nightlife a bit, while obviously it helps Jamming & The Apocalypse not inconsiderably. So far, we've had the disastrous DIRECTIONS/APOCALYPSE opener of Feb 22nd, where neither the SHOUT's drummer or the bar turned up; a far more successful event with THE BIRTHDAY PARTY/ZEITGEIST/APOCALYPSE on March 29th, though we only broke even; and on May 3rd, 400 piled into the black hole of Covent Garden (with 50 more turned away) to see GIRLS AT OUR BEST!/ARTERY/APOCALYPSE play in the hottest place since the Jam played the Marquee. At least everyone seemed to enjoy themselves....

By the time you read this, the ORGINAL MIRRORS/APOCALYPSE/MOTOR BOYS MOTOR bill on May 31st will have been over and done with, and in mid-late June, there will be a smaller bands night, with 4 or 5 groups for £1.50 - a chance to see the 'names of the future'? Hopefully, gigs with bigger names will make it financially worthwhile to do regular shows with a host of smaller names. There are fanzine stalls, NO age restrictions, terrible accoustics, & hopefully the smaller gigs will start to have a bit of variation in the way of poets or comics as comperes. It isn't the ideal place to organise gigs, but is certainly as near as you can get. Ads appear in NME & Sounds, and posters are up in most alternative record shops in London. Try & come along - the gigs have a good atmosphere if nothing else...

Then after Jamming! gigs, we see the arrival of JAMMING! RECORDS. (A bit of a joke this!). At long, long last it's set up, and at the time of writing, it's known that RUDI are going to be the first band on it. The single probably won't be out 'till late July, so in no. 13, we'll carry the full story, as well as a proper feature on Rudi. Since our article in no. 9, the band have been playing regularly in Belfast, but with the exception of a few north-England dates and Mike Reid's falling in love with them, have failed to get anything big happening. The single will change all that. They still have their massive following in Belfast, and when you look at it, where are all the other Belfast bands now, excepting the Undertones and SLF? As I said, the full story and news will emerge in no. 13, around the time of the record and some British gigs.

On other fronts, the SMART DISTRIBUTION company has been set up by Smart Verbal fanzine to distribute mainly cassettes (tho' some fanzines) through mail order and stalls. It will hopefully build up a network for the rapidly growing cassette revolution. The set-up is totally against the music business, and appears to be extremely well-run. Free catalogue-s & info from 104 Sandford Road, Moseley, Birmingham 13. It's only going to cost you a stamp for some alternative culture info, so don't pass it by...

... Another co-operative just started is the FEDERATION OF BANDS, with small aims of 1% deals, and £100 for a major support gig! You can use whatever facilities are going (cheaply), and get publicity as well. But looking at it, how will you ever get £100 for a support gig? We know this industry is full of rip-offs, but a band will always take the gig! 'cos they need & want to play. And also, who wants to follow the rules of other bands? In this business, it's you vs. the world, and though you may find similar-minded bands, it's up to each band to fight for what they can get. If my views don't discourage you, info is available from 5 Stanway Gardens, London W3.

DELTA 5 have got their long-awaited Pre Records deal, with a £40,000 advance. The contract is for 4 years, requiring an album & 2 singles a year, which means that eagerly anticipated album is just round the corner. But why (see letters-page 30) does everyone assume that by taking a big deal they've sold out?.....

LETTERS

(MOST ARE ON PAGE 30)

'The last 3 issues of Jamming (which we'd always previously thought was pretty good) have shown a gradual decline, highlighted by your appalling abuse of colour. Issue 11 did little to reverse the trend, with two pages of single reviews included not to state any particular opinions, but merely to maintain the steady influx of vinyl.

Unfortunately the clothing adverts reflect on your degree of compromise, & the gullibility of most youth cultures. It's difficult to justify helping to encourage readers to cough up pounds for mass produced 'fashion' clothing. Hopefully, they'll see through it.

As we get a steady stream of adulatory letters we know how easy it is to get complacent so hopefully this letter will serve as a much-needed kick up the backside and you'll get down to writing more articles like the interesting Beat interview. Hopefully you'll take these comments in the spirit they're intended.'

Ray (& Mick), Allied Propaganda, Northolt, Middlesex.

'I got Jamming 10 from Better Badges & just thought I should send you my view of it. Here's a simple but clear index:- GOOD: Venue Guide/Delta 5/DIY Records/Crass interview.
BAD: Too many ads/Directions/Singles (out of date).

I thought it was great to review 'Der Plan'; I don't know if German bands are well known in England, but most are really individual & not imitating the English stuff, so they're worth a listen at least.

...Keep up the good work & review some newer singles next time. Please excuse my bad English because I'm German.

Please plant a factory & have Jammings (what???!!-AF).'

Michael Prenner, Koen, Germany.

'This note is to set the record straight regarding the comments made in Jamming 11, 'Flexi Discs' & 'Fanzines'. 1) The idea of putting a flexi in Toxic Graffity by Crass was first thought out in Dec '79, so the concept pre-dates any of the other mags you mentioned. 2) Print & records are both forms of media... & as such they can be used with integrity, as I believe I have used them, or in a money-grabbing, childish way, like, say, Flexipop has; the choice is up to who writes it, it is not an inherent fault in the format of record/zine. (Besides, who draws the line between 'Teenybop crap' & 'The definitive popzine'? To me 'Pop' crap is pop crap.) 3) Although some people will, of course, buy TG 5 for the record foremost, only a very small (if existent) blinkered minority, would pay 50p then throw the zine away... 4) If I do a mag with a flexi, article or anything in it, I do it because of integrity & honesty, & the purity of a message of a band, be they 'small' & 'unknown' or 'big' & 'well-known'... 5) 50p is good value for 46 pages & flexi & NO ADVERTS, for what amounts to consumer crap to pad it out/subsidise the printing. 6) Just as one can use a record to 'sell copies', so can you use interviews with 'name bands' to 'sell copies', eg Who, Jam, Beat etc, who are the ones who are really into the business of shifting more boring product onto a gullible & impressionable young market....'

Mike Diboll, Toxic Graffity, Biggin Hill, Kent.

Yeah, & I suppose The Who, Jam & Beat only ever formed in the first place because they're part of Maggie's plans to grind down the youth of today, not because they wanted to make music they believed in; unlike bands that exist purely as politicians (eg C---s). The day TG gives £15,000 to CND, then you can talk about being more constructive than these bands.....

20

BACK ISSUES

Well if The Face can get rid of 5,000 of each back issue, we can shift up to a couple of hundred. All prices inc. p&p - take 5p off for each item added on....

No. 5 (Not many left) - Jam, Ants, John Peel interviews. Reading, Carnival ?, Ultravox etc. 40p.
No. 6 - Pete Townshend, Tom Robinson, Mark Perry, Scritti Politti, Rezillos, Sore Throat i'views. Loads loads more. 40p
No. 9 - After a year of sending back money, we found 100 at Rough Trade - Jam, Fall, Selecter, Shrink, Pack, Rudi, Ack-Ack interviews. Tribalism, radio, local scenes. 45p.
No. 10 - Danned, Au Pairs, Crass, Delta 5, Girls At Our Best!, Directions, Security Risk, Apocalypse interviews. DIY Discussion, more local stuff. A mere 44 pages. 50p.
No. 11 - Beat, Dead Kennedys, Zeitgeist, Shout interviews. Fanzine round-up part 1, Jam, 'rock'n'roll' etc etc. 45p.
Badges - 10p + sae or in order. Subscriptions - subscribe, you lazy buggers. £1.60 for next 3 issues, and we promise you'll never see your money again! All payable to A.Fletcher.

ADAM ANT

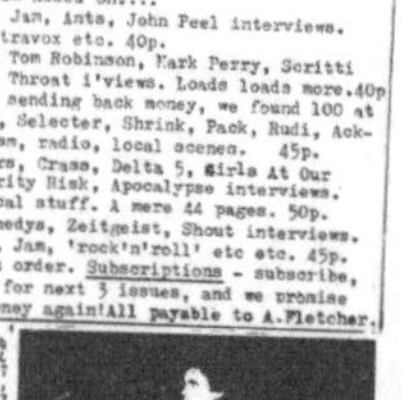

Seeing how quickly Jamming 5 was selling, & assuming it had something to do with The Ants, I thought I'd look it up & see what he had to say for himself in September '78. And I came up with some real gems....

'I feel very attached to punk, but I have to make clear to you what my defenition of punk is. Punk is destruction of one thing:- the supergroup situation.....'

'Kids say they like the band because...we're the only band the press hate. We're hated nationally, and that's great, 'cos it goes out on an underground level. We are - and always will be - an underground group.'

'I don't want - and I reiterate this to you - I don't want the singles to be on the album.'

'We like doing the small clubs, because we know that the kids can see and everything.'

'The fans have said 'Adam - screw the press'. And I am, I'm going to screw them. I will remember the names (of the people who insult me), and when they ask me to do an interview one day I won't do it. Or else I'll say I will & I won't turn up.'

Or the real jewel, out of In The City no. 13...

ITC: Are you influenced by the charts-do they bother you?
Adam: No they don't bother me, they just disgust me. They're just a big facade of crooked.... it's a ball-game.

This may seem like bitterness, but it's not as The Ants were never my no. 1 group. I personally think it's very, very wrong to lead people on by making promises you don't keep. Adam had the chance to change the music business when he hit it off - he had (still has) so much more power than a group like The Jam because his success was so sudden & so complete. For instance, he could have smashed the music press with a single blow - he didn't (doesn't) need them. But what happens? People like Dave McCollough call the band 'Wooftahs' (it sounds timid, but when your music's being reviewed, it isn't) & not only does Adam arrange an interview with him, but he turns up for it and spends hours talking rubbish. Still, Adam made one sensible quote back then...

'I think everybody wants to be famous, and everybody will be famous for 15 minutes, as Warhol said'. And as you said.

BRIXTON

A dodgy subject to write about in this mag, but what happened and what was reported made me so sick, I have to...

CLASSIFIED ADS

...a word, 6p if capitals. Addresses free.

SMART DISTRIBUTION CO. 'ZINE CASSETTE CATALOGUE (No. 2) AVAILABLE (WITH SAE), FROM S.D.C. 104 SANDFORD ROAD, MOSELEY, BIRMINGHAM 13.

POETRY! POETRY!

...WILL BE BRINGING OUT A ...Y BOOK ALONG THE LINES OF THE ... IN THIS ISSUE. IT WILL BE ... FROM THE 150 (& OTHERS) WE ...ED FOR PUBLICATION. IT SHOULD ... LATE JUNE). FOR A COPY, PLEASE ...5p (inc. p&p) TO NORMAL ADD... PAYABLE TO A. FLETCHER.

...arkham is an American mod... who would welcome any correspondence with English mods. Make a girl happy - write to 21917 Meridian Ave. SW, Bothell, WA 98011, USA. Tribalist!

ARMY STO...

BETTER BADGES

KILLING JOKE REQUIEM 1"
RED BEAT 1"
MALICIOUS DAMAGE 1"
SKI PATROL 1"
4 BE 2 1"
THE BEAT PSYCHEDELIC ROCKERS 1¼"
DELTA 5 DV 1"
SPIZZLES RISK 1"
STRAY CATS 1"
SPANDAU BALLET 1"
PERE UBU ART OF WALKING 1"
BLURT b 1"
THIS HEAT HEALTH & EFFICIENCY 1¼"
SECTION 25 SXXV 1"
TALKING HEADS RED STAR 1"
GANG OF FOUR 'HISTORY' 1¼"
GANG OF FOUR 'ENTERTAINMENT' 1"
CRASS NAGASAKI NIGHTMARE 1"
BOW WOW WOW 1" CASSETTE PETS
NEW ORDER CEREMONY 1"
THE CLASH SANDINISTA 1¼"
THE CLASH SANDINISTA 1"
FLUX OF PINK INDIANS GOD 1"
FLUX OF PINK INDIANS HEAD 1"
JOSEF K 1"
STUDIO ONE 1"
DENOB ANTI POLICE 1"
POISON GIRLS CROW B/W 1"
INNER CITY UNIT LP 1"
BARRACUDAS 1"
LUDUS 1"
23 SKIDOO 1"
WAH HEAT WAH! 1"
TEARDROP EXPLODES REWARD 1"

BETTER BADGES 20p EACH + 15p P&P

TRADE RATE: 10p EACH + VAT. MINIMUM 100 in 5's.
286 PORTOBELLO RD, LONDON W10.

IMAGE AS VIRUS DISEASE AS CURE

SALES TO SHOPS/DISTRIBUTORS

NO.	SHOP/DIST.	PRICE	P or SOR.
100	VIRGIN Megastore	26p	P
50	VIRGIN Marble Arch	30p	SOR
50	VIRGIN Oxford Walk	27p	P
10	SHADES	28p	P
20	FANS, Old Compton St.	33p	P
25	SMALL WONDER	28p	P
100	BONAPARTE	25p	SOR
15	PAPERBACK CENTRE,	25p	SOR
50	COMPENDIUM	26p	SOR
20	HONKY TONK	28p	P

PEOPLE SELLING CO

	10 RICHARD
PAID	10 Tom Collingridge, Devon
PAID	20 ALAN, for Devon
	30 Smart Verbal.
PAID	20 AL, Flipside, Los Angeles
PAID	20 Dave Jennings, Bradford & Birming
	100 Tony Perrin, Sheffield.
PAID	100 Deanna Shinde, Canada.
	100 John Lee, Leeds & Yorks
	20 Martin Carrigan, Hastings
	50 Kate Betts, Norwich
20	30 MARTIN, Coventry.

JAMMING 12

COPIES COLLECTED

13/6	313
15/6	513
	713
	843
16/6	943
18/6	1043
	1843
	2043
19/6	2163
20/6	2363
25/6	3363
7/7	3410
18/7	3510
13/8	3610
17/8	3810
20/8	3910
28/9	3960
12/10	4045
9/11	4931

FINANCE

AMOUNT OWED IN TOTAL TO BETTER BADGES 800
" " " TO DJ LITHOS: £299

(£350 BACK TO MUM)   TOTAL PRINTING BILL: 1100.

AMOUNT PAID TO BB:	AMOUNT PAID TO DJ
£800 OWED. MINUS	13/7 - £50
£ 50 200 JAMMING's	14/7 - £20
£ 16 ADVERT	20/7 - £80
£350 PAID UP FRONT	27/7 - £70
£384 OWED —	3/8 - £80
£ 25 100 JAMMINGS	OWED TO MUM: £350
£359 OWED.	PAID BACK:-
	15/7 - £50 10/10 - £10
	20/8 - £140

ACCOUNT SETTLED

SETTLED WITH
DJ: 3 AUGUST.
MUM:
BB.

DATE	NO.
15/6	200
15/6	50
15/6	50
15/6	10
15/6	20
15/6	25
15/6	200
16/6	15
16/6	50
16/6	20
16/6	10
16/6	30
16/6	10
16/6	10
16/6	15
16/6	10
16/6	100
18/6	100
18/6	800
18/6	50
18/6	50
	1745

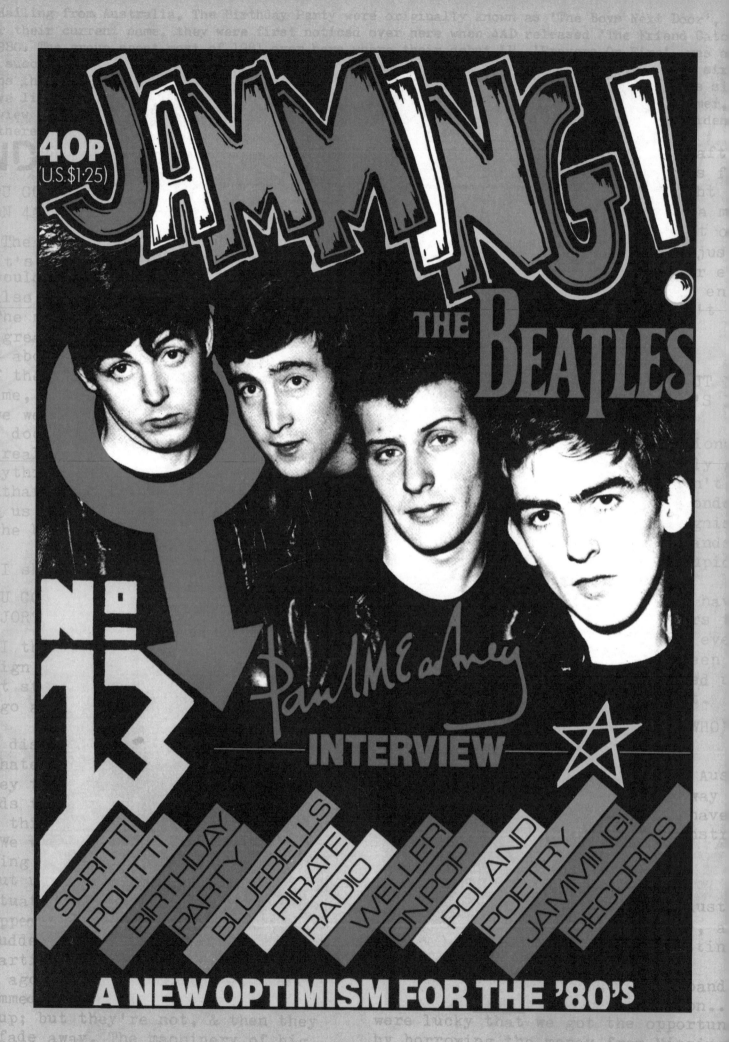

JAMMING!

40p
(U.S. $1.25)

THE BEATLES

Paul McCartney
INTERVIEW

№ 13

SCRITTI POLITTI · BIRTHDAY PARTY · BLUEBELLS · PIRATE RADIO · WELLER ON POP · POLAND · POETRY · JAMMING! RECORDS

A NEW OPTIMISM FOR THE '80'S

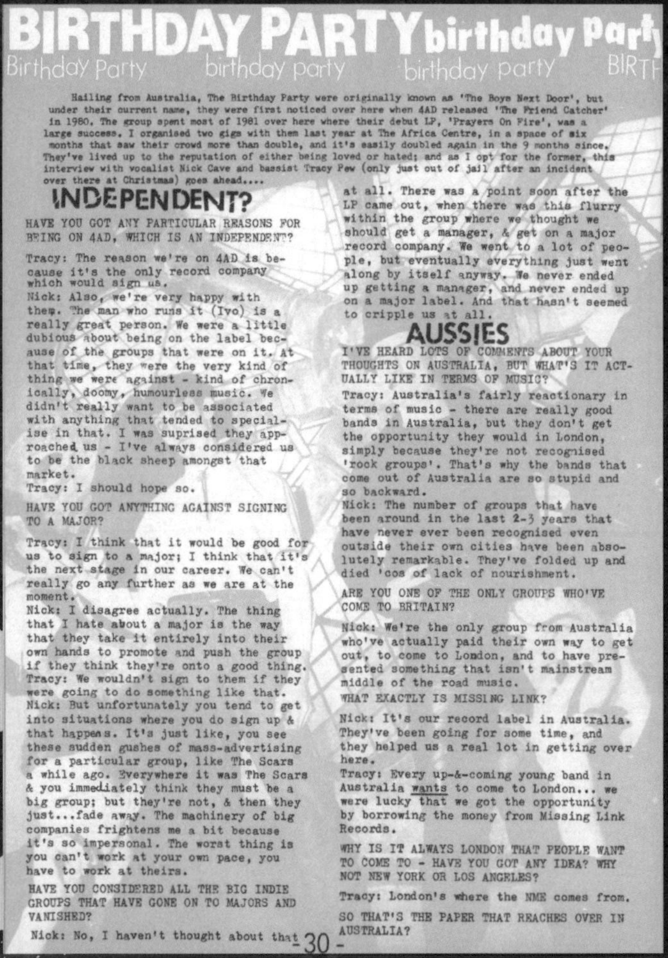

BIRTHDAY PARTY birthday Party

Birthday Party birthday party birthday party BIRTH

Hailing from Australia, The Birthday Party were originally known as 'The Boys Next Door', but under their current name, they were first noticed over here when 4AD released 'The Friend Catcher' in 1980. The group spent most of 1981 over here where their debut LP, 'Prayers On Fire', was a large success. I organised two gigs with them last year at The Africa Centre, in a space of six months that saw their crowd more than double, and it's easily doubled again in the 9 months since. They've lived up to the reputation of either being loved or hated; and as I opt for the former, this interview with vocalist Nick Cave and bassist Tracy Pew (only just out of jail after an incident over there at Christmas) goes ahead....

INDEPENDENT?

HAVE YOU GOT ANY PARTICULAR REASONS FOR BEING ON 4AD, WHICH IS AN INDEPENDENT?

Tracy: The reason we're on 4AD is because it's the only record company which would sign us.

Nick: Also, we're very happy with them. The man who runs it (Ivo) is a really great person. We were a little dubious about being on the label because of the groups that were on it. At that time, they were the very kind of thing we were against - kind of chronically, doomy, humourless music. We didn't really want to be associated with anything that tended to specialise in that. I was suprised they approached us - I've always considered us to be the black sheep amongst that market.

Tracy: I should hope so.

HAVE YOU GOT ANYTHING AGAINST SIGNING TO A MAJOR?

Tracy: I think that it would be good for us to sign to a major; I think that it's the next stage in our career. We can't really go any further as we are at the moment.

Nick: I disagree actually. The thing that I hate about a major is the way that they take it entirely into their own hands to promote and push the group if they think they're onto a good thing.

Tracy: We wouldn't sign to them if they were going to do something like that.

Nick: But unfortunately you tend to get into situations where you do sign up & that happens. It's just like, you see these sudden gushes of mass-advertising for a particular group, like The Scars a while ago. Everywhere it was The Scars & you immediately think they must be a big group; but they're not, & then they just...fade away. The machinery of big companies frightens me a bit because it's so impersonal. The worst thing is you can't work at your own pace, you have to work at theirs.

HAVE YOU CONSIDERED ALL THE BIG INDIE GROUPS THAT HAVE GONE ON TO MAJORS AND VANISHED?

Nick: No, I haven't thought about that at all. There was a point soon after the LP came out, when there was this flurry within the group where we thought we should get a manager, & get on a major record company. We went to a lot of people, but eventually everything just went along by itself anyway. We never ended up getting a manager, and never ended up on a major label. And that hasn't seemed to cripple us at all.

AUSSIES

I'VE HEARD LOTS OF COMMENTS ABOUT YOUR THOUGHTS ON AUSTRALIA, BUT WHAT'S IT ACTUALLY LIKE IN TERMS OF MUSIC?

Tracy: Australia's fairly reactionary in terms of music - there are really good bands in Australia, but they don't get the opportunity they would in London, simply because they're not recognised 'rock groups'. That's why the bands that come out of Australia are so stupid and so backward.

Nick: The number of groups that have been around in the last 2-3 years that have never ever been recognised even outside their own cities have been absolutely remarkable. They've folded up and died 'cos of lack of nourishment.

ARE YOU ONE OF THE ONLY GROUPS WHO'VE COME TO BRITAIN?

Nick: We're the only group from Australia who've actually paid their own way to get out, to come to London, and to have presented something that isn't mainstream middle of the road music.

WHAT EXACTLY IS MISSING LINK?

Nick: It's our record label in Australia. They've been going for some time, and they helped us a real lot in getting over here.

Tracy: Every up-&-coming young band in Australia wants to come to London... we were lucky that we got the opportunity by borrowing the money from Missing Link Records.

WHY IS IT ALWAYS LONDON THAT PEOPLE WANT TO COME TO - HAVE YOU GOT ANY IDEA? WHY NOT NEW YORK OR LOS ANGELES?

Tracy: London's where the NME comes from.

SO THAT'S THE PAPER THAT REACHES OVER IN AUSTRALIA?

- 30 -

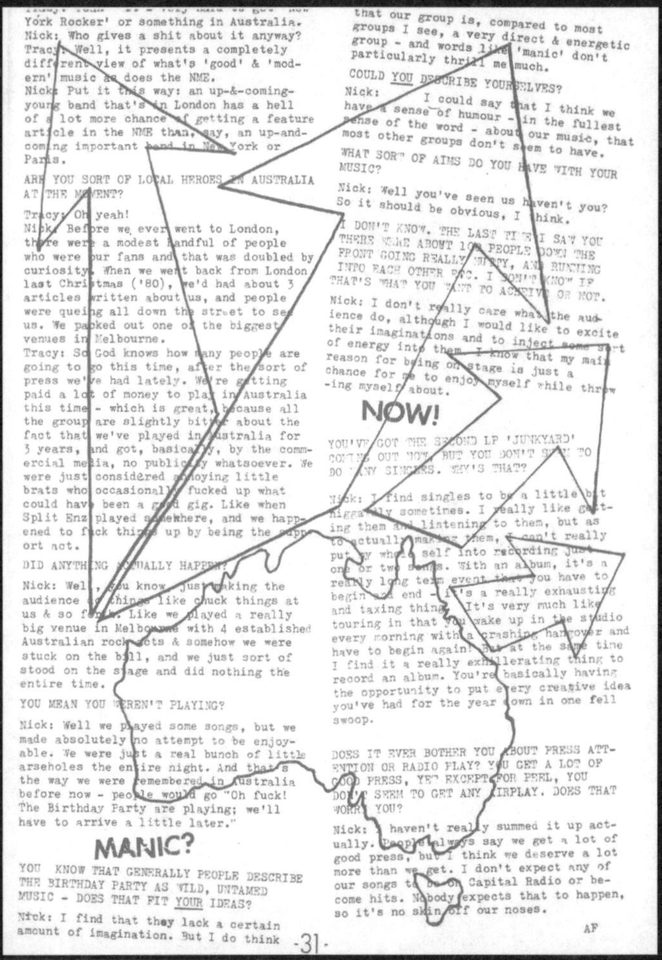

York Rocker' or something in Australia.

Nick: Who gives a shit about it anyway?

Tracy: Well, it presents a completely different view of what's 'good' & 'modern' music as does the NME.

Nick: Put it this way: an up-&-coming-young band that's in London has a hell of a lot more chance of getting a feature article in the NME than, say, an up-and-coming important band in New York or Paris.

ARE YOU SORT OF LOCAL HEROES IN AUSTRALIA AT THE MOMENT?

Tracy: Oh yeah!

Nick: Before we ever went to London, there were a modest handful of people who were our fans and that was doubled by curiosity. When we went back from London last Christmas ('80), we'd had about 3 articles written about us, and people were queing all down the street to see us. We packed out one of the biggest venues in Melbourne.

Tracy: So God knows how many people are going to go this time, after the sort of press we've had lately. We're getting paid a lot of money to play in Australia this time - which is great, because all the group are slightly bitter about the fact that we've played in Australia for 3 years, and got, basically, by the commercial media, no publicity whatsoever. We were just considered annoying little brats who occasionally fucked up what could have been a good gig. Like when Split Enz played somewhere, and we happened to fuck things up by being the support act.

DID ANYTHING ACTUALLY HAPPEN?

Nick: Well, you know, just making the audience do things like chuck things at us & so forth. Like we played a really big venue in Melbourne with 4 established Australian rock acts & somehow we were stuck on the bill, and we just sort of stood on the stage and did nothing the entire time.

YOU MEAN YOU WEREN'T PLAYING?

Nick: Well we played some songs, but we made absolutely no attempt to be enjoyable. We were just a real bunch of little arseholes the entire night. And that's the way we were remembered in Australia before now - people would go "Oh fuck! The Birthday Party are playing; we'll have to arrive a little later."

MANIC?

YOU KNOW THAT GENERALLY PEOPLE DESCRIBE THE BIRTHDAY PARTY AS WILD, UNTAMED MUSIC - DOES THAT FIT YOUR IDEAS?

Nick: I find that they lack a certain amount of imagination. But I do think that our group is, compared to most groups I see, a very direct & energetic group - and words like 'manic' don't particularly thrill me much.

COULD YOU DESCRIBE YOURSELVES?

Nick: I could say that I think we have a sense of humour - in the fullest sense of the word - about our music, that most other groups don't seem to have.

WHAT SORT OF AIMS DO YOU HAVE WITH YOUR MUSIC?

Nick: Well you've seen us haven't you? So it should be obvious, I think.

I DON'T KNOW. THE LAST TIME I SAW YOU THERE WERE ABOUT 100 PEOPLE DOWN THE FRONT GOING REALLY NUTTY, AND RUNNING INTO EACH OTHER ETC. I DON'T KNOW IF THAT'S WHAT YOU WANT TO ACHEIVE OR NOT.

Nick: I don't really care what the audience do, although I would like to excite their imaginations and to inject some sort of energy into them. I know that my main reason for being on stage is just a chance for me to enjoy myself while throw-ing myself about.

NOW!

YOU'VE GOT THE SECOND LP 'JUNKYARD' COMING OUT NOW, BUT YOU DON'T SEEM TO DO MANY SINGLES. WHY'S THAT?

Nick: I find singles to be a little bit niggardly sometimes. I really like getting them and listening to them, but as to actually making them, I can't really put my whole self into recording just one or two songs. With an album, it's a really long term event that you have to begin and end - it's a really exhausting and taxing thing. It's very much like touring in that you wake up in the studio every morning with a crashing hangover and have to begin again! But at the same time I find it a really exhillerating thing to record an album. You're basically having the opportunity to put every creative idea you've had for the year down in one fell swoop.

DOES IT EVER BOTHER YOU ABOUT PRESS ATTENTION OR RADIO PLAY? YOU GET A LOT OF GOOD PRESS, YET EXCEPT FOR PEEL, YOU DON'T SEEM TO GET ANY AIRPLAY. DOES THAT WORRY YOU?

Nick: I haven't really summed it up actually. People always say we get a lot of good press, but I think we deserve a lot more than we get. I don't expect any of our songs to be on Capital Radio or become hits. Nobody expects that to happen, so it's no skin off our noses.

AF

-31-

ISSUE #13

6/82

There was no satisfaction in taking a year between issues, but Jamming! Records almost immediately become a full-time (though unpaid) job. What few hours it did not consume were taken up by the increasing progress of my own band and the significant appearance in my life (at last) of girlfriends, all of which seemed to have more urgent deadlines than those of a self-published fanzine, regardless of *Jamming!*'s cultural popularity.

Interviews were nonetheless gathered, as with Australian expats The Birthday Party, the only band to have headlined not one but two of the *Jamming!* gigs held at the Africa Centre in Covent Garden through the middle of 1981. And then, in the New Year of 1982, while I was with The Jam at AIR Studios as they worked on their new album *The Gift*, Paul McCartney stuck his head in from the studio next door, where he was similarly completing *Tug Of War*, and responded positively to a request for an interview. Three days later, I had three hours of conversation with him on tape – which, considering that Macca had not been heard from since the assassination of John Lennon just a year earlier, merited the kind of exclusive the biggest tabloids in the country would surely have crowed about.

For various reasons, Joly had stopped printing fanzines at Better Badges, and as I struggled to find an equally amenable ally, those tabloids came a-courting. Presented with the prospect of financing the print bill by assigning first rights to the *Sunday Mirror*, I duly sold out. I then ploughed 90 per cent of what was, to a 17-year-old getting by on supplementary benefit, a small fortune, straight back into the magazine, and Issue 13 finally took shape.

There was something closer to a proper team in place now, with Anthony Blampied taking pictures, Robin Richards continuing to design, and a new friend, Pedro Romhanyi, during the many days he helped out at the office we now occupied underneath The Jam's in West London, offering considerable verbal impetus. Gary Crowley wrote about travelling behind the Iron Curtain with TV21, and Paul Weller himself dropped an opinion piece into my lap, which I titled 'Weller On Pop'. I conducted an interview with a shiny new pop Scritti Politti, unrecognisable from the scruffy band I'd spent many an afternoon hanging with at their Camden Town squat through '79 and '80, and also assembled a typically obsessive, all-inclusive round-up of the American scene; with poetry now a regular part of the contents, we had more than enough for a bumper comeback issue.

Robin Richards stayed up late several nights in a row as we closed in on deadline, but his meticulous nature rendered impossible his intent to design the entire interior, and even the most casual reader could readily recognise the difference between his layouts and mine. Still, by late spring, I'd found a printer who could handle Robin's unusual designs (Leighton & Lonsdale if memory serves correct), along with a distributor that would take most of what I recall to be a 12–15,000 print run off my hands and presumably into the newsagents: the trusty notebooks had been abandoned, and whatever paperwork may have once existed has been lost in the mists of time. The magazine itself, fortunately, has not.

'A STATEMENT'

A year and a half ago in Jamming! II, I wrote a one-page rant denying that 'rock'n'roll' /live music was dying. Those 18 months have proved me wrong - the first half of 1982 has been the worst period in ages for the clubs. But that doesn't mean I was wrong to say it was still alive - I just hadn't realised the surge of pop groups was so obvious, seeing it more as an alternative than a total coup. ABC, The Human League, Adam, Altered Images, Haircut 100 and more have all removed the importance of a group building up live - the music scene in the last 18 months has been totally different to what me and others had been used to or expected.

However, I'm not going to be despondent; in fact, I'm now more optimistic over music than I ever have been. Jamming! wouldn't really have been that valid over the last year - it would have been little more than an underground magazine pissing in the wind while the pop world, including it's press, rejoiced in cocktails, yellow shorts and good, clean fun. Jamming! missed the obvious okay, but the press are missing the obvious fact that this will all die and something new will emerge.

Pop music moves in cycles of four years alternating between energy/change and straight pop, making for 8-year cycles of such. Consider some facts:

In 1956, Elvis and rock'n'roll breaks loose; 'teenagers' appear and go mad at the new noise, doesn't seem to have been that effective with pop music dominating the charts. But eight years after rock'n'roll's outbreak, the whole thing goes wild again, as groups that were pre-teen in '56 have learnt their instruments and lessons, and 1964 sees The Beatles, Stones, Who, Kinks and more, more, more, appear, ready to storm virtually the world. The Sixties being what they were, everything moves at incredible pace and by 1968 we're back round with energy again - 'rock' music is born. Four years later (my earliest memories) we have another pop boom, perfectly worthwhile at the time, but ultimately fickle. A generation of kids get bored, they create punk, and in 1976 start to smash things up. Move on another four years, it seems to have been useless, and the nations obsessed with pop once more.

So what am I suggesting? Basically that (though the cycle might break and the above is open to dispute), there are a generation of youngsters about who were affected by punk, but were either too young to get out there and do something at the time, or were living in the country and again couldn't get involved quickly. These people have learn't over the years what punk meant; they haven't fallen for quick fashions (though media ruined those more than the kids) or 'punk' revivals, but have taken their time and are ready to start being noticed.

There's no doubt that the pop music boom is on the decline - sure it will last a while yet, but Depeche Mode and Altered Images are already slipping, with more to follow within the next year. We're somewhere round '74, heading for the horrible greyness of '75, with The Human League as the new Abba, willing to brighten the times with classic pop, and The Jam as the survivors (Long May They Reign). Of course, there are plenty others there, who we try and write about,

moving at their own valid pace, but then this is an article not a book!

You can shout 'Crap'! No one can predict the future, but I believe something is very gradually starting with people slowly returning to gigs to follow the groups that are beginning to emerge. It seems like the movement coming through this time won't be immediate, as punk was. Punk became a fashion, big labels signed the bands and they all attacked at the same time. But there were no independents in 1976; those have now built up to a commanding position, and that's the sort of thing I mean about learning from the last few years. Hopefully, the next surge will come through independently, starting to release singles now, though it may well be two years before they sell in large quantities. But the thing can be done ourselves, keeping control over what's going on. It's refreshing to see the number of groups about who consider themselves an idea in motion, determined to build it their way, however long it takes.

And it will only be a gradual thing. Though occasional records are emerging (notably the first Alarm single), it'll be the rest of this year and part of next before it really gets going. However if the groups do get as organised as I think they can, there's nothing to stop them coming through the moment the climate is right. People growing out of the current pop boom will hopefully get into this as their teens develop, (as I actually adore great pop music, please turn to the singles page for a closer definition of what this boy is on about). At the same time, these kids too young to remember punk could be affected by the next wave, ready to kick it over in yet another eight years.

So where does Jamming! fit into all this? I honestly believe it's time to put my neck on the line and say I can sense something just beginning, and that I want Jamming! there as a catalyst. I was too young to do anything in '77, but I've been involved for 4½ years now, and have learnt the history of the previous two. Jamming!'s been fun, it's tried to encourage, staying enthusiastic and committed. Yet even fanzines have died with the pop boom; I suppose it was inevitable. But we can learn from what happened and get it right from the start this time. Start working towards something NOW! Everyone! It won't be another rock'n'roll (1956), it won't be another punk (1976) but it could be something great (who said 1984???). What I'll say here and now in print is that if none of this happens, then I'm the wally and I'll get a nice, quiet job somewhere - BUT IT WON'T STOP ME TRYING!

Optimism! Hope! Those of you who thought mid-1980 thru' mid-1982 has been lacking something, read the above again. Start working towards your ideals, and let's see if we can create something together. Let us know of any young group you think has the suss, and we'll build up a network. Jamming! won't stop writing about what is happening now with music that's of any worth (because there's a fair bit about), but I want it to be there and encourage whats going to happen.

Welcome to a new Jamming!

Tony Fletcher

I can remember where I was when I read 'A Statement'. I'd come down to London from Glasgow. But my group The Laughing Apple had kind of fallen apart, and Andrew Innes, who I had come down to London with, had got hepatitis and gone back to Scotland, and I was quite lost, in London on my own. And I remember reading that issue of *Jamming!*, and it just spoke to me. I was never a particularly talented person musically, but I had a great fucking passion, and the passion in 'A Statement' got me. It was the reason I ultimately got Creation Records together.

It was, the way I remember it: Start a band. If you can't start a band, put somebody's records out. And if you can't put somebody's records out, put some shows on. But don't sit on your fucking arse, because you're just gonna get old and fat. Just get on with it, and try and put something in rather than take something out. I was 21 and it spoke to me. It's not even the words, it was the feeling it conveyed, that punk was still alive. To me, being a wee punk rocker from Glasgow and being there since '76, it was just: 'Ah! Somebody else gets it.' Because in music, everything else had gone pop! Even The Jam. The whole world went Haircut 100.

So I started a new band (Biff! Bang! Pow!), and I did a club (The Communication Club) and a fanzine (*Communication Blur*) all at the same time. Would I have started a fanzine and a club without reading 'A Statement'? I have to say I probably wouldn't have. That issue, that statement, fired me up and I thought: he's right, let's have a go. I was mortified when I sent *Jamming!* my first release on Creation, by The Legend, and Tony absolutely slated it. Still, when you try things a few times, you eventually get it right. By the eighth time I put somebody on at a club I was getting good at it. And by the twelfth record I put out on my record label, I signed The Jesus & Mary Chain. **Alan McGee**

SCRITTI POLITTI

THE INTRØ

A sunny afternoon in early summer, just off London's bustling Oxford Street; a meeting with an old (though never close) friend who I don't recognise. Would you?

Green Garfield, leader of Scritti Politti, had always been a thin, fragile creature dressed in black with tatty clothes, his looks tieing in with his group 'Scritti Politti', who specialised in left-field music and promoting the idea of DIY records. The group did a great job, producing some very entertaining music and influencing a LOT of people into making their own records through the heady days of 1979 and 1980. But Green had never appeared a well person and disappeared from London in 1980. This interview was the first time I had seen him for a year & a half, and though I knew well the changes in the group, I didn't expect to see such a different young man. The once straggly, depressed figure now looked bouncy, energetic, lively and extremely self-confident, even arrogant. It would appear that serious illness CAN, believe it or not, do a man good. Certainly Green has come out of it a happier, healthier and wiser person.

Anyone (un)lucky enough to have a copy of Jamming! 6 lying about their house might recall it featuring the first-ever interview with Scritti Politti, back in November 1978. Their debut single, Skank Bloc Bologna (with all the details of it's costings on the cover), had caused quite a buzz, and they were the darlings of the NME and Rough Trade. Three and a half years later they still are, but, as their critics will be quick enough to remind you, their music and image has undergone one hell of a change in that period.

'I don't think anyone could ever say we've bandwagoned. But a lot of the point of the DIY thing was spent. At any given time, there's going to be some group who's got the best information about it, and you can only pioneer that for so long. So we did that. After having done the three singles in that vein - the kind of aesthetics that went with the business - we wouldn't have been happy doing any more. It just so happened that there was along layoff while I was sick, and I came back to do the music this way. I think that the big switch to 'pop' and the white soul thing is really just a copywriter's invention more than mine, although there is an element of that in it. But it would be totally unfair to say it was contrived thing; it just genuinely does reflect my changing interests.'

WHAAM! - Green has just answered half my questions in one fell swoop. Maybe even the bright atmosphere of a cafe pavement for an interview (better than a pub, gig or press office any day) has made a difference.

D.I. WHY?

Green might have made it clear from the start that he'd sooner forget the old DIY days of the Scrits, but it's something that needs to be remembered. Scritti Politti used to be three live members - Green on Guitar and vocals, Nial on bass, and Tom on drums - with about a dozen people behind them supposedly making valid contributions to a communal organisation. One of them, Matt, certainly was useful as organiser and is just as much their manager now as he ever was. Green explains a bit more about how and why everything changed....

'In 1980 I spent nine months in Wales, and the reason I went away was not just because I was sick, but also because there was a bit of dissension in the group about me. I wanted to go very poppy, but Tom and Nial weren't very keen on the idea, so in coordinance with the old bookwormish Scritti Politti I decided to make some notes - which in retrospect is a ridiculous thing to do - about the theory and politics of it, and why it was a good thing to do, as opposed to keep slogging away at St Pancrass Records. So I went away and wrote an enormous amount of stuff for them as well.

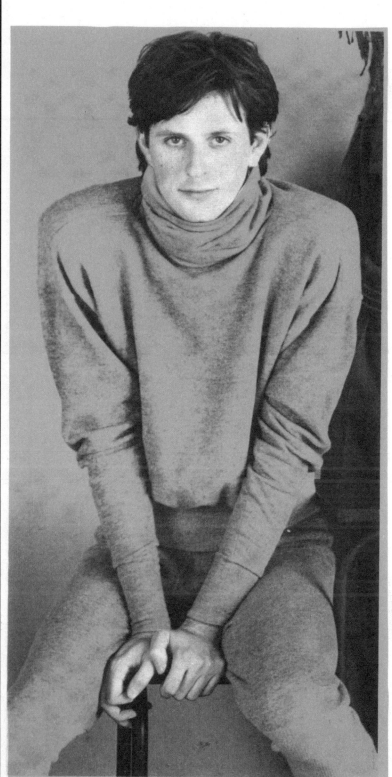

'I ended up saying"Right, from now on, when I've got a number of songs I want to do, then if you want to play on them, that's great; if you don't, lets forget the whole thing." That was the basic shift of footing, that I wasn't prepared to go to the lengths of all that intellectualising to justify the songs- it was crazy. And as it transpired, Nial happily and pleasantly left, and Tom was happy as long as he got to play the drums which (laughs)... well we could have saved a lot of time!!

'I think it took too long. And some of it was... well, the Peel sessions EP, I really can't understand what we were doing then. It was trying to juggle with too many things, and living that ridiculous lifestyle, trying to concoct this magic potion anaesthetic that reflected it somehow, and I'm not sure whether it was wholly successful. I personally would have made that shift late '79, but there was the whole thing of having to account to the other two - or three - and that was a ridiculous way to function.

'It was just that crazy way of living and working. We had such an arrogant, lackadaisical attitude towards the DIY thing. There was a lot of jaw-jaw went on about it, more than actually getting down to doing it. It was seen as some sort of tactical ballistical exercise sometimes.'

Do I detect a trace of bitterness there?

'Well I'm not bitter... (pauses) Perhaps I'm a little bit annoyed that, as I say, it dragged on for as long as it did. Because it had become a fair bit of a drag by 1980. That's why it took so long; there wasn't the freedom for me to write a song and take it to the others - there had to be a board meeting first! Stupid.'

Are you saying that it was always you who wrote the songs?

'Yeah, the bass lines and everything. But again the whole thing of having 15 people pose for group photos was part of this great collectivism thing. It really couldn't sustain itself - and it would have been terribly boring if it had - but people developed their own ways and at their own rates, and it just drifted apart. And as much as we tried to make that unit thing work, it was always the case that I wrote and arranged the stuff. For my sins! I wish some other bugger had written the early stuff (laughs) - no I don't really.'

SWEET

The change referred to here was almost immediate: in the gap between the group's I2" EP of late '79, and the emergence of The 'Sweetest Girl' on the NME/Rough Trade C8I cassette, Green developed anew taste and love of music, and the result was quite astounding. 'The "Sweetest Girl"' will remain in a lot of peoples list of all-time favourites; certainly a more emotional and better crafted love song would be hard to find.

When eventually released as a single in August, The "Sweetest Girl"' was not the great hit it deserved to be, though it was the first single on the actual Rough Trade label to chart. I remain convinced that it was too long in being released, leaving time for many imports and cassette copies to be bought by avid fans who might have given the record a much bigger initial push. But Matt esplains the reasons behind it's delay:-

'We wanted to hold it closer to the LP being ready. Although one can say that had it been put out in March, then everything might have happened, it doesn't really work that way. It takes a long time to wind people up about things. You need both the press and the shops and everybody else to be behind you to really have a hit and I don't think at that point they knew anything about the group'

Green: 'It was a good thing to do. The NME asked for it, so as it was a new track, we gave it to them. There are a number of other putatedly successful single on the album.'

Ah yes, the Scritti Politti album! In I979 they were planning it; in late I980 they started on it; in early I98I they finished the backing tracks; and in August they finished it totally. Considering that it's taken almost a year to see a very much in-demand record released, surely people are justified to accuse the Scrits of being a terribly laid-back, lazy group. That's what I'd been beginning to believe, until I heard Matt and Green justify their reasons for not putting the album out until now.

'We could have released it then,' explains Green, 'and it would probably have got some nice reviews, sold a few thousand copies and disappeared. But we thought that if we held on to it, put out 'The "Sweetest Girl"'

built on that a bit, took some more singles off the album, built up the interest and then put it out, it would do a lot more. Seeing as we were really pleased with it, I would much rather that happened. Considering it's almost a year old, I'm amazed at myself that I still love it. The next LP is going to be devastating but this one's a great start.'

RT

Of course, this is where we get onto the business side of music, the planning and organisation that goes on behind all successful records. And though to the general public, Rough Trade and Scritti Politti have probably appeared as inseparable as Paul Morley and cocktails, a large reason for the absence of the LP - called 'Songs To Remember' - has been problems with said record label.

Matt: 'We wanted to build up to the point where the LP would get the recognition and space it deserved.'

Green: 'When we finished it, we weren't very happy with the way Rough Trade were going, thinking "Oh God, is this going to go the way of all independent flesh?"'

Matt: 'But with things like Pigbag and Yazoo doing so well, there's certainly been a growth in expertise and distribution'

Green: 'There's still a lot of problems, as far as I'm concerned, fundamental matters of distribution and economics, promotion, marketing and a bias against their product at radio stations- which happens.

But surely things have changed recently with the success they've had with other stuff?

Green: 'Well I don't know what's on Rough Trade itself - apart from us and 'Faithless' at the moment- that's going to get near the charts, so it's going to be a bit pioneering in that respect.'

But are things like that going to stop you now?

'Oh no. Nothing at all is going to stop us now, I'm absolutely hell-bent on success.'

Chart success?

'Oh yeah. There's absolutely no point in making music,no point in having a bash at pop, and theorising about it, without actually having popular records.'

At this point I mention that Scritti Politti seem to have always been the archetypal Rough Trade group, from the days when they were both heavily into DIY and self-suffiency, to the current situation with both looking towards the charts; and ask whether this is a natural progression, or if one has influenced the other.

Matt takes the subject up. 'I think that we became interested in the charts long before they did, and played quite an important role in pressing them into going that way. The other important factor has been Mute Records, with Depeche Mode and Yazoo doing so well.

Green: 'Ican remember having discussions with them where we were saying that we'd want simple promotional devices on a record like someone taking it to the radio stations, that just wouldn't be contemplated.'

'They felt that things should sell - in some odd way - on their own merit,' says Matt.

In fact, Scritti Politti used to order Rough Trade not to give away promotional copies of their records, a far cry from the nicely packaged press kit Matt presented me with after the interview.

'The one thing that still worries me is Rough Trade's A&R,' continues Green. 'They missed a lot of opportunities to wise up to the new populism, but inst-

ead kept paying for more Pere Ubu albums, which weren't even selling. It's crazy, and I'm still pretty concerned about that aspect of it.' (Without trying to stir – I think I should point out that Green, along with Nial the old bass player, cited Pere Ubu as an important influence back in Jamming! 6). 'Although we are both purportedly interested in commercial success, they've still got this A&R thing that puts us away from other people on the label.'

Is there a plan these days? Three years ago it was very much 'release a record and see what happens'; how has it changed?

Matt: 'We're much more coordinated and thought out.'

Green: 'It's "Let's be the best group in the world" these days!'

Matt: 'Have a hit with Faithless, then a hit with the LP, then a hit with the next single.'

remember 'songs'?

With all this talk about the LP, people are going to be expecting something pretty remarkable. And they're not going to be disappointed: 'Songs To Remember is an album of pure class, a deeply emotional yet extremely commercial collection of nine songs, that is almost impossible to fault, by virtue of the obvious craftmanship that has gone into it. Although it contains four tracks available on singles, I don't think anythings going to stop this record being bought by different types of people all over the country. People can talk about 'new soul' or any other kind of hype, but when it comes down to it, this record is timeless and fashionless – certainly not many groups could leave their LP in the studios for a year and still sound contemporary when they release it.

'Songs To Remember' opens with 'Asylums in Jerusalem', a three-minute pop song with funk influences, and possibly my favourite on the LP for it's hooklines and wonderful flow. The importance of the new members is shown on songs like 'A Slow Soul', full of melancholy sax solos and beautiful backing vocals courtesy of Lorenza, Mae and Jackie. The title of the song must be a slight pun, as it's certainly very reminiscent of the old Aretha Franklin/Otis Redding sound Green claims to have been aiming for.

'Jacques Derrida', the next single, is once more a different sound, this time taken along by accoustic guitars and quick moving vocals, quite folky in some respects. Other songs are all equally varied, and almost all perfectly made. 'Sex' is a dance-orientated number; 'Rock-A-Boy-Blue' features a great double bass solo following Green's musings on pop, as well as a terrible edit; and Gettin' Havin' and Holdin'' is a leaf out of the lovers rock book, slow, smooth and decidely off-beat.

The numbers already familiar with some people are 'Lions After Slumber', in this case the 12" version, 'Faithless' and the albums finale, 'The "Sweetest Girls"', those three adding up 17 minutes playing time. Any record that can start with something as wonderful as 'Asylums In Jerusalem' and end with 'The "Sweetest Girls"', yet manage to keep the interest all the way through, has to be something special. In fact, I'd sooner the music papers stopped trying to adopt Green as their own little hero, and gave the group alot more space to appeal to Radio 2 listeners, soul-boys, the down-and-outs, and the well off businessmen. Music like this really shouldn't just be appealing to the hip readership of the music press, but should be accepted as high quality sounds that will mean something to anyone.

Person-all

Talking of which, the lyrical content seems very personal, in fact quite hard to get into.

'Yeah, they mean a lot to me,' explains Green, 'but they're not actually about any individuals. I mean, there isn't a 'Sweetest Girl', and there wasn't a girl or man in mind in 'Faithless'. It's more just the language, the sort of language one finds in soul or lovers rock records. Though they've obviously got a very personal feel, they're not autobiographical. They are very serious,' he concludes, and laughs while he says it!

Funnily enough it's Matt who very simply and sweetly sums up the songs, saying how 'Noone could have written them without having lived, loved and lost.' This is certainly very true– I can see 'Songs To Remember' providing the soundtrack to quite a few lonely days and nights of regret and sorrow, oneof those great records to be left alone with.

Green: 'The line in "Faithless" about the sweetest boy is a reference to the fact that in this song, I suppose it's the boy who kind of gets his comeuppance from knowing too much to ever be...' Green trails off

while trying to find the right words to convey the emotions felt on songs like his. 'The song's about what a pain in the arse it is to be enlightened! It's lovely to know what's going on, but when you do know, it's a shitty place to live. It makes for a tough life.'

Of course, noone could claim to have had much opportunity to see these songs live....

'Well for a long time, it was a mixture of being nervous about it; there not being a fixed line-up to do it, and then the kind of feeling more recently that it wasn't a hugely necessary thing to put a lot of time and enery into. It would be a better idea to get a whole lot of songs finished, do some more recording, work on some videos, and then ste p out when perhaps we've consolidated. Playing live isn't as important as it used to be for being successful. But we did a Peel session last Saturday and that was such great fun to do, the whole seven of us. We did it effectively live – one take, no practice – and it was something that I'd never experienced before, just to go in there and really enjoy playing.'

So how do you feel now: would you...

'Yeah, yeah, I would like to play live now,' interrupts Green, relaxed and answering my questions before I can ask them. 'But I'm obviously going to be careful about that; we're going to do a bit more recording, plus we've got to decide a bit more about what the future involves as regards companies and publishing, all that crap. Then when that's sorted out, we'll get some more stuff recorded, and maybe if we work fast, and get the second album done before Christmas, then'll be time then.'

Well Green, do you ever see yourselves as being the next big thing?

'Yeah! In an impeccably classy way, definitely, Particularly after doing this Peel session.'

Matt: 'I'd never want to be the next month's thing and then it's gone.'

'That definitely won't happen', retorts Green. 'Mainly down to the songwriting, which is quite classy, solid, varied.'

You seem very confident.

'Yeah, for a change!'

'We don't want to just hype ourselves up there', explains Matt. A lot of companies wanted to put The 'Sweetest Girl' out, confident they could make it a big hit. But we sent them away – we weren't interested in all that.'

Ah, talk of hyping. A little chat with Matt when arranging the interview had seen him offer some strange suggestions of promoting a record for the once kings of DIY, so I asked him whether he was definitely going to avoid that.

'Not necessarily, no. I don't disapprove of it morally, or think that it's wicked or evil, but you have to choose the right course for the right time.'

Don't you think it's possible to succeed on talent alone, then?

'I don't think it's impossible, but sometimes you can have talent but not have anywhere to display it.'

We work out exactly what we call hyping, then Matt continues with his explanation.... 'Even if you do give records away like that, all that the companies can really do is get the records into the Top 75, maybe the Top 50, or at a pinch the Top 40, but if people don't like the record, they won't go out and buy it to make that company's money back. More important to most record companies is getting radio play, and though you can buy the producers lunch, you can't buy their airtime.'

Green: 'Records are never going to make it on merit alone; we've established that. There's no way you can make a beautiful record and say 'Come and get it.' You have to actually go out and get people into it.'

THE EXIT

Green sits back contentedly, having pilfered one of my cigarettes, only to meet stern warnings from Matt acting the nanny at his side. Well, do you want to be a pop star, Green?

'Yeah, Yeah.' he sounds a bit lethargical, as though I should have assumed he already is one! 'Not as an end in itself, but as a reflection of interest and popularity, I guess yes, I must admit I'm extremely enthusiastic about it all.'

Enthusiastic must be the word. For all Green's arrogance, all the changes the group have gone through, the annoying fact of always being ultra-hip, the image of this one man 'rediscovering' soul; for all that, Green and Scritti Politti are certainly something to get enthusiastic about. They are pure class, creating true 'music of quality and distinction', and with Green Garfield as songwriter and leader, they could turn into a 'pop' group of the ultimate kind.

Tony Fletcher.

-14-

This piece was originally written as an introduction to an article in the NME that never saw print. Britain's largest selling music weekly had asked Paul for an interview before Christmas, but instead Paul suggested he interviewed the writers and do the piece himself. Unfortunately, despite writing this introduction, Paul didn't have time to finish the article. Therefore, what we've got here does lack a conclusion, but it still throws up many interesting ideas on pop, it's press and the idea of 'stardom'. This is not meant to be a definitive statement, so don't go accepting it just 'coz it's by Paul Weller- that's the attitude the article is largely against. We would really appreciate all comments on this as trying to get further than just listening to music, and actually understanding the reasons for it's existence, is a very difficult and untouched-upon subject. NB - Please remember when reading that this was meant to be in the NME, so certain comments apply to them, not us- AF.

"London, Paris, New York, Munich, everybody talk about - pop music." That's Pop Music spelt S-H-I-T! South Africa, India, South America, Middle East, everybody talk about....

Pop Music - The modern working classes art. Van Gogh, Cazano, Picasso Warhol, the whole of the Tate (half of which is shit), Dickens, Wells, Shaw, Lawrence, Burroughs, Keruac, William Blake, Shelley, Miller and thousands more I can't pronounce, spell or have never heard of.... these artists aren't for you! No, I don't mean you reading this in the 'dorm' (tee-hee), or you the pathetic neurotic struggling student with middle class delusions who regularly write to the NME to "tell them what I think" and believe that there's no such thing as the 'Class system'.

No, I'm talking to you, Joe Bloggs; you the hoddy, you the unemployed 16-year old who buys his piece of middle class (with proletariat sympathies) rubbish every week. No, the afore mentioned artists are for the intellectual public, the educated mass of literate thinkers. Pop music, along with radio, TV, and cinema is your art! All created especially for you. Great eh?

Pop(ular) music is viewed by the select classes as-
a) Cheap and vulgar
b) Mindless entertainment for the mindless working classes, but
c) Very profitable.

Most pop music is cheap and vulgar; a lot of it is fucking mindless; and certainly it is very profitable. Most of the time it stays this way because unlike 'Higher Art', the class that pop music rightfully belongs to and is directed at has no control over it. We have no control over it's media - TV, radio and the music papers - and obviously it's profits. I have actually earned a lot of money out of pop music but it's still nowhere near what record companies, publishers and promoters can earn. Even though since punk we have seen the rise of these people in the independent field (and good luck to you), it's still not enough. There should be a greater liason and structure nationwide for groups to work together. But then again, we are in a very competitive line of art - most groups hate each others guts. The 'Rough Trade' groups hate people like The Jam because they think we are crass because we are signed to a big label (which is a fucking joke!). I hate them because they're so drab and colourless, but I admire their independence. I especially respect groups like Crass who actually live the life and ideals they sing/shout about.

I also love groups like Madness, big label or not (and with little control over their output), because they bring real joy into my heart. I dislike the so-called 'Underground' groups who are happy to belong to an elite section until they realised they weren't getting anywhere, and so opted for the crass, vulgar and mindless pop-kids market(hi Adam, Teardrops, Human League, C.M.D., and a whole lot more):- the music is nice and pleasant, but the about turn in attitudes makes me cringe.

When the obligatory question "Do you think success has changed your ideals or watered them down?" arises, I can quite honestly say no it hasn't. In fact I've grown more idealistic in the last three years than when we first started. When I was 18, all I could think about was becoming famous and a star. Now the thought of stardom makes me feel sick. Pop stars are generally one of the most self-centred, unhealthy, big-headed bunch of wankers around, so why should I wish to be associated with people like that? Look at all the best pop groups - Madness, The Beat, TV21, Department S, etc etc - and you'll find that most of these people love the idea behind pop music, but loathe pop stardom. And quite right too. You can create good pop music, cultural and intelligent; you can get people's minds, feet and imagination going, without resorting to base gimmickry and mindless lyrics.

The pop papers supposedly exist to reflect what is going on in music, to introduce new groups, styles and to expose the musical charlatons. And hear hear I say. But whatever they say they are practically always innacurate, always just that bit too late (look how long it took them to pick up on punk and the Pistols), or otherwise just plain self-indulgent. All the papers are run by old men, certainly compared to their readership. Their criteria is limited and also unobjective.

Some of the writers are very nice people - quite real and honest - but I would say the majority are wankers. A lot worse than the pop stars they write about, and that's saying something! (By the way, It will be interesting to see who slates me/us after this as well!). Some I have met really believe they are something special, that you dear reader rely on them totally to give you the info and views that you desperately need - this is true! They honestly belive they are up there with the Big Cogs of the Wheels of Music. Fucking hilarious, innit?

Paul McCartney Interview PART ONE

'INTERVIEWING PAUL McCARTNEY is not some-something an everyday fanzine writer (or in fact, any journalist) tends to lose much sleep over. I mean, the man doesn't exist! Or if he does, he's protected by millions of bodyguards and is totally in-accessible to his public. WRONG! The Jam and Paul McCartney happened to be record-ing their new albums in the same studio back in January; with gratified help from Paul Weller, an interview with one of the world's most famous people was acquired quite simply - "Sure, do it tomorrow"!

Despite such a healthy start, I thought Paul would still be guarded, untalkative and act the superstar he undeniably is. Instead, I chatted with one of the warmest, most friendly people it's ever been my pleasure to meet. It's very hard to get starstruck with someone like Macca, when he is actually sitting on a sofa right next to you, constantly hitting you to force a point home! We had been warned countless times that Paul doesn't talk about the Beatles, and doesn't allow photos to be taken, yet we did both without any problems, so just for once in our lives we have a bit of an exclusive.

A lot of you might already have seen bits of this three-hour bonanza in the Sunday Mirror, but this is the full interview,

left in the manner it was conducted, as I believe it brings out Paul's character better, as well as explaining some sub-jects a lot clearer. I can't comfess to loving Paul's current material, finding Ebony & Ivory (for example) a sickly song with hopeful but naive lyrics; yet that didn't matter when talking to Paul, because for three hours it was like being in the sixties, talking to an idol who hadn't just been there, but had been responsible for most of what happened then. Many thanks to Macca for being so talkative and open, and be pre-pared for what the man himself described as 'THE PAUL McCARTNEY EPIC'....

DID YOU EVER THINK YOUR LIFE WOULD BE LIKE THIS? WERE YOU VERY AMBITIOUS AT THE START? THINKING "I'M GONNA MAKE IT AS A STAR"?

PM: Oh Yeah! When we were starting out, I remember standing at the bus stop where we used to live in Allerton in Liverpool, and thinking that if I won the pools - which was the only way you were gonna get anywhere - I'd get a house, a car, a guitar and an amp. That was as far as I could see - to me I thought that would cover it.

THERE HADN'T BEEN ANY BIG POP GROUPS AS SUCH TO SET THE WAY, HAD THERE?

PM: Well, The Shadows... but not really that big, no. We always used to have a joke, me and John, saying 'Where are we going?'; 'To the top,Johnny!' It was only a joke at the time, but it set the direction. It channelled our ambitions - 'Yeah, we're gonna do it, we're gonna get there, we're gonna crack America'. The great thing about us was we believed our-selves; we could see that what we were

doing was pretty good, but we never knew if it would succeed everywhere. We liked it, it's just we never knew if everyone else would like it.

SO HOW DO YOU FEEL NOW? DO YOU SIT BACK AND THINK 'CHRIST - DID THAT REALLY HAPPEN?'

PM: Yeah, I do sometimes. But then I'm still the ongoing story. Generally, I think its amazing, I can't believe the success we've had. But for me, I don't sort of sit around as though it's finished, I still think it's going on - even if it isn't. At seventy I think I'll stick the same way. I never really stop to look at it all - I haven't even got a record collection of The Beatles. I think sometimes I must be mad - why didn't I just buy a copy of every one as it came out and keep it?

DIDN'T YOU GET GIVEN THEM?

Yeah, I think you got one free one. I think that's all that engineers and

producers ever used to get off the record company - a straight salary plus one free record. If you look at EMI's figures and tally it up with The Beatles sales, the company suddenly balloons like mad; and when the Beatles split it suddenly takes a dive. But yeah, it's pretty crazy. It's that.... being Paul McCartney. I've always said in all the interviews that I feel about the same as I did when I was five. Inside I feel the same. I've grown up, and all these amazing things have happened around me, and to me, but it still feels like the same little fellow inside me!

I TAKE IT YOU ALWAYS WANTED TO BE FAMOUS? BUT DID YOU EVER WANT TO BE A GOD? WHICH IS WHAT YOU ARE., OR AT LEAST WERE?

No. You never think of that, do you? That's the trouble with all famous people: you've got your dreams of a car, a house, guitar - ooh! - but you forget about things like the press. You forget about people who automatically think they can take photos of you, or come up to you, and ask for your autograph. The thing is

-17-

though, that I was the kid outside the stage door. I used to hang around outside the Liverpool Empire, when I was about 12 with short trousers (in those days you didn't get long trousers 'till you were about 14), and I remember getting the autographs of the Crewcuts - this American group - and I was just knocked out, 'cos they were great fellas and didn't tell us to piss off or anything. So I've always tried to be like that with fans, with people, try and realise that they don't mean you any harm; it's just they freak out when they see someone famous.

DOES THAT EVER GET TOO MUCH?

It does sometimes, yeah. Like the other day, that thing in the Daily Star: I was just walking in to the studio, and there was a fellow there who was obviously going to take a photo; but as I didn't feel like having my photo taken, I just turned my back on him to make it obvious. He said 'What's all this? Hang on!' and I thought 'If he's cool, I'll turn round and he'll be alright; but if he's not, if he's a journalist, he'll be snapping away.' So I turned round and he was; I just turned towards him, blocking his lens, and pushed him over...

WAS HIS CAMERA SMASHED?

No, no, nothing! But then he goes down to the editor, who says 'Oh this is good, somebody famous pushes a poor photographer over. Now, what happened - did he punch and kick you? Well, we'll stick in "punched" and "kicked" anyway.' So it looks like I'm going round laying out photographers, and people are saying "This is really great for your image!" (laughs). But that's the kind of game you get involved in - there is a down side to fame.

WOULD YOU RECOMMEND TO OTHER PEOPLE TO WANT TO BE THAT FAMOUS?

I think it's okay to be that famous, but I think you've got to watch out for the things I'm talking about, because I think of the kind of people it freaks out - like Marilyn Monroe or whatever. A woman who's known for her beauty... when she starts to get old, she can't hold onto it, and the papers start saying this, and people start saying that, and it gets to her head. 'Cos till then, she's only been coping with being beautiful and famous, but now she's coping with being ugly. You have to be ready for that kind of thing; the pressures are immense. (Laughs). No, it's not that bad; there may be down sides, but really there's a lot of advantages to it.

YOU LOOK BACK ON IT ALL WITH A SMILE ON YOUR FACE?

Oh, yeah. I think it's great, absolutely. The advice is just to watch out for all the snakes ready to bite you and all that stuff, but as long as you keep your head..

IT'S NOT JUST ALL THAT FAME WITH THE BEATLES? BUT THE FACT THAT - OFFICIALLY - YOU'RE THE MOST SUCCESSFUL SONGWRITER IN THE HISTORY OF THE WORLD.

Well I don't know if that's true. But if it _is_, then that's great. Because that's the kind of thing that you are working towards; even when you're 15, you think 'I wish I could write a few songs.' So somebody telling me I'm the one who's done it most in the world is a slight freak-out, because... in fact, what it is is I don't really believe it like other people do. I can't take all that in. I just think 'Yeah, I'm winning. This is great, I'm getting what I wanted - prizes, rewards - and I'm chuffed. I don't really take it in. I do sometimes think 'Wait a minute, I must have been pushing pretty hard to get this far.'

YOU WERE IN THE FIRST GENERATION OF BRITISH TEENAGERS TO BE AFFECTED BY ROCK'N'ROLL, AND I WAS WONDERING IF THAT MIGHT HAVE AFFECTED WHAT MADE THE BEATLES. FOR ME, ALL I CAN REMEMBER ABOUT THE BEATLES IS 'LET IT BE' (THE LAST SINGLE) ON TOP OF THE POPS, BUT FOR YOU, IT MUST HAVE BEEN REALLY EXCITING, BECAUSE ONE MINUTE THERE WAS NO ROCK'N'ROLL, THEN THE NEXT MINUTE IT WAS THERE.

It was exciting, yeah. It was amazing. 'Till then it had been pretty slushy, you know - 'hits' and 'pop', Frank Ifield kind of stuff - then suddenly instead of hearing records you quite liked and tapped your feet along to, you were hearing records where your spine was going tingly. _That_ was the difference. But I suppose it'sthe same now - you must get that.

YEAH, BUT THE MUSIC HAS ALWAYS BEEN THERE FOR ME.

I see what you're saying; you're probably right - coming out of _nothing_. The nearest was just sort of Johnny Ray, Frank Sinatra, the girls would swoon over that, they were called bobby-soxers. But that wasn't our generation, that was people just a bit older than us. And then suddenly - for me - it was just seeing a pic of Elvis in the paper, a little ad in the NME saying 'Heartbreak Hotel'. All the kids in our street were going 'Did you see _that_? Who's _that_?'

DID YOUR ELDERS HATE ROCK'N'ROLL, LIKE SAYING 'CHRIST! WHAT IS THIS?'

YEAH! They worried about us all becoming hoodlums. Because 'till then my crowd had been going down the straight and narrow. You'd do reasonably well at your first school, good enough to get to grammar school, then you were going to be trained as teachers or doctors, trying to go down that path. George was like that. But the thing that freaked the parents out was when we started wearing tight trousers and winklepickers, blue suede shoes at school. You'd do your hair up a bit, and they automatically thought you were in a gang, beating people up - they didn't see it as just a fashion. My dad got me a pair of new school trousers, but a mate of mine knew a little tailor where we had them taken in, so I got home and my dad said 'Are those the same trousers you had on this morning?'. 'Yeah, course they are!' We used to have two pairs of trousers and change on the bus. You had to do all that just 'cos you didn't want to get into an argument with them, and you knew that if you were going to a gig or something you didn't want to wear school clothes .

YOU FIRST MET JOHN IN THE QUARRYMEN AT A FETE IN WOOLTON, JULY '57, DIDN'T YOU?

Yeah. A mate of mine at school had said 'Come along and see this group, they're great.' We used to go to the fair together with these great jackets with flaps here, light blue with flecks in them.... 'Whoosh! Sharp!' We really thought that was _it_, go down the fair, just at the age, you know? But I went to see the group, and loved it - it was a young group, instead of dance music. John was obviously leading this thing - he had an acoustic guitar, brown wood with a hole rather an F shape in it, and a bit of a crew cut, with a little quiff, a bit like yours (WOW! - AP.) He didn't know the words for anything, he'd obviously only heard the records and not bought them. But I was pretty impressed. I met up with John backstage in this little church hall, and just picked up his guitar (which I had to play upside down, 'cos I'm left handed), and played 'Twenty Flight Rock'. They were all impressed 'cos I knew all the words, then somebody played the piano, somebody sang 'Long Tall Sally', and later they asked me to join.

AT WHAT POINT - IF THERE WAS ONE - DID IT OCCUR TO YOU AS A GROUP THAT 'THERE'S SOMETHING HERE. WE'RE NOT JUST A BUNCH OF KIDS PLAYING IN THE STREET, THERE MIGHT BE SOMETHING GOOD HERE.'?

At the beginning we didn't really have much faith in ourselves, I don't think. Promoters weren't going particularly mad over us, we were just doing gigs and getting paid. We were always being beaten in talent contests by old ladies with spoons- they ALWAYS turned up! But then in Hamburg we started to learn how to interest the crowd - we had to, 'cos there was no one there to buy beer. On Fridays and Saturdays we started to build up a decent crowd, and then even in the week we started to build it up. And that was the _first_ time people started taking any notice of us, in Hamburg. We got back to England, and though they still weren't paying that much attention to us, we'd learnt our craft a bit better. Then it _really_ started to take off at the Cavern, and we built up a great little audience there. So in Hamburg we clicked, at the Cavern we clicked, but if you want to know when we _knew_ we'd arrived, it was getting in the charts with 'Love Me Do'. That was the one - it gave us somewhere to go.

WHEN YOUR TYPE OF GROUP WAS GOING, IT SEEMS THAT THE AIM WAS TO PLAY EVERY NIGHT - FROM 1960 THROUGH TO ABOUT 1963 YOU MUST HAVE PLAYED AT LEAST 300 GIGS A YEAR. NOWADAYS - I SUPPOSE IT'S JUST CHANGING TIMES - YOU FIND THAT GROUPS DON'T WANT TO PLAY EVERY NIGHT. THERE'S NO POINT, IT'S BETTER JUST DOING ONE GOOD GIG A WEEK. WAS IT SOMETHING YOU ALWAYS WANTED TO DO, SAYING 'WE'VE GOT TO PLAY TONIGHT, WE'VE GOT TO HAVE A GIG?

It wasn't being physically hooked on gigging. It was just we wanted to do it, we wanted to get everywhere, have every newspaper write about us, play every single gig, earn money, get famous. And the way to do it then seemed to be you'd agree to every interview, photo session or gig. But I do remember going up to Brian Epstein one day, after we'd done a TV show called 'Thank Your Lucky Stars', and saying 'Look, we've got to have a holiday, it's going to our heads.' We hadn't had one week off in the whole year. In truth, playing that much, getting that well-oiled - as athletes if nothing else - was probably what pushed us so far. You revved your engine up so much, that when you let them go, you just coasted. Like at Hamburg, I think we often played an 8-hour day! Playing like that you get to have lots of tunes if nothing else. So what we used to do, even on the 8-hour stint, was to try not to repeat any numbers. That was our own little ambition to stop us going round the bend. That gave us millions of songs, though some we could only just get away with - "Dum-da-dum-da-dum-da-dum" for half an hour! We'd shout out a title the Germans couldn't understand to keep ourselves amused, like 'Knickers'! But eventually we built up quite a programme.

Hamburg was a good exercise really in commercialism - a couple of students would stick their heads round the door, and we'd suddenly go into a piece of music that we thought might attract them. If we got people in, they'd pay us better. That club was called the Indra - which is German for India - and we played at that, the Kaiserkeller, The Top Ten and The Star, in that order. We were nicking left, right and centre off other bands there; we'd see something that we'd like, and after they left Hamburg, we'd put it in our set. Well you've got to, haven't you? We used to like going up and watching Tony Sheridan, 'cos he was a little bit of the generation above us; he used to play some blues, real moody stuff. Eventually we built up quite a programme. We could do a lot of American R&B stuff, quite a bit of pop and some

DO YOU ALWAYS WANT TO DO THAT THOUGH?

o, not really, that wasn't the side we
nted to do. But sometimes you were

llads. So if you got stuck in a pub
th a lot of old people, you could
st pull something out of the bag for

DO YOU ALWAYS WANT TO DO THAT THOUGH?

, not really, that wasn't the side we
nted to do. But sometimes you were
uck, so we wanted to be the band that
uld cope with anything.

**THINK OF YOU LOT IN LEATHER JACKETS
D IMAGINE YOU'D HAVE TAKEN THE
TITUDE 'WE'RE GOING TO PLAY WHAT WE
ANT, NOT WHAT THEY WANT'.**

those days, it seemed more
asonable to give them what they wanted.
did ballads anyway, 'cos somebody
ke Gene Vincent would do 'Up A Lazy
ver' or 'Somewhere Over The Rainbow',
d that gave it the authenticity for us
do it. We did a couple of soppy
ings, 'cos girls seemed to like them.
ere was a stage when we got cabaret
ookings, and when people there are
ssed at II.00, you've got to do 'My
ay' or else!

**TOOK FIVE YEARS FOR THE QUARRYMEN/
LVER-BEATLES/BEATLES JUST TO GET A
CORD OUT, WHICH PROBABLY WOULDN'T
PPEN NOW. DO YOU RECKON THAT WAS
OD FOR YOU, THAT YOU REALLY BUILT
UP?**

you're saying that being successful
good, which I would, though it's a
t dubious, then defenitely not getting
record out for five years was good
cause it's what contributed to all
nat. We were so desperate for it when
came, that we really knew what we
nted to get on record. It was such a
rill being let loose in the studio
at we almost OD'd on it! We'd always
nted to be in a studio, and in the end
stopped touring because we loved it
much. Maybe what you're saying,
ough I'd never thought about it, maybe
e reigns being held back for so long,
ant that when they were let go, we had
l that pent up.

**DON'T REALLY THINK GROUPS COULD DO IT
ESE DAYS; YOU MUST HAVE BEEN REALLY
DICATED TO GO THROUGH THOSE FIVE
ARS.**

don't know - I'm not a part of it
ymore. I don't really know how they
it these days. That's the truth, I
n't know what the difference is. I
ways think if there's a good group,
ey will do it the same way as we did.

**OM WHAT I'VE HEARD., HAMBURG WAS A
ETTY ROUGH AREA; WAS THAT AN
PERIENCE FOR YOU, OR DID IT COME MORE
TURAL, BEING FROM LIVERPOOL?**

. Even though we were from
verpool, we thought we were hard, but
weren't. We were pretty sheltered -
ne of us had ever really seen
ostitutes, never really seen strip-
ubs.

D YOU GET INTO RUCKS OR ANYTHING?

u tried not to, but sometimes you
uldn't help it. We'd all been living
home, and then suddenly we were in
is little room with a tiny bed, and
th the bog of this cinema we were at
e back of right next door to us. It
s just four cement walls, and we could
ell the bog of this cinema. It was
rrible, really cold. It must be pretty
milar to under the arches at Charing
ross; it wasn't as bad as that, but for
it was that kind of change. That's
w it started out, but obviously the
commodation got better; as we got a
t wiser, we just asked. At first it
s pretty rough, but it was great!
at more do you want if you're a fella,
d you're I7/I8, down in this dirty
rt of Hamburg with all your hormones
rking correctly, and you're getting
id to be there?! It was great!

**WHAT ABOUT THE CLUBS YOU PLAYED IN -
WERE THEY PRETTY ROUGH?**

They were gangster's clubs. Although we
didn't really know about that, it became
obvious, because they used to use gas-
guns, and they used to fire them off
occasionally. The waiters used to use
them when the customers caused trouble,
as the waiters were all big bruisers.
They were gangsters and all that but
they used to cry - big softies really.
But I find them to be the softest
anyway - the hard nuts. They didn't have
to act that way with us, 'cos we were
just the band; they knew we were a bit
girl's blouses. We didn't get that
involved, though from time to time you
couldn't avoid it.

**ALL THAT LIVING TOGETHER IN HAMBURG
MUST HAVE MADE YOU PRETTY CLOSE?**

Yeah, that's why it was a bit horrible
when we broke up in the end. We had
got tight with each other; that kind of
thing does tend to bring you together.
We'd be in a little Bedford van going up
the motorway in the fog, and the
windscreen would blow out - a stone
would smash it - and it was so freezing
with the windscreen out, that we had to
lie on top of each other, the four of us!
It was the only thing we could do - just
get a body heat sandwich! But you know
each other after that kind of thing. So
it was good that we could take the piss
out of each other, bring each other down
to earth, back to reality. And I think
of all that, when we were really going
as a team...

**WHY DO YOU RECKON IT WAS THE BEATLES
THAT GOT THE SUCCESS?**

I think it was because of all the stuff
we've been talking about. We practiced
up a lot in Hamburg, practiced up a lot
at The Cavern. We became the top group
in Hamburg - or one of the top
contenders anyway - and then got back to
The Cavern and became the top group there.
Gerry And The Pacemakers were our big
worry - were they gonna do better? But
I think it was all the practicising,
all that experience when it came to it.
If you'd had a diabolical night that
might make some other groups split up,
we'd just go - 'Ah sod it!'

**DO YOU THINK IT WAS ANYTHING TO DO WITH
BEING THE RIGHT GROUP IN THE RIGHT PLACE
AT THE RIGHT TIME?**

Yeah, I think it was a lot to do with all
that too. But we made our own luck with
all this stuff I'm talking about. You'd
get all the other groups until our style
of group, and though it wasn't just us,
we had to be in the foreground. Our
stage act was a lot of Shirelles, James
Ray, Larry Williams, Little Richard -
all the black American acts, it was all
their stuff. So that seperated us from
everyone - all the other groups were
doing Roy Orbison, The Shadows, or Cliff.
Then we started off the black polo necks
and suits, instead of ties and stuff. It
was a slightly different look - the hair
was different, brushed forwards. That
look was Astrid's - we saw it in
Germany. One of her mates Jurgend
Wollmer had it, and he and John went
hitch-hiking in Paris one time, when
he had some money. It was his birthday and he had got £100 off one of his
rich aunties. It was unheard of -
£100 in those days! That's the thing
about John - he did have the slightly
more well-off family than any of the
other people - he wasn't particularly
upper-class or anything, but there was
a bit more money in his family, and we'd
occasionally see it in the shape of a
birthday present. So we hitch-hiked
over to Paris, spent the time wandering
about... um, I've lost the track of
where I was there....

IT WAS ABOUT THE HAIRCUT....

Oh yeah. So Jurgen was in Astrid on
that trip - Fuck it, what am I talking
about?! He probably was as well! Sorry
Astrid! Anyway, Jurgen was in Paris on
that trip, and we said 'Do us a favour,
cut our hair like you've cut yours.' So
he did it, and it turned out different,
'cos his wasn't exactly a Beatles cut.
His was a bit like Paul Weller's, but
ours fell into the Beatles thing. We
didn't really start that.

**DID PEOPLE THINK YOU WERE REALLY
ORIGINAL?**

Oh they did. Expecially the British
newspapers. The impression that got over
was that it was just us, that we'd
started it all. We kept saying 'But
there's millions of people in art schools
who look just like this. We're just the
spokesmen for it.'

**YOU SEEMED TO BE TREATED TO AN EXTENT
AS REBELS BY THE PEERS OF THIS COUNTRY.
DID YOU FEEL THAT WAY?**

Yeah. We just spoke out a bit different
to the normal people that had gone before.
Traditionally if you'd asked a showbiz
fella about his views on Vietnam or
something, he'd hedge and say 'Well I
don't really like talking about that.'
We'd just say 'We think it's lousy; the
yanks should get out.' Then it was
'Well... outspoken... look at the hair..
look at the boots...'
    We did have a bit of an effect.
There weren't many people going round
likd us. So we stood out, that was all.
But as you say, we were the first lot
after the war, rock'n'roll and all that
- and it was different. It was
probably the first time anyone had just
owned up to being working class. 'Cause
up 'till then, actors and everyone had
disguised their voices (speaks posh)
'in order to get plenty of work.' They'd
have a nice rounded accent - 'I can go
for Shakespeare, or'(imitates cockney)
'I can do the heavy stuff'.

YOU JUST SAID 'THIS IS WHAT WE ARE'?

Well, there wasn't much choice with us!
We were abit the rebels. And John was
the more rebellious, 'cos he was more
outspoken anyway. I was a little bit
the P.R. man, because I knew somebody
had to take on that role. Plus it was
a bit to do with my family - ours was
like 'Come on in, have a cup of tea.'
Whereas John's upbringing wasn't so
much 'family', though last time I said
that his auntie never forgave me, 'cos
she brought him up, she though she'd
done alright. And she did, she was
great; she's a good skin. But he didn't
have the close family thing, which made
him a different kind of character. I
think the chumminess of my family menat
I took on that sort of role. Now John
was more... An Artist, A Rebel, more
obviously a Brendan Behan, Dylan Thomas
character, saying 'Fuck off! Get out!'.
Which is great 'cos in the end, someone
would do that if it needed saying. It
wasn't always John; George would often
come out with it, or Ringo, or even me.
But if there was a horrible ligger in
the room, it would be John who'd be most
likely to come out with it. Rather than
just saying 'Excuse me', he was a bit
more direct.

**'LOVE ME DO' MADE THE TOP 20, BUT WOULD
I BE RIGHT IN SAYING THAT IN THOSE DAYS,
THERE WASN'T SO MUCH MUSIC, THEREFORE
GETTING TO No.20 DIDN'T REALLY MEAN AS
MUCH?**

No, not really. I think the truth is, if
you got in the charts, in the top 30, no
matter where, it got you noticed. It made
you a chart group. We thought of ourselves as pop stars. You were in the
record business; now you could think about
the future, 'cos now you'd got in and
closed the door behind you. So we took

THE STORY GOES THAT AFTER 'LOVE ME DO', GEORGE MARTIN WANTED YOU TO RECORD 'HOW DO YOU DO IT?' AS THE FOLLOW UP, 'COS IT WAS A DEFINITE No.I: BUT YOU DEMANDED TO DO 'PLEASE PLEASE ME'. WAS IT BECAUSE YOU'D BEEN IN THE CHARTS THAT YOU SAID 'IT'S UP TO US'?

Yeah, we wanted to have the choice. Plus, we thought 'How Do You Do It' (which became a no.I for Gerry & The Pacemakers) was a bit of a cop-out. We had this reputation in Liverpool of being a pretty cool group, doing all this R&B stuff. We used to like playing for the fellas in the audience, 'cos they were the ones watching our fingers to see if we could play. Not putting the girls down, but for them it was all a bit 'Swoon, swoon' and they didn't seem so interested in the music. So we used to play to those hard fellas who actually came up to us afterwards and asked 'What was that chord?'

HOW IMPORTANT WAS GEORGE MARTIN?

He was good. The first time he started to take over was with 'Please Please Me'. John brought it in as a kind of Roy Orbison ballad (sings real slow and soulful... 'Last night I said these words to my girl...boom-boom-boom-boom-boom-boom') and George Martin said, 'Well I think it's too slow, you should whack it up.' We said 'Oh no!'

IT WORKED THOUGH!

It worked. That was him taking control immediately. And then he had a lot of control - we used to record the stuff, and leave him to mix it, pick a single, everything. After a while though, we got so into recording we'd stay behind while he mixed it, watching what he was doing. With the later albums, he started to have less control. But he was always a strong figure in there - he's done the new album. He's good,a technically strong and professional producer who knows what he's doing. Occasionally, we'd overrule him, like on She Loves You, we end on a 6th chord (sings it), a very jazzy sort of thing, and he said 'Oh! You can't do that! A 6th chord? It's too jazzy.' We just said 'No, it's a great hook, we've got to do it.'

WHAT ABOUT GEORGE HARRISON? DID YOU WANT TO KEEP HIM AWAY FROM SONGWRITING?

No, not really. It was just that normally he didn't write songs. He just didn't do it. When we came to do the first LP, we said 'We've got to get George in - he sings too. And Ringo.' Everybody wanted their tracks. So he did 'Chains' & 'Take Good Care Of My Baby' which were in our set.

and then pretty soon after that, John & I wrote him one. Eventually he started coming up with his own songs, but never that many. I don't know whose idea it was, but it soon became established that me and John were the main singers. It was just in as well in a way too because - not putting George down - I think me and John were better singers (laughs). He said modestly!

WERE YOU PLEASED WITH THE SONGS YOU DID THEN, WHEN YOU WROTE THEM? BECAUSE YOU BECAME SO BIG YOU KNEW EACH SINGLE WAS GOING TO BE A No.I, AND IT MUST HAVE BEEN VERY EASY TO STICK TO A FORMULA?

No, from what I remember we were just trying to improve all the time. Trying to get another hit, but trying to do something totally different. I don't think we ever really went for formulas. If you listen to it all it develops; we'd always be trying something different, like a string quartet or something crazy.

I CAN NEVER BELIEVE THAT THE LP 'PLEASE PLEASE ME' WAS RECORDED IN A DAY.

That was great, it was a real buzz. I don't know how it got to be done, or who suggested it, but the reason we could do it - which is something I say to young groups now - was because we knew everything. We'd been playing the songs for months and months and months before getting a record out. So we came into the studio at ten in the morning, started, did one number, had a cup of tea, relaxed, did the next one, a couple of overdubs.... we just worked through them, like the stage act. And by about ten o'clock that night, we'd done 14 songs and we just reeled out of the studios, John clutching his throat tablets!

BUT IT CARRIED ON THAT WAY: 1964-65 YOU WERE DOING WORLD TOURS YET STILL BRINGING OUT TWO LPs, FOUR SINGLES AND A COUPLE OF EPS A YEAR AS WELL AS THE FILMS. ALLTHE OTHERS MUST HAVE BEEN DONE PRETTY QUICK.

We didn't hang about, that's for sure. On this new LP of mine, we've really taken as long as we've liked - over a year - but that's just 'cos I don't feel like rushing it. But in those days, it wasn't a question of not having the time, it just took less time. We'd go in the studio at IC o'clock in the morning, me and John would play the songs through to George, Ringo and George Martin; we'd decide who was going to play what, run it through a couple of times and record it!

WOULD YOU LIKE TO SEE IT GO BACK TO THAT?

I'd like to see me go back to that, let alone music! But you've got to have a group that understands each other to do that. I'm not working as a group now, I'm working with different individual people, so it has to take a bit longer. But yeah I think it would be good, 'cos it's fresh, your ideas are more instant.

YOU MUST HAVE BEEN SELLING A QUITE INCREDIBLE NUMBER OF RECORDS PER YEAR AT YOUR HEIGHT.

Yeah. However it happened, the reasons were we got real practice, we really knew our shit, we knew exactly what we were doing, the effect we were having, we were getting a lot of gigs, working a lot. So there was no reason why it shouldn't work; it all just seemed to fit. As for the record sales - we just kept trying to sell more and more, trying to get another country - get America next! we'd seen all these guys go to America - Cliff and The Shadows etc - and never crack it, so what we did was get rather cheeky. We said 'We won't go to America 'till we've had a no.I', so we just played around Britain and Europe, built it up, until one day we were in Paris when the telegram came - 'You've got a number one!'

THAT MUST HAVE BEEN A BIT AMAZING.

Yeah -everyone leaping about. What we had only dared to think, almost joked about, had happened. And then no one could boo us because we could say 'We're number one.'

It was like being on a kind of yellow brick road; as you went down it, you were looking for fresh things to do. 'Yeah, we'll try that, sure!' 'They want you to pose for the Daily Express wearing these suits; will you do it?' 'Yeah!' We just kept trying everything. One thing that was very different from how it is now for me, is it was very varied. We were used to doing all kinds of stuff in the course of a normal day, - you might go and see a journalist, do an interview, do a photo session with someone; then you might do something that was totally unrelated, like a panel game on telly or judging a beauty contest or something, and then do a gig! We'd do everything - incredible! We must have been really desperate to do well, we must have been trying to prove something to someone!

IS THERE ANY WORD THAT CAN DESCRIBE BEATLEMANIA?

(Long, long, long pause).   Manic..... Crazy. I dunno - any one word isn't enough. For me it was just... buzz might be a word for it. 'Cause it was buzzing. But to me it's a bit of a haze.

THE WHOLE THING ABOUT THE BEATLES IS LIKE NOTHING ELSE IN THE WORLD... WHEN WE WERE COMING UP YESTERDAY ON THE TUBE WE WERE THINKING 'THERE WON'T BE ONE PERSON ON THIS PLATFORM WHO WON'T KNOW WHO PAUL McCARTNEY IS.' MY PARENTS CAN RELATE WORLD-WIDE EVENTS TO WHAT RECORD THE BEATLES HAD OUT AT THAT TIME. THAT SORT OF THING IS UNTHINKABLE FOR ME!

(Laughs). That's crazy, isn't it? I occasionally think things like that, but look at me sitting here - I'm a fella!

I remember we were in Scotland with the kids, and I was lying in some field - as is my wont - and one of the kids, who was very little at the time, said 'Hey dad, you're Paul McCartney, aren't you?' And it brought it home to me - 'Oh yeah!!!!! Sometimes it's like catching yourself in a mirror - WHAT?? But the thing is, it's not really what you think of yourself as. I said to someone the other day, 'I'm normal.' He said 'You're not, you know. Whatever you think, you're not normal.' And that's right, I'm not normal, because to be normal would mean I'd have to do all normal things....

AND YOU CAN'T REALLY CLAIM TO HAVE HAD A NORMAL LIFE.

No I can't. But I thought a better word for it is 'basic'. Not normal,but pretty basic.

(Going a bit over the top here to try and comprehend the Beatles' success) BEATLEMANIA LASTED SOMETHING LIKE FOUR YEARS - '64 THROUGHTO '67 - WHICH IS AS LONG AS GOVERNMENTS LAST, GOING FROM GOOD TO BAD TO GOOD ETC, AND I'M THINKING THAT, JUST IN THE PAST FEW DAYS, YOU'VE HAD YOU FULL PAGE   IN THE DAILY STAR, THERE'S BEEN A PLAY ON THE BEATLES ON RADIO 4, I'M HEARING THE RECORDS ON THE RADIO STILL, READING ABOUT YOUR EXPLOITS IN THE GOSSIP COLUMNS, HEARING THE BEATLES MENTIONED IN ALL TYPES OF INTERVIEWS....

It is incredible...... It must have been about a year before John died that I saw him, after we'd managed to get our relationship cooled out again after all the bitchiness, and he said he'd heard someone say somewhere 'Be careful what you wish for, because it just might come true.' And that's very true in the Beatles case, 'cos we really wished for all of this fame. And you know what? We got it! And it's crazy, because we didn't

MACCA CONT. | ALARM

really think we'd get it. People wish very hard to win the pools, and we wished very hard to be famous. As you say, go down the tube station, and everyone would notice me.

IT'S STILL - JUST TRYING TO EMPHASISE IT - THAT TO SOMEONE LIKE ME WHO NEVER LIVED THROUGH ANY OF THAT, THE BEATLES ARE JUST ABOUT THE BIGGEST THING THAT EVER HAPPENED TO THE HUMAN RACE?

Yeah, it's crazy! I don't believe it. You get that feeling of disbelief, and I'm very similar. It's like, I know it happened, I know we got really famous, and I know, as you say, people will all know who Paul McCartney is. And yet - I don't know why - I'm still working as though I'm trying to make myself more famous! It's crazy, I don't understand it at all. But all I think is 'Well, it's me job.' It's what I ended up doing in life, and I like doing it, so I don't see any reason to stop.

At which the tape-recorder uncannily clicks off, causing Paul to say 'That's not a bad way to end the interview.' I mumble an apology, and produce another C-90 from my bag, knowing we have to continue as We're only on to the mid-sixties. Paul agrees, and a few minutes later the interview is resumed. That will appear in Jamming! 14, covering all the pressures of stardom, Paul's image, the Beatles split, Allen Klein, Apple, Paul's solo music, Shout! and loads, loads more. Yes folks, we too deliberately spread the juicy bits over two issues so that you have to buy both episodes. Don't forget to ask your friendly Jamming! dealer to reserve you a copy of Jamming! no. 14, featuring part 2 of the Paul McCartney Epic!!!!!!!!

A group not interviewed in this ish because they wouldn't have got the space they deserve are THE ALARM. I got to know about them through that almost non-existent method of word-of mouth. Before Christmas, three totally separate people whose opinions I respect told me to look out for their debut single, 'Unsafe Building'. When I got a copy, I knew they were right:- at last, something exciting and meaningful. Now having seen the group 3 times I'm a hardened fan and honsetly think they're the most important group to have come through in years. Their big thing is the use of accoustic guitars, but miked so loud it's deafening - a raw and ready sound a.k.a. early Clash/ SLF. With incredibly dynamic songs in their set such as Marching On, 68 Guns & The Believer, they've rapidly built up a large live following in and around London, & look set for something special.

The group's spokesman Mike Peters, is one of those permanently energetic people with some really exciting andstrong beliefs; in fact, he's largely responsible for getting me to write my statement on page 3. I haven't been so excited by a group in ages, and all I'm saying here is go and see them ("You won't regret it"), and prepare for a proper interview in no. 14.

I suppose it was watching Antonioni's *Blow-Up* too many times as a teenager that drilled into my mind the idea that being a photographer in London was the most desirable form of existence imaginable. I received a 35mm camera for my 18th birthday and, back in the capital after a miserable couple of years living in a bleak mining town, I called Tony from a phone box (miraculously, a working one) and asked him if he needed someone to take photos for *Jamming* – to which I'd long been a loyal subscriber.

To my astonishment, he offered me a chance. It seemed like Real Life was finally about to begin for me.

But I couldn't kid myself: I was no David Hemmings, chatting up a string of dolly birds and leaping casually into expensive, open-topped cars. I couldn't even wear white trousers with the same panache as him.

Worst of all, I was stuck as a shop assistant, which seemed as far from the glamour of a photographer as you could possibly get. I think, though, that I secretly relished the Clark Kent-like dual identity aspect of it all: tedious, slow-moving days spent weighing screws and cutting lengths of chain in an ironmonger's – and then, on the stroke of 5.30, casting off my overall and heading across town to take photos of Pete Wylie or Steve Severin or Lindsay Anderson. Or, on one spectacularly unlikely occasion, Paul McCartney.

Did that really happen?? Well, yes: I still have the photographs to prove it. If not the negatives. These were borrowed and then subsequently "mislaid" by some oaf at the *Sunday Mirror* who were reprinting extracts from the *Jamming* interview. Never got them back; never saw a penny in compensation...

For some reason, Tony kept me on as occasional photographer, despite my regular failings with such basic notions as correct focus and adequate lighting. Alas, by the time I'd improved, the magazine had become slicker and was now able to draw on a wide circle of professionals rather than someone who was considered eligible by the simple act of owning a camera. Still, I continued to write the occasional film, jazz, and/or book-related article through to the bitter end. **Anthony Blampied**

POLAND

TV21 BEHIND THE IRON CURTAIN

by GARY CROWLEY

Another Christmas has gone by and didn't we have a nice time, what with all the booze, food and films on TV? But one country that didn't experience the same happy Christmas was Poland, currently suffering from the results of a military crackdown and everything that goes with it, ie. Martial Law, food shortages and general privation. You just can't avoid hearing about the country, it's people and their plight: reports that Solidarity leaders have been either jailed or put under house arrest; people being detained left, right & centre and placed in special open air camps (I don't have to remind you of the weather, do I?); strikes occuring with army intervention and arrest the outcome; and the Pope has been told to CANCEL his visit. As you can tell everything is NOT hunky-dory.

It's wierd to think of having been in the country only two months ago, when the authorities were actually planning all this, because it was in late October that I visited Poland with that up-&-coming Edinburgh group, TV21. With the trip organised through a man representing the Polish authorities in London (they were planning on bringing over groups like Rudgie & The Englbert, but what with the current situation I would imagine that these visits have been postponed), we arrived at the Warsaw Hotel after a flight which also stopped at the greyer-than-grey East Berlin, an airport with an atmosphere that set the example for the whole trip. Greeted at the hotel by Duffy (TV21's equivalent to Thunderbird's Brains!) and Sheila (their sound engineer and one of the few women in that role), we finally sat down to dinner and were officially welcomed by the organisers of 'Rock Estrada', the title of the tour that was the first ever to be undertaken by an English new wave band.

After the meal (very basic what everyone suffering from the food shortage), the party visited a Warsaw Jazz Club. Yours truly convinced one of the English-speaking organisers that TV21 were in fact a 'rock band working within a jazz format' & would take great pleasure in having a 'jam' with some of their guys. The bloke fell for it and soon TV21 were on stage tearing through a hilarious Pistols-influenced 'Johnny B. Goode' before having the plugs angrily pulled on them and being shown where the door was!

The morning after saw the tour officially begin with the journey to the opening date. Aboard the coach were Poland's premier pop band Crisis Brigade, an interesting bunch who musically resembled The Psychedelic Furs. A good relationship was quickly established (most of them spoke excellent English) - their lyrics were said to be very political, some of them were wanted by the police for draft evasion, while one was even certified insane to a doctor friend to avoid the call-up!

Stavolos was the first date and the audience reaction was similar to a Bay City Rollers concert. From the opening act Steal Baggage (an ageing heavy rock/hippy group gone punk overnight) through Crisis Brigade to TV21, it was fanatical with girls crying amongst continual crowd chanting.

The venue had a 3,000 capacity and as the tour continued we noted many things... The audience reaction was always the same for all three groups - even Steal Baggage who were a walking caricature of a cock-rock band. The audience's average age

-22-

must have been 16-17 but even younger/older attended; their clothes were always very dull while absolutely none of the girls wore make-up (Sheila stuck out in the street like a sore thumb). Very few could speak any English except for yes or no, so communication was down to sign language and much improvisation.

The travelling from town to town was exceptionally tiring; most of us spent the time reading, listening to cassettes and staring out of the window. Observing the countryside was something else - I just couldn't believe the backward agricultural methods still used on the farms and the thatched cottages with their wells in the garden. It all resembled scenes out of 'The Tin Drum'. Another sight which became normal after a while were the petrol queues as long as Blackpool's Golden Mile. The outskirts of the cities were normally full of vast housing estates (numbered in many cases) or factories, some with Solidarity flags flying, indicating that they were on strike or supporting the cause. The exception was the Pope's home town of Kracow, a charming historical town full of churches and tourists. But shops in the other town centres were so unattractive that you could walk past one without realising what it was. Most of them were virtually empty, so with little food came mammoth queues. Despite the shortages, we all ate exceptionally well as TV21 were paid handsomely in Polish money, while playing venues Genesis would play over here (only because there are no clubs in Poland).

The Polish concerts (Gdansk, Lodz, Kotowice) made TV21 work much harder as a group. Soundchecks were absolutely farcical, having to liaison with a PA company who spoke not one word of English, and with musical equipment even Glen Miller would have termed old-fashioned. The group just couldn't help but end up laughing most of the time, except once when the crew attempted to put two PA stacks on a couple of school desks, which even I could've blown over! Poor Duffy must have developed a string of ulcers after all he went through.

Live, the group were at a peak for me, working much harder than ever before, because they knew the Poles appreciated the energy. The last performance in Warsaw was worth the whole trip alone, performing at one of the top theatres (The Stones played there in 1966). The atmosphere was electric, and despite the handicap of it being an all-seater with a heavy police presence, the audience danced from beginning to end. TV21 capped it all by declaring it 'the best concert' they'd ever played.

Afterwards farewells were bid to Crisis Brigade and (even) Steal Baggage, plus some of the cantankerous old scruff's who organised the tour. We returned to the hotel for a meal then bed, rising at 4 O'Clock in the morning, we packed our cases and walked through dark, deserted Warsaw where we caught the bus which began our journey home.

Poland was an experience to say the least, one which I found very worthwhile, and I know the boys in TV21 feel the same. Some of the atrocities happening there now were obviously being planned when we were over (and it's very unnerving thinking of it), but here's hoping the country sorts itself out and the butchery and injustices stop. Here's for 'Solidarity' among the Polish people.

Tony's story wasn't too dissimilar to mine. Fired up by the burgeoning London punk/new wave scene of 1977, he too wanted to play a role, be a part of it somehow, and one way to do that was to start your own fanzine.

Jamming!, though, was everything my fanzine – *The Modern World* – would love to have been. It evolved from a simple, passionate black and white punk zine into a cool, passionate music magazine and was a must read for me and my pals. *Jamming!* was chock-a-block with interviews with Paul Weller and The Jam, The Smiths, The Beat, and Echo & The Bunnymen, among countless others, and of course there were those famous scoops with Macca and Pete Townshend, but what I loved most was the youthful energy that jumped out from its pages. When I was lucky enough to travel with TV21 to Poland, then behind the Iron Curtain, *Jamming!* was the magazine that sought a piece from me. After that, I was invited to write a couple of columns, too.

Looking back, it really was an eclectic, exciting time. And thankfully Tony and his merry band of Jammites were there to document it. **Gary Crowley**

STATE OF THE STATES

In 1976, music from America was a musical influence for the people who created punk. The Ramones, New York Dolls, Talking Heads, Patti Smith and others were all pretty unrelated but did have some sort of effect on England. Over the last few years this has all changed round, and the eighties so far have seen a new generation of group on the east coast, a massive HardCore scene on the west, and now even some interesting groups emerging from the vast mass of mid-US. The fanzines marketthere has also taken off healthily, and as Jamming! is getting a lot of material from the States, it seemed worth donating a page or two to the situation there.

REACH OUT INTERNATIONAL RECORDS (ROIR) is a cassette-only label releasing well-packaged albums of historical, if not artistic, importance. For example, they've put out possibly the first ever recordings of the NEW YORK DOLLS, an

album of various unreleased SUICIDE material, and a live recording of a DICTATORS reunion, three influential acts from NY. One of their more recent releases is a useful monument to what hit the West Coast:- 'Germicide' by THE GERMS is a live recording of a terrible group who couldn't play doing their third ever gig. So what? Well, The Germs were the first and most popular of the LA/San Francisco groups that have developed into Hard Core, while Darby Crash, their lead singer, died of a heroin overdose last year. The tape is worth nothing musically, but anybody involved in the California punk scene, will tell you The Germs were 'it'.

However, it's the DEAD KENNEDYS who made the impact in Britain. Jello Biafra, as you will know from the interview in Jamming! II, is an extremely intelligent and aware person full of energy, and the DKs have released some great material- powerful but with some special ingredient. Jello is a creative enough man to have set up a branch of their 'ALTERNATIVE TENTACLES' over here, which is now putting out US groups. But something has gone wrong...

It's not really surprising that the California punk scene should have been so violent, both musically and physically: to create change in the land of laid-back hippies, something totally chaotic had to come along. The sad thing is that nobody seems to have developed from this. Worst of all, that West Coast HC has now influenced British kids, via new punk etc, when they'd only taken their influences from what happened here five-six years ago any-

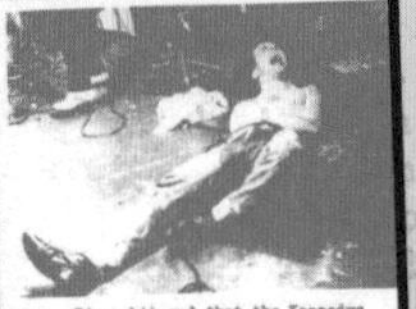

way. I'm a bit sad that the Kennedys last record-'In God We Trust Inc.' - was more basic than anything they'd previously done, as Jello seemed the man likely to take American punk a long way, rather than keeping it within it's own confines. However, the West Coast has produced some pretty exciting music, including 'Let Them Eat Jellybeans', the US compilation on Alternative Tentacles, which was a fine record full of promise and hope. But possibly a better introduction to the HC scene is a cassette entitled 'The Future Looks Bright Ahead'. It contains some really powerful yet accessible groups like SHATTERED FAITH, TSOL, SOCIAL DISTORTION, CH3 and SACCHARINE TRUST. It also contains the three tracks by BLACK FLAG that were released as an EP here by AI-'Six-Pack', 'I've heard It All Before' and 'American Waste'. Black Flag are certainly the biggest of all the HC groups on the West Coast, but don't seem to have the charisma of a Jello (or his intelligent lyrics) to take them any further.

Although the two aforementioned compilations are both well worth getting a lot of crap seems to be emerging from the West Coast as well - MAD SOCIETY might well have a cute II-year old Adam Ant clone as their frontman, but it would help if they were doing something

worthwhile, so forget their 5-track, 5-minute EP if you bump into it. Again I don't see any point in PLAIN JANE & THE JOKES20 minute LP, 'The Joke's on You'. All this horrible noise.. if you need to be loud and energetic, at least make it worthwhile like The Pistols, Clash or Damned did.

From further up the coast comes DOA - two of the tracks on their 5-song Alternative Tentacles EP, plus the one on 'Jellybeans' were reviewed in our last issue as being from their 'Something Better Change LP' so as you can see we can be the first with the news sometimes. Also-on Alternative Tentacles is a solo I2" by DK KLAUS FLUORIDE. Though I'm hoping the next DK LP (out in August, only 20 months after their first) will be more advanced, if it contains the boring electronics of 'Shortnin Bread' and 'The Drowning Cowboy', I won't be the only one giving it a miss.

The State of the American (ch) Arts

I know, I know, the American charts are pathetic, absurd, boring, predictable and caught in a time warp. All too true. To draw parallels between British and American music charts is ludicrous: just consider the size of Britain-about half that of California.

The U.S is so huge and before a record can chart, it must have achieved popularity in all those states between the coasts. When you consider the environment of such places (eg. Arizona, Nebraska, Missouri Alabama etc,) it becomes painfully clear that any diversion from Foreigner and Rush would bestotally anarchistic act. So when Blondie and Joe Jackson made the charts it was a real triumph!

Take California. Once outside of L.A. or San Francisco any 'new wave' music is considered punk, and is therfore subject to much jeering and insults, and sometimes threats of violence. And this is in 'liberal' California.

It's still hopelessly backwards here; there's no hope of ever hearing Radio I type music here, it's labelled 'underground'. Adam and the Ants aren't a pop band here, they're a cult band still outside the norm, while The Jam are unheard of on AM radio(and have only scratched the surface on FM).

The only beam of light is the college 'alternative' radio, of which there are about three in my area. College student D.J.'s do their own programming (along similar lines as your pirates, only legal). Frequently it gets a bit avant-garde but still beats any other form of radio. These stations don't have strong signals so they're hard to pick up, but it is the only way of hearing new British (and American) bands.

After racking my brain I have managed to come up with a few advantages. Since British chart music is still considered too strange for the mundane American palette, this makes for a smaller faction that actually follow it, (a definite effort is needed to have access to alot of records, especially indie singles). This brings me to a rather pleasant side effect: smaller venues and cheaper ticket prices. I recently saw Au Pairs at a revamped movie house: It wasn't even half full at the reasonable $5.00 admission. The Stray Cats and Stiff Little Fingers recently played the Old Waldorf (as have countless others), which is about the size of the Marquee. So in this aspect it may be just as well to keep the 'good' music out of the charts; mass success does tend to spoil the fun but it must be frustrating for the bands trying to break the States. It should no longer be a concern.

However, there's another side of the coin. With such a self-enclosed scene there tends to be a great deal of competition and elitism with-in it. With imported records being stocked in very limited numbers it often means a lot of people cannot buy what they want. The lucky few who either work or live in record stores jump on every shipment, and there is much snobbery when it comes to knowing every obscure little record on every one-shot label. So the scene does tend to be an elitist one that seems futile (and expensive) to compete with.

It's a sad state of affairs when local bands are unable to find venues to play in their own areas because out-of-town bands are being consistently booked for whatever price they ask. Perhaps one of the reasons for a lack of new American bands is that they are not being supported in their own community - for a local scene to thrive, there has to be more than one club willing to give a new band a chance.

Basically I view the music business as being interested in one thing; a well padded wallet. They want instant success, and don't feel it's worth their time or ample money to push alternative music (especially when the 'safe' crap is still selling in gold and platinum). Despite what a lot of Britishers say, your music scene is a healthy one by comparison. Enjoy it! - you could be here....

KIM WONDERLY

-26-

A couple more examples of HC, but this time from the East Coast, are again on ROIR. The BAD BRAINSsound like a typical thrash until they break into reggae songs and a photo of them reveals five rastas!

The idea seems quite funny (the difference between HC and reggae is pretty wide), and it would be good to see how they'd go down in California, home of nazi punks, but I did read in some fanzine that in fact they started playing hardcore as a joke, only they had it so off to a tee that they're a big success! The STIMULATORS are all young and apparently big news in the NY HC scene, and their live tape is of good quality musically, showing a lot of talent and energy that could see them get acclaim elsewhere.

Generally however, New York and the East Coast is the home of more arty music; asit's 3,000 miles nearer Britain than California, ideas swapacross the Atlantic a lot quicker. DON'T FALL OFF THE MOUNTAIN is the record label releasing the East Coast product both there and over here, and because of the wider musical range, I've reviewed the DEL-BYZANTEENS LP along with the WAITRESSES one, separately. Also on DFOTM is a I2" EP by BALLISTIC KISSES, a vaguely funky record that is likely to be picked up on by 'interested' people, but not to create

that much of a buzz. Which also goes for The BLACKOUTS single, out here on Situation 2, which is so heavily influenced by PIL it could pass for the real thing, and an album by and called SONIC YOUTH, which is dark though not too depressing. TV TOY have been going for years now - it was in 1979 we were presented with 20 copies of their first single - and their recent EP, 'Building with Assurance' is a very nicely packaged affair. It contains four tracks, of which the last, 'Steady Job', is the best, similar in some respects to Ballistic Kisses, ie. repetitive lyrics that wind into your memory with a fast tune to make the whole song very interesting. Once again we've got copies to give away - see page 2 for more details.

The West Coast scene is well-known, the East Coast one doesn't really exist; so what about that large space inbetween? Well it's that that made me do this article, because in the fortnight before going to press, we received five independent records - not HC - from that vast area, and although the quality is not yet particularly original, it seems pretty obvious that people are actually giving a v-sign to the large labels and doing things themselves...

The EFFIGIES come from Illinois, and are loud and fast but sensible with it. Their single is nicely packaged, featuring 'Security' and 'Bodybag', and though, like a lot of the other US new breed, they've got a long way to go before they get great, they've got their sights on it. The same probably applies to B-TEAM, who, like the title 'What Is This?' suggests, are well into Killing Joke. Actually, they come from San Fran., but it seemed better to mention them here as they're not part of the HC scene. THE C-NTS might have a 'slightly' punky name, but their music is in fact more reminiscent of heavy metal. It falls short enough to be enjoyable, but not to be memorable. THE HATES from Texas, don't seem to have much to offer musically, and with titles like 'All The Whites Are Going Negro', I'm not sure of their ideas either. START, from the vast depths of Kansas, are reasonably poppy, but I'm quite into what they've put down as the b-side, '(No More) Living In The Past'. I really hadn't thought states like Kansas could produce people who'd make their own moves, so all congratulations.

Possibly the best of these self-financed records comes from Canada actually: reviewed because Winnipeg is not particularly near anywhere except the border with the USA. The DUB RIFLES 5-track EP has a couple of good, dynamic songs in 'Production Of Funds' and 'Delicate Action' featuring saxes and good tunes, but it's still not earth-shattering (perhaps the West Coast is being sensible by causing a real explosion that people either love or hate). I'd also like to give favourable mentions of cassettes I received from WEDNESDAY WHERE NOTHING HAPPENS (friends of the Rifles) and the 4 IMPOSTERS, both groups sounding rather English, the former just in overall sound, the latter with defenite Buzzcocks undertones.

Vital to the blossoming American music scene are the fanzines. Without doubt the best and biggest(forgetting ones that have gone big business) is FLIPSIDE. The poor thing is currently only up to no.32 (!), coming out about every six weeks with around 50 packed out pages on all that's happening on the West Coast, as well as reports from throughout the world. It's team are extremely committed and together, and although most of the interviews with local groups are incredibley similar

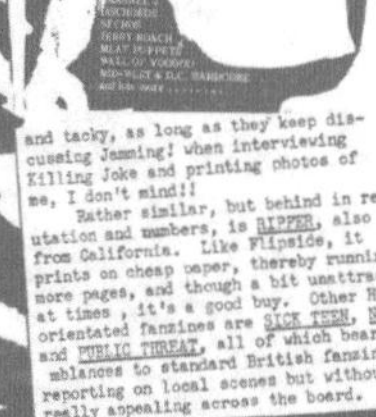

and tacky, as long as they keep discussing Jamming! when interviewing Killing Joke and printing photos of me, I don't mind!!

Rather similar, but behind in reputation and numbers, is RIPPER, also from California. Like Flipside, it prints on cheap paper, thereby running more pages, and though a bit unattractive at times, it's a good buy. Other HC orientated fanzines are SICK TEEN, NOISE, and PUBLIC THREAT, all of which bear resmblances to standard British fanzines, reporting on local scenes but without really appealing across the board.

America is largely the country of mail-art, and alongside many one/two pagers like SHORT NEWS, 2NE, EAR OF THE KAT and BE MY FRIEND are more provocative productions, such as BACK TO WAR, a great combination of imagery, poems and writing on a certain subject, much like what THE VALIUM ADDICT & PROPERGANDER try to do about life in general. These type of mags are generally a pleasure to be sent, and exist by the hundreds all over the States - the underground exists by post, with loads of pe ple on loads of mailing lists.

The OFFENSE is a long-running fanzine from Ohio that reviews more or less every British record it can get it's hand on (as well as quite a few American ones) and seems to print every letter it getsas well. A strange way of doing things, and somewhat intellectual at time but certainly a good read. Much the same can be said for THE COOLEST RETARD, a very good fanzine which I haven't seen for a while.

Stepping over the border into Canada, SCHRIK is a well-written though badly presented fanzine that's coming along nicely. It does alot to promote Toronto's music scene (which has a group called L'ETRANGER who sound most interesting) and if it could clear up it's layout would probably become the Flipside of Canada.

So that's it. As you can see the United States might still be dominated by crap in the charts (though the Go-Go's were one of the original West Coast punk groups) but all over the continent people are going out and doing something. When you consider that the product we're getting sent must just be the tip of an iceberg, the next few years coul see a large change for the better.

Useful addresses and costs -
(send US money if possible)
ROIR - 6II Broadway, Suite 2I4, New York NY I00I. All tapes £5 inc. p&p (a bit dear)
Alternative Tentacles - 49-53 Kensington Gardens Square, London W2 or PO Box II458, San Francisco, CA 94I0I, USA .
The Future Looks Bright Ahead available for £4 inc. p&p from Posh Boy, PO Box 3886I, LA, Ca 90038. (well worth it)
TV Toy - 70 Liberty Street, Dover, NJ 0780I,
Effefies - PO Box I458, Evanston, III. 60204-I4.
B-Team - 2642 22nd Ave, SF, Ca. 94II6.
Cunts - PO Box II463, Chicago, Ill. 606II
Start - I22I W. I9th Terrace, Lawrence, K 66044
Dub Rifles - PO Box 547, Wpg. gen. p.o., Winnipeg Canada R3C
Wednesday Where Nothing Happens/So Alone fanzine - 2I2 Parkville Bay, Winnipeg , Canada R2M
(Send £1.20 + 70p p&p for any singles).
Flipside fanzine - PO Box 363, Whittier,C 90608.
Ripper - I494 Teresita Drive, San Jose, C 95I29. 40p
Back To War - PO Box 26643 Dallas, Texas 75226. 40p
The Valium Addict - 424E 82nd St, NYC I0028 Free.
Propergander - PO Box I4846, MN USA 55414 40p?
The Offense - I535 N. High St, Columbus, Ohio 4320I, 80p.
The Coolest Retard - 2042 N Bissell, Chic III 60614. 45p
Schrik - 34 Longford Crescent, Agincourt, Ontario.
(send 60p&p each fanzine)

AF

-27-

BLUEBELLS BLUEBELLS BLUEBELLS

BLUEBELLS BLUEBELLS BLUEBELLS BLUEBELLS BLUEBELLS BLUEBELLS

Like it or not, fantastic/happy/birth/day is all the rage and while Altered Images and Haircut IOO have been the sweeping success stories of last year, there's been a more modest interest in five jock rockers who go by the proud name of the Bluebells. Bobby Bluebell (vcls/gtr) explained how things have changed for the group from being one of the acts on Postcard, the cult independent label, to being involved in the procedure of picking a major record company of their choice. Why the interest? Well maybe because they've recently supported both of the above mentioned groups, maybe because they impressed head haircut Hayward enough to want to write a song with them, and maybe because Elvis Costello believed in them enough to produce their next single "Everybody's Somebody's Fool". When I saw them they impressed me with their own instant but not disposable brand of three minute pop songs. My only doubt was whether they'd join Claire and Coco the Clown Nick Hayward in the more-grinning-then-singing brigade. After all, do we really need just another disposable pop group, no matter how good they are?

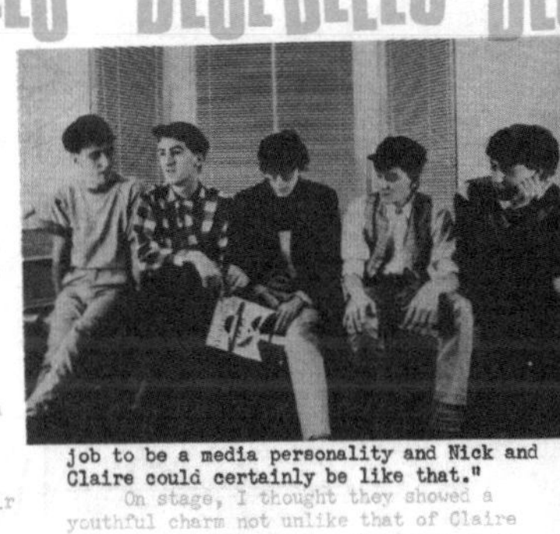

"That's the whole point though: we're not disposable pop music like Chas'n'Dave or DepecheMode," replies Bobby. "You see, if you write a good song and it coincides with someone's thoughts on a certain day, then that's going to last forever. Have you ever heard Simon Bates' radio programme, where folk write in and say play this record because it means so much, well they are just those type of records. I bet you've got records at home that you absolutely love, and it doesn't mean they're great songs but because of the day you heard it, they're the ones that are going to last."

Fair enough, but I wonder if the mass consumer appeal of groups like Haircut will make their records last?

"No one's going to know for another twenty years. Haircut IOO and Altered Images might 'cos Nick's dead charming and so is Claire. People like Lulu haven't got any talent but they last forever because people get to accept their faces and feel comfortable with them. It's their job to be a media personality and Nick and Claire could certainly be like that."

On stage, I thought they showed a youthful charm not unlike that of Claire and company, but whereas she drove me to irritation with her giggles and graces, the Bluebells warmed with their more restrained approach. Does Bobby Bluebell see themselves alongside those other groups as the so called 'new face of pop'?

"No. It's just that all these groups, and Orange Juice and the Jam are all really conventional with guitars, bass and drum and songs with a verse and chorus so we're not going to get it much past that. If they call us the new face of pop, I think it's better than being called the old face because you've got to keep things changing. You can't have things like the Who lasting for twenty-six years. I don't mind if in two years time people don't remember us because they'll have the records in their collection and in ten years time maybe people will appreciate them again. You should never consider the things you do for fun as a job but when you've been going for five or ten years that's what it becomes. If in two years time we've had a good laugh, made good records and had a bit of success, that's made it worthwhile hasn't it?"

So why do you think people compare you to Altered Images and Haircut IOO?

"I always thought people would think of us as neds or Johnny-come-latelys, and

-7-

dead sort of smarmy and confident, hoping that we'd fall flat on our faces."

But maybe that's also because when they hear you're a poppy Merseybeatish group who've supported two well known bands and have Costello producing your single, then they're going to think that you're just another manufactured group geared to making money out of mass trash music.

"There's nothing I can do about that. I care what people think about us, but not that much if they think the worst of us because it's so superficial. You're stupid to ignore what people say but you're stupid to think it's all that important. They can think what they want. This guy said that our songs were magical and naive - I think we're naive and that's a good word for us at the moment. All I can say is I think of music as good and bad, and songs as good and bad, and we're a good group with good songs, and when we start having bad songs we'll be a bad group but when that day comes we'll give up."

Music as good and bad, but maybe music can change things as well?

"Punk reflected change rather than created it and that's all that music can do: reflect things. Dexys and Kevin Rowland are the only ones that can possibly change the future of music because he doesn't want to do anything that's sort of conventional."

But you want to be conventional so aren't you just praising one thing and doing another?

"I'm not embarrassed or uptight about being conventional. I'm in it for altruistic reasons; he's in it for personal ones. You can praise something and not necessarily want to do it. He's really sincere but so am I too. I couldn't imagine him writing throwaway pop song because he'd be too embarassed, though he could probably write a great one. Look at Paul Weller: he's embarrassed by some of his songs which is really silly. He shouldn't write them or put them out if he's embarrassed about them - that's a shame because I think something like 'Boy About Town' is a great song."

So what type of people will like your songs. The same audience as Haircut have found perhaps?

"Ay, and other people too like Chris Burkham, Gary Kemp, Kevin Rowland, Weller, Bananarama.... folk that normally wouldn't like Haircut, if you see what I mean. I find it very important that my mum likes my songs too. Like my father and Russel's (gtr) father especially listened to everything like that for a long time, and what they remember are the classic songs, so if we can write a song and they think it's quite good, then that's a real compliment."

But why do you think the Kemps and Rowlands of this world might like you?

"Because sincerity's a big difference and we're not sort of namby-pamby."

Haven't people accused you of being namby-pamby though?

"Once they scratch the surface with us there's more there, but you do that with those other groups and you won't find anything more substantial."

Whereas Haircut have always meant pleasant music but nothing more, the Bluebells impressed me by being never flash though never trash. Pop music to me has always been absorbing though never demandingly difficult to follow, and has thrived on simplicity rather than languishing in it... a sort of pop sensibility you might say...

"That's funny because we've got this far by not thinking about what we've done, which is good 'cos I really resent that. You just do it and be what you are. If it's good enough it's good enough and if it's not too bad. It's awfully silly to go away and start planning what to wear. But people should make up their own minds and think for themselves. I'm not going to go on stage and say I'm dressed like this to reflect the new hedonism or glamour of the age. That's the trouble with groups like Haircut:- they're really superficial, I'm not."

byPedro

REMEMBER

PETE WYLEY, Walton, student: Before the punk thing got going I just hated the rock scene. It was a drag going to concerts. I went to see Supertramp and I just sat there, nothing happened, it was just like listening to an album.

But I went to see the Pistols and they were great. Johnny Rotten was great, y'know the music wasn't particularly educating, but it was just a great laugh to leap around to.

I saw them at Eric's. It's getting OK in Liverpool now, I wish more people would go to Eric's because otherwise it'll have to stop if they don't make the money. Racing Cars were on on Saturday and that was good, loads of people turned up.

Not enough of the big tours come to Liverpool — it seems to be just London, Manchester, Glasgow and Birmingham.

Manchester isn't so bad if you've got some money, but when I was at school I was skint, I couldn't go to Manchester.

I think all the records by the Pistols and Damned are great. In fact the records are better 'cos I went to hear the Damned and you couldn't hear Dave Vanian. It was great to see them though, and to talk to them afterwards...

Pete Wyley

Now would we stoop to the depths of running a Blackmail Corner? Would we? No, 'course not. We just just found these clippings & thought you might like to see them. Above, from National Rock Star Jan '77; right, first Questions single, 1978-79, called 'Some Other Guy'/'Rock'n'Roll Eight Days'.

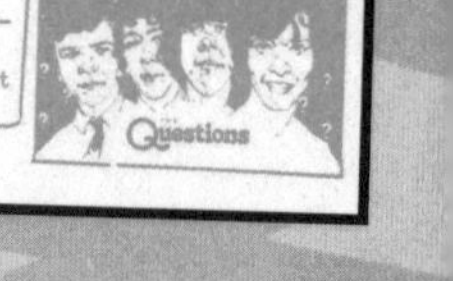

-8-

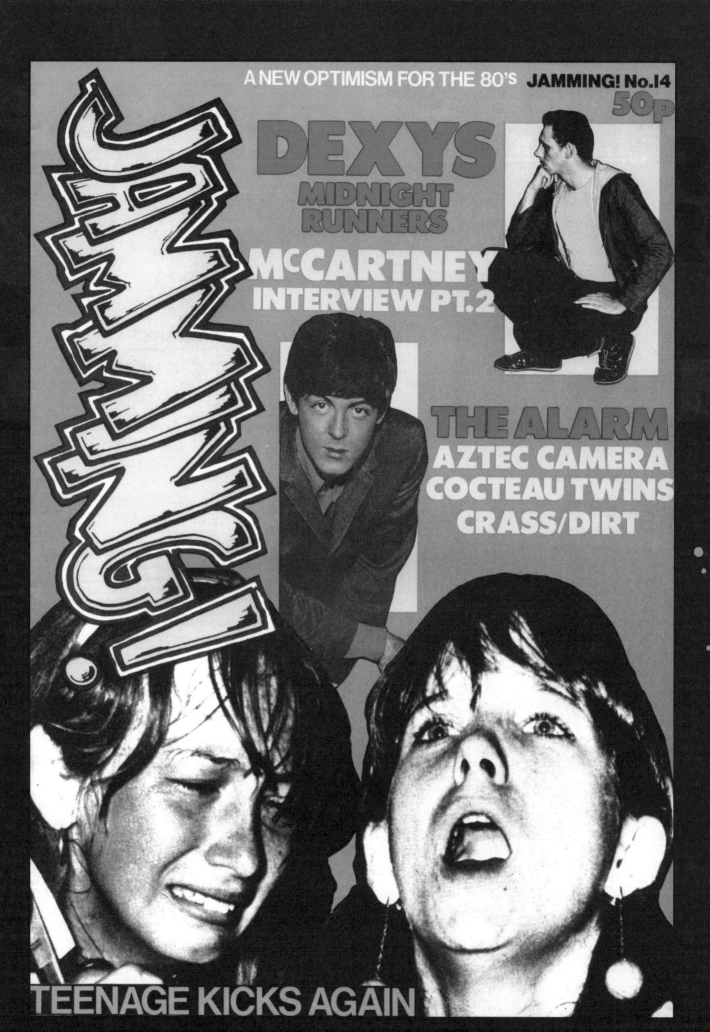

A NEW OPTIMISM FOR THE 80's **JAMMING! No.14**

50p

JAMMING!

DEXYS
MIDNIGHT RUNNERS

McCARTNEY
INTERVIEW PT.2

THE ALARM
AZTEC CAMERA
COCTEAU TWINS
CRASS/DIRT

TEENAGE KICKS AGAIN

The he delays between issues are almost as exhausting to describe in the 2020s as they were to live through in the 1980s. Through the rest of 1982, Jamming! Records continued to require 24/7 attention, which overlapped with the equally pressing demands of Apocalypse, who released their own single on the label and supported The Jam on (their

ISSUE #14

6/83

word of every draft article onto the page, combined with Robin's busy designs, ensured that much of the copy was minuscule. Nonetheless, the second part of the McCartney interview finally saw print, eighteen months after it was conducted, and there was a long-overdue, and suitably contentious, interview conducted by Pedro and myself with

DEXYS
LET'S GET THIS STRAIGHT FROM THE START

As explained in our last issue, Kevin Rowland and Dexy's Midnight Runners have been Top Of The Pops with us here at Jamming! for a couple of years now. Despite many futile attempts at interviewing the intriguing Kevin, we were eventually only granted the privilege when Kevin came out into the open last year to ensure that he didn't remain a cult figure for the rest of his life. Although this interview is now a few months old, we consider it particularly relevant in the light of Dexy's current phenomenal Stateside success and universal appeal. Despite the very lightweight quality of most recent Dexy's interviews.

Because of the very lightwight quality of most recent Dexy's interviews, we thought it would be more relevant to actually delve back a bit and see <u>why</u> Kevin ended up as The Celtic Soul Brothers, the piece therefore being more a history of the group than contemporary opinions. The interview was by Pedro and Tony, the write-up by Pedro:-

1979:- Carlo Rolan and his Mean Streets mob. A united gang with the intention to do something far more worthwhile than other 'rock' groups, be it through their music, their intolerance of the "cheery-beery" rock audience, or their disdain for the conventions of the 'music biz' and its press.

1980 :- Kevin and his boxing boots brigade. Emphasis on pride to "flaunt their emotions" and to combat "mainstream concert pat on the back", as the mission to create something passionate and absorbing continues.

1982:- Kevin Rowland, Dexys and the Emerald Express. "Kevin claims to be of Celtic origin" and once again they have major hits that, as often seems to be the case with Dexys past and present, win hearts while confusing minds.

After all, is Kevin Italian, Irish or both? Isn't it treading a thin line between being "ever changing and ever challenging" and change-for-changes sake. Oh Kevin, what do you think?

'It isn't that black and white. Alot of it's instinct. You don't wear the same clothes everyday, so there's a human instinct there as well. It's not totally 'Oh I'll wear that this year and this that year,' but I do believe in it as a way of putting things over. I think it's a waste of time to go on stage dressed up - that means fuck all - but I think these clothes (dungarees etc.) do. I think it reflects the music, and the music reflects the image, so it all ties up.'

SO WAS IMAGE A PART OF THE KILLJOYS (KEVINS GROUP BEFORE DEXYS)? THAT SEEMS TO BE ANOTHER EXAMPLE OF THE CONFUSION THAT SURROUNDS YOU,COS I'VE SPOKEN TO PEOPLE WHO SAW THE KILLJOYS AND SAY IT'S HARD TO BELIEVE KEVIN ROWLAND COULD TURN ROUND AND START ACCUSING OTHER GROUPS OF BEING SHALLOW WITH DEXYS. WHAT WERE THE KILLJOYS LIKE?

Useless.

IS THAT WHAT YOU THOUGHT AT THE TIME OR WHAT YOU THINK OF THEM NOW?

No, they weren't totally useless. They had a couple of good ideas, but were like in a stream and couldn't see their way out. I don't try and defend it and say it was really alright because I know it was no good.

DID THEY COME THROUGH WITH PUNK?

Yeah, but I must admit I was already in a group just before punk. It was like an awful similarity to punk

- I started to read about it and noticed the clothes we were wearing were exactly the same. There were a lot of similarities; with a group called 'Lucy and the Lovers' we did what we used to think was 'art rock' which then merged into being a punk band. Then with the Killjoys we went through about as many changes as Dexys but only in about one third of the time. It was changing every month and during the month of the most intense punk euphoria we recorded a single called "Johnny Won't Go To Heaven". That was a real punk single in May '77 and a month after that I hated punk. I hated it! I used to go around hating punks. I just thought it was a load of shit, and it made me angry that I'd been conned."

WHO DO YOU THINK CONNED YOU?

Well I don't know about being conned. I don't think anybody conned me, but I must admit I thought I could relate to it - and when I went to see the groups it may not have been that good but I thought 'Oh, it's great!' You know, I kind of convinced myself that I liked it, when I didn't really - I made allowances for it. I was really glad when I saw groups like the Clash at Barberella's - there was this heavy rock group there supporting that the audience pulled off the stage. I thought that was quite good, dead exciting, and a NEW thing - like loads of people did - and then I thought to myself for a couple of months "Oh we can be part of this movement and do something within it!" But by the time I realised that we couldn't, it was too late and we'd already recorded our single, so after that we changed and went the opposite to punk. We'd dress up really smart, have blow-dried hair, white shirts - not like power pop but with P.J.Proby shirts, jodphurs and boxing boots. We used to do Lionel Blair dance routines. Instead of doing fast songs we did slow ones, but we still kept the name 'The Killjoys' and that's why the audience hated us. There'd be punks at the front row because they'd heard the record and the name, and we'd come on and do Bobby Darin's 'Dream Lover',50's rock and roll and Country and Western!"

SO WHEN DID YOU THINK "RIGHT,I'VE LEARNED THIS MUCH FROM THE KILLJOYS, BUT NOW I'VE GOT THIS PLAN CALLED DEXYS."

January '78 I got the idea. I would still probably be going now with the Killjoys only the others left.

DID YOU ALWAYS WANT TO BE IN A GROUP THEN?

No, groups were nowhere. The kids I used to knock about with used to take the piss out of people in groups - who were student types. I still don't like other groups - I just think it's shit!

Why should I have to like other groups? People say to me 'You don't want to know. You're stuck up.'
Why should I want to go around with these people? I've got my own friends that I respect much more. They've got nothing to do with groups and I find them much more interesting, much more intelligent without a doubt, but because I'm in a group I'm expected to go around with other groups and be friendly when I see them and say nice things about them. I've got nothing in common with them and I can't think of anything nice to say.
I do believe in groups of people though - individuals coming together to do something, but groups, as in musicians - it's just a waste of time."

RETURNING TO THE FIRST TIME YOU GOT THE IDEA FOR DEXYS, WHAT WAS THE FIRST GROUP LIKE, BECAUSE I'VE HEARD REPORTS OF YOU PLAYING IN POKY BIRMINGHAM CLUBS WEARING ZENNIE SUITS AND WITH YOUR HAIR DOWN IN FRONT OF YOUR EYES.

Yeah, that was quite interesting really. It was a bit like Roxy Music, with early Dexys music, some soul covers.

DID YOU THINK THEN THAT THE IMAGE SUITED THE MUSIC?

Alot of people said it didn't but I thought it was alright.

OK, SO ONCE YOU HAD THIS PLAN FOR DEXYS, THAT AT THE TIME MUST HAVE SEEMED IMPRACTICAL, HOW DID YOU CONVINCE THE OTHERS OF THE IDEA?

I had to rope them in, sit them down for about 2 hours, and in return they used to keep leaving! There were loads of people in the group - we had about 10 keyboard players and 20 drummers. They just kept leaving every week!

SO YOU CREATED THIS JOKE ABOUT A GANG OF DESPERATE MEN RALLYING TOGETHER:- "THE REST OF THE TEAM TOOK A BIT LONGER TO RECRUIT AND SOME OF THE BOYS GOT IMPATIENT. ROWLAND AND ARCHER ASSURED THEM THIS SOUND WAS THE BIG ONE AND WAS WELL WORTH WAITING FOR."

It's more interesting if you put it like that. Nobody wants to know if 20 keyboard players left. I'm not kidding you but we used to discuss what we'd say in interviews:- We'd sit down and say 'You say that bit and when he...'. There's nothing wrong with that. It's how we used to operate.

I TAKE IT THEN THAT YOU DIDN'T ACTUALLY MEET HELEN O'HARA WHILE WAITING FOR A BUS....

Damn.... I have met her at a bus stop.... once!

TUT, TUT! ANYWAY KEVIN, RETURNING TO EARLY DEXYS, THERE WAS A LOT OF TALK ABOUT SOUL MUSIC AS YOU SAW IT. INFLUENCES SUCH AS ARETHA FRANKLIN, JAMES BROWN AND GENO WASHINGTON WERE SPOKEN OF, BUT I WAS WONDERING IF THERE WAS ANY NORTHERN SOUL INFLUENCES THERE.

No.

NOT WITH THE LATE NIGHT BEAT, THE DRIVE, THE GANG FEELING...

I've always hated Northern Soul.

WHAT ABOUT YOUR COVER VERSION OF 'SEVEN DAYS TOO LONG', A NORTHERN STANDARD?

Yeah, there's always an exception to the rule, that was the exception, and I thought a fucking idiot, a liar or a stupid twat that would think we were a Northern Soul group, because we were nothing like them! Alright, we had kit bags, but they never had wooly hats, donkey jackets, fuckin' leather jackets, or little taches! They used to wear trousers up to chests with waistbands with 26 buttons, really wide flares with pockets on the sides. I know people outside first one that's said it but I think they're all wrong. I just couldn't believe it - someone said we were Northern Soul mixed with a little bit of Soul music. It's really simple and clear cut. How the fuck can they get it so ridiculously wrong! I've always hated Northern Soul. I don't know what it is about it. I used to go and watch them in 1974 when I used to go to clubs, stand there and watch them and I used to get really angry. I just hated it! All it is up there is a load of kids dancing to records 15 years old, some of which are damn not good enough to get released in the first place, and they're paying extra money for them. I never really understood them.

ALRIGHT THEN, LETS TALK ABOUT INFLUENCES, BECAUSE IT SEEMS TO ME THAT YOU'VE ALWAYS TAKEN REALLY UNFASHIONABLE THINGS AND MADE THEM FASHIONABLE. LIKE 'SOUL', WHEN YOU CAME ALONG WITH YOUR FIRST L.P., IT WASN'T THE MOST POPULAR THING GOING, BUT YOU MANAGED TO SELL IT TO THE PUBLIC. NOW THERE'S TALK OF VAN MORRISON, WHO DOESN'T 'SHIFT UNITS' LIKE YOU'RE DOING. IS IT THAT SIMILAR?

Is it fuck! It's nothing like him. He sings totally different to me with an American Blues accent. He has used strings and brass but he used it in a totally different way to us - in the traditional sense with a classical string section like ABC.

I'D BE UPSET IF YOU WERE THAT SIMILAR. IT WOULD LESSEN YOUR IMPORTANCE TO ME.

I know. That makes me sick because I never had to say I liked Van Morrison, never had to. I thought it would be interesting as I think influences are quite important; you know, where you come from, and if there was a group I was interested in I would want people to know, but you tell someone that and they just use it against you. Danny Baker, when he reviewed 'Eileen' in the NME., said 'Look at the gypsy cover. Looks like they've been studying Van Morrison chic a little too studiosly.' It just shows these people must be thick, really thick, so the Van Morrison connection ends here and now. I respect him because he's the only artist that I know of that has done exactly what he wants over the last 20 years without any consideration for commercial success. However, I don't want to end up like him. I think I'm better than he is anyway but I respect him and I wouldn't dream of ripping him off. Plagiarism, I fucking hate! It's one of those things I really detest! That's one reason I hate musicians because they've got no ideas of their own. They just steal from each other. All I've had from him is inspiration like I've had from loads of other people.

IS THAT WHAT YOU WANT YOUR MUSIC TO DO? I MEAN, IF I SAID SOME OF YOUR MUSIC COMFORTS ME, MAKES ME HAPPY OR SAD, MOVES ME, IS THAT WHAT YOU'D CALL SUCCESS?

Yeah, I think it is really. That's what it does to me as well, but I don't think 'Oh this is going to fucking move them!' It's a natural thing you don't think about.

DURING THAT FIRST DEXYS NATIONWIDE TOUR, IT DID SEEM THOUGH THAT THERE WERE ALOT OF PEOPLE YOU DIDN'T WANT TO INSPIRE, LIKE ALL THE LADS DRINKING AT THE BAR OR ALL OF THE HECKLERS.

Yeah, I used to drive them away.

WAS THAT BECAUSE YOU WERE ONLY INTERESTED IN THE 50 PEOPLE OUT OF 500 THAT GENUINELY LIKED YOU?

Something like that. I actually went on radio and said 90% of our audience should go away, but of course that got turned around. The way I meant it was not the way it came across, and the next thing I knew was after I'd said it in June or July, they were playing it at Christmas on 'Rock On' with me saying it again, and the D.J. going, 'Ha, ha, 90% of his group have left now as well as the audience.'

DO YOU THINK YOU WERE BEING TOO HARSH THEN, OR WERE THE AUDIENCE TOO UNRECEPTIVE?

At the time I was in a very confused state. We had been planning to do a tour but I didn't realise it was 40 dates. I'd said I wanted to play in theatres and unusual venues

7

8

like St.John Ambulances or bingo halls, but the agents booked places that weren't right for us. We had a manager that was a total arshole, and I was doing everything and running the show as well. I had the group that were just sitting there stoned and I was saying, 'Look, he's nicking our money, we're playing in shitholes, getting nowhere, we're doing this all wrong and we've got to do something!' And they just went, 'Aah man, it's alright.' I was just going around scratching my head, doing nothing, and then on top of all of this we had problems with the record company. We'd nicked the mastertapes of our first L.P. so I was negotiating to sell them back for a better deal in London, and then playing in Bristol or somewhere every night. I had all these problems and a manager going round stoned and drunk all the time, telling everybody how he'd done this and that plus 'drinks for all my friends at the bar' on top of which I had to go out on stage every night. I could have gone through all that 'Oh yeah, clap your hands' routine but I didn't want to do that and anyway, I didn't like what I saw. They were sieg-heiling - the Madness audience and the Jam audience. I never wanted them so I wouldn't play to them. I'd challenge them. I never wanted the fucking rock people that came down the front every week and go mad, the kind of people that shout: never ever wanted them. I was always interested in the person that stays at home, doesn't come to see shows, is not interested in groups - the ones that don't seem to like music much.
They wouldn't come to the front and start shouting and grabbing at you. They're not that kind of person. They stand at the back or if they came in the dressing room to say hello they would never come up and start talking to you. It's so frustrating because 20 people might be talking to you, but the one at the back will say one word and you'll know they're the one you'd like to talk to but can't, because there's someone at the front with much more confidence, but nowhere near as much to say.

DID THAT TOUR SHATTER YOUR PLANS FOR THE FIRST GROUP, BECAUSE APPARENTLY YOU INTENDED TO HAVE A NUMBER ONE HIT WITH THE GROUP, THEN BREAK AWAY FROM THAT AND MAKE A FILM BEFORE FORMING A POLITICAL PARTY AND BLOWING UP PARLIAMENT. I'M NOT SURE HOW SERIOUS YOU WERE ABOUT THE LAST OF THESE, BUT WHY DIDN'T YOU DO IT?

I definitely had ideas for the group but they thought I was mad. I was still thinking of doing the film just before 'Plan B' (5th single) days, and we still might do it now, but I'll not burden D.M.R. with it. The Parliament thing, I can't comment on. Well, I must admit I didn't really know much about what I was going to do - I had thought about it but I didn't have a proper manifesto together.

SO, ONCE YOUR FIRST GROUP HAD SPLIT UP, IT SEEMED TO ME THAT YOU ADOPTED A NEW PLAN. AS YOUR FIRST GROUP HAD GOT TO NUMBER ONE WITH ONLY THEIR SECOND SINGLE 'GENO', YOU HADN'T BUILT UP A HARD-CORE FOLLOWING. BUT BY THEN BEING HOSTILE TO THE PRESS, TAKING THOSE ESSAYS OUT IN THE PAPERS, YOU SEEMED TO BE AIMING FOR A DEDICATED UNDERGROUND FOLLOWING...

Yeah, the idea for 1981 was to have and work to a small audience and do as much as we could within that framework, because I was just fed up, like the 1980 tour was just a joke.

WAS THAT IDEA PLAN B?

Yeah, it was an actual plan, though it had to be modified along the way; I'd resigned myself to the fact that if 'Eileen' wasn't a hit, then I was in trouble.

WITH THE NEXT GROUP THEN, DID YOU DECIDE ON NEW PERSONEL AND THEREFORE A NEW SOUND IN THE FORM OF THE FIDDLES?

I saw it before the first group broke up. Another of the reasons they left is that I asked them to learn to play violins. 'Liars A-E' (7th single) was an experiment in a way. That was the only one you heard but in 1981 we did a series of demos and they were all experiments. We were getting there and getting there and 'Celtic Soul Brothers' (8th) was the first one where I thought YES!.

THINKING ABOUT IT, DO YOU THINK THAT THE L.P. 'TOO RYE AYE' GOT CAUGHT BETWEEN 2 STOOLS, ONE OF WHICH WAS THE DEXYS BRASS BLASTS OF OLD, AND THE OTHER THE SINGING STRINGS OF TODAY?

No I don't - that's one thing I want to stress. It's been called folk music or Celtic but it isn't really. It's a mixture of the two things and it works best where we mix it, like 'Let's Make This Precious'. I don't think it's caught between the two; it's even

surprised me. When we started working on this I was really worried thinking 'Half the L.P.'s going to be new Dexys, half the old - maybe we should have one side for the old and the other for the new,' but I decided that'd be terrible. I just tried to put them together and it surprised me how well it worked - it really did.

Well it certainly seemed to work if you're talking in terms of popularity and sales figures, but when you see Kevin's face on every front page, just cos he's doing interviews again, taking 9 tracks out of 11 off the L.P. (though it could be argued that some of those were completely revamped, had been heard by relatively few people, and anyway Kevin believes they fit the mood and therefore have to be, there singles or not), I suppose you have to question whether it works in terms of the integrity of Dexys. Are they after all just another group? Were those essays just skillfully reworded adverts? Wasn't the hostility to the press simply a way of getting well known, albeit notorious rather than praised.

I MEAN KEVIN, YOU KNOW PEOPLE ARE SAYING IT'S ALL VERY WELL YOU HAVING THESE IDEALS BUT WHEN YOUR RECORDS STOP SELLING THEY SOON DISAPPEAR.

I just thought 'Fucking hell! It's 2 years since I've done an interview. I've made the point now. My attitude has changed towards interviews, but I still don't trust them. I think that I've put far too much work, time and sweat into a record to take it to someone and say 'Here, sit down for an hour and listen to this; I've spent two years on it, but you write at your whim what you think of it.' But we were suffering from it - not so much from the press but more the radio stations. They were getting like 'Oh, these Dexys are a funny lot' They don't do interviews, so we won't play their record - we'll play Soft Cell's' and we were getting a bad name all round. When I came up to Phonogram's T.V. promotion department about 3 months ago asking them to try and get us those T.V. slots like they were getting for ABC, the woman was genuinely shocked. She thought we were totally anti-publicity and that we didn't want to do anything.
I don't know what the hell people thought about us.

Seb Shelton

Helen O'Hara

Kevin Rowland

Billy Adams

Though Dexys will never be totally understood (and that's deliberate, for sure), it's obvious that they have been given a phenomenal vote of approval by the record-buying public all over the world. And it must be stressed that although Kevin does constantly backtrack and contradict himself (as he did frequently in the interview), though he does use image as no more than a selling device despite claiming it as his lifestyle, and though the last year has seen him play ridiculously safe, where previously he was the biggest risk-taker going, the end result is what matters. And that is a Dexys Midnight Runners who have been known to make staggeringly emotional music, a Dexys whose live shows are not only the most innovative and inspiring going, but also the most frequently changing, and a Dexys whose leader may not be trusted as a spokesman, but whose music has put a lot of joy into a lot of hearts. That's the rub.

McCARTNEY
INTERVIEW PART 2

Jamming! 13 saw the first part of our epic three-hour interview with Paul McCartney, covering the formation of The Beatles, the Hamburg days, the rise of the group and Beatlemania. Despite the fact that the interview was done over a year ago, it doesn't seem to have dated whatsoever, and this second part delves a bit deeper, into the actual person behind one of the most famous faces in the world.

DID YOU SUCCEED AT EDUCATION?

No, not really. I think none of us put enough time in really. We weren't that thick, but we always got reports saying 'Could do well if only he'd apply himself'. The year of my GCE's we were touring in Scotland with Johnny Gentle, which was one of the first big things we were offered. I had to miss my Geography exam, but I just thought 'Sorry!' We thought it was such a big oppurtunity - as it turned out, it wasn't - doing lots of dates with this guy, and if Johnny Gentle suddenly got famous, so did we. I got some 'O' levels; I think I got one the first year, then maybe a couple more the next... I stayed on into the Sixth form because I didn't want to leave school, I didn't want to have to get a job. I wasn't having too bad a time at school - it was a bit of a hassle having to go there, but I didn't hate it too much. Also, I knew this fella who was 24 and at the art college, and as I was about 17, the way I looked at it was that there was still seven years where I could lig around in the sixth form and go to art college! I thought I could put off the decision of having to choose what to do with my life!

A LOT OF THE PEOPLE WHO'VE MADE IT BIG THOUGHT LIKE THAT... 'ANYTHING BUT A JOB!'

And the joke is ... you get a job, like the job I've got now and it's a J-O-B! It's a real job, and I'm always trying to get out of it. But you know, I put in quite a lot of hours, it is a job.

WHAT'S THE STORY ABOUT BEING CHUCKED OUT OF GERMANY?

Well, like I was saying before, we lived at the back of this cinema, by the bog; it was like a broom cupboard, with a Push-Bar exit to get out. I think so anyway - this was twenty years ago, and I'm trying to remember what the door looked like! You know I never realised it was twenty years ago, I'm still talking about it as if it was yesterday!
Anyway, we were moving from this club (The Kaiserkeller) to a better engagement (The Top Ten)and Pete Best and myself were getting all our gear together, and one of us had a contraceptive - whatever you want to call it!- so just for a laugh we pinned it up on the wall as a goodbye gesture. It was just a cement wall without paint or wallpaper, and I think I set fire to it, and it left a little black mark. But the fella screamed 'Police!' He didn't want us to go to this new club, which would take his business away, so he thought 'This is a good excuse.' It was really just a harmless thing, but he managed to get us in nick. We were just going along the road, and the police pulled over.... 'Hey! come viz us!'

WAS THAT THE FIRST TIME YOU WERE NICKED OVER THERE?

Actually, it was the only time until Japan a few years ago, when I had a longer stay in there. And more fun! But anyway, the police dragged us to an official building, where we hung round for hours, and eventually a fella came up and said 'Come with us, we're taking you back to the club.' And no sooner said than done we were on the plane back to England.

HOW MUCH WAS BRIAN EPSTEIN RESPONSIBLE FOR YOUR SUCCESS? WAS HE SPECIAL, OR COULD ANOTHER MANAGER HAVE DONE IT?

Because he turned out to be special, I'd say he was special; you can't tell if another man would have done it. He wasn't a very good businessman - he used to undersell us - but we never wanted to be overpriced either. But I thought he was great. He was very keen, very showbiz, he was like we were saying earlier - just that generation before us. He may only have been a few years older, but there's a big difference. He'd studied at RADA (Royal Academy of Dramatic Art), but he hadn't done too well there, so he had this great longing to be an actor. He was living through us a bit, but he would see to it that we had a strong stage act or that the lighting was good, so I think he was a big influence. We used to slag him off a lot, as you do with managers, but I liked him; I thought he was great.

WHAT WAS IT LIKE BEING ONE OF THE FOUR MOST WANTED MEN IN THE WORLD BY VIRTUALLY THE ENTIRE TEENAGE FEMALE POPULATION IN EXISTENCE?

Terrific! You can't deny it - we were four normal fellas!

DID YOU ALL TAKE ADVANTAGE OF IT?

Oh Yeah, definitely - we had a great time! That's half of being in a group - or it was then. I remember my dad saying 'I wish I'd had as much experience as you, son.' We used to talk about it - he'd say that in his day, VD was the big scare,'cos by the time I was older they had a jab for it. It was definitely the biggest perk of touring-I cant deny that. It was only later I started thinking 'Shit - I probably broke somebody's heart there.' You don't think about that at first, but a little later you realise.... they are real people. But yeah, there was alot of ladies about.

WHAT ABOUT DRUGS,'COS EVEN FROM THE FIRST STAGE YOU MUST HAVE BEEN OFFERED EVERYTHING UNDER THE SUN?

Well, it was cigarettes to start with, then scotch and coke, then when we went to Hamburg it was pills-speed- and then later we went to America and it was marijuana, and that was about the size of it, except for a little bit of coke. For me anyway - John I think, later got a little bit heavier. But it came off it being available everywhere; all the gangsters in Hamburg used to have pills to stay up all night, so they used to give them to us. Preladin they were called:- 'Zu vant zome Prellies boys?Ia ya ya, schnatz und prellies?' They were just getting off on us silly Englishmen.

LATER ON THOUGH,AFTER BEATLEMANIA, WHEN YOU WERE A STUDIO GROUP, DID YOU NOT GO THROUGH HEAVIER STUFF?

No. Nobody got on to heroin.

BUT SEARGENT PEPPER'S WAS MEANT TO BE CONNECTED WITH LSD. IS THAT TRUE?

Yeah, there was a lot of LSD around at the time. It definately got into the music - it was the fashion. It became what everyone was doing - you'd go down clubs and people would come to you and say 'You want some acid? You want to back to our flat?' which you'd end up doing.

IN THOSE CASES YOU MUST HAVE HAD HEROIN FORCED ON YOU A LOT?

No. Heroin was the one thing you drew the line at.

I'D HAVE THOUGHT WITH YOU LOT HAVING EXPERIENCED EVERYTHING IMAGINABLE, YOU'D HAVE SAID 'WHAT IS THERE LEFT WE HAVEN'T TRIED?

The thing is, we were like anyone who plays around with drugs - you play around with them. Actually, I'm not saying like 'anyone',cos there's alot of people who are very different. But our approach was - as long as it's not really dangerous, we'll do it. I think a lot of people overdid acid; some of the people who took more trips still get flashes - they suddenly buzz without meaning to. I think we were very lucky with it really; it didn't get to us.

DID YOU SEE MUCH OF WHAT WENT ON AROUND YOU, 'COS I'D IMAGINE YOU HAD TO BE PRETTY WELL SHIELDED. YOU COULDN'T JUST WALK THE STREETS ON YOUR OWN.

Well you could- that's a myth actually. I used to go round a lot, and I still do. If I want to from here to over there, I won't do anything special, I won't panic - I'll just go out the front door. You'd be surprised - people may notice you, but what are they gonna do? They're not going to jump on you - it never happened even then. When we got to a gig, there would always be a gang of girls waiting for us, you'd expect that. But I've always felt that just normal living, I've always seen pretty much how people are. Like now, I wouldn't know what goes on down the 100 Club or anything - I see all the kids outside, as I go past, but I don't know what goes on. But half the people who walk down Oxford Street don't know either. So I don't know all the cult things, but just what goes on generally, I've always been up with. I'm a little bit out of touch with certain things, like I sent a fella out to buy some scotch, and didn't give him enough money! But generally, I think I'm more in touch than some people. For instance, I was always against the Common Market right from the off; people were saying 'Oh you're so out of touch' but they were wrong - I was pretty in touch. Nobody that I know really digs the Common Market, not your ordinary people like the milkman or someone.

WHY DID IT TAKE FOUR SOLID YEARS BEFORE YOU MOVED AWAY FROM SIMPLE LOVE SONGS, TOWARDS OTHER STUFF LIKE SERGEANT PEPPER'S? WAS THAT JUST THE WAY LYRICS WENT AT THE TIME?

I don't know really, I've never thought about it. I think the love stuff - 'You and me, boy and girl'- was just the early part of the development. To us, it was just the commercial songs, and we got hooked on little things, like we always had a 'me' or 'you' or an 'I', something personal, in the title:- Please Please ME, Love ME Do, Can't Buy ME Love, She Loves YOU, From ME To YOU...

BUT DID YOU ALWAYS MEAN THE LYRICS?

No, we didn't. I still don't always mean the lyrics - it's just not the kind of writing I do. They're not always personal, and sometimes they're just made up.

SO WHAT YOU WERE TRYING TO DO WAS JUST WRITE A GOOD SONG, AND SAY 'THE WORDS OF THIS SONG - LIKE SHE LOVES YOU - ARE GOING TO MEAN SOMETHING TO SOMEONE?

Yeah. Not all the songs were that, but that was the idea of it, writing something the people would want.

BECAUSE I WOULD HAVE THOUGHT THAT WITH THAT YOU WERE SAYING EARLIER ABOUT THE AMOUNT OF GIRLS AVAILABLE, YOU COULDN'T HAVE BEEN IN LOVE MUCH.

No, you're right. But you don't have to be in love to write a love song.

WHAT RECORDS BY THE BEATLES ARE YOU MOST PLEASED WITH?

Being sensible, as a record I probably like 'Yesterday'. That, 'Here There And Everywhere', 'Strawberry Fields', 'Hey Jude', and some of the other big ones. But if you said you can only take one, I wouldn't take 'Hey Jude' because I've heard it so many times; there's a crazy b-side I like, 'You Know My Name(Look up The Number)', the b-side of 'Let It Be'. I love that one - it's just an insane track, and what I remember from the session and all the laughs - we were just in pleats making that record, so that to me is one of my favourites. Another is 'She Said, She Said' - I just like those more off-the-beaten-track tracks. That's how we used to choose material; we'd never do the big hit by The Shirelles, we'd do 'Soldier Boy'. Even though they were girls singing to a soldier boy, we'd change the words a little bit.

WHAT ABOUT LP'S - DOES ANY ONE IN PARTICULAR STAND OUT?

I like Rubber Soul, Seargant Pepper's and Abbey Road. I listened to Abbey Road recently and thought 'Wow! That's good!' I like the White Album as well.

I KNOW THE OFFICIAL REASON FOR WHY YOU STOPPED PLAYING...

What is the official reason? I don't even know that.

I'M TALKING ABOUT WHY YOU STOPPED PLAYING LIVE...

Oh, that just happened. We did this one concert in America, when it was raining, with water coming in the amps, and we hated it - we did the show, but hated every minute of it. And then at the end of it, we were put inside this metal-lined van, and were sort of clattered about in there. And I think as we were sitting in there, John and George just said 'Sod this!' But they had been saying 'All this touring...' We were just shattering ourselves, And I think that was when I said 'Sod it - I agree with you.' That made three of us, so we went into recording. We decided to just keep recording, and if anybody said 'When are you going to tour next?', we'd say 'We're not sure.' We weren't going to announce that we'd stopped touring; we just decided to quietly pull out of it, and get into recording more.
Nobody noticed it for a couple of months 'cos we'd finished our live commitments, were doing some recording, and it looked fine. After a few months, people said 'Hey- wait a minute, when are you going on tour again?' Then after a year,people said 'It looks like you've given up touring.' And we said 'Well sort of, maybe'.

THE STORY GOES THAT IT WAS A PRETTY BIG THING WHEN YOU STOPPED TOURING. YOUR NEXT SINGLE -'PENNY LANE'/'STRAWBERRY FIELDS FOREVER' - FAILED TO GO TO No.1

FOR THE FIRST TIME SINCE YOU'D STARTED, AND THAT WAS MEANT TO BE A DIRECT REACTION TO YOUR NOT TOURING.

I can't really remember. It may have been that we were doing this quiet thing I was telling you about, and one of the newspapers said 'Are you giving up touring?' and we said 'YEAH!' and that hit the papers, making it look like we'd done it officially.

APPLE - WIDELY REGARDED AS YOUR DOWNFALL - CAME ABOUT PARTLY BECAUSE OF BRIAN EPSTEIN'S DEATH, DIDN'T IT? DO YOU RECKON IF BRIAN HAD BEEN ABOUT HE'D HAVE MADE THINGS GO MORE THE WAY YOU WANTED THEM TO?

I don't know - someone else asked me that recently. The thing is, his influence had stopped a couple of years before he died anyway. His influence, like George Martin's, had mainly been in the earlier days. As we grew up, into men rather than little boys, we started to want to make our own decisions a lot, so... It might have been okay if Brian had been alive still, but you can't really tell. It might even have been more disastrous, 'cos he was changing as well. I don't think it could have been done any different from the way it was done; it was just like a tree growing - if it's going to grow right through this wall, it will. We did it all naturally, you know; you can only guess at what might have happened if we'd done it all another way.

APPLE DID GO DRASTICALLY WRONG THOUGH, DIDN'T IT?

The thing is, that with a company that's gone drastically wrong, it's still got over a million in the bank, so it couldn't have gone that wrong! Yeah, it went wrong, but not as much as you'd expect - you'd expect it to be bankrupt. It's still got a lot of money in the bank, being The Beatle's company, having The Beatle's records, and having a lot of hits. It's hard to explain, but there's all sorts of company laws, you can't dissolve a company. Don't ask me why, I don't know. Ten years and we still haven't sorted it out! You wouldn't believe the stories on Apple. That's the new Beatle's story sometime, if anyone can get it together. But it didn't actually go that wrong: it didn't go as right as we wanted it to, like we wanted it to go smooth, never break up, make a lot of money and be terrific. Be good for people, be good for us and everything. But it was during the time we were breaking up anyway. So it wasn't actually the company's fault; it was us breaking up within the company. There's still endless negotiations, still meetings in New York to try and decide the fate.

DO YOU KNOW WHY YOU DID SPLIT IN THE END?

No, not really. The only thing I always reckon is.... You get teams of people, like a football team or something, and they go and do the big thind, but there's an inevitability they're not going to stay together. There's an inevitable break up of a team, by the very nature that you're holding on. I think we kind of did everything, achieved all our ambitions, cracked America, cracked the world, did everything we wanted to and then somehow we just wanted to start to split it up. Someone would want to do a solo thing, and then in the end, John started to get very strong with Yoko, and we started to get our own family things. We just kind of drifted apart. Then it got to be bitchy - we were drifting apart, and therefore the business had to be sorted out. 'That's mine - what do you mean?' That got very difficult, 'cos Allan Klein came in, and screwed us silly.

YOU'RE THE ONE WHO SAID FROM THE START THAT ALLAN KLEIN WAS DODGY?

(In quite a sad acknowledgement) Ummm.

Yeah. At first the word was that we were
going to go along with him, because maybe
he was bad, maybe he was good, but we
should give him a try. So we started to
negotiate his deal, and I said 'Well the
Beatles are a big act - there's not chick-
enfeed involved. We can get a really good
deal with this fella; he's lucky if he can
get 15%.' But everyone was so keen for him
that they said 'No, give him 20%.' So I
agreed, the idea being that we'd give him
a trial. But during the trial run, he'd
say one thing to me, then I'd see another
thing in the papers. So I started to suspect him, and at that point I tried to
get out of it all, but everyone said 'No,
we're going to sign with him.' It was
the first time in my life I felt I'd been
done the dirt with the other guys. I said
to them.' This is very weird, this is the
first time... we've been mates 'till now.'
But it was three to one, they agreed to
go with him, and I said no. No way. So
I started boycotting the whole thing, not
goin in, being on strike and having go-
slows! You know, anything I could to
hold him off. And at the end it was proved.
The worst thing was I had to sue The
Beatles. I said 'No, I want to sue Allen
Klein, I don't want to sue The Beatles, I
haven't got anything against them.' They
said 'But all these companies are in the
Beatles name - you can't sue Allen Klein
without sueing The Beatles.' It was just
the way it was legally set up, I had to.
So that was a very tough decision; I spent
a few months making my mind up whether to
do it or not. But the result was that I
either stayed with Allen Klein or did the
sueing - it was the only way out of it.
So I sued them in the High Court, and they
looked at all the evidence, and there in it
we proved that he'd been screwing us. Our
side won, and the judge said something like
'This man (Klein) has the patter of a sec-
ond-class salesman.' So that blew him out
a bit, all the other Beatles realised what
he'd been doing, and they tried to get out
of it. Then later, they came back and said
'Thanks, we're glad you really held it all
up.' But at the time of course, when they
didn't think he was wrong, I took some
stick.

HAS HE NOW GOT AWAY WITH HAVING RIPPED YOU
OFF?

Well this shows you how small-minded he
was.... he actually go $5,000,000 for man-
aging us for a year. There's me trying to
get him 15% and all that! Somehow he actually got paid $5,000,000 for one years
work. To which I said 'Come On, look at
that. You're kidding! You mean this guy
is straight? Why wasn't it $4,700,000? How
comes it's such a round figure?' And then
he wasn't content to just take the five
million and do something honest with it.
What he eventually did was... he's just
been in nick in America, and what they did
him for was selling sample records. He had
loads of people peel the little white things
off and sold them. He must have made a
little profit on that, but that was the only
thing they nicked him on in the end.

DO YOU BELIEVE ANY OF THOSE STORIES THAT
BRIAN WAS MURDERED?

No, I don't think he even committed suicide,
it was just accidental. I mean, I don't
know, nobody knows, not even the man who
says he was murderd, Norma Phillips - it's
Phillip Norman really. I think it was
just accidental, 'cos he used to booze a
lot, and he used to take pills a lot. I
think the two caught up with him some night
- he probably forgot he had so many drinks
started taking some pills, and if they were
tranquilisers, he'd probably forgot how
many he'd had. 'I can't sleep, I'll have
another.' I don't think he particularly
wanted to die. But we were a little bit
removed from it anyway - none of us saw
him, none of us found him, we just had to
believe whatever we were told from the
people in his house. I don't think he
committed suicide and I don't think he was

murdered - that just fits in more neatly
with recent sensationalism about The
Beatles.

THE THING TO SELL THE BOOK ('SHOUT!')
BASICALLY?

Yeah, this Albert Goldman, who wrote that
book about Elvis, is supposed to be warming up to do a book on John. But seeing
where he's at, you know what to expect.
He's going to dredge up all sorts of thing
that he's going to tell us about John,
some of which I don't even know. General-
lyI think it will be pretty much bullshit.
John got a little heavier towards the end
of his life.... no actually, he cooled out
totally towards the end of his life. Five
years before he died he wasn't on any drugs
or anything, he was just totally together.
But when he and Yoko first met, they were
pretty crazy. So there may be little secrets from those days. But you always get
those things.... 'Beatles Pissed On Nuns'
is one story which wasn't true at all.
All it was was we were staying in this
place where you had to go down about five
flights of stairs to go to a toilet, so
sometimes we'd piss out the window - good
old English medieval habit! And of
course, what happed was, one day, right
down the road from where we were pissing
there happened to be some nuns. They
didn't see us, but somebody did; the papers picked it up, and it went from being
a joke to being a fact. All that hell-
raising stuff wasn't half as bad as it
was made out to be. John saying we were
bigger than Jesus - it was just a small
little quote out of a whole big interview.

WASN'T IT JUST A SMALL QUOTE IN THE EVE-
NING STANDARD, BUT THE NEW YORK TIMES OR
SOMETHING PICKED UP ON IT AND MADE IT INTO
A MASSIVE ISSUE?

Yeah, they made it sound like John was
really boasting about it, which he wasn't;
he just happened to say it, it's just a
manner of speech. But of course the Bible
Belt in America weren't going to have that
as a manner of speech, thank you very much.
They were going to have that as a major
controversy. I remember some young ten-
year old kid banging on the window of our
coach - 'YOU BLASPHEMOUS FIENDS!' He was
really possessed, like a little Omen kid-
we really thought he'd get us.

SO WHAT DON'T YOU LIKE ABOUT 'SHOUT!'?

'Shite!' as I call it. I couldn't believe
some of the facts in the serialisation in
the Sunday Times, so I read the book. The
trouble is, there's some bits of it that
I'm not in that suddenly seem very believe-
able, like a really good story. Then I'll
see a fact that I know not to be true, and
I'll think 'Wait a minute! What am I doing
believing these other bits about Brian
Epstein's youth, and John's family background?' I think there are certain facts
in it that are quite fascinating, and certain things that it gets over, that aren't
too bad. But the crime is for him to call
it 'The True Story Of The Beatles', and yet
he never interviewed any of the Beatles.

I DIDN'T THINK IT WAS TOO BAD.

My problem is to me, I come over as this
very together guy, always got his finger
on top of everything; the man with no
problems. School - a doddle, got all the
exams. This is the sort of image of me.
Actually I had murder getting through exams, like I was saying about being on
tour during my GCE's. I was like the kid
who was getting the cane. Just like John
was, but he makes me the very shrewd, al-
ways-going-to-succeed guy, and John is the
kind of cute, working class hero. In actual fact though, John was just as shrewd
and ambitious as I was. What does me in is
he adds to this image I've got; I resent
that, because I know I'm not that, and I
know I've never been that.
Like in the book, I almost kill Stu Sut-
cliffe. The way it comes over is that I

used to really put Stu down, wheras in
actual fact, I had a little bit of a thing against Stu, but that was for one
reason - he couldn't play bass. I had a
purely musical thing about it - 'What
are we going to do about a bass player
who can't play bass?' And the other great
legend is Pete Best - 'Why did they get
rid of this poor lad?' Because George
Martin told us - 'Your drummer can't drum
Get rid.' What are we gonna do, try and
pretend he's wonderful drummer? We knew
he wasn't as good as what we wanted in
the group, so we got another drummer
that we wanted. He was called Ringo.It
had got to the stage that Pete was holding us back.
You can't help it, if there's somebody
in the group who doesn't click. Like
Stu. Stu was a great guy, a lovely guy,
and I didn't understand him, it's true.
There's a lot of people in my life I
haven't understood; I'm not the world's
most psychic person. I make a lot of
mistakes, and I misread people, I've
read a lot of stuff about Stu since that
I didn't know about; I was taking him all
wrongly. But it certainly wasn't just me
who was getting at him, everyone had their
little goes. But I suddenly come out as
the 'go-getter' and the ambitious one in
the group. And John's portrayed as the
kind of nice guy who always falls into
situations. And he has George standing
there with his plectrum always waiting
for a solo. Now that does George an injustice - there 's a lot more to George
than just this idiot waiting for a solo.

PAUL IS DEAD.

That's right. I'm really an imposter -
but the money's good! This mafia-style
operation has been paying me to be Paul
McCartney; as you can see, I've learnt
the history quite well, and I've got the
accent just about off!
No, what happened was a guy from our
office called Peter Brown rang me up, and
said 'Paul, there's a rumour in American
that you're dead. What do you want me to
do about it?' I said 'Is there Peter? Oh,
really. Well, what can I do about it; tell
them it's not true.' And that's how I
dealt with it. It all happened over in
America, so I didn't see it, I didn't
hear about it at all. People were telling me 'All the DJs in America are
building this rumour that's sweeping
the country. They say you didn't have
any shoes on on the cover of Abbey Road,
therefore...' But if you look at the
photo session from Abbey Road, you see
me sitting on the steps with sandals on.
It was a hot summers day, so I took my
sandals off to walk across the road.
Now that's the truth, but the rumour was
that bare feet was the sign of a dead man.

DID YOU MIND IT THOUGH?

Oh no, it was hilarious! There was nothing I could do, I just couldn't take it
seriously.

ONE THING THAT HAS BEEN PROVED WRONG BY
MY MEETING YOU IS I'D ALWAYS BELIEVE
THAT THE IMAGE OF PAUL McCARTNEY THESE
DAYS TO BE TRUE.... THE MULTIMILLIONAIRE
BUSINESSMAN SURROUNDED BY BODYGUARDS AND
AIDES.

Well how do you think I feel about it?
It's incredible, but there's nothing I
can do about it. They write in every
single article they do that I make £20
million a year - that's the figure they
have got hold of. I don't know where
they got it from, but what am I gonna do-
write up to everything and say it's not
true? When I walk out of here, I walk in
the street - and on my own, not with
millions of people. I've got an office,
yeah, but so have you. Ok, mine's pretty
ritzy, but I wanna do it like that. It
leads to an image that comes out, but I
honestly don't know where half my image
comes from. If I tell you some of the
true facts about how I live... I mean
some of them are just too true, too far

20

out, the true story.

YOU MEAN DOWN TO EARTH?

Yeah. Like Harvey Goldsmith came down
once, in his chauffer-driven car,. He
saw my house and said 'No no, keep driving - he couldn't live there. That must
be just the little lodge house.' Because
he believes that image too. Well the
thing with me is that you'd expect me to
live in a mansion, but what I like about
how I do it, and how I am - one of my
sources of satisfaction - is that it
isn't like that at all. Would you believe that I've got four kids and we
live in a two-bedroomed house? That
freaks me out, whether it freaks you out
or not. Ok, we're building a new house,
and the kids are getting a bedroom each,
which is what you'd expect. I mean, it's
not going to be a mansion, because I'm
not like that.
You see, I've tried all that big lifestyle. I've had chauffers, and I hate
being driven - I'm the driver, and I like
to drive myself. I've had live-in coup-
les which I've hated, 'cos they take over-
it's like living with your bloody auntie
or something. When I had that, I thought
'Bloody Hell! This is worse than living
with your parents!' So I'm off all of that
stuff, I don't do anything like that. The
big thing I'll use my money for is really
for jibs and perks, instead of taking a lousy flight, instead of taking a lousy flight somewhere
on Plummet Airlines, I might hire a jet.
I'll do that kind of thing, just to make
it more comfortable, and a bit flash.
Actually, it's not being flash, it's doing the practical thing - getting a really
safe plane that'll get me down in half
the time. That's the kind of thing I go
for.
But you know, I'm not really into flash
stuff. I'm not a jewellery man, I'm not
a big house man, the kids don't go to private schools. Another reason that I'm
quite proud of myself is that the kids so
far aren't basket kids, they're real good
kids. They're kids you can sit down and
chat with, like you can go out with the
older one, and find out her interests;
they're just very normal kids. There's
nothing snobbish about them.
It's quite funny, I remember once thinking 'If I have a kid in their teens,
there's nothing that would freak me out.
Long hair I wouldn't mind, 'cos I've been
through that; crazy fashions I wouldn't
mind, 'cos I've been through that;' And
yet when my kid started going punk, I
suddenly realised what my parents had
thought about me. Which is like 'Is
this gonna mean she'll get onto glue or
something that I'll sit up worrying about?
If I give her total freedom, and say
'Yeah! Go with all the fashions!' is that
gonna mean I'm pushing her onto heroin?'
And then I suddenly realised: 'Oh God! I

thought I'd never do this!' I always swore
that I was going to let them do whatever
they wanted to, but in the end I found myself realising 'So this is how my parents
felt!' Because one thing parents are,

THE KIDS MUST GET A LOT OF STICK AT
SCHOOL THOUGH.

They get it all, yeah. But the thing is,
they've got to learn to live with it, because there's nothing I can do about it.
What can I do - unmake myself? Turn the
video backwards? They are Paul McCartney's kids. All we do is just treat it
real normal. I don't open fetes or anything at the school; if I ever go down
there, it's just as a real ordinary par-
ent. I buy my coffee for 10p at the school play, natter about school stuff. I
don't feel famous. I know I am, and sometimes I'm proud I am and all that, but
in my ordinary day-to-day life, I like to
be the way people are- just what I am.
That's one of the wierd things that does
happen - your fame destroys you. We started off with you saying 'What would you
advise people?' and you've got to watch
that. You might get a bunch of money and
think 'Now I've never allowed myself a
bloody great car, but I would love a black Cadillac, so I'm gonna do it.' A
lot of people just do it for fun like
that, but then you've got a black caddie, and you're a black caddie man. You
don't realise it's changing your lifestyle, but it is.

ARE YOU PLEASED WITH ALL THE MUSIC YOU'VE
MADE SINCE THE BEATLES SPLIT?

Not all of it. I mean, the obvious thing
after you've been in a big group like that
is how do you follow it? I just went back
to square one, got a little group together
again, and went back to playing small
halls. So some of the music was done
under a lot of pressure, me trying to figure out what I was going to do etc. So
some of it was a bit duff. But on the
whole, looking back over it, I'm amazed
at how I've hung in there - every so often
there's been a good little record come
out.

DID YOU THINK WHEN YOU DID 'MULL OF
KINTYRE' THAT IT WOULD BE...

That huge? No. No way. I didn't even
think it would be a hit. We did it in
Scotland in our barn, and pipers who
played on it, all had their cans of
McEwans, getting tanked up, and they all
said 'Oh this is a hit.' From 16-year
olds up to 50-year olds, they all agreed
it was a hit. But we put it out at a
time when there was a lot of new wave,
punk stuff starting, and I thought that
it was just going to get left out. It's
funny - there's me in the height of punk
putting out a Scottish waltz. But it was
one of those records that just appealed
to people - you can't tell what it was,
but it just did.

THE THING THAT I WOULD SAY IS THE
BEATLES... WHILE I WASN'T THERE WITH THE
MUSIC I CAN STILL LISTEN TO IT AND LOVE
IT, THINKING 'THIS IS TIMELESS'. BUT
WHAT YOU'VE DONE SINCE THE BEATLES I'VE
NEVER BEEN ABLE TO GET INTO. DO YOU
THINK MAYBE AS YOU'VE GOT OLDER YOU'VE
WRITTEN STUFF...

Not as good, do you mean?

OR MAYBE IT'S A PRODUCT OF SOMEBODY WHO
IS OLDER?

Yeah, well that would be true. The last
thing I want to do is thingk ' Yeah , well
I did all me best stuff with The Beatles,
and there's no way I can do anything good
anymore.' I'd have to take up gardening
fulltime! But I think the public look at
it like that, like 'I've heard everything
by The Beatles; now if I'm going to check
out everything by Wings, it'll be duff in
comparison.' I think The Beatles stuff is
better, because as you say, it's younger,
it's a group,... all that stuff we've been
talking about. But I think there is stuff
I've done since that is as good... I mean,
I've heard 'Mull Of Kintyre' myself, and
you may not like it but I thought 'Yeah,
that's a good record.' Band On The Run,
as well.

MAYBE IT'S THE DIFFERENCE THAT 'SHE LOVES
YOU' SOLD TO PRACTICALLY EVERY TEENAGER IN
BRITAIN, AND MULL OF KINTYRE TO PRACTICALLY
EVERY HOUSEWIFE...

Yeah, that's what you'd think, but when
you look at it, there was millions of
young kids bought that record. I mean,
8-9 year olds. That's the thing about
it... it's a British record. It's got
weird appeal, but even not going on sales
I think that one does something.
The way I look at it is that I'm hanging
in there. I couldn't possible do The
Beatles again, I couldn't keep up that
standard. That was The Beatles, that was
me writing with John Lennon. I think if
you look at it now, you'd think 'Did the
Beatles, end of story, nothing from then
on', which I don't agree with. I think
if you look, and search a bit more, you'll
find there is some good stuff in there,
that you might not get into until later in
your life.
So really, you know, I've always thought
of myself as hanging in there. My motto
is 'E for Effort'.

And so the interview ended, Paul going off to finish some
recording, me left marvelling at how frank he'd been.
Whatever you think of Paul McCartney, hopefully this
interview will have opened your eyes a bit. My main reaction
from meeting the man was one of astonishment at just how
HUMAN he's remained despite living such a remarkable life.
He still does what he wants, has built a normal family, and
can joke about his life as though it were never him involved. Whether or not Paul is still a relevant force in music
is not really the issue: over twenty years, he's been largely responsible for the most popular songs and best known
group ever, and has come out sane; that is an acheivement in
itself.

©TONY FLETCHER

AZTEC CAMERA

AZTEC CAMERA: the Milky Bar kids of todays music with their cowboy shirts, young smiles, pale faces and toe-tapping tunes a-plenty. Witness the class, character and charisma of their Rough Trade 45's, and you'll find more hooks and catches than a year's supply of 'Angler's Weekly'. Lend an ear to that woeful waxing 'Pillar To Post', listen to the relaxed 'Oblivious' and enjoy the restrained 'Walk Out To Winter', & you'll find songs worthy of (and which nearly got) national success. Success?

"Well I do want to be successful but on my own terms," argues Roddy Frame, singer/songwriter of the Aztec beat and an authentic young gun at the tender age of 18. "When I say my own terms, I mean I'd rather put out a record that I was proud of but which only sold a mere few copies than release something that I hated which sold a million."

Whether or not he achieves success on these terms, I believe that Roddy and his sidekick Campbell Owen have made a debut LP to be justly proud of. Entitled "High Land Hard Rain", the Batman and Robin partnership have produced ten impressive tracks that include remixes of both the singles, as well as the new 45,'Walk Out To Winter'. Moods chop and change from the raunchy 'The Boy Wonders' to more reflective numbers like 'Bugle Sounds Again'. At one point, it's all light harmonies and accoustic guitars, the next all energy and venom, but this modern Simon and Garfunkel dont stop there. A Stax-type ballad, complete with '60's keyboards, mouth organ and gospel singers, means that if variety is the spice of life, then the debut Aztec Camera album is available from your local curry-house!! So, is Roddy deliberately searching for more variety, digging harder and deeper than the majority of safe middle-of-the-road music we're subjected to daily?

"I don't know about that, but I think there should be music that makes you think twice. I know people have accused us of being background music, but I think they're wrong-yet that's only my opinion. In one interview I accused groups like ABC of not making you think twice; I could have said that they do what they do very well and all that, but I didn't want to. I just gave an opinion because I think you should and that there ought to be more people around who think for themselves and have opinions."

A wise head on young shoulders maybe, but Roddy already has a couple of year's experience to draw from. The legend of the Aztecs begun two years ago with their debut disc 'Just like Gold' and it's successor 'Mattress Of Wire'. Both received critical acclaim - for what that's worth - as they and their label Postcard rose to cult status with a reputation for producing 'The Sound Of Young Scotland'. It was all as easy as a child playing hop-scotch (or should that be pop-scotch?) but no sooner had they been heralded as the next big thing than they were out in the cold, victims of an ever-fickle media. Unsuprisingly, Roddy now takes any praise without getting carried away. He's also keen to answer any criticisms laid at their door.

"Wimpy? Us? I don't think that's true. You're talking about a concert at the Venue that was just a bad gig for us. But when we play well, we're quite energetic, so I can't really see us as wimpy. Maybe it's got something to do with the Country and Western clothes that we wore. They were supposed to be a bit camp actually, but that's only an image and nothing more".

As it is, the Aztecs sound and image has been springing up in other places recently. Take the Pale Fountains, all big guitars and smiles of yesteryear, with their shiny new Virgin Records contract, rumoured to be worth £150,000.

"I went to see that lot actually," picks up Roddy, "and although I don't think they ripped off any of our songs or anything, I felt there was a definite influence there. In a way I was really quite flattered that they regarded us highly enough to be influenced by us."

Innovators or imitators, I hope these two talented Aztecs don't become part of another lost race. Let those cameras start clicking!

Pedro.

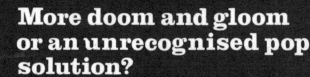

More doom and gloom or an unrecognised pop solution? JONH WILDE investigates......

Being used, as we are, to bands verbalising at length about their motivations and inspirations, it is unnerving at first to encounter Falkirk's Cocteau Twins. If you have been charmed by their intoxicating shadowed spell, you might presume that behind that vast swirling haze would be an eagerness to lift the veil from their enticing mysteries. In the Cocteau Twins though, there is a glaring absence of any worldly aim:-

'When we formed' explains guitarist Robin. 'There was no contrived idea about the kind of sound we wanted or the ideas that would be in the songs: it began as a gentle, melodic, sparse sound and developed from there. It's always difficult to discuss the band in any other way than the obvious BECAUSE we think so little about it really.'

In the attempt to define the might of the Cocteaux, there is the risk of being caught between two extremes - treating them as casual fun/entertainment on one hand or as a too serious and elusive creating on the other. Between these extremes lies a lifetime and the Cocteaux sometimes get speechless between the two poles. Quite simply, they offer preciously few clues. Their strength and infectious vitality hover between truth and fantasy and its great fascination lies in its misty, fragile form. The attraction of the indistinct images that they throw into the air lies in their inpenetratable STRANGENESS. It's the kind of strength that the Banshees should have maintained after 'Staircase' but they lost the EDGE; the Cocteaux though are one of those rare one-offs, sounding like nothing too particular.

Robin again: 'Up to now, the three of us have kept fairly anonymous, but thats not of our own making. The whole question of a mystery/intrigue in what we do is not something that we are aware of. We've not bent over backwards to give anybody an angle...neither have we deliberately tried to remain obscure. A lot of the time we've been written about as some dark brooding noise but we don't see ourselves like that at all really. It's more a mix of light and dark, if anything, but it's impossible to pin down. It's not as if we strive to create something that is different, any more than we try not to sound like anyone else.'

The Cocteau Twins fascinate me because they can be good pure fun, while at the same time, they can capture the nervous edge of love, hope and a dark sense of fear. They have the sinister spell of desire and the milling chaos of wide-eyed confusion. Their three releases so far on 4AD have been a convincing demonstration of their potency and spirit.

In 1982, their debut LP 'Garlands' and their first twelve-inch single 'Feather-Oar-Blades'/'All But An Ark Lark'/'Alas Dies Laughing' were amongst the best releases of the year - their inspiring, uplifting dense cloud of sound intermingling light and dark with shattering effect. This year has seen another twelve-inch single 'Peppermint Pig'/'Hazel'/'Laugh Lines' which has rightfully been a regular feature near the top of the Alternative Charts. The mighty sound revolves around the constant thud of a drum-machine; coiling around that is Will's bass, sombre and introspective, providing the shades of grey in extreme contrast to Robin's sharp, jagged, discordant guitar shapes that splash about haphazardly. Elizabeths strained vocal provides the final element - disrupting the random order as she knocks language out of shape with her strange inflections, and their subtle sense of grave beauty.

Will points out that 'The lyrics have been termed "obscure" and "vague" but we've never seen them like that. We get quite a lot of letters asking us to write the words down; they seem to be difficult to

grasp, but that hasn't really been intentional -
it's just Elizabeth's style.'
    Perhaps not intentional, but The Cocteaux do some-
times seem guilty of a wilful elusiveness - one of my
few doubts.
At the time of writing, they are half-way through a
tour of Britain and Europe as guests of OMD. I wondered how much they hope to have gained by the end of
it.
    'We'll probably be wondering that ourselves', answ-
ers Elizabeth.'The effect will probably be that the
whole purpose of what we are doing and where we were
heading will be confused somewhat. We were invited on
the tour as OMD liked our records; we agreed at first
simply because we thought it would be good exposure.
We haven't gone down too well in a lot of places, but
it's been a good experience.'

Perhaps one reason why they have not overwhelmed the
crowds on the tour lies in their lack of immediacy.
Bearing in mind the kind of audience that OMD attract
these days, the Cocteaux perhaps lack that abrupt pop
appeal. On 'Peppermint Pig', producer Alan Rankine
(of Associate fame) seemed to work on commercial potential in their sound, aiming for a more precise, coherent whole, but unfortunately achieving something

just a little less distinct than their previous releases -
much to the bands displeasure.
    One other problem that the Cocteaux might face if they
want to broaden their appeal is with self-imposed confines of their format. For the moment, the way in
which the entire sound relies on the perpetual beat of
the drum-machine gives their swirling, dizzy, bewildered Dance its driving energy. For the long-term
though, won't that format prove restrictive?
    'We wouldn't rule out the possibility of changing
our format at any time', concedes Robin, 'But we
don't consider it restrictive at present. But then
we never think that far ahead anyway...'
    The problem with using a drum-machine is that it tends
to limit a live bands spontaneity. The current Cocteau's set varies little from night to night, and though the songs themselves are strong enough to transcend any barriers it will be interesting to see how
far they can extend the sound within their limits. At
the moment EVERYTHING has to revolve around that drum-
machine thud.
    'We don't see that as a problem really, as long as we
continue to bring in new songs,' Robin argues. 'But
that is where we are falling short at the moment, because there never seems to be time to write new material, everything is happening so quickly.'
    As the Cocteau Twins have played virtually the same
set for six months now, it is crucial that newer,
stronger material is introduced to push them forward
again.
    Hail the Cocteaux.... part of their charm is their un-
conscious sway from the typical, conventional 'rock'
approach with not a trace of pretentiousness. They
have been careful to avoid jumping aboard the 'race
against rockism' bandwagon, to consciously avoid a
'Rock' influence/inspiration (W lie's 'rockism' notion
being taken far too literally - because if Blood And
Roses, X-Mal Deutschland, Zerra I, the remnants of Southern Death Cult and Spear Of Destiny career right
across the area that represents the fading rock dream,
picking at the scattered debris, then they, along with
the Cocteau Twins, surely hint at a brand new restora-
tion period - a healthily perverse renewal). The best
'Rock' music has always been that with an unsettling
perversity, a corrupting insinuating sense of challenge,
a malignant cancer. The thrill of the chase from the
Doors, the Velvets, Syd Barrett Floyd throught to Bowie,
Television, Banshees, Magazine, Joy Division and The
Fall... All have had that 'Lurking Doubt'- a disrespect for the banal , for complacency, for the squalid
decay in the refusal to move on. Sometimes, it is a
heart of darkness, sometimes a glorious exorcism of the
senses, sometimes a shimmering celebration of love, life
and a lingering excitement. The Cocteau Twins often
suggest that kind of acheivement, but for now, my faith
lies in their present potential blossoming in the
future.
    Robin: 'There is a sense of challenge in being in the
band and it is exciting to be in the Cocteau Twins but
always for differeent reasons:- A year ago, the prospect
of rehearsing in a proper studio was thrilling, then
other things obviously became more important. But at the
moment, the actual purpose of what we do and what mo-
tivates us to do it is not often considered - perhaps it
will begin to be questioned more as we develop. There
always has to be an element of challenge to make it worthwhile though, to spur us on to the next step. At present, we can never talk too much about the actual content
of the songs, their mood, themes, their whole angle. It's
not as if we worry about being misinterpreted anyway -
perhaps there is something good if people interpret the
songs their own way.'
    After the OMD tour, the Cocteaux will be busy writing new
songs and recording a new album which should be ready for
their own tour in mid-October. There's this strange kind
of perfection about them that has nothing to do with a
technical cleaness but something to do with a vague feeling of discovery, innocence and a secret, smiling knowledge of the mystery of fascination. They balance(perhaps
precariously) on the threshold of their enigma... their
sound nervously teeters and tremors on the brink of its
own potential.... and you wonder how far they can take it...
and if you love the magic of the Cocteau Twins like I
do.... you worry because you sense that they must break
loose.... break new ground, recapture the beauty and purity that has already passed.
    Therefore, they arrive at the crossroads edging closer
to exhausting the possibilities of their present sound
and approach, needing now to forge ahead, to toy with new
ideas. At the moment, they just might take your breath
away with their flood of potent, magical agitation, that
nervous, flickering flame of sweet desire. They will
grow stronger and instill the BITE in their music which
at the moment, only whispers. We are left, for now,
with the hidden promise, while the rest is left to them...
and their curious, fascinating noise.

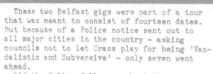

Following last issue's article on TV21's tour of Poland, TIM and LOU BELL of DIRT (now in Flux Of Pink Indians) offered to tell us about their journey to Belfast with CRASS and ANNIE ANXIETY. Groups rarely make the effort to cross the Irish Sea, particularly those with as strong views as Crass. Although the visit happened some months ago, it was, as ever, unreported in the media, which makes this account all the more interesting. It must be stressed that we are not trying to glorify the violent image of Belfast, and realise that life goes on there quite normally for many people, but ignoring the situation would be even worse.—AF.

CRASS & DIRT IN BELFAST

These two Belfast gigs were part of a tour that was meant to consist of fourteen dates. But because of a Police notice sent out to all major cities in the country - asking councils not to let Crass play for being 'Vandalistic and Subversive' - only seven went ahead.

Did the Police follow us about the country as well?

On one occasion our (Dirt's) van broke down and we got the AA to relay it seventy miles to Manchester, where we were staying. But as the relay service only takes five people, and there were eight of us three had to hitch. While thumbing a lift the police stopped us and asked why we were hitching at this time of night (midnight); we explained, they said "Oh! You're in that band aren't you?" As we hadn't mentioned any band we presumed that they had been talking to the others in the van, waiting to be relayed. On getting back we found that no-one had spoken to the Police....

Then on arrival at Dublin, the customs greeted us with the words "Oh, you're Crass aren't you!" In all, during the tour Dirt got stopped five times, once by the drug squad who searched all our belongings for three-quarters of an hour. We were also stopped on the North Circular Road (London) where we were told that "If you drive a hire van along the North Circular Road on a Tuesday morning you must expect to be stopped"!

FRIDAY 10th SEPTEMBER
DIRTY UNDIES AND PADDY REA'S

We left Manchester and got to Holyhead just in time for the 9.30 am ferry to Dublin. On arriving at customs everyone was ordered out of Crass's van, but as we all laughed at them the official told us to get back in. Dirt's turn came next,(Dirt's vehicles kept changing because we went through a van, car and a hire van during the tour). We were told to empty our bags. The first thing Fox (guitar & vocals) took out was a dirty pair of spotted pants which didn't please the official, especially when Fox held them up in front of his face! They searched the car and took away a pot of parsley and a pot of salt, thinking they were dope and smack, for tests. After taking the P.A. van apart without finding anything they let us all go.

The drive through Eire was pretty boring until we got to the border, where we got a shock. Seeing as we were on the main Dublin to Belfast road we expected quite heavy security at the border. Instead, all that met us was a tatty little shed with a small barrier and three people standing about who waved us through! We were later told that everytime a proper check point is built it gets blown up, so now it's just left as a shed.

It wasn't long though,until we went through a proper check point. We didn't have to stop but there were a series of ramps meaning we couldn't drive faster than 10m.p.h. On one side of the road stood a green pill box. It was quite high so that it could look down on lorries. There were a couple of RUC men (Royal Ulster Constabulary) standing about with rifles and a big "NO PHOTOGRAPHS" sign.

When we got to Belfast we headed to "Just Books", which is an alternative book shop situated just outside the city centre. It has lots of literature on Anarchy, Marxism, Communism, Gay and womens rights, and is run by several people who get a lot of stick from the authorities. These people organised the gigs and put us up for the nights we stayed. After we had eaten and found out where we would be staying a band called Stalag 17 came in and asked us if we wanted to go down to the local pub. So along with Fox and Steve Ignorant we took up the offer.

To get to the pub (Paddy Reas') we had to go through the City Centre, which is a bit like London's Oxford Street with all the major stores, but is surrounded by a wall of barbed wire. To get into it you have to go through a checkpoint where you get stopped by civilian searchers; to get out you have to go through a turnstile that only lets one person out at a time. All along the street are the RUC who wear a green uniform and carry rifles, and tend to be very big men. Some are on foot and others travel about in armoured land rovers.

Apart from the civilian searchers and the RUC there are also the UDR (Ulster Defence Regiment) and the British Army. They both look basically the same but the UDR have a harp on their berets.

We got to the pub which had a back room for punks, all sitting on beer barrels. The drink was cheap (50p per pint) and everyone was very friendly and noisy. Because it is near the City Centre the doors are locked at 8pm and no one is allowed to come in. At about 9.30 pm we had to get the barman to unlock the door for us to get out.

As soon as we got outside some winos tried to ponce off us. Just before the City Centre we drew near to a big group of Mods and Skins (Protestant Mods wear a red, white and blue target, Catholic Mods have a green and white target, Skins are usually NF and strong Protestants). We were shitting it as we got closer to them but they started fighting amongst themselves, and after being searched we got into the City Centre.

To get out a punk led us down a dark alley with the warning "Watch it down alleys coz sometimes skins jump you." Down the alley next to the turnstile there were several large figures; with our hearts in our throats we ventured nearer, but it was only the army. Our pace quickened as we made our way back to Just Books. That night we stayed at a house near the University, intrigued with our first day in Ireland.

...BUT AFTER THE GIG

SATURDAY 11th

We set off to meet the others who were staying a few streets away, but on turnign to go down a certain road, found it was taped off. The UDR told us to go the long way round, as apparently there had been a shooting. When we eventually met up with everyone, we found that someone had taken our car for a hoy ride and smashed it up: the back seat had been nicked, we had one burst tyre, bent steering and a wing missing. Maybe the British number plate was the cause? No one really had time to worry about how we were going to drive it back to Manchester because we had to set up the gig at the Anarchy Centre.

The Centre is a small building just inside the City Centre. It holds 3-400 people and is split into two low ceilinged rooms, one for a concert hall and one for a tea room. The gig was due to start at the unearthly hour of 2 pm as the buses stop early in Belfast due to the violence.

Unlike most bands, at a Crass/Dirt gig we all help set up the stage and P.A., which takes a few hours. This keeps the cost down as well as giving us more contact with the people who come to see us. When the doors opened the hall was soon full up and there was a great buzz of excitement:- Crass gigs are extremely professional, for there is always something happening.

First was a Mick Duffield film about the effects of nuclear war which was followed by a local band called Just Destiny. Although I didn't really get off on the music they were really together and went down well. Annie Anxiety was next and her poems and tapes kept the crowd tran-

...sfixed. She really is an amazing performer, often playing the parts of three people at once. As soon as Annie left the stage "Choosing Death" another Nick Duffield film, began. This film brilliantly links the arms race to the slaughter house to materialism to marriage etc. It's not a nice film to watch - it makes me feel disgusted with the falseness and deceptiveness of society - but it does make you think and that's what proper entertainment is about.

After the film Dirt really got the crowd going with their fast sharp music - well, what did you expect us to say?

Following another poem by Annie it was Crass! turn. Watching Crass is always exciting - behind them are various backdrops, either side of them are TV screens which show footage of different events, and above them is a film screen showing slides and photographs. Crass launched into their set which draws from all their records. Steve and Eve take turns on vocals, Joy leads a poem & songs like the brilliant Nagasaki Nightmare make sure all eyes are on them. See them do Rewel Tribal Rivals and Securicon & you'll never believe that Crass lack humour. The intensity of the whole package is stunning. See it.

After the gig while we were giving away badges and handouts, we heard someone had been put in intensive care after a beating by skins. Our moods changed immediately from elation to anger. The RUC arrived soon after and started telling everyone to leave the building, cordoning the area off with jeeps and beating up a punk who called them fascists. Someone got on the stage and warned everyone to "Take it easy because the RUC are in a nasty mood". At this Chief Inspector McCorrack of the RUC, told the organisers that he wanted the name of the speaker. The organisers refused and a heavy argument followed in which McCorrack asked if the place had a fire licence: on being told "Yes", he said "Bollocks I'll see to it that the concert tomorrow will have the press, maximum policing, the dogs and the drug squad." After this a punk told us that he'd once had his skin smashed in during an RUC raid. We filled in an official complaint, but saw the futility of this when the RUC called...

round his house every week for a month to beat him up.

SUNDAY 12th

Today everyone felt nervous because of the RUC threats. As we got closer to the Anarchy Centre three armoured cars went roaring past us and we expected the worst, but when we arrived there was no one to be seen.

Belfast on a Sunday is deserted. Apart from a few newsagents everything is shut, even the pubs. Religion takes priority here. As everyone was setting up the stage I went off in search of some milk so we could all have a cuppa. After walking about a hundred yards up the road I was confronted by a hippy and a skin. The skin asked me what I thought of "All these fucking punks about"(!!). Forever the diplomat I answered "It depends what they're like as people". I'd thought they might get nasty but as soon as they heard my English accent I was asked where I lived and how I was keeping etc. It can pay to be British here - and to have cut off your spikey hair!

The gig was roughly the same as Saturday, except the atmosphere which was more serious and controlled. I think the message got through better. Stalag 17 replaced Just Destiny and went down well, although I thought they lacked a bit of punch.

And so the weeks of planning and speculating came to a close. The gigs had proven an important success, and for the bands, organisers and the people who came it had been a much needed visit. The money was given to "Just Books" (Who are doing a great deal of necessary work and who's hospitality was over-whealming).

FINAL NOTE

When we left N.Ireland a new wave of sectarian murders begun. Although only spending a few days in Belfast, we all felt much more aware of the worstening crisis. It still doesn't look like the Government will try to improve torn relationships now or for the future, and so appalling conditions high unemployment, bad housing and widespread discontent worsten.

THE REFLECTIONS

THE REFLECTIONS

Though it never does an area any good to have a 'scene' built around it, it has to be said that all Scottish bands might not sound the same, but there are those that sound undeniably Scottish. Aztec Camera, The Bluebells and Friends Again all have that instantly recognisable accoustic '60's pop feel, and now, dear readers, you can add THE REFLECTIONS to that list.

At present, The Reflections number just two, those being George Williamson and Skip. In a tradition that always seems to end up for the best, these two have been best buddies (and making music) for a mere seven years now. Putting together and disbanding groups rapidly as they searched for their own style in the wake of punk, the duo soon became bored with the vanguard of Scottish music - Orange Juice, Simple Minds and Aztec Camera - and went back to 'discover their roots' by playing folk clubs, jazz clubs, and taking up the wonderful art of busking.

Looking back at it, English anarcho-punks playing Belfast in '82 was always going to be a little interesting. The Troubles were on and we got more than a touch. Our car (English plated – rookie error) was joy-ridden and smashed up, and the RUC made a point of interrupting the gigs and abusing audiences. But we also got a different sort of joy-ride: the intensity of the gigs, an audience deprived of overseas live acts, the hospitality of our hosts, and seeing Belfast, an education and experience. It was great, properly so. Tony Fletcher asked us to write an account for *Jamming!*, so we did.

Jamming! set the bar. Most of us were making fanzines for ourselves and our direct community. Literacy, production, distribution, audience reach and so on were backseat values. We were hobbyists. *Jamming!* aimed higher, in its writing, its production quality, its distribution (it was in W H Smith's, for God's sake!) and its aim for an audience. It smelt of ambition and professionalism. In the fanzine world, it was like one of the then iconic British indie labels. Getting an article into *Jamming!* felt like hitting the big time. **Tim Kelly**

50p U.S. $1.50

A NEW OPTIMISM FOR THE 80's

JAMMING!

No. 15

ELVIS BREAKS OUT!
THE MAN AND THE MYTH: ELVIS COSTELLO INTERVIEW

ECHO AND THE BUNNYMEN

BRUCE FOXTON

CARMEL   U2/ALARM IN AMERICA   THE TRUTH

"There's been punk, funk, pop, rock and reggae . . . and now there's Carmel!"

Carmel in action at Ronnie Scotts.
Photo: Jason Pevovar.

It's a rare occasion indeed when a record you initially think you're going to hate, you end up wanting to rush out and buy. You must know the sort of song: all wailing vocals, off-beat drumming and awkward rumblings, then, bit by bit, it all falls into place. A glow of emotion erupts in that high, ferocious vocal, an abrupt rhythm arrests your body, and that pounding double bass irresistably leaves an expression on your face that says one thing: you've been converted.

Such an event happened a year ago when a song by the name of *Storm* literally blasted from my radio. It turned out to be the debut single from a three-piece group called Carmel; further investigations revealed a six-track mini LP imaginatively entitled *Carmel*, on Red Flame Records, and further proof of what a highly promising and exciting group this was; put simply, both records had

just that. Strengthened by the use of keyboards and backing vocalists for the first time, it is a pillar of strength and emotion. These additions have done nothing to take away the raw edge and its inspired urgency of the group either; the song lifts where it should lift, moves exactly where it should move, but ever importantly, it touches the listener throughout.

That early sound of Carmel has evolved and sounds as strong as ever. At the same time, so too has the voice and focal point of the group, to the extent that comparisons to the likes of 1940's singing legends Edith Piaf and Billie Holliday, or the evergreen Aretha Franklin have been made. But are they really getting it right?

"I think there's been far too much made of this sort of comparisons already," responds Carmel. "It's true to say that I admire all of those singers but I'd never dream of copying them, ever, and anyway, we sound nothing like them. I suppose it's just because they're females and I've gone on about them that people have compared us, but it's about as accurate as saying we sound like Michael Jackson; who we all love!"

"It always happens," picks up Gerry. "Whenever people start writing about a new group, they compare it to this and that, but let me get this straight. There's been punk, there's been funk, there's been pop, rock and reggae . . . and now there's Carmel!"

All three maintain that Carmel are at their best playing live, and also point out that they don't consider "Bad Day" as truly representative of what they're about; in fact, they consider the B-side, "Rue De St. Denis", (whose unconventional

rhythms and sparse melody make even the A-side sound about as daring as Abba) closer to what they're trying to achieve. Personally, I hold both in very high regard, though I'd always prefer "Bad Day", as there is nothing more exciting to my mind that a truly genuine hard and uplifting record invading that area infested by rubbish, but nonetheless scrutinised by all: the dirty thirty! Imagine a hit parade where records of the calibre of The Grandmaster's "Message", The Clash's "Cashbah", Jackson's "Wanna Be Startin' Somethin'", Echo's "Never Stop" and, of course, Carmel's "Bad Day" were the order of the day and not the occasional oasis in the desert. It's an exciting prospect, and why shouldn't the line from the last of those classics, "Bad day, you better go away now", come true!

Pedro Romhanyi

guts where other had mere groves. In addition, there was an undeniable spirit of adventure – a genuine attempt to give the listener a new sound

to embrace, to not adopt a tired and conventional style of music, to challenge that listeners heart and brand it with music of quality.

Inevitably, the outfit gained the attention of one of the bigger fish in the sea and soon London Records and Carmel were wed. Time passed, and other than a few occasional live shows, little was heard from the combo. Why the silence - were the record company remodelling the act for their first proper voyage into the stormy seas of pop music? After all, mightn't that same challenging and exciting sound find no harbour whatsoever in the minds of the Great British Record Buying Public, so often weaned on a diet of tasteless slush? Won't Carmel have to dilute that unique sound and style and succumb to the cheap surrender?

Thankfully, Carmel's debut single for London, the rousing Gospel - inspired *Bad Day*, has done

"Look," insists double bass basher Jimmy Paris, angered by the very notion, "we've been together for some time now, and we intend to be around for a lot longer, *playing the type of music we want to hear*! If that appeals to other people, then great. If not, well, I don't think any of us really care because we couldn't see the point in working on something that we had no heart or belief in."

"AMEN!" holler the other two thirds of the group, namely the lady with the golden vocals, Carmel McCourt, and her percussion pummelling sidekick Gerry Darby. Refusing to let the subject lie however, I suggest that with public tastes being as slow and unadventurous as they are, won't the group have to dilute it's sound and song writing approach if it's ever going to approach a mass audience?

"I've already told you exactly how we felt about what we do and we don't intend to change that at all, if we can help it," repeats Jimmy with more that a hint of feeling insulted. "All along the line, we've had people coming up to us and saying that sort of thing, but we've simply got on with what we wanted to do, and I think we've gained admirers exactly because of that. Of course, things are somewhat different now that we find ourselves on a label alongside the likes of Bananarama and New Edition, and I'd be a fool if I pretended that making music we thought was great but nobody bought would get us by. All I can say is that we intend to make music we're proud of and let's wait and see if it sells."

The SMITHS
Reel Around The Fountain
b/w   Jeane

OUT NOW ON ROUGH TRADE RECORDS

PAGE 12

No longer having the full-time distraction of a record label, I decided to take the plunge and commit *Jamming!* to a regular timetable and a new degree of intended professionalism; such requirements were also part of the formal agreement with Seymour Press, a mainstream distributor in Brixton who were lovely to work with and seemed genuinely committed to making a success of the venture. For the launch of this new bi-monthly schedule, the magazine was typeset and printed in full colour for the first time – in Finland, no less, which saw me take a vodka-laced junket to Turku – and in September 1983, after I watched the pages roll off a press about the size of a house, something close to 50,000 copies duly made their way into newsagents nationwide.

If all the above suggests that *Jamming!* had jumped the proverbial shark and transitioned from scrappy fanzine to slick magazine, the content and, especially, the layout, confirmed otherwise. The latter, at least, was not entirely intentional. Robin Richards, perhaps still not caught up on sleep after designing the interior of Issue 14, balked at the thought of continuing further, but perilously late in the metaphorical day. Still operating out of the windowless cubby I had constructed in his company's basement, I approached Pete Barrett, the Dexys designer with whom I had been sharing many a lunchtime cappuccino in Soho alongside contributors Gary Crowley and Pedro Romhanyi; Pete instead recommended his assistant, Russell Tate. With almost no time to recruit anyone else, and unwilling to delay the new schedule, I took Barrett's recommendation. Russell was great fun to be around, had the youthful energy necessary for the late night deadlines and

ISSUE #15
9/83

was full of colourful visual concepts – so colourful that the 'What's Cooking' section on pages 4–5 confirmed that national distribution would not immediately hinder *Jamming!*'s reputation for illegibility!

Hidden behind that puce design were short features on the new record labels Kitchenware and Blanco y Negro, indicating that *Jamming!* maintained its finger on the trendy pulse. So, elsewhere, did Pedro's piece on Carmel and a soon-to-be collector's edition ad by the Rough Trade label for The Smiths' single that never was ('Reel Around The Fountain'). But the main thrust of this debut colour publication was the exclusive and relatively feisty interviews with Elvis Costello (conducted by Dave Jennings), Echo & The Bunnymen (by Jonh Wilde) and the newly solo Bruce Foxton (by yours truly). Along with a personal tour diary by Mike Peters of The Alarm recounting his group's first excursion to the USA, opening for U2, this was all sufficiently mainstream to ensure healthy sales of around 30–35,000. Whether the heavily discounted income from all these newsagent sales (income that now arrived 60–90 days down the line) and the few advertisements we could muster (being a publication too big for the indies and too small for the ad agencies) would cover the cost of those Finnish printing bills, the frightening typesetting costs, *plus* the sudden request from contributors for payment given that this was now meant to be a professional operation, all remained very much open to question. As for how I financed all this in the first place, that answer was simple: by securing an overdraft from my mother's bank, the security being collateral in her name, of course, given that I had none. What could possibly go wrong?

hotos: Bleddyn Butcher

THE ELVIS COSTELLO INTERVIEW

by DAVE JENNINGS

"I think it would be really pretentious of me to try and write an anthemic song for the downtrodden people, which a lot of writers try to do and look really stupid."

WHEN TOLD that I would be interviewing Elvis Costello at the television studio used to make Channel 4's *Switch*, my first reaction was one of simple excitement and pleasure; the reaction of a fan given the chance to meet one of his favourite artists. Costello has been responsible for some of the most literate and incisive pop songs of recent years, from 1977's *My Aim Is True* set right up to the present *Punch The Clock* collection which was to be previewed on *Switch*. When I considered the prospect of the interview rather more calmly, I began to wonder what the *Switch* studio would be like, imagining some starkly modern building made entirely of concrete, red brick, glass and neon. I could hardly have been more wrong – in fact, the home of *Switch* is more like a small mansion, complete with spacious gardens, and it was in this elegant setting that the following conversation took place . . .

I'M VERY GLAD that you've agreed to talk to us – how did it come about that you broke off diplomatic relations with the music press? What was the reason for that?

I think I just got a bit tired of the way every article was writen with a huge preconception, and I didn't really feel that anything I said made much sense, because it was written with this preamble before it, assuming that I had this one attitude. So I thought, "Well, they're going to write nonsense about me anyway, so why should I contribute?"

What kind of audiences have you been getting recently in Britain?

Mixed, really . . . I was quite pleased with the attendances on the last tour – we did about 75% at most halls. We hadn't had any hit records, which bring in the kind of people that are not really crazy about you, that just saw you on *Top of The Pops* last week. When we had *Oliver's Army*, and things like that in the charts, we got a lot of those kind of people, and now it tends to be a different crowd . . . more people that know a lot of the songs, know the album tracks. So I suppose it's a more dedicated crowd, though I'm not sure that's necessarily a good thing, to only play with those people in mind. Certainly, it's not a good idea to make records with only those people in mind.

Are there any of your records, that are other people's old favourites, that you wouldn't want to perform now?

We don't do (*I Don't Want To Go To*) *Chelsea* very often, we just dig it out occasionally for a bit of fun. It was the mainstay of the set when we didn't have very much material, so we kind of exhausted it. Some of the older numbers we can still do . . . we still do *Pump It Up*. Now we do it with the horn section, it's a different number, y'know . . . it's got a whole different character to it. It's a sort of anti-rock'n'roll song, that's the joke of it, really. And I still enjoy the perversity of playing it, and people all leaping around, and acting just like they do to a regular rock'n'roll tune, when the song is actually . . . the opposite of "Satisfaction", if you like! (*Laughs*).

At one point, when I was a little bit more serious – I took things maybe a bit *too* seriously – things like that used to annoy me. Now, I see the humour in them, and I can appreciate the irony of it, rather than get wound up about the fact that people are *not understanding my Art!* Just 'cause you write a song with a certain thing in mind, you can't demand that people listen to it with that certain frame of mind. They've got to listen to it with whatever frame of mind they've got – if they've got one at all! I know I've done my job properly if I'm happy with the song and I'm happy with the recording. And if you want to seek it, there's stuff put in there deliberately so that people can get out of it whatever they want. I don't demand that people sit there with a set of rules on how to listen to our records!

Wouldn't it worry you, though, if you wrote one particular song that a lot of people seemed to take the wrong way?

Well, I'd think it was a badly-written song, then. I think there are a few songs which are so obscure that the lyrics don't mean anything to anybody.

I would never, even though I'm personally unemployed, have guessed that ". . . And In Every Home" was about unemployment, if I hadn't read the NME interview . . .

Yeah, that was deliberately . . . you see, I think there are plenty of other people that write very specific songs about social problems, in very, very bald, very cold terms, and do it very well. They have a kind of relationship with the audience which allows them to do that, like Paul Weller, and UB40 to some extent at the height of their powers, anyway. And that's not a relationship that I've ever cultivated – I've never pretended to be A Man Of The People. I'm an individual – I'm not masquerading as Joe Ordinary, so I think it would be really pretentious of me to try and write an anthemic song for the downtrodden people, which a lot of writers try to do and look really stupid.

To try and write something which *even they* will understand . . .

Yeah, it's really patronising! So I wanted to write a song that is a story, and it's about some of the crueller ironies of unemployment rather than just the bald facts which everybody knows.

I did hear a story about that song, that you'd done a fairly simple demo of it, given it to Steve Nieve to do an arrangement, and he'd come back with this enormous widescreen production . . .

Yeah, well, it was just a simple piano tune . . . not *that* simple, the chords are all a bit peculiar. 'Cause I ramble around the piano a bit, I don't really play it properly, so some of the more eccentric tunes are written on the piano! The straight forward ones are written on the guitar, normally; I play neither really well, but the piano leads me to odder things! So I had that, and Steve did write the rest of the arrangement. I said to him, "just go mad" and he did!

How much of a role do the Attractions normally play, then, in how the songs sound on the records?

It's hard to say, really . . . I come along with an idea of the general rhythm, and sometimes that's the way it goes, and everybody works out their parts, like, Bruce and Pete work out a rhythm pattern, which you have to do to propel the song. Bruce is very good on harmonies, he's not just a good rhythmic bass player. In fact, his strength is really the melodic lines that he thinks of; he often adds really interesting notes which help bring the melody out. Steve is an excellent musician, he's capable of all that as well. Then sometimes I'll bring a song along, and I've got the idea of the rhythm, but it won't sound right, so we'll play nine different arrangements, you know! We'll play it as a tango, play it as a waltz, play a reggae arrangement, and we go through all the comical arrangements! Sometimes you might hit on something really interesting; more often, you come round to some variation on the original idea.

The trouble with "Imperial Bedroom" was that I took a lot of the vocal ideas to an

extreme; I was working with just Geoff Emerick in the studio, and making a lot of the production decisions myself. That's my only criticism of "Imperial Bedroom"; I'm really pleased that I did that record, it has all of these almost experimental ideas on it; but a few of the songs are maybe over-developed. They'd gone past the point where they were good; and I got bored with them, and did something else to them, and it wasn't always a good thing.

DO YOU THINK that the other media, apart from the press, have treated you reasonably well?

Er . . . I think there's always been the people that have kept an eye out for what we've been doing, particularly on the radio There's other people that, whenever we're having a success, will always tell you that *they* played that record, when in fact, they probably didn't! With TV . . . well, we don't really have a relationship with TV! The only way you

build up a relationship with them is by having lots of hits! I think that overall, television does treat pop music rather shabbily. Pop music programmes are all shoved on at dodgy times, or they're given tiny budgets . . .

You think that's still the case, even with the new ones on Channel 4?

I still think there's a way to go. I think they are getting better; just the fact that there's more of them, means that hopefully there has to be more exposure for bands. I think it's good that there are magazine programmes where you get live bands *and* videos; I wouldn't like to see an innovation like MTV, the American system where it's just 24-hour videos. Musicians are an uninteresting bunch of people to look at anyway; loads of people miming to their records, over and over again over the space of 24 hours – I think it'd drive you right round the twist, to watch it!

"I was talking to one of Duran Duran and he seemed to give the impression that they were considering making the video first in the future, and then putting the music to it!"

There were some people, not very long ago, who would have had you believe that making a video was, in the future, going to become part of the creative process of making a single, and that bands with no visual ideas wouldn't be able to succeed.

We did some videos in late 1978, when we were on our way from Canada to Japan – that was just where we were touring, we weren't being flash! – and we stopped in Hawaii, and did some videos on the beach there, a sort of a parody of "Help!", if you like! It was great, because it was so unusual then – everybody was standing up

against brick walls and snarling in leather jackets, and there we were on this beautiful sunny beach, and running into the Pacific Ocean! I thought they were really humorous, but you compare them to Duran Duran videos, where they're taking themselves so seriously – or at least I think they are; maybe they are really sending themselves up all the time, but I suspect they're taking themselves seriously – and they really look like Bounty adverts to me, y'know! I happened to bump into one of them up at AIR Studios where we were recording, and I might be wrong here but he seemed to give the impression that they were considering making the video first in the future – that there might be some future date where they would make the video first, and then put the music to it! Which seems a really odd way of going about making records, but then maybe they're not making records! Maybe they're a new innovation – they're video makers, like . . . singing male models! If that's the future, it might just be the future of that one particular branch of it, 'cause obviously people like me wouldn't fit into that at all; so records would be one thing and videos would be another. I think it's stupid to have an attitude against video, on the basis that other, good-looking groups do better with video – that's just a childish attitude.

Yeah, because good-looking groups do better with pictures in the paper . . .

Yeah, right!

On the subject of television, how did the Breakfast TV Appearance come about – when you were on reviewing the newspapers?

It was just one of those things – the researchers on those kind of programmes looking for people that might be a bit different. Generally, they have journalists, or actors, or politicians . . . The one thing about news, or current affairs programmes, on the rare occasions I've guested on them – or even chat programmes – they always seem amazed that anybody in a group can string three words together! I think they always think we're all illiterate, y'know, and all our speech is obscene! And of course, a lot of groups would probably confirm their prejudices – they probably *are* inarticulate, and illiterate, and profane!

You'll probably never get a good review from Julie Burchill again, after what you said in the hanging debate . . .

Why, is she pro-hanging?

Violently so.

That girl's got problems!

Was that what you were getting at in *Pills And Soap* – the lines about, "Give me the needle, give me the rope"?

Er . . . no; that's a very cynical song. One night, I was watching the television, and saw coverage of a funeral . . . it was somebody in Northern Ireland, it might have been a soldier or an IRA man or an innocent, I honestly can't remember. It was just the insensitivity with which the camera dealt with the mourners – it really made me angry. Prying into people's grief – I mean, abject grief – and at the same time, matters that really should concern us are trivialised or hidden away, and replaced with cute articles about dogs and cats, and children – and not really about things that matter about kids and animals – but the nice, cute stories that fill the newspapers. And it was a rather nasty suggestion that we did away with them all – what would they write about then? (*Laughs*) It was a very black song – and I was watching a film called *The Animals*

Film, and I just wrote down the title 'Pills And Soap' – it transpired that that's one of the by-products of the misuse of animals. And then I started to expand the idea to the misuse of the human animal, in all its many ways . . . particularly with reference to misplaced sentiment, including patriotism – misplaced emotion along those lines.

So that was why you felt you had to get that song out in time for the Election Campaign?

I just wanted it out. It wasn't going to make the slightest bit of difference to the election; I thought it was, as much as any song I've ever written, pertinent to that moment. Had things gone the way they were supposed to, in terms of our business arrangements, our album would have been out by then – but, as it was delayed it suddenly dawned on me that there was nothing stopping me putting that record out on its own, as a single, under another name and on my own label. So that's what I did!

What made me think of the connection with the Election was the fact of it being deleted on June the 9th . . .

Well, obviously, there was a suggestion there . . . I wasn't going to get up and make a big political speech; I left it open to people's interpretation, and if they can't work *that* one out, then there's no point, y'know!

What was the legal position that forced you to put that out as "The Imposter"?

There was no legal position that forced me to put it out as The Imposter; I simply put it out as that to distinguish it from, "a new Elvis Costello And The Attractions single", because, strictly speaking, it's only Steve and I on the record; and I knew that within a month we would be releasing *Everyday I Write The Book*, on one record label or another.

The first thing I thought of, when I saw that you were going to put this record out under an assumed name, was the line in the "NME" interview where you claimed that you were seriously thinking of dropping the name "Elvis Costello", at least for Britain . . .

I think I said that fairly flippantly . . . and of course, in cold print, it looked quite dramatic! I *did* think that there is a possibility that you can get tied to a time, in people's minds; people associate us, and The Buzzcocks, and The Clash, with 1978. And to some people's minds, they're only interested in The New Thing, and whatever kind of record we make, they're not going to give it a chance. But then they cheat themselves out of a lot of great music, because I know a lot of stuff that's a damn sight older than what I do, and still gives me a lot of pleasure.

So I can take it that you haven't got a lot of time for the current crop of punk bands?

No, no . . . they're tired and boring. Rage is one thing, but it doesn't age very gracefully! You can only shout for so long at somebody, and you either lose your voice or they stop listening! And that's something I learned pretty early on . . . there was quite an aggressive in-tention behind a lot of our early records, and it's not something I left behind; I've just found new ways of saying things with similar intent. I don't think there's any song on my first or second album, which purists can hold up and say, "*That's* when he was good, that's when he was really young and angry". There's no song on there that's in any way as vitriolic as "Pills And Soap". I have learned better ways of putting the point over – and you don't always have to shout! In some ways, the most frightening threat you can make to somebody is to whisper – if you go right up close to them, and (*whispers*) "I'm gonna break your neck!" – that's a lot more threatening than suddenly going wild! A threat, or anything aggressive, done quietly, is much more sinister than anything done like a ranting idiot.

COULD YOU TELL me what *The World And His Wife* is about?

Yeah, it's about a family of exiles – it's not any particular family I know, it's just based on certain people's attitudes. I set it in almost like a play situation, about a family gathering of exiles, constantly moaning on about going home to "The Old Country". It's just a sort of cynical view of them, really, I suppose.

This is something that Siouxsie and The Banshees have touched on in about three or four songs; people idealising a foreign country, and imagining it to be like heaven . . .

Yeah, well, what's worse is when it's some place that you're talking about going *back* to; as if it were The Homeland. People do it all the time, I think; I'm sure people that are abroad from England do it; but certainly Irish people do it. Lots of nationalities do it, and sometimes it's a positive thing, it sustains you, but I'm writing the song about the negative side of it, because it builds up a lot of bigotry. The last verse goes: "*But late on in the evening, through the tears and fol-de-rol/ Come the sentimental feelings for the lure of vitriol/Longing thoughts go hankering for the old home overseas/With a blindfold and A National Anthem sung in different keys*". So, obviously, I've got Ireland in mind more . . . not to take one side or the other, just the nationalism on both sides. Idealising any country is going to lead to grief.

Do you still feel that the extreme right in this country is a serious threat? It seemed you did around the time when the "Rock Against Racism" thing was quite big . . .

Yeah . . . I think they've made such fools of themselves that only people of very limited intelligence give them any credence anymore. The thing is that they had a kind of caravan rolling at one time which looked rather dangerous. But I don't think you can ever write people like that off, because when you least expect it – and when things get very grim for everybody – it's very easy to persuade people who are easily persuaded that "*These* people are the cause of all your problems". It's easy to manipulate the public using those kind of arguments; I think you've always got to be on your guard for those people, and never give them the chance to gain a foothold. I don't think there's perhaps quite as imminent a danger of them taking hold of a lot of people's lives, the way it appeared about four years ago; but all the time there is that feeling – and there's an underlying racism, not just against black people, but against lots of races in this country – inherent in the national character. It really came to the fore during the Falklands War. If they'd been Germans, or something – well, not the Germans, because we hate the Germans as well! But if they'd been Canadians – if it had been the French Canadians it wouldn't have been so bad! But they were *dagoes*! That the attitude! It's like, go and kill the wops! All that "let's bash the Argies" attitude we saw in the papers – there's no doubt it had a lot of sympathy with people, you've got to accept that that's part of certain peoples character. The extreme Right can mobilise that kind of ignorant bigotry, because it's in a lot of people.

It was very clear that the "Falklands Factor" played a tremendous part in boosting Thatcher's popularity . . .

Oh yeah . . . she took full advantage of it. I think you don't need to look so far to find the Right now – the Right's in power! I think you've got a very cunning Right-wing Government, so every day of your life is affected by their decisions, and their lack of compassion. They're content that they seem to hold half the population in. Now I don't think you have to look so far for the people that are threatening your freedom of choice, and freedom of life . . . particularly children. They're just gonna grow up to a completely different society if the Tories have their way.

So did that recently motivate you to start writing more obviously political songs, like "Shipbuilding" for example?

Obviously, it reflect what I see about me, the same way as all the songs do, but they're about different things. Some of them are much more light-hearted; there are songs on the new album like "The Greatest Thing", which are much lighter. That's another song about pride, but in a different way. Instead of being a cautionary tale it's a celebratory tale. You know . . . *"Everybody stopped when she walked into the room/Isn't this the greatest thing?"* It's *I Saw Her Standing There*, if you like . . . a 1983 version of *I Saw Her Standing There!*

You are one of those performers who have a very devoted following – does that ever get unnerving at all, when you know that people are wanting to know every possible little detail about you?

Only if it's in any way sinister; fortunately, it's usually fairly positive. Some guy that wrote some magazine about us was pestering my father – I thought that was a bit much. I don't personally draw a distinction between work and life, but I think it's wrong that people allow anybody's work to dominate their lives to the point where they feel they have to seek out these really pointless pieces of information, y'know.

I promise this is the most trivial question *I'm* going to ask you; but nobody knows when your birthday is . . !

It's funny, that, isn't it? Even the BBC get it wrong! It's the 25th of August 1954. People always seem to have been lying about my age, saying I was older or younger – usually older!

Have you ever come close to parting company with the Attractions? There were rumours to that effect circulating around the time of "New Amsterdam".

Yeah . . . there wasn't a rift between us, I quit the group. At the end of the "Get Happy!" tour I decided I didn't really want to do it any more. That was the tour – not the "Armed Forces" tour, funnily enough – where a lot of people that had only seen us on "Top Of The Pops" and didn't know anything about us, just came to hear "Oliver's Army" and "I Can't Stand Up For Falling Down". And it got a bit frustrating . . . I just felt that I hadn't really got the bulk of the songs over to a lot of people, I'd just got one or two; and I didn't just want to be one of those one-or-two-number singers, like Gene Pitney or somebody! I quit, and we went our seperate ways, but we had a European tour to do! And then Steve had gone over to America, and he was in a car accident; and while he was recovering, I had second thoughts – I didn't want to go out and cancel tours and everything. Martin Belmont came in, and we played as a four-piece, with two guitars and no keyboards, and we did a whole European tour like that. It was very odd – I played a bit of organ on a

"I'm in a very privileged job to play music and make records for people. Sometimes you get a bit depressed that your record didn't go up in the charts, instead of which, you should be glad that you're even making a record."

"The Ivor Novello Award? You must be joking!"

couple of numbers, terrible organ, y'know! But we muddled through, and we had some good gigs; and it re-activated my interest in doing it, somehow. When I was actually faced with the reality of quitting, I realised I was being a bit spoilt, really.

I am in a very privileged job, to play music and make records for people. Sometimes you get a bit depressed that your record didn't go up in the charts – instead of which, you should be glad that you're even making a record! And now if we have a massive success, I think I'm much better equipped to deal with it than I was at the time. I always thought that I handled it pretty well, but looking back at some of the things – particularly personal matters – I didn't handle big success at all well. I don't think very many people do. And if the records aren't massively suc-

cessful, as long as I'm happy that I'm making the best record, and not wilfully trying to make obscure records . . . I wouldn't put out shoddy records, or I try not to. I can only think of one record I really dislike – "Party Party".

Really?

Yeah . . . I don't like the title. I like the bridge, and I quite like the horn part; but it was written in ten minutes, and it sounds like it. It wasn't really *our* new single, it was for a film. That's the only one I really hate; some of them I feel awkward with, 'cause they're that much longer ago. You change, and you think you're getting better, but you might just be getting different! I think it's more likely that I'm geting better at songwriting. I don't know physically how much better you can sing. I mean, I've only got the voice that I was born with; I can stretch it, and push it, and mes around with it, but i can only achieve so much with it. I just can't sing certain ways I'd love to be able to sing; like Marvin Gaye . . . like Chet Baker . . . like Frank Sinatra . . . like Stevie Wonder . . . to have that kind of dynamic range, and for all this to be effortless! The way you can improve as a singer is just . . . more care for the song. Trying to reach the feeling . . . the voice will do what you want it to then.

You've now got this deal by which F-beat is licensed to RCA – is that a deal you're happy with? Have you got as much control as you'd like?

Yeah, we were in negotiations with all of the companies up to a point, and RCA just simply sounded the keenest. They certainly didn't offer the most money – that was Virgin! I think Virgin reckon they can buy everybody, but that just proves them wrong; 'cause I dislike the company, I dislike their attitude. And they once offered me a 5% deal, before I signed to Stiff, so I thought, "You had your chance there, mate"! We've never gone with the biggest money offers; when we re-signed to CBS in America, we were offered much more money by Arista. Record companies are very impersonal things, so we've always tried to keep some identity. That's why we've got F-Beat, so that we can make the decisions about packaging, about releases, and videos, and all of those things; whereas, if you're in the hands of a big company, you're passed along a conveyor-belt of Departments. So I am happy – I've got my own label now, the IMP label. I'm going to keep it for one-off things; it's not going to be like Respond, where I'm actually seeking out new acts. If a lot of things turn up, then I'll release a lot of good records!

Do you intend to produce anyone?

If something presents itself, and I think I've got something to offer, then I would get involved. I'm not very technically-minded as a producer; I'm good at getting performances out of people. That's one thing I know I *am* good at.

So, is there anything planned after this extensive tour that you're doing?

More touring!

IN THE WEEKS since the interview, I've had the chance to get properly acquainted with *Punch The Clock*; and I can only say that I think that's a chance you should take, too. Elvis Costello continues to shine, to confuse, to excite and to frighten; and I hope and believe that he will still be doing so for some considerable time to come. As he says; even in a perfect world where everyone was equal, he'd still own the film rights – and be working on the sequel . . .

Visions of America

Among the British bands currently invading the higher reaches of the American charts are Dublin's favourite sons, *U2*. For part of their mammoth tour there earlier this summer, they brought over *The Alarm* as special support act. What's it like for an up-and-coming British group in The States for the first time, where the people may be jumping at anything remotely British, yet are still in such a different country? *Mike Peters* of The Alarm kept a diary of the trip specially for Jamming!

JUNE 1st LOS ANGELES

To the strains of '68 Guns' sung by our ever-present, ever-faithful, self-titled Family Of Fans, we left Heathrow Airport at midday bound for America, our plan to beat jetlag (stay up all night and sleep on the plane) failing miserably as we were too excited to even blink, never mind sleep. As we flew over North America, all of us trying to look out of one porthole at the back of the plane, we imagined what the Beatles must have felt as they flew over for the first time. Nowadays every household has head of The Beatles, yet we were coming in to no screaming girls, only some old man muttering "Holy Mackerel!" at the sight of Twist walking through the airport doors!

JUNE 3rd SAN FRANCISCO

After an eight-hour drive from L.A., we had our first taste of what we had all imagined was America. Driving over The Bay Bridge into San Francisco the view was unreal – the high rises all reached up for miles, and with Alcatraz Prison on the right and behind it The Golden Gate bridge, you've got to be there to really feel the power of the view. We headed for the Civic Centre, an almighty venue of 10,000 capacity unseated, where we were third on the bill with a band called Romeo Void appearing before U2. As we prepared to go on stage for our first ever gig in America, the tension in the air was tremendous, especially as we hadn't done a soundcheck or even had time to change our guitar strings – it really was into the unknown. The light of experience filled the hall and we ran on to the largest audience we had ever faced in our lives. The feeling of performing in front of all those people, who had never heard a note of music by The Alarm before, was a great experience. It was such a challenge to reach to the farthest corners and try and win every single soul, that it brought some fantastic moments for us. We found ourselves playing a lot more powerfully than we'd every done before, and after the gig we talked for hours with people about America and music, learning a lot to carry to the next show.

JUNE 5th SALT LAKE CITY

We drove all night from S.F. to Salt Lake City and I took the wheel about midnight. There was a terrific thunderstorm that I thought was literally beautiful; to see it light up the whole sky, I was really taken in with it and ended up driving all the way into Salt Lake. Just as dawn was breaking we could see the white of the salt flats all around us, and reached S.L.C. around 8.00. On arrival everyone went straight to bed except Redeye (part of the Alarm road crew) and myself, who decided to get something to eat. We set off up the road but had to turn back after only 200 yards due to all the locals (in cars and on foot) freaking out over our haircuts. In Britain people may be conservative, but over here they're *wild*.

JUNE 7th DENVER

Red Rocks Auditorium is a venue cut into the mountains in Denver, Colorado, and is designed to give perfect accoustics. It was here that U2 performed the set shown on The Tube special. The gig itself had to be cancelled due to rain and another gig was hastily arranged in Boulder about 30 miles away, but so many people turned up at Red Rocks that U2 decided to perform a few numbers without a support. Once they hit the stage everyone knew that something special was about to happen:– the rain continued to fall as U2 turned in one of the most spectacular and honest performances I have ever witnessed. The entire show has been captured on film, and with band and audience battling against the elements, it makes essential viewing.

JUNE 10th TULSA

Travelling overnight to Tulsa, we decided to take Route 44 rather than the Interstate so as we could enjoy a more scenic journey. At about 10.00 pm we stopped in a town called Craig to get something to eat; upon entering the restaurant, the man behind the counter said, as though in a typical Western, "Boys, have you picked the wrong town!" We calmed him down enough to be allowed to eat there, but were told that in some places in The Bible Belt – the mid-West of America – we could end up getting arrested for looking wierd!

JUNE 11th AUSTIN

Saturday night in Austin, Texas, and after the gig the only place to be is Sixth Street which is packed with bars, discos and restaurants, and teeming with young people. We met lots of people who came to talk to us, asking where we were from etc. – everyone was very friendly, even though they were taken aback by our appearance, which, as I've explained, receives a more fierce reaction than in Britain.

The advent of MTV – a 24-hour music TV station – has put the grapevine back into action in the USA, something which has been missing since the Sixties. Although the effect is only slowly beginning to emerge, once again its roots are based in music. Before MTV, bands used to have to play America state by state, the only real exposure being the radio, which only caters for a local city or two. Obviously, it was very hard for bands to have an impact on the American public all at once, as there was no real national focus such as NME or Radio 1 etc. However, MTV has provided exactly this focus – and a talking point – across the nation. It can be boring and mind-numbing after watching for a long time, but when a good band like Dexys or The Clash come on you certainly feel the effect.

All the kids here want to know what's happening in Britain because they can now compare the good British bands with established American rock, and we all know the impact that British groups are making over there. It's also having a positive effect on young American music; some good bands are emerging, such as REM or The Violent Femmes and I don't think it'll be long before we see something really exciting coming from America again.

JUNE 16th LOS ANGELES

While in L.A. we did our first headline show at The Club Lingerie after playing with U2 the night before in the sports arena. When we arrived at the gig lots of people were being turned away, including all of U2. We managed to persuade the management to let our Irish pals in but most people were being turned away as they didn't have ID to prove they were over 21 (as in U2s case) or simply weren't old enough anyway. It was unfortunate that we weren't informed of this in advance, but American clubs are really strict about the legal drinking ages, which, though it varies state to state, is generally 20-21, thus forcing groups into playing concert rather than club tours so that everyone can get in. As a result, young audiences never experience the closeness of a good club gig.

JUNE 29th   NEW YORK

The last night of the tour:– 18 dates for us, 50 for U2. The scene:– Pier 84, Hudson Bay, an aircraft carrier moored on Pier 83. The gig (an open air concert) had completely sold out and was a marvellous setting for the last night of the tour which was a triumph for all concerned. We carried on to do three more shows of our own, finishing with a sell out gig at the Ritz Ballroom. We left New York on July 3rd, the day before Independence. We knew that it would take us a while to assimilate everything that happened to us personally and musically, but what we all do know however, is that we all had the time of our lives, and are looking forward to returning again later this year.

Alarm pics: Jason Pev

SALT LAKE CITY

SAN FRANCISCO   DENVER

TULSA

LOS ANGELES

FLORIDA

AUSTIN

NEW YORK

JUNE 20th   FLORIDA

This is where we first felt the heat, everything else paling into significance in the mad rush for cold drinks or escape indoors to the comfort of the air conditioning. By this part of the tour the travelling, playing and so on really hit us; as a result, we saved all our energies for the stage and interviews, which were starting to come in thick and fast as news of the Alarm spread.

CROCODILES AND STRINGS?

A TALE OF DETERMINED YOUNG SCOTS

The days when every indie release was a possible classic are sadly over. But every now and then there's a bolt from the blue, a true piece of homegrown talent that turns up from nowhere, occasionally leading the group onto greater things, but just as often getting totally ignored.

One such single is 'Pleasant Dreamer'/'Stop The Rain' by the ridiculously-named **Suede Crocodiles**. Along with **Del-Amitri's** 'Sense Sickness', their single is the first fruition of a new Glasgow label, **No Strings**, which has the dubious task of following in Postcard's footsteps, but that, on these initial outings, seems every bit as capable.

able but a bit stubborn. The Suede Crocodiles, however, rely on pure, old-fashioned pop, and carry it off to perfection. Both sides of their single marry great tunes with lovely harmonies, a huge amount of soul, and just the right touch of energy. Anybody wondering what happened to the sons of Orange Juice need look no further: here we have a band capable of competing with the best.

Having actually got the music onto vinyl, Graham and Nick are now faced with [ling the damn things. Airpl[healthy on the hometown Ra[rest of the country, a bit o[

When The Alarm were invited to play America with U2 back in June 1983, no one could quite believe it – least of all us, as we were virtually unknown outside of a small following and the occasional non-committal live review in the music weeklies... The only person who realised the importance of an unknown British band going to the USA so early in their musical journey was Tony Fletcher at *Jamming!* Tony didn't have the big budgets of the music weeklies or the funding from a major record label PR to be able to travel with us, so he asked me to write a diary of the tour instead. I'm so glad about this, because it meant I hit the mental record button from the moment we set off (I didn't have/couldn't afford a camera at the time), and attempted to capture every second of this most pivotal life experience by writing it down in long hand. When we landed in California, our lives changed in an instant, and my memories of this time are burned deep because of my commitment to write the piece for *Jamming!* I can still picture every moment, and if you read the diary, I hope it gives you a sense of being with us. This was a coming of age in every respect. **Mike Peters**

A PROMISE FULFILLED?

After almost five years steady growth, Echo and The Bunnymen have at last laid claim to the crown of being Britain's no 1 rock band. But in doing so, have they strayed from the path they originally set out on? *Jonh Wilde* trailed Ian McCulloch to his Liverpool kitchen to find out; all photos by *Paul Cox*.

'Perhaps the one constant in Mac's lyrics is a sense of betrayal, of a promise broken, of the disappointment that comes from seeing humans betray their potential over and over'.
Mark Cooper in the Bunnymen/Teardrops biog 'Liverpool Explodes!'

It jarred me and worried me when I thought of that idea again, for the first time since 'Porcupine'. I suddenly realised that Echo themselves were falling *short* of their sizeable capabilities and that smouldering potential. I considered, just for a moment, why 'Crocodiles' still seemed quite unique, sometimes so pure and absolute, ultimately such a convincing pop masterpiece. I was knocked sensible with the recollection of how 'Heaven Up Here' sl.ook me with its insinuating power and how it ... up my imagination with its subtle ironies, twisting and crawling through some unexpected truths.

'Porcupine' provoked great expectation but proved a crushing disappointment and an opportunity lost. Perhaps it was only when it was compared to the best of this year's releases that 'Porcupine's' real weaknesses began to shine quite so hard. It talked of 'pain' but never realistically stabbed at the heart of its possibilities, only hovering indecisively at its edge. Perhaps Echo's greatest shortcoming has always been the tendency to merely hint at a depth of emotion, rather than evoking extreme feeling (lacking the blood lust turbulance of Joy Division, The Birthday Party and The Doors when it has been needed. They lack, perhaps, that savage intensity and the strength of exorcism).

It seemed to me that something – an element that had made the first two LP's such fascinating prospects – was missing and maybe this was their pained transition. Curiously, this artistic falter coincided with Echo's greatest commercial success yet; it was a strange irony.

I thought of the power of a violent, desperate love that they only hint at. I feared that they never take their music to the brink of emotions and wondered why I ended up like that, falling in love with their absurdity and their swirling Northern haze. I thought of the sheer guts and passion in 'Heaven Up Here' and the way they can breathe fresh life into ROCK. I reflected that they seemed to know that the last LP was a step to the side, neither advancing nor regressing. Perhaps we had begun to expect the world from Echo and they might have just missed the force of inspiration with 'Porcupine'. After all, the self-disarming irony is very clearly set down:–
'Missing the point of our mission.
Will we become misshapen?'
('Porcupine'.)

Ian McCulloch – just out of bed at nine in the morning – greeted me on the doorstep of his Liverpool home and once settled down with a much-needed coffee, he addressed his thoughts to the last album. The impression of a wilfully oblique soul quickly crumbled to ashes . . .

Around the time of 'Porcupine', you seemed dissatisfied and it was almost as though a forced optimism prevailed in the band . . .

The interviews that I did around that time might have given the impression that I was totally dissatisfied with it but, on the contrary, I feel that it was definitely the best LP we have done in many ways, despite certain shortcomings. It did rely too much upon atmosphere and less upon the real strength of the songs, which is something we are getting away from now. It lacked *directness* I suppose. For a start, we spent a hell of a time on the record (a very harrowing time in many ways) and eventually, perhaps, we started to think too carefully about the direction of it. The first two were a lot more natural, I suppose. I wish we were good enough to just work very quickly with inspiration, but we always seem to spend so much time labouring over songs. On the new material, we'll work everything out before we get into the studio so that should work better.

On 'Porcupine', there seemed a problem with lyrics – the fine balance between humour/seriousness seemed to have been exchanged for a disillusioned self-examination that overshadowed its true strengths.

The LP was a kind of autobiography on vinyl and it worked well in that way. It didn't really break any new ground and perhaps it failed to aim beyond 'Rock' but that wasn't the aim – we've never pretended to be anything more than a rock band. When a lot of other terms were floating about, we just came straight out and said that we were just 'Rock'. Since then, it's been treated in a very derisory fashion as though it has to mean 'stale' and 'complacent'. I encourage it because I know that, however much I encourage it, everyone will know that the Bunnymen are not Rock in a mundane sense.

Accepting that the LP was autobiographical then, it more than hinted at a struggle for direction at that time.

"We are the funniest band going! I would like to get that across more."

Lyrically, most of the songs were concerned with knowing what was happening to us at the time – almost like a confession. Musically, it was very different from the first two LP's but it fits in that sequence somehow. I believe that it was a very honest album but strangely, it seemed to be misinterpreted because people assumed that we were unaware of the ironies in the songs but we WERE! *It was about falling short of our potential.* It was the first album that we have done where we actually questioned rights and wrongs, where we questioned the whole purpose of Echo and the Bunnymen. The LP is a good autobiography of that struggle to come to terms I suppose.

All that determined self-examination – and for what? Did the Bunnymen worry so passionately to break on through to those bluer skies?

We talked about losing that ripeness – and it was partly about people not achieving everything that they are capable of; it is the idea that Mark Cooper was talking of in 'Liverpool Explodes!' but that was mainly directed at ourselves.

Yeah! Just at the moment, I have that faith in our *greatness* again and the new songs are a lot more positive in addressing that question of potential. There's a lot more belief now.

About the lyrics though, I find it just as healthy if someone interprets a song as I meant it when somebody reads it completely different to how I meant it. The last LP hopefully could be understood as a personal idea of 'betraying potential'. It isn't necessarily about Echo.

While accepting that 'Porcupine' had serious intent, though, the press generally turned it into an idea with great pretentions and pretences. Were you being taken too seriously perhaps?

Of course, because the humour in the songs is all too often overlooked. There is both seriousness and humour in what we do and generally the humour balances everything. There was a great deal of misunderstanding about the seriousness of some of the last LP. The song, 'White Devil' for instance, talks about the poet John Webster but I only used his name because I had no other lyrics for that song. I just discovered the line in a book of my wife's that just happened to be lying open. But it was taken so seriously, as if there was a great depth of literary influence! I mean, *we are the funniest band going!!* I would like to get that across more.

Perhaps it is that subtle humour (aimed at meeting the Echo darkness half-way) that is often misconstrued as the elusiveness or vagueness (even pretentiousness) in the band?

I find that quite curious but we have no interest in that kind of wilful obscurity. I would agree that there is a certain elitism, the kind that I enjoyed at school, perhaps, when I was the only kid who loved Bowie. I suppose I don't like sharing something that I've discovered myself, it's a strange sort of pride. In the same way, perhaps that kind of elitism has worked against us in the way that certain sections of the pop press dropped us when we began to break through to a new and wider audience. Everybody has a certain kind of elitism about them but it doesn't have to be about striving to be best. Maybe it could be about that potential again – there's nothing wrong with aiming at that. About elitism though, one thing I always wanted to avoid was an audience/performer barrier and I'm conscious of that all the time because I'm not interested in that kind of elitism.

PAGE 25

Stars are stars and undeniably McCulloch was always an inevitable pop 'idol'. However, he always appeared to remain identifiable and Mac seemed too aware of the possibilities of his image to allow his intentions to be reduced to a shallow gloss or a throwaway half-truth. Around the time of 'Porcupine' though, there were times when he seemed content to let that partially eclipsed image loom larger than real life . . .

Ian:– "In the last interviews, I concentrated on the idea of the image of 'Mac' being outside what I really felt about everything. Maybe it was a convenient mask, but I did that because I needed to at the time – it was to escape paranoia really. Generally, I don't treat what I put into the songs as being outside my own experience. Basically, Echo is not a pretence, a fantasy or a lie:– it's very real, y'know."

'Back of Love' was the first great hit; personally, I was anticipating a 'Porcupine' that would sway positively towards that abrasive, sweeping pop sound, rather than the flawed excesses that did characterise the LP.

'Back of Love' is probably the best song that we have ever done. It was the sheer *energy* of that which restored an element that had been missing for some time. I basically wanted an album full of songs in the vein of that one. The basis of most of the songs were very strong but they lost some of their edge when they came to be recorded. I think we were all a little confused and worried at that time and although it was a great LP, it could have been greater.

How do you see Echo in terms of appeal and audience in view of the massive commercial success over the last year?

I think it's been quite unique as far as the audience goes because few people that followed us at the start have lost interest. It shows that we were never just a cult.

I still believe in that idea about the amount of people that come to our gigs, about the potential of that mass to change something or to achieve something. I think about that a lot, it's almost frightening.

With the Bunnymen's steady but impressive rise, was it proving difficult for you to retain a sense of challenge and maintain the spirit that was at the heart of the 'mission' in the earliest days?

It is a challenge trying to surprise people or still being able to make people feel great through the music. It is crucial to find new reasons for satisfying our *own* demands, as the original challenge of just being in a band gradually becomes routine.

Last year, I didn't personally achieve all that I wanted with the Bunnymen; I really needed to escape from everything a lot of the time.

I wondered about influences and about the lyricists that you particularly admired.

I think more about the people I like, rather than 'influences'. Leonard Cohen has always impressed me, more because of the atmosphere in his songs than his words. I don't believe basically that sad songs have to naturally be 'depressive' or 'depressing'. 'Sadness' can be treated in a song and the song can still be uplifting.

Bowie I've loved for ages of course . . . Scott Walker has a great voice but I've always found his lyrics too naive.

"I still believe in the amount of people that come to our gigs, about the potential of that mass to change something. I think about that a lot, it's almost frightening."

The mere mention of that godlike dreamer directed my thoughts towards that ultimate Scott Walker enthusiast, Julian Cope. I reflected for a moment on the curious year it had been, all in all, for the original Crucial Three. 1982 witnessed Wylie's surprise commercial breakthrough, Cope's struggle to recapture the awesome spirit of 'Reward' (he will, I am convinced, return with a vengeance) and finally McCullough's continued upward advance . . .

"It was an interesting year in that way. I'm wary these days, though, of discussing Pete and Julian because the whole thing is already out of hand. This idea of rivalry started to be taken seriously by people who didn't know us and couldn't understand the humour. When I used to see Julian a lot, I'd say to him, 'What crap have you been writing today then?', and it was all very light. Then it started happening in public and it was blown out of proportion".

Our discussion drifted back to Echo and Mac's motivations . . .

"There's just a few fascinations that I always seem to return to – I like catch-phrases like 'Read It In Books' and standard cliché phrases, twisting them around to mean something else. Some of them deal with the idea of that betrayal of potential but there's others too. There's

no one theme really, sometimes it's just clues . . .

My motivation? I have a pride in honesty, simply because I always believe that I'm doing this for the right reasons and with the right motives. There has always been that morality in the Bunnymen, recognising the difference between 'right' and 'wrong'. If anything, I love doing this more now than ever. *Then* we might have done it for the sake of doing it, *Now* we want to make it matter."

'How can you pretend when there's so much at stake/When it's a different world and everything shakes'.
'Gods Will Be Gods'.

"The reason we are using other musicians on the tour this time is purely and simply that we wanted to see how a nine-piece worked. It is just an experiment and because we've been working as a four-piece for so long, it was necessary to have a change, just a fresh approach. Working with the same format over a long period, it becomes increasingly difficult to motivate each other. We haven't decided to what extent we will use the nine-piece on the next LP but it probably won't be as extensively as on the tour.

The tour itself was designed to break off the normal gig circuit, to avoid the usual places. It was aimed at regenerating the excitement, the anticipation and the love of involvement again. The feeling is very, very positive now.

'Never Stop' restores a lot of the bite I think, although it is a lot more subtle than 'Back Of Love'. I'm just satisfied that we're steering away now from the idea of 'atmosphere' and we're concerned with *songs* again. For the last LP, we found that we had lost the ability to be decisive and intuitive. The newer songs are closer in structure to the 'Crocodiles' period if anything and that is definitely a good thing."

Although 'Never Stop' perhaps failed to completely re-activate their spirit and restore the old sense of adventure, the Peel sessions were to unveil the Bunnymen with new-found simplicity of approach, a brave directness and a blooming pop vitality. Live though, they were to lapse on tour into that all-too-familiar tendency to clutter ideas, stray into (rock) self-indulgence and lose the *sting* that they are capable of provoking. Quite simply, for the most part, the experiments on the British tour were bold but failed to add any real strength of character to the Echo mist.

In our interview, Mac successfully highlighted the drawbacks that they faced with 'Porcupine', yet still Echo and the Bunnymen seem to struggle to regain the pure brilliance of 'Rescue', 'Villiers Terrace', 'A Promise' or 'Back Of Love'. They have always been about great fleeting moments of inspiration but it is that sporadic splendour, that worrying inconsistency that may always threaten them.

'Silver', 'Seven Seas' and 'The Killing Moon' (the new songs showcased on the tour) nevertheless hint at a re-adjustment and a period of new positive recovery.

Post-Joy Division rock has seen too many heads going down, too much despair, too little eager hope, too little promise. More than ever (with a 1983 music scene so obsessed with image, hollow pretence and gloss, with music's lack of spirit and lack of conviction) WE NEED GUTS AND PASSION.

The gauntlet is down . . .

"Echo is not a pretence, a fantasy or a lie:– it's very real, y'know."

Throughout the middle, arguably 'golden' age of *Jamming!*, the poetry section was a regular feature, sometimes taking up as much as three pages. Contributions flooded in from far and wide, and the process of selection and commentary was commissioned out, first to Mark Stowe and then to Richard 'Kool Knotes' Edwards. From top left: Issues 12, 14, 17 & 20.

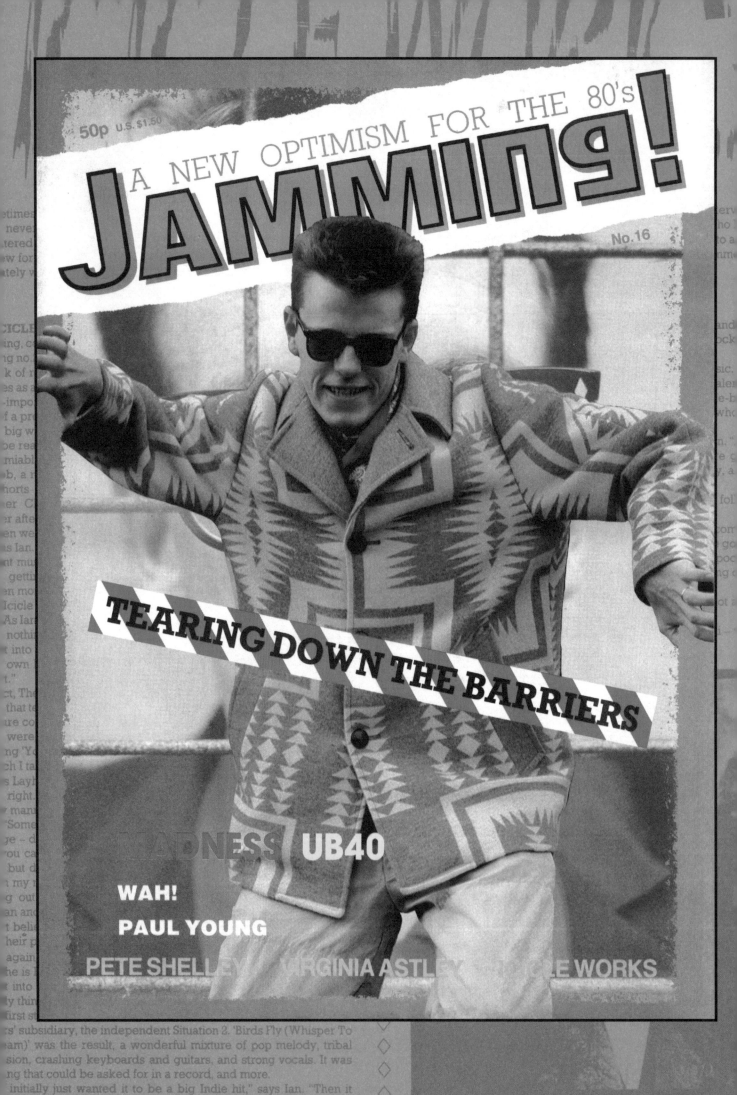

A NEW OPTIMISM FOR THE 80's

JAMMING!

50p U.S. $1.50

No.16

TEARING DOWN THE BARRIERS

MADNESS   UB40

WAH!

PAUL YOUNG

PETE SHELLEY   VIRGINIA ASTLEY   ICICLE WORKS

Jamming! 16 arrived on schedule (though requiring a couple of sleepless nights to do so) exactly two months behind Issue 15. It delivered a solid combination of pop stars (Madness, UB40, Paul Young), borderline rock stars (Pete Shelley, Wah! and The Icicle Works) and promising debutantes (Virginia Astley, Big Sound Authority and Skeletal Family), although how we could claim that such a generally commercial list of artists could be 'Breaking Down The Barriers' is now beyond me. Still, Russell Tate's enthusiastic designs suited the positive editorial mood of this particular issue, some even flouting our general requirement for either reading and/or sunglasses. All this was progress.

It was therefore quite a shock to receive 50,000 copies from Finland and find that somewhere in the printing process the Paul Young interview had swapped places with the first page of the Madness cover feature, despite all pages being clearly numbered. It felt like a calamity, an insult to all our attempts at professionalism, though hindsight has tamed the pain and it now looks defiantly amateur, even zine-like. (It also almost certainly secured a reduction in the printing price.)

In the meantime, friendships were fast being formed as new contributors came on board. Most consequential among them was photographer Russell Young (UB40, Virginia Astley), who would stay through to the end, contribute more cover shots than anyone without ever pulling rank, and go on to artistic greatness. Among others who would assume permanent residence on the masthead were Mark Stowe, who took over the poetry section, Ross Fortune, who offered up his first written contribution, and Jason Pevovar, who submitted his debut photos.

On a separate note, I had started appearing on *The Tube* as an occasional presenter, a role hopelessly beyond my capabilities given the exclusive authority cast by primary (male) presenter Jools Holland and the genuine chaos of a show that went out 100 per cent live on Friday evenings. Still, many were the times that I'd jet off to Newcastle by plane or first class train, stay over at the same hotel as Kevin Keegan, interview the likes of Elvis Costello and Wham! live on air (and, on one especially memorable occasion in January 1984, Morrissey live from the balcony of The Haçienda in Manchester), and share transportation to London back after the show with a rogues' gallery of pop stars, comedians, media figures and record industry moguls alike, all of whom made the most of British Airways' copiously generous alcohol policy. It was a long way from the impoverished fanzine lifestyle, that's for sure – though the minimum union fee seemed so generous to someone recently on Supplementary Income Benefit that I forewent a salary from *Jamming!* during this period, even as others (specifically, Jonh Wilde, Russell Tate and Alan McLaughlin) received one, however paltry.

Been invited to Rome by the Arts Council of the Italian Communist Party (*ARCI* – Archie to you). They organised an International Youth Culture Conference, and all the international delegates ended up in the same hotel. Swedes on the landing, Germans in the bar, Icelandic punks parading, and cool New Yorkers rapping in their rooms, all for the benefit of the Italian national press. The communist party were pleased with the turn-out, but unfortunately their enthusiasm did not make up for their lack of organisation. I had flown out with Steve Lewis (Animal Nightlife manager and ex-Le Beat Route disc-spinner); the purpose of his attendance was to play records at the Saturday-night soiree. We arrived on the Thursday, and stumbled into town with a grey-worthy City Limits hack. What was going on? No one seemed to know. A bubbling Berlin couple warned us of the confusion – Germans like things ordered and could not cope with the Italians raising their hands in the air like they just don't care. Frankly I didn't:– I was in Rome, it was sunny, the hotel was paid for and I had time to wander about.

Steve and I met up with a local radio (*Citte Futura*) DJ, Marco Militell, who was an afro-funk fanatic and useful guide. Marco instructed us in crossing the road Roman-style ordering food and searching out clothes. Radio Citte Futura is a communist sponsored legalised pirate station. In Italy, if you set up a radio station and pretend you know what you're doing, the government issues a licence and you're away. A trip along the crowded FM band is an education:– Latin stations, national radio (RAI) playing Euro-pop, disco stations, funk vendors and the usual sports, News and politics. The local stations are not plugged, so the DJ's buy the records they *like* and their playlists are bizarre. Dolce Vita, Viva Zimbabwe, Nina Simone then Culture Club. Even the eclectic English find this hard to comprehend.

Back to the meeting. This took place every evening for a week under the banner 'Love you, Fuck you' – really radical man. The venue was a disused, open-air slaughterhouse, the area of Wembley stadium. Once in the place, most of the time was spent either wondering around trying to find out what was going on, or propped up at the bar staring at videos. Films were shown while bands played (strange watching Scum with a soundtrack from Icelandic and Yugoslav punk bands). The spirit of '77 still lives in isolated pockets all over the Western World, where blue spikey hair and leathers is not passé but a protest of some sort. Die Toten Hosen (Dead Trousers!) from Dusseldorf were the stars of the week, fighting with the local punks and flashing their paisley flares to a curious crowd. All the groups were either Euro-Ramones, spitting out Clash-type songs about the price of Levis in Lubiana or records in Reykjovik, or Banshee types droning on about cubist haircuts.

This meeting seemed to suggest that Europe has little to offer the contemporary music scene, and London is still the focal point for what's new, although New York is fast catching up. The Latin language does not lend itself to rapping, but the crowd lapped up the second-rate chants of Phase 2 and his scratch partner Whyz Kid. I helped Steve Lewis with his turn on the tables of the open-air dance floor (a basketball court). About 1,500 people were getting down to Herbie Hancock, Hot Streak, James Brown etc. until a gang of local punks decided they had had enough of the 'Funky stuff'. Spitting and shouting they surrounded us, the security men disappeared in true Italian fashion, and just as I started to panic and wish for the latest waxing from Watty and the boys, Don Letts appeared like the cavalry, with his '*Clash At Shea Stadium*' film, and the seething spike-tops settled down to strangling each other.

Leaving the gathering I realised that the organisers had attempted something on a scale which was too adventurous, but although the proceedings were disorganised, the opportunity of seeing groups and films about young people from Germany, Yugoslavia, USA, France, Spain, Finland, Sweden, Holland and Italy was well worth the effort. Europeans who can be bothered to dress and think differently from the mass, seem to take elements from English and American style and music and reassemble it to suit their own taste. Skinheads wearing Clark's desert boots, Van Halen T-shirts and riding Vespas may not be common in Basildon, but the sheep in Italy are not so easily led. *See you soon Alan Marke*

P.S. Rome Girls are like the ice-cream. Probably the best in the World.

SUNSET GUN

An excellent double cassette package that has just wound it's way from Glasgow is 'The Angels Are Coming', put together by Klark Kent and Robert King, with help from Sunset Gun, and under the banner of 'Pleasantly Surprised'. Confused? So was I. But it's the music on the tape that's important, and there is no shortage of that – artists included are Bauhaus, Fiat Lux, Nico, The Blue Orchids, Gene Loves Jezebel, The Suede Crocodile (raved about in Jamming! 15), The March Violets and many more. Pride of place however, must go The Alarm's 'Unsafe Building', now a distinct rarity.

The cassettes come with a little info booklet, although unfortunately, the tapes themselves are rather shoddy. And although some of the music is unlistenable – such... Department live – most of it is good-to-great... If you can't find it locally, it is £4 inc... 614 Pollokshaws Road, D...

TROJAN

Credit this if you can:– *Trojan Records*, once the thr... hive of British reggae, is now down to a one-man operation, go... over by an 80-year old with no interest in pop music. Patrick... ads is the man with the unenviable task of trying to get the whole la... back on it's feet from nothing, but also the man with the envia... task of spending hours in the basement digging out rare tapes.

Patrick has managed to uncover seven unreleased Bo... Marley tracks, produced by Leslie Kong of '007' fame, and which... ill be coming out as singles over the next few months. Caught in a... cious circle of having no money to push records, and hence no bi... ales, the Marley singles might not do as well as the man's last... ity, 'Buffalo Soldier'. But one record that is unlikely to be ignored... '20 Reggae Classics', due out before Christmas.

"The idea was to release reggae tracks that have... en successfully covered by modern-day artists," says Patrick... 'It includes '007' just covered by Musical Youth, and 'The Tide Is H...', made famous by Blondie. Then just when I was wondering if I h... enough tracks, UB40 released 'Labour Of Love'."

No less than seven tracks on that current... owned by Trojan, includ...

The summer of '83 had been a crazy time for me booking bands on SWITCH (a Channel 4 music show) as well as helping Gary Crowley with his legendary Tuesday club night at Bogarts in South Harrow, and later at The Wag in Soho. Gary had been invited to DJ at a festival in Rome, but when he couldn't go, he suggested I attend with Steve Lewis, Le Beat Route DJ and Animal Nightlife manager. I ended up staying there for a fortnight with the family of Marco Militello, the young RAI funk DJ who had invited us over. Being mates with both Gary Crowley and Pedro Romhanyi, both of whom were matey in turn with Tony Fletcher, it was suggested I write about the trip for *Jamming!* I was happy to say yes: *Jamming!* was a great magazine that was all about the music, without the egos of *NME*, *Melody Maker* and so on. Tony also invited me to contribute some other pieces for the magazine, and I did my best to push at its edges, writing about black music and visual media and occasionally reviewing some rock records too! The 80s music scene was a vibrant one all around, and I was glad to be a part of it, forming lasting friendships, with Gary Crowley and I coming full circle to work together on TV documentaries about The Jam and The Style Council. **Alan Marke**

UB40

When UB40 topped the charts a few months back with 'Red Red Wine', it came as a great relief to them as much as anything else. For the Birmingham eight-piece, who are the most successful reggae band this country has seen, had lost their golden touch. Their singles were missing the Top 20 by a long run, and their live album was a unanimous failure, disappearing almost without trace. However, the uptown tempo of 'Red Red Wine' showed a new side to UB40, as did the whole of the no.1 album, 'Labour Of Love'. With almost every track a dance floor classic and prospective hit, it has put UB40 firmly back in the public eye, and in fact, in a more commanding position that ever before.

To coincide with this success, the group played a rather safe tour venue-wise (Odeons, Apollos and Gaumonts not being particularly designed for dancing), and I travelled to Ipswich to see the group. UB40 have never felt the need to play here before, but still the gig was sold out well in advance, as was most of the tour.

Anyone already acquainted with UB40 may know that the most talkative member of the group is drummer Jim Brown. To newcomers, this may seem unusual, as it's normally a hard enough struggle to get sticksmen even to talk, but in this case, not only is Jim one of the best and most influential drummers around, but also, the nearest to a leader the group have. Jim writes half of UB40's controversial lyrics, and as their self-appointed spokeman, is possibly responsible for giving the group such a misunderstood image. I have always been suspicious of any group than comes close to calling for revolution, while happily admitting that their main priority is to become as rich as possible, and running such a determinedly capitalist machine as DEP International, their own label. The reputation of this financial house runs well ahead of a group who have always stated that being tough businessmen is part of their job.

It's easy to see how this image has been created because Jim is too bloody honest. An instantly likeable, well-spoken and clever

man with violently strong opinions, his openness gives plenty of room for the critics to jump in. Hopefully, this interview can help redress the balance a bit, because if some of Jim's comments seem pessimistic, unexpected or controversial, remember that honesty is a virtue second to none . . .

Has the audience been different on this tour, following on the back of a No.1 hit?

Yeah, it's been more of a pop audience, obviously. The most popular numbers tend to be 'Red Red Wine' and the newer tracks, because we've caught a new audience, although the old audience is still there as well.

How do you define that old audience?

Well, it's always been a real cross-section, like all ages, all races, and that's still there. It's just there's a lot of young girls as well.

Is being 'pop stars' as you are now, something you've always wanted?

Oh yeah. We want to sell as many records as possible, that was always the aim, and if we've got screaming girls as well, which is something I don't understand fully, then it's not something I'm going to lock myself away and feel terrible about, because it's part of being in a pop band.

Up until 'Labour Of Love', your popularity was dropping rather dramatically. Do you know why that was?

No, I don't really; I think there was a bit of a backlash probably. But I thought the single which sold the *worst*, 'I Got Mine', was really good. I don't know the reason for it all – if I did I'd never have let it happened.

The Live LP was a bit of a disaster . . .

Yeah, that didn't happen, but then there's all sorts of reasons why live LPs don't happen. But the last studio album, 'UB44', went gold before it was released, on top of which, 'The Singles Album', which we didn't want released, was out at the same time and sold really well – together, we'd done a platinum album. Sure, the sales were a little bit down, but I think the market's a little bit down as well, and the singles, up until 'I Got Mine', were still going Top 20.

So how does DEP International work?

We lease the label, not the group, so that DEP is, at the moment, leased to Virgin. They manufacture and distribute the records, and we run everything else. At the moment, we've got about six people working for us in Birmingham, which is not counting the press agents and pluggers that we employ, who are down in London.

There's a reputation with UB40 of being very, very hard with business.

We try to keep a track of everything that's going on. We've got a basic approach to business whereby we want to make money, without outlaying money for no reason. We're always getting cash flow problems, which you get, whatever business you're in. But in the music business, you can earn up to two years behind – the money we're earing now abroad with 'Red Red Wine' being no.1 all over Europe, we won't see for another year-and-a-half to two years.

What about your plans for DEP as a label for other groups?

Well, it would be really nice if we could make DEP into a new Trojan.

Yeah, I keep hearing that said, but why haven't you started yet?

Because we want to be able to promote a band the way that we promote ourselves. We actually want to go into it in a big way, and get bands into the charts, but that takes money. We don't see the point in releasing a record and making a small profit, when if we invest in it, we can release the same record and make a big profit. But at the moment, we can't afford to do that.

Do you know what groups you want to do it with?

Yeah, we've been talking to a few quite big reggae acts. We're hoping it'll happen next year. We've got a projected plan for ourselves right up until the end of next year – it never works out exactly like that, but you need to have a skeleton plan worked out.

Will the next batch of songs you write be as political as before?

The next album we make will, I suppose, be just as political as the last one, 'cos we'll be doing our own lyrics again.

How political do you actually consider yourselves?

I'm political enough to be really pessimistic about almost everything. I've become really cynical, because I've had a lot of time to think about things, just travelling about on the coach on tour. When I was in my little backstreet in Birmingham, I thought that you could possibly change the world; you think 'Yeah, if we get this momentum going, things could really change.' But the more you travel, the more apathy you see, and the more you realise that you're not actually going to change anything.

So have you given up?

I've given up on the idea of change, but I haven't given up on the need for change.

Do you think politics has got a proper role in music?

I don't see why not. I don't think you can really separate them. I think things are a direct result of whatever political views you've got – if you're apolitical, that's reflected in your music, and if you're political, that's reflected.

You were saying earlier that you don't think your exposure has been reflected by your political stance . . .

Yeah, I really don't think people take it that seriously. Really, if you could change anything or have any influence by singing, it wouldn't be in pop music, because it wouldn't be exposed on the radio. And yet it is all the time. Especially when politics was fashionable, there was a lot of political records being played on the radio. If the powers that be considered it serious, they wouldn't allow it.

So you're saying that what you do is having no effect?

Absolutely. I don't think it has any effect at all. The only effect we have is that if people are open to ideas as a result of listening to our music, then they were open to those sort of ideas in the first place.

Do you think part of your decline was due to politics going out of fashion?

Well, politics has definitely gone out of fashion, but I don't think politics is enough to make people either buy or not buy a record. I don't feel the reason we were so popular was because of politics, just like I don't feel that a lack of politics will make us unpopular. Nobody really takes it seriously when you're in a pop band.

You don't think you've gained the image of being a political band?

We got an image as a political band to people that were susceptible to politics, but I think most people aren't.

I know the songs on 'Labour Of Love' were from your youth, but whereabouts did you used to hear them?

Well I've said this before, but it's like our version of 'American Grafitti', the real teenage nostalgia thing, discovering girls, discovering music, going to local clubs. We were mainly around 13-14, and just discovering life.

Was 'Labour Of Love' something you were always going to do?

The only reason we got round to doing it was because we'd just built our own studio in Birmingham, and we were experimenting. Having our own studio gave us a chance to demo everything, and just mess around; we were getting a good feeling there, and it was sounding really different, so we thought 'Yeah, let's put this together'. There was never a conscious decision that we were gonna do it, it just happened.

Do you think you've achieved much with reggae, in terms of broadening people's tastes?

Yeah, I think so. We were really naive about how naive our audience were, because it turns out a lot of people aren't exposed to that sort of thing. There's people who've never really heard reggae, and think that we're the same as Gregory Isaacs because they can't differentiate between the two. Just like I don't know the difference between Journey and Rush – they all sound the same to me.

The reggae influence in current music seems to have dropped off a bit . . .

Well, I don't know, I think it's probably more subliminal than it used to be. It's not as trendy as it was, but it's sneaking into all sorts of wierd places you don't notice, like adverts and TV signature tunes. It's become a standard form of music now, and people like Black Uhuru and Gregory Isaacs can get albums in the charts, even if it isn't as trendy.

Are you going to be doing another dub album?

Yeah, we've got one half done already, that Mikey Dread's mixing. That should be out quite soon, and then we wanna start experimenting with some of the tracks on 'Labour Of Love'.

You seem to be always changing distribution for DEP International, your own label . . .

Not really. Ever since we left Graduate, at the end of the first year of our existence, we've had our own company which is DEP.

We were distributed by Spartan in England and CBS abroad, then we started being distributed by Virgin, which was CBS as well, and then Virgin switched to EMI, which is what we're doing now. So really, we've only changed twice.

Why did things get so heavy with Graduate in the first place, that you had to go to court?

Well, there were niggly things, like 'Signing Off' being released in South Africa without 'Burden Of Shame' on, which is the track that mentions Soweto. But the main reason was that it was becoming the record label we

studio time, recorded it, took it to be cut, and took it to the distributors as well, which was all record company work. So we actually said 'Let's keep the 50% that we're giving him' for ourselves.'

That's the point I was trying to make earlier about you getting taken up as a group for the trendy liberals.

Yeah, but that doesn't have much of a bearing on mainsteam pop audiences anyway. It's only people who are aware of trendy liberals and aware of politics that can make that sort of assumption – like the music press for instance. But I don't think 13-year old girls that have bought 'Red Red Wine' are saying 'They're a trendy liberal band' because they didn't know that we ever were.

By saying that you're admitting that you're a trendy liberal band.

We were only a trendy liberal band to other trendy liberals, who were trying not to be. If you came to our gigs you'd find that our following is a very very basic working-class following, most of the people that come to see us are just normal kids. Certainly we don't get the same sort of audience as Crass do, even though our politics are very similar.

On 'Love Is All Is Alright' you follow that line by saying 'But you've got to find a little more hate'. Why?

Well, we're not pacifist. We believe that pacifism gets you nowhere, and there comes a time when you actually have to fight. I don't object to a violent act just because it's violent; I object to the reasons – if I object at all. The song is very metaphorical, but it's saying that if you've got the problem of having the NF on your streets, then you've got a responsibility to fight them off. Saying 'Please don't' won't get you anywhere. However, saying all that, I still think that acts of political violence are just as much a part of society as anything else. Terrorists are a good enemy to bring people together. Society needs enemies – it needs people to be blamed. But I think there will come a time when you will actually have to fight.

Can you see that happening in this country?

No, I can't really see it happening anywhere. I don't believe that capitalism will eventually decay; it will just change the way it is.

Would you call yourselves capitalists?

(*Incredibly long pause*). Theoretically, no, but in practise – of course we are. Because we're living in a capitalist system.

How does saying 'yes' and 'no' answer it? People end up thinking, "It's alright UB40 making all these strong political statements, but they're off making as much money as

money to be able to retire. It's quite possible in the pop business to earn enough money to never have to work again, it just depends how much money you want. I want enough to never have to do anything, and as soon as I have got that I'll retire.

Isn't there the argument that as soon as you've reached one goal, you want more?

No. Because I don't feel that I'm a competitive person, and I don't feel the need to strive for a goal as a way of moving me into doing something. For people to reach another goal, they've also got to work that little bit harder, and give themselves a reason to carry on, because they enjoy what they're doing. I don't actually enjoy what I'm doing that much.

You don't enjoy the group?

Yeah, I do, and I enjoy playing music; I wouldn't like to do anything else. But I don't much like being in a pop band, I don't like the life much.

Well, what do you think the life is, 'cos people have different ideas?

It's hours and hours of sitting on a coach, and sound-checking, and doing gigs. It was all really great for a while, but then you want something else. A lot of bands do it because they think that's the reason for doing it, to be on the road, take a lot of drugs, go with a lot of girls, and have a good time. I don't see that as the reason for doing it – that's like a side-effect of it. It's something that you can enjoy doing – and of course I'm better off than almost anybody I know – but that still isn't enough to want to keep doing it all the time.

As a group, are you thinking of changing your role at all?

Yeah, we're all working to the point where we don't have to tour any more.

Does that mean not playing live at all?

Yeah, I suppose it does.

Don't you think that's an important, integral part of music.

Not necessarily, no. Even though we're still better live than we are on record, there's only so much of it you can do without it becoming automatic. At the moment, it's not automatic. This is our fifth year now, which I think is quite a long time to do the same thing.

So you're seriously thinking about not touring anymore?

No, not in the near future, but it is uppermost in our minds. You see, I don't particularly like being on stage – it's alright while you're up there I suppose, but a lot of the time, I'd much sooner be doing something else.

That's strange because the public always gets the idea that people love being in pop bands.

And some of our band do. It's just a difference of opinion. If I was a front man, and I was getting the response that the front men do, then it might make me change my

Photos: Russell Young

didn't want it to be. We always kept a track of our own information, and when we asked the bloke who ran Graduate for some accounting information, he said 'There's no reason why one artist should have any more information than any other.' And yet we were the only artist on the label! He was making a lot of bread for things that we ended up doing anyway. With 'Present Arms', we booked the

possible."

Of course. The thing is, we're living in this system, and there's a lot of things we do where we have to compromise. Because I don't believe there will be change overnight – I think it will be more gradual – I've got a responsibility to myself to be as happy as possible, while doing as little harm to other people as possible. I want to earn enough

PAGE 17

mind. Because I'm part of the background, I get the crowd response, but to get a good crowd response all you have to do is reproduce what you do well. That may sound a bit cynical, but it's *not* that difficult.

So what are your ambitions?

I like studio work, I like producing. I really enjoy being at the mixing desk; I think that's where most of the band will head.

Do you think pop music can ever work as rebellion?

No, it's all just a good way for people to let off steam, it's really shallow. That's the thing that used to get me about punk – everybody would let off steam in a punk gig, then let it build up again, so then they'd go to another gig. It's a terrible thing to say what people should and shouldn't do, but I believe that letting off steam in a riot is more constructive.

But you got a right slating for playing Lewisham the night of the Brixton riots, where the lyrics you were singing had absolutely nothing to do with what was going on in the streets.

Oh yeah, of course. Pop music isn't in the real world, and remember, we're just a pop band. We're not martyrs for any cause.

You do seem really cynical . . .

Yeah, I've become more cynical in the last couple of years. That's because I've realised how impotent you really are.

Is there any chance that you might give up?

No, I'll never give up. I mean, I'm actually more extreme than I used to be.

Some of Jim's comments will undoubtedly get a lot of people's backs up, as it certainly is daunting to find a group who can balance virtually anarchist principles with a desire for retirement in their '20's. Yet I think it's only fair to say that just about every question seemed to have been answered by Jim in his own head prior to the interview. He is neither some new rock'n'roll upstart or an ungrateful pessimist, but a man who is sure enough of what he is talking about, to answer all questions on the matter.

Later on in the evening, UB40 took to the stage at the Ipswich Gaumont to a crowd that had already been on their feet for an hour. Most of the 2,500 people here had never seen UB40 before, but there were certainly enough who knew every song. With an unusual and highly functional stage set, and the group in strictly casual clothes, they quickly got into the swing of things. All eight members have a natural affinity with reggae (yeah, I know it's been obvious for five years!) and are simply superb on their instruments. Ali and Robin Campbell are the mellow duo, occasionally skanking with each other but doing little more, leaving Astro to do the honours and shake the hands of the hundreds of awe-struck girls at the front of the stage. He follows 'One In Ten', with an awful 'Hello Ipswich' cry and a promise to get everyone dancing tonight. He reminded me of Eddy Grant's dreadful corn with these old cliches but as Jim Brown had earlier pointed out, this *is* the entertainment business.

The UB40 set, an impressive 1½ hours long, took in a wide range of material, revolving around a five-number stretch from 'Labour Of Love' in the middle. This included a rousing rendition of 'Johnny Too Bad' with Brian Travers on vocals, and a rather dull 'Red Red Wine' (possibly due to the crowd's over-expectations) that still featured the superb toasting fade-out from the album. Elsewhere, UB40 avoided an obvious Greatest Hits show, with 'Love Is All', 'I Got Mine', 'Don't Let It Pass You By' and 'One In Ten' the only old singles in the set.

Jim Brown's drumming was nothing short of superb through-out the set, leaving me even more confused with the idea of him not enjoying himself, and most members of the band found themselves swapping instruments at least a couple of times. They went out with a strong version of 'Tyler' to an ecstatic crowd so obviously starved of live music. I've always found out-of-London gigs so much more refreshing than the inverted snobbery of the big smoke, and in Ipswich the kids knew they were getting a good deal. The demand for an encore was, quite literally, perhaps the loudest I've ever heard.

Reappearing with support band Winston Reedy for an enormous jam session, the night finally ended with an incredibly hard version of 'Medusa'. At times, UB40 are far removed from roots reggae, but this was the real thing, an unbelievably mighty sound. They unfortunately then spoilt the night by bringing the houselights on immediately, almost before they had left the stage. Music, to me, is meant to be about spontaneity and I found such a blatant sign of dismissal to the crowd rather insulting.

But nay worry – UB40 had been and done their job, and the crowd had been and done theirs. Jim Brown might be right when he talks about music being futile, but occasionally it also brings moments of magic. And that makes it all worthwhile.

Tony Fletcher

I bought *Jamming!* over the years because I bought all fanzines. And so, after I put together a portfolio under fashion photographer Christos Raftopoulos, who was my mentor and the only person I ever worked for, *Jamming!* was on my list of magazines to approach. I remember coming to the office and thinking there was a lot of energy and a lot of authenticity there, and I thought 'I really want to work with these people.' Tony commissioned me almost immediately, to do a shoot with Virginia Astley. We did it at Kew Gardens, which is a place I loved, so I don't know if that was my suggestion or not, but I do remember totally falling in love with her and her music. I still play her album, *From Gardens Where We Feel Secure*, some nights when I go to sleep or when I wake up. And every time I do, I remember, 'She was my first professional photograph.'

Around the same time, Tony asked if I wanted to photograph UB40 in concert, so I offered to drive us both to Ipswich where we'd have more time with the band and fewer photographers to get in the way. The stepped stage that UB40 had seemed so slick and professional, like something you'd expect from Frank Sinatra in the old days. I took a whole load of photos, *Jamming!* used them, and it all marked the beginning of a beautiful and long relationship. **Russell Young**

VIRGINIA ASTLEY

"IT WASN'T MEANT TO BE A SAD RECORD," says Virginia Astley of her debut LP, *From Gardens Where We feel Secure*. "The mood was just meant to be reflective, but it's hardly a miserable record. It's just the way I am, always thinking how everything was this time last year or the year before. I don't dwell on it at all, I just tend to recall memories quite a lot. There's this feeling I get, it's like when you remember an old smell, but you can't define what it is. I sometimes think that if I can grasp what this feeling is, then I would understand everything."

Virginia Astley's records are a lot like that – sketchy landscapes of sombre tone with that subtle sense of secrecy, almost entrancing in their grave beauty. It is important not to think of her records as *quaint* but we might allow for *charming grace*. 'From Gardens Where We feel Secure' is an instrumental impression of a country summer, a slightly subdued reflection with an underlying method of a harsher nature. It doesn't shout at you and it doesn't really want to fit into any world but its own, amongst loss, regret and an ideal love.

"As usual", she says, "it was accused of being twee or over-sentimental although next time, I DO want to make an album with a much harder sound. There was this idea to do a 'Winter' instrumental album to compliment 'Gardens'."

Virginia was formerly one-third of The Ravishing Beauties (which also featured Nicola Holland and Kate St.John). A growing need for three individual creative paths saw their eventual demise. As Kate left to pursue a modelling career, Nicola began to contribute to The Fun Boy Three, leaving Virginia to aim at her own solo ambitions. The Ravishing Beauties finally disbanded in the summer of last year, leaving us just two radio sessions and a track ('Futility') on the NME's 'Might Reel' compilation cassette.

"The 'Mighty Reel' contribution was our own interpretation of a poem by Wilfred Owen," she explains to me, "and 'Futility' is probably the most direct song I have ever done. Usually, my intention is to express a feeling in the songs rather than a view or an opinion. 'Futility' is more straightforward in a way – having an anti-war sentiment."

Her first solo release was an ethereal collection of songs on a ten-inch EP entitled *A Bao A Qu*. It seemed that she now possessed a sense of freedom that was never evident in her Ravishing Beauty days.

"Well," she agrees, "there is probably that greater sense of freedom now – the Ravishing Beauties just turned into a nightmare in many ways. I know now that if I make mistakes, at least it will be down to me. I just want to be careful about what I do. At the moment, I want to play live a lot, and I'm quite happy with the area I'm working in. Sometimes, it has been treated with a little confusion when I play live, but the response generally has been very varied. I tend to prefer supporting people because it relieves the pressure somewhat. There's still this problem, though, of being treated as a classical-pop crossover, like something of a novelty. It's label I could do without. I also wish it wasn't mentioned that I had a classical training – it's quite a long time ago and I never finished college, anyway."

It was at college that Virginia met Nicola and Kate. Losing interest in academic life, she left abruptly to explore new possibilities, working for a while with Richard Jobson and Troy Tate from The Teardrop Explodes. When offered the chance to support the latter, she decided to get back in touch with her two college-mates. 1981 also saw her work with brother-in-law Pete Townshend on 'All The Best Cowboys Have Chinese Eyes'; his daughters were later to contribute to 'A Bao A Qu' on backing vocals.

Her only other release on Why-Fi, apart from 'A Bao A Qu' was this year's single, *Love's A Lonely Place To Be*, essentially a pop song with an effective air of drama, desolation and the kind of haunting sadness that seems to be a part of almost all her songs. Virginia admits that it did sound like a commercial release although it certainly wasn't intended as such.

This year has also seen her performing live with a strictly flexible approach. Her gigs have been quite rare during 1983, but have included a support to The Armoury Show and as Pure Sex (with Anne Stevenson, Audrey Riley, Kathy Seabrook and Josephine Wells) in a one-off at London's 'Venue' in August. Live, perhaps she has yet to capture the wistful, dreamy intimacy of her records, but she is, nevertheless a quite endearing performer – her voice slight and soft but with an insinuating power.

Options loom in luxurious abundance for Virginia Astley at present. Having completed work with poets Anne Clark and Patrik Fitzgerald on a film called 'Isolation' for Channel Four (which should be broadcast before the end of the year) she is undecided about her next moves, but there seems to be no shortage of possibilities.

Having played with Paul Simpson on the B-side of his latest single, she is toying with the idea of a tour with him ("perhaps doing the occasional gig on a canal"). There is also a possibility of writing a film soundtrack, although it is too early in negotiations to go into detail.

As far as records are concerned, she explains that "There are a lot of different options available because there are a couple of major record labels that have come up with offers. I'm a little wary now though, because of my experience in the past. It all depends on how much control I would be given. I was happy to put the album out on my own label so I'll work within that set-up unless the right offer comes up."

Virgina Astley might make music that speaks in a whisper, but it is music that is close to a pure classicism, music of natural, rich beauty. Virgina Astley's music is irresistible, not least because its breath of life exists beyond the restraints of fashion, current conducts and our expectations of what should fit in our pop world. Most of all though, her music is compulsive because it is about the muddle of memories and the force of love, sensed with an innocence that is perhaps *eternal*. Her songs and instrumental sketches, in the final analysis are concerned with our impressions as much, perhaps, as her own.

"I always need a new challenge, I suppose", she concludes, "The excitement gets lost if everything is too familiar. I still love being in the studio, but it isn't the same feeling as I had in the beginning."

Virginia Astley will continue to discover new forms of beauty, and the possibilities seem endless. If you've missed that pure heart in her music, it's not too late to change your minds.

Jonh Wilde

Photos: Russell Young

●THE ETERNAL FICTION ROMANTIC

It's six and a half years since The Buzzcocks became, with 'Spiral Scratch', the first ever punk group to put out their own record. Quickly establishing themselves among the vanguard of the "new wave", songwriter Pete Shelley soon became the first true romantic of that generation, 1978 bearing witness to five slices of some of the most energetic, emotive pop tunes ever. Despite eventual chart success, The Buzzcocks eventually lost direction, and split after three albums and a dozen singles, reserving a niche in pop history. Pete Shelley has since established himself at the forefront of computer technology, mixing raw emotions with banks of synths. He no longer has hit singles, but he does sell albums; *Dave Jennings* went along to Spirit Studios in Manchester to see than man at work . . .

PETE SHELLEY
● ● ● ●
▷ ▷ ▷ ▷

I IMAGINE THAT a lot of people were quite surprised when you came out with a first solo album that was almost entirely electronic . . .

Yeah, because with The Buzzcocks, there were just four of us, and three of us played guitars! None of us were keyboard players, so synthesisers were out of our scope, really – unless you could actually programme a synthesiser to play something, to play a pattern or a line.

Did you get fairly bored with The Buzzcocks towards the end?

It wasn't so much boredom, it was just . . . lack of whatever it was that we started off having. We didn't adapt when there was a change in the musical climate, which put paid to our chances of getting records into the charts; we did some things which were uncommercial, but which . . . released at any other point in time, were commercial! So it's really the luck of the draw whether or not you get chart success.

Of the later Buzzcocks tracks, which are the ones that now mean most to you, which you feel should have got more attention?

Well . . . (laughing) . . . all of the later stuff which didn't get into the charts! There's some parts in *A Different Kind of Tension* which I think, in some ways, were beyond their time; but we were trying to do as much as possible with two guitars, bass and drums. I was straining at the leash to get into a new way of doing things.

Presumably, since you did end up leaving the band, there must have been a degree of tension involved in that . . .

When we did the *Love Bites* tour, that was when I first thought, "I want to do something else". All groups are basically doomed, they've got a brief life span, and that's it, that's when the group can work. Beyond that, you've got to get into a different way of working; and I think we got into one which didn't actually work out for everybody in the band.

You think perhaps there's an initial period of work in a group where there's spontaneity, and you're excited about working with each other, and then after that there's a period of thinking "Well, this group has been successful, so how can we keep it going"?

Yeah, it's like that. It becomes more of a business relationship . . . you don't phone everybody up and say (enthusiastically) "I've got this song, we should do it!". The Buzzcocks were losing that; and once it loses that, you think . . the only thing to do is to leave! So I went down to Martin Rushent's studio to do demos for what would have been the fourth Buzzcocks album, and the first one we did was *Homosapien*. We were using machines, because it was just me and Martin in there. And we sat back, after fifteen hours spent working on Homosapien, and we listened to it again and again and again – we spent three hours just listening to it! We didn't believe that me and him could have done something like that! And the day after that, we did *Pusher Man*; and the day after that, we did *I Generate A Feeling*. And it seemed that there was no obstacle in pursuing this – the only obstacle was that I would have to go back and tell the band that . . . either I'd already recorded the album, or that I wanted it doing exactly like this!

Do you, then, still have anything to do with the former Buzzcocks?

Well, about eighteen months ago, when I was on tour, Steve Garvey played bass; but he's over in New York now working with his band, Motivation. And also about eighteen months or so ago, I had a phone call from John Maher; he was asking whether I was going to do anything, but there was no definite plans. So then he got in touch with Steve Diggle again, and they're doing Flag Of Convenience.

Do you still know Howard Devoto?

Yeah!

You're still friends with him, but not planning to work together – is that it?

Well, we've often talked about getting together again. But the general consensus is that unless there's something specifically which the two of us want to do, with the same initial fervour as with The Buzzcocks, then it'd be pointless.

Have you enjoyed any of his work with Magazine, or his solo stuff?

Yeah, some of the stuff from Magazine I like; I haven't actually heard his new album. He's a talented individual; what more can you say without getting into petty details? But the last Magazine album is one of my favourite cassettes.

Magic, Murder And The Weather? That's interesting, because that was perhaps the least popular of all Magazine's albums . . . but you like it a lot?

Yeah . . . I've been working with Barry Adamson for the last year now, and he said that when they were doing that album, they knew that that was going to be the last one; and therefore they made the album that they wanted to make. It doesn't have to be a commercial album to be a good one!

Who else are you working with now, in your band?

Well, basically, at the moment, it's just me, Barry, and Francis Cookson on drums.

Are you doing anything like what Yazoo did live, then – using computers and backing tapes?

Well, the first time I went out, I used backing tapes; the next time, I want to do something more "live". Not that I found any limitation in using tapes; it's just that I've already done it, therefore it wouldn't be as much of a challenge to me. The only thing you've got to worry about with backing tapes is that the tape doesn't snarl up, or something like that; we were on tour for three months, and that only happened one-and-a-half times!

○ ○ ○ ○ ○

ONE SMALL DIFFERENCE between *Homosapien* and *XL1* was that there were a couple of songs on XL1 which relied more on acoustic instruments. Was it just that you were wanting to try something different again?

Well, when me and Martin got together to do XL1, our intention was to get something which expanded upon the knowledge we had of the machinery, and to explore some more areas. The electronics are secondary to the actual songs; if you don't get the song there in the first place, then all the electronics in the world won't help you.

Do you consider yourself, then, to be a songwriter rather than a musician?

I don't consider myself to be a virtuoso musician. That's why I don't mind giving the credit for, "who plays that synthesiser part?", to "this computer"! So therefore, me doing a solo album isn't like someone like Mike Oldfield doing it, because he's approaching it from a musician's standpoint. The XL1 album isn't as synthetic as "Homosapien", although a lot of the things which sound like they've been played by live musicians weren't at all. There's no live druming on the album.

Whose idea was the computer programme at the end of XL1?

Oh, that was my idea, 'cause I'd just got my ZX Spectrum as I was doing the album. The idea was that you'd have the line of text coming up as it was sung. So I worked out a way in which I could record that; and so I proved to myself that it could be done!

Did you consider the question of what proportion of the people who might buy your album would be able to take advantage of the computer graphics?

Yeah, and I considered that to be high enough. As well as having more video recorders than any other country in the world, we've got more home computers; and the Spectrum is a high-selling computer. It's also one of the cheapest ones.

Have you now used up all your old songs? Because I believe that on *Homosapien* there were one or two things which were relics from your past?

I don't think I've used them all up. The fact that they're old . . . I don't just wait until they're old before I do them, they might just have a growing period. "Telephone Operator" is the oldest one so far; that's ten and a half years old, I wrote it in 1973! It's always good to do the old stuff, because you know that's one less thing to worry about.

HAS YOUR ATTITUDE to relationships, that you reflect in the sings, changed a lot over the years?

Well, I've never been one for writing "moon and June" type lyrics; therefore, what I'm trying to do there is to come to a nice, easy understanding of the fact that most problems are caused by the way we think about things, rather than the things themselves. Desires in a relationship are more likely to make the relationship fail than any other, outside circumstances.

You think it's one's expectations of another person that are more likely to ruin a relationship than, say, economic circumstances, or anything like that?

Yeah, it's your expectations, and I think that you start fraying at the edges if you're not getting the proper results!

So that's something you've always believed in, that's always been there in your songs?

Mm . . . although sometimes I've been into areas which aren't really personal statements and testimonies. Like, *What Was Heaven*; that's a story-telling exercise, not an actual experience.

I think that one of the things which made the Buzzcocks have an impact was the fact that, although you were identified as being part of the punk movement . . . one of the main commandments of punk was "Thou shalt not have emotions, thou shalt not love people". Did you find that you were ever held up to ridicule by people from that sub-culture?

I suppose so, yeah. But I never let if affect me deeply. Some people believe that all life's problems can be solved by political means; some people think they can only be solved by terriorist means. Some people think you can't solve them; I'm one who happens to think that by understanding the other people in the world better, and the relationships between them, you can get things to run more smoothly!

Yes, I do think that a lot of political theories fall down because they seem to be based on the assumption that human beings are rational . . .

Yeah. Politics is a mass thing, but at the end of the day you've still got the individual! I think individuals are more adjusted than the mass, and society.

As someone who's played to thousands of people at once, have you ever felt intimidated by "The Mob Mentality" – you know, the way people behave in crowds that they don't behave in as individuals?

I think that's one of the reasons why some people go to gigs, actually; just because you can get that release from everyday constraints. In some ways, you can stand

I HAVE A couple of quotes written down from XL1, which I'd be grateful if you could expand upon, and explain exactly what you were getting at. From *You And I* an excellent line, I think – *"What's the point of reason, anyway?"* . . .

Er . . . love is a very irrational thing!

Yeah . . . it always surprised me that you played so many gigs with the Au Pairs, because while I had a lot of respect for them, they were people whose view of interpersonal relationships were quite radically different from the one which came over in Buzzcocks songs; they really did seem to view it all as a science, and all based on power and selfishness and so on . . .

Yeah; it's always good to give the opposite view, or complementary views. A live situation is not meant to be like an evangelical meeting, where only one point is put forward, and Billy Graham gets his two penn'orth in! Just cause I've got an idea about how things should be, I'm not naive enough to think that that's the only way it can be looked at! Sometimes I put in contradictory views to what I hold. If the songs are to work, then they've got to have contradictory elements in them, because there's nothing in life which you can look at which doesn't have a contradictory element. I mean, they don't make things perfect!

The second quote *From Many A Time: "Why must we wait until a revolution before we drag it down?/It's not too late to dissolve the old solution/And then we'll drag it down"*

Why wait until a revolution when you can do it yourself? You don't have to wait for everybody around you to go through a dramatic change, because there's . . . small things! The earlier lines set the idea of it being a song about putting things off until the right occurrences happen.

What are you working towards now?

In a commercial sense, a new single soon. I'm doing these demos, and trying to work out a real plan for the future. I should have been in America now – we were supposed to be going at the beginning of September, but we changed record companies.

You have sold quite a few records in America, haven't you?

Yes, there's still interest in what I do, even though I've never gone to great heights of stardom. I'm not sure I'd really like it up there if I got there! So it's good being allowed to do what we want to do, and to have all the help, advice and financial assistance to be able to do it.

there and look at a crowd of people, and think "My God, how dumb!". The reason I like playing live is 'cause afterwards, you get to meet people. During it you get to meet people! I usually concentrate on the first ten rows, 'cause those are the ones I can see – and you can see them in very good detail! There used to be sporadic incidents of crowd violence, and on a few occasions I'd stop what we were doing, and say, "Look, you – yeah, *you!*" So being on stage isn't just an opportunity – you have to knock these people who are really close to you!

PAGE 21

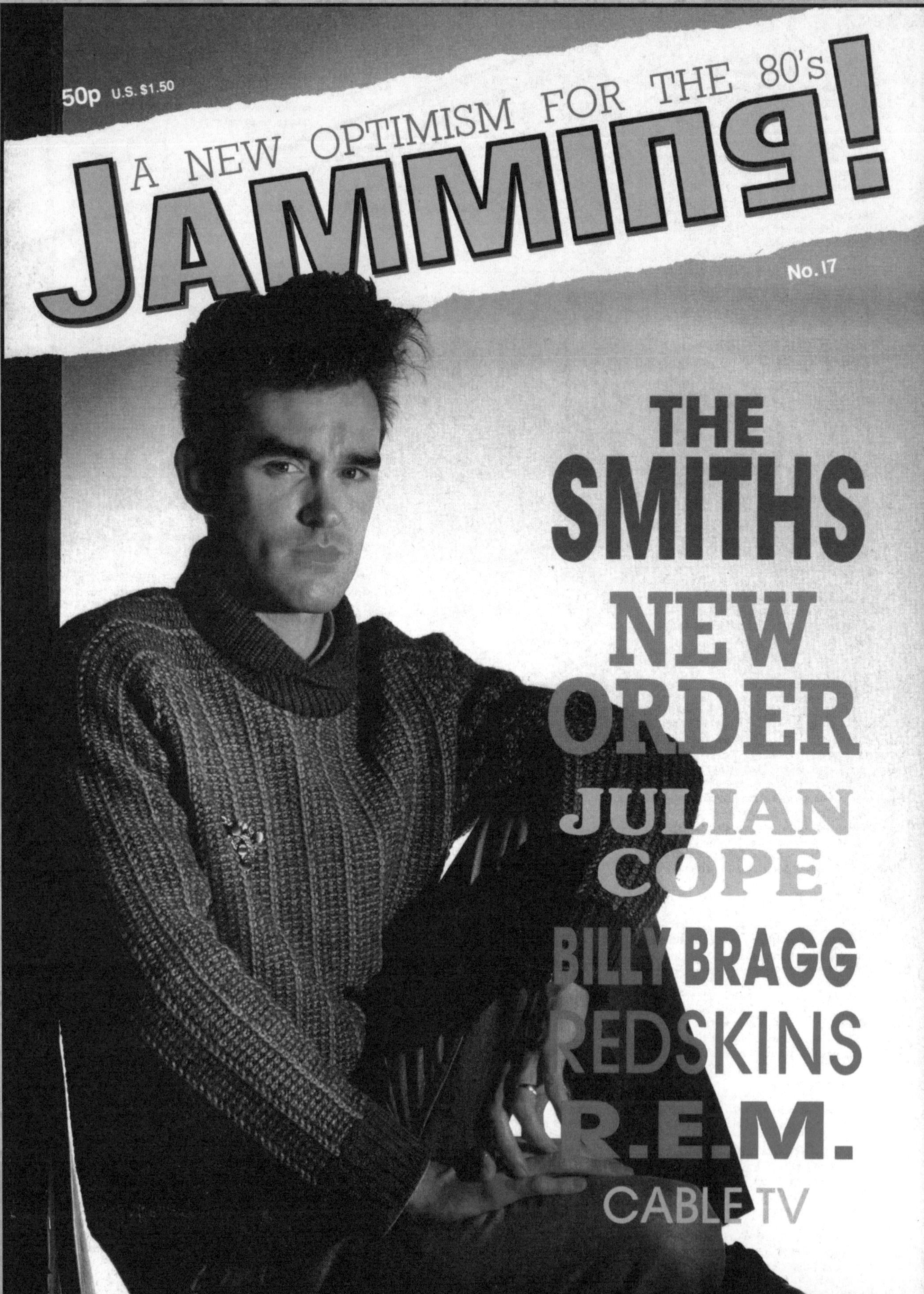

50p U.S. $1.50

A NEW OPTIMISM FOR THE 80's

JAMMING!

No. 17

THE SMITHS
NEW ORDER
JULIAN COPE
BILLY BRAGG
REDSKINS
R.E.M.
CABLE TV

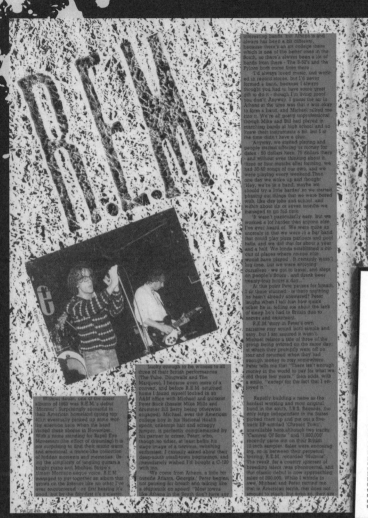

The most painfully hip issue of *Jamming!* was SO painfully hip it even included 'The Billy Bragg Guide to Being Hip'. It also came with a Morrissey front cover perfectly timed for the release of The Smiths' debut LP, an interview with New Order, an early R.E.M. feature, the agit-rock of The Redskins and the psych-pop of Julian Cope.

ISSUE #17 1/84

Some of this was the fortuitous timing of *Jamming!*'s bi-monthly schedule; it would have been much harder to find so many great acts to feature had we been publishing on the fortnightly frequency of, say, *Smash Hits*. But much of it spoke to the fact that we did, largely, have our collective fingers on some sort of pulse. While Jonh Wilde's questioning of generational spokesman candidate Morrissey (misspelled from start to finish as Morrisey, such was our lack of copy-editing or simple fact-checking) seemed stage-crafted after the event, the Q&A format, as also utilised with New Order (by Dave Jennings) and Julian Cope (Wilde), generally served *Jamming!* readers well. This forthright approach additionally cut through the crap of what was becoming an increasingly pretentious weekly music press. Also working in our favour was Russell Tate's design, a little less poptastic this time around, a little more zine-like, ensuring that *Jamming!* could still not be confused as a mainstream magazine despite its content.

Hipness was one thing. Inclusion was and remains something else. It shames me that Issue 17 also included a full feature on Pauline Black (ex-The Selecter and an artist in her own right) and an introductory piece on punk-poet-singer Joolz but that neither woman, the first of whom was also the magazine's only featured person of colour, made the front cover list, not even in lieu of the words 'Cable TV'. The fact that no one commented on this while we were working on said cover was probably the result of an inside masthead now twenty-one people strong – every one of them male, and notably none of them a person of colour either. (While I would keep Pedro Romhanyi's name on that masthead in hope of further contributions, his feature on The Redskins proved his swansong; he moved swiftly sideways into the world of television, advertising and award-winning music videos.) Much debt is therefore owed to Alan Marke and Alan McLaughlin, whose reviews veered into the kind of Black American music that many of us (e.g. myself) tended to belittle if it didn't operate within our home-grown cultural reference points.

The cool quotient ensured that, for now at least, *Jamming!* nonetheless continued to sell north of 30,000 copies. We had even taken the bold step of moving back into Nomis, where the Jamming! label/fanzine had previously held court and where, on the ground floor, pop stars who had never heard of *Jamming!*, let alone sought its approval, routinely rehearsed for *Top of the Pops* or upcoming global tours. One of their future compadres made the back cover in the form of a full-page ad for Nik Kershaw; such were the printing bills, office rentals and assorted Christmas party expenses that we didn't turn away anyone from paying for that privilege.

THE SMITHS

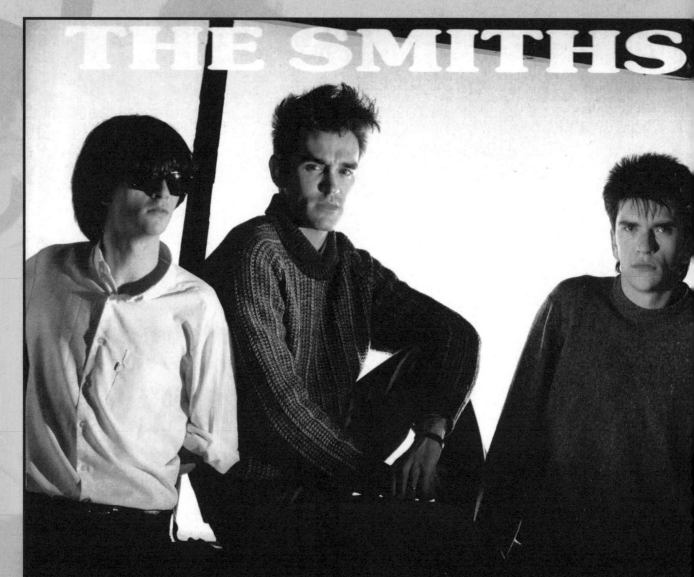

PAGE 16

LET ME BEGIN MY DREAM, and let's be abrupt, not only for the moment. Can music reach the stillness? How much is worth all the fuss, the dressing up and the expectations? To consider the highest and the best here is to weigh up, in all seriousness, our favourite moments, transports of delight and the glory of melody sweeping in upon our daze, opening us to the prospects of a new thrill, transition and the winds of change. Surely nothing less? And therefore, between the quality of the pop single that gleefully disrupts the balance of our days and the merit of the three minutes that entertains but leaves us unaffected lies the *genius* of the great pop record. We could hover just there, believing that the imagination *must* dance . . . what is sure?

Last year, amidst the mass of music that was all too much of a muchness, too tolerant and unobjectionable, there *was* The Smiths, thank Christ. Their second release of '83, 'This Charming Man', the follow-up to 'Hand In Glove', contained almost everything essential about the modern pop song, its go-full-tilt READY TO BURST panache having the agitating edge that is sudden, contorted in motion, its grace ingrained in its unpolished, unfinished surface.

No illusions. The Smiths are the first great *aesthetic* pop band since The Buzzcocks, at least, transforming our expectations of how much energy could be conceived in three minutes of song and dance. The Smiths, translating vision into sound, are not far from life, not just concerned with singing about beauty, sorrow and love but ultimately intent on capturing the first nervous bursts of them all in every three minutes.

They obviously knew the value of beauty and were aiming at the highest, recognising that alongside the problems of time and death and God should exist the image of the girl of our dreams, insisting that the imagination MUST dance, with a sudden sway.

'This Charming Man', let's not pretend otherwise, was heart-melting, fidgeting about, forgetting oneself. We've come so far since, what difference does it make? What happened next? I don't want to be too accurate. Trembling with pleasure, a twinkle of the eye and everything held back (just for the moment), another burst of speed, a clean pair of heels and away. Laugh? I didn't waste a moment. It was time to clip their wings, heckle and haggle, pull the rug from under them. Me and Morrisey met somewhere. It might have been a bus-stop.

Jamming!: Persuade me.

Morrisey: We seem to have some incredible depth of character. I believe that I have a great deal to say, so I would never shun an interview. Especially now in such desperate times! I think it is crucial to say as much as possible. I hate the way that people shun it all – it just foxes me.

Thinking aside . . . how concerned is it all? Don't be too accurate.

It's not so much political as common sense. It just seems that sense is not very common anymore. Everybody is waiting to hear a voice *saying something* – either musically or politically. I just don't hear it. It's just like grinding out sausages; we never grind our sausages.

You seem quite close to perfection. I wanted to know just how close.

To me, at the moment, it feels completely perfect. I feel that if the group was accepted by the entire universe tomorrow, it wouldn't surprise me. We do have everything. I think you must have that attitude or you will be swept under the door. I cannot think of any limits, I feel I'm a completely open book in every way. As a wordsmith, though, I feel as though I've just written a comma so far. I feel as though it has hardly begun. I believe that we've just started to chip away. It's more important than breathing.

> **"I won't rest until 'Hand In Glove' is in the heart of everything. It should have been a massive hit."**

So what makes you shout and jump and write and how close are The Smiths to real life?

Most of my inspiration does come from outside music – especially literature and particularly Oscar Wilde. But I am incredibly fond of popular music. My first record was Marianne Faithful's 'Come Stay With Me' which I bought when I was very young. I remember it had a profound effect on me, and from that time, I was totally obsessed with all aspects of popular music. I like Sandie Shaw and The Marvellettes. Within current music, I can only think of people who have chased their own tails, then crumbled.

I wasn't going to ask about your sex life but . . .

I think I try to be very unsexual/asexual about the way I write. I haven't pinned any gender on the table and been very forthright. I think by being completely sexless, it has caused some degree of attention, so people believe I'm totally obsessed with sex. It's a strange paradox – if I wrote about breasts, people would probably ask me about The Clash all the time. Because I've said publically that I'm not interested in sex, people are always asking me about it.

So much rock'n'roll is masturbatory in a way, very phallic at times – sex is almost completely linked with it. But I can't help that – it's just the history of the entire syndrome. I think it *is* very masturbatory because it is the height of glamour. It's just like somebody standing on stage saying, 'I'm up here, this is what I can do, you must worship me now'. I think that sex element does come into it.

So where do The Smiths fit in amongst the sex, the glamour and the star-spangled world of rock'n'roll?

We have a very traditional line-up. It's nothing special but it's very special. We are four individuals; we just simply open our hearts and open our mouths. If that isn't enough, we might as well go home. We don't have any metaphysical plan – there is nothing gimmicky that we want to rope people in with. We are four individuals, naked before the world – people will either react, or not.

It strikes me that many people who are stars are shallow individuals. It is rare that you get anybody *up there* who has incredible depth or value. It seems that there is a shallow veneer to so many people. I prefer to think of us as

accessible rather than commercial. Obviously, we want to be very popular. We have this particular intelligence that means we will never get swept away with the mundane and moronic popular groups. There is an attitude that if you are strong-willed, then you will turn your back on the charts, television etc. But we want to utilise all those avenues. If you are weak, you will take those avenues, have a hit record, get swept away and people will dominate you. But if you are sure about what you do, it won't happen.

What is important? What is sure? You talk about the depth of The Smiths and I wonder.

The records have to be memorable – it's not just an instant fad thing, the flavour of the month or whatever. If I thought we were going to be in vogue until February or March, then the whole thing would be repellent to me. It *has* to be memorable.

These terms like 'charming' and 'handsome' that we cling to – it *is* a positive calculation. So much music in recent years has been such an inverted, dour and depressing atmosphere thrust upon audiences. I just became so tired of the attitude that seemed to be riddled through groups and writers. I wanted to inject a new attitude into everything, that people don't have to be cool and monotonous any more – they can just relax, do anything they want, follow their hearts in every direction. There is that entire non-human feel with the use of synth in so much music now. The Smiths are an argument against that.

I cannot imagine what I would be doing if I didn't have this group. It is so essential to me.

It's such an emotionally edgy thing. It seemed before that everything I wanted to say was just locked away. I just couldn't communicate with people. The Smiths is my mouth-piece and it's also my dream. It's such an immense gratification when we get so many letters saying exactly what I want to hear. People seem to be affected by the slightest lines and the slightest gestures.

> **"At the moment, it feels completely perfect. I feel that if The Smiths were accepted by the entire universe tomorrow, it wouldn't surprise me."**

Would it be fair to say that you write love songs (with a difference)?

In many ways, they *are* love songs, though in my case they would be concerned with self-love. I would say that they were complete celebrations – even celebrations of sexuality if people want to take it that way. They are all concerned with making use of what you are and what you've got.

The 'classic love song', for me, was never a love song – it was just a statement. We are probably writing classic love songs. They are very open about falling in and out of love, expectations, love and hate. Because they are so to-the-point, they can be quite brittle.

Do you not recognise a measure of obscurity in the songs, a kind of ambiguity?

I get very annoyed when the word 'obscure' is brought into the whole context. I feel that I go to great pains to be very direct and precise. I don't want to be misunderstood in anything I say. I think it has been a trend in recent years

PAGE 17

to be very obscure and very surreal. The Smiths must be understood on every level, in every way.

You've talked before about tragedy.

Most of the songs are about my own life, which has been quite tragic, so most of the songs are concerned with tragedy in some way. I treat tragedy in a very personal and real way. I speak from direct experience, as down-to-earth as I can. Ultimately it is very optimistic. I feel that I have been very explicit in all the songs I have written. I really have to write very personal, I can't hide behind things -I can't join in the short-sightedness of modern lyricists.

There seems that there is this messy, unwritten law that you cannot say certain things. I have to be open, but I find it impossible on a 'friendship' level. Because of that, it is all channelled into The Smiths. Because I was silent for so long, it is now quite easy for me, just to express everything.

I'm not interested in painting my personality in the songs – that sounds a little artificial. I'm totally immersed in the whole idea of this group – 25 hours a day. I'll stand by it to the death.

Does it all overawe you sometimes, the sudden sweep to success with 'This Charming Man', TOTP and the hungry attention?

It doesn't overawe me because I believe that what we do is so special – therefore I expect us to attain the highest degree of success. We do expect more – when I see the songs that got higher in the charts than 'This Charming Man' or when I think of the songs that will get higher than 'What Difference Does It Make', there is no way I can sit back.

Your climb to acclaim has been almost meteroric and there's no pausing for breath. Is it all so sudden and splendid?

Up to now, it has all been marvellous. The only tragedy for The Smiths has been that 'Hand In Glove' didn't gain the attention it deserved. I won't rest until that song is in the heart of everything. It's been given another lifespan because it's been re-recorded for the LP. But it should have been a massive hit. It was so URGENT – to me, it was a complete cry in every direction. It really was a landmark. There is every grain of emotion that has to be injected into all the songs and it worked perfectly with 'Hand In Glove'. It was as if these four people *had* to play that song – it was so essential. Those words had to be sung.

Persuade me (again).

We want to reach as many people as possible We've hardly begun. We try not to comply with any other attitude – whether it be the attitudes of groups on major record labels or on independents. We *will* appear on The Russell Harty Show and Cheggars Plays Pop. We think we can do these things and walk away with enormous credibility because we are very strong-willed characters and our belief is very deep-rooted. We just have immense strength – the musicianship is quite special. There is a great deal of depth that just hasn't seen the light of day, yet. It's self-evident really. It's all in those songs. Believe me.

Is there anything else? Don't be too accurate.

Here's my bus. What difference does it make?

I DON'T WANT TO get carried away but. We've come so far and The Smiths burst into life, accidently and out of context. I don't want to get carried away but. The Smiths breeze in, wasting no time with an acute sense of beauty. How can you resist? The secret is . . . *don't give in to grief*, be enraptured by a single smile and this is the year of The Smiths. Full of life and from birth (Sept. '82) to just a moment ago, they have been concerned with a complete lyricism and a constant flux of emotion. One eye on perfection and the other on the next nervous burst. Can we ask for more? Not yet.

I don't want to get carried away but. I had this dream. There was me and Morrisey at a bus-stop. We agreed on one thing. They were worth the fuss. *But*. I forget to ask. Can music reach the stillness? What happened next?

Main photo: **Paul Cox**
Live Shots: **Russell Young**

THE BILLY BRAGG GUIDE TO BEING HIP

Billy Bragg tells the secrets of how, in one year, he came from working in a second-hand record shop to being guest writer in JAMMING!

"I don't want to be hip and cool" sung Howard Jones in 'New Song' and proved himself to be the true spokesman for his generation as a multitude of young executives, bank clerks and newly weds sang along. But "I don't wanna live by the rules", the line that followed, threw a whole nation of hipsters into disarray. Surely, *not* 'living by the rules' was *the* definition of being hip and cool?

To clear up this ambiguity, Jamming! have asked me to define once and for all who and what is 'hip'. Is it you or is it Howard Jones? Read on if you dare . . .

WHAT IS 'HIP'? Well brothers and sisters, hip is something that you can never actually be. Hip is something that other people think you are. When first approached to write this article I was informed that I was 'hip' and so should be an authority on the subject. I thought "How can I be hip? I only own one pair of shoes and I go to bed most nights with only a hot water bottle for company, and I don't have enough *pants*". But Tony Fletcher assured me that I was undoubtedly 'hip' and that I would be paid for every single word I wrote and so after much research, I can now invite you all to come with me and look into the Myth of 'Hipdom'.

HIP or TRENDY? The dividing line between hip and tendy is very thin. Most people who actually *try* to be hip are merely being trendy. For instance, which of the following are 'hip' and which are 'trendy':

a) Going to Camden Palace
b) Not going to Camden Palace

a) Steve Davis
b) Alex Higgins

a) Buying a Drum Machine
b) Paying no more than £2.50 for a haircut.

If you answered a) to everything then you are a trendy. If you answered b) to everything then you are a closet trendy because its really unhip to answer these stupid questionnaires.

"STREET CREDIBILITY": Now this is something that a lot of people crave but it is very hard to define. For pop stars it basically boils down to whether you can change the tyre of your car in the East India Dock Road whilst wearing your stage clothes without getting beaten up. You can? Then you are "STREET".

CLOTHES: The predominant dress style for February 1984 is going to be warm clothes. It is always better to be warm than to be hip as any hyperthermia victim will tell you.

POLITICS: Well here we are in 1984 and if Mrs Thatcher hasn't made you *all* hip to what's going on by now then you must be buying The Sun. Working for the Clampdown is *very* unhip.

PEOPLE: It's very important that you steer well clear of those you consider to be hip because if you start coming together in little groups of hipness then there is always the possibility that you will form an elite. The Oxford Dictionary defines an elite as a bunch of wankers who think they are the bees knees. Not very hip, I'm sure you'll agree. Similarly, its rather unhip to be involved with anyone vaguely 'Sloane Ranger-ish' as they are all incurable trendies and are also a further manifestation of the continuing failure of the upper classes to come to terms with reality.

STYLE: It's very important to have some eccentric quirk that singles you out as hip amongst your crowd. For instance, leaking government secrets is becoming quite hip. Tax evasion is a perennial favourite and I think in the New Year a lot of people will become involved in the abduction of prominent media personalities for sexual purposes. Another hip pastime is, after a bath, drying your private parts with an electric hair dryer. That's very hip. I do it anyway and the way I'm going I'm so hip I'll be back working in the secondhand record shop by next Christmas, but who cares? Being hip won't solve any of your problems. The important thing is to suss out what everyone else is doing and deviate!

Still buying the Sun every day? Forget it. Join the New Hipsters and become a mataphysical hod-carrier in the building of the New Jerusalem!

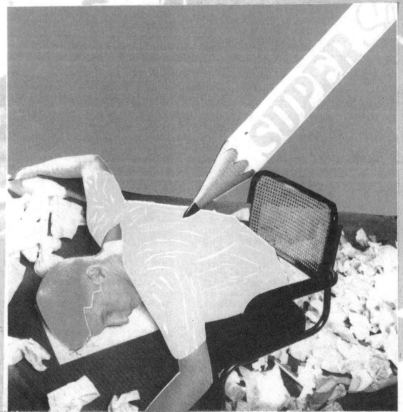

'The pen is mightier than the sword.' Billy Bragg gives up trying to write a hit song.

PAULINE BLACK

THE MANY STAGES OF A CHEQUERED CAREER

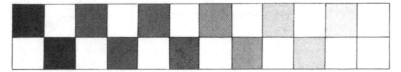

It was as a singer with The Selecter that **Pauline Black** first came to prominence. Since their split she's broadened her horizons, appearing in three plays, hosting 'Hold Tight' (a children's T.V. programme) and more recently Channel 4's 'Black On Black', as well as continuing in music. **Ross Fortune** talked with her in Liverpool.

1. THE SELECTER.
PUTTING THE PAST AWAY:

Looking back on those heady days of Two-Tone, when ska was king, and black and white did truly unite, I wondered what Pauline's feelings were now towards that first success, and clearly she viewed it with affection.

"The Selecter was probably the best thing that ever happened to me. I'd been working for five years in the NHS as a radiographer, and if you've ever had to do night duties you'll understand why . . . The Selecter was my start and I loved it and hated it all in one. I was still naive enough to wonder why people wanted to give us money for something we all enjoyed. It got pretty heavy between us at times, even coming to blows, and I liked to be involved in all of that! Looking back, I loved it and that's that."

Like the other members of The Selecter, although the one who has remained most in the public eye, Pauline still lives in Coventry, remaining in touch with most of the others:—

"'H' is in a band called 'Kangaroo Court', and Charlie is involved with getting youth facilities together for music workshops and recording. Neol Davies and I are not the best of friends, but he's teaching guitar in Coventry schools".

All thankfully show no indication of wanting to live off past glories, Pauline plainly recognising that it is all very much in the past, with her suitably blunt and to the point appraisal of the recent 'These Are Two-Tone' LP which, as far as she is concerned, "Is a piece of nostalgia, and a way for the record company to make money." Indeed, she seems genuinely much more keen to look to the future, revealing that aside from her solo work, she has been having long dawntime conversations with Brad from The Specials of late. "I'm really interested in his JB Allstars and he's interested in what I'm doing, so you might see a collective hit vinyl sometime in early 1984 . . ."

Of all the other Two-Tone/Ska groups that emerged from that period Pauline singles out The Specials and, newly formed from the ashes of The Beat, General Public, to wish the most luck to "because I really like the people involved," and also presumably because of a political affinity between them and the views espoused on The Selecter's second LP 'Celebrate The Bullet'. It was a political awareness incidentally that went largely unnoticed amidst the band's fall from grace.

2. POLITICS AND MUSIC

As a fan, I'd initially liked The Selecter for a string of great singles, but didn't care too much for the first album and saw little future for them beyond the ska days. So I was very pleasantly surprised when the second LP 'Celebrate The Bullet' came out, with its definite musical progression and integration of strong political comment. Unfortunately the great British public seemed rather less than impressed, and sales and interest dropped off, resulting rightly or wrongly in the band going their separate ways.

Bearing in mind the three songs Pauline wrote for the 'Bullet' album then the subject of politics would seem to be quite near to her heart, her attitude being realistic, yet optimistic, countering doubts about whether anger or expressions of morale and political views are, or can be, worthwhile when channelled through music.

"I can only write what I think or feel, and since that is a reflection of what is going on around me, then I think that to channel it through music is both relevant and necessary, particularly at the time we're living in now! Anyway, I don't know how to write any other way' . . ."

Agreeing that she too likes the second album but not the first, she goes on to say that "The new album, when my record company decide to let it see the light of day, is a mixture of politics and my own personal feelings about what happens or has happened to me. And though I don't think as an individual I can change anything, I do know that I'm not the only person who thinks the way I do, so who knows what might happen."

However, this optimism and concern being not too much in keeping with current musical trends, I point out what Jerry Dammers has said about politics, sexism and racism now being unfashionable. Pauline agrees, but does stress that "It's not all depressing, and there is still good music about, it's just it has to be searched for, and I'm content to be just in there still pitching."

So I wish Pauline all the very best amongst pop's current crop of stale, flat and very profitable dross. And move on to the actress within her.

3. ACTING

Pauline first got into acting in January 1982. "Trevor Laird, an actor and director with the Black Theatre Co-Op first turned me on to it and gave me the confidence to do it", she says. And of the three plays she has since appeared in, she explains that "First was 'Trojans' in which I sang and acted, and the second play was 'Love In Vain' which was about (legendary bluesman) Robert Johnson in which I played a straight role as his girlfriend; that was my favourite play to date. And then most recently, the Blue Angel production which is the only thing I've acted in that hasn't had an all-black cast".

'The Blue Angel' was a stage adaptation of Josef Von Sternberg's film of the same name starring Marlene Deitrich as Lola Lola, and so I asked her if she had any trepidation about taking on the role made famous by Deitrich's film portrayal.

"No, because I felt I was right for the part. In 1929 I'd probably have done exactly the same, and I thought it was great casting the part as black. When little old ladies come backstage after the matinee and tell you how they enjoyed it, then I think it was a success and very worthwhile. Those saturday afternoon matinees were the best".

It is apparent that Pauline takes her acting career very seriously. "I love acting, and it's become as important an outlet for me as singing. My ambitions are to be the next black woman to win an oscar, as nobody has done it since Hattie McDaniels in 'Gone With The Wind'. I want to be as good as her and Dorothy Dandridge. Who knows . . ?"

And though that may seem to be aiming high, after having seen her impressive performance in 'The Blue Angel', then as she says – Who knows?

4. MUSIC (AND THINGS)

But back to her singing and the future of that particular aspect of her career. Where does she see herself heading?

"Well, you've probably heard the single 'I Threw It Away' featuring a fifteen piece gospel choir, which I incidentally wrote in January and recorded in March last year, long before the current trend of gospelites got going. What I want to do is use the conflict of my political beliefs and the choirs religious beliefs to spur us on to find that common ground where we have to agree. Our arguments are long, frantic and sometimes brilliant, but strange as it may seem we all know what we want, and even stranger it's the same things. Performing live is a problem and I use seven of the choir then, but the buzz that gets going on stage between us is exactly what I want, cos they're real people who are not afraid to show their emotions, which is the most important thing".

And emotional sincerity and strength is a criteria prominent in those she admires and cites as having been influenced by. "My earliest influences were men like Mick Jagger and Marvin Gaye. That was at about fourteen, and I knew that I wanted to get on stage and do exactly that. Then it was Janis Joplin and Aretha Franklin, followed by Joan Armatrading and Billie Holiday, who is my spiritual influence – she was a fighter and knew how to live, and her style was hers, and whatever anyone else was doing she stuck to it and ended up paying the price. But she'll live on long after the Ella Fitzgerald's and Lena Hornes are dead. Oh dear, I'm getting

heavy again! I admire Warren Beatty for his acting and directing of 'Reds', Helen Mirren as an actress, Vanessa Redgrave for her politics, and Bob Marley for showing that you can marry politics and music together (but then only the good die young)."

One final point and a niggling contradiction that I'd wanted to clear up was that bearing in mind her political awareness and the fact that her signature features the feminist circle and cross, I wondered how she reconciled this with the so-called sexist single sleeve of her a while back, and indeed what her views on feminism are:

"The sexist single sleeve . . . that's a laugh. It was for 'Shoorah Shoorah'. I thought it was good. I was wearing a white shift which showed my legs and one bare shoulder. I was depicting, albeit badly, a New Orleans black girl hanging around a shack in the delta. That was the sound of the song, and just having played a character called Betty Mae in 'Love In Vain' I thought it was great. The women's movement is important but I think a bit misguided in some of its thinking. I'm a woman and nothing's gonna change that, and if all we've got out of it is Margaret Thatcher as Prime Minister . . . what more can I say? I still use the feminist circle and cross as a punctuation mark after the word 'Black', then everybody knows that I'm a black woman and what they're dealing with.

A talented singer, songwriter and actress, it'll be interesting to see the future developments of Pauline Black's career. In the meantime I look forward to her LP, though Chrysalis now tell me it probably won't see the light of day until spring. However, with or without the aid of her record company, who seem more interested in milking Two Tone's past than pushing her future, Pauline Black's many talents should ensure her the security to pursue her own ideals and directions on both record and stage. Temporarily out of the limelight maybe, but there's enough movement in the shadows to ensure that her progression will be both steady and on her own terms.

Ross Fortune

THE RISE AND FALL (AND RISE AGAIN?) OF JULIAN COPE

In typical Jamming! style, we now have the pleasure of informing you of an exciting series just as we reach the end of it! *John Wilde* had spent many months tracing Julian Cope for a feature; in the meantime, he interviewed Ian McCulloch of The Bunnymen for Jamming! 15, and Pete Wylie of Wah! for no. 16. When the ex-Teardrop Explodes singer became available for this issue, we suddenly realised we had a series on the Crucial Three, a now-legendary, if over-discussed, Liverpool group for 1977 comprising these three eratic, but magnificent musicians. Mac's permanent tongue-in-cheek attitude has been evenly balanced by Wylie's optimism, and now the overwhelming confidence of Julian Cope, following his previous rise and fall. Photos are by *Paul Cox*.

I'd been trying to corner Julian Cope for over twelve months now. He wasn't quite ready, quietly plotting a return to his finest moments. 1983 swept by but the only hint of movement was the release of the last Teardrop Explodes single, 'Disappear From View' that Cope barely approved of and which, if anything, spoiled an ending that was just perfect. In November of last year, he finally returned with 'Sunshine Playroom', a single, that sounded like a false re-start. Me and Julian Cope had at least one thing in common though. We both believed in the genius of Julian Cope and secretly knew that his finest moments (yet) were close upon us.

With Xmas also pressing upon us, we finally met for an afternoon in a cafe close to his publicists to marvel at those little things that keep us on edge, fit to burst and in love. 'World Shut Your Mouth', the next Julian Cope LP, would soon be with us, telling us, in some uncertain ways, that there should be room for simple pleasures and small sins amongst the worries, whys and wherefores of our everydays. I wasn't going to argue – after all, Julian Cope was picking up the bill for the coffees. I was there to pick up the pieces, capture the mood, play with words and you hum it, I'll sing along. We were both in love (a coincidence) and, as ever, in love with inconsistency. After all, we could hardly get the words out, such was our excitement.

TO START WITH, I see an importance in re-evaluating the past briefly. Listening to 'Kilamanjaro' of late, it's struck me how ageless it is and how underrated it seemed to be at the time of release (especially by yourself).

Yeah! I listened to it for the first time in two years the other day and it sounded great. I was perhaps too close to it at the time; there's nothing on it I'm too disappointed with on it now. A few of the songs sounded too '1979' perhaps but it has proved to be a lot more innovative than I imagined at the time. I *do* see The Teardrop Explodes in a lot of bands now. 'Kilamanjaro' did get bad reviews at the time, but what the hell.

When 'Reward' elevated you from cult status to star, you handled the role of glossy pop hero very awkwardly, always steering just clear of naturally accepting it. The chart success was most brief – not lingering long after 'Treason'. Was there something self-destructive in not maintaining that momentum?

I did enjoy seeing my face everywhere around 'Reward' time, but it's like a light you want to switch on and off when you feel like it. You get mobbed at the wrong times – you always get mobbed at Euston station when you want to get somewhere!

There has always been this irony in most of my songs. Most of all, it's been this irony of me as a pop star – like girls being into me when I always used to get slagged off. There was this whole 'spazzy' thing I used to feel – just walking from window to window checking that I didn't look like a spastic. I always felt like that in Liverpool before the Teardrop Explodes happened. The reason why we couldn't get a deal for ages was because all the record companies thought I was a crap front-man. Bill Drummond and David Balfe, who were managing us, thought I should do something about it. Even after 'Bouncing Babies', all the rest of the band thought we needed a new singer but I wanted to be *it!* When we were forming groups in Liverpool, nobody took us seriously. Even when we were gigging, people thought we were going to finish.

A lot of the change was simply circumstance, just chance really. I grew my hair longer and bought myself a flying-jacket and all of a sudden, it just happened. Perhaps I started to look cuter or something. In all the early photos, I just *didn't* look good.

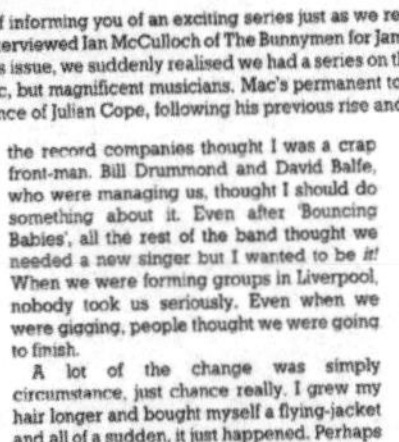

"Insanity is obviously based on what society will accept."

Feeling uncomfortable in the role of pop star did you consciously try to shatter the image, force yourself away?

Oh yeah! I said to all the pop papers at that time not to expect us to keep going like that for years and years. The Teardrops were like a train in a tunnel that came above ground once in a while. I wasn't really bothered. I did break it all down. I remember doing a horrible sex rap at a gig in Nottingham. There were all these fourteen year old girls at the front of the stage, so I took my top off and everyone stopped playing, except the synth wailing out. So I started doing this Indian dance and shouting, 'This is the part where I weird out!' Then I started this rap, asking who was fourteen, and all these girls were going beserk so I started shouting "Wet your pants" and stuff like that. It was just gross and I was thinking, "There's mothers and fathers in this audience." People came backstage afterwards and I just sat there with my hands down my trousers. People were just speechless. I was just saying, 'Sorry man, but we're not a pop group y'know. We just happened to have lapsed into this pop ethic. Don't expect the same thing.'

There must have been so many little girls who either loved it or never bought another Teardrops record again. Personally, I couldn't give a shit. I care about the one in two thousand who can dig it for what it is.

With The Teardrops, one thing I prided myself on was a kind of spontanaiety. If live, it was a stream of consciousness, sometimes it would be pure, unconscious drivel. Other times, it might be illuminating stuff, but I would never do the same thing.

'Wilder', the second LP, was almost the most uncommercial follow-up you could have made. It was also a very difficult LP to appreciate because it was so obviously personal, so much of it being relative to your own domestic struggles at that time.

There was a weird force about when we were doing 'Wilder'. The strange thing is that when I was writing those songs, the actual writing was very coherent. I would go to pieces though when we were recording them.

When we were doing 'Tiny Children' and 'The Great Dominions', I just cried all the way through them. I would do a verse, then lie in the corner for a while. There were so many vocal tracks that we couldn't use because my voice was cracking up with the whole emotion of it.

It was a pity that 'Tiny Children' as a single was relatively overlooked. I still look upon it as one the Teardrop's greatest moments. It's in the same league as Scott Walkers 'Angel Of Ashes'.

Oh Yeah? That's great! That song was written at a strange time, when we were really successful but I was living in this squat in Islington in complete chaos, and I had just broken up with my wife. It was weird because, on one level, I was an incredibly successful person and on the other, I was a complete failure. I knew that I had to forfeit one for the other. I suddenly realised that if I wanted to live the next fifty years, I would have to forfeit the commercial aim.

So how do you feel about 'Wilder' in retrospect?

Well, Mick Houghton, who does press for me and The Bunnymen, was saying to Max Bell that 'Wilder', is as good as Love's 'Forever Changes'. Now whether it is or not, it's great that someone can say that. Brilliant! That keeps me going more than if ten million people bought my records. Just brilliant!

In November 1982, you broke up The Teardrop Explodes forever which didn't surprise many people, as it had been expected for some time. But how difficult was it to make that decision?

Simply, it was the *right time* to break up. It had to happen. With all my favourite bands, I feel the same. Love should have finished after 'Forever Changes'.

It would be dishonest to continue as The Teardrop Explodes. I wasn't The Teardrop Explodes, I just happened to be the main person in it. At the end, we might have gone down commercially but *not* artistically. It was as pure as ever, at the end. If anything, it was more pure at the end because I was so sure of what I wanted.

I'm overwhelmed at what we did as a band. I DO believe that we had a lot more peaks than (say) The Bunnymen who could have taken a lot more risks. Well, I hope that we have taken more risks. At least, there was a lot of uncertainty all the way through, which is how I wanted it.

DURING 1983, YOU disappeared almost completely, returning at the end of the year with 'Sunshine Playroom', such an uncommercial single. It seemed quite a departure from your past. How then is 'World Shut Your Mouth' different from your work with The Teardrop Explodes?

When I did this LP, I just wanted it to be so different from anything that had happened in 1983. I'm just so anti-soul at the moment. I hate the way that anything that is 'soul' is cool now. It just devalues all the great soul there has been. There's just so much bad 'white soul' about. At the moment, it's so cool to be mediocre again.

With this new LP, it was the first time that I have enjoyed recording for a while. It's not that important how well it sells, so long as I have enough money to do another album. We did this one very quickly, in about eighteen days, altogether. There's that Lou Reed line – 'Between thought and expression lies a lifetime'. Well, for me, the aim was to make the time between thought and expression much shorter. When I used to give the group a song in the past, they felt a compulsion to *do* something with it. On 'World Shut Your Mouth', I played bass, rhythm, guitar and keyboards, Gary Dwyer did drums and Steve produced and played lead guitar.

At the moment, everyone is going right over the top with production so I just went in and *did it*. It was as exciting to do as the first Teardrop's single – that kind of freshness about it. I honestly feel it's the best LP I've done. I was finding out how to use trashy guitar sounds and get away with it. All the guitar and organ was recorded incredibly loud – that was very necessary to me.

The most important thing is that it starts with such a bang. The opening song is 'Bandy's First Jump' which is the oldest song I've recorded, it comes from the pre-Teardrop period.

The songs seem to address themselves to typical Cope themes – morality, irony, love, melancholy, pure idealism.

As usual, I think they're very subjective. I do think there is a tremondous lack of morality in my songs though, quite honestly. That is only because my morality is such a personal thing and a very, very strong thing. I used to think that there was an 'amorality' in the songs but 'amorality' is perhaps just a euphemism for 'immorality'. It's a little like the way we define 'insanity'. It might be that we're just so horrified by dissenters in The Soviet Union, for example, being put in lunatic asylums because they are 'insane' as far as the rest of The Soviet Union is concerned. Insanity is obviously based on what society decides; insanity in Britain is basically an unawareness of what society will accept. You can only get a state of insanity when there is a society to define it. It's perhaps the same with the idea of morality.

How then have you dealt with that idea of morality in your songs?

What I was trying to do was quietly challenge the morality of society and quietly challenge the way I had been brought up. I got very pissed off, for instance, when people became very against the acid thing. I got into all that purely because people abhorred it so much; it then became a compulsive thing. It has always been a kind of quiet idealism, like venting my spleen on a small scene of society.

It has always been a very personal kind of idealism though, hasn't it – it has never been explicitly, say, political?

That's true, my idealism was always such a personal thing. Perhaps it was safe in a way because I could never sell out. The whole idea of idealism though can become hideous. I loved the way The Pop Group, for one, came out with all this *belief* but Mark Stewart had to work for Amnesty International before he felt better about it. Then, he wasn't just writing about it, he was doing something about it.

You were always accused of being obscure or elusive in your writing weren't you?

Yeah! But I saw our elusiveness as another form of coherence. I'm not very good at being direct but the people who are good at being direct do it very well. Mark Smith is direct; occasionally he's so prosaic about what he says that he overshoots and misses the mark. He refuses to have anything but a graphic description of something. Ian Curtis, for example, used to deal with much more of an expressionist lyric; 'To the centre of the city' and all that kind of imagery. It was probably more extreme than it needed to be, but then again, it was the only way he could get across the incredible emotion he was putting into a song.

Personally, I would rather use a broad and allusive image, an image that is going to sink into people slowly. Occasionally, it will be obtuse, but it is bound to be if you use lyrics like that.

But Christ! T.S. Eliot was more obscure than anyone in the world but it didn't stop him being great. It is probably presumptuous to allude to anything that great but I'd rather do that than aim at something so mundane.

You have always been very open about your influences. Especially on your newer material, you seem to have no hesitation about wearing them on your sleeves.

I have to wear the influences on my sleeves – it's the only way I can do it. My influences are basically the same now as three years ago – Scott Walker, Jim Morrison, John Cale and a lot of 60's psychedelia. By talking about these people publicly, it gave me the urge to try and do something as good as those people, although I think I can be and have been at certain points. I don't mind if I can be occasionally bad as long as I am so good when I *am* good. I can forgive my favourite people when they are bad. 'Reward' is like a great rush isn't it – like an incredible speedball.

You have always had this interest in the perverse side of pop music. Perhaps it has been this perversity that has always prevented great commercial success, bar 'Reward' and 'Treason'?

I do like pop songs a lot. I always thought there was a mess about *my* pop songs though. Perhaps that was part of their charm. There is that edge in my songs that has always kept them a step from being commercial pop songs. I used to think that maybe I was copping out twenty miles from commericality, thinking that if I got any closer, it was like selling out. But you can go much closer and still have a cutting edge to a song. Obviously, I am trying to make popular music but perhaps there's something too fucked-up to make it pure. It's cancerous pop music.

Most of what I've done has turned out as I intended. I've never tried to do anything as serious as say Tim Buckley's 'Sweet Surrender' (that is *way up there*). It is something that is going to take time.

This new LP though, loses any politeness that was still left after The Teardrop Explodes.

Did you miss anything during the last year?

Not really. Perhaps, I just missed touring. There was a great feeling in being miles and miles from anywhere, say like playing Texas where we made so little sense. But last year, I didn't like a lot of music that was coming out – except Alan Vega, Dalek I Love You, Matt Johnson. They all made good records in 1983. I also liked The Bunnymen's LP – that was good.

Where now is the sense of challenge that keeps you creative?

It pleases me in those one-off situations when someone will pick up on something cryptic and understand what I meant in a song; equally, when someone see it *not* for what it is, but when their interpretation is more interesting than I intended it to be. There was this fity year old woman who asked me if 'Treason' was about the menopause. That was great. But there's no right or wrong.

There's two ambitions. One is to be incredibly famous and so successful that people are sickened by it. The other is simply to go on making albums. The side that wants to be sick about it, just to be bloatedly successful, is more like a quiet dream for me; I don't really want to be that successful. I just wouldn't be very good at it. I'll leave that to Adam Ant who is good at immediate self-parody.

After 'World Shut Your Mouth', what can we expect from Julian Cope?

The unexpected.

I should have known.

John Wilde

PAGE 25

The relentless energy and enthusiasm that had carried *Jamming!* through three successful bi-monthly issues finally ran out of steam with Issue 18, as exemplified by a decidedly uncommercial and disastrously unattractive cover photo session in which The Special A.K.A.'s Jerry Dammers posed as a vagabond against a brick wall adorned with the graffiti 'Burnt Out Stars'. If it was a genuine oversight that the photographer (Jason Pevovar?) remained (thankfully?) uncredited (until now?), it was an equal lack of focus that led any of us – and there were now all manner of people buzzing in and out of our Nomis office – to believe that Dammers, the first person to grace *The Face* magazine's front cover back in 1980, carried anything like the same cachet in 1984. Then again, nor did General Public's Dave Wakeling (ex-The Beat), nor again Big Country's guitarist Bruce Watson, each of whom also submitted to the seemingly regulation Q&A format. (Watson's interview was printed in authentic dialect which, over a decade before Irvine Welsh's *Trainspotting*, was considered patronising rather than authentic, according to some angry letters we received.) Smaller articles on the likes of New Model Army and Under Two Flags hardly broadened the readership. An acknowledgment in the editorial that we were lacking for female contributors was countered in part by Sabina Sinclair's article on the state of the performing arts, though that was a piece better suited to something like *City Limits*; similarly, an overdue celebration of British reggae with Steel Pulse floundered on leader David Hinds' unapologetically anti-homosexual stance. It was 1984 after all, the miners' strike was digging in, and things were about to get worse. As such, the collective comedown was entirely apt.

ISSUE
#18
3/84

THE SKARS H...

"WHO IS HE ANYWAY?" enquires one of the tastelessly coiffeured punkettes of Jerry Dammers as the main man poses for photos in Soho's Chinatown. Jerry points to the grafitti on the wall that reads 'Burnt Out Stars' and proudly declares "That's me!"

Three years ago, no self-respecting citizen would have needed prompting to identify Jerry Dammers. His toothless grin perfectly encapsulated The Specials, whose rapid rise to fame in 1979 sparked off the 2-Tone legend, the label which The Specials, and particularly Jerry, used to pole-vault Madness, The Beat, The Body-snatchers and The Selecter to fame in an eight-month fire of such ferocity that it always had to burn itself out. From the ashes of 2-Tone rose The Fun Boy Three, The Belle Stars, General Public, The Colour Field and Pauline Black, with Madness alone maintaining that initial impetus. When The Specials first split, ironically while sitting at no. 1 with the most poignant political song of a decade in 'Ghost Town', Jerry Dammers continued working on the third Specials album, still to see the light of day some three years later. The album has now become an albatross around Jerry's neck; it's impending release will free him of a yoke that has made him increasingly uncomfortable over recent years.

With talk of the album costing over £500,000 to record, it is hardly surprising that both Chrysalis and Jerry's management were none to keen for the toothless wonder to start doing interviews that might upset the master plan. And although Jerry had been determined to do Jamming!, the man who sat opposite me in a central London cafe made it clear from the start that he was distrustful of the interview situation. We both agreed not be be menacing.

By the time you read this, 'Nelson Mandella' will either have been the long-awaited – and much-deserved – hit that Jerry, and particularly Chrysalis, have been waiting for, or else it will have unfortunately gone the way of the last three Special Aka singles, and disappeared quietly amid a distinct lack of airplay. The latter point is hardly surprising when one considers the sentiments behind the songs:- 'The Boiler' was a terrifying tale of rape, 'War Crimes' obvious in it's stand, and 'Racist Friend' equally blunt, while the new single is a tribute to the leader of the African National Congress who has been in a South African jail for 22 years already, because he wished to peacefully better the down-trodden black man's life in the ever-fascist South African regime.

"I don't know what's happened to Terry Hall; he's just changed. You expect some of the audience not to get the point of what you're doing, but when the lead singer of the group doesn't get the point ..."

Jerry, choosing his words carefully, explains why he wrote the song: "I went to a concert at the Alexandra Palace to celebrate his sixtieth birthday [five years ago] and at the time I didn't know anything about him. However, since then, I've read a few books about him, and I just think that the situation in South Africa is going on and on and on and nobody's doing anything about it. The rest of the world has got to do something about it, otherwise nothing's going to change, because the people in South Africa haven't got the power. The point of the song

is really just to say what I feel about it, in the hope that other people feel the same."

As a record, 'Nelson Mandella' is particularly intriguing because it sees Elvis Costello at the controls for the first time since that historic debut Specials LP. Jerry explains the circumstances in which Elvis resumed the producers chair: "In an interview he did, he said he thought 'Racist Friend' was an important record, so I just thought 'Right! We'll get him involved.' I think it was good to have an outsider, because I'd been producing everything and it was getting very bogged down, so it was like a fresh pair of ears."

With Jerry already hinting at his dissatisfaction with the time spent on the new album, it seemed appropriate to ask him why he

ever decided to complete the third Specials set.

"Well it all happened over a period of time," he explains. "The Fun Boy Three left first of all, and Roddy went about the same time; then Horace left, and it was like everyone abandoning ship [laughs]. At that time we'd already started on some rhythm tracks that were intended for the old band, so then we were left with the choice of abandoning it completely, instead of which I decided to carry on and find new people over a period of time.

"It was a difficult decision to make. One of the only things that has held it together all this length of time is the ideals of the original Specials, and trying to keep to those ideals, and therefore the name stuck. And also, there was

national djs, has not done much for the success of The Special Aka's recent singles.

"It's very difficult to get airplay on records like ours, because a lot of the djs want something that's really bland – there're not willing to stick their necks out. If you try and compromise too much you end up not saying what you wanted to. Even 'Ghost Town' when it came out didn't get a lot of airplay."

Suggesting that a lot of this may be to do with the current musical climate – Dammers summed it up himself on 'Bright Lights' – Jerry makes a distinct effort to be more positive.

"The new single is definately more 'up'... I don't want to get too miserable! This one's got a better chance, if they play it. It seems ridiculous to me that those djs on radio 1 have got so much power; it's like with Frankie Goes To Hollywood – although everyone's said it: why should Mike Read be the person to decide what millions of people should listen to? It's just ridiculous."

"I wish they'd ban our songs, but they don't – they just ignore them!"

Of course, we soon come round to the Beeb's equally farcical refusal to play recent Specials singles, appallingly highlighted in it's silent protest against 'The Boiler', as though intimating that rape was not a problem. Jerry, however, laughs it off: "I wish they'd ban our songs, but they don't – they just ignore them! The best thing that can possibly happen is to get a record in the charts and then get it banned. If you get banned before you get into the charts however, that's a different thing altogether."

Our talk turns to the current Special Aka line-up and it's workings. Jerry points out that "This new single is really the only one that has been done properly as a band, because when we started the LP we didn't have a band. Looking back on it, it would have been better when the original Specials split up, to not do anything for six months to a year. Instead of which, because I had all these ideas, we just carried on, which in a way was a mistake. And then you find that the songs were written for the old band, and that the new people coming in have got different talents... the whole thing's been a bit of a ..."

Jerry trails off, obviously frustrated at the never-ending saga of the album. I ask him just how pissed off he is.

"I'm not really, because I know that the public don't see ... The first Specials LP took two years to get together; the band were going two years before that came out. This band is a completely different band, and we're really just at the stage of the first Specials LP. It's hard because you can't just go down the local pub and do gigs and develop naturally because there's so much attention."

But despite his misgivings, it's good to see that Jerry still maintains that wicked sense of humour, opting to call the new album 'In The Studio' to drive the point home, even to the extent of doing the sleeve photos there! How have Chrysalis kept their patience?

"Well halfway through the album, when everyone realised it wasn't going as good as it could

have been, Chrysalis stuck us in Wessex studios, which they own anyway. So they're just taking the money out of one pocket and paying it into another."

Having established that Jerry is perfectly happy with 'In The Studio' – it's just he wants it out of the way – it seemed an appropriate point to talk about 2-Tone. When the chequered black and white flag was initially raised to such roaring approval, it was always apparent that the bubble had to burst one day. If Jerry Dammers didn't realise it, you can bet your life that everyone else involved with the set-up did. Why has Jerry decided to single-handedly raise a sinking ship?

"Because I've always had this sort of dream or ideal from the

start that eventually when the Chrysalis contract ran out, 2-Tone would go independent. Obviously that's taken a lot longer than intended, because the contract with Chrysalis is for five LPs . . . . 2-Tone had such a strong image and style about it, that a lot of people think that 2-Tone is that certain style of music, so that when we decided to move on, people thought 'This isn't really 2-Tone anymore.' I always thought of it as just a record label; I never put that much importance on it; obviously the public did."

Jerry's humour, however, is never far behind this reminiscing, and he suddenly declares that the new album will bear the 2-Tone logo 'with cobwebs and cracks and everything! Bits falling off it ... Walt Jabsco in a bathchair!"

Remembering, however, Jerry's earlier pronouncement of 'ideals' I wonder aloud whether 2-Tone ever achieved anything, recalling that just as it united kids in a time of trouble, it also gave vent to a particularly moronic following at times. Jerry is typically philosophical, though proud of his achievements:

"Obviously you can't say what it would have achieved, but I think that whole skinhead revival would have happened anyway, and I think that if it hadn't been for 2-Tone, it would have been a lot more right wing. I think we did diffuse the situation a bit; the way things were heading it could have got really bad. Music can't change everything, but from the letters we got it obviously changed some people. I was talking to a kid only

no definite point in time where we could have said 'This isn't the Specials', although, looking back on it, when the others left, we had to really start from scratch all over again, and it takes a bit of time to realise that. I thought that we could carry on, and a lot of other people did as well."

Jerry's talk of ideals made it apparent that the new Special Aka would have just as firm a manifesto as the original group. "It's not that definite," says Jerry, "but there's the whole thing about racial unity, and some of the political ideas of the original band, and the idea that the songs are about important things rather than just pure pop."

Of course, Jerry's determination to write about matters close to his heart, rather than that of the

The New Look Special A.K.A. – Photo: Paul Cox

a couple of months ago, who told me that, at the time of The Specials, he was 14-15, from the East End, and he said he would definitely have gone into the National Front and everything if it hadn't been for 2-Tone. We got so many letters from people who said similar things – it had an effect, though you can't claim it had that much.

"I thought what Terry (Hall) said recently in an interview was really stupid, that there was no racism in Coventry before The Specials started talking about it. I though that was really pathetic. I don't know what's happened to him; he's just changed. Maybe he never believed in it in the first place. You expect some of the audience not to get the point of what you're doing, but when the lead singer of the group doesn't get the point . . . . it wasn't true at all." .

As Jerry gets firmly into his stride, I comment that he does have a very serious public image. This he is only too aware of:

"Sometimes it comes across as being a bit miserable, but it's difficult because it's not as if I can just sit down and write a silly sort of pop song. I've tried to do that and they're just terrible! If I try and write really happy songs they're just not convincing."

I thought The Specials did some convincing happy songs . . .

"Well they weren't written by me! I can only really write about things that make me personally angry, or that I feel strongly about."

Page 10

Does the new album bear witness to this?

"No, there's two sides to it really. Some of it's political and some of it's more personal. I was really upset over The Specials splitting up and everything, so there's a lot of quite miserable songs on it. We had to wait till we got something a bit more positive like 'Nelson Mandella' to finish it all off with, otherwise it would have been all miserable! A lot of the tracks are great in the context of the LP, but they're not great singles; maybe we're more of an LP band."

Jerry wisely saved his pennies from the days when he was one of the country's hottest song-writers, with the longterm intention of building his own studio. Following the money spent on this LP, he is cursing himself for not having followed that one through earlier. But the man with the toothless grin, the unlikely pop star with a conscience, does not walk round with a permanent scowl on his face. As we set off round Soho to do some photos, Jerry comes alive with increasingly ridiculous ideas for the shots. By the time we end up with him impersonating a tramp under the 'Burnt Out Stars' sign, it is obvious that Mr. Dammers has never really changed; 'In The Studio' is but a nightmare that must be exorcised from him, following which, anything is possible.

And then the passers-by might remember who he is.

Tony Fletcher

I joined *Jamming!* in early '83. I had built up a relationship with Tony by mail initially as I lived at the other end of England. I called him one day and asked to come in and see him as I was coming to London. At his windowless basement office, I asked if he needed any support for the magazine. He went away and thought about it for a few days and came back with a yes. And with that, I moved from Buxton to start a new life.

I'd never met anyone like Tony before in my life. I'd travelled the world in the Royal Navy, lost a father at 8 years old and received a thoroughly working-class childhood of poverty, dust and grief. This guy was five years younger than me but five years ahead of me in a strange way. His ferocious intelligence totally intimidated me and I struggled to keep up at first.

There was no use competing with him so I decided to create my own world and represent *Jamming!* by just being myself, and being nice. This worked very well and I managed to secure lots of people to appear in the magazine.

I also took the role of both defuser and comedian during the days in the office, as when deadlines started to appear, obvious tensions did too.

Before we secured full distribution, I hand delivered all the magazines throughout London, as Tony and his friends had done before me. No mean feat.

There were some great perks to my role at *Jamming!*, not least taking up residency at Ronnie Scott's Jazz Club. It felt like I saw everyone that came through there between '83 and '88.

It was a memorable part of my life and I look back now with fondness for all I achieved for the magazine during difficult social and political times.
Alan McLaughlin

A NEW OPTIMISM

As promised in the last issue, this time round we are bringing you a special offer, Jamming!'s own compilation album, entitled 'A New Optimism'. The idea behind this record is to say to people "This is what we've been writing about over the last couple of years," and to that effect, we have mixed well-known bands with total unknowns. In fact, when we started putting this album together before Christmas, the only bands to have got anywhere were The Alarm, & Wah!, and Billy Bragg, and so the subsequent success of The Icicle Works, and Billy Bragg, and the growing stature of The Redskins, R.E.M. and Zerra I proves that you'd better get in quick before the other groups become chart-bound as well!

'A New Optimism' is almost totally comprised of tracks either unreleased here or recorded especially for the album. It has been put together with the help of Situation 2 Records, to whom we are most grateful. We are offering this album to Jamming! readers at a special price of £3.45 (inc. VAT) plus post and packing. 'A New Optimism' is available as either record or cassette, both with a full colour cover and informative sleeve notes. 'A New Optimism' is not a shabby compilation tape or record-company assisted promo album; it's a quality compilation that we expect to stand up on it's own merits.

'A New Optimism' will be released on April 2. At the time of going to press, the track listing is as follows:—

THE ICICLE WORKS: Waterline. — A new version from that on the b-side of 'Love Is A Wonderful Colour', this is the way it was always meant to sound. Not featured on the group's debut LP.

THE CLIMB: A Wanted Man's Woman. — The first vinyl offering from this much talked about, and potentially enormous band.

WAH: Body And Soul. — This is the first new material from Wah! in a year; unavailable elsewhere, it's a taster from their long-awaited second album.

ZERRA I: The Banner Of Love. — The hit that wasn't. Now signed to Phonogram, we've included Zerra I's last single so that more people can hear this great song.

THE ALARM: Unsafe Building. — Their first single, of which only 2,000 copies were ever pressed, is now changing hands for £15 a head. This gives you all a chance to hear it.

SUPERHEAVEN: Stronger. — Ex Rudi, this is Superheaven's first vinyl offering and shows a marked change from Rudi's well-known sound.

BILLY BRAGG: The Man In The Iron Mask. — Recorded especially for the album, this is Billy's first non-solo vinyl release, a noticably different version from that on the 'Life Is A Riot' mini-LP.

APOCALYPSE: Don't Stop. — Their first vinyl in over a year, this shows the sound one can expect from their future EMI releases.

R.E.M.: Gardening At Night. — The much-talked about group from Georgia, USA, have given us this, their first release, previously unavailable in Britain.

THE REFLECTIONS: Flower Girl. — Again, recorded especially for the album, this is a promising sample from the up-and-coming Scottish group.

UNDER TWO FLAGS: — Although the actual title is yet to be confirmed, Under Two Flags, with one big indie hit already behind them, are recording their song especially for the album.

THE SMITHS: Wonderful Woman. — At the time of going to press, this track is still unconfirmed, but we hope to be bringing you this unreleased Smiths classic from a Radio I session.

THE FIRE: Mothers And Sons. — A much-talked about Liverpool band, this is The Fire's first vinyl release, recorded especially for 'A New Optimism'.

THE REDSKINS: It Can Be Done. — Again previously unreleased, The Redskins have given us this track from a popular BBC session.

All in all, 14 acts, 14 different songs, all for only £3.45, and available only through Jamming! To [...] below and send it to us. Please allow 21 days for delivery.

I enclose a cheque/Postal Order* for £3. made payable to 'Jamming! ([...] record/cassette* of 'A New Optimism' and will allow twenty-one days for deliv[...]

*Delete as appropriate.

NAME...

ADDRESS..

Jamming! Publications Ltd will make every effort to ensure that the track listing of 'A New Optimism' is as above. If you do not w[...] listing that may occur please state clearly on your order and we will send a refund. We regret we cannot offer refunds (except[...]

Despite the generally grey pallor to Number 18, I clung to the notion of *A NEW OPTIMISM!* Accordingly, that issue's biggest exclusive was probably the news of a *Jamming!* compilation LP of the same name to feature The Smiths, R.E.M., The Special A.K.A., The Alarm, The Icicle Works, Wah!, The Redskins and Billy Bragg, alongside a host of lesser-known acts, most of whom had been featured in *Jamming!* along the way. (These included my own Apocalypse who, rather than break up due to the other demands on my time, had instead signed to EMI, creating yet more demands on my time!) With all of us now feeling the pressure of multiple deadlines and other creative outlets, the artwork suffered accordingly, and the biggest disappointment about the compilation LP was not that The Smiths ultimately bailed, but that Russell Tate used a mediocre and largely unrepresentative image as the cover shot – only for that image to get lost in return transit, causing the stock photo company to sue our label partners Beggars Banquet for an insultingly high reimbursement, all of which led to my one and only time in court and a rather unhappy conclusion to what was meant to be a celebration. **Tony F.**

BREAKING DOWN THE BARRIERS
JAMMIng!

60p U.S. $1.50 No. 19 *Now With More Pages!*

FRANKIE GOES TO
HOLLYWOOD

WITH

CAPTAIN SENSIBLE IN
THE RETURN OF THE DAMNED

ALSO STARRING

ASWAD ● THE WATERBOYS ● RED GUITARS ● THE SOUND
NEWTOWN NEUROTICS ● THE QUESTIONS ● TONY PARSONS
THE G.L.C. AND MUSIC
SPECIAL GUEST STARS
★ **THE CLASH** ★
EXCLUSIVE INTERVIEW CENTRE PAGES

It's hard to imagine a much bleaker place than Harlow. A drab new town just off the M11, it was built to house London's post-war excess population and is noted for its Gin Factory and very little else. The Newtown Neurotics (along with Attila the Stockbroker) hope to change all that.

A band with their roots and inspiration in 1977-78, but with their hearts and heads firmly in the eighties, the Newtown Neurotics have become one of the most respected bands to be classed in the increasingly meaningless category known as 'punk'. That respect was further enhanced by the release of their debut LP 'Beggars Can Be Choosers' last October. I spoke to three 'Newtown People' in a Newtown pub about the public's expectations of the Newtown Neurotics.

"People expect different things" says Steve Drewett, the band's guitarist, vocalist, song-writer, and not surprisingly, spokesman. "I think that on the whole the way people perceive us through the media is through what we deliver on stage. We haven't hid many complaints."

The LP was a big step forward for the Neurotics, but aren't they rather restricted as a three-piece?

"If a song demands it then extra instruments can be brought in," explains Steve. "There is so little money about that we have just been able to include horns on the next single. There's not a lot of Rock and Roll instruments that you can use, everybody moves onto saxes eventually."

So you are still prepared to work within the 'Rock and Roll' structure, unlike Weller who claims to have rejected it?

Steve again: "Let's halt this now. The line 'Rock and Roll is dead' has been going around for so long that it's become another cliche. It sounded great in 1977, but today even the worst Rock and Roll bands are still going. I even saw an ad for Barclay James Harvest the other day!"

The other two nod in disgust, while Steve explains further . . .

"You can't just eradicate a sixties-based type of music overnight by saying it doesn't exist. Music, and the music industry, is a continual cycle based on only a limited form; it goes through phases. It's been a long time since guitar-orientated stuff was really popular, you can't say that it's dead and buried."

Of course Weller got good mileage out of R'n'R before he decided to drop it, and nobody could accuse the Neurotics of being the next Pink Floyd, but don't they ever feel that they are in danger of getting in a rut?

"Our sort of Rock and Roll is probably nearer to that of Chuck Berry and Eddie Cochran than the massive rock bands of today" declares Steve. "We try to balance out the influences, it's like a cake mix y'know. No, that sounds terrible, like we're playing stodgy."

Isn't there a danger that in trying to appeal to such a wide audience you end up appealing to nobody?

Steve: "We won't be like the Clash who are progressing with the few few EP's, then they just went 'Blam' over the whole broad spectrum of music."

Colin interrupts in agreement. "Now they can play ten different types of music badly instead of one type of music well."

Steve: "We don't want to be like that, we'll have influences creeping in here and there."

Colin: "I don't think we are stuck in a rut, although some of the old numbers are beginning to sound a bit stale. I find most of the new stuff we are doing vital and exciting."

"The only way we will get stuck in a rut is if we are labelled as a certain type of band," declares Simon. "Some people expected that every record we made after 'Kick Out The Tories' would be the same."

Well, maybe that's just a reflection of the popularity of that classic gem, but while we are on the subject (of being stuck in a rut. . . .

Colin: "Maggie has done one good thing in getting a nice safe Labour Party to stop squabbling and remember what they are supposed to be about in the first place. She has created a situation where they are getting back to the grass roots of Socialist policies."

But with the Tory press insulting the country's intelligence by offering them the journalistic equivalent of BO sandwiched in between soft porn and a forty million to one chance of winning a bingo prize, can the Neurotics see any hope for the future?

Steve: "Despondency is something that we are fighting against. The Neurotics and Jamming! – a new optimism for the Eighties. We as a band can't change the government, but we can draw attention to the fact that people are becoming despondent and that they have got a lot more fight in them than they realise. Can you imagine not having any hope? Strip a person of their optimism and they will become just a shell and fade away to nothing."

Colin: "There are a lot of kids who were too young to vote and now have to live under a government they hate."

"There are people fighting in every way
To protect the freedoms you enjoy every day
Your opinions have a familiar ring
Nothing I do or say will change anything
You say politics are boring, boring and grey,
But would you rather see Cruise brighten everyone's day?"

At a time when it's rare to see a band take a firm political stance it's inspiring to see the Newtown Neurotics (soon to be Neurotics AKA) charge in head first. Yet the Neurotics offer much more than empty slogans; for them it's a matter of pride and a belief in their fellow human beings. All presented with snap, crackle and pop. What more could you ask for?

Richard Edwards

THE CAPTAIN STRIKES BACK!

Was Geoffrey Boycott right?
No. I would never play in South Africa in a million years. I used to admire him because he plays a game whereby he's got one eye on the ball, and the other eye on his batting averages. And I think that's amazing. I think that's really weird. I've got a kind of grudging admiration for him, rather like the grudging admiration I've got for The Damned, surviving eight years. One eye on the music, and one eye on the history of the group. And that's why we won't split up.

The first day of spring had arrived late but in style. While Captain Sensible relaxes in the corner of a grotty Fulham pub, I get the drinks in. I once made a vow not to do any more interviews in pubs, but with The Captain, it just seems . . . . logical.

During the photo session, the Captain patted me on the back and called us 'survivors'. His reason was a certain fondness for the funniest interview ever to grace Jamming!'s pages – a classic repartée between me, The Captain and The Damned's vocalist Dave Vanian, back in issue no.10. He refers to it as 'the best interview I've ever done, because you just printed exactly what was said', and I agree with him. That night four years ago, The Damned were very much The Damned, at an artistic and successful peak, somewhere between the riotous 'Machine Gun Etiquette', and the magnificently varied 'Black Album'. That night in a Crystal Palace studio, Captain Sensible would have put Keith Moon to shame, with his incessant post-taking, imitations, slaggings, practical jokes, and outright threats of violence. That was how I've always remembered the Captain.

But that was four years ago. These days a lot of people have forgotten who The Damned are (despite their ability to sell out major venues easier than this week's upstarts could ever hope for), while Captain Sensible himself is an eccentric pop star. If somebody had told me then that in four years time Ray Burns would be a protest singer, I'd have laughed. But then times change. And I wanted to see how the music world had changed it's own favourite loony.

So where are The Damned?
Well, by the time this goes out we'll be in the studio. We've got a deal, it's all agreed, and we're just waiting to sign it.

Why did it take so long to get a deal this time?
I've been thinking about this, and I think it's the fact that the Pistols have split up. The Who have split up, and everybody's looking for the new bad boys of music. And the stories that get told in Dingwalls about Keith Moon and Sid Vicious, they now tell about me and Rat Scabies. I believe that everyone in the music business thinks The Damned are trouble, and that's the reason we haven't been offered a deal.

Isn't it true though?
Absolutely not. You know me, and you know Rat. You don't know Rat? I can vouch for him, he's an eminently nice bloke. I'd give him a character reference in court any day! In fact, when he was in court, I offered to give him a character 'reference, and he told me "Help like that I need like a hole in the head"

How do you balance The Damned and your solo career at the moment?
Well, quite easily at the moment, because last year, 1983, was quite a lean year for me. I was doing nothing, and The Damned were doing nothing. We were all trying to pay the rent, everybody had to sell their cars, it was lean all round. We've learnt one thing though – the money you pay for damages comes out of your own pocket in the end.

Following the commercial and creative disappointment that was Issue 18, we were faced with a quandary. Did we put The Clash on the cover, given that we had an exclusive interview with Joe Strummer (and that it was our first *ever* piece on the most internationally important of all British punk originators)? Did we go for Captain Sensible, of fellow punk originals The Damned but also now with a notable solo career? Surely we would not betray our roots entirely and, alongside every other magazine of the era, opt for Frankie Goes To Hollywood upon the launch of their long-awaited and predictably overblown first album? But of course we did!

In fairness, our decision was made in part because we knew that the new-look *Cut The Crap* era Clash was, well, crap; because the Captain was beloved by all who met him but not someone who would 'sell magazines'; and because the Frankie image we had on hand loaned itself to a surprisingly strong overall cover design, and Jonh Wilde had secured an equally commanding interview with Frankie's 'other' frontman, Paul Rutherford. Plus, photographer Russell Young, talking himself out of a potential (first) Captain cover, insisted that Frankie were the new Doors – a group that could balance teenybop appeal and number one singles with critical and credible respect from the rock audience. Hey, we were all fooled for a while there.

Regardless, these headline interviewees were joined by Aswad (thankfully free of homophobia), The Newtown Neurotics (both by Richard Edwards), The Sound (Johnny Waller), punk journalist turned pulp novelist Tony Parsons (Alan McLaughlin), and Mike Scott, re-emerging in *Jamming!* all of two years on from Another Pretty Face with his new band The Waterboys. A feature on 'The GLC and Music' confirmed that this was 1984, a full page on the 'Future of British Cinema' marked the debut of Bruce Dessau, and Chris Heath made his debut with a short profile of Andy White that went widely unread due to *Jamming!*'s continued and seemingly unrepentant error of printing black upon blue. Talking of which, the third page of the Captain Sensible interview was somehow reversed into a negative image, an entirely unintentional but suitably serendipitous throwback to *Jamming!* 10 and the ineligibility of that famed interview with him and The Damned's Dave Vanian in a Thornton Heath 8-track studio. You could keep the punks off the front cover, it seemed, but you couldn't quite take the fanzine out of the magazine.

ISSUE #19
5/84

Since Mick Jones, who was always such an important part of The Clash, was rather less than ceremoniously booted out last year, the remaining two original members – Joe Strummer and Paul Simenon – along with the latest in a string of drummers, Pete Howard, have formed a new Clash, with the addition of Vince White on guitar and Nick Sheppard on guitar and occasional vocals. And while the old Clash were never the most proficient gang in town, they were one of the main instigators of punk, and occasional purveyors of some of the most varied, vibrant and important records to emerge since '77. So The Clash 84 have quite a reputation to live up to, and bearing in mind the very strong political stance so closely associated with them, quite a daunting manifesto to follow. Namely to change the world . . .

However, the driving spirit that pulled them through then is still very much in control now. Joe Strummer, wise and foolish, bloodied but unbowed, sincere and enthusiastic, spoke to me about The Clash past, present and future, after their recent British tour and a couple of days before they flew out to America to continue their assault on that nation's youth.

THE CLASH

BORN AGAIN

Following two years of internal troubles without so much as a sniff of a new record, the addition of three new members, and a tour greeted with a largely unenthusiastic critical response, how happy is Joe Strummer himself with the new band, and does he think it can be a long term thing in its present form?

"Well, we put it together with that purpose and that intention – to make it something that was going to last. We didn't just get some old mates in or something. And so far it's been pretty good. I mean what I want is not very exensive: I don't want any sulking, I don't want any hippiness, I don't want any drug-taking and I don't want any moaning. But apart from that I'm willing to let someone exist and let them become what they want to become. I don't want to have them all hemmed in with expectations, just those few things really. Everything works so much better when there's no sulking and nothing festers."

You seem to be talking from past experience . . .

"Yeah, there was a lot of festering with Mick. Things would fester for months and months, and even after you'd forgotten what started it all there would still be festering left, and that's terrible, because at the bottom of it all this has got to be a laugh. We do so much roadwork that there can be so much pressure and mental strain, it's really tense, so if you can't have a laugh with your mates who you're doing it with then everything can get on top of you, there ceases to be any sanity in it all, and

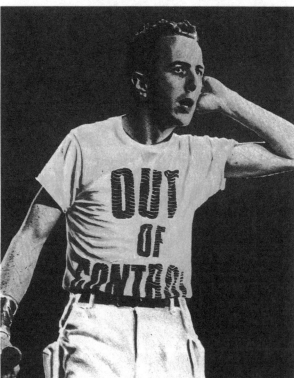

you go over the edge. At the mome[nt] anyone's got anything to moan about we [get] it right out, there's no bad feeling . . . it's so much healthier."

How do you feel the British tour went [?]

"Well I think it went pretty good. Mo[st of] the people I meet and talk with, people [who] aren't going to bull me, say that it's the [best] they've seen us, and prefer it now becau[se it's] so much more lively. I mean there's [more] people falling over and twisting their a[nkles] and breaking things."

Not that the critics have seen it quite [like] that . . .

"Nah, that's just mealy mouth. I don't [care] what they think. We got some stick from [the] 'Melody Maker' for example, but that w[as] a particularly good gig anyway so I can't r[eally] moan, but a bad review lasts as long [as a] packet of fish'n'chips really, same with a [good] review.

But the criticisms that have been level[led at] the new Clash do have some founda[tion.] When I saw them in Liverpool, although [they] played for over two hours, performi[ng a] commendable 32 songs, 20 of them were [from] pre-79, and this coupled with videos o[f Sid] Vicious beforehand, all made for a very h[eavy] nostalgia. I pointed out that this so[rt of]

"What I want from The Cl[ash is no] sulking, I don't want any hip[piness,] I don't want any moaning."

reliance on the past could be seen as q[uite a] dilution of what punk had originally be[en] about, and that two of the main protago[nists] from that period, Johnny Rotten [and] Strummer himself, could, and indeed [have] been, accused of living off the past. Stru[mmer] agreed with my comments about Rotten [but] stressed that he had no intention of cash[ing in] on the past.

"Maybe there is a lot of the past in wh[at we] do at the moment, but only because I [realise] where I went wrong, and I want to tou[ch the] true things again to find a forward direc[tion. I] don't think you can just wash your han[ds of] the past. I think you've got to [take] everything on its merits, and when I com[pare] 'It's A Miracle' to some of our songs I c[an see] which is going to be remembered in ten [years] time, and it ain't going to be 'It's A M[iracle] for a start. I read the other day that [Billy] Bragg joined The Redskins for an enc[ore of] 'Garageland'. It just shows that if we do[n't do] those songs other people will. And I thi[nk we] can do them best. I mean, we wrote the[m."]

As manager Kosmo Vinyl (the band['s] own travelling press agent) is quick to [point] out at this stage, although there is a lot [of old] stuff in the set, they do play about si[x new] songs as well –

". . . Songs that aren't even recorde[d yet,] but because the other stuff is so well kn[own it] just seems that there's a lot more old mat[erial.] I don't think when 'Combat Rock' cam[e out] we played six off that."

Bearing this in mind then, and the [four] years deafening silence on the record f[ront,] what's the situation on any new [Clash] records? Strummer aga[in:]

"Well, we've a fair amount of new mat[erial,] but I don't want to actually record until w[e've] got the group as a unit. I don't want the[re to] be any kind of session feel where you ju[st get] strangers in. That's why it's good to play [with] the new band because that soon sorts you [out,] you're faced with all kinds of emergen[cies.] Like with a few thousand people star[ing,] looking at you something fucks up, it test[s the] mettle of each other, and the unit has to [come] unit in order to get through these times, [and] the only way to do it is to go out on the [road.] We'll probably go in the studio in the sum[mer] some time, though I'm not sure whethe[r it'll] be early or late."

CBS AND THINGS

After so long without a record, with nothing new in the can, and with a tour of Britain lined up, I was quite surprised not to see a Clash Greatest Hits or live album suddenly rearing its enterprising little head. Surely they must have been under pressure from CBS to put one out?

"Well not really, because I think we've hit them a bit by surprise by hitting the road so fast – so they were still trying to figure out whether to go with Mick's thing or us. They were confused, probably phoning each other up all the time, and we just ignored them and went out on the road. I'm still not sure what their attitude is yet. They are probably working on a Greatest Hits thing at the moment, which I actually wouldn't mind so much now as it would close one chapter before we begin another."

Kosmo again: "It's not really the right time for them now, they probably wish they'd put one out before Christmas sometime, that would have been perfect, but they didn't know what was going on. You see, the big thing with CBS is that finally after all the trouble and aggravation they feel they've had with us, The Clash get a big selling record

...very extensive: I don't want any ...don't want any drug-taking and

('Combat Rock') and they think that at last it looks like we're going somewhere for them, and then out of the blue what they consider to be a winning partnership splits up. They just didn't understand it and probably didn't think it was a permanent split until now when they can actually see it."

Talking of relations with CBS, Strummer's attitude to the corporation appears to have gone through quite a marked change since the late 70's, when just about every interview with The Clash seemed to contain a hefty proportion of anger and bitterness directed towards the record company. I sense the distaste still remains, but the past conflicts have resulted in a more resigned approach and a subsequently greater willingness to compromise.

"I think we used to look at it in the wrong way. We used to spend a lot of time winding them up, but really it's a waste of energy to do that. 'Sandinista', for example, was a three album set not for artistic reasons, like 'Oh we've got 36 great tracks, we've got to put them all out,' but more like, 'Ha ha hee hee let's do them over, let's play silly buggers'. I think it was a good joke for us, but it was a bit silly really."

Although I don't think it worked particularly well at the time, I point out that I do really like 'Sandinista', perhaps because of, rather than in spite of, its sprawling fusion of various styles . . .

"Yeah, a lot of people seem to hold that opinion now, but I think it should have been a double album. Kosmo thinks it should have been a double, I think you've got a responsibility when there's people interested in you and your music. You've got a responsibility to make decisions for the right reasons. Now I see it as a side issue playing silly buggers with CBS, but at the time it seemed to be a main issue. When I realise that the independents use the CBS distribution network then it seems to me that the difference is pretty slim really. With CBS I'm just trying to look on them as a tool – I've got something to say and I want it to be simultaneously available in the shops if people want it, and they can do that for me. That's the way I think we should look at it."

Although in terms of the actual contract, Joe sighs wearily:

Naive to the workings of the music industry, I had got hold of legendary Clash manager Kosmo Vinyl's number and bugged him for weeks trying to arrange an interview with Joe Strummer. Although I intended to submit the feature to *Jamming!* I don't think I actually told anyone at the magazine what I was up to. I knew nothing of editorial planning, photo shoots or print deadlines. Never even considered the possibility they might have already had an interview arranged. I was young, passionate and stupid, but somehow it all worked out.

I interviewed Joe Strummer on March 17 1984. He was magnificent. We sat together for over an hour, just the two of us in the dressing room at Brixton Academy before the rest of the band arrived. It was the runt of The Clash, post Mick Jones. Between our chairs there was a galvanised steel tub filled with drinks and ice. Nervous, I took up Strummer's offer to help myself. By the time the interview was wrapping up and the other band members were traipsing in, I reached in for a last beer. No go. I sifted and trawled the ice till my hand was numb. No more beer, just Coke and bottled water. Strummer wasn't drinking. Jeez. I had drunk all of The Clash's beer. That was a badge I wore proudly for a while.
Ross Fortune

"We've got about another 5 albums to do because they took up an option on page 94B, Clause 44 . . ."

And on the five albums they've released so far, and 'Sandinista' in particular, The Clash have incorporated many different styles of music with varying degrees of success. So what can we expect from the new band in the future?

"I think we're going to do a Clash style; I feel that's something we've ignored in favour of other styles."

Do you think you got back to that more with 'Combat Rock'?

"Well probably only by accident rather than by design, but yes, some of it might be Clash style. I think it's important once you've got a sound and style that you pay it the proper respect and not abandon it. That's something I've learned anyway. I mean you point out that we just about ignore 'Sandinista' from the live set, but what could be played off that? You see that's another thing I want to do, and that's use what we've got in the studio, rather than putting additives on, because if we're so essential we'll have it with us now, we'll travel with it, which means guitar and drums. What I'm thinking now is that why not just use that to record with?

"We used to know that but obviously somewhere along the line decided that 'anything goes', which I now think is a sloppy attitude. I think it's much harder and much more creative to just use your limitations – if you can get something great out of just guitars and drums then that's surely a finer achievement

"Watching Top Of The Pops is like having your face gaffa-taped to the front of a pinball machine – it's all ping! dong! clash! whoosh!"

then dolling it up with a brass section and the two black female backing singers that everybody goes on the road with these days. I'd rather go down the drain with guitars and drums really. I don't see why we should use anything else. Of course, when we get in the studio we'll probably overdub elephants stampeding down the Nile or something!"

PLASTIC POP AND MUESLI YOUTH

At a time when the studio orientation to pop music and producer is king mentality is so predominant, Strummer seems not surprisingly unimpressed with the state of music in general

at the moment, citing Pogue Mahone as one of the few new bands he's impressed with.

"They supported us in Brixton recently, very interesting and different. They play a lot of traditional Irish music which is a kind of relief after watching a thousand identikit electro groups and a thousand identikit punk groups coming at you on the TV."

And The Clash have always held strong ideas about music on television, as well as sticking fast to their refusal to ever appear on 'Top Of The Pops', a programme which Strummer still holds in contempt, though he's none too impressed with 'The Tube' either . . .

"'Top Of The Pops' . . . it's all too easy to sway around and mime to some pre-recorded masterpiece, but let's see how it sounds if you've really got to bash it out in front of our eyes and ears. I think it would not only be much more entertaining but probably hysterically funny as well. What I do like about TOTP though, is that you get one song and a quick turn around, like they allow the djs about four seconds to do their spiel at the miles. What's wrong with 'The Tube' is that it's all muesli-youth, hey man TV presenters for the kids, all that sort of syndrome of 40 year old guys deciding, and presenters trying to be hip or funny. Well we don't want them to be hip or funny, we just want to see groups come at us – bang, bang, bang. No group seems to do themselves a favour on that programme, whether it's because of all the scaffolding or what I don't know, it's like a TV presenter's dream. I'd like something that was more out of control than that, something a bit rougher, there's too much extra going on. I think you could pack something into half an hour that would be better than The Switch or The Tube. I do quite like it when they do reports from other places but that could be another programme."

Also the lighting – if you watch old clips of 'Oh Boy' or 'Ready Steady Go' they knew how to get drama, they knew how to get atmosphere out of very little, but on 'Top Of The Pops' it's like having your face gaffa-taped to the front of a pinball machine, it's all ping! dong! clang! whoosh! . . . and in the end there's no atmosphere or drama there. Sometimes I watch TV clips from the 60's where they have a dark studio with one singer, one spotlight, and then another one – bang! – illuminates the backing singers, and then it goes out. It's very dramatic, quite riveting just using a couple of lights – yet Top Of The Pops have got every damn thing all going on at once, and the sum total is about as exciting as these three naked light bulbs here.

What I'm saying is there's no artistry. People want something dramatic and atmospheric but they've gone right over the top and we're getting nothing now."

It's all very easy to sit back and criticise this sort of trashy Top Of The pops glitter-pop mentality, but if Strummer doesn't feel The Tube presents a suitable alternative, can he come up with anything more positive. Like whatever happened to the talk about opening their own club where they could put their idea(l)s into practice?

"Well it's something we've mooted, and I think it's something that we would have done as well if Mick hadn't frozen all the money with his law thing. I don't know if he's trying to make his lawyer a millionaire or something, but he's going the right way about it."

There's clearly a lot of bad feeling . . .

"We were willing to give him his share of the dosh but he never even asked for it, he just got his lawyer out and slapped an injuction on us. The writs started arriving at my door thick and fast. I haven't got time to bother with that, he obviously has."

Not wanting to dig too deeply into what is clearly still an open wound, I'll just say that Mick Jones is currently forming his own group and he and his girlfriend are expecting a baby. And move on to . . .

ABHORRED BY THE USA?

Perhaps the most common criticism of The Clash nowadays concerns their seeming infatuation with America. Though it is probably a little too easy to just cite 1977's 'I'm So Bored With The USA' as evidence of their hypocrisy in spending so much time and effort there. After all, The Clash hardly embrace Americana or advocate world 'democracy' Reagan style, although they have been accused of making capital out of what some see to be empty political sloganeering.

"People say we're pre-occupied with America, but I think that's sour grapes really. For a start there's this myth that we live there when in fact I doubt if I've spent more than two days there when I wasn't working and when I didn't have to be there. I don't think we've done any more tours of America that we have of England, in fact we've almost certainly done more shows in England. We have done a few tours there, sure, but at times that was keeping the group alive when Europe wasn't. Without that we'd have gone down somewhere between 'London Calling' and 'Sandinista' because we had a load of debts then. 'London Calling' got us out of debt, 'Sandinista' didn't make us a penny and then 'Combat Rock' sold a million and a half."

What do you actually feel about America then?

"I don't like it. I don't like the food there, I don't like television there, I don't like the way everywhere looks exactly the same, I don't like the signs all over the place, I don't like the plastic buildings, I don't like the imitation muzak dribbling out of the speakers, and I don't like the way they let the government get on with things. They don't even care about the way they're stamping through Central America. Most people haven't got a clue what's going on, don't even know where it is. I wouldn't care if they all went 'Yeah, yeah we believe that's right', but they don't even try and acquaint themselves with the rights and wrongs of it, they're too TV-gone."

Joe Strummer strongly believes that music can play a part in effecting change:

"Stevie Wonder's done it for a lot of blacks registerring to vote in the USA, and Jessie Jackson is reaping some of the benefits and doing his bit for it as well. I think music can definitely do something."

He also believes that the best part of

'Sandinista' was its title. Something not generally known about The Clash is that the catalogue numbers on 'Sandinista' and 'Combat Rock' – FSLN and FMLN respectively – stand for the Sandinista Front for National Liberation ("that's the one in Nicaragua") and 'Farabundo Martí Liberation National' ("that's the Salvadorean rebels").

Small gestures maybe, but Joe Strummer is sincere and genuinely believes The Clash can do something, to which end they are trying to help by creating a greater awareness amongst people who, in America in particular, might otherwise never extend their brains beyond trying to understand the deep and meaningful lyrics trotted out by The Police or worse. Strummer has always attempted to integrate The Clash's music with the areas of social and political concern he feels so strongly about.

"My politics lie with justice. In Nicaragua the Somoza family kept everyone in a feudal state, no one reading or writing, living in a patch of mud, and one in three children dying all over the country, while they were creaming off all the dough. I'm for anything that turns that around and teaches everyone in the country to read and write, gives everybody self-determination to be able to think for themselves, stops the money being cleared off to Swiss banks and puts it back into the country. I want justice and I don't want a few to pocket the gross. I reckon there's enough for every person in the world."

O.K., but how do you see your role in actually trying to change such things?

"Well, because I've got half an ear of some young people who will have a say in the destiny of the world. My role is to use that opportunity the best I can, though I do always have to bear in mind that if I go too far I'll get less and less ears to speak to. I'm treading a fine line, but my role is to use the opportunity I've got by sheer luck really."

THE MESSAGE

Outlining a Clash 'manifesto' several years ago, Strummer said that The Clash were prepared to concentrate more on America to try and change things there as he thought that people in Britain had more sense. Now, one war, intolerable unemployment, a crippled welfare state, rioting in the streets, a strengthening of police powers, and undermining of local democracy and trade union rights later, I wonder about that comment . . .

"Yes, I was obviously wrong. I hadn't really realised how disorganised the Labour Party

and the Left was. Like they'd elected Foot as a traditional deference to his seniority, almost like a golden watch – you can be leader because you've put in so much leg work over the past forty years. But really you've got to be harder than that, especially fighting Saatchi and Saatchi and Thatcher. OK, Foot was a pretty humane guy and had done his bit, but maybe they could have used him as a senior adviser or something . . ."

Do you believe in organised politics then, like say the Labour Party in this country?

"Well, in this case I do, because for a start the Labour Party *is* a labour party now. They're not right of centre, or centre-centre, they've gone left and they're going to unilaterially disarm, or so they say, so I'd say that was a radical alternative compared to Conservatism and Thatcherism. You've got to be serious and you've got to work with what you've got, and they're about the only ones who've got a crack against Thatcher. You know, if Kinnock can keep dancing with Tracey Ullman we might have a goer there! I would urge anybody to vote for Labour, because let's start somewhere. I mean the alternative to voting Labour is not voting at all which is what happened at the last election . . . apathy because people felt 'What's the difference really?' But now I feel that for maybe the first time in our lifetimes there is a difference and it should be noted. I don't like to follow the same old guidelines, I like to really perceive anything freshly just in case it's changed, and now I think it has."

Perceptive and aware, Strummer remains optimistic. Although he half-jokingly states that "We'll be around until we're irrelevant, though God knows it looks like about 1999 at this rate" he does believe he'll be able to see his aims through:

"Especially if we can keep banging away at it. The trick is not to get dissuaded, because I've been dissuaded from my aims in the past by people going 'nah, you're mad' and 'why don't you just shut up and get on with it like everybody else'. Sometimes you tend to believe these people, but now I realise that fatalists and cynics are the worst kind of people, and I'm never going to listen to them again. Even if it's the most respected hip scribe, if the guy or girl is a fatalist or a cynic they're no use to my dog let alone me."

I put it to him that perhaps the message he is trying to get across is falling on deaf ears:

"Well I'd rather preach to deaf ears than to the converted, because who knows when their hearing might come back? But also the whole situation now with The Clash is so much healthier, like we can afford to be a bit more outspoken because as a group we've got nothing to hide. After the gig the other night we were talking to some people and they had the Drug Squad in, pretending to be normal people, sniffing the atmosphere out, then they took their drug dogs out and went through our coach, looking in all the ashtrays and sniffing, and then they searched the roadies coach as well. We could afford to laugh and treat it as a joke, but when you're taking drugs you get all paranoid and wound up. I think if you really want to speak out against things you can't afford to have that kind of liability if your cupboard. So I'm glad that nobody in the group cares for drugs, which was a bit of a lucky stroke really because by all rights Vince and Nick could have been any of the drug taking population, but it just so happened that Nick was sick of it, and Vince thinks it's stupid anyway."

And the message?

"Well, the message really is . . . whatever destiny we have is dirctly dependant on your actions, or anybody's actions. Even in the face of such overwhelming cynicism, the whole 'don't vote' thing, the deep rooted view which is easy to see that politics is a load of bullshit, the state of mind where everybody wants to party and nobody wants to get boringly serious; in the face of all this what is really exciting is that the world could be changed, we could change the world, and when I say 'we' I mean anybody's who's interested. It could be done y'know. I like to read about revolutions in Central America because then I realise that not only once upon a time but *still* that is possible, that people take their own destiny in their own hands and re-make it in their own way."

> *"I like to read about revolutions in Central America because then I realise that it is still possible for people to take their own destiny in their own hands and re-make it in their own way."*

"I feel that youth in the western world feel that's such a long way off because they see the traditions, the Monday Club, the House Of This, The Civil Service, the whole beauracratic machinery, all the multi-national corporations, stock exchanges, cotton markets, double deals and the banking system, and it's all just so incredibly complicated and they just feel like a flea in the face of all that, but there's so many people in the world, and something can be done. You've got to feel like you can get involved, because damn it, you're not watching it on TV – life is not on television."

Joe Strummer – clumsily articulate, passionately sincere with a heart so big, pumping so true, that if points were awarded for sincere rebel spirit the contest would have been over long ago when The Alarm were still The Toilets and when The Clash were everyone's favourite band. But all is not fair in love and war and the fight goes on. And while Strummer deserves success on his own terms, it looks like we're going to have to wait a lot longer to see whether the new band can help him achieve the dream. For though The Clash have always cared and they're now needed as much as ever, on the recent tour although they showed very clearly where they've been, they appeared less sure about where they're going. I still have faith in Joe Strummer, but do confess to feeling less sure about the new Clash as a group and as a vehicle for his aims. All I can do is hope that they can stay true to his ideals, work their hearts out, and just possibly achieve something quite remarkable.

Ross Fortune

THE WATERBOYS
THE WATERBOYS
THE WATERBOYS
THE WATERBOYS

THE WATERBOYS

Mike Scott of The Waterboys has a passionate belief in the music and values of Patti Smith. Ross Fortune of Jamming! has a passionate belief in the music and values of Mike Scott . . . .

Only 25, but with the most impeccable of pedigrees behind him, a comprehensive rundown of Mike Scott's career would be impractical, so briefly – pre-Waterboys, with The Bootlegs, Another Pretty Face, the Noise! the Jazz!, Funhouse and The Red And The Black, he created, with John Caldwell, quite simply the finest, most vital and exciting music I have ever heard.

The great pity is that only a fraction of it was ever released – a single by DNV (The Bootlegs), four singles and a cassette by Another Pretty Face and one single as Funhouse. Fervent ideals independent spirit, plain bad luck, and a strong, ultimately self-destructive attitude of no-compromise accounted for the mass of unreleased tracks that include an album for Virgin, an LP recorded with 'top' producer Hugh Jones, and more recently several tracks in New York with Lenny Kaye, as well as probably at least three to four albums worth of other quality material.

Since a certain bitterness and understandable disillusionment sent John Caldwell back to Scotland, where he's now playing with The Collector (see 'What's Cookin'), Mike has signed to Ensign, formed The Waterboys, and finally made a start at releasing much more

actual 'product', albeit mainly old stuff in order to clear the decks. Last year The Waterboys released two singles – the excellent 'A Girl Called Johnny' and 'December' – and a fine LP that still only really hints at the potential yet to be fully captured. The singles b-sides, incidentally, contain seven previously unreleased tracks, a policy that continues with the best and most recent single, 'The Big Music', a song that captures for maybe the first time the essence of The Waterboys, where Mike Scott is at *now*, and the direction we can perhaps expect him to move in the future.

With the second Waterboys

LP due out in June, there has again been quite a delay in it actually seeing the light of day, a situation Mike is understandably unhappy about. "There's nothing I'd like more than to go into the studio, record eight songs, put them out on an LP, and then start writing some more." For various reasons this method of working has never happened as yet. Indeed, struggles with

record companies have become quite a feature of Mike's past, but he's hopeful things can be different in the future, though he also points out a certain irony in his present situation: "I used to hate record companies so much, and here I am on about six!", with Ensign, who are distributed by Island, who are joined with Stiff – "Then there's all the ones for overseas . . . "

Of all the unreleased material he's amassed over the years, Mike says: "I'm not interested in any of the APF stuff now, that's all pre-history, but there's a lot that I've done since which I think should have come out that hasn't."

Mike does believe however that old material will see the light of day, even if only through b-sides. "But so many of those tracks should be on LPs not on the back of a 12"."

All the same the position does seem to be more hopeful now. So does Mike feel he's learned from his experiences with APF?

"Well I don't underestimate my capacity for repeating all kinds of mistakes. I'm good at that, but I guess I have learned quite a lot."

Indeed, where once honesty, integrity and com-

mitment burned through his veins, creating words of hot fire, his attitude now appears possibly more mature, and interestingly more realistic.

"I think in APF there was far too much energy expended in trying to do idealistically sound things all the time, like playing gigs that under 18's could get into, playing gigs that didn't cost much to get into, playing gigs with no bar

and selling fanzines at the door. These are all quite laudable things that I don't disagree with in principle, but they took up so much energy. Y'know, there were gigs when me and John, or Willie the bass player were on the door selling fanzines! It was great fun, but it just wasn't the sort of thing we should have been doing. There was not nearly as much thought going into what we were doing musically, it was far too much like a campaign."

Such comments are indicative of Mike's change in attitude, for though the values remain essentially unchanged, his passion is now harnessed to the realisation that to preach or sloganise is not necessarily the most worthwhile form of communication. What he has to say now is conveyed in a more subtle way – an integration of music and lyric – whereas before the music may have sometimes been used as something of a battering-ram for the message. What Mike Scott appears to have learned is that it is ultimately far more positive and beneficial to actually promote independent thought, than just dogmatically hurl messages at people.

"I think things are going to sweep the whole of society away – that's what I live in hope of, that we're going to have an expansion of consciousness, and there'll just be no need for all this, people will realise they're just being silly, to put it mildly. That's why I make records, that's the purpose of the records I make now – it's all to do with the mind."

It is a musical and lyrical passion, a positive and uplifting direction encapsulated brilliantly on 'The Big Music'.

Clearly aware, however, of the snug position the music business occupies within a world he holds so much in contempt – orientated around capitalism, exploitation and hollow consumerism – he plays along only so far as he has to in order to get his music heard. Another lesson learned perhaps, bearing in mind the lack of compromise in the past by APF. Though then again, he still by no means embraces the record company ethic.

"I'd like to be happy, but the record business doesn't make me feel happy at all. I mean I tend to be fairly cheerful most of the time, but overall I'm not very happy. I'd really like to get far away from everything. I just get freaked out by the world, the world's just terrible – mankind, what an arsehole! – and I don't like being part of that world. I get to think that all I've got is a career, and I'd rather have a bit of a life. I don't think that living in a white, western society you get much chance to feel alive.

MIKE SCOTT

Everything takes life away from you. I wouldn't mind some experience, some mental stuff happening to me that isn't just to do with making money and making record company people rich and things. I mean they've every right to get rich by their own standards, but those standards aren't mine."

Mike Scott is a very talented musician, a man with an astute awareness and sharp insight, looking like anybody else for happiness and fulfilment and finding it to a certain extent through music, but always aware of the frustrating alliance this necessitates with the very system he seeks to undermine in the guise of the music business.

After so many years of hassles, struggles and disputes with the record industry, he is clearly not totally happy working within its strictures, now setting his ambitions outside this sphere.

"I'd like to get a book published; I could write a book on Patti Smith, I think she was the voice of the female species at its zenith, it was completely anti-everything; she was the first person who actually lived publicly, through music, the kind of attitudes that I'd been thinking about since I was a small boy. I could do a poetry book, or a number of poetry books, or various other ideas

I've had for books. I'd like to see my name on the spine of a book. I'd actually feel that I've achieved something. Any arsehole can put an LP out, I don't feel proud about that at all ..., though I guess if I had to spend five years demoing books then the sheen would go off it just like it has with records."

I wondered whether in the face of his distaste for a musical 'career' he would ever envisage leaving music and going on to do other things. "Well it's funny, I get more and more pissed off with the professional side of being a musician and what it involves, but I get more and more into music, I like music much more; I think that APF were musically complete rubbish compared to what I'm capable of now. I really like music and I think you can do amazing things with it, and everytime I play guitar I can feel it now, it's like real, so I'd like to be able to continue exploring music."

Finally I was interested to hear Mike's views on the new Clash, a band APF always cited as a strong influence, and wondered whether he thought that Joe Strummer and Johnny Rotten were still of any relevance.

"Well, I think that Strummer's alright. But I think Johnny Rotten's just an idiot. They are both relying pretty

heavily on the 70's, but they're doing it in such different ways with such different motives that I don't really notice any connection between them. Johnny Rotten's obviously got nothing to say, while Strummer obviously has, and he's pulling all these old songs out of his old chest, a real treasure-trove. I mean nobody criticises a folk musician for playing songs that he wrote ten years ago, or Muddy Waters for playing 'I've Go My Mojo Working' twenty years after he wrote it, because those guys have got roots. Well so has Strummer, so I think it's alright".

But back to Mike Scott and The Waterboys, and from a past studded with fine musical achievements, to a future which promises further progressions, more musical and literary challenges, and hopefully the respect he deserves. For, intelligent and talented, he retains a love of, and feel for, a music he has chosen to make his life. A music that is both inspired and inspiring, way above the fickleness of fashion, and far beyond the barriers so many bands are currently too easily satisfied working within. Mike Scott, passionate and sincere, still enthusiastic after all these years, deserves success and respect. Nobody else comes close.

Ross Fortune

When my first band, Another Pretty Face, found itself in the wilderness, *Jamming!* was one of the few magazines that championed us. We hung out with Tony, did an interview in his mum's high-rise flat and saw his band rehearse in a hall off Streatham High Street. A few years later, when the karmic wheel came round and I was up and coming with The Waterboys, Tony gave us coverage again. Not just a bad-weather friend! **Mike Scott**

I had been a regular reader of *Jamming!*, and published seven issues of my own fanzine, *Cool Notes*, between 1981 and 1985. It was named after a London Lovers Rock group and we regularly featured reggae and soul music. I was elated to contribute to *Jamming!* and jumped at the opportunity to bring my love of reggae to a magazine that had no one else writing about it. My first assignment was to interview Steel Pulse. I was a huge fan and so I was disappointed as well as shocked to hear David Hinds' anti-gay sentiments. Maybe I was a bit naive given that Rastafarian beliefs are based on the Old Testament, but I must have equipped myself well in responding to them, because I was invited to interview Aswad for the next issue. I was born in West London so had a soft spot for the area's top reggae band, and still recall their epic live performance at Notting Hill Carnival, later released as an album. I remember telling Tony that much of their interview was delivered under a cloud of ganja and I feared we couldn't use it. He sent me away confident I could deliver some usable copy and I think it stands the test of time, as does much of British reggae music of that period. **Richard Edwards**

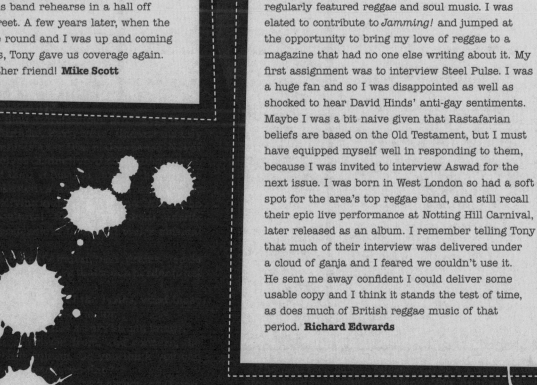

A·S·W·A·D

Britain's top reggae band explain the problems of selling their music to *Richard Edwards*. *Jason Pevovar* clicks the shutters.

For a good few years now reggae has played second fiddle to the endless variations of popular music that arise in this country; not even the syrupy melodies of lovers rock could change that. When reggae is left to fend for itself in the make or break world of the music business it very rarely gets a look in. It is brazenly black, usually openly militant, and as it normally sells to a minority market it won't be making anybody's fortune. In short, by its very nature it is not likely to attract the attention of the big decision-makers within the music industry.

Despite these set-backs it has managed to develop into an industry of its own, catering specifically for its own needs. Reggae has produced its own labels, studios, clubs, radio shows, distributors, press, and of course, its own superstars! Most of the people working within this undercurrent industry will earn a pittance compared to the takings of the mainstream music business, and although the likes of Musical Youth or Eastwood and Saint occasionally strike it lucky, most of the time the decision makers will play it safe by offering the masses their ration of roots in the form of identical Eddy Grant singles or a posthumous release of everybody's favourite – Bob Marley.

Sometimes people of fair skin like myself will stumble across the cultural border, discover what they have been missing for years and curse the world for not sharing their devotion.

Sadly it is upon these rules that Aswad must compete.

Aswads present success has certainly not sprung up overnight, it's been a long hard struggle since their Ladbroke Grove beginnings in 1975. Drummie reminisces about others that were around at the time. "We had Eddie and the Hot Rods, Brian Ferry, Suzi Quatro . . . then we went right through punk, two-tone, and New Romantics to get where we are now. Most of the bands that are around now, if they had come out in 1975, do you think that they would still be around?"

I very much doubt it, but then that's no great loss. Nearly a year after forming Aswad were signed by Island, and since then have released records on C.B.S. and Grove Music, before recently returning to Island. Brinsley explains why Island succeed with reggae music when so many others fail.

"They seem to take the music more seriously. They respect it more because their connections with reggae go right back to Chris Blackwell," a Jamaican (and heir to the Crosse and Blackwell empire) who started the label in the sixties.

Drummie nods in agreement. "Chris had more feel for the music coming from Jamaica, rather than somebody growing up in this country. You have to have faith and enthusiasm in the music. A lot of people will just try to use reggae to make money, and if it doesn't happen the first time they will just give in and forget about it."

So it was these thoughts in my head that I trekked down to Island Records to interview the lynchpins of the group, vocalist Brinsley Forde, bass player Tony

Tony, Drummie, Brinsley

Robinson, and Drummie Zeb whose name no doubt speaks for itself.

Despite this faith in Island Aswad continue to run their own label, 'Simba' which is used to release records with less commercial appeal such as 'Thirteen Dead, Nothing Said', or the dub version of their 'New Chapter' LP.

Strange though it may seem, there are probably more reggae bands in this country than in Jamaica, yet nobody seems to have stepped forward to take the place of the Wailers or to challenge Black Uhuru.

"Well most people can't afford the equipment to start a band up, guitar strings and drum sticks aren't easy to get in Jamaica" declares Drummie. "That's why you find so many groups here; even though it's hard to start, at least they can get the instruments. The reason that Black Uhuru are so popular is because they have got Sly and Robbie behind them, and they are session players. There are a lot of session studio bands like The Roots Radics, Sly and Robbie, High Times, and We the People."

"You'll always find more singers, toasters and DJ's than bands in Jamaica, because all they need is their voices," suggests Brinsley. "You'd be amazed at how quickly they make records over there, they have to work on a very fast turnover. A record that might take a week to make over here can be made in less than a day in Jamaica. There is very little formal organisation within the music industry, one producer and session band might work for a number of artists. A lot of the records are exported to this country, which means that Britain often gets to hear a record before the place where they made it does. That's how forward Britain is with reggae compared to Jamaica. They even play reggae more often on the radio."

Well that certainly doesn't give our radio stations anything to boast about, for reggae music has always been denied the airplay that its popularity deserves. One of

the things that might be inadvertently holding it back is the fact that most reggae records are sold through specialist shops that aren't included in the chart return calculations. Maybe if all the people of Brixton and Handsworth went into their local Woolworths and W.H. Smiths and demanded the latest Gregory Isaacs single . . .?

Brinsley shakes his head. "That would close all the independent record shops and the big stores would refuse to take orders for records that wouldn't meet their sales quota. We know that massive numbers of people in this country love reggae, so what is needed is for reggae to be accepted on the radio and given a fair chance."

Our conversation then turns to a side of Aswad that is not so commonly known, Brinsley's early acting career. The mere mention of the words 'Double Deckers' is enough to produce roars of embarrassed laughter all round. "Yes, that was a long time ago, I hope you all enjoyed it, now can we get onto the next question please?" For those of you too young to remember, 'Double Deckers' was a children's TV programme featuring the adventures of a gang of tearaways on a stationary double-decker bus. Did he enjoy being a child actor? "Yea, it was OK, it just happened that I got into the audition for it. My acting started before that. I was in a show called 'The Magnificent Six And A Half' with Derek Gyler, and that's where they got the idea from."

Brinsley's modesty prevents him talking in detail about further acting roles in 'Please Sir' and 'Babylon'. After such a successful start a career in acting seemed in order, but as with so much of our conversation, all paths lead to Africa.

"That was one of the things that brought me to where I am now. At that time there was nothing really serious for black actors. Now it's different, but then you were just used to make up the numbers. I began to check for Rastafari and there was no position for a dread actor so it was music for me."

Aswads militant Rasta beliefs play a major role in their lives, yet whilst nobody but the most reactionary bigot would deny

them the justice and equality they demand, there might be people like myself who doubt the wisdom of the 'Back to Africa' policy.

Brinsley sees it as an essential part of his faith. "Africa is the home of the Black race, without question. Now it might be divided into different countries and islands but basically the Black race comes from Africa. In order to play your part on earth you have to know where you are coming from. Take black kids in America, most of them believe that they are Americans, which in reality they aint. When I was a kid I sometimes felt that everything black was bad and everything white was good. So I tried to be like them and get accepted – it really hurts you until you find out who you are."

I asked Drummie if he sees any hope for a peaceful multi-racial society in this country, and his reply shocks me. "No, not really, in reality it's a racist country. You talk about having racial equality in this country but in Africa there is still Apartheid. It's people here who are controlling it, that's why Zola Budd can come and run for this country. In reality South Africa and England are the same."

Brinsley is rather more lenient. "It's not a matter of race or colour, it's a matter of good and evil. Society is run in a certain way; there are people who are willing to keep the masses ignorant, because we the workers are here to generate their whole power structure. We were kept in the dark and the only thing for us to do was to argue with each other, it's only through things like music and going to school together that we actually had communication with each other. When you get down to it the things that we are going through now, like food prices, and places to live, . . . it doesn't matter if you are black or white, you're going through the same things."

Isn't there a danger though that the separatism of Rasta will breed hatred and mistrust?

"I understand what you are saying and I agree with you," answers Brinsley. "But it has to be equal on both sides first, before you can eradicate it. Basically, the ordinary people in the street don't hate no-one, you put them in a fifty-fifty situation in the street and they will probably end up helping each other."

With so much emphasis on a return to Africa, what is Aswad's relationship with their present base in Ladbroke Grove, an area that often comes up in their songs? Drummie: "We feel happy there. We know of our roots and we know of our culture. Africa is our home but it's not as if we are saying 'We can't wait to get out of this place', because we know that we have got a lot of work to do here. That area has inspired us, our vibes come from there."

Aswad's connections with West London were further increased by the release of a live LP featuring their performance at last year's Notting Hill Carnival. And what a show it was. Successful live LPs are none too common, yet 'Live And Direct' couldn't be nearer to the real thing. A hard and crucial sound that has managed to capture the whole mood and atmosphere of that hot sunny day last August. Strangely Brinsley is rather reluctant to disclose details of the next LP, simply stating that "It will be a progression from our past works."

Well if it's half as good as their last LP, then we're in for a treat, but where does that leave Aswad? Having further secured their position as the country's top reggae band, they now look set to put their nine years of experience to good use. As I said before, all paths lead to Africa, and so it seemed, did most of our conversation, which meant that quite a bit went unsaid, but no doubt Aswad's future success will speak volumes for them.

Page 33

BREAKING DOWN THE BARRIERS

JAMMING!

60p U.S. $1.50 **No. 20** *Now With More Pages!*

WELLERS
SUMMER
SNAPS!

Everything But
the Girl

Difford & Tilbrook

George Best

**THE BLUEBELLS ● LINTON KWESI JOHNSON ● BLACK
● KING SUNNY ADÉ ● FLESH FOR LULU ● MAD PROFESSOR**

In the wake of 'Eden', Ben Watt and Tracey Thorn tempt us with their next move entitled 'Mine'. Meanwhile, they whisper to Jamming! about real life and romanticism, pop stardom and the dilemma of escaping their past.

EVERYTHING BUT THE GIRL

No Longer So Naive

Keeping his distance: Jonh Wilde
In focus: Russell Young

Ben and Tracey sit in one corner and I keep my distance in the other – hurling words like 'provocative', 'subversive' and 'beautiful' against the walls and watching them bounce back without retaliation. What is it that sends them swooning, fading, dissolving, dreaming, twisting and turning? These and other stories.

Look!", stresses Tracey. "We're not interested in telling people what to think. I want to make it clear how I see the world and people can make up their own minds. At this point, I don't think many people have any idea how we look at it at all. So, that's a bit worrying, but it means that we have that to strive for. It's as though all the reviews of 'Eden' were trying to define how it should be listened to. I don't think 'background' is the word . . . but, anyway, we walk about the house while music is playing – we put on an 'Eddie Cochran' LP when we get up; I like jumping up and down when I'm brushing my teeth. We're not like wallpaper muzak or something."

Although her lyrics are never too direct, there is always room for ambiguity though, ideally, she would want the song to be understood as it was meant.

"Look! we don't lose any sleep at night worrying what interpretations people are going to put on the songs. On the other hand, I don't stop thinking about any song when we've finished recording it. Like 'Each and Every One'. I thought that was my first political lyric but it got such 'nice' reviews. Y'know, 'What a lovely love song'. Well, it's political to me, although I doubt if anyone could work out where I stood after hearing it. But you can't spell it out every time – this is what I'm saying and this is what I think about everything. You have to make it more subtle to make it interesting, to provoke some response. Probably, nobody but Ben knows what I put into a song . . . and that's a shame."

Ben, meanwhile, breaks out of a sulk to tell me that Everything But The Girl are neither complex not matter-of-fact, neither naive nor worldly. Just hovering somewhere inbetween, neither too old nor too new. Their songs dance a muted, drowsy delight – sometimes sounding almost disinterested in the agonised romance that fills their dreams. Tracey, at the same time, can stir herself up when those songs are put down for the same kind of lightweight, faintish sentimentality that The Marine Girls were always accused of.

Eden

I've never looked at the world through rose-tinted glasses", she protests. "Especially now, 'naive' is the last word I would use to describe my songs. Maybe, in the past, I've not been so concerned with comment, but that will probably be more evident from now on. In the past, I've gone out of my way to avoid very clear-cut statements, because I've assumed that people dislike anything too obvious. So, maybe I've been too optimistic."

"If we have been misunderstood in the past", continues Ben, "The fault probably lies with us, because it comes back to the problem of communication. For a start, I've always steered away from the idea of putting lyrics on the back of sleeves, which we did for the first time with 'Mine'. I feel that, in some ways, the actual words are qualified and their meaning determined by the form of the music. If you write down the lyrics to 'Light My Fire', they might look incredibly banal, but in the context of the way they're sung and delivered, they work. A meaning comes through which is very different from the way it might look on paper. In terms of our own lyrics, I've never wanted to write them down but it seemed inevitable because of all the misinterpretation. We're probing about in the dark as well y'know. We're trying to get through to people."

Are Everything But Fun And Fear really as detached, as private, as delicately pained as we are fooled? Are they really twisted in knots?

"I don't mind ambiguity", snaps Tracey, "but nobody even gets the meaning that is there. The original importance of the song just doesn't seem to get picked up on at all. It's always the positions being stated in the songs that are the importance. The last single – 'Each' – was just a strong feminist song about a woman standing up for herself in a world that doesn't want her to be strong. If people knew what I was really like, they would understand the sentiment of that. As I've been tagged this sweet, precious, romantic girl, people read that into whatever I write about."

For Ben, it's the pre-conceptions that people hold (especially for Tracey) that prevents them establishing an identity beyond the pale of slush-slosh sentiment that characterised her previous work with The Marine Girls and even her solo work on the mini-LP, 'A Distant Shore'.

"I think people listen to something like 'Each And Every One' with that pre-conception of Tracey Thorn as this 'sweet young thing'. It's like if you were to listen to the next Robert Wyatt single, you would automatically listen to the lyrics from the stance of 'What is this saying politically?' because Wyatt is recognised as a potent, populist figure. Chic can do 'At Last I Am Free' and it's a love song. When Robert Wyatt covers it, it's automatically regarded as a political song. Tracey can sing a political song and it's treated as trivia."

They are confident of shaking off the 'wet' connotations that automatically punctuate their every step, rightly or wrongly. They also care little for most of the reviews of their recently released debut album. They admit, meanwhile, that the personal, intimate nature of their work always leaves them open to the usual taunts of pubescent self-pity. Tracey shouts at me from the other corner and swears that she doesn't inhabit the same world as Lionel Ritchie, that even when she was writing 'straight' love songs – they were still concerned with the ironies, the complexities that make it real (life). Ben insists that 'Eden' is an impossible LP to dislike.

"Even if you're talking about a record that you're going to play while you do the washing-up, it's the one record that will not grate."

Ironically, he might have unwittingly exposed their greatest downthrow. The dexterous, candid Latin amble of 'Each And Every One' might have drawn me into its light mesh of supple twists with little difficulty. 'Eden', subsequently, must rank as one of the year's most crushing bores – leading us past their closed doors in an undramatic confusion of bossa nova, ripples of whispered jazz and muffles of undistinctive, introspective pop. Like all Thorn's previous work, her limitations – as an artist with the potential to move – are only totally betrayed stretched across a full album's worth of soft sighs. As a lyricist, she's had her moments – often pinning down the fragile nature of human situations with perception and a ready wit. That rare touch has always been hampered by her tendency towards the kind of self-absorbed control that will always be between her and truly great pop music. Their voguish jazz dabblings always sound just like that – just a slight veneer. It forgets all the dark edges.

Argues Tracey:– "But, to me, one of the worrying things about pop music is that people think that anything 'provocative', anything with any 'subversive' quality in it, has to be grating in some way. Well, I just like music that is listenable and I think you can be subversive within that format. We've got no intentions of upsetting people's notions of what music should be. Anybody who does that just ends up being elitist. The word that's always thrown at us is 'pleasant'. Some things that we've done, as solo artists, in the past, have been unbearably pleasant and we recognise that. 'Eden' was made and treated simply as a pop record – it was intended as something more than pleasant. Some pop can even be pleasant, yet still have a beautiful power about it. Billie Holiday or Ella Fitzgerald were never grating but their songs are moving. People might not think that we offer any challenge at all, but, if we are concerned with romance at all, it's hardly the traditional idea of boy–girl."

Ben, meanwhile, chooses to put it this way:– "I think if you see your role as a musician in some way educative, then you're trying to put over a view of the world. So, the last thing you want to do is alienate people. In some ways, perhaps you have to pander to their preconceptions and once you coax them into that, then with a sharp uppercut, you make it count. Of course we regard what we do as special – we wouldn't be doing the f-ing thing if we didn't."

Ideals

Tracey, though, is a little more idealistic, viewing her idealism as close to cynicism as you could get. "Basically, they're the same thing though most people see them as opposite ends of the pole. Most idealists tend to be very cynical and we're fiercely idealistic because we feel there's plenty to be cynical about. We definitely don't cut ourselves off from reality, though we're often seen that way. Obviously, we feel that what we have to say is of value to the world so we're 'special' and at the same time . . . we're really quite ordinary. That's why I think what we say will interest a lot of people, rather than a small minority because we don't want to express our views to some crazy, eccentric few. While all our songs are written from the point of view of the individual, they're also bearing in mind the majority.

Ben and Tracey – No more brooding behind locked doors.

"I've never looked at the world through rose-tinted glasses." (Tracey)

Everything But Fun And Fear?

ISSUE #20 8/84

A summer issue came with a summery feel: Paul Weller as the Style Councillor of Cool, sporting not one but two sets of sunglasses for a cover shot in Hyde Park (the additional pair, to be fair, were loaned by photographer Jason Pevovar) and, though their appearance with Weller at that ICA *Jamming!* magazine show in January 1983 went unnoted in our pages, Everything But The Girl. A long overdue interview with two other great British songwriters, the former Squeeze frontmen Chris Difford and Glenn Tilbrook, was joined by the return of The Bluebells. In a less overtly pop mode, *Jamming!* could take some pride in featuring future indie stars like The Three Johns, Black, The Farm and Flesh For Lulu all reasonably early in their admittedly staggered trajectories, while also introducing yet another new contributor in the form of Leeds-based fanzine editor James Brown.

The Poetry section was handed over to Richard Edwards, who immediately promoted the 'Ranting Verse' of people like Atilla The Stockbroker, Swift Nick, Seething Wells and Porky The Poet. Edwards also interviewed dub producer the Mad Professor, Ross Fortune sat down with dub poet Linton Kwesi Johnson and Hugh Morley spent time with Nigeria's King Sunny Adé. Alongside a major interview by Jonh Wilde with footballing icon George Best (the only access we ever paid for, though I believe it was merely a matter of principle and unlikely to have covered Best's bar bills for an evening), a feature on the 1984 Olympic Games, and full pages dedicated to long-form video releases (they were the new thing!) as well as to new books, it was as decent a cultural range as we had mustered. *Jamming!* was finally – bold-faced names aside – walking like it talked its 'Breaking Down the Barriers' motto.

All this good work was nearly completely undone by the politics of the times. The dockers had come out on strike in support of the miners, and given that *Jamming!* was still being printed in Finland, that meant the entire run of 40,000-odd copies sat on a British dockside for at least two additional weeks past Issue 20's due publication date. Despite public assertions to the contrary by members of certain red-skinned groups that we featured in *Jamming!* nonetheless, we accepted our fate without public complaint nor any attempt to circumnavigate the process. But with cash flow and sales impacted, the delay felt interminable to the point of ruinous.

However, time had already been called on the overseas printing process; it was too long a turnaround even without the potential of dockers' strikes, and especially for a magazine that was about to go monthly. Yes, the good people at Seymour Press had been whispering steadily in my ear, claiming that 'bi-monthlies' like *Jamming!* caused nothing but confusion in the distribution chain, and that we would be better served joining the monthly circuit. And so, in a familiar display of youthful exuberance that cast financial and bureaucratic considerations to the wind. I went along with them. A monthly we would be.

Russell Young

SELF DESTRUCTION SENSE & STYLE!

A Profile of George Best by Jonh Wilde

He was just one of those incomparable individuals – a timely opportune genius. A sixties child. If anything, George Best was style, pure and simple. Furthermore, like all truly great stylists, he found his place in time and created his own legend, encompassing a breathtaking wealth of controversy, intrigue and wonderment. Best took football in the early sixties – when the game was beginning to give in to tactical, back-room lukewarmness, as imagination submitted to big business – and almost single-handedly provided its life support of character, colour and unconventionality.

He made his Division One debut for Manchester United at the tender age of seventeen. Within two epic, eventful years, he was being hailed as football's 'new wave star' – the fifth Beatle. In an era when pop became *the* art form, Best was a symbol of a new way of football. Just as the game was ready to sell out to theory and 4–2–4 gambit, he appeared to knock it sensible, with his flair for the unexpected. More than anything else, he brought the surprise back into League Football – showing up the academics for the ageing, lowbrow bores that they really were. He made the 1960's his own party, crowning the decade with the 1968 European Cup win over Benfica.

Like most of the 60's dreams it was to fade rather dramatically. The first years of the new decade were to prove his most eventful and led to his departure from Old Trafford. The newspapers revelled:– alcohol, late-nights, IRA threats, Miss Great Britain, Eva Haraldsted, club fines . . . at the end of it all, Best was telling the Sunday Mirror that he was close to a physical and mental wreck. At the end of '73, following a 5–0 trouncing by Crystal Palace, he scribbled a note of resignation to United, threatening never to play football again. At the time, he meant every word. Even if he wasn't completely finished, most people didn't need convincing – as he drifted away from the glamour and

splendour of life at the top, only the notoriety seemed to remain for a while. For those who had never marvelled at his dazzling genius on the field, only the scandal and self-destruction in his private life mattered.

As Manchester United plummeted spectacularly to Division Two, he chose the escape route, the lucrative lure of football abroad. While the British gutter press were still scraping the barrel for one last sordid story, he told them to rearrange the words "Off Fuck" to make a well-known phrase or saying. Then he was gone.

British football had lost its most eloquent player and its most fascinating personality. Best drifted from thereon, rarely capturing even a flash of the brilliance that he would be remembered for.

Ten years on, he sits before me in the lounge of London's plush Cavendish Hotel, telling me all about his current involvements. He still plays fairly regularly, mainly abroad or exhibition games. Most of his time though, of late, has been taken up with TV work and personal appearances.

He flashes me a typically cheeky, self-confident smile.

"When I played over here, it was always fun and that's the way I played it. To be quite honest, if I was playing today, I couldn't possibly enjoy it in the same way. So much fun has gone out of the game and it's become more of a business. The greatest difference is that nobody wants to try anything different anymore. The players are frightened and the crowds are too busy fighting each other. It's a bit sad really and in a weird sort of way, I'm glad I'm not playing in it at the moment. I'm still doing it for fun, playing where I want, when I want.

"I'm just glad that I played for United when they were the best team in this country. I was so used to success there, almost from day one, even playing for their youth team when I was fifteen. I signed professional after they won the FA Cup in '63, so in 1965 they won the League, 1967 they won the League, in '68 it was the European Cup. So, in all honesty, I miss the success and I miss playing with great players. Manchester United in the sixties were such a great machine with great individual parts."

If Best ever lived with comparisons, it was being drawn up to the level of other footballing legends like Matthews and Finney. Like them, he had the kind of ability that went beyond technical efficiency and all-round capacity. Best was one of those

George Best – no longer a shadow of his former self

preciously rare sportsmen that took their versatility, their ingenuity and their innate ability and converted it into an art. He might have always seen the game as fun, at all costs, but he was always aware of the originality in his performance.

"Basically, I regarded myself as an entertainer, first and foremost, so the field to me was like a stage. That's why I used to love night-time games, because it was just like being under the footlights. I was aware that I could do things different to other people, so I purposely played up to that, deliberately making people laugh, I knew I could keep people on the edges of their seats. I knew that from the start so I always tried to *entertain* people. I've always looked upon it as theatre or art.

"Finney and Matthews both had tremendous class and charisma. Len Shackleton, though, probably had the edge over them – because he had the cheek to bring a little more fun into it. You can talk about brilliance in anything – theatre, music, films – and you can take two people with identical ability, but one might have that extra cheekiness or nerve and he would have the edge.

"My own style obviously owed much to the sixties, which for me was such an exciting time to be around – clothes, hair, music, money. At that time, particularly in the North, the music business was going through an unbelievable uplift – The Beatles, Gerry And The Pacemakers, The Hollies – and I was a part of that. All those people were growing up in the same time, in the same surroundings as me. At that time, my face was appearing in more pop magazines than football papers, just because of how my image fitted into that scene."

Just as pop was beginning to become something like an established way of life, Best effortlessly fitted the role, his style conjuring up all the necessary 60's elements – flash, rebellion, non-conformity, originality. Christened 'El Beatle' by the Portuguese, his exhibitionism and flagrant ways were to win him as many enemies as friends. Gradually, it became apparent that he could always be relied upon for some controversy and a quick, newsworthy note. To many, he was pushing the 'birds, booze and never-second-best' image too fast and too far.

"For me, the start of the decline was after the World Cup in 1966. Everything became too serious after that. I suppose everything had been too good throughout the early part of the decade. The kids at that time were doing rebellious things, but they were fun things.

"I was always cast as the 'playboy' of the football world, but it was all blown out of proportion. To me, there's no such thing as a playboy. There's nothing wrong with having a drink or going out with women, but I wasn't supposed to do things like that. So unfortunately, that started to take over from the football side and I became the playboy who also played football.

"A lot of that was down to me growing out of my teens, I suppose. I was growing away from an era that meant a lot to me, so I could see everything changing in all areas. The fun was going out of everything, and I just wanted to remain a teenager. There was always pressure and 'good' advice all around me, but it never really affected me at all. It was just that I was getting advised in every area but football and that was the only area I was really worried about, because it meant so much to me."

Suddenly, it all began to work against him, as his private concerns began to be claimed for public property. As Matt Busby's highly successful reign at Old Trafford ended in '71, Best entered that stormy period where the pleasure-seeking, reveller image began to

turn back on him. His private life was front-page fodder for the Sunday Scum rags and, suddenly, all Best's dirty washing was hauled out for public view. The headlines were unforgettable . . . 'I've Had A Thousand Women', 'George In Night-Club Brawl', 'Bestie Disappears Again' . . . and so predictable. Simultaneously, his form began to disintegrate.

"I was like most kids. I like to see my name in the papers, particularly when good things are being written about me. But, at some point, it began to change for me, when people didn't want to write good things, but began to dig for all the dirt. The press started to pester my friends and my family to find some new scandal. There were so many lies told about me around that time and they tried to give me a hard time. They would dig and dig until they found something."

For so long, during his riotous sixties days, the taste of success was as sweet as the dreams he held when he was kicking a ball about for the boys' club, Cregagh, as a lad in Belfast. Then, he could hardly have imagined the high-drama that lay ahead of him.

"I always used to dream about being a great football star, but deep-down, I never had that much faith. Even when I came to Manchester for the first time, in 1961, I just imagined I'd get a trial, then come home. Even that would have been like an incredible achievement for me at that time. I wasn't really equipped for

what happened – playing for the best team in the world at seventeen and winning trophies. Of course, I wonder, if it didn't all come so quickly, whether I would have done any of it differently, but I definitely don't regret any of it.

"It was quite strange though, being so young and going through all that. It was frightening to the extent that I would be detaching myself from everything that somebody else my age could get into."

Once his personal downfall began, those dramatic moments of unpredictable genius *on* the field became rarer and rarer. Best was aware that few downfalls are graceful and he remembered the old maxim, 'the bigger they are . . .'.

"I think, at the time I stopped playing for United, they also declined – so I think a lot of people presumed that I contributed to their downfall and that saddened me a little bit. I wish that they could have kept winning things after I left them. I had nothing to do with their relegation to Division Two but I've been blamed for it so often. I was under no illusions though because I knew that I was the single most important factor in them winning all those trophies."

In 1974, after a spell in Canada, he made one last attempt at a comeback with United – with Tommy Docherty then at the helm – but it was too late. He didn't have the appetite any more. He had other pressures – both of

"I know that I *was* the single most important factor in Manchester United winning all those trophies."

15

"There were times when I was so depressed that if someone had given me a bottle of sleeping pills, I would probably have taken them. What kept me going was the thought that I might miss something the next night."

which were to lead to more trouble – alcohol and the latest Miss World, Marjorie Wallace. Best was on the rocks, broken and disillusioned, and a lot of shit was hitting the fan.

"I missed a lot of opportunities to get back into the game at that point, because of my problem with drink. The only solution, at the time, seemed to be to run away from it all, which is what America amounted to really. Here I was, hurtling downhill – gambling, drinking, getting into fights, smashing cars up – I was living such a debauched life, I had to get away. All I was doing was transferring my problems from one country to another – instead of staying here to fight my way through them.

"I needed the anonymity that the USA afforded me. Out there, I could make friends with people who weren't interested in my name and my first few years in LA were terrific. Eventually though, the alcohol caught up with me there. The nightmare had only moved from England to America."

Excluding a brief spell at Fulham, teaming up with his old mate Rodney Marsh, Best was to stay away from England for many years. He's actually only settled again fairly recently.

"What amazes me is that after all I've been through – good and bad – I'm busier today than I ever was, in all areas. When I came back to this country in 1982, I had nothing, I was bankrupt. It was hard work at first to get back into everything, but now, it's totally enjoyable. I tend to have very busy months followed by quiet ones. It's only the quiet ones that worry me, because of the temptation to indulge in a few old habits. Unfortunately, I've always been the sort of

person who gets bored very easily and I still do. I just need new challenges all the time. I've been travelling around the world for the last two years, so I've not had too much time to sit back and think about it too much. I get offers coming in every day, so I can just pick and choose really."

At 38, looking as fit as he's ever looked over the last ten years, he tells me there's still something of the wide-eyed bundle of mischief in him now, the same kind of thirst for adventure that he had as a fifteen year old apprentice.

"I try to look at everything with my tongue in my cheek and that's probably how I've survived all this time. I've been in hospital three times for alcoholism treatment, but I try to make light of it – even though it is a serious matter. I've always been able to laugh at myself and if you can do that, you have a chance at the end of the day.

"It reached a point where I had enough of taking myself seriously. There were times when I carried the weight of the world on my shoulders and I tried to solve it all by drinking. In a way, I'm still the same. I still get into trouble but that's just the way I am.

"If I've ever had one principle that's always been adhered to, it's been honesty, because I've found over the years that I was always lying to myself, but I was always getting into trouble being honest to other people. I still don't know if that was a good or a bad thing. I still don't know whether it's right sometimes to hurt people in order to help them. I still get into trouble because of my honesty, but I really have to believe in it.

"I was working on Saturday night football on the TV up until last year and the producer was always saying to me, 'I can't understand what it is about you when you come in, but

there's something that you have that I can't put my finger on'. Well, I didn't really know what he was talking about. Then about six months later, we finished a good show and he said to me, 'I know what it is now. I'm on the edge of my seat watching you because I never know what you're going to do or say next. I never know what to expect.'

"Well, I'm always like that. I never rehearse, I just always ad lib. That's what gives me the buzz. I just like those spontaneous moments. It's the same when I'm on the field. I always liked the spur-of-the-moment decisions. Football was always very simple to me. I never thought about my next move. I just *did it*. I've always relied on instinct basically. It's often been those instinctive moves that have got me into a lot of trouble, but I've never thought about good or bad before I've gone for something. It's always been from the heart."

Best, before anything else, was an original with no precedent. As football's first 'Pop' figure, he was perhaps the first to realise that privacy was always going to be fainter a possibility, the more far-fetched his public image was to be be. As Michael Parkinson was to write in his entertaining study of the man, 'Best was the first athlete to straddle the line between showbiz and sport and the first to discover the difficulties of having a foot in both camps.'

He will be remembered a million different ways, because most people who recognised the genius in him will cherish their own favourite moments. For me, he was almost football's last hope – a last defiant two-fingers up to the backward looking bores who would kill the vitality of the game with rationalisation and tactics. Amongst many other things, he should be celebrated for his irresponsibility, his imagination, his impish moments of scintillating brilliance. His greatness lay in his will to reach for the extremes. It was at the edge that he met his greatest glory and his most crushing destruction. The pressures were endless.

"The private George Best was always going to be different from the public version. To some extent, there was always the need to put on an act, just to protect myself. I hate not being myself, but often it was essential to get by. I learned very quickly that you sometimes have to be a good actor in public.

"Nobody was interested in the private personality because all those details wouldn't sell newspapers. Nobody was interested in the other interests I had – movies, books – because there was always the scandal to turn to.

"But I can't pretend that I didn't like a part of that image which built up around me. I think people really love the fact that I always did what I wanted to, regardless of anyone else. Whether it's Jagger, McCartney or Boy George, you can drag them through the dirt but you have to respect them for trying something different.

"The people who I've always admired have been those on the outside, the people who have had the spirit of adventure. People like James Dean and Terence Stamp. Well, Stamp especially was a brilliant actor and he could have gone on and on. But he wanted to do it his way and went for what he wanted in the end.

"As for myself? Well, I could have taken the easy way out in the 70's and settled down somewhere. But, I've always been something of a gypsy. I always want to try something different. There has to be an element of self-destructiveness in there somewhere. There were times when I was so depressed that, if someone had given me a bottle of sleeping-pills, I would probably have taken them. What kept me going was the thought that I might miss something the next night."

16

More than anything, he (understandably) wants to be remembered as a footballer and not for the booze, the fast cars, the ladies. Curiously and paradoxically, his late-teens ambition was to be a millionaire by the time he was thirty.

These days, though, he describes himself as the least materialistic minded person imaginable, considering his chief concerns as his three year-old son and his own health.

The riotous, frivolous days might be over to an extent, but, these days, a sense of self-control replaces the unshackled indiscipline of old. Best is still searching for the next thrill and the next situation. Only now, he doesn't let it get the better of him.

"In the past, I used to play up to that image so much. I used to think, well . . . if they want me to do something outrageous, they'll get it. I'd just do it for effect. That idea is OK to a certain degree but you can go overboard.

"If you have that idea, you can take it to the ultimate. You can begin to believe it if people say that you're going to end up a certain way. Someone's going to find you in a hotel room with your throat slit or a bottle of pills beside you. It's almost too easy to take it to extremes like that – to believe in what people expect of you to that extreme. You have to come to a point where you know your own limits – how much of an act to put on and how much not to.

"I wouldn't mind if the next twenty years were as dramatic as the last twenty because it's not been bad. I find the drama now, but in different ways. I still do crazy things but I do them with a clear head. I think of some of the crazy things I did when my head was full of booze and it's frightening to think how little control I had over myself.

"I know that I pushed myself to the limits, but when I look back on it now, it's as though the bad times never happened. I always wanted the extremities and I know that the great times couldn't have happened without the bad times. Again, it's just as a footballer that I'd choose to be remembered – for some magic moments. Some will never be forgotten – the European Cup Final in 1968, the six goals I scored against Northampton in the cup – but there's thousands of little ones that I'll never forget. All my friends recall one special one; it might be me kicking the ball out of Gordon Banks' hands, or some time when I'd stop in front of a defender and tell him to come and get it.

"We'd played Ipswich in the League one Saturday and I'd scored direct from a corner. Bobby Robson would refuse to believe it wasn't a complete fluke. Anyway, we met them in the Cup the following week and I nodded to Robson when we won our first corner. I swung it in and it went smack against the post. Moments like that – with some character to them – will always stick in my mind vividly.

"They're not all old memories either. I volleyed a ball in from thirty-five yards when I was out in America three years ago. That was voted Goal Of The Century in a TV competition. It meant a lot to me that I could do something like that when I was 35 and not 20 or something.

"The memories won't be when I went out and got pissed or any of that. There were too many good times. It doesn't really overawe me when I consider how much I crammed into those years. Maybe, it just surprises me that I survived it all. These days, I have a lot more respect for myself at the bottom of it all. I always used to worry that I wouldn't be number one in whatever I did. That was so important to me because I was so used to success. Now, I feel that there's nothing wrong with finishing second so long as I enjoy it and I'm honest to myself.

"Now, I feel a pressing urgency to get everything done. There's still so much I want to achieve; I'm definitely not short of ambition. Not yet! If I think about the realities of nuclear war, for instance, I can only think in terms of what I'd miss if it all ended tomorrow."

It's difficult to ignore the tragedy that wrenched Best from the good times throughout the seventies – a decade that saw his ingenuity give way to that self-destructive urge for excess. He stood alone, for most of his glory years, as the one footballer who could always be relied upon to transform a game with one sudden, unexpected burst of masterful control. Best, more than any other from his generation, was capable of making football a beautiful, elegant craft.

He admits himself that, currently, the game languishes in a sorry, dejected mess – lacking wit, anticipation and personality – while singling out Nicholas, Hoddle and Clive Allen as the lone causes for optimism.

Part of that tragedy rests with the niggling knowledge that nobody will ever appreciate how much more George Best could have realised, if he hadn't chosen the path of ruin instead. When his genius peaked, as it did so often during the sixties, it was inconceivable to imagine that it could ever end. But, despite the premature end of a career that amounted to an astounding feat of athletic spirit, I presume few would have wanted him any other way.

Best gave in to the glory and mystique of glamour, forsaking his wealth of natural *style.* He left behind him enough drama to fill many lives with a dash of impudence, a riot of controversy, a flash of that genius.

Just a flash of that genius. There was *style.*

Jonh Wilde

Neil Fraser, alias the Mad Professor, is this country's leading exponent of Dub music and he also manages the independent Reggae label Ariwa. His language is that bizarre distortion of Dub which often defies description. It is built around a backing rhythm, in which the drum and the bass are given prominence, then passed through a maze of special effects. Imagine yourself trapped in an arcade of continuously playing space invader games, then add a vibrating reggae rhythm interspersed with pulses, echoes, fadės, and chants. This might give the unitiated some idea, but as the technical variations are endless, you can never be sure of what is coming next. This is particularly true of the Mad Professor's work. In a rather shambolic Headquarters in the heart of Peckham I spoke to him about his work and Ariwa records.

"I was born in Guyana and came to this country in 1970 to finish school and study electronics. After a brief spell in the Caribbean I returned here and worked in various electrical jobs. I was often repairing mixers and my interest in Reggae music led me to build my own recording studio, using a four track machine. That was very basic, and it often picked up the noise of passing cars. I progressed to an eight track machine and in 1980 Ariwa had its first release. 'Come Back Again' by Sergeant Pepper, which was not very successful."

Things improved as 1982 became the turning point with releases by Divina Stone, Ranking Anne and Mad Professor's own debut LP, 'Dub Me Crazy Part 1'. Since then he has released 'Dub Me Crazy' parts two, three and four, as well as a host of releases by artists on Ariwa. The Mad Professor's reputation has spread dramatically and his skills on the mixing board are now in great demand.

His own distinctive laboratory of sound soon became a focal point for all those artists who wished to include Reggae music in their repertoire. Among those in need of his talents were Rhythm Collision, Ruts DC and the militant Reggae ranters The Anti Social Workers. The Ariwa label also attracted its own artists like Johnny Clarke and Ras Bombo. With so many people seeking his time, The Prof has to be selective.

"I prefer somebody who is eccentric, a little bit weird. Like Ras Bombo, although a lot of people can't digest his stuff, or Ranking Anne who is a liberated woman."

That eccentric streak is clearly apparent on the Professor's own Dub LP's which take rather more chances than your average reggae production. But is he ever worried that his work will lack that commercial touch and be unpalatable?

"Every three or four months, I go through a period where I question myself about compromise. Either the political content is too strong or the music doesn't fall into any easily recognizable pattern. A lot of records don't get played because they don't fit in with the trends at the time but I don't think that my work is on the same parallel as the mass of reggae music."

Ample evidence of that last statement is available on a recent single by Scottish country singer Doug Veitch – a unique amalgamation of country music and Dub rhythms.

For all his work, technical PROF-iciency is an obvious requirement to master the endless variations available on the mixing desk. Of course, the Professor's previous experience in the electronics industry is put to good use.

"Because of my background, I lean more towards the technical side rather than the musical side. When I play something it is usually for the mystery and excitement that it causes. I don't tend to work in keys. Dub is just an extension of your moods. Errol T. and Dennis Bovell are more musically orientated but Lee Perry is like me and tends to go by the vibe."

Photo – Valerie Bosser

Does the Professors 'Vibe' result in a distinctive Ariwa sound?

"Well, because all the tracks are recorded in our own studios, we do tend to develop a recognisable sound, but it will vary from artist to artist."

With so much talent on his hands, the Professor is obviously a very busy man . . . but what has he got planned for the future?

"I'm a shifting sort of person who tends to get bored with the same projects. I hope to spend less time in the studio and more time running the label. We have just released Ranking Anne's second LP and an Ariwa Posse compilation LP. Next I'll be working on records for Benjamin Zephaniah and the Anti-Social Workers."

Well, that's certainly enough to be going on with. Those of you who would like to see the professors protégés live should look out for the Ariwa Posse: Ranking Ann, Sister Audrey, The Wild Bunch, Mother Nature and the Prof himself, when they hit the road later this year.

Richard Edwards

19

Pool of Young Blood

Paul Davies finds a new breed burning on Merseyside

'A conspiracy of silence speaks louder than words', said John Lennon, in what could have been a direct reference to the answer given by certain groups when asked to appear at a Miners Benefit in Walton Hall Park, Liverpool, organised by the Merseyside Young Socialists. It's no great surprise to learn that the tacit Tories of Tin Pan Alley would rather keep schtum, keep a clean nose and get their flabby features splashed across the pages of the teen trivia magazines, rather than make any kind of contentious or political statement. It is, however, thoroughly heartening and uplifting to discover that there are groups and individuals who will stand by what they believe in, and take part in events such as these. So, hats off if you please for WesternPromise, The Faction, Newtown Neurotics, Billy Mayell, Pete Wylie, The High Five and The Farm, all of whom donated their services free.

THE HIGH FIVE – Glorious Bursts

Before the concert I spoke to Rob Jones, drummer and founder member of **The High Five.** The rest of the group are Phil Hayes (guitar/voice), Mark Braben (guitar) and Phil Jones (bass). The High Five are not part of any Liverpool scene, sound or second coming, but Rob Jones does feel a definite kinship with other local groups Ellery Bop and the Farm:

"It's an attitude more than anything else, in the sense that it's very un-rock'n'roll. The bind is politics really. Us, the Ellery Bop and the Farm all help each other out and lend each other's stuff."

The group's first single, 'Cold Steel Gang', was released last year on the independent Probe Plus Label. It's a glorious burst of brash and buoyant guitar bluster topped off with a brilliant impassioned vocal. The 'Cold Steel Gang' of the title is, as Rob puts it, "any authoritarian power who seek to govern by the politics of economics rather than the politics of the people." Its obvious specific application is to the axe-wielding monetarist bootboys of the Tory Cabinet.

A sharp political edge and awareness informs several of the High Five's songs and consequently they have been tagged as a bolshie bunch of Liverpool lefties by pasty-faced music biz plantpots. Unperturbed though, Rob Jones dismisses out of hand any suggestion that they may have to compromise their beliefs in order to achieve further success. In the future, he assures me, there will be no dilution of politics. No film flam. No compromise. No sell out.

"I'd like chart success, I'd like the High Five to be the biggest thing around but I wouldn't want the group to bend towards being chart orientated . . ."

The High Five believe what they believe and they'll stick by it, whether it's to their detriment or not. The best of their songs weld their radical stance to a stinging, vital pop attack – it's the sound of a hundred careering guitars crashing into each other in an exuberant trebly collision of noise. Their new single, 'Working for the Man', will be out at the end of August. You have been warned.

THE FARM – Life Beyond the Bunnymen

After picking up some extremely heavy-duty press coverage in the last twelve months, **The Farm** are currently being heralded as the next BIG thing. The seven members of the group are John Melvin (guitar), Steve Grimes (guitar), Carl Hunter (bass), Andy McVann (drums), Tony Evans (trombone), George Maher (trumpet), and Pete Hooton (vocals). Visually anonymous to the point of invisibility, the Farm are a bunch of untutored roughnecks whose music is fired by a smart arrogance and a righteous anger. They specialise in a scruffy melodic dance pop, and amongst their best songs they have a brace of potential hit singles ('Memories', 'Rules of the Game', 'Information Man') which would grace the higher reaches of any chart. Although still without a deal, the group plan to release their first single in August, come what may.

As well as singing, Pete Hooton writes all the Farm's lyrics. He cocks a derisory snook at bands who shy away from reality and shroud their songs in obscure verbal camouflage.

"We wouldn't write lyrics like 'the flowers are screaming' or 'cucumber this, cucumber that'. A lot of lyrics from Liverpool bands are just nonsense. You just have to look at China Crisis – their lyrics are hilarious. Groups like that are in the public view and they've got a chance to say something . . . that's why I had a big mad argument with McCulloch a few weeks ago. He just makes statements that he doesn't qualify, like 'I want to make Liverpool a Bill Shankly Liverpool'. He shouldn't even mention Bill Shankly in the same breath as Echo and the Bunnymen. It's a disgrace to the great man. As a matter of fact, all weirdoes are known as Billy Shanklys now, all Bunnymen fans."

The Farm have a vociferous local following, but 'Hooto' doesn't feel that their popularity will be confined to Liverpool.

"No, because since we've done the Oxford Road Show we've had loads of letters from people all over the country who saw us. I think there's a certain type of people everywhere who'd be into our music."

He does admit though that the Farm/scally/football connection may be putting some people off going to see the group.

"If a punk heard a session of ours and liked it, he'd probably think twice about going to see a concert of ours. But it would be the safest concert he could go to. We've never had any trouble really. The last concert we played was at McMillan's (in Liverpool). There were about four thousand people there, and it was just chaos, everyone dancing, like an early Madness concert."

The motion which inspires most of the lyrics is anger, the starting point of one of his songs comes to his mind immediately: "When Michael Foot was at the Cenotaph, he was getting slagged for having a donkey jacket by some cheeky bastards. I mean, what's it matter that Michael Foot didn't have what you're supposed to wear on? I wrote 'No Man's Land' after that, it's about when the Germans and the British played football together. And then Paul McCartney stole the idea for his video, the bastard! It would have been the perfect video for 'No Man's Land'."

With or without the video, it's another one of The Farm's many great songs which should be available on vinyl. The only obstacle to their continued success is the distinct possibility that their future record company (whoever they turn out to be) will try to market them on the basis of 'Hooto' being some sort of bogus 'Voice of Youth' figure, leading the scallies towards some fake promised land. If this happened it would be an unforced error of truly Grobelaarian proportions.

The 3 Johns

The Three Johns – John Hyatt, vocals, John Langford, guitar, and John Brennan, bass – have, over the last two years, won themselves much praise with their fast dance tunes and gritty stupidity. Tongue in cheek they have clocked up five excellent singles and shown how with fleshy guitar riffs, imagination and a good splattering of wit you don't have to be wimps to be good.

Having been treated (too?) favourably by the media – five Radio One sessions and front cover of the NME – they are in a position where they are quite probably going to get dumped on. Sitting a hundred yards away from Leeds' urban motorway the three grown men were visibly worried as they discussed the highlights and pitfalls of the music business . . .

"They're all bastards at the NME, especially Mat Snow," grins the fat guitarist. "Despite his belief, neither the Fall or the Birthday Party have ever influenced us musically. Our biggest influence has been inability, learning to get our instruments."

"Naah, we're all good musicians, but secretly we just pretend to be inept." Brennan rolls over and continues with his rush of verbals. "He's a good guitarist, the only thing he lacks is economy. That's his one failing as a musician but at the same time it's not really a failing because the medium we're working in, 'rock n roll', is all about breaking the rules. So if his technique offends me in anyway it's . . ."

"Probably because I don't sound like the Smiths."

Brennan: "Nah don't be . . . I don't want you to sound like the Smiths."

So what about the Smiths and the other bands currently clogging up the Independent Charts?

Brennan: "In most of those bands, there's one person in the group who is the major force. With the Johns, we thrive on the conflict between the three of us, and because we've all got different ideas the conflict comes across when we play."

Langford: "I think we're getting more extreme as we go along though we were quite tame when we started. We've reversed what most bands are doing, like they're quite raw when they start but they mellow as they progress. We've gone the opposite way which is what we wanted to do. Three chord rock 'n' roll is a lot of what we do. We're not breaking down any musical barriers or re-inventing any sort of musical structure."

Brennan: "Changing the structure of music isn't what it's about. The point is how the music is being played and how it applies to what is going on today."

The last two Johns singles have been vicious stabs at the Tory re-election of last year and the current state of popular music. On stage they bounce, career and pose in the most ridiculous of rock's stereotypes while Langford puts fire into his mighty exaggerated guitar licks. Three Fatboys with idiotic grins, trying hard to look rebellious. Meanwhile their ability and stupidity crash through, only matched by their ever so sincere awareness of the responsibilities they have inherited as 'rockunrowll heroes'.

"Yeah, I think it's very important that there's no barrier between me and the kids . . .!"

James Brown

LONDON

WPL
WHITEWAY PUBLICATIONS LTD

3 WHITEHALL LONDON SW1 Tel: 01-839 6519

THE HOLYHEAD & LIVERPOOL Mails 828

Dear Mum + Sally
being really good down here.
Look in "JAMMING" mag:
in RSMcColls or Woods for my article
on 3 Johns. Tonight I'm
playing 5 a side football against
THE ALARM for "Jamming".
That's something to tell your friends Sally
– the photographs might be in the
next issue of Jamming! If not I'll
get copies anyway
See you today JAMES

MUM + SALLY
1 GRANBY GROVE
LEEDS
LS6 3BE
YORKSHIRE.

PHOTO: JOE CORNISH
© WPL 1984
W 40
Printed in England

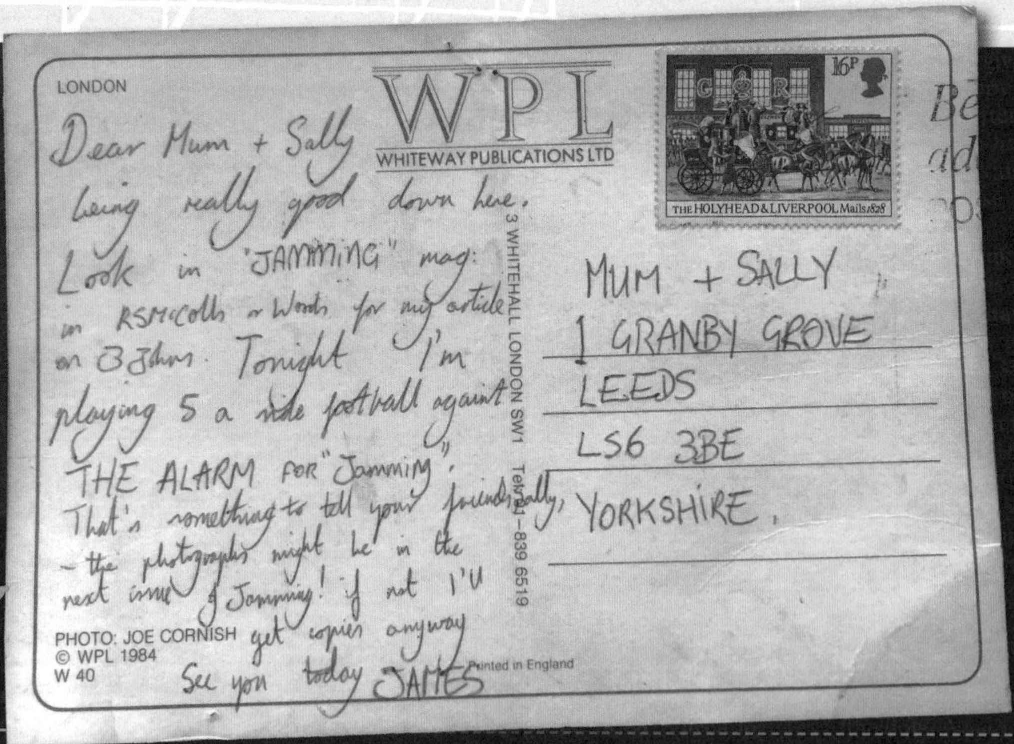

Jamming! was really important for a lot of us fanzine writers. First it showed that with ambition we didn't need to stay in our bedrooms publishing. And secondly because it actually paid us a little bit of cash and reviewed our fanzines. Like *ZigZag* it was an independent title that existed between the fanzine world and big weekly music papers.

I wrote a few pieces for it: on The Three Johns, Big Flame – and That Corporate Feeling, whose lone single now sells for about £200 even though hardly anyone has heard of them. But that's what *Jamming!* did: it gave space and a platform to people – be it bands or writers – trying to be heard. My memory of the Three Johns piece was they were very upset that I documented where they light-heartedly referred to an *NME* writer as a bastard. I was doing it in the same jovial light as themselves, but it looked much worse in print. I also played for the *Jamming!* football team once at the Michael Sobell centre in North London, where we hammered The Alarm, and was so excited about it I sent my mother a postcard to tell her! **James Brown**

WELLER WELLER WELLER!

Tell me more, Tell me more..

"It always seems easy for 'The Young Ones' or 'Monty Python' to take the piss out of the establishment, 'cos a lot of them are from the middle classes."

As Paul Weller walked away from The Jam in December '82, he was forsaking the comfort of guaranteed success that they had become. While Foxton and Buckler faced a difficult evolution from thereon, Weller merely picked up where he left off – enjoying a first year with The Style Council, tentatively flirting with various forms and new directions. His first year away from the security of The Jam was rounded off with the release of the debut Style Council LP (Café Bleu) in April this year – a hazardous cacophony of contrasting ideas that, despite an all-round critical backlash, proved commercially successful at least.

Whatever the reactions, The Style Council showed us a new side to Paul Weller – revealing a new thirst for experiment, a quieter public profile and a flair for self-parody.

To probe a little further into the 1984 version, *Dave Jennings* (our very own) met Paul Weller on a long, hot summer day at Hyde Park.

Jason Pevovar gleefully snapped away.

I get the impression that, since you started The Style Council, you've regained enthusiasm for the music world which you lost towards the end of The Jam . . .

For the actual music business itself, I've got nothing but contempt; that hasn't really changed for a long time. But for what I do – yeah, definitely. That's down to playing live, as well – I grew really disenchanted with that, I felt it didn't really get me anywhere. That's changed for me now – the gigs we've done this year revived my enthusiasm. It's more of a loose thing now – there's not that same kind of tension either.

Yeah . . . Although I'm sure there were a lot of creative and intelligent people in The Jam's audience, there were also the little miniature thugs who'd throw missiles at the support band if they weren't wearing the right uniforms, weren't there?

Yeah. That's definitely changed, because of the way we geared the shows this time. We went on first, then the Questions came on, then Billy Bragg came on, then The Questions, then Billy again, then we finished off the evening by doing a second set. And with The Jam, we'd never have got away with something like that – the support bands would have been slaughtered. A Style Council audience is far more open-minded.

You think it is different people?

I think it's probably half-and-half. I think there's probably 50% who used to like me with The Jam, but I think there's a lot of new people as well. Some of the things we've done have been quite different – some of the images we've put forward have been a bit contrary to my public image.

In your songwriting for The Jam, you wrote a lot that was social observation; observation of different types of people. The Style Council LP goes from one extreme to the other – a lot of the music is very gentle, and yet there are two songs on the LP during the course of which you call for the immediate formation of lynch-mobs! Is that a deliberate change of policy? Did you come to the conclusion that the observation songs, like 'Man in the Corner Shop' and 'Mr. Clean' were useless?

Well, I don't know about useless . . . I feel I exhausted that, that's what it comes down to really. I done that to death in The Jam. I don't think I'd ever write those kind of songs again. At the moment, most of my songs are just my own personal thoughts – not really using the environment, or characters, or vignettes.

There are some fairly startling lyrics on 'Café Bleu'. Like, from 'A Gospel' – "I can't wait for the day they do the lamppost swing/ and no mercy should they be shown/for you cannot reason with the Devil's own". There's something familiar in 'The Whole Point Of No Return', as well . . .

Well, I don't think you can reason with someone like Thatcher, or someone like Reagan . . . or a lot of prominent people from the Establishment, which everyone tries to say these days doesn't really exist, but of course it does. And even if you get your Thatchers and Reagans, or the bankers and the people who really control us . . . I mean, I'm not sure if you can change it any other way, I'm not sure if you can change them through a gentle process of socialism. They've been used to that – they've been used to having that same kind of power for years and years and centuries and centuries. I don't advocate shooting every rich person, but I think the people in control, with the power – and for that you have to look past the politicians, you've got to look at the real core of it, which involves the whole Public School thing – I think that's where all of it comes from, that whole Old School Tie network. Those people ain't gonna give up their power that easily – so if they're not gonna give it up, they've got to be forced to.

HOW DID IT COME ABOUT that you chose Mick Talbot as your partner in The Style Council? Why him rather than anyone else?

I suppose because he's the only keyboard player I know who's more or less the same age as me, and plays those instruments. He still plays piano and Hammond organ; most young keyboard players today are brought up on synthesisers, and the new electronic keyboards – which we use, and I think can be used in an effective way – but still never, ever, as far as I'm concerned, beating the pure sound of natural instruments. There aren't many people playing in that style, either – in a kind of R'n'B style.

I've been led to believe that Mick is more of an extrovert, carefree character than you . . .

He's more *carefree* than me, yeah; I wouldn't say he's an extrovert. He doesn't think about things as constantly or as deeply as I do; that's not to say he doesn't think about things in the same way, but . . . he said to me that he thinks I think too much!

Has he made any attempts to write actual songs, as opposed to instrumentals?

I don't think he'd write a lyrical song – he freely admits himself he has trouble writing lyrics. But he's written lots of other tunes, which we've had around for a long time, which we just haven't got around to putting any lyrics to. Like *"The Big Boss Groove"*, which is the other side of this last single, where Mick wrote the music and I put the words to it afterwards.

Do you socialise together?

Me and Mick? Quite a bit, yeah; not as much as we used to, because he's got a girlfriend.

What's your idea of a really good, fun night out?

I had a good night out the other night. I went to a club one of my friends was doing, where he played all 70's soul – I thought that was really good. My ideal night would have been something like that, for it to be as warm as it was last night . . . just to stay out 'til four or five in the morning, just wander and maybe go to an all-night café or something.

Is it possible that anyone else will be recruited as a permanent member of The Style Council?

Steve (White) more or less is anyway – it remains unsaid, but he's played on almost all the records. He's just so good as well, and his attitude's really good. It all depends; if we found the right people, I guess we would do. But I'd be reluctant to have a whole band, because then I'd be back to square one, and I like this freedom – getting new people in every time, it does keep things fresh for us. There's a couple of people I'd really like to get on some of our records, like – you know the little guy out of Bronski Beat, the singer? I'd really like to get him to sing one of our songs. And there's another singer – have you heard of David Joseph? He's really good, I'll have to get him to do something for us as well.

Do you intend to carry on doing a lot of instrumentals?

Yeah, I do, definitely – 'specially after some of the reviews we had, even more so. 'Cause I personally think they work, I think it's just that people ain't used to it. We work within pop music, where instrumentals are kind of unheard of, so I think it's all the more reason to do it – to open up pop music a bit more. I think they're really effective. It was so powerful live; despite not having any lyrics, there was a kind of lyrical feel there anyway.

Do you have any favourite comedians, or comedy shows on TV?

I've got some favourite comedy shows – I don't like any comedians really, like Jim Davidson or any creeps like that.

Are there any of the newer ones; like Alexei Sayle, or 'The Young Ones' . . .

No, they're not funny. They're too smug for me. I do laugh when I watch it, but it's all smug, student . . . I really like **'Only Fools and Horses'** – the characters are so good, and the acting's excellent. I really like **'Minder'** – or I used to, anyway. One thing I do like about the English race is that kind of irreverent humour. 'Cause, like, a lot of those – 'Young Ones', and 'Monty Python' – it always seems a bit easy to take the piss out of the Establishment, or this or that, y'know . . . It's easy for them, in a way.

Why particularly easy for them?

'Cause a lot of them are from the middle classes. I always think it's a bit like a sideline for them.

How about your record label, Respond? Are you happy with the way that's gone so far?

It could be better; but anyone could say that, really, so . . .

You have taken quite a bit of stick over your choice of acts . . .

That's on the critics' side. I couldn't really give a shit.

Do you really never pay any attention to what people say about your records in the press?

Sometimes it gets to me, it all depends. One thing that really got to me was the review of the Respond compilation LP, which wasn't that hot, admittedly. Dave McCullough from **'Sounds'** reviewed it, and just used it as a tirade against me. I thought that was just really unprofessional, to take out on the Respond bands the fact that he dislikes me.

Have you got any other areas of creativity you'd like to go into?

I'd like The Style Council to make a film – I don't want it to be like 'A Hard Day's Night' or 'Help!'. I'd like to be able to make a really good film, for a band to be able to pull off a film. I'm not saying I can act, but if we can make the overall thing good . . . we've got to find a story, which is what we're trying to do at the moment. We've got three different people working on a script for it, or an idea for it; maybe we'll even put all three together. I don't think I would be any good in it, quite honestly – I don't think I could act to save my life! But I think Mick will be good in it, and we'll probably get two other people involved as well. If people relate to it, and it has some meaning to them . . . I think that'd be quite successful, really.

What other projects have you got in the pipeline?

21

Did you get very far?

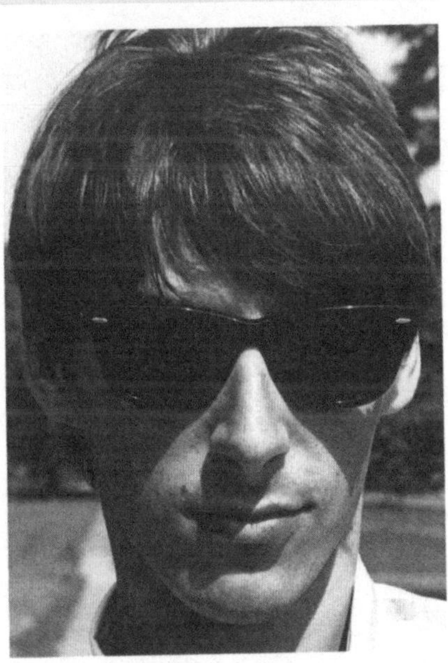

Well, I wanted to put another LP out this year, but everybody seems to think it's a bit heavy going to have two LPs in a year. So we'll probably make it, and keep hold of it, and put it out next year. Do you remember that Wire LP, the first one they ever did? It had 23 tracks on it, or something . . .

'Pink Flag'.

Yeah . . . I'd like to do an LP like that. I want to go back to writing really short tracks . . . two minute songs. So that's something I shall probably work on; and we are going to do some dates, as well.

IN AN INTERVIEW he did for us last year, Bruce Foxton remarked that you never seemed interested in succeeding in America. Is it true that you're not interested in working there?

I saw that, and I thought it was a load of bollocks. I put the same amount of time into going over there and playing as he did . . . But what it comes down to is that I'm not prepared to go and live over there for a year, or to go and tour there for six months, which is what most bands do. To me it's just too much compromise.

Bruce seemed very proud to have been in The Jam; he said that, in his opinion, The Jam did achieve an awful lot. Do you feel that way?

I do, yeah. I think stopping it when we did really encapsulates that. Our relationship with our audience . . . I don't think many bands have had the same kind of relationship. It got more and more dissipated towards the end, just because the whole affair became so much bigger – but I always felt there was such a kind of intimacy . . . I found it really unique in pop music, that kind of communication. Also, the fact that records like *'Going Underground'* and *'Town Called Malice'* got to no. 1 – to me it kind of proved that you haven't got to be Wham! or something to do it. You haven't got to sacrifice everything for commercial success.

Out of the people who get in the charts regularly, is there anybody you like?

Well, I quite like (Boy) George, or I did do anyway; but they seem to have softened up a lot, become a little bit slick. Around this time last year I went to see 'em, and I thought they were really, really good; and I thought George seemed to be really natural, he seemed to be very honest. But American success always seems to spoil people.

There is one aspect of your stance over the years which I've always found rather irritating, and that's the great obsession with "youth". I agree that often young people are more idealistic than people over the age of 30; but people have children, and then they need more money to look after them; and it's more difficult for older people to stand up and be optimistic and idealistic, because when you're 16 to 20 it's expected of you! People write it off as just youthful rebellion . . .

Well, I just think . . . as young people *are* the future, then they should be given a hand in devising their future. And as they're always thwarted in that, you can't expect anything else but frustration from them. I think there's a lot of positions of power which youth could do far better in. I *have* got a romantic vision of it, but I'm not particularly worried about justifying it – that's just the way I see it. You were saying then that once people get over a certain age they have kids, and settle down, and look for a comfortable lifestyle – just because that's the norm, that doesn't mean to say it's right, does it? That's not life, is it? If it is, that's pretty depressing!

The point I'm making is that it's perfectly possible for people to carry on being brave and idealistic up to all kinds of ages –

Of course, yeah! I wouldn't disagree with that. Maybe some remarks I've made in the past have done, but I wouldn't disagree with it as I sit here now talking to you. I just think about people who I know – people my age, from where I used to live – who really, by the time they're 20, have given up; not because they haven't got a job, or anything like that – they've just given up in every way, because they *are* happy with just going to the same pub, night after night, year after year. And they're quite happy just to settle down, and have their kids, just because that's what everyone else does. That's what I find depressing.

Do you think our generation – or Tracie's generation – is in any way really different to the ones that have gone before?

Well, every generation is unique, isn't it? You have the same kind of frustrations, and the same kind of aspirations, but . . . I think it was easier for me, for my generation – when we were 15 or 16 there was much more money around, for a start.

That's true, yeah . . . It does seem a cruel irony when you look back and think that people described early punk as "dole queue rock" – and now there's three times as many unemployed!

I thought about this the other day, actually. Every band had a song about how bored they were; everybody had a song about being on the dole. *Now's* the time when you'd expect it – and now's the time when nothing seems to be coming out that way. The 60's were a bit like that as well . . . it seems that only in times of affluence does youth rebel.

Maybe Paul Weller's public countenance, as that grim, humourless kill-joy, still lingers even now. Sometimes it can be difficult to conclude otherwise when confronted with a man who uses a question about comedy as an opportunity for a spot of attempted class-warfare.

Neil Kinnock, Billy Bragg, Ken Livingston and Captain Sensible are all living proof that ideals can mix with a dash of that essential humour.

And Paul Weller?

The Style Council is still in its infancy – with a youthful zest for adventure on its side. If that genuine inspiration of old is still lacking, there's still time.

There's always time.

22

Singles

Tony Fletcher rounds up the recent crop of releases.

Summer always sees a lack of major releases, as most major acts tie up their holidays in the Bahamas with recording their new album, timing it for the Christmas market and that period's lucrative sales. Therefore, the summer is always a good time for new acts to come through – who knows, they may strike big enough to rush out an album and also join in the Christmas fun! Most of the singles here are by unknown acts on independent labels; as people were quick to point out last time I claimed otherwise, the independent scene is not dying, but a thriving, ongoing concern. Where it has fallen flat on its feet is that the current climate allows little or no media coverage, and no money for people to buy records on spec as they did in the late '70's (and who'd have thought we'd ever say *that*?).

It is no surprise, at the end of it all, that the three best singles here, out of over a hundred that were ripe for reviews are all on majors – they can *afford* to sound good.

ECHO & THE BUNNYMEN: Seven Seas (*Korova*)

'Ocean rain' may have been the Bunnymen's worst-received album to date, but for me, it was the first time they had yet made a decent long-player, and beyond that, I could almost start to believe its ludicrous claims to being 'the best album ever made'. Never before has an orchestra been used so well on a rock record, and for once, The Bunnymen concentrated almost entirely on a stream of emotive good tunes, only occasionally resorting to self-indulgence. 'Seven Seas' is a perfect example – all cascading chords, strong vocals and a stirring orchestra – that should notch up another Top 10 hit for

them. However, watching The Bunnymen's career now is like watching the downfall of a group in action replay – when will McCulloch realise that the day you start believing your own press is the day the public stop believing in *you*? Grow up and just carry on making great music, and maybe you'll be more successful than ever.

THE COLOURFIELD: Take It (*Chrysalis*)

The long-awaited second single by Terry Hall's new outfit comes as good news after the disappointment of the first release. 'Take It' is the most commercial song I've heard Terry sing since 'Our Lips Are Sealed' and although the primitive sound of the Fun Boy Three is still there, this time a real tune comes careering happily through. Both b-sides ('Pushing Up The Daisies', a noisy collection of ideas as opposed to the mellow 'Windmills Of Your Mind') are also well worth your attention.

THE KANE GANG: Closest Thing To Heaven (*Kitchenware/London*)

Until now, I have been silently unmoved by the fuss surrounding Newcastle's untrendy soulboys, 'Small Town Creed' sounding too forced to be pleasant for these ears. This though, is the real McCoy, a delightfully sweet tearjerker, with soothing voices and hooks a-plenty. It's been a steady build-up for The Kane Gang (which is probably the way they wanted it), and this should be the one to see them launched into the upper reaches of the charts.

THE JUNE BRIDES: In The Rain (*Pink*)

As Bruce Dessau pointed out when he reviewed this lot live last time, just how do you pinpoint what makes a great group great? The June Brides have *the touch*, mixing their influences into a scorching cauldron that comes out with a mutant pop song of startling originality yet seemingly derivative – an art in itself.

THE WOODENTOPS: Plenty (*Food*)

From the opening four bars of crescendo, 'Plenty' is a winner, mixing psychedelic Beatles with loud choruses and Northern jangly pop. Despite the awful name, The Woodentops prove here – in a song just that big too long – that they too have a healthy future ahead of them.

THE ROOM: New Dreams For Old (*Red Flame/10*)

Though this has been out for a while, it seems to have gone a bit by the board, which is a shame as The Room have knocked out an energetic and innovative record that should really have done them more justice. The vocals are Bono/Kerr, but with strong brass and more of that jangly guitar. Is this the same Room that have been knocking about for years and never getting anywhere? If so, it's time that was changed.

LAW LORDS INTERNATIONAL: Livingstone Rap (*Cherry Red Ken*) 12"

Where would we be without the occasional gimmick, and what better than a record in support of, as the press release says, 'London's sharpest leader since Cromwell'. Though this certainly doesn't possess the best dance floor track known to man, lines like *'He is loved by everyone/Everyone except The Sun'* do show a sense of humour which will serve to make Ken Livingstone a bigger pop star than Neil Kinnock.

FAITH BROTHERS: Tradesman's Entrance (*FBI*)

This cruelly ignored single has been out for months now, but is simply too special for me not to write about. It is rare indeed to hear a political ballad these days, but though 'The Tradesmen's Entrance' leans almost towards Barry Manilow, it wins through *pure emotion*. Relying on a beautiful soul voice and some magnificent piano playing, this tale of unemployment and recession hits as hard as any frantic guitar-dominated attack on the Establishment could ever hope for. In the right hands, this could have been as controversial a hit as 'Relax' – because it is *that* commercial – but although others may ignore this, expect to read more about the Faith Brothers in Jamming!

FUN 'N' FRENZY: Fallen Down In Love (*Boiler*)

More mutant pop, the weird effect being lent by the weak production. A strong pop tune that bodes well for the future, flip over to 'Untouchable Divine' for some lighter, though equally strong, music. So much talent about, so little attention.

THE HIT PARADE: Forever (*JSH*)

A new label that vows never to release a song of more than three minutes in length (!), The Hit Parade launch it all with a strong number dominated by recurring piano lines. This really does sound like it was recorded in a box, but they say that great tunes always come through, and this is no exception.

VARIOUS: What A Nice Way To Turn Seventeen (*Glass*)

A fanzine or a record? For a mere £1 (plus 30p p&p from 4 Coniston Road, Leamington Spa, Warwicks CV32), you can obtain not just a well-written fanzine, but an EP featuring **Nikki Sudden** (ex Swell Maps leader, for those of you under 30!), a relaxed psychedelic jaunt by the **Rag Dolls** entitled 'Sparrows', a disappointing ballad by the **Jazz Butcher**, and an unworthy contribution by the aptly-named **Sad-Go-Round**. All in all, exceptional value, and only a fool would ignore this in favour of the new Thompson Twins single. (But then so many do . . .)

BELFI & BUNKER: 12" EP (*Next Wave*)

Two people making weird music, one of them (Bunker) formerly lead singer of Optimax, a group I never expected would end up this way. After a few hearings, the omnipresent beat and synths, with uncomfortable vocals, develops from interesting to intriguing, with a likeness to Throbbing Gristle, but I would still sooner leave this to those who are used to experiments.

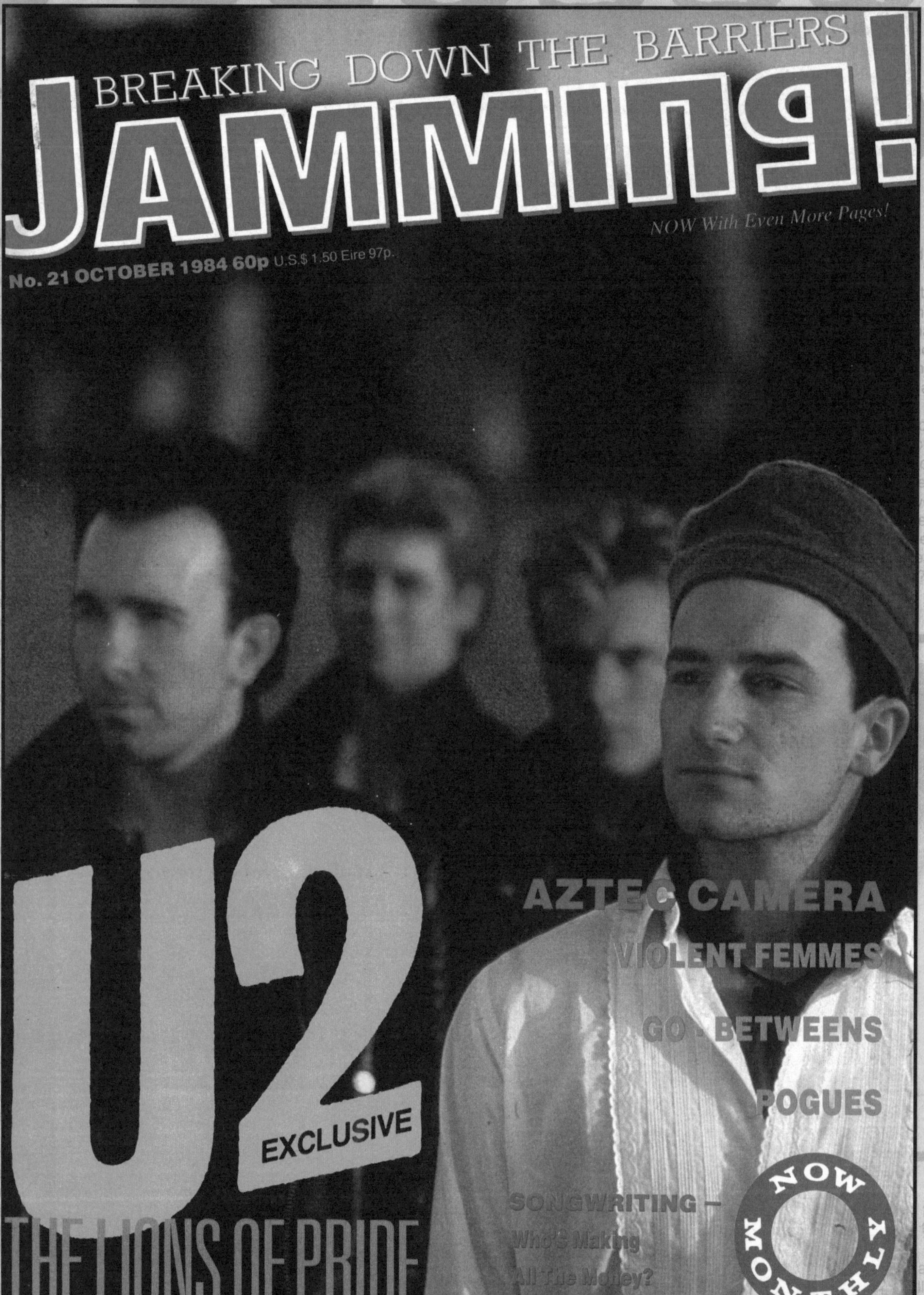

BREAKING DOWN THE BARRIERS

Jamming!

NOW With Even More Pages!

No. 21 OCTOBER 1984 60p U.S.$ 1.50 Eire 97p.

U2

EXCLUSIVE

THE LIONS OF PRIDE

AZTEC CAMERA

VIOLENT FEMMES

GO - BETWEENS

POGUES

SONGWRITING –
Who's Making
All The Money?

NOW MONTHLY

self. Then we might end up playing it in front of a crowd. That's pretty ironic. Also, the whole idea of playing rock'n'roll to a live audience sometimes feels totally absurd. There is always this indelible air of the ridiculous that pervades their live performances and their recorded work, born out by the exaggerated methods that they use. Gano feels it, most of all, when they

hatred, which is taken from The Old Testament. Originally we wanted the Scripture to be written on the sleeve, to show people that it wasn't something I had written myself. Strangely, the record company left it off at the last minute, which I find difficult to believe was... we wanted to make it clear that the song was intended to be taken literally.

much talked about folk element exist no way quaint or gimmicky. Their qu in their manic pace, their ec naughtiness, their fresh inventivenes lack the unhealthy self-control o modern pop, instead falling back expert minimalism – Gordon's jabbin Brian's fluid bass and Victor's percussion. The folk lies embedde

Jonh Wilde encounters America's latest hot export.

THE VIOLENT FEMMES

"If we enjoy the absurdity of one aspect, it has to be defying all these descriptions." (Gordon Cano – voice, Telecaster)

Violent Femmes are used to the pressures of categorisation – their brand new provocative pop already tarred with the brush of everything from 'folk punk' to 'Ramones go skiffle'. Logically, they endeavour to avoid being revivalists or revisionists, too busy taking it all in, screwing it all up into some whirling ball of thinking-fun, emerging with something seductively new.

Gano, just twenty, is a third of the all-male Violent Femmes, joined by Brian Ritchie (acoustic bass guitar) and Victor De Lorenzo (all sorts of drums). The Femmes, building a frantic reputation over here, are most at home when playing live – their hectic, eccentric vitality as likely to find its release in a cinema-queue as a standard rock venue. Their penchant for spontaneously setting up in the street apparently stems from their early, difficult days in home-town Milwaukee when it was impossible to gig properly. These days, they have few such problems, but even so, busking remains an essential part of their repertoire.

The Femmes' reputability, with the recent release of their second LP, is finally dragging them out of the constraints of cult appeal to wider, more profitable horizons. 'Hallowed Ground', the successor to their eponymous debut, also breaks new ground. Along with their first Slash release, its strength lies in homespun, folksy melody and cleverly suggestive lyrics. Whereas the first album obsessed itself with the comical agonies of love and lust, 'Hallowed Ground' ebbs its mad way into more sinister territories.

Gordon and Brian bundle me into a London cab – en route to Victoria – and attempt to explain where the fun ends and the suggestive truths begin. Amongst the chaotic rumble of rush-hour, the tale unwinds.

Two extremes are usually in evidence when people react to The Femmes' jarring, hay-wire pop-art:– love and hate (inevitably). Gordon admits that they tend to attract those strong elements.

"People have come up to each one of us and said, 'When your album came out, it saved my life', and even to a lesser degree, people seem to be enormously affected by what we write. There's all kinds of ways that people see us. I like the idea, for instance, that we're totally open to interpretation. I particularly like the irony in what we do because that's always around us in whatever we do. Some of the songs might have been written with a very sincere feeling, just for myself. Then, we might end up playing it in front of a crowd. That's pretty ironic. Also, the whole idea of playing rock'n' roll to a live audience sometimes feels totally absurd."

There is always this indelible air of the ridiculous that pervades their live performances and their recorded work, drawn out by the exaggerated methods that they use. Gano feels it, most of all, when they play to an audience. "You're singing something that was written out of your own pain and people are standing about laughing and drinking."

Prophets & Fools

The Femmes occasionally tread thin lines between the whimsical and the less playful. 'Hallowed Ground' in particular features material that Gordon is forever explaining away the pre-conceptions of. 'Jesus Walking On The Water', as a breezy, spiritual knees-up, is easily interpreted as parody whereas it was intended as nothing of the sort.

As Gordon points out, "Especially in England, people seem to see the lighter side of what we do, to the extent that something serious is taken the wrong way. The religious references on the latest LP have been read as tongue-in-cheek, but they are completely sincere. The title track has also been treated that way. The song, 'Hallowed Ground' features a spoken intro which is completely serious, but most people thought we were just making fun. It reads, 'The prophet is a fool/The spiritual man is mad/For the multitude of thine inequity/And the great hatred', which is taken from The Old Testament. Originally, we wanted the Scripture to be written on the sleeve, to show people that it wasn't something I had written myself. Strangely, the record company left it off at the last minute, which I find difficult to believe was just an oversight. We wanted to make it clear that the song *was* intended to be taken literally."

So, presumably, the song was written from the point of view of a traditional Christian belief?

"It would *have* to be", Gordon replies, "Because that is my belief. The song, 'Hallowed Ground' is about how the spiritual man is considered to be insane because society is full of so much sin and hatred. Well, those lines were written thousands of years ago, but the fundamental reason of it is still true today. It has been true all through mankind."

Or, as Brian reasons, "People can be prophets and still be fools. You only have to look at somebody like Hitler. Some of the things he said were brilliant, but he was also a madman. Anyone can be those two extremes at the same time. There's prophets in every religion and Christians hate people from other religions. So, does that mean that the only true prophets are Christians?"

"It just depends who you talk to," drawls Gordon, bringing the digression to a close, "because I don't hate people from other religions."

Brian, Gordon & Victor: The Femmes themselves.

The Femmes are composed of a distinctive looseness which finds time for all the subtle nuances necessary to drag you back. Their much talked about folk element exists, but in no way quaint or gimmicky. Their quality lies in their manic pace, their edge of naughtiness, their fresh inventiveness. They lack the unhealthy self-control of most modern pop, instead falling back on their expert minimalism – Gordon's jabbing guitar, Brian's fluid bass and Victor's restless percussion. The folk lies embedded in the earthy honesty of it all. Gano writes from an autobiographical viewpoint.

10

THE GO·BETWEENS

Photo by Tony Mottram

"Success doesn't come to bands in Australia who are good as easily as it does here. After a while you begin to realise there's no money in it so you start to write and play songs that only you like. No-one's going to give you £50,000 to make an album like they do here. You realise it's a dead-end to an extent so you might as well please yourself, and write the songs that you want to write. That's what we do; that's where we come from."

Thus Robert Forster accounts for the individuality of the Go-Betweens' charmingly edgy pop music. He, along with the group's other founder member Grant MacLennan, contrived to escape the situation of their formation – Brisbane, Australia, 1977 – and so, after two local independent singles, they flew for England in 1980. Eccentric Scottish music enthusiast Alan Horne, then the toast of the music press for his Postcard label (Orange Juice, Josef K, and Aztec Camera), bumped into them in London and took them to Scotland to gig and record a single 'I Need Two Heads'.

Though they soon returned to Australia they were back the next year with new drummer Lindy Morrison after Rough Trade picked up on their debut LP 'Send Me A Lullaby'. Two years of odd jobs and sleeping on floors followed, while they continued playing and recording, releasing the inspirational 'Before Hollywood' album early last year. Robert Vickers (absent from the interview) an old friend from Brisbane days, subsequently took over bass duties, freeing Grant to play second guitar.

Despite their growing stature, as last year progressed relations with Rough Trae became increasingly strained. "There was a desperation to find a hitmaker," explains Robert. "First it was Scritti Politti, then the Aztecs, then the Smiths. We were caught while Rough Trade were shifting from co-operative to corporation." The label expressed displeasure at the bands "Uncommercial" 'Man O'Sand' single, and finally Geoff Travis (Rough Trade chief) met them in New York over Christmas and announced that there was no money for their third album as arranged. That was that.

"The thing that really grated," says Robert, "was the acclaim that 'Before Hollywood' got." Still, their saviour soon appeared in the form of Sire records, thanks to recommendations from Warners America, and Geoff Travis, to Sire boss Seymour Stein. They were sent to Cannes, France to record a new album (to be released soon under the title 'Spring Hill Fair'), though they still remain somewhat reluctantly based in England. According to Robert "You only need to see two or three other places to realise that London doesn't come up to scratch."

The prospective tracks for 'Spring Hill Fair' are extremely impressive. Thankfully they haven't suffered from the typical major label psychosis of embalming their music in a suffocating gel of synthesiser and brass – if anything these new recordings are probably more sparse and spacious than their predecessors. There are occasional keyboards though, like the haunting contribution from the famed Jacques Loussier (who owns the Cannes studio) on the new single 'Part Company', a stream of bitter recrimination that will be the first single. Its prospective follow-up is 'Bachelor Kisses', according to Lindy "our first stab at a hit single", an elegant ballad of melodic morality – the crucual line in it seems to be the plaintive part-advice, part-question, part-accusation of *"faithful's not a bad word"*.

For me the attraction of The Go-Between's brittle pop lies in its prepondency to disappear in unexpected directions, avoiding the simplest positions, while relishing in the honesty of its inconclusiveness. The corollary of this is that their songs often eschew obvious melodies and can, as they have themselves acknowledged in the past, relish in a slight perversity. Robert warms to my suggestion that his most instant compositions have been 'Lee Remick' and 'Karen' way back on their first Australian single but otherwise parries my thrust.

"To me a band that is awkward and perverse are Prefab Sprout who have

36

ISSUE #21
9/84

From a publishing perspective, Issue 21 proved bittersweet. Having taken the plunge to go monthly, and having brought the printing process back to the UK for a faster turnaround, another dock strike now halted the import of paper itself (probably from Finland!), and our new printers presented us with a fait accompli: our flagship monthly issue would have to be printed on cheaper paper stock if it was to be printed at all. So much for competing in the world of glossy magazines.

This was bad news enough, and it certainly seemed like the printers were taking their supply chain problems out on their newest and weakest customer, but the print itself was appallingly off centre, for which there was no viable excuse. Furthering this visual disaster, designer Russell Tate was overwhelmed by the deadline demands; the layout lacked its usual urgency. It's a tough issue to flick through all these years down the line.

Fortunately, this rather dismal backdrop was brightened by the front cover: a (then) exclusive photograph by Anton Corbijn promoting an equally exclusive interview with U2 on the eve of *The Unforgettable Fire*. This interview came at the band's own request, and it was conducted by Yours Truly, also at their behest. (Not being a big fan, I was happy to send our eager Christian rock correspondent Martin Wroe, but word came back that they insisted on the editor.) The experience was daunting, this being *Jamming!*'s first corporate excursion outside the country; it was rendered more so when press officer Neil Storey's stomach ulcer kicked in before take-off at Heathrow and he tried to disembark and leave me to my own devices in Dublin! Somehow, I convinced him to stay on board (or perhaps the plane just took off!), and at the other end I was treated like royalty by a band that was already considered as such, at least by their fans. Indeed, when Bono, referring to a previous *Jamming!* I brought with me, commented that 'If U2 was a magazine, it would look something like this', it was the highest compliment possible – unless you hated the band in which case it confirmed *Jamming!*'s commercial sensibilities. Bono's sweet-talking aside, the interview itself was conducted almost entirely with The Edge, a trade-off of sorts in this delicate dance in which U2 sought *Jamming!*'s credibility and we sought their selling power. Still, The Edge had plenty to say for himself, eloquently so, and without any pretensions to grandiosity, at least by comparison. It seemed too good a story to waste on just one issue, so we didn't.

Elsewhere, Chris Heath furthered his résumé with modestly composed pieces on The Go-Betweens and The Woodentops, Jonh Wilde wrote with typical wide-eyed zeal about Violent Femmes, and Bruce Dessau had a few rounds with The Pogues. Plus, future media star Phill Jupitus rendered his debut in suitably memorable fashion with a cartoon strip entitled *Hamming!*, under his ranting nom de plume, Porky The Poet. There were further book, film, label and media profiles, none of which was likely to set the world on fire, though credit is due to writer Hugh Morley, who had worked his way up from various 'What's Cooking' profiles and LP reviews and was rewarded now with a commission to write… a three-page piece about the glories of music publishing (i.e. songwriting). Finally, a full-page Faith Brothers feature served as an unintended warning of yet another impending distraction: having raved about this Fulham duo's self-pressed single 'The Tradesman's Entrance' in the previous issue, I'd found myself besieged by A&R people and was effectively serving as a gate-keeper for the act. But there was little time to think of where this role might lead me, let alone sleep on it: with the new monthly schedule upon us, we were fast on to the next issue.

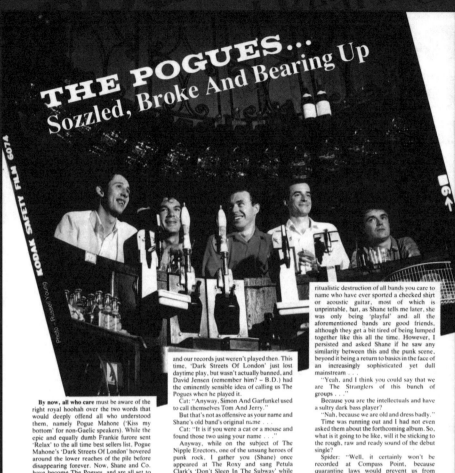

THE POGUES…
Sozzled, Broke And Bearing Up

Photo – Russell Young

KODAK SAFETY FILM 6074

By now, all who care must be aware of the right royal hoohah over the two words that would deeply offend all who understood them, namely Pogue Mahone ('Kiss my bottom' for non-Gaelic speakers). While the epic and equally dumb Frankie furore sent 'Relax' to the all time best sellers list, Pogue Mahone's 'Dark Streets Of London' hovered around the lower reaches of the pile before disappearing forever. Now, Shane and Co. have become The Pogues, and are all set to inflict their particular brew of footstomping folk melodies onto an eager public with a soon-come album and an imminent national tour supporting Elvis Costello. I rendezvoused with Shane (guitar + vocals), Cat (bass + vocals) and late arrival Spider (titanic tin whistle), fifty percent of the ensemble, in yes, you guessed it, a public house, to discuss punk rock, singing postmen and other things that really matter . . .

While Spider was absent from the opening questions, and Cat played the world weary cynic, Shane played the steadying influence and sage in the inteview. All this from a man who was once a Nipple Erector. Just to clear the subject up once and for all, I reminded Shane that The Nipple Erectors had also been forced to shorten their name (to The Nips), asking him if he saw any similarities in the circumstances . . .

"Well, in those days, people thought the name was sexist, which was pretty stupid since it was thought up by our girl bass player. We couldn't even get gigs as The Nipple Erectors

42

and our records just weren't played then. This time, 'Dark Streets Of London' just lost daytime play, but wasn't actually banned, and David Jensen (remember him? – B.D.) had the eminently sensible idea of calling us The Pogues when he played it.

Cat: "Anyway, Simon And Garfunkel used to call themselves Tom And Jerry."

But that's not as offensive as your name and Shane's old band's original name . . .

Cat: "It is if you were a cat or a mouse and found those two using your name . . ."

Anyway, while on the subject of The Nipple Erectors, one of the unsung heroes of punk rock, I gather you (Shane) once appeared at The Roxy and sang Petula Clark's 'Don't Sleep In The Subway' while pulling petals off a daffodil. Is this true, and if so, would you consider yourself as some kind of forerunner to Morrisey?

"Yeah, I can remember something like that happening, in fact I think The Jam were supposed to be playing that night. Except that I think I sang 'Downtown'. As for Morrisey, I don't think he's half the performer I am."

What about these raw onion sandwiches you were renowned for eating, not to mention the infamous tomato sauce fights?

"This is all lies, I deny it all!!! (laughs). They were just days of your youth, we 'ad a great time and although we never had any money, we somehow managed . . ."

A lot has been made by the media about some kind of new music which is a return to basics in the same way as punk was, linking bands such as The Shilleleagh Sisters, Boothill Foottappers and The Pogues as some kind of 'punkabilly' movement. As soon as the subject was brought up, Cat entered into a lengthy, but predominantly obscene,

ritualistic destruction of all bands you care to name who have ever sported a checked shirt or acoustic guitar, most of which is unprintable, but, as Shane tells me later, she was only being 'playful' and all the aforementioned bands are good friends, although they get a bit tired of being lumped together like this all the time. However, I persisted and asked Shane if he saw any similarity between this and the punk scene, beyond it being a return to basics in the face of an increasingly sophisticated yet dull mainstream . . .

"Yeah, and I think you could say that we are The Stranglers of this bunch of groups . . ."

Because you are the intellectuals and have a sultry dark bass player?

"Nah, because we are old and dress badly."

Time was running out and I had not even asked them about the forthcoming album. So, what is it going to be like, will it be sticking to the rough, raw and ready sound of the debut single?

Spider: "Well, it certainly won't be recorded at Compass Point, because quarantine laws would prevent us from leaving the country."

Shane: "It'll be about half originals and half covers, which I think is probably taking liberties because there are so many songs better than the ones we have written. But give us another twenty years and we'll be up there with The Wolftones and The Dubliners. This is just the start of a long career."

With the mind-boggling thought of The Pogues at forty, and with last orders being called, I just have time to squirt out the hack's chestnut, heroes/influences . . .

Cat: "Elvis Costello, but he's a bit fat at the moment, like Robert De Niro in 'Raging Bull'."

Shane: "Christy Moore, and The Dubliners, good authentic Irish stuff with that real rebel spirit."

Spider: "Berni Flint, the singing postman, or was it milkman? But where is he now?"

Aaah, the transient, fickle world of modern music. Let's hope that The Pogues are still around at forty. By then maybe they'll buy another round . . .

- Bruce Dessau

In 1983, I briefly dated someone who took a shine to my leather biker jacket somewhere between Forest Hill station and East Croydon. Her name was Pennie, she was a neighbour and friend of Tony Fletcher and a fan of his band Apocalypse, and following a gig we attended together in Forest Hill, she took me to meet him at his mum's place in nearby Crystal Palace. I knew Tony's band and his magazine *Jamming!* and so we got chatting. I think our friendship sparked the idea of me writing about music. Something I'd never even thought of before.

The brilliant thing about Tony was that he was really fired up by the music scene and really supportive of anybody else who felt the same way. And so, in 1984, I found the number of *Jamming!*'s office, phoned him up and asked to come in and meet him. He immediately commissioned me to start writing for the magazine. He also gave me a lift back to South London.

Just before jumping out of his car at the lights on Camberwell Green, I asked Tony why he had taken me on without seeing any of my writing. He simply replied that he could see by my enthusiasm for music that I could do it. Maybe he saw a bit of himself in me.

Tony gave me all sorts of breaks. He even made me the magazine's first regular film critic after I interviewed esteemed movie journalist Barry Norman. Best of all, *Jamming!* gave me the chance to interview terrific bands. I got to profile the very young and very talented Roddy Frame. I went on the first Creation Records tour of Europe and stood in for one of The Jesus & Mary Chain on stage in Germany. I probed Dr Robert of the Blow Monkeys at RCA Records HQ, finishing up by raiding the office mini-bar, impossibly thrilling back in the day. And on the subject of drinking, a taped interview with The Pogues in a pub off Oxford Street proved almost impossible to transcribe because of the sound of clanking beer glasses. Theirs, not mine. **Bruce Dessau**

U2

Excepting live albums and video, U2 have been silent, both on record and in the media, for a year and a half. Now back with an Eno-produced album and a world-wide tour, they give an exclusive interview to Jamming! to explain what makes them tick.

Words: Tony Fletcher.

Photos: Anton Corbijn.

the pride of lions

23

Chapter 1:
Stranger In A Strange Land

Dublin in the middle of a summer heatwave is a fair city indeed. A long, narrow town that hugs the Irish coast preciously, it is full of wide, spacious streets that exhibit its glowing architecture. A warm and friendly city, with equally vibrant people, it seems so much further than just a short hop across the Irish Sea. Follow the River Liffey – with its putrid stench in the summer heat – down to the docks, and you come to Windmill Lane, a back alley surrounded by the crumbling buildings now familiar to any city's docklands. Here are U2's offices, conveniently placed on the same premises as the studios they do almost all their recording and mixing in.

In a country of only three-and-a-half-million, U2 must be virtually Ireland's biggest export – only Guinness springs to mind as a more popular commodity. And I find it hard to believe I'm here – invited by the band who simply *don't do* many interviews, and in this case, have decided not to do any others to coincide with their new album release in Britain. After eight months of negotiations and tentative dates, I'm finally here, the man they requested. Which is a bit ridiculous, because U2 have never been my favourite band.

When they made their first visits to the British shores and the London centrepoint around the turn of the decade, U2's boisterous enthusiasm and unashamedly rock approach was at odds with the hardline independent mood of the time. Then it seemed as if they were part of the old order; but as the anti-heroes of the day either simply faded away or opted to cop out and become pop stars, U2 became almost a last refuge, still powering on through self-motivation, pride and an undeniable sense of purpose.

In 1984, U2 stand loud and proud above almost the whole music scene, trading on emotion when others couldn't define the word in a month of (bloody) Sundays. Any band that can still have two platinum albums in the charts fifteen months after last releasing a single have obviously got a very special relationship with the public, even if that very same feat brings back memories of the Pink Floyds and Led Zeppelins of yester-year. But it is not enough to simply love or hate a band for their actions; if they can play such a vital role in peoples' lives, it becomes a necessary task – for myself at any rate – to find out *why*.

And so I am sat down with The Edge, U2's brilliantly individual guitarist and occasional keyboard player. In typical U2 fashion, Bono had decided it was time someone else played Vox Pop. The idea that the others would join the interview was scuppered by the late night just spent in the studio, The Edge having to be woken to be told I was ready and waiting. An intensely likeable man and a happy new father (the first in the U2 camp), The Edge made his introductions, sat down and waited for the cameras to start rolling (more of which later). Island's amiable press officer, Neil Storey, had informed me they were building up for this – "They are going to *talk* and *talk*", he said. Of that, there was no mistake.

Chapter 2:
Tell Us About The New Album, John. . . .

Jamming!: After finishing the World Tour last Autumn, with this big success around the world, did you find yourselves at a crossroads, having achieved massive ambitions, having no. 1 albums, and actually being a *big* band?

The Edge: Yeah, it was an interesting time, having climaxed – certainly commercially – in that way. But those sort of ambitions have never been important to us; we never set out to make number one.

But it must be a thrill – 'War' came in at number one.

Yeah, it was remarkable. But the thing that really has kept us going, kept us fresh, has been an artistic ambition. We didn't climax on that tour or with that album. We're getting closer with every record, but I don't think we'll really meet that ambition, which is one of the reasons I think we've a few years ahead of us.

Is it as a lot of people say, 'Once you think you're perfect – that's the time to give up.'?

I think so. It must be very depressing to find yourself at the pinnacle of whatever it is. The top of Mount Everest must be a very depressing place. You're there so, you know what's next? But with us, we've never come close to peaking creatively, so although 'War' was a milestone for us it never gave us the sense of "We've arrived!", or "This is it!"

Most people are going to be very interested to know why you've changed producer.

We've been trying to change producers since 'Boy'! You might not believe that, but Steve (Lillywhite) had said, "I've been doing a couple of albums with bands and just at the moment I'd like to cut it down to one album and then a gap of a couple of records." But we tried, and couldn't find anyone we were as

confident with as Steve, so, on two occasions at almost the last minute, Steve came back and agreed to do the album.

I thought it might have been something to do with the recent spate of bands coming along, using Steve Lillywhite, and sounding exactly like U2.

No, that wasn't really a contributing factor. We just felt that to get into any sort of a rut is a bad idea, so we like to change the things that are variable as often as we can. The fact that we failed to find someone we were pleased with on October and War was a shame. But I think those were albums no-one else could have produced in the end. Because Steve has a particular style – he's really good in the studio at maintaining the momentum of work, at not letting things go off the boil. Keeping morale high. And those two albums were extremely difficult to make. I think in a sense that was one of the factors that made them the albums they are.

The Edge: "The primary motivation behind the group is our own integrity is what we *believe* to be right."

So why Brian Eno?

Well, Eno is somebody that we've thought highly of for a while. Not only because of his own work, but also because of his work with Bowie and Talking Heads. We just really enjoyed what he did, so we met him and Danny Lanois – who's also worked on this record – and there seemed to be a lot of common ideas between us.

It wasn't until we met the guy that we were finally committed to the idea of him producing, because he is a very, very honest, no-bullshit kind of person. He's worked with some of the most obscure avant-garde artists, but I think that's just because he's a little bored with some of the mainstream things. We felt maybe he was a little too contrived in the people he works with, but not at all.

It seems a strange choice.

I think the album will answer all the questions people have about Brian Eno's production. He's a really solid guy, and he also agrees with so many of our unwritten rules about music, the axioms upon which we judge our music and other music. He seems to have so many common feelings about things, it's remarkable.

You changed studios as well, didn't you?

Yeah. We'd been toying with this ambient music idea, which was one of the common music ideas in fact, because Brian Eno has a label called Ambient that a lot of his records come out on. The idea being that instead of going into a dead, acoustic atmosphere, which is the usual studio sound, and then trying to revitalise the recorded work using effects and reverberation and all the standard music trappings, we would go into a very live room and try to do the opposite – try and tame what would be a wild sound, something with natural excitement.

I've just seen some photos of the place – Castle Slane – with this enormous ballroom where you were recording. That looked quite strange.

That turned out to be almost too wild for us because the roof was about thirty foot high and it's just a huge oval dome. We did a lot of work there, for that wild sound. It worked in many ways, because I think there are sounds on this album that we just couldn't have got from a studio.

Have you ever felt caught at having an identifiable sound? Despite what I've said about Steve Lillywhite's production, a U2 record is instantly recognisable.

Well certainly we've never wanted to create a sound we couldn't diverge from so I suppose we have reached the point when we wanted to try something else. But in a funny sort of way, we're not really in control of the sound, because the sound is us. If we were David Bowie or someone, we could bring in a whole new set of session musicians and they could play the album and that would be fine; it would have a different feel. We could do a country album, a soul album, or an African album. But really the sound of the group is us – so although we can influence ourselves in what we're listening to, ultimately it's not really within our control! Which has been proved from this album – we've changed the producer, the studio, everything that we could, but there is still that sound that is *us*.

Chapter 3: Rewriting History

The biggest criticism of U2 is about being – to coin an old phrase – blatantly rockist. You're known for playing stadiums, doing fifty-date tours across America, not doing many interviews and so on. It's a criticism that's commonly levelled – does it bother you?

Well, obviously it's not something we relish, being thought of in those terms. I suppose I can understand it because we haven't done many interviews, but the reason

we haven't isn't because we're boring or anything like that. It's the opposite. Interviews for us are like a total thing. It's not good enough for us to do a fifteen-minute interview and talk about our favourite clothes shops and what films we've seen lately. For us, every time we do an interview, everything comes out. And what was happening was that every interview, because it was done like that, was the same. So we just felt that until we decided that there was something important we wanted to say that we'd avoid doing interviews, certainly with papers we'd done lots of interviews with in the past. And unfortunately that was perceived as "We no longer need the exposure, so we're just not gonna bother", but that wasn't the thinking behind it at all.

On the level of the stadiums, I think there's a certain sort of naive idea in England that stadiums are bad, that if a band has really got any credibility they stick to the small theatres.

band that played the Hammersmith Palais, we're far bigger than that now.

Do you as a group, agree on a limit on how many people you can play to and still keep that atmosphere?

We haven't found that limit yet. We've played open-air festivals of fifty-thousand and managed to create the sort of atmosphere that one associates with a club. That's the way we approach *every* live show and I don't think we would compromise that. If it's not going to happen, I don't think we'd do it. But I really believe we can make the stadium work.

Isn't it a case of, someone comes along and because they're paying the money, they're gonna enjoy it anyway. You're back to that thing where the group is right up there on the stage, and they're paying however much it is to possibly be a long distance from the group. So they end up thinking, "Because I've paid my money, I'm going to make sure I enjoy it.?"

Well I don't necessarily agree. If you're in a

Later on in the day, I have plenty of time to talk to the rest of the band, or more precisely, Bono and bassist Adam Clayton, drummer Larry Mullen being notoriously distrustful of the press. Adam is a genial, well-spoken man (his public school voice is more Prince Charles than Terry Wogan), who, like Bono, is happy to sit down over a cup of tea and talk about things in general.

The Edge: "We're just gonna rewrite history concerning the stadiums."

He tells me of U2's first two releases, brought out on CBS Ireland, the first of which catapulted them to no. 1 there, but the second of which apparently almost finished them off. Remembering never again to put out music they weren't satisfied with, they haven't looked back since. Adam laughs when I ask if they're the biggest band in Ireland. "I don't really think The Wolftones are much competition," he boasts. Rephrasing the question (are Van Halen more popular? in essence), he tells me, "Well, we've built up to the extent where yes, we are the biggest band here. Last Summer we organised the Phoenix Park Festival, where we played with The Eurythmics, Simple Minds and Big Country. We drew thirty thousand people to that, which is more than Bob Dylan on his recent visit. I'm quite confident that if we decided to do that again, then we'd get 60,000 next time. And to be honest, I don't really feel you can pull more people in Ireland." Unless you're The Pope of course.

Adam's tale carries a valuable sting. In Britain, Culture Club are (unarguably?) bigger than U2, but in Ireland, where if you sell 500 singles you're a hit band, 30,000 people at one concert means *there are no contenders*. And realising that when you walk the streets of your town you are a Folk Hero, has affected U2 only to the extent that their obvious sense of pride often tumbles into apparent ignorance. If they weren't important in their home country, then why else would Bono be appointed to a committee on unemployment? Why else would Smash Hits suggest he is a future Irish Prime Minister? Why did I forget to ask him about this?

Chapter 5: I WILL NOT FOLLOW

Jamming!: I saw U2 twice at The Lyceum on your first visits to London – once sandwiched between The Bunnymen and (vastly different) Thompson Twins – and both times the bill was full of hip independent bands. Then U2 were suddenly onstage with Bono clambering all over the PA, and you looking like a guitar hero, and it seemed so different from other music around then. Was that something you were deliberately doing?

The Edge: It wasn't something we could help. When we go onstage, again it's a total thing. If things are going well then I think we maintain some sort of level-headedness and some sort of calmness. But if anything starts happening which we don't have control over, then anything can happen. Bono's probably the most extreme in that case, and I've seen him literally stop the show, bring the audience onstage and just totally lose his head. And that's the dangerous side of the band live. It's one of the attractive things about us – you really don't know what's going to happen. People used to think it was a contrived thing, that you knew Bono was going to do a certain amount of jumping around the rigging, and the lights, what-have-you, but he's never planned it. In fact we used to sit him down in

Which is the way I think

Yeah, but that argument doesn't hold any water when you analyse the logistics of it. If we were to go to, say, England at this stage in our career and play theatres, we'd be doing three weeks at the Hammersmith Palais, which would mean – even with three weeks – we wouldn't meet the demand for tickets. That would mean you'd have scalping – people paying thirty, forty, fifty quid for a ticket, which we certainly don't want to happen; and you'd get a kind of elitist thing where only people who happen to be first to the ticket outlets get the tickets and not everyone who wants to see us will be able to. And then I think after two weeks of playing in the same venue, I'd be going mad.

Surely there's a compromise between being able to meet the ticket demand and playing somewhere where, to the people at the back, you're just little dots on stage. Have you not been to festivals yourself where you have seen the band as a little dot and maybe felt "This isn't close enough," or "There's not enough atmosphere."

I know what you're saying. I've been to a few shows like that, but I've also been to one or two shows where I wasn't particularly close to the stage, and I *didn't* feel isolated. And I think that would be the only way we would take on a stadium, if we felt we could do that. We avoid stadiums where there is this huge gap between the stage and the back of the audience; we try and do them where there is some sort of distance we feel can handle. I've seen Bruce Springsteen in Wembley and I was just knocked out! And I wasn't close to the stage.

Is that what you hope U2 can do?

That I think is what we're setting out to do. It's quite a brave thing to try. It's far better than just admitting that this can't be done and deciding to stay with a venue like The Palais, which would be a total *lie* in a sense, because we're not that band anymore. We're not the

club, it's far more difficult to be objective about a band that's onstage because you're almost onstage yourself, but if you're at a stadium and it's not good it's very easy to just turn away and get yourself a Coca-Cola. To catch people's attention and keep them with you for a whole show is far more difficult in a stadium. So if there is that atmosphere, you can assume that you've earned it. As opposed to sweeping a small venue into a tide of emotion which I think is a lot easier.

I really think that of any band making this transition to arenas or stadiums from theatres, we have the best chance, because I know that the people in the stadiums wil be the people that we've seen in all the theatres. I've no apprehension about them – we're just gonna rewrite history concerning the stadiums.

That's a big claim to make

I think people will change their minds about them when we play them. In the past Wembley has had this stigma of being a bummer. I've seen a few bum gigs there, I can understand.

The Jam bowed out by playing Wembley and it didn't work. They were very similar to you, being the archetypal live band, building up their following from nothing without really needing the media. It's quite a claim to make isn't it? Saying you're going to rewrite history over the stadiums?

Well that's the way we feel. It's not necessarily that U2 are so far ahead of everyone else. It's really that I know the people that are gonna be there. I virtually know them by name, so I really am not worried about us being in a stadium.

Half the argument about Wembley is that it's seated and I wouldn't imagine U2 are the sort of group that would want to play seated venues.

No, I don't like seated venues generally. I think it's possible to take out the seats at the front – and I'll certainly be arguing for that.

the dressing room and say, "Bono! You are *not* gonna do this tonight!", and he'd say, "No, I've decided that's over. I'm not going to do anything." But in a given situation onstage it's just he can't help himself – this is his only release.

Going back to when you first came over to London. . . . I know you were going for a few years before doing those sort of concerts. Did you actually feel very different from the other bands around you? You certainly looked it.

Yes we did feel very different. Coming from Ireland, I think we had this gift of objectivity which was something nobody else around seemed to have. They were so immersed in this kind of music and this whole idea that nobody seemed to see it from the other idea and see how ridiculous it all was.

What do you think was so ridiculous about it? It was all very anti-stardom and very down-to-earth.

Well, everybody seemed to be saying that but I never really saw that to be the case. I saw everybody perceiving themselves as a star in their own right. We would go backstage after a show and talk to some of these groups, and really, the attitude was so negative, so elitist, that I soon lost respect for a lot of these bands and that movement generally. They were playing and recording under this banner of anti-the-old-order, but in fact they were falling into the same traps, on this star thing.

Although I'd agree with that to an extent, people were saying we thought we'd learnt the lessons about stadiums.

I can see your train of thought but that's based on the axiom that stadiums are bad – I don't necessarily think they are. I've seen some really successful gigs in stadiums. It's the bands attitudes to stadiums that can be really bad – you're talking about the bands of the seventies and their attitude. I think live performance had become almost a way of life to them and it was nothing to do with the audience and contact with the people that were buying their albums. It was all to do with a totally unnatural way of life where they were the centre of attention. Their feet were not on the ground at all.

Is that, for example, why Bono often pulls somebody out of the crowd to dance?

Well one of the reasons . . . . A lot of the time it's just trying to think of something to do! He's always saying "If I could only bloody well play guitar I wouldn't have to do all these stupid things." But the guy onstage has got so much to let out he just pulls up what he can.

Chapter 6:
KEEPING APACE OF THE BONO VOX

Ironically, Bono arrives within five minutes of the two-hour interview winding up. A firm handshake, a warm smile and there can be no denying his depth of character. Four years ago, in one of the band's first interviews, Bono recalled how, as a child, "I really felt I had something to offer the world." This he must feel he has proved; he also seems to feel there's plenty left.

Sitting down next to me on the sofa, he immediately picks up a copy of Jamming! and delivers an incredible compliment. "If U2 was a magazine, It would look something like this," he says in his soft Irish brogue. Mumbling thanks and something along the lines of we do what we believe in, like them, he warms to the subject and raves about the positiveness of it all. "But really, when you think of it, you haven't even started. When you think that U2 sell half a million albums in Britain, and that all these people should be reading something as positive as this . . ."

Longing to jump for the tape recorder but frightened of missing the next vital burst, I let Bono continue. "To me, there's two types of groups – those who use everything positive

about themselves, and those who pull from the negative side of themselves. I find the latter deeply disturbing.

"I always think that one's self and one's music should be part of each other. Whenever I hear someone say 'This is me, and my music is something else,' then I feel something is very wrong."

Jumping to his feet, Bono offers to give me a guided tour of the impressive Windmill Lane set-up. Past the control room where Brian Eno is busy mixing and forbidding intrusion, he stops me by the reception, pointing at the stairwell. "See this?", he says, standing in a small cube of space under two flights of stairs. "This is where we recorded the drums on our previous albums. Steve Lillywhite found he get the most incredible ambient sound from putting the drums here and getting it all reverbing from the stairwell. I think he's searching the world for somewhere else he can get as brilliant a drum sound!" Before I can comment, Bono is finished with this and is whisking me up the stairs for more delights.

"There's always been two sides to U2," he says as we climb the stairs. "The energy and atmosphere. With Steve Lillywhite, it was always the energy that showed, but now, Brian Eno is helping bring out the atmosphere again."

Windmill Lane, it transpires, is more than just a studio, boasting film, animation and video facilities amongst other things. Upstairs, somebody has been experimenting on U2's behalf, putting snippets of old Japanese Samurai films and speeded up day-to-night city sequences to a demo of 'Wire'. Elsewhere, a documentary is being made about Sean McBride, the founder of the IRA and the only ever receiver of both Nobel and Lenin peace prizes. "A great man," says Bono, but before I get the chance to seize on this line of talk and try and clear up some of U2's Catholic views, Bono is back downstairs and leading me across the car park to the band's own offices. Here the group is run with military efficiency, and while all around us stage sets are being designed, equipment mended and Visas obtained, Bono takes me into manager Paul McGuiness's office to play me a tape of 'Pride', the only song finished at this stage.

Bono: "We've done very few songs – normally we just make music."

Immediately striking me as probably the most commercial thing U2 have done, I stand taking it all in with Bono enthusing next to me. I almost expect him to jump on the speakers and start singing, but he seems to restrain himself. Just.

"'Pride' is the best song we've ever written," he says. "But we've done very few songs – normally we just make music. 'I Will Follow' was a song, but then the next one wasn't until 'Sunday Bloody Sunday'. It's very different from the rest of the album though – there's nothing on there as straight as this."

I suggest that such a commercial number must be the obvious choice for next single, commenting that it would sound great on the radio.

"I know, but we've never really had any airplay. It would be weird if suddenly we did. It might be too easy to put out something we know will be a hit – maybe we should put out something a bit more *wild*." Bono's eyes light up again. "Do you know we're the only band to have done Top Of The Pops whose single went *down* the charts the next week?"

Yes I do. The Edge was very proud of that one too.

Bono was right when he said there was no other song like 'Pride' on the album. Anybody new to U2 and buying 'The Unforgettable Fire' on the strength of the single is in for one hell of a disappointment – this is not an album full of hits. What it is, however, is a forceful collection of atmospheric ideas and themes, forgettable at first but strangely haunting and soon firmly implanted. Eno's production has succeeded in withdrawing some of that overpowering force that put U2 in the bracket of Heavy Metal and placed them firmly back to a land where emotion is the driving force, challenging knowingly for the attention it deserves.

Though 'Pride' is undoubtedly the stand-out track, other delights soon follow. For example, 'A Sort Of Homecoming', a throwback to the U2 known and loved by many, or 'Wire', with its awkward guitar line and insistent chord changes. Likewise 'Indian Summer Sky', often reminiscent of U2's typically brash approach before throwing itself into haunting choruses or vaguely tribal fillers. These tracks are perfectly complemented by the more gentle songs, the best example being the title track. A full orchestra of strings for the first time on a U2 record hover in the background, with piano and guitar back up Bono's soft yet firm voice. 'Bad', possibly the only other single on the album, starts gently with its amalgam of guitars before building up to a firey finale.

The album ends with another ode to Martin Luther King, star of 'In The Name Of Love', simply titled 'MLK'. "Sleep tonight and may your dreams be realised", laments Bono to an almost folk melody over nothing but a simple synth.

With its many strengths, 'The Unforgettable Fire' only slips when falling into the trap of self-indulgence. '4th of July', assumedly another attempt at atmospherics, passes by on even the tenth hearing without any ado, while the strangely-titled 'Elvis Presley And America', though captivating, wanders around in its box-like sound without achieving anything. Apparently, Bono made up the words as it went along, and it shows.

'The Unforgettable Fire', when put alongside 'War' for instance, shows how an instantly recognisable band can sound different with a new producer, and Eno, originally such an unusual choice, has proved capable of putting over the pure emotion of U2 much more successfully than Steve Lillywhite. What he's missed out on, however, is in getting the melodies that so often hover around into a straightforward form. U2 deliberately shy away from the commercial, but they don't realise how near they are to achieving it stylishly at their best. 'Pride (In The Name Of Love)' is the perfect example of U2 mixing all their attributes together, it's a shame they don't go for it more.

Ultimately, however, it isn't worth criticising. U2 would have made 'The Unforgettable Fire' if their last album had sold two copies – having never followed anyone's rules before, they aren't about to start now. The spiritual side of U2 shines through on this record more than ever, and it will be a lasting memory to me of Bono, staring me in the face, declaring that "The more this album has gone on , the more we've found it's been writing itself, or something's been writing it for us. It's fallen into place of its own accord."

Next month: U2 on religion, wealth, Ireland, and why it all matters.

27

BREAKING DOWN THE BARRIERS

JAMMing!

NOW MONTHLY

No. 22 NOVEMBER 1984 60p U.S.$ 1.50 Eire 97p.

IS THIS MAN A...
GUITAR HERO?
Billy Bragg tells all!

The Unknown Face of Culture Club

The Lions of Pride
U2 – Part Two

★ **Feargal Sharkey**

◯ **The Fall · Gun Club**

★ **10,000 Maniacs**

◻ **Blue Nile**

★ Tony Parsons on Bruce Springsteen

It's a year since we've heard from the man with the quivering tonsils. Paul Davies finds out what he's been up to.

Feargal

What a difference paper stock could make. *Jamming!* 22 felt much more like what the previous, "flagship" monthly edition was meant to be: a shiny glossy music magazine that nonetheless retained a fanzine's edge. We put Billy Bragg on the cover for what was actually his first interview in *Jamming!* despite considerable prior coverage, and it coincided with an excellent agreement made with pop photographer Paul Cox, whereby *Jamming!* set up a session and got exclusive first rights at our own low rates before Paul sold the rest of them at market rate. I love Paul's cover shot as much as I do any that we commissioned, and am glad that we followed up the U2 exclusive (which continued into this issue) by pushing someone properly independent and proudly political.

Bragg's cover status helped offset a piece on Culture Club's guitarist (just, *why*?) and a centre-page spread on the newly solo Feargal

Sharkey (two of his former Undertones bandmates had been included in much less glamorous style in Issue 21). Features on The Fall, The Gun Club and 10,000 Maniacs confirmed Jonh Wilde's excellent indiecentric taste, as did Martin Wroe's piece on the much more polished The Blue Nile, but collectively the line-up suggested that we were slipping back into the all-white all-male content we'd otherwise spent much of 1984 trying to escape. Viewed with such hindsight, asking Tony Parsons to wax lyrical on Bruce Springsteen was hardly the boat-rocker it seemed when Alan McLaughlin first suggested it, but Parsons obliged – for the same fee as everyone else – and his article was superb, one of the best we ever published.

Sales were solid, maybe in the high 20,000s, but the monthly turnaround already felt suicidal. Still, on we soldiered. After all, as far as the public was concerned, *Jamming!* was a proven success story.

ISSUE #22
10/84

BRAGG'S Potent BREW!

Tony Fletcher meets the mobile mouth

•

Paul Cox snaps him pulling poses

Billy Bragg is in a difficult position and he knows it. For the last year he has been everybody's favourite musical underdog: one man, armed with only a guitar, crusading around Britain as support act, firstly to anyone brave enough to be upstaged by him and later, to his own choice of some of the country's biggest bands. Any Jamming! reader who regularly goes to concerts can't have failed to miss him on their travels – the big-nosed Cockney with the gruff voice, scratchy guitar and a suitcase full of clever, heartfelt and frequently energetic little numbers. By the end of October, Bragg will have clocked up over 114 live gigs this year alone, playing to at least a quarter of a million people.

And all thanks to one mini-LP recorded in three days flat in July 1983. A last-ditch effort by a man who'd done the rounds in the dodgily-titled Riff Raff, joined the army for something to do, and left after three months to happily while away his time in a second-hand record shop. Seven songs, with just a voice and a guitar and no great aspirations. If Billy's been quoted on his line *"I don't want to change the world, I'm not looking for a New England, just looking for another girl"* once, then he's been quoted a thousand times. The subsequent success of 'Life's A Riot With Spy Vs. Spy', released first through Charisma and then on Go! caught Billy by surprise. A place in The Top Ten of John Peel's Festive Fifty, two appearances on The Tube, a front cover of the NME, and an indie no. 1 with 50,000 sales under his belt later, the Billy Bragg Success has still refused to release a single, still failed to record with a band and still avoided becoming a headline act.

None of which makes it any easier. With a new album 'Brewing Up With Billy Bragg' just released as part of Go!'s new deal with Chrysalis, those people who have been wondering what the fuss is all about will be looking for a work of art. Which puts a bit of a weight on the poor man's shoulders.

"There's no Godlike Genius of Billy Bragg", he says forcefully. "All people are gonna get with the new album is eleven songs as best as I could play them in July 1984. I've only ever looked upon myself as being able to do what I know I can do. I know I can do gigs. If they get reviewed, that's alright – if they get good reviews, that's great, and if they get bad reviews, well . . . what can I do?"

What indeed? Part of the undeniable charm that is Billy Bragg comes from his self-effacing modesty. The man's never asked to be a star, and he may well never become one. If his musical career was to finish tomorrow, you know he'd be happy with what he's achieved up until now. Which is not bad going by anyone's standards.

Billy Bragg lives in a one-roomed Barrett's house in deepest Acton, "something I wouldn't wish on my worst enemies." It's not exactly spacious, that's for sure – the front door leads into the only room, cluttered as it is with guitars, amplifiers, cassettes and copies of The Beano. A bed will later that evening unfold itself from the wall, while the bathroom is only big enough to swing a newt and the kitchen forms part of the main room. When I arrive on a windy Sunday afternoon, I'm graciously offered a cup of coffee. What could be better? What could be quicker?

The rise to cult status for The Billy Bragg

Collective, perhaps, which was both swift and unexpected. As he says, "It wasn't as if I was schooled by a manager or a record company, under some big campaign 'Billy Bragg is coming'. When I made 'Life's A Riot' I thought 'This is it, this is the very last thing I'm gonna do.' And so I thought 'How am I gonna do it – do I get loads of session musicians in or do it alone?' So I just went 'Sod it', and did it live. And now that in hindsight it's sold all these copies, it looks as if I went in and made a conscious decision to make this really ace album. And I assure you," he stresses, laughing wildly as he does, "it was nothing of the kind. It was three days of losing my voice, my fingers hurting, and, at the end of it, not being sure that we'd got even one or two good tracks!"

In fact he had seven. And most readers will be familiar with them. From the anthemic 'A New England' to the uncompromising 'To Have And Have Not', through the softer 'The Man In The Iron Mask' and 'The Milkman Of Human Kindness', coming out at the other end with 'Lovers Town Revisited', 'Richard' and 'The Busy Girl Buys Beauty', Bragg quickly found himself the darling of the underground. Through Peel's support, press hysteria and an arduous amount of gigging, the word spread and Billy found himself proudly at the top of the indie charts with a national Top 40 album. Not bad when you were just about to jack it all in.

The Billy Bragg Backlash has thankfully stayed away for now, but I put it to him as he fills the kettle that he must be wary of media overkill.

"Yeah, but what can you do about it? I can only refuse you an interview. I've had nothing in Smash Hits or No. 1, and they're the big circulation papers. Alright, so I've had loads of gig reviews, but I do loads of gigs! Likewise, I do lots of fanzine interviews, but I just feel that I'd much rather sit down with some kid and his tape machine, whose fanzine is the most important thing in his life, than do an interview with The sun."

As possibly the busiest solo artist in the country, The Billy Bragg Suitcase has just returned from its first visit to American, as invited guest of Echo & The Bunnymen. The idea of the USA getting Billy Bragg Fever seems most unnerving, and not surprisingly is a way off yet.

"There was a bit of a 'buzz' about me in New York, but I get the feeling they read their NME religiously. In Houston, Texas, there was no buzz whatsoever but I went down the best on the whole tour. Some nights you could feel the hostility coming off the audience. In Salt Lake City I got 46 dollars worth of small change thrown at me – I went round afterwards with a plastic cup." To prove the point, he shows me a half dollar piece, collected on stage – bearing more resemblance to a discus than any coin available in this country.

I put it to him that this might be due to the Britishness of The Billy Bragg Experience?

"What's British about The Milkman Of Human Kindness?" comes the immediate response.

Milkmen? say I hopefully.

"Rubbish," he says with a smile. "They have milkmen in America. I personally would expect it to be very British, but you meet people after the gigs and they talk about a song like 'To Have And Have Not' exactly the same as someone over here. Maybe we underestimate the record buying public in America's ability to be able to take a song with strong social content. All the American record companies offer them is crap. I hate to write

off so many American bands in one go, but the companies think they know what the public want, so they just water everything down, and make it all as inoffensive as possible."

Warming to the subject, Billy quickly gets into his stride. The kettle is still waiting to be filled.

"You see, I'm really surprised that people in *this* country bought 'Life's A Riot'. I thought it was for a really small minority. I was genuinely surprised by the way people reacted. The letters I get – some of them scare me. I got one from a girl a couple of weeks back, who explained the way that 'The Man In The Iron Mask' affected her, and it's exactly the way Tracks Of My Tears affects me. Now when you're a songwriter, you hear a song like Tracks Of My Tears, and think 'God I wish I could write a song like that', and then someone says you have. Maybe I should give up now! They'll probably be saying soon 'If only he'd died after the first album!'"

As the kettle at last finds its way to a running tap, Billy talks about how he found the youth of America thankfully more aware than the dumb Reaganites we paint them as. "I met a lot of very intelligent people who could see that there were definitely things that their country were doing wrong, and that they didn't believe in. But there's no focus for them. What's the point of being a Democrat when the difference between Mondale and Reagan isn't really all that great."

Ah, politics. Anyone already aware of the Billy Bragg Phenomena will be only too aware of Billy's eagerness both to put gigs where his mouth is and argue the toss with any unsuspecting interviewer who happens to drop by for coffee. For a man whose new album includes only two political numbers, it

might seem unusual, but I'd caught the Bragg just after his return from three miners benefits – in miners towns, and on two occasions, in their clubs – and the man wasn't about to be stopped.

"I'm not a political activist by any means," he declares, (just looking for another girl?). "I've never been on a picket line,. I'm not someone who goes out pamphleting and leafleting – I didn't even bother to vote in 1979. But society's become politicised in the last four or five years – the two extremes are coming apart. I couldn't really tell the difference between Heath, Wilson and Callaghan in the '70's – I don't really think it was there to be seen. But I read in a newspaper about five years ago where some Tory minister had cut school meals, and when someone complained about it, his reply was 'What good are school meals if they're being fed to you by the Russians?' That was him justifying taking money from school meals and spending it on missiles. I realised two things from that – one, that they were gonna take the welfare state apart, and two, that they really believed the Russians were gonna come. All that led me to take an interest in politics and see how the Conservatives could be defeated. I always thought that Thatcher would defeat herself until the Falklands War."

Pausing to switch the kettle on at last, he's soon back in full flow. "I've become incredibly politicised since doing these miners gigs. I got a real grilling from this guy in Corby, a middle-aged fellow who obviously wanted to know what motives I had for doing the gig. And I was surprised by the really good coherent argument I put up.

"I think at the end of this – whatever the outcome – we're going to come out with lots of bands who are less shy about dealing with politics in their songs. It's become really unfashionable, and anybody who writes about it immediately gets no end of stick, but there's nothing disrespectful in writing what you feel about. And if you come into contact with the miners strike – and let's face it, who hasn't in this country one way or the other? – then it's up to you to reflect it in your songs. Politics and music are related to each other, because politics is life."

(Here I should say just how welcome it is to meet someone who can talk coherently and passionately about political issues. He's correct when he says it's unfashionable to bring it into music – certainly at Jamming! we get letters both telling us to leave the politics out, and accusing us of being too trendy or sitting on the fence. Luckily, the vast majority realise it is purely a matter of trying to make people aware without forcing it down their throats. Billy's own grasp of matters comes as a refreshing change after the regularity of bands who either throw in a cheap comment, do benefits for the kudos, or simply don't care. But I digress . . . .)

"This last week I've met women who are running three food funds, and they are ordinary people who have never done what they're doing now" continues The Billy Bragg Spokesman. "A woman in Sunderland went up in front of nearly six hundred spikey tops and they listened to her. And they applauded her. So there is a bond to be forged between music and the labour movement. In which some aspects of music stop being about going up to Camden Palace and taking loads of drugs."

At this point I dare to suggest that miners gigs are becoming trendy (more a stab at peoples attitudes than at Bragg himself). As the kettle boils over, so does Bill.

a reasonable day, he remarks. 'I'm really glad this
interview came off. I always wanted it to
happen, but then the more I thought about it . . .

the more stilted . . . The fact that it does appear in the
lyrics I suppose . . . I won't get . . . up a couple
no reason, not just the fact that it's there . . .

"Why should they be trendy? The only people who are going to say they're trendy are the people who won't fucking do them. I have no fear – the bands that are doing miners gigs are standing up to be counted for something else than what the record companies want us to do. We are pointing out that there is more to this than making records and being on Top Of The Pops. Alright, so we're in the entertainments industry, and I've never believed that by joining hands and singing 'Imagine' we'd ever change the world, but if I can do a gig and pull 600 people to raise money for miners families' food funds, then that's what I'll do."

A pause. The kettle's almost cold again now and while Bill warms it up, we somehow broach the subject of The Redskins; not an easy one.

Like Billy Bragg, The Redskins are 'trendy' (a sad fact of life), uncompromising and put their money where their mouth is; more than this both acts are the best of friends. But those who've seen them will be well aware of The Redskins' SWP connections and outwardly militant stance. A subject to be argued with them at a later date, but someone ought to play them The Beatles' 'Revolution' in the meantime. Billy, stressing that he doesn't want to talk about them behind their backs, still gets his point of view over.

"I believe that Labour must win the next General Election and that's fundamental to why I'm a member of the Labour Party, whereas the SWP think there should be a workers revolution as the end of Margaret Thatcher. Now I can't be bothered to go down to pedantics with the SWP about revolution. If they want revolution then let them work towards it, but the things I want to come don't involve us all running up the street and getting shot."

The spoon is hovering between the coffee jar and the cup now but there's not much chance of it finding a home. Billy has a point to prove.

"The only people who would survive a revolution in this country is the army. We've got the best counter-resurgent army in the world – Northern Ireland to here is only an hour away, and they wouldn't hesitate, if they thought there was gonna be a workers revolution. All it would mean is a lot of dead workers. It would put troops on the streets of Gwent and there's no reason to imagine they'd be gone in a week. The Emergency Powers Act would come in, the Suspension of Democracy would come in, the Americans would come in . . . Now does someone who's got a mortgage and two kids want a revolution in this country on those terms? No, but with two kids and a mortgage they're going to want to protect the welfare state and avoid their children being blown up in a nuclear war. So I can see the Labour Party will appeal to the voters of this country, where the SWP won't.

"Having said that, I still think the Redskins are one of the most important bands in Britain today."

I don't believe it. Not about the Redskins, but that the coffee and water have come together in a mug that's being brought over to where I've been patiently sitting. Brewing Up doesn't come in to it!

A ttempting to change the subject, I ask The Billy Bragg Persona if he's happy being a big fish in a small pond.

"Am I?" he inquires, surprised.

Most certainly. You're a real cult, if you don't mind my saying so.

"Well, when I was no. 1 in the Indie Charts, I thought 'Great – there's all these people I really respect, and according to this I'm

selling more than them.' But when you see someone like The Smiths or New Order sit at the top for six months, you think what is the point?"

Trying to prove that I'm not really talking about independent-versus-majors (an argument I've found particularly trivial in recent years), I change tack and ask if he's really set against being a pop star.

"What's a pop star? Does going on the Rock Trivia Quiz make you a pop star? If so I'm a pop star. Does going on The Tube make you a pop star? If so I'm a pop star. Does having a no. 1 LP make you a pop star? If so I'm not a pop star. Does making a single make you a pop star? If so, I'm not a pop star. Does going up to Camden Palace make you a pop star? If so, I'm not. It's totally intangible, Tony. It's like fame. What does fame mean? It means I can go up to Camden Market and if they're selling a Billy Bragg cassette I can go

up to them and take it off them and say 'Thanks, I'm Billy Bragg'. Then I can go to the next clothing stall and they've never heard of me."

It's something a lot of people need.

"Maybe they do. Maybe I need miners benefits to justify what I do. Personally, given the opportunity to play 'To Have And Have Not' on Top Of The Pops, I'd take it. I don't think The Clash proved anything by not doing Top Of The Pops. To become a star, I think you've got to want to – you can become a cult by accident."

Another gem from The Billy Bragg Phrasebook.

But Billy Bragg is still in a difficult position. Finding myself subject to a role reversal, I'm intimately quizzed as to my reaction to 'Brewing Up'. It's a difficult record to make quick judgements on. What do you, dear reader, expect? Another seven songs by one man and his guitar? 'Lover's Town Revisited' accompanied by The Royal Philharmonic? Or a selection of future singles featuring The

Billy Bragg Backing Band. In the end, you'll get none. He's cautiously moved one step further, introducing acoustic guitar here, a trumpet there, an organ over there and yet the same old rough guitar throughout.

Kicking off with a knee in the groin, 'It Says Here' pulls no punches, launching a loud and angry attack on the press. Along with the other outwardly political song, 'The Island Of No Return', it sticks out not so much for its lyrical content as the equation that anger must automatically make for a lot of shouting and loud guitar. I prefer the subtlety of 'Love Gets Dangerous' or 'The Saturday Boy' myself, the former featuring backing vocals for the first time (shock! horror!) and the latter a wonderfully baroque trumpet line. Meanwhile, there are more Braggesque numbers to be found via 'In A Vauxhall Velox' or 'Like Soldiers Do', songs of growing up and teen romances, the side of Billy's writing so

rarely brought to light.

B ut then that's because he enjoys a good argument. And we all enjoy nothing like a good cup of coffee. Unfortunately, The Billy Bragg Cookbook makes nothing like a good cup of coffee – probably something to do with the number of times the water boiled! Still, it proves he's only human, something the Bragg would like everyone to remember as he's raised unwillingly onto a pedestal. Billy Bragg is not a man on a mission, but he's bloody good entertainment, and he can make you think. He can also touch you now and then. That's good enough for me.

Not for some people though. On the bus back, I read a fanzine that's apologising for its non-appearance over the last year, and detailing some of the more exciting events to have occurred in their absence. They end with the forboding . . . .

'The world gained a new Messiah . . . Billy Bragg.'

Don't let him know you said that.

FRONT ROW TICKET

Bruce Dessau reviews the latest film releases.

Sometimes the cinema presents for us a desirable world, one of beauty, flowers and buses running on time. But occasionally a film crops up as a timely warning of how things could turn out if we are unfortunate. **1984** (*Virgin*) is one of those films, not so much entertainment as a cautionary tale. As everyone who has not been locked in a cupboard all year should know by now, '1984' is the tale of Winston Smith, one man alone in a terrifyingly totalitarian state known as Airstrip One (formerly England). Written soon after the last war, George Orwell set his novel in April to June of this year – the precise time that the film was shot. But this does not mean that we can take comfort from the fact that things really are not as bad as the book/film shows. The choice of date is arbitrary, that this could be actually real remains a definite possibility, albeit at a date in the future.

Director and writer of the screenplay, Michael Radford has drawn on already existing images to put the possibility of reality over, and at the same time demonstrate that Fascism need not be of the Nazi variety, but can just as easily arise from the left, being any political system based on authoritarianism. Big Brother as he appears on the TV screens resembles British Fascist Oswald Moseley, while the children run about in pseudo-Hitler Youth uniforms. But the dark uniforms worn by all the workers echo Mao's China and The Inner Party, with their privileges of wine and the ability to turn their screens off are undoubtedly an Orwellian view of the Soviet leadership.

Meanwhile, the overriding feeling of Smith's position is one of being in prison without bars, except for those that serve Victory Gin, a cheap spirit to dull the senses of the workers and keep them down. The sets are as one would imagine – a post-holocaust London of grey decaying buildings (as featured in Culture Club's excrutiatingly naive 'War Song') while the crowd scenes echo Queen's 'Radio GaGa' video, row upon row of faceless drones in dumb salutation of their (in)glorious leader.

The politics, "If only they realised it, the strength lies in the Proles", may be a little obvious in these ideologically informed times, but just because Orwell's 'prophecies' have not yet been realized does not mean we can relax.

John Hurt puts in a suitably vivid realization of Smith, while Richard Burton, in his last film role, wallows in the sadistic voyeurism of O'Brien, particularly in the infamous Room 101 scene, but really does not have a great deal to get his teeth into. Suzanna Hamilton as Smith's lover, Julia, successfully renounces her membership of the Anti-Sex League but delivers possibly the most unconvincing on-screen "I Love You" this year. Movie of the year, more by virtue of its title than its execution, 1984 is always overshadowed by the book, but still well worth seeing – as long as you go with someone who will make you laugh afterwards.

World War Three Starts Here

Another alternative view of the present is offered by director John Milius in **'Red Dawn'** (*UIP*). Milius has been responsible for the original screenplay of 'Apocalypse Now', the recent view of macho surf culture 'Big Wednesday' and 'Conan The Barbarian', so in direct contrast to the emaciated visions of '1984', one knows that Milius movies mean muscle. Sure enough, 'Red Dawn' opens with a Mid-America class being lectured on Genghis Khan (!) when parachutes begin to land outside. Thinking it is a training mission off course, the class go out to investigate, only to find themselves under attack from Communist invaders (!!). In fact, wait for it, World War Three has ensued and America has been invaded by the Soviets and their allies . . . and this film is about how a group of American teenagers fought back . . .

Like a survivalist version of 'Lord Of The Flies', a group of teenagers take to the uncaptured mountains where they learn to fend for themselves. In fact this film is so macho that even the girls become men, which makes a change from having them in a film like this merely to do the laundry and for the love interest. Familial loyalties are given up for personal survival and when a brother gives away their position, he is executed because he can no longer be trusted. Harsh justice indeed.

Gradually the group get organised into a guerrilla force (there is only about a dozen of them) known as 'Wolverines' and follow the quote from American hero Teddy Roosevelt, "They can have my gun when they pry it from my dead fingers" . . .

Hearing of events in Europe, "Only England got involved and they didn't last long", they battle to defend their own land against the might of their invaders.

As a dramatisation of one's response to being overrun by the enemy, this is what one would expect from Milius, lots of guts 'n' bleeding. There are some amusing touches in the way American institutions are utilised – MacDonalds becomes the army canteen, and the drive in cinema becomes a prison compound, permanently showing, Big-Brother-like, propaganda films. 'Red Dawn' has its moments, and is a fair bit of fun, but the ending is all too obvious and rather oversentimental, the kind of cinematic denouement which '1984' avoids in the extreme . . .

Another Sixties Trip

Indeed, after films that take a disturbing look at the possible present, **'Baby It's You'**

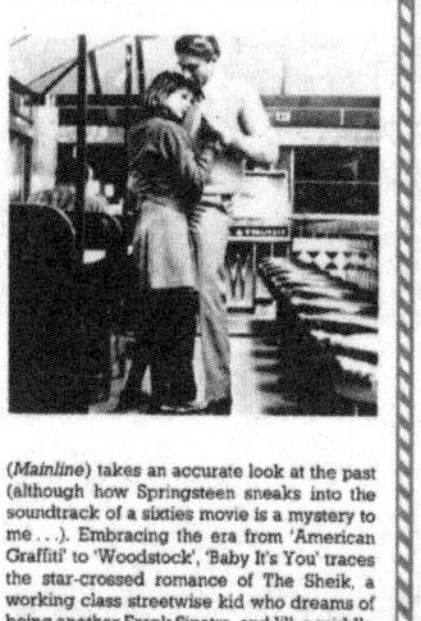

(*Mainline*) takes an accurate look at the past (although how Springsteen sneaks into the soundtrack of a sixties movie is a mystery to me . . .). Embracing the era from 'American Graffiti' to 'Woodstock', 'Baby It's You' traces the star-crossed romance of The Sheik, a working class streetwise kid who dreams of being another Frank Sinatra, and Jill, a middle class girl with academic aspirations. Although she finds him desirable, she is convinced that their relationship will never work and continually tried to break it up, but when she moves away to college he follows, earning his keep by pathetically miming to his hero's discs in low down dives. As they move to the late sixties she is destined to drop acid while he just drops out, but they are also destined for one final touching reunion . . .

A poignant, and occasionally moving movie, 'Baby It's You' managed to avoid the usual sixties movie clichés, underplaying cars, bars and guitars and replacing them with dialogue and feelings, giving it a fresh, but tragic air. Still, any soundtrack that features 'Chapel of Love', 'Venus In Furs' and 'Strangers In the Night' is alright by me . . .

Save the World

Finally, for anyone that saw 'Streets Of Fire' and is still wondering whether its star Michael Paré can act, go see **'The Philadelphia Experiment'** (*Columbia-EMI-Warners*) in which he plays the sailor who fell through space, switching times from 1943 to 1984 and finding it hard to choose between a modern blooming love and his duty to mankind by going back to 1943 and saving the world. At the end of the day there is no real choice is there? Is there? 'The Philadelphia Experiment' is lots of fun and excitement, repeating the most tedious joke in the world about The President being an actor quite successfully. A worthwhile picture . . .

the pride of lions

part-two

In part two of our U2 exclusive, *Tony Fletcher* talks to *The Edge* about religion, wealth and why it all matters. Photos by Anton Corbijn.

Chapter 8: THE STAND

Do you see yourselves as essentially a live band or studio band, or do you see them complementing each other?

They're different mediums for sure. I think we've built up a reputation as a live band 'cos there are very few bands who make a success of their live concerts. I think if we were in a different set of groups as our peers, I don't think there would be that same emphasis on our live performance. It just seems that nobody is interested in communicating anymore. All they are interested in doing is arriving at the show, playing their songs and maintaining their own haircut as intact as they can for the duration of the show. And that whole way of approaching live work holds no fascination or interest for me. I just think it's conceited, it's vanity. That's basically it.

U2 were one of the first examples of groups from the late seventies that just built up and built up; you were years getting a hit single, but you were always popular. Is there a sense of pride in doing it that way?

I'm sure we would have liked a hit single early on. I always thought that 'I Will Follow' was going to be a hit and '11 O'Clock Tick Tock' a near hit, but they weren't. Maybe that was a good thing, I don't know. We didn't plan it.

But a lot of bands in that position sit back and think, "What's gone wrong? What can we do for a hit single?"

We never really judged things like that. If we believe in a song, believe that it works as a 45 release, we go ahead. If it doesn't happen commercially, that's something else. The primary motivation behind the group is our own integrity in what we *believe* to be right. I just couldn't release something that I didn't think was us, no matter how good a shot it was as a hit. The whole idea would just sicken me.

So why, when 'New Years Day' and 'War' came out, did it suddenly happen then?

I don't think New Years Day was a hit because it suddenly got played on the radio and suddenly loads of people went out and bought it. I think it was a hit because our following had grown to the size that when they went out and bought it, it just made the charts. We are the only group who did Top Of The Pops and our single went *down* next week. At that time we were so thick we didn't get that point for a few times. We're not going to do Top Of The Pops anymore. It just doesn't work for us, it's not the right arena for this group. I don't think the people who buy U2 records want to see us on Top Of The Pops – I don't think they're particularly *interested* in what's happening on Top Of The Pops.

If I felt that we had a release that fitted into the Top Of The Pops field maybe we'd do it. But that's such an unthinkable situation, because Top Of The Pops for me, is like the ultimate advert. TV is about selling things generally and Top Of The Pops is just the ultimate sales platform, one that I don't think we suit at all. We'll probably put videos on if they'll accept them.

What about if they let you play live?

That would interest me – if, again, I felt that it worked. We did a re-recorded live version of 'Two Hearts Beat As One'. You had to re-record the track for union reasons, but a lot of groups would just pretend to, while really they'd be using the same tape. I hated that whole deception – I just thought that was sickening. So when we did 'Two Hearts Beat As One' and 'New Years Day', we actually went ahead with the re-recordings, even though we only had three hours to do it, and it had taken us maybe a week when we had originally recorded them.

This discussion about Top Of The Pops raises the point that you're known as more of an LPs band. Is that deliberate?

No, it's just us. What is a singles band? I always think of a 45 as a more easily marketable product. For me it conjures up something that is more throwaway, more of a one-off. For us the whole 45 things doesn't work generally.

Looking up at the blackboard here (with the track listing and timings on it), you've immediately got a problem in that there's only one track on your new album which is the normally acceptable length for a single.

That's never really been one of our priorities. When we're in the studio we're very single-minded about things. We know what we want, we know what we don't want and we'll go to any lengths to get what we feel is right. Until we finish the album, things like singles and interviews are really the last thing we're interested in. The only reason we're doing Jamming! now is because it's a magazine we wanted to do and we realised that we wouldn't get the issue that coincides with the album unless we did it now.

Nothing against U2, but I've always liked bands that somewhere down their schedule go in and record a single that doesn't appear on the albums. Do you find that you don't get the time?

A mixture between that, and, the funny thing about this group is that it takes us a few weeks to switch from a live footing to a recording footing. So the first two weeks of recording are *terrible*; and the first two weeks of touring is like, mayhem. That's when Bono starts losing his head totally, 'cause the set is in tatters. There's no flow or continuity so we go out on stage and we're really hanging on by our fingernails to the atmosphere in that hall. When people want to see some personal fireworks, that's when to see us.

CHAPTER 9: HEALTH AND EFFICIENCY

Amidst all the talk about a band that sets itself a world apart from the daily capitalist actions of the pop elite, it should be firmly stated here and now that U2 are run with a military precision that I, for one, have never seen matched. None of the band are prepared to take the credit for this, putting it quite rightly down to manager Paul McGuiness.

Previously an assistant director for a film production company and with no experience in the music business other than having secured another Irish band a record deal many moons ago, McGuiness, much older than his partners, initially seems a strange man for the job. But he possesses a knack as manager of one of the world's leading bands that has fallen into place as naturally as all the other elements.

"Paul has managed to grow with the group," says The Edge. "I've never felt at any stage that we had somebody in the management position who wasn't up to it. Anything he didn't know he quickly found out. And also he's got his own individual way of doing things which works. So it's not a corporate management company thing, where he manages ten other acts, including a country artist, a cabaret singer and a heavy metal band. It's again a very individual relationship."

And one that has kept the group in that enviable position where to the public eye, nothing seems to go wrong, as the group go from strength to strength, and profit to profit. Certainly McGuiness has an eye for keeping the cash flowing. As The Edge explains later, it was he who realised that a concert at Red Rocks would be ideal for filming, managing to get it shown twice on The Tube (over six months), thereby preselling the 'Under A Blood Red Sky' live LP and making even more meat out of it as a separate video. Likewise the recording of the new album has proved an opportunity Paul couldn't resist. On my arrival, I was politely asked if I minded the whole interview being filmed as part of a documentary the group were making on a group making an album! Calm and collected, he has obviously secured the group's financial future with a tie-up between them and Windmill Lane Studios (unless it is pure coincidence that they share premises), and yet at the end of the day, he understands the band perfectly, never selling them short. As I prepare to leave the studio at the end of an arduous day, he remarks "I'm really glad this interview came off. I always wanted it to happen, but then the more I thought of it, the more I realised that to only do Jamming! would be such a typical U2 thing to do!"

I can't help but ask Edge if Island Records, who reputedly almost bankrupted themselves breaking U2 in their early days, are also part of this close-knit unit. His reply is typically grandiose.

"I see Island Records, not as a lot of groups see their record companies – as something to be battled with, a necessary evil – but as an extension of us. I feel just as passionately about what they do as I feel about what Paul our manager does or what we do. Though we're not in control of it, it boils down to a faith in the individuals involved."

Chapter 10: THEY COULD NOT TAKE YOUR PRIDE

Jamming!: The Red Rocks concert was meant to be one of the most special you've ever played. What's the full story about it?

The Edge: We'd always wanted to play Red Rocks because we knew it was one of the best venues in that part of the world, so we were finally in the position to do it, and then Paul said "Look, it's bound to be an incredible concert, let's arrange for it to be filmed." We got other people involved financially, but it quickly became a far more serious proposition because Paul made a few enquiries and discovered The Tube and various other video-orientated TV people were very interested, so it became more of a production thing. We ended up spending quite a lot of money on doing it. The only problem was, the day we were doing it, it was pissing with rain and had been for two days. So we had a choice – we either cut our losses, move to a nearby stadium and set everything up inside; or we take a chance and just do it in the rain, which is what we did.

One thing on the film that really comes over is at the end, when you do '40' . . . There's nine thousand people there and Bono can come back on and without using a microphone get the whole crowd to sing along. Is that something that's happened much?

No. A few select gigs. It's such a great way to leave stage, it's one of the most special moments of the tour for me.

Does it ever move you to tears?

Occasionally. That Tube appearance was really emotional for me. I don't know why. I think it was one of the first times we'd played Sunday Bloody Sunday, and that really got me. It was really moving. And sometimes onstage there is an atmosphere . . . I believe it's a mixture between the audience and the band, that what happens is bigger than both of us. It's just a union. I'm a spiritual sort of person, so I really am very aware of the atmosphere, of the spiritual mood of a place.

Do you ever feel that U2 have been persecuted for those spiritual/religious beliefs?

Oh yeah. People don't understand it, so they lash out. It doesn't bother me though – I'm past caring what people think about our beliefs. The people that really matter are not going to judge you on an interview or some smart comment made in a review of an album. They're going to listen to the album or see you live, and make up their own mind. That's good enough for me.

Isn't part of the reason that people have a go because it's in the lyrics so much? In the way a band always putting politics in their lyrics come in for the same sort of stick?

Well that isn't really the case – The Clash were never criticised for being political, nor was Bob Dylan originally. I think there's something peculiar to spirituality – or Christianity in particular – that brings on that sort of stick. The fact that it does appear in the lyrics, I suppose, is what gets up people's nose. It's not just the fact that it's there, it's the way it's presented in an extremely challenging, extremely powerful way. It demands a response, and I don't think people generally like that.

At times it looks like you're on some sort of crusade.

Well we've never sat down and decided to do that. It's just, again, that when Bono's singing, I don't think he has too much control to be honest. He writes the lyrics, but I always feel there's something else in there as well, something that he's really only being used as a medium for. I really believe that. There's an undercurrent to most music, be it ultimately positive or negative, and you open yourself up to that. Sometimes without even knowing it you can be a medium for something positive, something good. But by the same token you can easily be the opposite, be used as an outpouring of something that's far darker, more sinister, more negative. It's not something easily explained.

There's got to be thousands of U2 fans who are atheists dancing along to your music. Do you think about that at all?

I'm not really interested in people's religious beliefs. I think the sort of spirituality that I believe in transcends religion, leaving it looking *stupid*. Religion for me is like politics in a sense – something to belong to. It's a set of values that people accept a lot of the time without thinking about it.

There is a parallel between very religious people – as in the church – and political people, in their infallible belief in what is 'right'. That's why I asked about your audience, because some political groups don't want people in their audience if they don't share their viewpoint.

That's far too small-minded for me. The whole concept of religion . . . I think religion was originally a framework for spirituality. It was something that was man-made to enable people to relate better to that positive force, Spiritual Being, whatever you want to call it . . . . God. But it's become something else, and I don't really have much time for it. But I think everybody's different. There's so much diversity in this world that it doesn't bear thinking about the diversity that there lies in God. I'm certainly not going to make up my mind about someone else. All I'm interested in is producing something I believe in that has positiveness to it . . . . and anyone else really has to look after themselves. I'm not interested in judging anybody.

You must feel quite misunderstood on the whole matter.

Very much so. People get the strangest ideas. A lot of people seemed to think we were a fanatical Catholic group which is laughable, because, well Larry's from a Catholic family, but none of the rest of us are.

Is it something you were taught when you were young or something that you *felt*?

Certainly nothing we were taught. I reacted very violently *against* organised religion. I think every one of us did in a sense. It's a very personal belief, something I really do see in people. I think you either deny that deeper spiritual side of yourself or else you encourage it. A lot of people inhibit themselves or play it down and therefore they're not sensitive anymore. I can see it in people, in their work and in everything about them. I can feel it. It's so often people who aren't Christians, people who know nothing about Jesus Christ, it's so often the last person you might think of that has it. So I've given up thinking about Christianity or spirituality in terms of religion. A lot of times it bears no relation at all to it.

I realise now that where you've been misunderstood is that people thought of you – like you say – as some sort of Catholic fanatics,

or as having a certain manifesto to put over, whereas what you're actually saying is it's something spiritual rather than an organised religion.

That's the key to it. It's only an extension of the individual. I think everybody has it, everybody has some sort of awareness and it's a decision to follow one or the other path. I think the world generally is travelling one way and it's almost up to people to decide not to follow.

What can U2 as a band do about that?

Consciously, nothing. But I think if you make yourself available you can be used for something totally different. And that's the thing I feel passionately about music, that it's not me, it's not U2 that's creating this great art. That's why I can be so arrogant – or seemingly arrogant – about what we do, because I really don't think it's us essentially. There's something that works through us to create in this way.

. Talking to Brian Eno, who has no spiritual beliefs at all, he relates *exactly* to what I've just said, that the most talented people he's worked with are people that worked intuitively, instinctly or subconsciously. That they themselves, their conscious mind, is very rarely involved in the creative process, but there is some other thing that comes in . . . and takes over, if you like. And that's why I hate bands that come across like 'We Are Geniuses', because I don't believe it. I don't believe that the greatest art in the world has been created by Man, consciously – I think there's something else, a far deeper thing, that comes out and does the work. If we try and work consciously on something, we just get in a mess. You really have to relax with what you're doing and let it almost write itself. And then you start to come into that other way of working which is, I believe, the most creative method.

With what you're saying about your music coming from inside, what can you give, at the end of the day, to your audience?

We can give *ourselves*. I don't want to get into too many seemingly ethereal philosophical concepts, but that's really what I think you must do, you must give yourselves; ie, hold nothing back, yet at the same time be honest and try not to present something other than yourself.

What, in turn, can your audiences take away from U2?

Good question . . . I get a lot of enjoyment from our music, because I discover things about it that were not thought about, that occur within the music. Lyrically and musically, there are trains of thought, ideas in the music that I know I won't understand until a later date. So in a sense I can relate very closely to what people see in our work. I can relate to their first listening, and I enjoy it. I think it's very rich. So I think that really is what we offer, an extremely rich music.

Chapter 11: THE CELTIC FACTOR

Irish people have always got a certain fire in them and a certain love of their country that so many other people don't have. How easy was it for you to stay living here at the stage when I expect everyone was saying 'Come and live in London', when you were first breaking?

It was actually very easy. Because everything made sense here. The problem in being in one of the media centres like London or New York is that everything is super-real. In fact, sometimes Dublin to me seems super-real, and I go off to Kilkenny or somewhere, a really small town where you can see how lives are lived in a normal situation. Cities don't allow you to do that, especially the big cities, the media centres, and I think an artist must keep in contact with that seemingly, apparently, mundane, normal way of living. Because if he doesn't, he's commenting on something that needs to be put in context, the context of the big city. A lot of dance music that's coming from New York is so short-lived because it demands to be placed in the absolutely precise context of New York or the big city, before it can be understood. I think really good music, really good art, is something that can be related to, no matter where you are, no matter what time. That's why all these pop bands go out, because their time has passed. What they're doing is locked so closely into that era, that particular location, that it makes no sense six months later, or somewhere else in the world. What I think we try and do is make music that can cross over any geographical or time barriers.

Do you think if you were living in London you'd still be the same band?

No, not at all. I've seen so many Irish groups go to London and just lose touch with whatever vein, creatively, they were locked into at one stage in their career. I think it's tragic. In a sense that's why people were freaking out in places like Manchester, Liverpool, Glasgow . . . it just seemed like instinctively, people were aware that these cities provided a more sane backdrop for an artist to work in. Hence their work was more easy to relate to.

Maybe this ties in with the reason you tend to get a lot of bad press. You're not on their doorsteps to be seen at the right spots, to give quotes all the time and go to the gigs where the journalists are going . . . You're not part of what they consider *their* scene.

Yeah, I think that has a lot to do with it. I think it works for other creative areas as well – the fact that The Tube isn't recorded in London is quite important. Not that I don't like London – I think it's one of the most beautiful cities in the world – but for an artist I think it's absolutely the wrong place to be. It really is. You might think that living in isolation in some Scottish island would be terrible for somebody in music, because they'd be so out of touch, but as far as I'm concerned it would be exactly the right place to be. It would be real. I think you have to seek out some natural surrounding – to inspire you.

And you find it easy to get inspiration?

Yeah, definitely. It's very important to me, as an individual, that we don't lose a sense of normality. I know a lot of groups who've managed to get over that problem – The Beatles for instance. There was nothing normal about their life but they still managed to create something really special. Sting's life is nothing to do with normality, yet he's producing some of his best work now. The previous albums I wasn't very interested in but the last couple have been nice. And that's a guy who's managed to do it in a totally unnatural situation.

This all ties in with the question of wealth, because the other argument is that once you get money, you're no longer living a normal lifestyle. Obviously at this stage you must have done quite well, so do you find that's a bit of a myth?

That is the biggest single threat to this group: Money. I've struggled with that, I've thought I'll give it all away, I'll just put it somewhere and forget about it, but it's something you can't run away from, it's something you've just got to respect. You've just got to be so aware of the dangers of losing what you've got due to this thing called money.

Do you think you can avoid it?

We have done up to now, but then again, we haven't really experienced wealth up to now. If this album does well this'll be the first time where there'll be any chance of us taking anything other than a medium wage from the operation. But I think the most significant thing about our new position is that we can do what we want creatively.

Wouldn't you say you always have done?

Yeah, but we've always had financial limitations. And the fact that our goals have always been creative goals means that that hasn't really been changed by our financial position. I don't think we'll ever reach those artistic goals and that's important.

Are you still as close friends as you were at the start?

Yeah. I think we probably piss each off more than when we first started but there's pretty healthy relationships within the band. I think when we were younger there was more of a band opinion. It seemed to be that the best opinion prevailed. I think now that we're a little older we're developing more individually.

Chapter 12: AND FINALLY . . .

If there was a new punk movement tomorrow, would they respect U2 as Godfathers or reject them as dinosaurs?

It depends what you mean by 'punk movement'. If you mean what I think punk is about, which is the individual – honesty, a rejection of image-based *pap*, music with no soul and no real commitment to it – then I think they'd certainly respect what we do. On the other hand, if you mean a revitalisation of the safety-pin movement – all the clichéd political views and images that go with that – then I don't think they would because I think we are too individual to fit into that category. We really are defining our terms in so many areas, going against what those sort of bands feel is the way to go, that I'm sure we wouldn't be their favourite group. But I think it's far weaker to pander to images of what people feel you should be, than to go your own way. And that's certainly something we've always done. For better or worse we've always done it our way.

THE END

BORN TO BE *BOSS*

A Bruce Springsteen Fan calls no man Sir and one man Boss. Tony Parsons author of 'Platinum Logic' and other best-sellers is among them. Here, he tells why.

In 1984, the world turned mulatto. On the cover of every magazine, under the cover of every Dansette, the Maginot line between black and white was overrun time and time again.

Anyone who bought 'I Want You Back' and 'The Love You Save' found it tough to come to terms with the fact that Michael Jackson – with his radical cosmetic surgery, heavy metal guitarists and quiet lunacy behind closed doors – was these days about as black as Barbara Cartland. Even someone who had suspected Prince of latent genius since 'I Wanna Be Your Lover' and 'When You Were Mine' found it hard to think of him as black, what with his gloriously seamless music and a line like, *"I don't care if we spent the night at your mansion."* 'Take Me With You' was great – but it sure wasn't Gil Scott-Heron.

And these were the two faces everywhere. Prince Rogers Nelson and Mad Mike, set up from Fleet Street to The Face as young pretender and reigning champ. *Can Prince take Michael's crown?* The question never really arose and Prince knew it, he knew where his real competition was even if James Brown didn't ("Watch out, Michael"), and he checked it out live every chance he got.

He sure wasn't sitting in the front row of the Jacksons show.

"We busted out of class/Had to get away from those fools/We learned more from a three minute record/Than we ever learned in school . . ."

Born In The USA' is The Boss stripped bare of all superfluous imagery and self-serving myths, both of which were fine – quite beautiful, in fact – when we were all growing up, but are now best put aside. 'Born In The USA' cuts right to the core, it hits you – knows you, lifts you – right where you live. It is Bruce Springsteen in his prime. Overwhelming.

The first thing that hits you about 'Born In The USA' is how un-American it is. It is so good, so real, it is totally international, beyond borderlines, stateless. The lines in the title track, *"Got in a little hometown jam so they put a rifle in my hand/Sent me off to a foreign land to go kill the yellow man,"* could just as easily be, *"Sent me off to a foreign land to protect the Orangeman,"* and Khe Sahn could just as easily be Goose Green.

It is an Internationale of the underclass, an anthem for lives that are not controlled by the people who are living them – it brought back to me the faces of young soldiers I had seen on the streets of Belfast, faces I had not thought about for seven years. In Steinbeck's *The Grapes of Wrath* disfranchised farmers run off their land by corporations and banks in mean mood squat in the dust – figuring. In 'Born In The

USA' squatting in the dust – figuring – is a luxury that nobody can afford and the line, *"Came back home to the refinery/Hiring man says, 'Son, if it was up to me',"* tells more about unemployment than dole queue rock ever did. As I say, there is nothing specifically American about any of this – these are songs for here at the Western World.

Springsteen puts his cards on the table with the opening track, and he's holding all the aces, but the song is untypical of the album. His *real* strength is documenting the agony, ecstasy and tedium of personal politics. The rest of the world *wonders* about us Springsteen fans, ponders exactly why we are so batty about the man's work – here's the reason why. He makes us believe our emotional backgrounds are identical, that he has suffered exactly the same pains, tasted exactly the same pleasures as we have – your life flashes past you but instead of drowning, you're dancing in the dark. Add to that the fact that the noise the boys from E Street make is one of the most exhilarating sounds you will ever hear and you have it. *That* is why a Springsteen fan calls no man Sir and one man Boss.

Ten years ago I broke up with – well, I guess you would call her my childhood sweetheart. I bought the 'Born To Run' album and . . . it connected. It helped me to remember, mourn, forget about it and begin again. Ten weeks ago my marriage broke up and I bought 'Born In The USA' album and it did exactly the same thing for me that 'Born To Run' had done ten years earlier. Ten years from now, when me and my fifth or sixth wife are breaking up, if Bruce Springsteen is not in my corner, still rooting for me after all those years, waiting in the record racks to console and uplift, then I will be very disappointed.

Springsteen understands that true love invariably does two things – conquers all and wears off.

In three consecutive songs on 'Born In

The USA' – 'Darlington County', 'Working On The Highway' and 'Downbound Train' – he just about writes the book of love. 'Darlington County' is probably the greatest song ever written about . . . pulling. There is a swagger to the music so young and cocky that it breaks your heart, there's a grinning, boastful quality to the lyrics that recalls every dumb chat up line that you and your best mate ever came out with when you were both as green as you could possibly be and imagined yourselves to be the hottest thing the world had ever seen.

"Girl, you're looking at two big spenders – the world don't know what me and Wayne might do/Our Pa's each own one of the World Trade Centers – for a kiss and a smile I'll give mine all to you."

If 'Darlington County' is a hunting song – that's not sexist because some girls are *brilliant* hunters – then 'Working On The Highway' is a having song – it feels even better. *"I met her at a dance down at the union hall/She was standing with her brothers, back up against the wall/Sometimes we go walking down by the union tracks/And then I look straight at her – and she looks straight back."*

The final part of this carnal trinity, 'Downbound Train', is about losing, a losing song is what it is, and no matter how dumb or hard you are – or pretend you are – there's nothing in heaven or earth that can stop it hurting like hell. *"She just said, 'Joe, I gotta go. We had it once, we ain't got it anymore'."*

A sad, sour note to end on – but then boys and girls, men and women, will always hit a sour note when they go their separate ways. What stops you reaching for the razor blades and giving your wrists a close shave is what will always stop you – not the very next girl, but the next girl you like *more*. The three songs are sandwiched – either by coincidence, act of God or the infinite wisdom of the Boss – by salvation in

dication

the shape of 'Cover Me', which looks like being the next single over here (believe me, CBS – it should be 'No Surrender') and the quiet fever of 'I'm On Fire'. It is here at the last exit from danger and desperation that the careers of Springsteen and Prince cover the same waterfront – when Prince howls, *"Baby, baby, baby – what's it gonna be?"* he is staking out the same territory, running from and to the same dreams and realities that Springsteen gives you a glimpse of – again, that shock of recognition again – in 'I'm on Fire'. Pillow talk and the promise of release, relief, about being ready – and still able – to believe, a hymn to some sweet smelling Seventh Cavalry of the soul . . . baby, baby, baby . . .

"Sometimes it's like someone took a knife, baby, edgy and dull and cut a six inch valley through the middle of my soul/At night I wake up with the sheets soaking wet and a freight train running through the middle of my head/Oh you – you cool my desire/Ooooh-oh-oh, I'm on fire."

Ooooh-oh-oh indeed. The internal massage is the message. Sometimes a relationship breaks up and you feel poleaxed – time and the touch of another can make you feel like what *really* happened is that you were let out of prison after serving a seven year stretch. Bruce understands.

O ne of the greatest things about the Fender Bender is that he has mastered his art to such a degree, he is so concise, is able to go straight to the heart so accurately that after telling you what is wrong with the world – making you want to stick your head out of the window and shout at the neighbours that you are not prepared to take anymore – and after telling you your own love stories – making you wonder if he was hiding under the bed – there is plenty of space left for him to manoeuvre, room to explore, ruminate, celebrate and sigh knowingly. Subtle is not a word often used in connection with Bruce Springsteen – epic, heroic, all the Ben Hur words are usually used – but subtle is what he most certainly is.

There's nobody better at writing about feeling pissed off with a woman. *Not* hating her – not, if you were the only girl in the world and I was the only boy, I would still spit in your eye. But just feeling *pissed off*.

"You let out one of YOUR BORED SIGHS," he bitches with a weary familiarity, too tired to be real contempt, in 'I'm Going Down'. *"Well, lately when I look into your eyes/I'm going down . . ./I pull you close but when we kiss I can feel a doubt/I remember back when we started/My kisses used to turn you inside out . . ."*

It's these nuances that animate his work, that sustain every line with flesh, blood and bone. In 'Bobby Jean' he aches at the loss of an old friend, in 'Glory Days' he pines for the prime time of old friends who have now peaked and in 'Dancing In The Dark', which you know about, what his world

needs now is a new friend.

'No Surrender' roars with the will to take another breath – Springsteen as life guard, something he excels at. Survive – despite every doubt you ever had, *because* of every doubt you ever had.

The album closes with 'My Hometown' – 'Independence Day' expanded all the way to the city limits. Anyone who has been both a son and a father must find it almost unlistenable, it comes that close to home. The only thing that *makes* it possible to listen to it . . . Jesus, it's beautiful.

B orn In The USA – *that's* the score to beat, the man in the front row with the wispy moustache. You drew level with 'Purple Rain' and now, year after year, you have to do it again and again and again. Because that it exactly what Bruce Springsteen has done.

Eight years ago, when he stood tall as the floodtides of 1976 and all that washed all around him, he seemed like the man linking the past with the future, the old

with the new, and he still seems like that, I think he always will. It has been a career of constant renewal, of constant reaffirmation of all the things that make you know you're alive and glad to be that way. I hope he doesn't fulfil one of his own fantasies – ah, come on, Bruce, own up – and get killed in a car crash. If he died – after what he did for me with 'Born To Run', 'Born In The USA' and whatever the next one is called – and I'm sure there *will* be a next one – then I know that, as some bunch of brothers crooned in the Sixties, I'd feel like I'd lost my guardian angel.

I know he comes in for a lot of stick but – aw, hell . . .

"Now some folks say it's too big and uses too much gas/Some folks say it's too old and that it goes too fast/But my love is bigger than a Honda, it's bigger than a Subaru/Hey man there's only one thing, and one car that will do . . ."

No retreat, no surrender. Ah, c'mon, baby – take a seat on the fender.

Tony Parsons

blue nile

A river in the Sudan and probably green. Or brown. Three Glaswegian experimentalists who quite by accident earlier this year released an LP by the title of 'A Walk Across The Rooftops'.

It was in May this year and I only wanted a dip, just ankle deep to see if I liked it. I drowned in the Blue Nile like all the others. Never in history have so many people enjoyed such a good drowning. The classical atmospheres and eery, lethargic vocals – a powerful seduction. With music like this, who needs to come up for breath? Get some gills.

"We didn't know if anybody would recognise it as music. We'd pursued our logic and were happy with it but we didn't know what it was; we weren't sure that anybody else would."

So confides Paul Buchanan, vocalist, and like him I'm not sure what "*it*" is either. But then you don't have to know what something is to like it – take babies and ice-cream or four million readers of The Sun. Still, as Buchanan continues, "what happened is that people have injected their imagination into it." And liked what they've imagined.

So, without using words to cross-breed bands à la "Tom Waits – meets – Japan – meets – Gallacher and Lyle" (meets meaningless) – what does this particular river sound like?

The Blue Nile are possessed of a lazy power but a surprisingly forceful flow. Occasionally they appear laid back to the point of falling over, the Nile looks suspiciously tranquil . . . and then come the rapids. The driving chorus of 'Stay', their first single, (excepting 'I Love This Life' an early independent foray onto vinyl); the stubborn insistence of 'Heatwave' and the vaguely sad philosophising of 'Tinseltown'. But the overwhelming impression of The Blue Nile is one of poise and class, of grandeur and maturity. That first album 'Rooftops' refuses pigeonholing or comparison. Specifically intent on "coming up with music that doesn't draw from influences but from personal expression", the record, perhaps inevitably, runs against the current currents of pop, a deep Blue vein in a sea of fluorescent oranges and yellows.

Their surprise at the warm critical reception and substantial sales the LP has garnered is only matched by their surprise at having made a record at all. Quite by chance Linn Products, a Scottish hi-fi hardware company who had never signed a band, heard some material the band had put on tape. Despite normally catering for specialist interests only, they were so impressed that they immediately contracted the band and financed the album.

As Paul Moore observes, without a trace of immodesty, "They were interested in getting a good recording and we were interested in making a good recording."

Linn Products' enthusiasm was the pay-off at the lucky end of a big gamble which had involved each member throwing in thriving and lucrative careers and completely immersing themselves in their music. For years their work had been a mutually shared secret, the product of late nights and self-indulgent experimentalism: the trouble with making an album is that other people have to hear it!

Paul Moore: "The night we let people hear

the album in that big eerie studio with everybody coming and going . . . it was purgatory, dreadful. None of us could cope with anyone else hearing it. It just seemed so inappropriate."

Like taking your clothes off for the Face?

"It was just so odd for other people to hear it – it was like a private thing, a passion belonging to the three of us. For once in our lives we wanted to focus on something and to do it absolutely right."

Absolutely right it was done. An album of seven songs, or perhaps they should be called 'pieces', being delicate compositions of weight and balance. No sign of the three minute popette but equally little trace of the pre-punk pose and pretension, the classical synthesizer lesson in pompous self indulgence that we all loved to hate.

There is a certain space and grandeur about the music of the Blue Nile but it has nothing to do with Brahms and Beethoven, as Moore is keen to assert.

"Of all the music we listen to, we know least about classical music. If we use violin it's not to sound classical but because they're acoustic and will give us a space which using organ won't. We're fairly studied about remaining amateurs, none of us wants to be clogged up with thinking we know about things. It's an exercise of the imagination and by and large the things we react to musically are the things that make you tingle."

Tingle. Yes, that's the word. A tingle sends

a shiver up the spine and the best music shivers the spine into temporary frost bite, if not hypothermia.

But to drop for a moment into the language of academia, 'A Walk Across the Rooftops' is an exercise in empathetic self-projection. It's about putting yourself in the other person's shoes.

Buchanan: "It's about imagining what it's like, sitting at your window at night, in a house a mile away or in another country and wondering what that person's feeling. That person is really just going through exactly what you're going through . . . you know?"

Yeah, I s'pose so. Sounds a bit nosey, but there you go. Are you offering solutions, have you got a manifesto, where do I put my X?

Buchanan: "We're not making a political statement in terms of being in favour of or against any one party; our concern is with more basic things like 'why is anybody hungry'? The album is an artistic thing not a political thing even if it contains politics. It's about worth and dignity and what it's like to be alive."

We are talking serious philosophy. Isn't that a little pretentious? After all, how much can a tune hold?

Moore: "A band shouldn't be afraid to make records that address large subjects without being pretentious. If we can achieve minor goals like that, then it's great."

The Blue Nile flows on. A re-released and re-mixed version of 'Stay' in the shops this month and a return to the studio to record the follow up album. They still don't feel competent to grant the dozens of requests to play live dates and they certainly don't feel part of the music business. Interviews, for example, are only as regular as trips out of Glasgow, not very. The Blue Nile may be flowing against the pop-tide but the tide may turn given the success of the new single. At the very least they're a rich new colour flowing into the ocean of 1980's music. I for one hope the colour runs.

Martin Wroe

CALL FOR ESCAPE ROUTE

10,000 MANIACS

10,000 Maniacs are telling me where they grew up, where they grew from, where the hell they think they're going. Their home is Jamestown, New York, spells small-town limbo, wasted ambitions, cover-version bands, no-where to play, insularity, intolerance, snoozeville u.s.a.

"Everyone was always wondering what we were trying to do – they still are!" says guitarist John. "Even when we started out, we were doing strange versions of 'Love Will Tear Us Apart' and 'Part Time Punks'!! We just let our own songs evolve. Like any band, starting out, it was great to just be avoiding work. Jamestown is 30,000 people – somehow we all fell together and 10,000 Maniacs grew beyond our wildest expectations."

And still growing fast. 10,000 Maniacs are ready to leapfrog to the front of the growing queue of U.S. contenders, having just returned from a lightening visit to this country that squeezed in three, sell-out London dates. They were totally unprepared for the riotous reception that greeted them here, pivoting on the verge of mass acclaim. Though their debut LP, 'Secrets Of The I Ching' was recorded as far back as March 1983, their progress over here has owed everything to John Peel's unrelenting enthusiasm. 'My Mother The War', the single taken from 'I Ching' was played constantly throughout last year and steadily, their reputation was to spread. In June of this year, they released 'Human Conflict Number Five', an EP which further demonstrated their rich, strange promise.

Their records and performances reveal a deceptive sense of musical crossover and subtle innuendo. Maniacs might be seen as frail and unadventurous, which would be understandable but unfortunate; their bright, occasionally frantic pop is not necessarily 'new' – its elements are fairly familiar – but their execution is completely individual. Taking calypso-reggae, punk pace, folk charm and a slightly perverse pop sensibility . . . they take it all, screw it all up, stare hard at the world and spread it thick over their shiny eighties surface. Maniacs are (sometimes) musically restrained. They are also spooky, sensational, unpredictable, dramatic, capricious and pained (which makes up for it). Their star is Natalie Merchant, anxious and angelic – who performs with mischief, magic and temptation tangled in her heart.

"It's because people are watching, so I get very nervous and the music is so emotional. If I think about what I'm singing, I get angry or cry. Some of the words I can detach myself from, but most of them are confessional. We like to bring up things that are buried. It's a shame that so many beautiful words have become archaic. I sing a lot about death . . . that seems like the most glorious moment . . ."

Photo Mad: Russell Young   Word Mad: Jonh Wilde

Her words – artful, abstract and armed with the thrill of personal discovery and political feeling – are sung with a distant passion. Natalie seems immersed in the wonder of their sounds and images, their simplicity and their loose associations. It is hardly surprising that she rates The Smiths and The Cocteau Twins as her favourite British bands; both Morrisey and Elizabeth Frazer, in their separate worlds, are among the few to actually re-invent the possibilities of the pop lyric in recent years. Maniacs deplore the constant barrage of banal images that pop regurgitates – through politics to sex. Instead, they bring ingenuity and poetry into their tinkling, thrilling harmony. Submerged in all their songs is Natalie's jumble twists of imagination, words that glare with sensitivity and an (almost) hallucinatory, haunting flow.

> 'Greta's cedar hope chest
> Is full of pamphlets
> Glass shelves of romantic
>   vignettes
> A journal laced with
>   sedimentary prose
> Norma gathers and collects
>   vintage photoplays
> Hair combs valentines'
>   (Katrina's Fair)

Besides their own lyrics, they have also adopted the poetry of Wilfred Owen (in 'The Latin One' and 'Anthem For Doomed Youth'), setting his tragic war scenarios to their quirky backbeat. In that, and in their own words, the images are unsettling.

As Natalie suggests, "Especially in America, the images used in pop music stick with one, tired old formula. Maybe the bright people stay out of rock'n'roll? We never think of ourselves as unique but people say we are . . . I sometimes think that what we're trying to do within a rock'n'roll format is totally absurd."

John: "So many people decide what they're going to do first. Y'know. 'Let's form a rockabilly band and call ourselves something with cat in the title.' They set themselves perimeters within which they can operate."

Maniacs meanwhile, incorporate a wealth of styles, sometimes too literally. Their expansive vocabulary of styles works best in a live setting, their performance simmering to the last gasp of 'My Mother The War' – one nervous shudder of edge and elation. Maniacs are not necessarily a straightforward concern, all their eccentricity and angularity working beneath the surface of their noise. Twin guitars (John Lombardo and Robert Buck) etch out fine-grained melodies – Dennis Drew's organ patterns purr delicately, bass (Steven Gustafson) runs fluid and frictional – Jerry Augustyniak's drilled percussion holds everything solid and controlled. Meanwhile, Natalie's wavering, featherlight vocal floats above it all like a tidal rise.

Maniacs have tension, have thirst, have time on their side. Pop orgasm, here we come.

BERNTHOLER

Berntholer are from Belgium, more Brussels than Prefab pop. They have a singer **Drita Kotaji**, and a single, 'My Suitor', on Blanco Y Negro. But what is 'My Suitor'? A wistful half smile? A playful shaft of sunlight through a crack in the bedroom door? Another music in a different cuisine?

I'm sitting opposite Drita Kotaji discreetly wiping the sweat from my brow, having had my plea for an explanation returned to my court? *"My Suitor* is finished for me now. You tell me what it means."

Hellfire, it's going to be one of those interviews.

"But you can ask me some questions about it if you like," she adds.

Well, is it animal, vegetable called contrived since the singer is a Belgian of Albanian parentage, there are echoes of a younger, more optimistic Nico or Marianne Faithful, rather than the twee, less than precious pop of a Grogan. Its relatives in pop are few and at the same time many. Meanwhile, from the lyrics to the Percy Byshe quotes on the sleeve, poetry is written all over this product in Frankie-size letters. There is simply nothing quite like it at the moment. And yet . . . and yet . . . there friggin' well ought to be. In the course of our discourse, I did also discover 'My Suitor' to be about the difficulties of assuming relationships of all kinds, and the problems of clearing the confusions which are all in one's mind.

"Live, I like to sing this song acapella, because it is really a very personal song, and if I am on my own I can sing it at my own pace, depending on how I feel. It is all just fancy." Why make a record rather than join what letter I have received in the morning, the weather, where I am. Sometimes I love it when it rains, it gives me an excuse to stay in when I do not want to go out, and then sometimes, I feel sad when the sun shines and I cannot go out. London makes me happy. Compared to Paris or Brussels, it is a very peaceful city. When somebody asks me for a light I do not think they are going to attack me as I do in Paris, where people are very agressive. Music affects me. I have just seen the new version of 'Metropolis'. Most of the music is not very good, but there is one moment where it is used to represent the heartbeat of a machine which is very affecting, very tragic."

When you sing you sound a little unhappy. What would make you very happy?

"Real happiness comes from inside, not a big car or house. Happiness is the realization of truths, self knowledge, self-expression. This band started because we were friends and

Jonh Wilde took me to see 10,000 Maniacs down in Brixton, and Natalie Merchant was singing a song on stage, crying. Just crying, this song was so emotional to her. I always had a love for her from that moment onwards. We did the photo session at the Italian Gardens by Kensington Gardens. They were staying in a hotel by Bayswater, as all rock bands did, so that was an easy walk. And I remember when she lifted up her trousers she had hairy legs. I thought, *'That's* pretty cool.' **Russell Young**

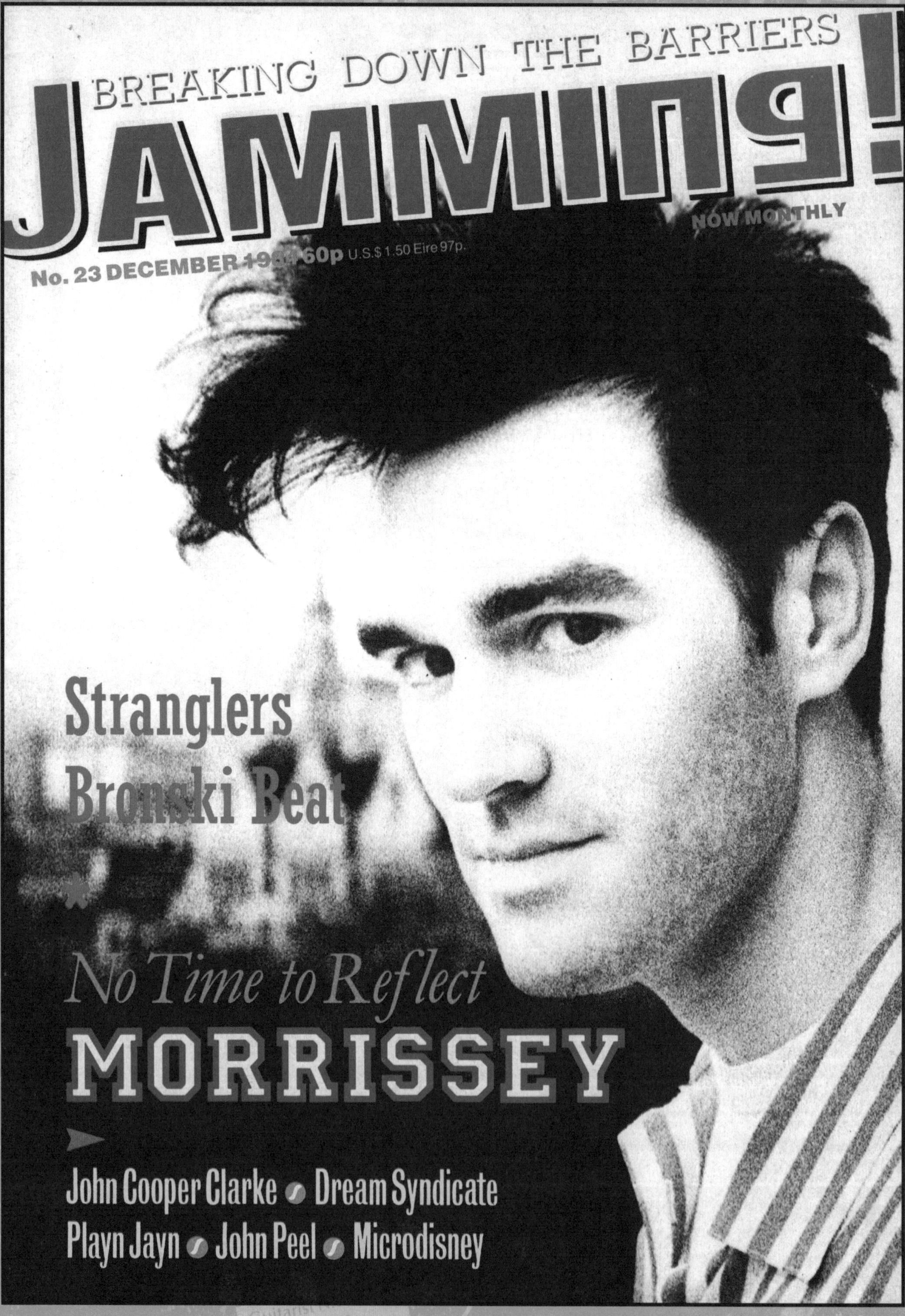

BREAKING DOWN THE BARRIERS
JAMMING!
NOW MONTHLY
No. 23 DECEMBER
60p U.S.$ 1.50 Eire 97p.
Stranglers
Bronski Beat
No Time to Reflect
MORRISSEY
John Cooper Clarke
Dream Syndicate
Playn Jayn
John Peel
Microdisney

Building on a Strong Foundation

As we all know, there are times when interviews can be boring. And, as they say, a picture can tell a thousand stories. So we sent intrepid lensman Jason Pevovar to see one of the country's liveliest bands – The Playn Jayn – on a typically wild night at their fave stomping ground, The Marquee in London.

The Playn Jayn have only released one record to date; a low budget, live album recorded at The Marquee on July 13th this year, and therefore, accurately called 'Friday The 13th'. Reaching the lower positions of the LP charts, it was living proof that if a band is exciting enough, and works hard enough, they can earn the sort of live following that will sell their records for them. Often accused of being reactionary, it is true that the Playn Jayn don't make the most original sound going. But their brand of mutant psychedelia creates its own little anthems in numbers like 'You Weren't Born, You Were Created', and 'I Love You Like I Love Myself', while the crazed actions of dual vocalists Mike Jones and Craig Lindsey make for one of the most entertaining live shows going – as the following pictures should prove . . .

Going through the motions at soundcheck time. The most restrained photo ever of The Playn Jayn!

Mike Jones and Craig Lindsey burst into another chorus.

Guitarist Nick Jones (yes, they are brothers) proves that the long hair comeback isn't confined to members of King.

Erol Suleyman, the calm lynchpin vital in every bunch of loonies, at his most active! Drummer Clive Francis is hidden behind his thingies.

The crowd don't seem to be having too bad a time either.

Craig on the verge of re-enacting some of the nastier scenes from 'Friday The 13th'.

I f *Jamming!* was rightly associated with The Jam back in its adolescent, late 70s fanzine days, the 1980s young adult colour magazine firmly attached itself to the phenomenon that was The Smiths. And why not? They ticked all our boxes, being a guitar band signed to the fiercely independent Rough Trade, profoundly provocative, frighteningly prolific, delightfully photogenic, incredible in concert and, thanks to a fanatically dedicated following that made that of The Jam look almost pedestrian by comparison, sold shitloads of magazines. For Issue 23 then, Morrissey, Weller's son and heir for all Spokesman For A Generation purposes, duly made his second front cover appearance of 1984, with Jonh Wilde receiving his own encore interview honours, and Russell Young finally securing his well-deserved first cover with a memorable session that would become the most widely seen of any *Jamming!* photographic commission.

Morrissey may have been tight-lipped about his sexuality, but Bronski Beat helped change the cultural conversation by being openly gay, and Chris Heath came into his own with an excellent profile of the trio that discussed homosexuality's place in pop music without

ISSUE #23 11/84

apology or embarrassment. It could be argued that such a feature was long overdue in *Jamming!*, but it should also be noted for those who were not around at the time that a 'don't ask, don't tell' policy had long governed musician and media comments alike, Tom Robinson's prior agitpop notwithstanding, and I had never felt it was our job to 'out' musicians who were not ready to come out for themselves.

On the subject of 1977's heroes, Issue 23 felt at times like an unintentional throwback, with Hugh Morley tackling Hugh Cornwell of The Stranglers and Paul Davies profiling John Cooper Clarke, for each act's long-overdue debut appearance, plus Jonh Wilde interviewing John Peel. One-page pieces on The Sid Presley Experience, Microdisney and The Dream Syndicate, and a double-page spread of in-concert Playn Jayn photos, shared space with features on playwrights, cinema, video releases, poetry, books, fanzines and even Christmas movies. *Jamming!* was covering multiple cultural bases, but as with Morrissey's first cover appearance on Issue 17 back in the New Year, only the white male musicians made the front-page masthead.

BRONSKI·BEAT

Chris Heath meets Bronski Beat, finding that sexuality and music go hand in hand.

Photos: Paul Cox

> f you're brought up for 16 or 17 years being told you're supposed to settle down and marry some woman and have kids, that you're supposed to lead this life where a man doesn't cry, doesn't do this, doesn't do that . . . . then you suddenly realise that's not what you are. You're something else, but you don't know what it is because someone's never told you, no-one's ever given you any education about what being gay is, everything's geared towards being straight. You've got a lot to discover."

I

Sexuality and music go back a long way together. Long before it was deemed decent only to show Presley's upper half on TV for fear of what those suggestively gyrating hips might do to impressionable youth, music and sex have been virtually inseparable. And not only in the obvious ways, in that most pop lyrics deal with love, passion, desire, and sex (or more often than not the lack or loss of these). They are also entwined even more closely in the actual way they interact in our lives as we live them. For instance, the places music are played in are traditionally also places of courtship. Furthermore, the age at which most consumers (particularily the only casually interested ones) listen to pop as part of their lifestyle is during the years of sexual adventure and discovery.

In all this the music is not neutral. It is not merely the backdrop to sexual ideas and endeavour. Music and its associated styles and personalities are part of all that forms and articulates our ideas on sex (as on other things; e.g. politics). Obviously it would be stupid and naive to imagine that it simply has the power to shape them, as if our thoughts on these matters were putty in the music's writhing hands. Nevertheless, music is important. The children of Frankie, Iron Maiden, Prince, and Smokey Robinson are all receiving, storing, experimenting, rejecting and assimilating very different ideas to each other from their conflicting sources. Music isn't innocent.

II

Homosexuality has, until recently, been camouflaged and denied within this mêlée of dancing, kissing, singing, and loving. Perhaps because its potential existence threatens the culture's dominant male ego, the idea of two men's emotions interlocking has been obscured, never allowed out of its closet – nor indeed was it usually even possible to admit that the closet existed. (Lesbianism, you will

I'd had nothing published anywhere, aside from a few local publications in Cambridge where I was then living. So, I'm not quite sure what even gave me the nerve to put myself forward to *Jamming!*, nor whether I said or did anything in particular to make anyone receptive, beyond just asking. But I think maybe I'd glimpsed an opening in its sense of possibility and belief and lack of judgement. (I mean, it was *full* of judgement, as it needed to be, but it didn't feel like an unapproachable world where the only protection from being poisoned was to poison someone else first.)

After a few shorter pieces went well enough, I was asked to write about Bronski Beat. I remember that I was pretty sick that day, but didn't want to lose the opportunity so told no-one, and that for the interview Bronski Beat and I sat on note, is typically totally excluded from these scenarios; I suspect because the naive male response to it is not one of particular disgust or threat but one of *puzzlement*: how can they *do* anything? What *with*?)

That silence ended, we are often told, with glam rock. On the day that Bowie admitted that he was bisexual the barriers apparently simply dissolved. At last this *other voice* could be heard.

We should be sceptical of these claims. As the nauseatingly condescending inventor of 'Sloane Rangers', Peter York, noted in one of his more lucid moments, 1972's bisexuality

was little more than that season's stylistic cliché. Journalists would queue up to ask bands about it as in other times they had quizzed them on their favourite food (1966), drugs (1967), tax exile (1975), or political stand (1977). Furthermore academic sociologist Mike Brake has pointed out that the bisexual pop star of glam rock was not one who embodied a liberating, open, sexuality. Quite the converse, he was one who reaffirmed traditional macho values. Bowie and Bolan were in fact super studs. They weren't just ordinary men, they were such great men that they could not only get off with girls but with boys *as well*. Millions bowed their heads in admiration.

III

Recently though we've had Frankie, and also Morrisey and Boy George, those pioneers who have forced the pop scandal writers in the daily rags to learn to spell the word 'ambiguity'. Musically I find at least two of these performers irresistible, more so in fact than the group who are the subject of this piece. However I want to suggest that, despite the claims that have been frequently been made for them, none of them has successfully portrayed a gay sexuality in pop music.

For instance, Morrisey's avoidance of sexual stereotypes has been very valuable, but the lyrical devices he uses to preserve the songs' mysterious seductive power also render them, more often than not, gender*less*. He finds a world where the sexuality 'we' have is one that *is* free of the common constraints – but he only achieves this at the expense of us never knowing who the 'we' in question ever might be. Sex without a subject and object is an enticing prospect in theory, but in practice we are left with no conception of what its realisation might be, or how we might attain it.

Boy George has a similar problem. His drag queen appearance does (or at least did for a while) turn heads but again he deals with the most difficult questions by avoiding them. Echoing Johnny Rotten he tells the press that he'd "rather have a cup of tea", but is careful not to let slip what he would actually do if sadly tea was off the menu and he had to make do with sex instead. Bronski Beat (yes, this is a Bronski Beat interview) still think George is great. As their singer, the weeny Jimmy Somerville, says: "He changed a lot of attitudes. I actually like George, and I hope someone says that for once."

Larry, the bespectacled one, adds that he looks great on telly! "He should take over Russell Harty".

"He's so powerful," continues Jimmy. "He'd just rip them all apart. I think he's fab – even though he's a mad drag queen!"

But they don't counter my main point.

What about Frankie though? Haven't they been the gays to thrust gay sex in the public's face, to make it acceptable and visible? All those sperms on record sleeves, Bernard Rose videos, Mike Read wetting himself – isn't that progress? Well yes, but I see two problems.

Firstly, by living their (and Paul Morley's) outrageous fantasies out in public, Frankie have in fact reinforced gay stereotypes. To be outrageously explicit and perverse is a challenge, and to be openly gay is a challenge. To be both together is unfortunately to give people the chance to explain away the one by the other – Paul and Holly can simply be seen as conforming to the stereotypic pervert, both excessive in action and unconventional in object: "that's what gay people are like – odd, aren't they?"

Secondly, as Jimmy points out, "there's just the two gay ones. The rest of the band, they're the *lads* – as in 'these are the *real* lads'. So Holly Johnson and Paul Rutherford aren't real lads because they're gay. That's not very positive."

IV

So what about Bronski Beat then? Biba Kopf (Chris Bohn), in the NME's review of their debut LP 'The Age Of Consent', portrays them as the worst of the lot: "professional gays, full time victims complicit in whatever misery it is that sets Jimmy off moaning his interminable white boy blues". I think he's wrong.

I should say at this point that I come neither

to exalt or insult Bronski Beat. Most of their music is good, but then again I've heard much better. Their album is promising, but too much of it is stylistically uninteresting and musically undramatic.

I should also say that any value that I shall claim for the sexuality embodied in the Bronski's pop is not an enduring one. *Nothing* can long survive pop's powerful assimilation of anything that threatens or undermines it. Look for example at how cliched already ZTT's bold symbolisms seem, despite the efforts of their brilliant propagandist, Morley, to stay one step ahead. And even if their music could remain uncontaminated, Bronski Beat themselves will soon turn to pop stars, whereas it is exactly that they aren't yet that I am drawing attention to as significant.

Their importance lies in the fact that they are simply so normal. Perhaps even to the extent of being boring. They're not good looking, neither do they have the spectacularly gross deformities that always make a good substitute for classic beauty in the pop world. They're not stylish, nor are their clothes fashionably uncool (as are Morrisey's). As they point out when I suggest that they will soon be plagued by copy-cat Bronski Beat haircuts, "they're so ordinary that people are doing it already."

It is for similar reasons that their gayness is so important and striking. They don't write songs about giving head, leather or transvestites, but about loving men. The most physical thing that happens in a Bronski Beat song is a kiss: "*the contempt in your eyes as I kiss his lips*", which would have meant, as Jimmy points out with some amusement, that if the BBC had decided to ban it they would have been taking the strange step of declaring the word 'his' obscene.

What I'm suggesting is that in a very imperfect way Bronski Beat are perhaps the first real, plain, boring, gay band; that consequently, they are the most threatening to those who find such things awkward/ unsightly/obscene. Bronski Beat videos and records can be the musical equivalent of two men kissing in the street. The real weight of this to those who are offended by either is that the band could be anyone. They shout a silent message so loudly that it scares the prejudiced: gays don't have to be outrageous, perverted, tight-lipped, limp-wristed, or pale-faced; the only significantly different thing about gays is that they are gay. And perhaps what frightens some people about the idea that gay can be normal is the way it undermines their own shady sexual self-assurance.

Of course I would be lying if I denied that Bronski Beat are a little 'camp' in the classic sense, but more important than that is the general point that they take gayness out of the nightclub or the bedroom or the bathroom and bring it into the living room, into the mundanity of normal life, (gays are just as boring as anyone else) where it belongs.

V

"you and me together / fighting for our love"

"Everybody's got their own idea of what love is. Some people don't believe in love, some people do. But the point is that everybody's got the right to actually have that thought, and if you're going to be denied those thoughts, then of course love is something to fight for."

But is it particularly a fight if the love is a gay love?

"Yeah of course, because we're actually not *allowed* to be in love. Love entails a lot of things – emotion, affection, and so on – we're denied those."

Before signing to London records Bronski Beat were offered a deal by ZTT ('£250

13

opposite sides of a desk in one of London Records' basement offices. In the article, you can tell how young I was by how old I'm trying to sound. I was 22, and pretending to know with certainty things that I'm barely beginning to understand thirty-six years later. It's excruciating, now, to witness all the fake-confident posturing and pomposity that I thought was required (pity, too, that I couldn't spell "Morrissey"), but I can also see myself just beginning to realise how to be honest and curious, and learning how to describe small things in a way which might make them just a little more than they at first seemed. *Jamming!* allowed me that. At its best, it was a great gift of *permission* all round – to its readers, to its subjects, to its editorial staff and, here, to a writer making his first hesitant newborn steps. I'm grateful for that. **Chris Heath**

advance') but turned it down. As Steve explains, they saw how Trevor Horn works. Did he like a particular song?

Larry: "Yeah, the most outrageous one."

Jimmy: "'Hard Rain', which is about bombs and fascism."

Steve: "There was this line he picked up on, 'when the fascist calls' . . "

Larry: "That's what he keyed in on. And the fact they we were gay. You could see it clicking over in his head – outrageous song, gay band."

VI

The first ever song Jimmy wrote was 'Screaming', which he recorded alone to a drum machine for a video project he and the others were working on. Lyrically, it comprises a list of mostly painful possessive remembrances from the opening *"my man love my first love / my closetness and pain"* to the closing *"my loneliness my aching brain / my pounding in my head . / machismo my manhood / my wanting just to scream"*

"It's the most personal song we do. It's about frustration and anxiety – about having to keep things to yourself; about the thoughts that go through your head – confusion."

While the plodding synth pop that makes up the backing doesn't take the imagination anywhere particularly exciting, the lyrics are a chilling re-enactment of an adolescence of guilty secrecy. As they admit, the song borrows its form off Scritti Politti's 'Lions After Slumber', but in comparison, Scritti's appears an indulgent catalogue of possessions – 'Screaming' has instead a chilling vulnerability.

VII

"money is the root of all evil"

"'Love and Money' is about how much money dictates. Like your sex life, what you can and can't do. And so many people have such a love for money that they would kill, exploit, or abuse for it", explains Jimmy.

But is money really the root of all evil?

"Yeah, I think so" he replies. "In the wrong hands. All those millions of pounds spent on nuclear arms – that is the root of all evil. Capitalism is the problem, it's becoming so outrageous. And it couldn't have come about without money."

But shouldn't you then be writing songs directed at capitalism?

"None of us are that politically intellectual", he answers derisively. "I can't write a song like that. I can only write one as it comes into my head, and that is quite simple."

But doesn't what you sing suggest that only the poor can be good?

"No!" he answers in exasperation, "but most capitalists are bad."

But won't you be reaping lots of profit and having a good time with it?

"Yeah", he says defensively.

So money can give you a good time. Things aren't so simple then, are they?

"No, but the line in the song explains what money is about at the moment. We'll take money, but we'll do good with it. We'll be *angels* with our money."

"Promise!" adds Steve in a Mickey Mouse falsetto.

But what will your fans think when they listen to the song but also see you raking the money in?

"I think they'll sing along" replies Steve. "It's a dead catchy tune."

VIII

"junk is all he'll ever know"

What's the junk? I ask Jimmy.

"Everything"

But what causes it?

"Capitalism. Commercialism. We all depend on it, we actually need it. That's why it's so depressing."

So are Bronski Beat junk?

"Everything's junk really. But you've got to pick out the best junk. But most people don't get the chance to do that because there's so much junk thrown at them. It's hard to find the good things. They're all smothered by the bad things, and it's getting worse. They make things that don't last as long as they should, so you've got to buy more often, so you spend more money. And they change the product all the time too."

But isn't the record industry you are working in perhaps the perfect example of a source of capitalistic junk?

"We're doing good stuff. We're not going to end up doing trash."

He adds later: "You're trying to go so deep – we're saying something so simple. How can you be looking so deep at something so simple? You've lost me about what you're going on about. We're not intellectual. We don't think in such deep ways."

IX

Before Jimmy arrived, I asked Larry and Steve about the music – about songwriting, influences, aims, intentions, methods, similarities. That was the only time in the interview they looked ill at ease. Finally Larry exclaimed with a bemused look on his face: "We've never been asked about the music before."

(the bit for the record company)

Bronski Beat's album, 'The Age Of Consent', features their first two singles, 'Smalltown Boy' and 'Why', both of which you should have swooned over in their far preferable 12" forms. It also features a weak 50's pastiche 'Heatwave', featuring a tap dancer on percussion, and a gay male voice choir (the Pink Singers) on the excellent smooth version of Gershwin's apt 'Ain't Necessarily So' (probably the next single), and on a poor cover of Donna Summer's 'I Feel Love' which totally misses the original's orgasmic intensity. Its only redeeming feature is the introjection near the end of *'Johnny Remember Me' . . . 'Johnny I love you. Why don't you come back?'*.

"That's an old cowboy song I think," remarks Jimmy.

Is it any Johnny in particular you're referring to?

"No" he replies, "It's just a line I sing."

"He's met so many Johnnys" adds Steve, sniggering.

X

I have argued that Bronski Beat have made their small contribution to widening horizons of thought and breaking down prejudice by trying to give a glimpse of the lifestyle and passion of some gays who are fairly average people, without purporting to directly represent anyone. But, the cynics cry, isn't all this gay stuff a marketing ploy?

Obviously it's impossible to stop a record company highlighting your saleable features (and representations of sex have always sold well, perhaps due to a lack of the real thing) but the Bronski's don't think they've been misportrayed at all and feel safe in the hands of London's marketing division. In fact they successfully managed to keep their pictures off their records – initially in a bid to maintain an anonymity which they soon discovered the pop machine wouldn't allow.

Not surprisingly Jimmy gets heated at the suggestion that they might be casually portraying a gay sexuality to sell records: he says with exasperation, "We *can* only write about and perform things as the emotions of gay men."

Within a few months, all these over-important judgements will seem stupid and ill-advised. By then, though their music may be better, the Bronski's life will inevitably be permanently interrupted and distorted by stardom. Because of that, however hard they try to retain it, their normality will have gone, and with it the most potent threat they pose. As soon as they're pop stars they can easily be marginalised again; 'wacky people; wacky habits'.

But it's still worth speaking now. These things do matter but the purpose of pointing them out was never so that it could be possible to reach out and grab them and cherish them at your leisure in a private place. Instead we must try to help, appreciate, and understand them as they bloom, knowing, but not regretting, that they will soon turn to dust in our fingers.

14

MORRISSEY'S YEAR

Then, he was just an insecure Mancunian Celibate.
Now, his every move thrills thousands.

STARRING **THE SMITHS**   DIRECTED BY **JONH WILDE**   SCREENPLAY BY **RUSSELL YOUNG**

My second date with Morrissey this year. And what a year. In January, there I was, carried away, The Smiths were worth the fuss. I had this dream . . . The Smiths were not far from life, not just concerned with singing about beauty, sorrow and love but ultimately intent on capturing the first nervous bursts of them all in every three minutes.

Our second date, wondering just where we are. Within the opulent walls of Liverpool's Adelphi Hotel, Morrissey and I munch cucumber sandwiches, sip tea and sigh softly. One year of The Smiths — what a serious world.

Our second date spent looking back — Morrissey eyeing me somewhat suspiciously, debating whether I've come to bury the ghost of The Smiths — in twelve months which has seen them tread the tightrope separating nervous bursts from burlesque.

1984 watched The Smiths edge dramatically away from that pure pop aestheticism (see 'This Charming Man') and nearer to a damaging self-parody. If anything, Morrissey was the living proof that intelligence does not breath easily in the pop whirlpool. Even excluding the unqualified embarrassment of the Sandie Shaw saga, The Smiths failed to burst. Their debut LP offered little of the glorious, shimmering brilliance of their previous singles (too self-conscious and clean-cut for its own good). Furthermore, their subsequent releases teetered along a little uncertainly.

Most importantly, Morrissey (now a household pop name) seemed bored with being Morrissey — the effete, ascetic aesthetic, the little charmer, life's burdens resting squarely upon his lonely shoulders. All his obsessions seemed exhausted, all his lifelong misery carefully chronicled. He sat next to Alvin Stardust on Pop Quiz and wriggled

uncomfortably, wondering quite what he was doing there. Maybe Morrissey was beginning to long for his solitary room again . . .
Time for the next cucumber sandwich, time for the first novel.

Maybe you've overexposed yourself this year?

All the interviews were becoming completely predictable, because everybody was asking me the same questions. When it appeared in print, it seemed as though I was very boring and that I could only talk about a limited number of things. That wasn't true; it was just that I was answering the same questions. I needed to step back, so I've only done one in the last four months, which for me shows great restraint.

Was it the probing, personal nature of the interview that unsettled you?

Well, I initially gave the impression that I would answer questions on any given subject, regardless of how personal they might be. So, people began to probe into the depths of the old soul, as a matter of complete course. Having to go through it several times a day . . . it's like staring at your own reflection in the mirror for twenty-four hours in a day — it's quite daunting. It was like constantly being on the psychiatrist's couch, people coming in asking, "Well, how ill are you today, how miserable are you now," like I was making a miraculous recovery from some great illness.

"It depends how heavily you want to probe into things. On the face of it, the Sandie project was a tremendous success. I felt, at that time, that what we were doing was the absolute envy of the entire industry. It was The Smiths, these relative newcomers, and Sandie Shaw at the other extreme. Just the way we came together, the combination was almost perfect; it had virtually never been done before in the history of music. I know that, if it had failed, the failure of the idea would have been given massive publicity, but it didn't fail. For that reason, I'm pleased. I just thought that the press treated it all like some Punch and Judy curious double-act. Everything, but the record, is immaterial, because you have to live with the record for ever, it will always be there.

"The whole Terence Stamp-Albert Finney attitude was so petty, even though I really like those people . . ."

Is that the danger in treating 'heroes' as something more than human?

I don't really believe that — I can't believe that even personal insult can corrode that adoration. I love those people, regardless of what they say, regardless of how disinterested they can get. I'll try to understand it and I'll still

23

love them. It is quite real, really.

Have you realised that there's a limit to how far you can push the public face of Morrissey?

(unclear) There are no limits and I intend to make full use of that fact. Lots of detractors have suggested that The Smiths have become very 'ordinary', very poppy. It always seems that, once you are accepted in artistic terms, then your records have no value. That seems most absurd, downright deceiving criticism.

When you get close to this industry, you see how it is so hostnamed by utter apes. When you're a member of the audience, sitting in the stalls, the whole idea of making records is incredibly wonderful. When you get into the thick of it, you realise that the subject being examined by cult...

You told me, last time, that you never wanted The Smiths to milk a formula dry. Weren't 'Heaven' and 'William' just ridiculously familiar?

I don't think the format of the songs become...

> "All the daily tabloids treat me as a dangerous figure and that pleases me. At least it means that I'm a strong person and I'm not Andrew Ridgely."

The cover with Morrissey was taken on the steps of Liverpool Town Hall. It was a windy day; I remember my cameras and films getting blown by a gust of wind and Morrissey getting down on his hands and knees to help pick it up. And then he said, 'Oh, I'm going to do the interview at the Adelphi Hotel,' and we had an amazing conversation walking over there, which we continued afterwards. I remember thinking, 'OK, you're the first genius I've met in the music business.' And to be honest, even since then I've not really met anyone with that peculiar intellect and humour in the music business. And rarely in life, ever. Our paths crossed over the years: I did the 'Everyday Is Like Sunday' single sleeve and he used photos of mine in *Peepholism*. That cover of *Jamming!* has always stood out to me. Somehow LFI got hold of that image and it was used in various unauthorised biographies. And I had to let him know through someone else that I did not give permission and nor did I get paid and if he wanted to sue them, go ahead, I don't do that, but good luck. You never know if Morrissey is miffed at you.

Russell Young

---

normal pop band"?

Only once, and that was coming off the set of Pop Quiz, because that was so depressing. It's easy to say that now, but as I sat in that chair next to Alvin Stardust, I thought, "My God! I've really lost control". Before the cameras rolled, Alvin Stardust told the audience a joke which was incredibly depressing and everybody laughed. I just thought, "Oh no! I shouldn't be here". I had nothing to talk to, that's the only reason I did it.

Do you think The Smiths, as a band, push themselves to the limit?

Totally. I see them as very extreme and in very positive ways. We never listen to everyone else. I think the only thing to do with advice is to ignore it because people will never understand the real you. They're never there when your group begins — they're never in your room when you're writing lyrics. So, I don't presume that they're going to understand my music and they don't. When people say erroneous things that are positive, I just smile. When they say erroneous things that are

negative, I feel very strong about it.

There was all that fuss about 'Suffer Little Children' in the newspapers, all these comments and opinions from people who knew nothing about the group and nothing about music. I felt very sad and angry about that, so much just being headlines. Nobody had approached me and never ever wrote long, inflated comments, "Morrissey says this . . ." and "Morrissey wrote it for this reason . . .". All of it was totally untrue and I couldn't understand why nobody had asked me. At one point, someone from The Daily Mail rang up, giving me the chance to give my side of the story. Of course, they weren't interested that I got on famously with the parents of the victims. So, they wouldn't print the story. Well, that really upset me.

We've never deliberately set out to court controversy but I think it is quite natural that we always will. The lyrics are intellectual and that's too easy in modern music. You can't write anything serious. When I wrote an ineffectual line such as "I was looking for a job" And then I found a job/And Heaven knows I'm miserable now", that outraged people which pleased me. All the daily tabloids treat me as a dangerous figure and that pleases me. At least it means that I'm a strong person and I'm not Andrew Ridgely.

Morrissey talks, you can't help thinking that he plays a cunning game — a pop's public face; you can't help wondering what's left of the real Steven Morrissey — introverted, solitary Manchester boy. He aims at being just the tiniest bit improbable, his talk littered with maxims and ironic wit. If Morrissey is his mask, it's a most fascinating presence. Meanwhile, I'm left wondering what remains of Steven Morrissey.

"It was really easy to lose my past, because I was so determined. I wanted to move on and forget. To an extent, I'm the same person, though I do tire of being Morrissey from time to time. Joining The Smiths was like a purging for me — it's been like a life-raft. Otherwise, nobody would have cared what I said about anything, which is quite sad. It means that, if you're an anonymous person, and you have very strong views, you're considered insane and you're closer to an asylum than a knighthood. But when you cross over and you become quite

famous, everything you say is quite interesting to people, then you're never considered insane. If I had stood in the middle of a Manchester housing estate and announced, 'I'm celibate', I probably would have been shot. I find it very difficult to be complacent. When somebody says something nauseating, I'm ready to attack — I'm not incapable of violence and I'm not incapable of being undiplomatic. I'm not a delicate flower by any means.

"I get angry when The Smiths are talked about in such short-sighted terms, the very fundamental, nonsensical things."

Didn't you bury all that this year — appearing on TOTP with a bush up your backside? Weren't you parodying the image of yourself?

It was the end of a stage for us and, in a way, it was parody. But also, to me, it was high art. Now, you can snigger, but in a hundred years . . . people laughed at the Pre-Raphaelites, remember that I did think it was quite artistic. For one thing, it had never been done before and to me, it's quite serious.

> "People stop me in the street and say 'Where's your bush?' which is an embarrassing question at any time of the day."

I mean, people stop me in the street and say, "Where's your bush?". Which is an embarrassing question at any time of the day. I mean, what do you say to people? "I've left it behind on the mantelpiece". I can't even mind if people remember me for my bush or my bearing-aid — as long as it's for artistic reasons. It was all done in being some life into TOTP and other programmes. I don't do anything just to surprise people. I'm not thinking, "Now, what will fox them next?". It's not a circus and I'm not some trapeze artist. I think The Smiths are an irregular group, regardless of what we do.

'**H**artial Of Hollow' seems like the perfect way to map the fluctuations of The Smiths so far, contrasting the sweeping grace of the early sessions with the later recorded works. Did Morrissey intend it as some retrospective summing up of The Smiths so far?

"There seems to be a few aspects to it," he replies. "We wanted it released on purely selfish terms because we liked all those tracks and those versions. I wanted to present those songs again in the most flattering form. Those sessions always caught the very heart of what we did — there was something positively messy about them, which was very positive. People are so nervous and desperate when they do those sessions, so it seems to bring the best out of them."

You've talked before though of losing your excitement for life. I mean . . . you're still very young. (I watch him smile)

It's like what I mentioned before about things seeming so wonderful from a distance, but when you go to Rome, you're bored and you want to come straight back home to Scunthorpe. It's a bit like that. When you're doing television programmes every day, interviews every day, being whisked up and down the country, you begin to get a headache. You just want to sit at home and do nothing, and you're made to feel that when you lose your zest for those 'glamorous' activities, there's something wrong.

Have you exhausted most of your ambitions this year?

No, because we still want to make lots of records and ultimately, that's the only thing that matters. Other things we can do without,

they're not important.

Do you never feel you've given it all away — exhausted all your passions?

I've given up a lot of my obsessions and some of that comes back to age, I regret to say. With almost everyone I've ever met in the music industry, they have music and success, but they also have their private lives — family or whatever. They can switch off, do something that is totally unrelated to music. But I've never done that, for me it's this way off the time, it's just music all the time. Besides that, I never think of my limitations, I just can't consider them because I can't consider failure.

I don't see that The Smiths have to change, it's just not necessary. People have got so used to modern artists changing so much that they expect it. To me, that just hints at massive insecurity. I have to say this again — I still feel that The Smiths have hardly begun, we've just scratched the surface. We'll last for a very long time. Because we entered the industry with such a furore, people thought it stank of hype and imagined we were a temporary attraction. I think people are beginning to come to terms with the fact that we will be around for a very long time.

Also, I must say that the material on the second official LP, which we're recording right now, is stronger than ever. We're still using the traditional, fundamental instruments and keeping it very basic. We still get such dramatically passionate feedback from Smiths' devotees and that makes me even more secure about the situation. I can't feel passionate about any one thing, besides The Smiths. It's like my most consistent fantasy throughout life — that we're of some value, feeling that we were here and we did something. Now, I'm pleased to say that I have.

26

BREAKING DOWN THE BARRIERS

Jamming!

NOW MONTHLY

No. 24 JANUARY 1985 60p U.S.$1.50 Eire 97p

THAT WAS THE YEAR THAT WAS!

BIG COUNTRY · R.E.M.
KANE GANG · SIMON FRITH
COOK DA BOOKS · ZERRA 1
── MINERS STRIKE ──
THE GREAT BRITISH FILM REVIVAL!

THE KANE GANG

From the hip to the thinking tank. Paul Davies catches the Kane Gang living it up.

'We've got to live with everything we do, so therefore we might as well be as true to ourselves as possible.'

ISSUE #24
12/84

Devoid of an obvious A-List act for a cover, we opted to create a collage that best summarised our 1984, which Russell Young brought suitably to life with the addition of his cat Jim.

The assorted images reflected Issue 24's varied contents. While a deeper dive with R.E.M. (Hugh Morley), a return interview with Big Country (Martin Wroe, who got a free trip to Paris out of the deal) and an introductory piece on The June Brides (Bruce Dessau) demonstrated our continued commitment to some sort of New Rock, this was tempered by Chris Heath's considered argument on the subject with Zerra 1, my drunken escapade to Zürich with Liverpool's anti-punks Cook Da Books, and a piece by Paul Davies on the decidedly funky Kitchenware Records act The Kane Gang. Nikki Sudden and Felt also made an appearance.

But the best pieces were those far removed from regular musical profiles. With the miners' strike now entering a desolate winter and with 'scab' workers returning to the pits out of desperation, I took a trip to Pontefract with my best friend (and bandmate) Tony Page and my oldest friend (and early *Jamming!* contributor) Jeffries Briginshaw, where the depressing scenes played out on my psyche in a way that no manner of Redskins anthems or Billy Bragg ballads could ever match. Recognising that there was a low-grade civil war going on across parts of the country, I wrote about the experience with something approaching real journalism, and we all regretted condensing the resulting article down to three pages instead of four (especially as the issue contained a surplus amount of festive filler). Elsewhere, esteemed *NME* cartoonist Ray Lowry was recruited for an end-of-year review that revealed him as an equally gifted writer, this being

one of the sharpest and most acerbic pieces *Jamming!* ever published. Phill Jupitus delivered a meticulously drawn and suitably hilarious full-page comic strip; we collectively assembled a humorous (and not entirely far-fetched) look at the prospects for 1985 (further illustrated by Jupitus); there were features on films, the record label Fashion, another poetry page and a rare collaborative article warning of 'The Death of the Independents'. Amidst all this lively debate, a profile of academic music critic Simon Frith seemed superfluous.

Behind the scenes, however, *Jamming!* had fallen apart. Financing a monthly magazine from an overdraft at my mother's bank was insane at the best of times, but with interest rates in the double figures in 1984, it was nothing short of suicidal. We were selling magazines, but not enough of them. We were getting ads, but not enough of them. The money was only just coming in from the first monthly issue, and there was not enough of it to bring down those interest charges and an ever-growing overdraft. Barclays of Dulwich Village finally realised they'd backed the wrong horse and shut down the pipeline. I couldn't pay the printing bills, and Issue 24 stalled on the presses. I was all of 20 years old, with no business training, mentors or managers, having operated for seven years on enthusiasm and energy, and readily distracted from what was obviously now a full-time job by the allure of television and my equally long-term band. Frantic phone calls finally found our saviours in the unlikeliest of corners: a pair of Jewish South African émigrées running a successful business magazine called, *What Telephone?* (Yes, really.) *Jamming!* 24 finally rolled off the presses around Christmas Day, barely making it to the stores before the cash-flow crunch end-of-the-month; the so-called 'holidays' remain a permanent personal blur.

UNDERMINI

Tony Fletcher visits Pontefract, the Yorkshire heartland of the Miners Strike, to see what life is like after nine months on strike.

I CAN THINK of more *comfortable places to be at 5.00 am on a freezing November morning than on a picket line outside a Yorkshire pit for the first time. We're waiting at Prince of Wales colliery in Pontefract – an area prominent in the news for its violence during the strike – for the 'scab bus' (as it is unanimously known in the area) to bring in the morning's working miners. Today, Friday November 23, is the last day available for men to go back to work and claim the various bonuses and holiday pay on offer from the National Coal Board in their massive publicity campaign. The previous Monday had seen the largest single 'surge' back to work since the dispute started, but at Prince of Wales, the number had only just reached double figures out of a work-force of around 1400.*

By any outsider's standards, the morning picket is a large one. Over a hundred miners mill around trying to keep warm, half of them crowded around the bus shelter opposite the pit, the other half to one side of the entrance. The official NUM picket – limited to six by Tory industrial laws – huddle around their fire by their makeshift hut, behind police lines. The road is blocked off from all traffic, with police vans dotted all over the area. A few hundred yards down the road, the M62 – the motorway that links the industrial north – draws out its straight line parallel to a railway track, that has seen many a miner receive a beating at the hands of riot police in the past few weeks. Up towards the town is another railway line and a road junction; it is from here that the bus will come.

All of a sudden, and without warning, the pickets by the colliery gate disappear up the road towards the town. They call the others, but before we can follow them, a police line has blocked the road, throwing back any picket trying to get through. But by now at least fifty pickets are on their way casually up the road, totally to my bemusement. It's a good two or three minutes before two riot police vans – as surprised by the move as anyone – set off after them.

Five minutes later, a series of headlights appear blazing over the crest of the hill, the police escort for the 'scab' bus that comes careering in at 30–40 miles an hour, carrying what seems to be around a dozen working miners, in a darkened bus that makes counting almost impossible. The remaining sixty pickets make a token shove forward, screaming 'Scab!' as the men are driven in. Immediately, everyone disperses, as an incident starts with the other half of the picket further up the road.

Dejected at the futility of simply watching the bus shoot in every day, the splinter group had gone to meet it at traffic lights up the road, where they now realised it stopped every morning to get ready for the sprint into the pit. The pickets had just missed the bus, held back by riot police; in fury and frustration, they started stoning their adversaries. As a mounted charge by the police split them up, a chase ensued down the railway line and a few men got an early morning beating at the hands of truncheon-wielding riot police. No arrests were reported.

It's a typical morning in Pontefract.

1984 WILL BE remembered as the year of the Miners Strike, one of the most historical industry struggles in the history of Britain, whichever side you are on. Though dominating the news for the past nine months, for the vast majority of people it has become a strangely taboo subject, considered part of the three matters never to be discussed for fear of argument, politics, religion and money. Sooner or later, somebody is going to 'win', and the larger part of the country is prepared to take a stand seat until that day, confident that the miners strike has nothing to do with them.

Which couldn't be further from the truth. The Miners Strike is the crucial event that is going to settle the route this country follows for many years to come. In one corner is a Government whose monetarist policy puts profits before people, believing that a Coal Board with a healthy balance sheet is more important than the welfare of whole communities, and who see Trade Unions as annoying structures aimed at disrupting the economy and therefore harming the monetarist policy. In the other corner is a group of workers and their union renowned throughout history for being the most hard-lined in the country. In this instance, they have chosen to be the first section of the working class to refuse to accept the Government's policies, affecting them and their communities as severely as mass pit closures will do. The battle-lines are drawn, and it was obvious that with the two extremes at war, no-one would 'win' overnight.

The media has pointed out that the NUM moved its money out of the country three days before calling the strike. The Economist, not a particularly liberal magazine, printed in 197_ details of a secret Conservative paper that admitted to expecting the miners to be the group to respond against Tory policy should they get in, and disclosing measures to ensure they (the Tories) would not be caught on the hop. These included mass stock-piling of coal at power stations and the training of the police force to prevent at all costs, industrial action having any effect.

Many of Jamming!'s readers are likely to have at least some sympathy for the miners, and being among them, it no longer seemed good enough to sit back and take the facts from the TV and National Press, which has, with the smallest of exceptions, presented only one side of the argument. So it was, with two active union friends, that I journeyed to the battleground of Pontefract, not attempting to come back with the definitive word on the Miners Strike, or even hoping to cover every aspect involved, but to capture the feeling of the people and the world they are living in, in what has proved the heartlands of the strike.

Our host was a miner we shall call Tom, a worker at Prince Of Wales, currently under a 1_ m – 4 am curfew after his second arrest of the rike. Though, through his militancy, Tom is not ypical of the striking miners, he was an ideal guide r revealing the other side of the coin.

AT THE START of the strike, Yorkshire was solid. So much so that picket lines were irrelevant – the pits simply stayed losed and unattended – while the hard-liners like om went off to picket other areas. Tom was urned back on the Nottinghamshire county line nore times than he can remember, but it failed to op him being on a picket virtually every morning nce day one. Only in the few weeks before our isit had men started going back to work in the rea, tempted by the enormous bonuses being Tered and the poverty they themselves were in.

"There was a surge," admits Tom of the revious week's growth in 'new faces'. "But ney're family men. They're desperate. Some of nem, who haven't been around the strike, wanted get a Christmas bonus. But that's dropped now we think we'll have them out by Christmas."

The two per cent at work in the area were at least aving one positive effect for the striking miners, in otally stretching the police force. Working miners re being given quite incredible police protection s they arrive for work, which creates animosity nat can only lead to violence, and this has retched the West Yorks police to the point where ney had had to, on the morning we set off, draft in utside police. "They've announced a programme hereby they're going to take in scabs on a aggered basis," says Tom. "5 O'Clock one pit, 6 'Clock the next. But if they can transfer the cops om one pit to another, then so we can transfer the ickets."

Tom's attitude is uncompromising – "We love king on the Tories," he announces – but it is one orn out of the miners pride and commitment to eir cause. "The base line for us is jobs. *We've got where else to go.* As far as we're concerned the only ing we can do is fight. What can you do if you aven't got a job? Have this woman put us all on oody youth training schemes? We're not having ommunities wiped out. We're not having mass b losses. We're not having old traditions wiped ut. This is us, this is our tradition; it's like music black areas. *It's culture.* You can't erode these ings away from us."

Tom keeps telling us that we've got to feel the ood of the area ourselves to understand what the ruggle is about. So the next morning, we do.

FROM PRINCE of Wales (which is where you joined us), a modern colliery not used to the amount of support it has been getting late, we drive to Fryston and Wheldale, two old astleford pits which had seen their most fierce enes of violence at the start of the week. We had drive along a totally unlit stretch of road where mp-posts had been uprooted by striking miners form a barricade along with cars from a nearby rapyard and a JCB. This had been the strikers action to men coming in for the first time, bribed the NCB's money and under heavy police otection. The local NUM official claimed it was e work of outsiders, but Tom knew different. "It s the work of local people. Whether or not you ree with all that happened, they did deal with e problem of people going in at that pit. And so e people that were going in at Wheldale are now ing taken in at Kellingley."

The mood at the Wheldale and Fryston llieries is harder, but sparser than at Prince of ales. Twenty odd pickets roam around at each of e pits, as we try to establish whether the strike- eakers have gone in or not. At Fryston, a pit lage that was later to provide my most vivid emory of the trip as a whole, an older picket

(teenagers and old men are side by side on the picket lines) asks which pit we're from. When he hears of our circumstances, he breaks into a jovial mood. "London, eh? Cor, farking' 'ell," he says, hoping to imitate us. "I knew a bloke from London once . . ."

Little more needs to be said; the isolation here is such that we could as easily have been from Aberdeen, Belfast or Mars. As we leave, the pickets are still staring sullenly at the pit across the road, the source of all their pride and all their hatred, all at once.

Any astute observer of the miners dispute knows that it will be won or lost at the power stations – or more precisely, in transit between the coalfields and the power stations. These get 80% of their fuel from coal, and were the workers to take action in sympathy with the miners, the country would grind to a halt, and the strikers be victorious virtually overnight. However, with their union leaders giving only verbal support to the miners, the power stations have been able to continue running, albeit using a 50% oil mixture and suffering voltage cuts. Now the afore-mentioned stocks of coal are dwindling, and the miners' task is to prevent the coal being transferred from stocks at pits and eventually, from the Midlands. Union leaders, anxious to prevent any kind of national strike, have refused to call out the power workers in sympathy, but rank and file support is strong. The previous night, we had met a shop steward from the local Egborough Power Station, trying his best to build up support for the miners cause, and at least ensure his men would not accept 'scab' coal when the time came. This morning was to see miners' wives picket the power station to try and win the workers' support. But when we arrive, the only people at the gates are the SWP, busy leafletting the incoming workers and annoyed to know that they will have competition later in the morning.

By now, the rain is coming down and we go to Kellingley, Britain's largest pit with a workforce of 2,400. Surprisingly, there are a mere fifteen pickets, others hindered possibly by the colliery's position off the beaten track and the weather, but more so by sheer despondency. The police however are taking no chances – Kellingley was the scene of violent clashes a few weeks back, and Tom shows us the mushroom farm next door used by the police to show the miners a lesson or two. This morning, in the face of this pathetic turn-out of pickets, the twenty uniformed men on the gates are backed up by *twenty-three* (count them) Transit vans full of riot police in the courtyard. It would take a thousand pickets to so much as contemplate challenging this number of police, and there's little sign of that. But like ourselves, the police have no idea where this morning's mass picket will be – it is a word of mouth event that has failed to reach Tom – and so throw out every man available to every pit in the county to avoid being caught short.

Being the biggest pit in the country, it is probably no surprise that men have gone back, but as three buses sped in at 7.00 am – the middle one blacked out and the outside two full of jeering, insulting strike-breakers – there is little chance of a head-count. The NCB claims 90, and as the coaches are driven round the back of the pit for the first trip, there is no chance of disputing this. But the whole issue of the number of 'new faces' claimed by the NCB each day was causing widespread anger at the time of our visit. On November 20, three days before our visit, The Sun's early editions reported 47,631 miners at work. For some reasons, later editions had this at *62,631.* Coal News, the NCB's own paper, claimed 57,000 men working in their July issue, 'more than 60,000' in August, and in November, a

massive . . . 53,000. The Daily Telegraph, on November 10, let slip that there were '150,000 men still on strike', meaning that, even if workshops and cokeworks were taken into account, only 46,000 men could be at work. A lot of confusing statistics, but for many miners, all that mattered was the depressingly regular count of 'new faces' declared on the news each day.

We adjourn to the Kellingley Strike Centre, a venue that should be a hive of activity after the morning picket, but instead has only a few disheartened men drinking tea and peeling potatoes for the days kitchen work. I couldn't help but wonder, that with 90-odd men going in, and 15-odd on the picket, that there were 2300 men at the Kellingley pit taking no active part in the stike. If they had wanted to, they could all have walked into work with no fear of attack. At the same time, if they felt strongly enough, they could all have been on the picket.

According to Tom, Kellingley is a possible centrepoint in the region. "What we think they'll do," he says, "is take the people in from different pits to a pit like Kellingley and get them to operate the washing plants there. With a skeleton force of 100 you could work a coal preparation plant, and that means prepare coal for the power stations. And at the same time, with a real concentrated effort from the state, really going mad – which they've been doing – they can reduce your pickets through fright. You've got men in the group operating t'washing plant, and then, what's happening in the Barnsley area, is that the only jobs available are for HGV licensed men. They can get people who've been on the dole for years, to move the coal to the power stations, to give them this final kind of injection to keep them going through this real hard period. Because they're knackered – honestly, there's no coal stocks there. So then they can keep this front going, that the .strike's having no effect, and the demoralisation process will set in . . ."

Sad to say, it already had at Kellingley.

BACK AT Tom's house, *Breakfast TV informs us that the morning's mass picket was at Askern – only ten miles towards Doncaster – and of the spilling of thousands of tons of coal, by French miners before it could leave their country for Britain. This at least is good news. "If they can do that for us all those miles away, why can't the bloody power workers up here do something?" challenges Tom. We're soon joined in his house by five more people, just off the picket lines, this time members of the Revolutionary Communist Party, the third and final far-left party we'd met within two hours this morning! Only two are actual miners, joined by a woman teacher from Leeds and the spitting image of (Citizen) Wolfie Smith's dumb partner, who's from Huddersfield. How far is that, we ask. "No idea," he replies. "I don't even know where I am."*

The reason for the abundance of far-left political organisations in mining areas at the moment is neither because they're running the strike or particularly striving to win over the miners' allegiances. The miners at the moment need little persuasion to desert a Labour party that has already deserted them. Founded in the interests of the working class, history may prove that no Labour Government has done much for its supposed kind. But even so, the common miner and his wife has been surprised at the total lack of support given them by their leaders, in this struggle. When Neil Kinnock condemns picket line violence every time Thatcher demands him to, it is obvious that he has never spent so much as one morning of the strike on a picket line to see where that violence comes from. When the Labour Party and TUC give verbal support for the miners but not one iota of practical support, it is obvious that the miners feel alone. And when the NUM are told by their so-called allies to follow the law, then that isolation turns to frustration and direct action. For the law has been the tool used by the Government to attempt to totally destroy the miners in this dispute, either by its petrifying use of a state police force, making indiscriminate arrests and beatings whilst spending valuable public money protecting a minority of working miners; by getting Tory lawyers to act for working miners, declaring the strike unofficial, fining the union large sums of money and then attempting to sequestrate its funds; and finally, by appointing a Receiver who just happens to be a Tory Party official. As many of these outcomes have stemmed from the Tory Industrial Laws – which the TUC refuses to recognise – it is ironic that the one union prepared to stand up to them is outcast because of it.

At the same time, the fringe parties calling for a national strike live in a dream world. Most Britons have been trained to look after themselves and noone else; though many may be prepared to put 10p in a collection bucket, asking them to sacrifice their own wage for what they see as someone else's struggle, is, at this moment in time, futile.

All of which only serves to make the miners feel more isolated than ever. And if nobody else who claims to be acting for them will help them, then they'll damn well help themselves.

THE PERFECT EXAMPLE of this is the Miners Support Groups, run predominantly by wives to ensure that noone is starved back to work. As Tom remarks, "The support groups are like extra-union activities. The women go everywhere, they're all over the shop. These things are based on need, not on rules and regulations of the Trade Union movement.

"Before this strike, a lot of miners were quite backward in ways. But now, the wives are down on the picket lines, saying 'This is our strike – it''s our community that's at stake.' If they try and prevent their wives getting involved, they'll have a bloody riot in the kitchen, let alone on the picket line!"

Up in Pontefract Town Hall, the kitchens are better equipped and more organised. But the struggle and effort is the same. We arrive shortly after mid-day, with a queue reaching down the stairs, and a larger kitchen covered in steam as half-a-dozen women attempt to cook for 300 people at once. Across one wall is an enormous sculpture of Nelson's death throes, accompanied by the legendary line, "England expects every man to do his duty." The irony of this was probably discussed when the miners first came here to eat; now it is simply ignored.

But the lack of drive shows itself when a cook shouts out for help to wash some dishes before more meals can be served. Noone volunteers, so five minutes later silence is called and the kitchen is announced closed unless people come forward immediately. The men look round wearily; two or three raise a smile and head off for the kitchens. "If they can go on strike, we can go on strike," says Linda Walsh, treasurer of the Pontefract Miners Wives Support Group.

Linda spends all her time running the support group, sprinkling the newsletter with quotes from Shakespeare, Shelley and Churchill to give historical references to their struggle. She explains how they can now provide 1200 meals for under £250 a week, all of the food being bought wholesale. The local (Labour) council consider it a favour letting them have the hall, so money has to come in from collections, donations and raffles – today's prize for a 10p ticket being a joint of beef for Sunday lunch. So much for the prosperity of Britain in 1984.

With so much talked about Social Security money paid out during the strike, I ask Linda how much her family of four live on a week. "Oh, we're fortunate," she says. "We get £32.50 a week, plus child benefit." Making a grand total of £45.50 to pay for everything for four of them. Wondering how she could dare call herself fortunate, she tells me about a young striker who came in, having just had his electricity cut off. With a boy of five, a little girl of two, and a baby expected in eight weeks, he was living on £11.85 a week plus child benefit of £13, and the Electricity Board wanted £6 a week off him to reconnect the power. To prevent more cases, the Support Group gave out duplicate letters to send to the local Electricity Board and Director of Social Services. Linda herself hasn't paid her mortgage for three months, but were the Building Societies to attempt to reclaim one

miner's house, they'd have to reclaim nearly a hundred thousand, an unthinkable proposition.

LINDA'S HUSBAND Terry, and his mate Eddie, are the last men out of the kitchen, around 2.00 pm. Both were at Prince of Wales for the picket, and have spent the rest of the morning helping the Support Group. These two are hard-working miners, committed to their job and their community – and therefore to the strike – but both must now go through life with a criminal record. Eddie served an eleven-day stretch in a top security Leicestershire prison for allegedly assaulting a policeman. His lawyer, brought up from London by the NUM, called it the 'worst example of a kangaroo court' he had ever seen. Despite their records, both want to play the strike by the book, which is why they disagree with the decision to picket Egborough power station on Monday.

The Fryston picket 'hut' (a generous description) has 'Fryston A-Team' sprayed across its corrugated sides.

The village itself consists of half-a-dozen rows of red-bricked back-to-back terraced houses literally a stone's throw from the pit, a permanent reminder to the families, of who owns them. Some houses are boarded up, and cars are far and few between. Eddie points to a field behind the village where the sight of kids searching a slag-heap for traces of coal is a sad one. Four children have already died at Upton, a few miles away, when heaps had collapsed on them, whilst looking for coal. "They glossed over that pretty quick in the media didn't they?" complains Terry. Eventually, upon production of a union card, we get to take photos, but my visual memory of Fryston was already implanted on my mind for ever. It was one of pitiful poverty, of frustration that had escalated into wanton violence in the area, and of suspicion born out of desperation.

The story at Wheldale was much the same. Here the pickets apologised for not being able to take us into the pit itself as they could have a few weeks back, but the sight of the abandoned JCB, uprooted lamp-posts and damaged bridge told its own tale, as did the white paint on the colliery wall declaring 'Scargill 84' and the 'scabs' names. The pickets told us of the one-armed man arrested for throwing stones (?!), and of the picket who with two broken knees had still demanded to be on the lines. Given the thermos flasks and told to stay at the back, when trouble had broken out he was hand-cuffed helpless to a lamp-post as an easy arrest. In police custody, he had refused to be photographed or have his fingerprints taken – both basic civil rights – and had seen his charge altered from breach of the peace to assault on a police officer. Which isn't bad going for a man who couldn't walk!

THE PREVIOUS night we'd asked Tom at what point the miners could claim victory. His answer went off at tangents, but still painted a picture that shows a long wait before peace returns to the area. "Obviously, the thing that stays in everybody's minds is the withdrawal of pit closures. But things have changed since the strike developed. I think if we can come out of this strike with our organisation intact, without becoming cynical about all the things we've learned about these fringe groups; and about organising ourselves at rank and file level; and being able to defend all the people who've been done . . . 'Cos they're sacking people who've been done a few times, and especially, they sack instantly people who've been done for pinching coal. We dealt with our coal stocks very early on. We descended on them – they went out to pensioners and everybody else. There's a man across the street, an ordinary bloke, and he said to me the other day, 'I'll never go back to that pit if they sack people who've been active in this strike.'

"They're not gonna withdraw the pit closure list, and on the other hand, we're not gonna be forced back to work by the state or any bugger else. In the middle of that there's going to be no negotiated settlement. I leave you to make your own minds up . . ."

The pictures shown on these pages were mostly taken in Yorkshire and Nottingham. Not one has yet been printed by the National Press, despite the disturbing scenes they show. They might go some way to proving that not all picket line violence comes from the miners.

Orgreave May '84

Maltby

Cresswell

Photos used by kind permission.

Credits:– The News Line, Martin Jenkinson, International Freelance Library Limited.

Boasting a bucketful of hooks, heart and highly articulate ideals, **REM** spearhead the revival of American rock. In conversation with *Hugh Morley*, guitarist *Peter Buck* sheds light on their upward ambitions.
Photos: *Russell Young*

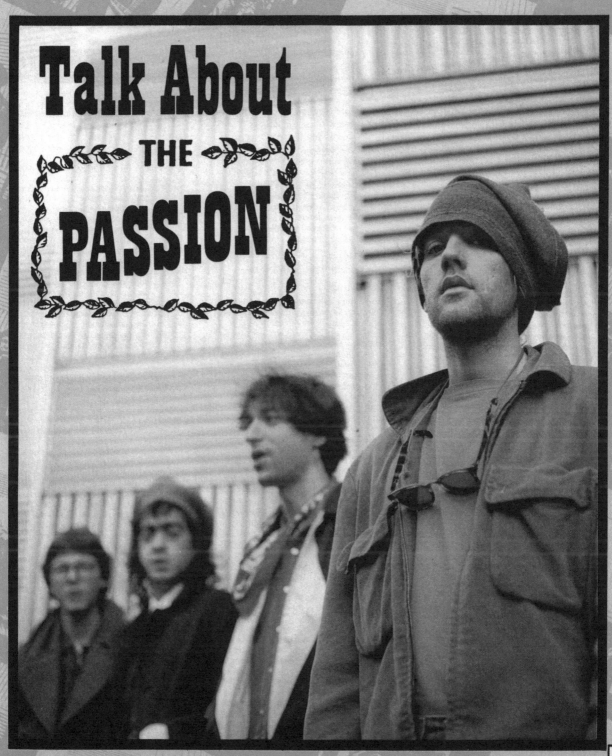

Talk About
THE
PASSION

Anyone who lauds the briliance and intensity of the second REM album, 'Reckoning', can understand the problems of interviewing the band. Clutched full of hooks, riffs and the melancholic achings of Michael Stipe the album is not perfection, for no such thing exists in the world the REM's strive for, but is a supreme example of a perfectly orbicular pop-album that stands alone on its own merits. What more need be said?

At the same time the members of the band come from the grittily down to earth region of the Deep South of the United States. An area steeped in traditions almost totally at odds to their sweet soaring melodies, savage invention and arrogant disrespect for the old ways.

I met Peter Buck, REM's highly articulate guitarist, in a Baker Street hotel. A man so choked with enthusiasm that his speech is emitted in spasms at twenty words per second. Half afraid that this brief chat would dispel the aura surrounding the band's music, I probed him to find more about one of the few bands to keep the torch burning in the rush for pop-wimpery, bug-eyed foppery and the consumption of a mass melodic opiate to soothe away the depression.

In his first blast, he exposes the tangential path REM are taking away from British pop values; ironically, some would say, a return to the old ones. Having been nurtured in an atmosphere where you live and die on the night, and not on the front of a magazine, REM think THEY'RE doing it differently!

Certainly, if the success of their recent Uk tour is anything to go by, they're doing it successfully too. With this being their last visit to this country for twelve months, their next LP will not arrive until mid-'85.

"I just think The Smiths are the English REM."

I start by wondering how the singles sell? REM always seemed like a pop band to me – a natural 45's machine.

"I like putting out singles but I don't have any hope that we'll have a hit. In the States they get to number eighty or something, but we're not really a singles band. 'Reckoning' sold a quarter of a million copies which is good for a band that doesn't have a monstrously huge video. We've found ways to short circuit the rock and roll business. We tour a lot rather than putting out videos. We do every interivew, every radio station, every teeny video station and every live TV show that wants us – building a following of people who trust us and are willing to take chances

on going out and buying a record before they've heard it."

So how do people look at REM in the States? Over here, 'rock' music has been swept away by synthesiser and dance music to an extent, but in the States it never went away.

"It's strange but you're right. Over here, we're more against the trends but in America 'rock and roll' never really left. Bands like us – if there were any – still weren't on the radio, but in America we're perceived as 'Hey, this rock and roll band that doesn't have hair down to their waist, doesn't have a monster light show and who aren't jerks. It's seen as an alternative to rock and roll – stripping away a whole lot of excess.

"Because it seems like once any band gets successful they have smoke bombs, light shows, boring albums, videos, with naked girls . . . so we're seen as how to do it without turning into a cliché!"

So do you think you're actually different – aside from the trappings etc, the music itself?

"I think the reasons for doing it and the results are a lot different from bands in say, the top forty. In America now there are a lot of bands who are really good but who aren't getting accepted because they're on a small label or they're uncompromising and we feel an affinity for those bands – mostly regional bands. Suddenly an audience has sprung up who don't listen to the British Invasion bullshit and are slowly returning to American groups. Three years ago there wasn't anyone making interesting records in America, but in the last year a lot of bands have come up from nowhere.

"Things like the mutated hardcore stuff – Huska Du, The Replacements, Black Flag. There's a lot of pop stuff coming out of LA whether it be The Dream Syndicate or The Rain Parade or the Gun Club – though they're not a pop band. In the North East there are the DB's, The Raybeats, Mitch Easter's Band (Let's Active), & Jason and The Scorchers. Every city has a scene just now and every scene is filled with bands, some good, some bad, but who are trying to do something outside the American music business."

How is the radio now? When you started it must have been really stiff.

"Yeah it still is. The first EP and 'Murmur' were played by the college stations and then with 'Reckoning' we made inroads into the commercial stations. But the whole way we've gone about this is to prove that we're an indispensable band. We're trying to prove that they can ignore us for so long but we're not going to go away. We're going to keep making records and you're going to keep hearing about us, so sooner or later you've got to play us."

So what kind of music did you listen to when you were young? Is there a big country influence in there?

"I heard country all the time but I never liked it up until the last four years. In the South you grow up with it and your parents listen to it and it's like, 'christ that old Okie stuff, whining in his beer'. But now I've realised that it's working class white soul music. The good stuff that is – Hank Williams and George Jameson. And although I'm not an expert I've started listening to it more.

"When I was young it was really obvious stuff – The Beatles and The Stones and The Supremes. When I was thirteen or fourteen I guess I was different or I was trying to be different – I really liked the Velvet Underground, T. Rex and Slade. I also really loved The Raspberries and The Beach Boys. I probably didn't own a record by a black person until I was sixteen and I suddenly fell in love with Al Green. Then it spread until I was listening to Howling Wolf, The Cramps and The Sex Pistols. All that stuff from '76 and '77 was very exciting."

"I think there are good things to come from every era – the past is the beginning of the present."

Were you isolated from punk being down in Athens?

"We got it second hand. I started reading about it in '75 and I couldn't figure heads or tails of it. I mean it was like 'The Ramones and Blondie and Talking Heads are all punks huh?' So you buy the albums when they come out and it was 'That's really weird!' In Athens, everyone was really into the punk thing, but it didn't mean that you got a spikey haircut and a leather jacket – it just meant that anyone could do it. So the B-52's were directly inspired by punk and the same with us."

So how important was it that you came from the South? Of the main bands who came out of that area, B-52's and Pylon, you have a more traditional 'Southern' sound.

"It's more of an American sound. We didn't just want to be real trendy – we didn't know enough how to be – we just had to pick up the instruments and learn to play. We started up and we were musically primitive, but we weren't ready to throw away the past and start over afresh. I think there are good things to come from every era – the past is the beginning of the present.

"Whereas I don't think the people in Pylon I ever really listened to music until 1977 and then they just picked up the instruments and started playing. You can tell there wasn't a whole lot of knowledge of blues and soul."

So how did this unique sound come about where the bass and drums hold it together and work really hard so that the guitar and singing can do whatever they want?

"Well Bill and Mike had worked together before so they were real tight and Bill especially loved that Motown and soul stuff with the bass and drums locked in. When I first started, I was a pretty inept guitar player and I'd do anything to fill up the spaces – all these weird guitar parts. And it was a conscious decison to go freeform. That the instruments would call and respond and work together as an ensemble."

Someone compared REM recently to The Smiths – have you heard them?

"Yeah I can understand the similarity. People on this tour have said I've been influenced by Johnny Marr but I hadn't heard one note of the Smiths until about four months after 'Reckoning' came out. There are probably things we have in common, I just think they're the English REM."

Listening to 'Reckoning' and especially, 'Don't Go Back To Rockville', although it's a love song, it's like this Southern boy trying to get out; a desperation to get out of this place where nothing happens?

"In a way, yeah! Nothing really does happen in Athens and it was a way to enliven the boredom. It was definitely an attempt to try and break away from the norm. We didn't look ahead and say, 'well, we'll be going to New York and England and we'll make records.' But it was the only way we could really grasp at the time to change our situation immediately. We didn't expect to be a good band, we just thought we could do it and tour a bit and it would be something worthwhile to do with our lives."

"Except for Carter, America's elected Nazis for the last fifteen years."

In New York they have this attitude about 'oh down there in the South, closed minds and rednecks' and this sort of stuff. Now that you've travelled, do you think it's changed the way you look at things or is that just a myth they create to elevate themselves?

"Well the South has always been the whipping boy. I mean there have been a lot of real bad things in the South – racial problems and everything – but it's not hidden. The racial problem is a lot worse in the North than the South. It's certainly less sophisticated than say New York or Los Angeles, but if you go thirty miles out of New York, it's just as hick as anywhere in Georgia.

"It's this myth about the South being backwards but I really like it there. Scotland and Wales remind me of the South a lot. The audiences are a lot less 'let's dress up', less money, less pretentious. They just want to have fun and people are friendly.

"When we first got to New York people would come up to me and go 'Well I'm glad there's a good band in the South because

"The whole way we've gone about this is to prove that we're an indispensable band."

everything is so stupid and the Civil Rights problems . . .' and it's like, 'fuck you!.' Two years ago in Boston they tried to integrate the schools and it was almost like a war. All of us have gone to integrated schools all our lives and that's the way it goes."

How much of that is left – the traditional problems of racism etc?

"Sure its still there, and everywhere in America too. In the big cities its not so bad. The main problem is a kind of secondary racism in that black schools still aren't up to par. And though there's integration, there's still schools that are predominantly black and aren't so hip and so you don't get a good degree and you don't get a job if you want it. Like in Athens, even with the schools integrated, you still don't have a chance because there's no jobs."

In the past, you've said you write songs lyrically obliquely, and they are mainly just personal. Are there any themes running through them?

"Well we tend to write the songs in one bulk. We'll be on the road and we'll have two weeks to write the songs. Without meaning to, a lot of the same themes will multiply around. Like the first album was a time when a lot of things were changing in our lives and we had a record deal and we were getting to a point where we realised people would listen to us and there's five or six songs where it's not really elucidated on but it's about travel and change and leaving things behind, whether it's 'Pilgrimmage' or 'Catapult' or whatever.

"With 'Reckoning' there's a whole lot of weirdness about lost love or lost friends because we've had a couple of suicides and car wrecks and stuff like that which happened to close friends. And communication – there are a number of songs about communication."

Does it bother you that some of them are difficult to decipher whether it's through the language or Michael's accent or whatever?

"No, I think emotionally you get the correct thing. I mean I don't have to tell you that 'Camera' is about a friend of ours who's dead – you can pick that up from the 'will she be remembered' bit. Sure there's some obscure imagery, you know, book stuff. But it's like Dylan, a lot of stuff is filler to fill a line emotionally. Sometimes it bothers me that

people are so used to having it delivered on a plate that they don't try."

So what's 'Little America' about?

It's this weird perverse view of us driving around the country seeing things that are really nice and really horrible. You know, 'What's our country coming to?' About being a performer – having your soul caught and killed for commercial display and the fact that America does make the most noise. 'The biggest wagon is the empty wagon' – sometimes I think America is bankrupt but it's not. I mean, there are plenty of good things there but sometimes when you're feeling bad and you think 'goddamit I've got Reagan back again and the moral majority is running this country – what's going wrong with this place?' It should be great. America should be the greatest country in the world. And it's not the worst but there's a lot of things wrong with it. The selfishness. The fact that we keep electing Nazi's. Except for Carter, we've elected Nazi's for the last fifteen years.

Does it ever motivate you to sing about it specifically?

"We do talk about it but we're not that kind of band. Those things come through but I can't tell you how bored I get hearing how bad Reagan is. There isn't enough time in a rock and roll song to tell the world what's going on – even if you're qualified to do it. Most rock and roll protest stuff is so vague that right wingers and left wingers can agree with it."

REM are the essential peoples band; the essential Jamming! band! They don't preach, pretend or pose around to stroke their ego's. They struggle to keep their pride and they play. Coincidentally they're the best at what they do. So what do they want out of this?

"We want to be an important band to people. Not like the Thompson Twins where you buy it if it's a nice single and that's it. I want people to think about the albums and be moved by them. And we want to do it by the business changing to accommodate us, not for us to change to fit the business. We always assumed that if we were a great band that money woulc come along – it hasn't worked out that way but money isn't important. It's nice when you're old, but when you're young, you need a place to sleep and a place to eat and after that? – who needs it?

Jefferson, I think we're winning . . .

BREAKING DOWN THE BARRIERS

Jamming!

MONTHLY

No. 25 FEBRUARY 1985 60p U.S.$1.50 Eire 97p

Fink Wink!

THE MADNESS EMPIRE STRIKES BACK

Steve White: The Junior Councillor ★
Redskins ★ Michael Palin ★ Jazz Butcher ★
Winston Reedy ★ Prince ★ The Men They
Couldn't Hang ★ Big Sound Authority

READERS POLL: SMITHS SWEEP IT!

GROUP

1 THE SMITHS
2 U2
3 The Style Council
4 The Cocteau Twins
5 Echo And The Bunnymen
6 The Redskins
7 The Alarm
8 Lloyd Cole And The Commotions
9 Frankie Goes To Hollywood
10 R.E.M.
11 Everything But The Girl
12 Big Country
13 Aztec Camera
14 The Special A.K.A.
15 The Fall
16 Elvis Costello And The Attractions
17 The Pogues
18 The Stranglers
19 The Waterboys
20 Simple Minds

THE SMITHS: Group-1; Album-1&2; Male Vocal-1; Lyricist-1; Tunesmith-1; Public Hero-1; Idealist-2; Singles-5, 6&7; Band To Split Up-9.

Morrissey: "I know lots of people are desperate for The Smiths to be a fad. We didn't show up in the Smash Hits and No. 1 polls and I seriously thought we'd been blacklisted, but that was probably me just being neurotic! So this means a great deal."

VOCALIST (Male)

1 MORRISSEY
2 Bono Vox
3 Paul Weller
4 Billy Bragg
5 Ian McCulloch

VOCALIST (Female)

1 ELIZABETH FRAZER
2 Tracey Thorn
3 Alison Moyet
4 Siouxsie
5 Annie Lennox

THE STYLE COUNCIL: Group-3; Album-5; Singles-11; Band To Split Up-9. PAUL WELLER: Idealist-1; Male Vocal-3; Lyricist-3; Tunesmith-2; Public Hero-8. RESPOND: Non-Event-6.

SINGLES

1 PRIDE (IN THE NAME OF LOVE)   U2
2 Keep On Keepin On   The Redskins
3 Nelson Mandela   The Special A.K.A.
4 Pearly Dewdrops Drop   The Cocteau Twins
5 What Difference Does It Make?   The Smiths
6 William, It Was Really Nothing   The Smiths
7 Heaven Knows I'm Miserable Now   The Smiths
8 The Killing Moon   Echo And The Bunnymen
9 Two Tribes   Frankie Goes To Hollywood
10 Relax   Frankie Goes To Hollywood
11 My Ever-Changing Moods   The Style Council
12 Kangeroo   This Mortal Coil
13 Come Back   The Mighty Wah!
14 The Power Of Love   Frankie Goes To Hollywood
15 Forest Fire   Lloyd Cole & The Commotions
16 The Green Fields of France   The Men They Couldn't Hang
17 The Chant Has Just Begun   The Alarm
18 Peace In Our Time   The Imposter
20 I Wanna Be Loved   Elvis Costello And The Attractions

Adam Clayton, U2: "It's great that we won, but I'm actually more proud of our involvement in the Band-Aid single, which is a much more important record. I hope it becomes a Christmas classic and each year raises money for Ethiopia: I presume their problems won't be over by next year."

U2: Group-1; Single-1; Album-3; Male Vocal-2; Tunesmith-5; Album Sleeve-2; Video-2; Event-6; Idealist-4; Public Hero-6.

TUNESMITH

1 JOHNNY MARR
2 Paul Weller
3 Billy Bragg
4 Roddy Frame
5 The Edge

Johnny Marr: "Oh wow, I'm dumbfounded. Do I get a front cover this year?"

LYRICIST

1 MORRISSEY
2 Billy Bragg
3 Paul Weller
4 Elvis Costello
5 Roddy Frame

Morrissey: "This means more to me than anything else."

ALBUMS

1 THE SMITHS   THE SMITHS
2 Hatful Of Hollow   The Smiths
3 The Unforgettable Fire   U2
4 Brewing Up With . . .   Billy Bragg
5 Café Bleu   The Style Council
6 Rattlesnakes   Lloyd Cole And The Commotions
7 Treasure   The Cocteau Twins
8 Ocean Rain   Echo And The Bunnymen
9 In The Studio   The Special A.K.A.
10 Declaration   The Alarm
11 Knife   Aztec Camera
12 Goodbye Cruel World   Elvis Costello And The Attractions
13 World Shut Your Mouth   Julian Cope
14 Steeltown   Big Country
15 Reckoning   R.E.M.
16 A Pagan Place   The Waterboys
17 Born In The USA   Bruce Springsteen
18 Welcome To The Pleasure Dome   Frankie Goes To Hollywood
19 Aural Sculpture   The Stranglers
20 The Wonderful And Frightening World Of . . .   The Fall

Johnny Marr: "The readers of Jamming! obviously don't see us as something that's disappeared. It's nice to be there with a lot of other good names as well. My message for 1985 is that The Smiths haven't even scratched the surface yet."

Adam Clayton, U2: "In other words we came second!"
Billy Bragg: "Next year I will definitely start wearing the old flowers in the back pocket."

BEST NEW ACT

1 LLOYD COLE AND THE COMMOTIONS
2 Bronski Beat
3 The Pogues
4 The Colourfield
5 Smiley Culture

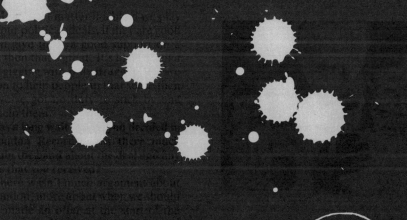

LLOYD COLE AND THE COMMOTIONS: Best New Act; Group-8; Album-6; Single-15;

Lloyd Cole: "I suppose it's very flattering. But the polls don't really bother me because they're always won by U2 and Big Country. Oh, The Smiths won, did they? That's nice! It's quite nice to know you're being appreciated."
Morrissey: "Is that for his act onstage or offstage?"

24   25

Other than a rather evasive editorial on the subject of our new ownership, the casual reader could have been forgiven for thinking it was business as usual at *Jamming!* HQ. And there was, admittedly, a certain familiarity to the contents of Issue 25: Suggs of Madness was back on the cover, The Redskins were back in a supporting role, The Style Council's boy wonder Steve White got a profile, Tony Parsons offered up another enthused star turn, this time profiling Prince, and I waxed enthusiastic about The Men They Couldn't Hang and Big Sound Authority. It was all very blue-eyed soul (apart from Prince, of course) and, along with such genuinely varied artists as The Jazz Butcher, Winston Reedy, Hurrah!, The Jesus

ISSUE #25 1/85

& Mary Chain, The Flowerpot Men, Christy Moore and The Screaming Blue Messiahs, would make for a damn good 1985 playlist. A separate article on Creation Records and a half-page on African music further hinted at a broad purview. It was, perhaps, a mark of *Jamming!*'s relative establishment that for our Reader's Poll Results, swept by The Smiths, we were able to secure post-poll reactions from the likes of Morrissey, Johnny Marr, Billy Bragg, Lloyd Cole and U2's Adam Clayton. But the fact that these results were printed in the centre pages confirmed that there was no definitive interview, no solid attention-grabber, and let's be honest, the cover was rather too pink and oh so very *Oh Boy!*

The Jesus and Mary Chain

CURRENTLY TOUTED AS THE NEXT BIG THING THEY RELEASE THEIR SECOND SINGLE, 'NEVER UNDERSTOOD' THIS MONTH. RON ROM VOTES IN THEIR FAVOUR.

THE JESUS AND MARY CHAIN are the band where most attentions are attached to at the moment. Rave reviews, in most quarters of the prestigious music press, have given rise to a sold-out London concert, a debut single which poisoned the top of the independent charts, and many major labels thrusting large amounts of readies to get their scrawled signatures on their clammy contracts. All in all The Jesus and Mary Chain can be considered as a very important band, which is an amazing position for a band who age no older than twenty, have played only sixteen gigs and had their demo-tape rejected (un-listened) by most of the people who are now queueing to sign them up.

Someone who did listen was Alan McGee, entrepreneur of highly acclaimed ventures such as The Living Room and Creation Records. As for the Jesus and Mary Chain, they grew out of the squalor of East Kilbride, consisting of four members – Jim Reid (vocals), Douglas Hart (2 string bass), William Reid (guitar) and Bobby Gillespie (drums). They play what can only described as a polemic musical maelstrom creating a malaise of feedback guitar, imprecated drums and improvised vocals. This being dependable on Jim's mood.

Their debut single– 'Upside Down' –was a chaotic unleashing of what their embittered hearts possesed and stands out as one of the highlights of 1984. The singles' unorthodox sound created one or two problems in the studio, as Jim describes:

"The problem was we spent more money and time on these idiots who run the studios. Like we would put the guitar in the corner and let it make noises and the engineer looks at us as if we're mad or something. Then we spend two hours telling him that's what we want on our record and he says, 'I've been doing this job for twenty five years and you can't do that boys.' It's quite funny really, we got into the studio and cracked open some beers and his eyes popped out of his head."

So do you think you're tearing up rule books?

Jim: "Yeah like Sham 69! No, we're just doing what we want to do that's all. I mean there's just a load of earholes in the music business, we haven't been in it that long but we've discovered that already. Like on every corner, there's someone getting in your way. PA men not turning your sound up and so on."

Douglas: "So you say 'turn the sound up'. Then the bloke waves a knife and says 'you're dead pal!' They're just stupid and petty."

The Jesus And Mary Chain are going to put a vehement buzz of excitement back into the impoverished music scene. They are not the progression of anything, as Jim points out: "We just want to make the music we make with as little messing about as possible, whether people say it's great or otherwise. It's up to them. We're not the next anything, we are The Jesus And Mary Chain!"

In this land of conformity, boredom and depression we enter 1985 with the exit of the tunnel being ominously sealed. Darkness envelopes us, misery beseiges our souls and time for love, enjoyment and other such things we once read of is now filled with repressive fear. It's a time when we need music more than ever, it's a time when we need The Jesus and Mary Chain. For no others can seize our hardened hearts and fill them into a zest for living again and create an atmosphere where. . . yes. . .everything is possible. 1985. . . the year of The Jesus!

CLOSE UP

THIS MONTH, *BRUCE DESSAU* PUTS *CREATION RECORDS* UNDER THE SPOTLIGHT.

● THE REVOLVING PAINT DREAM: Flowers In The Sky

● THE X-Men: Do The Ghost

● THE LEGEND: Destroys The Blues

● BIFF BANG POW: There Must Be A Better Life

● THE LOFT: Why Does It Rain

● THE JASMINE MINKS: Where The Traffic Goes

There was a kind of poetry in my meeting with Alan McGee to discuss the emergence of Creation records. For almost one year ago to the day, I had been drunkenly accosted by a young Scotsman in a London alehouse, touting a tatty, but well meaning fanzine, 'Communication Blur'. Under duress, but swayed by the free TV Personalities flexi enclosed, I purchased a copy and was drawn into conversation with its editor who then regaled me with his plans to start the latest, last and best post-punk indie label, *Creation*. Big ideas I thought. Big dreams, I thought. Blame it on the booze. But one year later those dreams are becoming, and rapidly so, a reality. For Alan McGee, they were never anything but. Now read on . . .

Creation has not only put out a string of consistently high quality singles, but the majority have been by, until then, unknown bands, just showing that there is still plenty of young talent out there if only, in Alan's words, "Major labels would get off their fat arses and go out to gigs occasionally". One can but wonder where The Jesus And Mary Chain, latest signings to Blanco Y Negro (see elsewhere in this issue) would be today if Alan McGee had not taken the trouble to listen to their demo and follow that up by viewing a live performance in an East Kilbride dive, at which he was suitably stunned. To say that Creation has the identity of a Motown or Stax might be taking things (only just) a little too far, but like those labels it does have a high quality turnout which means if you like one Creation disc, you can be pretty confident that any other will also brighten up the dullest of days. So, what exactly does Creation have to offer the fun starved no pap, pop consumer today?

Sadly, the early singles, by The Legend, Revolving Paint Dream and Biff Bang Pow ('73 in 83', 'Flowers Are In The Sky' and '50 Years Of Fun') are already unavailable (highly prized collectors items in fact, as is that reluctantly purchased T.V.P's flexi of mine, also bearing the Creation Artefact logo), but a sample of what has been missed can be heard on the recent 'Wild Summer, Wow!' compilation.

Since these singles, sales have picked up considerably to the point that all Creation discs top the thousand sales mark, at a time when most indie records do well to sell half that amount. To date, The Jesus And Mary Chain's 'Upside Down' has passed the seven thousand mark, only kept off the number one indie spot by the eminently risible 'Toy Dolls' effort.

But as satisfying as indie chart success may be, Alan's real aim is to see Creation records in the big boys' national charts. "With The Cartel handling distribution, there's no reason why Creation shouldn't have the same national success as, say, Rough Trade have had with The Smiths. By the end of this year Creation bands should be appearing on TOTP. Of course it would be nice if The Jasmine Minks got a deal with a major label, but what I'm saying is it isn't

42

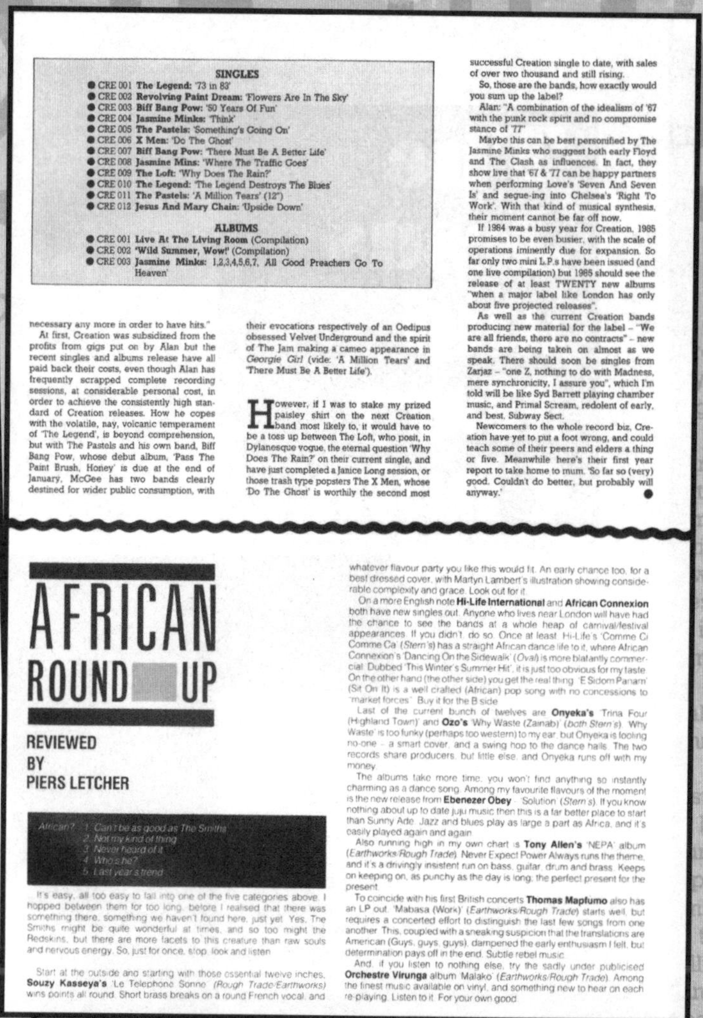

SINGLES

- CRE 001 **The Legend:** '73 in 83'
- CRE 002 **Revolving Paint Dream:** 'Flowers Are In The Sky'
- CRE 003 **Biff Bang Pow:** '50 Years Of Fun'
- CRE 004 **Jasmine Minks:** 'Think'
- CRE 005 **The Pastels:** 'Something's Going On'
- CRE 006 **X Men:** 'Do The Ghost'
- CRE 007 **Biff Bang Pow:** 'There Must Be A Better Life'
- CRE 008 **Jasmine Mins:** 'Where The Traffic Goes'
- CRE 009 **The Loft:** 'Why Does The Rain?'
- CRE 010 **The Legend:** 'The Legend Destroys The Blues'
- CRE 011 **The Pastels:** 'A Million Tears' (12")
- CRE 012 **Jesus And Mary Chain:** 'Upside Down'

ALBUMS

- CRE 001 **Live At The Living Room** (Compilation)
- CRE 002 **'Wild Summer, Wow!'** (Compilation)
- CRE 003 **Jasmine Minks:** 1,2,3,4,5,6,7, All Good Preachers Go To Heaven'

necessary any more in order to have hits."

At first, Creation was subsidized from the profits from gigs put on by Alan but the recent singles and albums release have all paid back their costs, even though Alan has frequently scrapped complete recording sessions, at considerable personal cost, in order to achieve the consistently high standard of Creation releases. How he copes with the volatile, nay, volcanic temperament of 'The Legend', is beyond comprehension, but with The Pastels and his own band, Biff Bang Pow, whose debut album, 'Pass The Paint Brush, Honey' is due at the end of January, McGee has two bands clearly destined for wider public consumption, with their evocations respectively of an Oedipus obsessed Velvet Underground and the spirit of The Jam making a cameo appearance in *Georgie Girl* (vide: 'A Million Tears' and 'There Must Be A Better Life').

However, if I was to stake my prized paisley shirt on the next Creation band most likely to, it would have to be a toss up between The Loft, who posit, in Dylanesque vogue, the eternal question 'Why Does The Rain?' on their current single, and have just completed a Janice Long session, or those trash type popsters The X Men, whose 'Do The Ghost' is worthily the second most successful Creation single to date, with sales of over two thousand and still rising.

So, those are the bands, how exactly would you sum up the label?

Alan: "A combination of the idealism of '67 with the punk rock spirit and no compromise stance of '77"

Maybe this can be best personified by The Jasmine Minks who suggest both early Floyd and The Clash as influences. In fact, they show live that '67 & '77 can be happy partners when performing Love's 'Seven And Seven Is' and segue-ing into Chelsea's 'Right To Work'. With that kind of musical synthesis, their moment cannot be far off now.

If 1984 was a busy year for Creation, 1985 promises to be even busier, with the scale of operations iminently due for expansion. So far only two mini L.P.s have been issued (and one live compilation) but 1985 should see the release of at least TWENTY new albums "when a major label like London has only about five projected releases".

As well as the current Creation bands producing new material for the label – "We are all friends, there are no contracts" – new bands are being taken on almost as we speak. There should soon be singles from Zarjaz – "one Z, nothing to do with Madness, mere synchronicity, I assure you", which I'm told will be like Syd Barrett playing chamber music, and Primal Scream, redolent of early, and best, Subway Sect.

Newcomers to the whole record biz, Creation have yet to put a foot wrong, and could teach some of their peers and elders a thing or five. Meanwhile here's their first year report to take home to mum. 'So far so (very) good. Couldn't do better, but probably will anyway.' ●

AFRICAN ROUND UP

REVIEWED BY PIERS LETCHER

African?
1. Can't be as good as The Smiths
2. Not my kind of thing
3. Never heard of it
4. Who's he?
5. Last year's trend

It's easy, all too easy to fall into one of the five categories above. I hopped between them for too long, before I realised that there was something there, something we haven't found here, just yet. Yes, The Smiths might be quite wonderful at times, and so too might the Redskins, but there are more facets to this creature than raw souls and nervous energy. So, just for once, stop, look and listen.

Start at the outside and starting with those essential twelve inches. **Souzy Kasseya's** 'Le Telephone Sonne' *(Rough Trade/Earthworks)* wins points all round. Short brass breaks on a round French vocal, and whatever flavour party you like this would fit. An early chance too, for a best dressed cover, with Martyn Lambert's illustration showing considerable complexity and grace. Look out for it.

On a more English note **Hi-Life International** and **African Connexion** both have new singles out. Anyone who lives near London will have had the chance to see the bands at a whole heap of carnival/festival appearances. If you didn't, do so. Once at least. Hi-Life's 'Comme Ci Comme Ca' (*Stern's*) has a straight African dance life to it, where African Connexion's 'Dancing On the Sidewalk' (*Oval*) is more blatantly commercial. Dubbed 'This Winter's Summer Hit', it is just too obvious for my taste. On the other hand (the other side) you get the real thing. 'E Sidom Panam' (Sit On It) is a well crafted (African) pop song with no concessions to "market forces". Buy it for the B side.

Last of the current bunch of twelves are **Onyeka's** 'Trina Four (Highland Town)' and **Ozo's** 'Why Waste (Zainab)' (*both Stern's*). 'Why Waste' is too funky (perhaps too western) to my ear, but Onyeka is fooling no-one – a smart cover, and a swing hop to the dance halls. The two records share producers, but little else, and Onyeka runs off with my money.

The albums take more time, you won't find anything so instantly charming as a dance song. Among my favourite flavours of the moment is the new release from **Ebenezer Obey** – 'Solution' (*Stern's*). If you know nothing about up to date juju music then this is a far better place to start than Sunny Ade. Jazz and blues play as large a part as Africa, and it's easily played again and again.

Also running high in my own chart is **Tony Allen's** 'NEPA' album (*Earthworks/Rough Trade*). Never Expect Power Always runs the theme, and it's a drivingly insistent run on bass, guitar, drum and brass. Keeps on keeping on, as punchy as the day is long; the perfect present for the present.

To coincide with his first British concerts **Thomas Mapfumo** also has an LP out. 'Mabasa (Work)' (*Earthworks/Rough Trade*) starts well, but requires a concerted effort to distinguish the last few songs from one another. This, coupled with a sneaking suspicion that the translations are American (Guys, guys, guys), dampened the early enthusiasm I felt, but determination pays off in the end. Subtle rebel music.

And, if you listen to nothing else, try the sadly under publicised **Orchestre Virunga** album 'Malako' (*Earthworks/Rough Trade*). Among the finest music available on vinyl, and something new to hear on each re-playing. Listen to it. For your own good.

Somewhere along the way I became *Jamming!*'s unofficial Creation Records correspondent, charting the new releases on Alan McGee's independent label. I'd been going to his Living Room club in Central London since it started and loved the groups that had a scruffy punk spirit but a more accessible pop sensibility. Bands such as The Jasmine Minks, The Loft and the pre-'Loaded' Primal Scream. My coverage of the label prompted McGee to invite me on a short European tour with a few Creation bands in October 1984, with a view to writing an on-the-road feature. The line-up was his band Biff Bang Pow!, The Jasmine Minks and a new outfit who had just released their debut single, 'Upside Down', The Jesus & Mary Chain.

I don't know what happened to that feature (Ron Rom got in first with a profile on the Mary Chain; see left.) Instead, Tony commissioned me to write an overview of the label so far. I brought in my entire Creation Records collection so that the sleeves could be used in the page design.

Somehow all of the sleeves got mislaid and I never got them back. I distinctly remember saying at the time, 'Don't worry about it, I don't think Creation Records is ever going to be that memorable or collectable.' **Bruce Dessau**

Flower Power

Jonh Wilde meets the flowerpot men

January's Jamming! rounded up the events of 1984 on a comfortless, disconsolate note, our writers unanimously deciding that the previous twelve months painted no rosy picture. Reflecting the bleak political background that we find ourselves swamped in, British music sank to sluggish, desolate new depths.

In a year of crumbling expectations, pop could only manage to internalize the despair that emerged behind it. Most distressing of all was the further decline of the underground/independent cause – its descent speeded up by the distribution collapse at the end of the year. In '84, it appeared to move further than ever from the raw vitality and spirited simplicity of its birth phase. Increasingly, the so-called alternative to chart glitter began to resemble a quaint, hippy cottage-industry collective; this reflected by the backsliding reactionary air that pervaded John Peel's shows throughout the year.

There were exceptions; amongst them The Flowerpot Men. Their debut EP, released in December on Compost, was voted Single Of The Month in these pages. Recalling the better moments of Suicide, DAF and the rest, its swarming swell of electronics made it one of the most unnerving releases of last year.

Its makers, Ben Watkins and Adam Peters, have dabbled together in various forms for two years now. Their first vinyl collaboration appeared earlier last year, both of them contributing to 'The Empty Quarter' (Illuminated), with Ben offering keyboards, drums and guitars to Adam's cello. Properly, a Youth-Watkins creation, it was nevertheless to bring Adam and Ben together to bring The Flowerpot Men into existence.

Comments Ben:– "The Flowerpot Men is an established band, but it aims at being as flexible as possible. It's like an umbrella operation, in a way – under which Ben and myself are able to do whatever we want."

That first release has already demonstrated the diversity and breadth of their capabilities. Aside from the dark dynamics of 'Jo's So Mean To Josephine', there was the harder, more brittle 'Rapids' and the languorous 'Ug' to consider. So how multiform can we expect it to get?

"Well, there will be no one Flowerpot Men sound", promises Adam. "Really, we want it to be as many-sided as possible. The difference between us and many other 'experimental' bands is that we place a lot of emphasis on limits and limitations. Other people try to create something totally *open* but we state our limits and aim to play within them as extremely as possible."

Adam, himself, who previously played with The Drowning Craze (a band that also featured Simon Raymonde, now of The Cocteau Twins), has also been involved with The Bunnymen for the last year, playing cello on tour, as well as contributing to the 'Ocean Rain' LP.

Ben, outside The Flowerpot Men, will also be collaborating with Youth on another, 'Empty Quarter' very soon. Meanwhile, both of them will be busy building up the reputation that 'Jo' has begun rolling.

Adam:– "The kind of terror that was screaming out of 'Jo' – people don't expect that kind of edge on a pop record any more." I think The Flowerpot Men are a few years ahead of their time and 'Jo' is the sort of record that will be hailed a couple of years from now."

In the throng of the monochrome swamp of indie-land, The Flowerpot Men are struggling to stand ugly pop on its head with a wide-open sound. Breath deeply now.

45

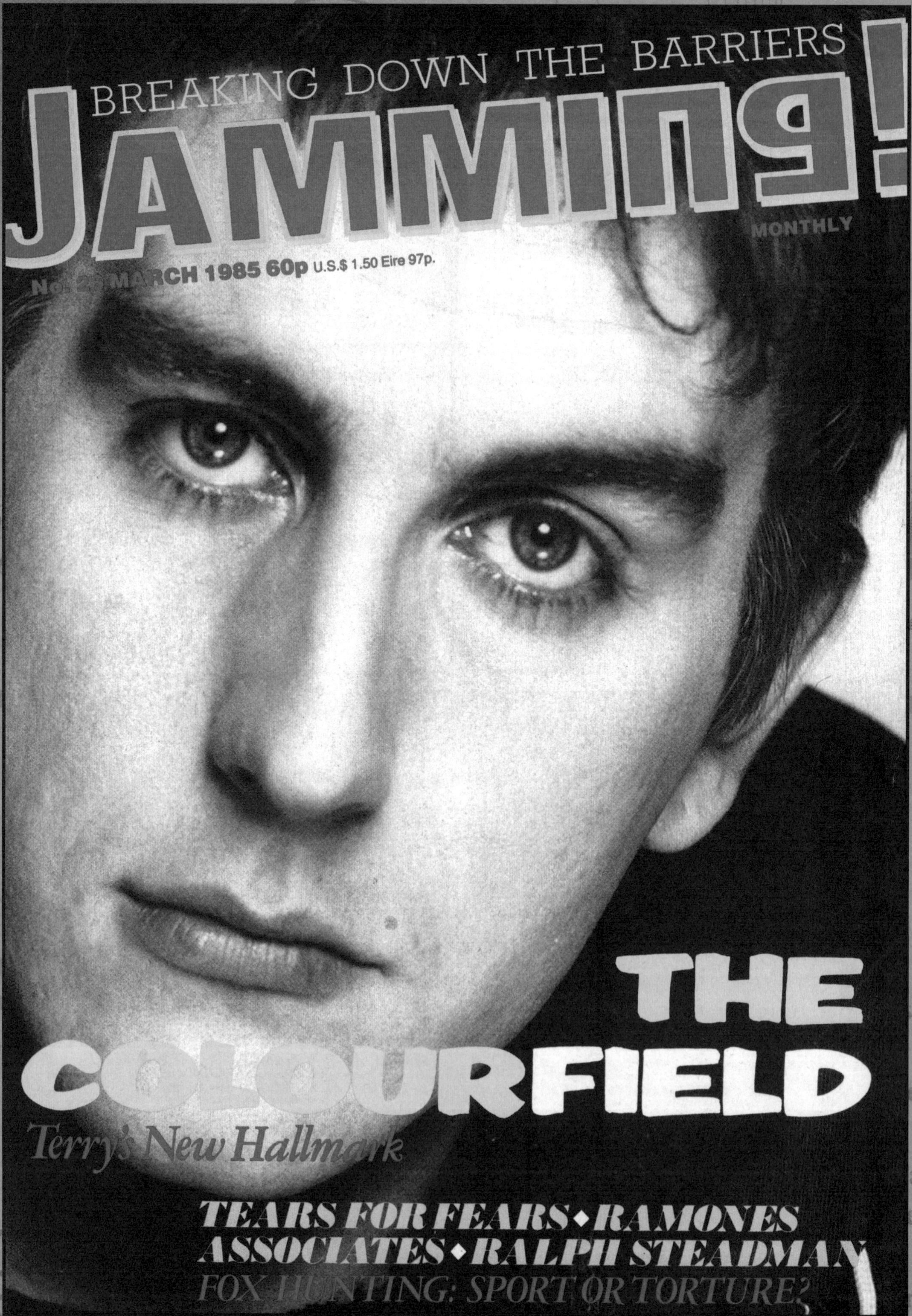

BREAKING DOWN THE BARRIERS

Jamming!

MONTHLY

No. 26 MARCH 1985 60p U.S.$ 1.50 Eire 97p.

THE COLOURFIELD

Terry's New Hallmark

TEARS FOR FEARS • RAMONES
ASSOCIATES • RALPH STEADMAN
FOX HUNTING: SPORT OR TORTURE?

and loathing.

PROFILE: Jo

PHOTOS B

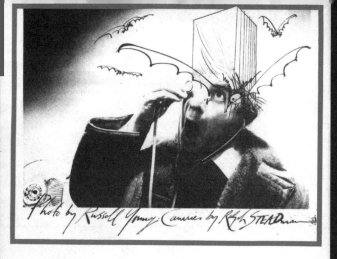

Photo by Russell Young. Canaries by Ralph STEADMAN

Jamming! 14

RALPH STEADMAN
Between The Eyes

In twenty-seven years of cartoon and illustration, Ralph Steadman has proved himself to be Britain's most distinctive and consistently innovative artist. Always aiming between the eyes, he has raged against injustice and celebrated the beauty beyond the fear and loathing.

● PROFILE: Jonh Wilde
● PHOTOS: Russell Young

Danielle Dax's first solo LP is re-released this month, just as her dusky, blurry experimentation is beginning to creep stealthily into the public eye. 'Pop Eyes' is more of her characteristically opaque, though illuminating displaced pop.

Danielle was previously with notoriously perverse post-punk moodists The Lemon Kittens and 'Pop Eyes' was originally released in June 1982. Typically obsessed with sparse, surreal deconstruction, it maintains the melodic complexity that Lemon Kittens were infamous for - weaving their abstract invention into more immediate, more urgent shapes. Its innovative maelstrom of erotic/exotic chants and shards of broken melody come from a four-track recording, employing a large array of unusual instruments: windchimes, banjo, sitar and synth are all played by Danielle - she also designed the sleeve herself.

Its current re-release arises following the critically favourable reaction to last year's 'Jesus Egg That Wept' album and Danielle's growing reputation as a performance artist. 'Pop Eyes' - almost a marriage of Eastern contemplation and Western conception - is released this month by Awesome Records (through Rough Trade outlets).

Besides her musical involvements, Danielle's career in acting has borne fruits over the last twelve months. Already she has appeared in Jordan's 'Company of Wolves' and Warburton's 'The Chimera'. With both performances receiving hefty critical encouragement, her film career should open up this year.

Variety is the spice! As they say ...

● photo: Coneyjay

Jamming! 36

NNew ownership did not appear to have changed *Jamming!*'s MO. Former male 2-Tone star gazing into the camera from the front cover? Check. (Terry Hall.) Major pop band profile to confirm critical approval? Check. (Tears For Fears.) American punks afforded long-overdue coverage? Check. (The Ramones.) Borderline pop star(s) given the classic Chris Heath investigative profile? Check. (Billy MacKenzie.) Suitably edgy up-and-comers afforded one-pagers? Check. (Danielle Dax, Easterhouse.) Black/world music artists? Check. (Orchestra Jazira.) Sports profile? Check. (Boxer Colin Jones.) Enduring artistic outsider profile? Check. (Ralph Steadman.) Political reporting from the field? Check. (Fox Hunting.) Content, then, was reliably solid and varied, photography increasingly excellent, and *Jamming!* was establishing itself as a credible alternative culture monthly. But individual stand-outs – a reason to buy the magazine above any other – were, at least this time around, lacking.

ISSUE #26
2/85

Colour Me Pop: Karl Shale Toby Lyons Terr

Tony Fletcher spoke to . . . and Paul Cox photographed . . .

THE
COLOURFIEL

Jamming! 20

Terry Hall has never been the ideal candidate for an interview. From his earliest days as lead singer of The Specials, he appeared an uncompromisingly dour, dead-pan young man. Anyone who ever saw that most vital of late seventies groups will recall the motionless singer stage centre, surounded on all sides by a riot of constant movement. Leaving The Specials at the time of their greatest glory, the optimistically titled breakaway faction The Fun Boy Three did not really provide Terry with any more sense of enjoyment. While the music bounced a bit more and a less depressing picture was painted, Terry still managed to look permanently bored, an image possibly proven when he left at equally short notice.

Then, in 1984, following a brief period of silence, Terry emerged with The Colourfield, an undeniably exciting proposition. Yet it seemed as if his automatic pass into the charts had been cancelled, as for some reason (certainly not lack of quality), the eponymous debut fell short of the mark while the follow-up 'Take' missed altogether. Had Terry over-anticipated the public's reaction to his continual change of groups?

Maybe it was just temporary amnesia, for in early 1985, the lilting sound of 'Thinking Of You' has been dominating the airwaves, busy putting The Colourfield where they belong – among the leaders. Though the group openly admit that after the failure of the first two singles, this one was planned to be a hit, that honesty does not belie the fact that here is a pop song of the finest calibre, a Harrods amongst the street traders of the charts.

More than anything, Terry is now being projected as a more genial, even humourous young man, the days of sarcasm and belligerence transformed into an optimistic and clean-shaven approach. Or so I'd been told. Throughout our conversation, it proved hard work getting more than a sentence out of Terry at a time, his attitude plainly contemptuous to the interview process and the character painting exercise it can undoubtedly tend to be. Perhaps Terry has never learnt that by putting some thought into it, an interview can be (and frequently is) used to project exactly the image the artist requires, or, as is more likely, Terry can't be bothered. Like it or leave it is the order of the day.

The Colourfield would like it known they are a group, that's for certain. And it is quickly apparent that Karl Shale (bass), and in particular Toby Lyons (guitar and keyboards) are providing valuable input into a trio where nobody is a self-elected leader. There was some serious consternation at Jamming!'s decision to put merely Terry on the cover, but at the heart of it all, Toby and Karl – who aren't even signed to Chrysalis – accept that they would not be gracing the pages of any magazine were it not for the public face of Terry, the man who walked out on the Specials, one of the most important groups this country has ever produced.

And there our story begins. Bursting onto a post-punk scene in desperate need of rejuvenation, The Specials reintroduced the multi-racial ska sound before launching the likes of Madness, The (sadly-missed) Beat, The Selecter and The Bodysnatchers into our homes, hearts, and consistently, the charts via their legendary 2-Tone label. Mixing dance music with a message, they seemed an ideal soundtrack from the times, a point proved when they hit the no. 1 spot with 'Ghost Town' at the exact time this fair isle exploded in riots, July 1981. And lo! it was seen that good pop music *could* make accurate statements and the public rejoiced at such a wise choice of pop stars. But then suddenly, and without warning, Terry left, taking with him fellow vocalist Neville Staples 'and bassist Lynval Golding to form The Fun Boy Three. The Specials – or Special A.K.A. to be precise – have never been the same since, despite songwriter Jerry Dammers' consistent, and occasionally successful, efforts. And yet just as the myth of this short-lived burst of 2-Tone fire has been entered into rock's rich tapestry, here's Terry Hall busy unweaving it.

The ball started rolling when, around a year ago, Terry declared that there was no racism in Coventry, 2-Tone's hometown, until The Specials started singing about it, a statement hotly denied by Jerry Dammers in Jamming! 18. It had to be asked – does Terry genuinely believe this?

"Definitely. Before The Specials started, there was a fair amount, but once we got going, it was terrible, really bad."

Last year, not having any success did me a lot of good – Terry Hall

However, the trouble that accompanied the heady 2-Tone days in '79 and '80 (generally with skinheads in the starring role) had, I put to Terry, been brewing since the days of Sham 69, a year before The Specials made the grade.

"But nobody out of London knew about that," he hotly denies. "I went to see Sham 69 in Coventry and there weren't any skinheads there – there just weren't any up north."

But The Specials had certainly seemed the right group for them, not just with the ska sound, but in the cropped hair and button-downs, gestures to the uniform.

"But all that came after a Sham 69 gig, where we saw all these skinheads, and Jerry suggested we were the group they all came to see. 'They need a group' were his words. So we all had our hair cut. It was at Crawley – The Clash, Suicide and us," he rounds off, totally unaware that he has just changed the details of exactly where all this was decided upon.

Nevertheless, all went well with the band until the fateful tour to accompany the second album 'More Specials', where the group were greeted night after night by an army of seig-heiling skinheads. Terry's conciliatory attitude was thrown to the wind one night in Cambridge when Jerry led a charge into the crowd to drive the fascists out. Suprisingly, this was virtually the last straw for Terry.

"Was that really preaching unity and racial harmony?" he demands. "Leaping out into the audience and bashing people with guitars?"

What would you do? Let them continue?

"Well I certainly wouldn't bash a kid who didn't know what he was seig-heiling for round the head with a guitar. I just couldn't work it out."

Toby Lyons, who was in the support band that night, recalls the skinheads placing their champion, a black lad, onto the stage to take on a Specials roadie. "It wasn't a racist thing, it was more like 'Let's have a fight," he recalls.

"It turned into football violence," declares Terry flatly.

But isn't that an inherent danger of live music, putting thousands of young people into the same place for hours on end, and leaving them standing around waiting for action?

"But there's no need to provoke it," says Terry. "You can calm it down. We were setting up concerts to go and talk to people who were kicking shit out of each other. Without those concerts they wouldn't have had anywhere to do it, 'cos they only fought at Specials gigs, Clash gigs and Sham gigs."

But surely they'd just fought on the streets otherwise?

"Yeah, but we didn't need to organise it for them. Half the people who were dressing up as skinheads in The Specials didn't know what skinheads were about, never thought about it."

Didn't that include you though?

"No, because when I was ten, I was a skinhead, and I was in gangs and stuff, so I knew what I was on about. I knew what paki-bashing was, 'cos I used to do it." Realising his admission, and possibly baiting the issue, he adds "Which is fair enough."

What, that you used to do it, or that you know what it's about?

"I knew what it was about. I knew the reasons, and the reasons were that there were no reasons. Like football violence – there are no reasons."

Terry's fighting phase (which included once facing Lynval when in opposing, white and black, gangs) ended rather suddenly – "after getting a kick in the balls one Saturday at Stoke City" – and thus explains how the gang appearance of The Specials never appealed to him. Even so, he stuck it out long enough to provide the vocals to an uninterrupted stretch of seven Top 10 hits, including the number ones 'Too Much Too Young' and 'Ghost Town'. Even this, however, now embarrasses Terry.

"I just don't like the idea of holding up a gold disc when it's got a lot to do with unemployment. It's a bit odd, like people on the Band-Aid record who turn up in Rolls Royces. I didn't feel Jerry was on my level when he wrote 'Ghost Town'."

But surely the acclaim . . .

"I just thought it was obvious what people were gonna say. That was fair enough, but I didn't really wanna be a part of it, I didn't want to be Paul Weller. But it was a lot easier to sing it than to leave the group at that time," he says with disarming honesty. "I was getting wages for doing sod all – it was quite good. It gave me time to breathe and think."

(In fairness, it should be pointed out that relations between Dammers and Hall are not as bad as they may sound. Though the two have not crossed paths for three years, the mere fact that they share the same manager must prove something.)

With that breathing space, Terry decided to get out, though in hindsight, not enough to ensure he formed the group he wanted to. Taking Neville and Lynval with him – "I thought they were the closest to me in the end" – The Fun Boy Three's debut single, 'The Lunatics Have Taken Over The Asylum' was in the charts before the remaining Specials had started licking their wounds.

"We didn't give anyone time to question it. They still thought we were The Specials, that we'd chucked everyone out and started ourselves." A pause, and then another poisonous dart. "Which we did really."

While never emulating the success of The Specials, The Fun Boy Three released some erratic singles before the excellent second album, 'Waiting'. Bar one cover, the only track not credited to the group was 'Our Lips Are Sealed', a song co-written by Terry with one of The Go-Gos. Their version had leapt to no. 1 in America, providing Terry not only with a comfortable nest-egg, but also the confirmation he needed that he was *the* songwriter within the group. When I point out that Terry has never been credited for writing a song on his own (bar one Specials b-side) he is quick to the defence.

"I did but I never credited myself with it – 99% of what The Fun Boy Three did. But I just wanted to be fair and just. It didn't affect me until money crept into it, and then it annoyed me, because I just wanted it to be a fair set-up. Nobody could be bothered, and I didn't really want to sink with everybody. So rather than having a group meeting and saying 'That is what we should be doing', it was easier just to say 'Fuck Off'. . ."

Words that Terry spits out with enough venom to convince me I wouldn't like them aimed my way. Lynval and Neville didn't have to hear them; they merely returned from holiday to find there was no more Fun Boy Three. Does Terry keep in touch with any of the vast number of musicians he's worked and abandoned?

"Some of them, but I don't go out of my way to keep up with things. I left them for a reason, and that's enough. I don't want to explain to them why I left."

And so a brief lull before the launching of The Colourfield. This time, Terry really did try and catch his breath before returning to the public eye. And with his new partners – which is what they stress they all are – it seems inappropriate to argue Terry's claim that this is the first time he's really got on with his fellow musicians. I ask if they were disappointed by the lack of success last year.

"Not with the first single," says Terry. "Because it was a test for us how we could work together. It was the first time we went into a studio and tried to write anything together. And that was enough. 'Take' was bit more disappointing, but even that was ..... so what?"

Defiant words maybe, but the result was nevertheless a conscious decision to make 'Thinking Of You' a hit.

"This single took four weeks to make," says Terry, "Because we wanted it to sound like a pop record. We needed this one to sound right, and that's why we got Katrina (who shares the vocals) in – it all gets a bit obvious but it seems to work. We need to sell singles to sell LPs to play, just like any other group."

Toby continues this unashamedly mercenary stance. "After all the crap that surrounded 'Take' and it floundering for the most stupid reasons, we just thought 'Right – we'll go for it.' Just to establish ourselves."

Which has certainly been achieved, to be enhanced when the debut LP, 'Virgins And Philistines' is released within the month. None of The Colourfield are proclaiming it as a classic, but their modesty would seem to owe more to the short time they've been together than any lack of quality in the songs.

"When you hear the album," says Toby, "I think you'll notice that some of the songs were done in a more advanced state of work than others. The Colourfield' was done quite naively, with a lot of cloaked references to issues. It was a bit token really, but it seemed to concern us at the time."

"And it was like finding our feet as well," reiterates Terry. "Like 'What kind of group shall we be?' From the album, we'll be able to pick our own favourites to decide which way we wish to go in the future."

For all intents and purposes, 'Virgins And Philistines' sounds like one would expect a Colourfield album to – the surprise is not so much in the sound as the quality, at the worst promising and at the best, redolent of the greatness of 'Waiting'. And much as Toby and Karl may hate these constant references to previous Hall-marked outfits, it's Terry's distinctive vocal tones that dominate the album from start to finish, his once flat approach is now gaining the quality of a first-class crooner.

'The Colourfield' itself is missing, at odds with the more relaxed feel of the album. At times, matters get too laid-back and on 'Sorry', 'Castles In The Air', and to a lesser extent 'Hammond Song', the mood gets depressing and only contributes to the 'miserable' tag Terry disowns. Elsewhere, it is the gentle pop song that is the order of the day, from the last two singles to 'Yours Sincerely', 'Armchair Theatre' and in particular, the LP's highlight 'Cruel Circus'. Based around an almost nursery-rhyme tune, it is a lyrically ferocious, yet musically polite, denunciation of man's treatment of animals. "*If we could talk to the animals, to the animals, could we justify our reasons, to the animals, isn't it enough to eat them?*"

Particularly worthy of mention is the contribution on drums from exiled Bunnyman Pete de Freitas, who, on the bold 'Faint Hearts' pushes the song firmly into Echo territory, no great surprise when one considers this is the *only* band any of The Colourfield could bring themselves to approve of in an hour of discussion. Toby wonders if it shows – "that we aren't bothered what anyone else is trying to put in the charts" – and I say it is. On the whole, 'Virgins And Philistines' sounds drastically out of place with the pop scene of 1985, and that can only be a good thing. The Colourfield are off to a healthy start.

But what of the future? Certainly the prospect of a live Colourfield is growing nearer, the lack of a touring band and full set being hurdles now jumped. The eight-piece featured on the Whistle Test is apparently close to what we can expect from them live.

In the meantime, they continue in their blasé, devil-may-care manner. With no contracts between the band members – something Terry claims ruined his previous groups – it leads me to ask Toby and Karl just what is to stop Terry getting up and walking away if he gets fed up. After all, he's done it twice before.

There's no easy answer. Terry believes that this really is *the* group – he's with friends, and excited about the prospects. Toby meanwhile, cites Terry's American Express card as ample reason to remain friends, joking about 'the delicate web of trust going on in this group', but then commenting, "If we wanted to, it's easy for us to part company. There's no point being precious about it."

"We really don't know what we want to do yet," repeats Terry.

Is that the greatest thing about this job, that you can do what you want the next day?

"Yeah, you can sometimes. You can have a lot of days off, which you can't in any other job."

Ah, but then you go out of the public eye.

Terry looks me in the face, to emphasise that he means what he's about to say. "Which is good. Last year, not having any success did me a lot of good."

As I think the saying goes (and I should know, as I've just made it up!) a man hungry for success will no doubt have a few good recipes up his sleeve. The Colourfield menu looks mouth-watering indeed.

For Fox Sake, Stop Hunting!

● The hounds' reward. The fox is tossed into the fray to be ripped apart by the surging pack. From the Beaufort Hunt, Gloucestershire

Fox-hunting is part of a die-hard British tradition. As the art of sabotage becomes more cunning, the hunt means confrontation. **Janine Booth** travels to Aylesbury to assess the right and wrongs.

● Special thanks to the League Against Cruel Sports for their kind permission to use the photographs on these pages.

1984 saw the first major media coverage of the rights and wrongs of the art of sabotage, as applied to the ritual of fox-hunting. The season is in full swing, the redcoats are out on their horses, the saboteurs are out in their vans, and the foxes are out in the cold.

The hunting of foxes is an English countryside tradition, continued through the ages, surrounded by an image of ladies, gentlemen, leisure and sparkling wine, attended by an army of foot followers, land-owners and aptly named hostelries. Yet, beneath the Christmas-card exterior lies the truth of the hunt – it is a cruel and unnecessary pastime, practised by depraved sadists whose great joy in life is to cause an animal revolting pain and suffering.

So, one chill Saturday morning, I joined around ten members of Cambridge Hunt Saboteurs' Association in a trek to Aylesbury, there to join up with other HSA groups, to disrupt the activities of the Vale of Aylesbury Foxhounds. Armed with wellies, Thermos flasks, maps, binoculars, garlic water and anti-mate sprays, we set off in the 'Sabmobile' – a self-drive hire van.

The hunting fraternity would have you believe that the van-load of saboteurs is a crack team of highly-trained commandos, in the employment of the Kremlin, bent on causing as much hassle as possible, merely because they get their thrills from getting up the noses of the upper classes.

Also, sabs are 'townies', who do not understand the ways of the country, and do not appreciate a good day's 'sport'. I always thought that 'sport' was a contest between two willing opponents, roughly evenly matched, not harmful in their intentions. Y'know, Liverpool versus Spurs, that sort of thing. How a pack of over-excited hounds, followed by charging horses, carrying yelling and horn-blowing huntsmen, versus one small fox, can be construed as 'sport' is beyond me.

Anyway, I digress ... The Vale of Aylesbury has a rather nasty reputation for being more than a little on the violent side, so sab Shaun gave me a thorough briefing on what to expect:

"Trouble from the hunt usually comes from one of two sources: the foot followers, who go out to see the hunt in action, and hopefully to be in at the kill; and also from the terrier men.

"Terrier men are usually people who are attached to the hunt formally. Their job is this: if the hunt hasn't flushed a fox by 'normal' methods, the terrier men will find a fox's earth, dig it out, and release it in front of the hounds. They're a particularly nasty piece of work, who will even go so far as to get the fox and cut its pads to slow it down, to make sure there's a kill . . .

". . . Or leave it sweating in a sack for a few days to make it nice and smelly; or soak it in strong-smelling liquid, or cut off the tip of the tail to get the scent glands working overtime; or cut the tendons in the fox's legs, so all it can do is stumble round in circles.

Back to Shaun: "This sometimes happens when the hunt has an important visiting guest with them – like Prince Charles – and they want to ensure that they have what they call 'a good day's sport', with a kill at the end.

"So the violence comes from the foot followers and the terrier men. At the very least, their tactics are to disrupt the saboteurs' vehicles by letting down the tyres, putting sugar in the petrol tanks, smashing windscreens or using their own vehicles to block us in, and make sure we can't follow the hunt. At worst, they'll in fact not be too reluctant to bring out a couple of pickaxe handles and set about us."

As you can imagine, I was feeling very comfortable and secure as we pulled up outside the Cock and Rabbit, scene of the meet. Unfortunately, horses, riders,

hounds and followers had already moved off, and we had missed that traditional country scene of milling dogs, snorting horses, and the drinking of the stirrup cup. More importantly, the chance to delay the start of the hunt had been missed.

We leapt back into the van and shot off down the road, knowing that we weren't far behind the hunt. Sure enough, we caught up with them on their way to drawing the first covert.

The hunt reached a small wood, known to be the site of several foxes' earths, and sent in the hounds, in an attempt to drive a fox from its earth. Unfortunately, they succeeded, and a fox was 'put up'.

Now was the time for our intrepid bunch to spring into action! We drove round to the far side, and intercepted

● The aftermath of 'a good day's sport'

the hounds about half a mile down wind of the covert. The pack was 'speaking' well, meaning that the dogs were obviously on a strong scent, and were make a lot of noise about it.

Sabs blessed with the rare skill of being able to use a hunting horn well, blew the right calls and behold! The hounds immediately stopped hunting, and came rushing towards us.

Foxhounds are specially-bred slow-runners, designed for stamina rather than speed: they are thus the ideal breed to prolong the chase, and give the horses a good gallop. Thousands of healthy hounds are killed every year by hunts – either as puppies with 'unsuitable markings', or as middle-aged dogs, too old to keep up with the hunt.

As the dogs swarmed around us, out came the

tools of the saboteurs' trade – spray bottles – and the dogs found themselves being doused with garlic water. Contrary to huntsmen's claims, this tactic causes no harm to the hounds – garlic water acts to temporarily impair their sense of smell, and prevents them recognising the trail of a fox.

Meanwhile, anti-mate was sprayed over the scent of the fox, disguising the trail, and making it impossible to follow. Sigh of relief. One fox saved.

The first tactical battle had been won by the saboteurs, and in the chess game of sabotage, we had taken the upper hand. The initiative was with us, and a quick conference decided that the next move would be an attempt to out-manoeuvre the hunt. However, we succeeded only in getting lost, and as we sped round frantically, there was time to reflect . . .

During a previous sab, I had asked a huntsman to justify the manner in which he passes his Saturdays. The man, a tweed-jacketed, retired-colonel type, replied by turning the question, demanding our justification for spoiling his fun. When I suggested that it's quite easy to justify saving the lives of innocent animals, he replied that there weren't any innocent animals in the locality. "The fox is a lamb and poultry-killing pest."

This is a belief that has long held back people opposing foxhunting – the

acceptance of the image of the fox as a conniving, bloodthirsty rascal. An image that it does not deserve.

Foxes, nocturnal animals about the size of domestic cats, live on a staple diet of rats, mice, voles, carrion and other such mouth-watering morsels, and control their own population to a level of around four adults per thousand acres.

Many farmers find lamb remains outside foxes' earths, and blame the death on the jaws of the fox. However, survey after study has shown that, in the vast majority of cases, the lamb had been either dead or dying when taken by the fox. In fact, the Ministry of Agriculture does not even bother to keep statistics of lamb losses to foxes, whereas they do tot up killings by dogs (including foxhounds).

It is reckoned that a mere 3% of lamb deaths are attri-

butable to predators, and the term 'predators' covers dogs, crows, snakes, birds of prey and others, as well as foxes. The other 97% die from disease, under nourishment, exposure, abandonment or birth complications – with all those dead littering the hillsides, what fox needs to kill one for food?!

The farmer who tends his flock well, and knows the ways of foxes, will feel no concern at seeing a fox prowling near lambing ewes – he knows that the fox is waiting to make a meal of a still-born or sickly lamb, or to enjoy the treasured delicacy of afterbirth!

Much publicity goes to the odd 'rogue' fox that takes the occasional healthy lamb or chicken, but it has been shown that such a fox is often in an emotionally-disturbed state, having narrowly escaped the hunt, or having lost its mate or cubs to the hunt.

Consider the situation . . . Sheep in this country are kept on hillsides or in open fields, with no protection from predators – if foxes were really inveterate lamb-killers, there wouldn't be any sheep left! And of the few chickens that are still kept free-range, all would be safe only so long as the farmer kept the gate shut!

And tell me this – if huntsmen are so concerned about controlling the fox population, then why do they openly admit to encouraging foxes to breed, protecting their coverts and rearing cubs in artificial earths?

The 'pest control' line has

we undoubtedly are, we sped round to the downwind side of the covert, where the fox should break.

Once again, the horns came out, and, accompanied by a great deal of shouting, the blowers succeeded in persuading about half of the hounds to abandon their gruesome pursuit, and come rushing out of the wood towards us, tails wagging, followed by a somewhat angry-looking huntsman. Quite some time passed as he attempted to round up the dogs.

This amusing incident was to be the last of the day's action. For the remainder of the afternoon, we followed the hunt, as it wandered around aimlessly, with seemingly little idea of where it was going or what it was doing.

At about 3pm, the fog descended, visibility fell to about ten metres, it became impossible to hunt, and the Vale of Aylesbury Foxhounds boxed up. They had killed no foxes, which represented a successful sabotage – not the greatest of days, but an effective exercise while achieved success with the minimum of effort and the maximum of enjoyment.

The justification for sabotage lies in a principle lauded by the great Martin Luther King – that it is valid to commit small crimes to prevent a greater evil. That obstructing the legally-permitted crimes of unnecessary cruelty, assault and murder justifies the trivial offences of trespass and 'anti-social behaviour'.

While some of the human race treats animals despicably, it is good indeed to see others doing their bit to protect our fellow creatures. And while some work at the painful necessities of campaigning, educating and lobbying, that one day this barbaric pursuit may at last be criminalised, the hunt saboteurs are saving foxes NOW.

Back to Buckinghamshire, where we rediscovered the hunt as it was in the process of drawing a large wood. Jumping out of the van, we found ourselves being approached by a group of hunt supporters, rolling their sleeves up! Being the brave, fearless people that

. . . practised by depraved sadists whose great joy in life is to cause an animal revolting pain and suffering

Photo – Russell Young

● Contact:
The Hunt Saboteurs' Association, PO Box 19, London SE22
The League Against Cruel Sports, 83-87 Union Street, London SE1

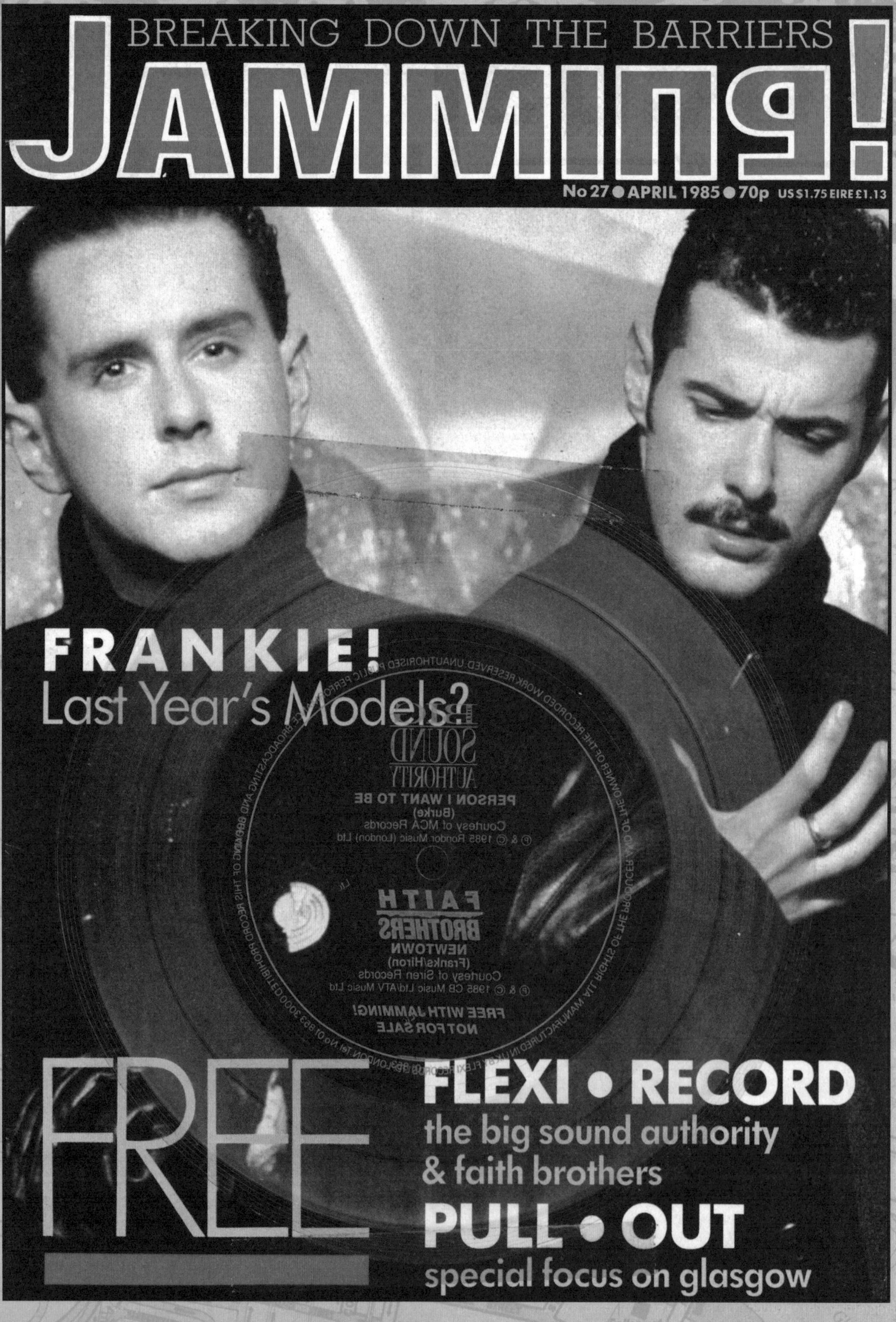

BREAKING DOWN THE BARRIERS

JAMMIN9!

No 27 ● APRIL 1985 ● 70p US $1.75 EIRE £1.13

FRANKIE!
Last Year's Models?

SOUND AUTHORITY
PERSON I WANT TO BE
(Burke)
Courtesy of MCA Records
℗ & © 1985 Rondor Music (London) Ltd

FAITH BROTHERS
NEWTOWN
(Franks/Hiron)
Courtesy of Siren Records
℗ & © 1985 CB Music Ltd/ATV Music Ltd

FREE WITH JAMMING!
NOT FOR SALE

FREE
FLEXI ● RECORD
the big sound authority
& faith brothers

PULL ● OUT
special focus on glasgow

ocus on Glasgow was produced by Jamming! Magazine and given away free with Jamming! No. 27. We would be keen to receive all comments and suggestions on how to impr___ ___us Special Reports.

dited by Tony Fletcher. Designed by Tim Brown.

ontributors: Finbar Burrows, John Dingwall, Andrea

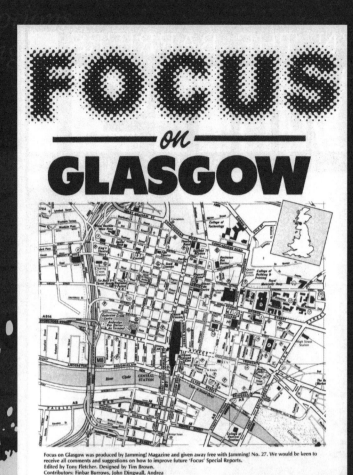

Focus on Glasgow was produced by Jamming! Magazine and given away free with Jamming! No. 27. We would be keen to receive all comments and suggestions on how to improve future 'Focus' Special Reports.
Edited by Tony Fletcher. Designed by Tim Brown.
Contributors: Finbar Burrows, John Dingwall, Andrea Millar, Alastair McKay and Stuart Straight.
All photos except those on the band section: John Logan

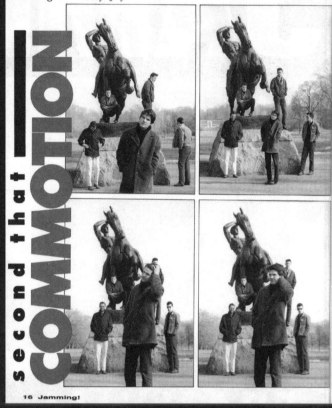

Jonh Wilde *in pursuit of the frantic pop of Lloyd Cole and the Commotions.* Zooming in:– Coneyl Jay

16 Jamming!

The error of putting an increasingly tiresome Frankie Goes To Hollywood on the cover again – rarefied *Jamming!* territory shared only with Morrissey – was compounded by failing to even mention any of the other more interesting and credible names on that same cover: Lloyd Cole & The Commotions, a readers' favourite already; Run-D.M.C., interviewed on the snowy New York City streets by a wanderlusting Hugh Morley; fellow New Yorker, the electro-sample pioneer Keith LeBlanc, a first contribution by Tiny Fennimore; the Boothill Foot Tappers, featuring Wendy May, who'd bought in the schoolboy fanzine *Jamming!* when managing Virgin Notting Hill several years earlier; the Poison Girls, fronted by the indefatigable Vi Subversa; the young Manchester band James; and a second Liverpool act, The Pale Fountains who, when Ross Fortune took ill, were advised by their publicist to show up at his hospital bedside – such, apparently, being the importance of a feature in *Jamming!* circa 1985 for a new band!

What were we thinking by not trumpeting these bands from the front page? We were, perhaps, over-excited by Chris Heath's adroitly understated excavation of Frankie's conflicted psyche, following an interview that concluded with a scene of considerable physical

ISSUE #27 3/85

violence. But I can't say for sure because, after months of pleading on their part and resistance on mine, I had taken on management of Faith Brothers at what turned out to be the peak of the act's short-lived success. The work – and it *was* work – kept me out of the office more than it had me in there, but I did combine my dual roles for at least this one month by securing a flexi-disc, attached to the *Jamming!* cover, that featured both Faith Brothers and Big Sound Authority; we needed marketing gimmicks to stay in the game, and offering free music to our readers seemed as good as any. So did putting together a series of localised pull-outs as an (unintentionally patronising) attempt to decentralise our London HQ, beginning with a 'Focus on Glasgow'.

On the subject of HQs, the masthead revealed a new office address for the first time in two years; along with the staff of *What Telephone* and its assorted communications special issues, we had moved into new offices just off Camden Road, where *Jamming!* staff were wisely sequestered in their own sound-proofed corner. A certain amount of sitcom activity duly took place in the inevitable culture clash, though it was somewhat diminished by the fact that *Jamming!* staffers typically eschewed the conference room for their meetings, preferring the pub located almost directly underneath.

Run D.M.C.

♦ **Words and pictures: Hugh Morley**

Like everything else in New York, if you're going to do it, then you do it BIG! At this point in time for RUN D.M.C. it's a film, next week. . .who knows? You realise just how seriously they take this business when the band sit down opposite and a smooth dude in a black kneelength woollen coat slips in next to you, smiles, and slides out a second tape recorder next to yours. Just for the record you understand!

But who are this band?

RUN D.M.C. are a garage rap band. While the rest of the world is loosening up to insipid electrobeat twelve inchers and cod breakdance feature flicks, RUN D.M.C. are planning a different movie. For them, rap is not a fashion or a fad, it's what they do! "We're more *street*, more with our culture than anybody else," they tell me. "We don't want to get rich. We'd like to get paid for what we're doing, but that isn't the main point behind it. We just want to show people that we can rap and perform."

Their sound is basic, as in BASIC! The 'streetbeat' they call it and it rolls along underneath the diving, weaving rap like a steamroller. A snatch of handclap, a morsel of melody, possibly the barest tug of bass. But ultimately it's the BIG drumbeat. Like the first time you heard the intro to Iggy's 'Lust For Life' at full volume. Barrel drums, booming around in an echo tunnel. Wam bam bam, bam bam ba lam!

"The name of this band is RUN D.M.C. I'm RUN, he's D.M.C. and he's our band Jay!" announces RUN with bombast. "He's our DJ so he scratches the records for us during the show."

Being rappers, they talk too much and listen too little, swopping sentences in conversation through rapping. It's very confusing. It

also gives you neckache, like watching a tennis match from the net! Somewhere underneath I get the inkling that they are not just another dodgy showbiz band!

Both RUN and D.M.C. who formed the band, have rapped intermittently since the early days of the movement. "When I was twelve years old, I used to spin and rap with Kurtis Blow, billed as the 'Son of Kurtis Blow'," RUN tells me. "That was about the time he put out 'Christmas Rapping', which was the second rap record ever made.

"We started RUN D.M.C. in '82 when we put together our first single, 'It's Like That'. Before that, we were in college. Neither of us knew what we wanted to do and I was in class writing 'It's Like That' when I hit a slump. I tried to think of what was going on in the world, what everything was like. So I gave the words to D.M.C. and he looked at them and came up with lyrics like 'War's going on across the sea'. So I wrote half, he wrote half and then he wrote 'That's the way it is."

'War's going on across the sea / street soldiers fighting the elderly / whatever happened to unity / it's like that – and that's the way it is!'

'It's Like That' was the first RUN D.M.C. single, released along with 'Sucker MC'. Both lyrically poignant and rhythmically colossal, it towers above their later records. It created a lot of attention in the States and made way for the follow up, 'Hard Times' and 'Jammaster Jay' which sold 370,000 copies there.

Both singles showed a strong streak of social awareness, along with another track on the later released album, 'Wake Up', which seemed to doff a sublime nod and wink to the Martin Luther King 'I have a dream' speech.

"I try to stay away from the 'garbage in the

that they were the hardest, meanest, most aggressive rappers around. The album shows them both intensifying their penchant for snappy interchanging wordplay refining their crucial meld of minimal rhythms and stray spiralling guitar riffs. The final track on the album sees them venturing into reggae territory with a joint rap/toast between the boys and Yellowman, a cultural collision that seems well overdue given the emergence of the fast

near documentary, film shot 'in situ' in the Bronx). The other two were too polished."

So how about the accusation that the whole thing has run its course? (A jibe that admittedly looks a little foolish alongside the failure of 'I Feel For You' until the rap section was added, and the consistent presence of Grandmaster and Melle Mel way up in the charts). A lot of people thought rap had died even before 'The Message' came out?

"No I don't think so," counters DMC.

RUN D.M.C. strip their sound to a minimum and put their faith in the rap.

street and poverty' raps," explains RUN, "because everybody knows about it, they've heard it. Now I like to go for more witty things so you can put on a rap record and laugh and don't have to talk just about the nuclear war or something. If you think about it, times aren't that bad. So the record ('It's Like That') talks about war and poverty, the government's in the garbage can, but it also talks about what the world's like. It's not an optimistic or pessimistic record."

Until recently the only UK release was the 'Rockbox' single, a step away from their rhythmic minimalism towards a neo-heavy metal feel, brain-graunching fuzzed guitar supplied courtesy of Quiet Riot's Eddie Martinez.

This situation was remedied last month with the release of the 'Kings of Rock' album which along with an electrifyingly energetic live show confirmed the opinion

MC style of the likes of Smiley Culture, and its similarity to rap. Run explains the situation.

"We wanted to make a reggae record and we were going to use a guy in the neighbourhood and we thought 'why not use a proper toaster', and we thought of Yellowman. But also 'Time' magazine ran an article on 'rapping goes pop' with us and Yellowman in, where they considered him a Jamaican rapper."

With one eye on the spectre of big business sat next to me, I test the water around the theme of business exploitation. Whether it be the graffiti in the galleries or the breaking on the screen, 'hip-hop' has been sanitised and served up to America like breakfast cereal. Take the films for instance.

"I don't like any of them," says RUN. "Neither 'Breaking' or 'Beatstreet'. The only one I liked was 'Wildstyle' (a small budget,

"They don't have to play it on the radio, and they don't even have to promote the shows or make the movies, because it's always going to be there. It was there before people found out about it. You don't have to have anybody controlling it.

"Some people make their records commercial but we don't care what people want to hear. It really depends on what you're going to say over the music.

"When Grandmaster and Melle Mel make records, someone else makes the music. But we produce ourselves. So we don't want harmonies, no girls singing in there. No song even. We want our records to sound loud with beats. When 'Sucker MC' came out, it was the biggest street record in the United States. No radio plays but in every town it was the biggest record at every party. When it comes on, everyone screams. Bam Ba lam bam. . . . .AaaaaaaaaahhhhhhhH!"

AGE OF REASON

Last year saw the release of the POISON GIRLS retrospective compilation, 'Seven Year Itch', which succinctly summed up the first stage of their existence. Now, with a refreshed line-up and a new album, 'Songs Of Praise', their music appears to be taking on a new shape. However, singer Vi Subversive claims no soften up!
● Interview: BRUCE DESSAU

14 Jamming!

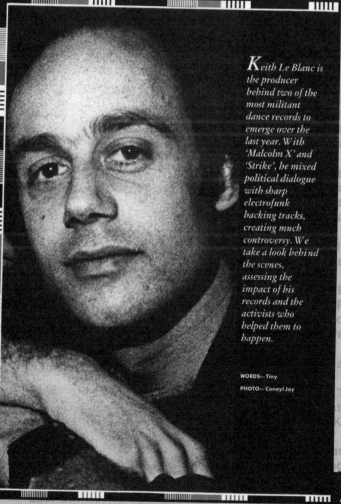

Keith Le Blanc is the producer behind two of the most militant dance records to emerge over the last year. With 'Malcolm X' and 'Strike', he mixed political dialogue with sharp electrofunk backing tracks, creating much controversy. We take a look behind the scenes, assessing the impact of his records and the activists who helped them to happen.

WORDS:– Tiny

PHOTO:– Coneyl Jay

● After a year at the top, Frankie Goes To Hollywood have got a reputation to live up to. CHRIS HEATH finds that they're only too happy to oblige.

Join us for an evening of conversation, insults, sex, and, in the end, violence.

FRANKIE
TALK · DIRTY!

● photo, Jason Pevovar

"**H**ello," says the reclining figure on the sofa in front of me, "I'm Holly."

Nervously I smile. As I clumsily lower my shoulder bag to the floor I try to acknowledge both the faces greeting me in this empty Brixton Academy dressing room, but as Holly and Paul are on opposite sides of the room it's difficult.

Paul rises. "You can do it if you like," he says to Holly, as if referring to an earlier contingency plan that has just been confirmed by their first impression of me. "I'll go on to the pub."

"OK," Holly replies, and Paul quietly slips out the door through which, only seconds before, I had entered. I sit down tentatively on the edge of Holly's sofa, rummaging in my bag for my tape recorder, my excuse for being there. Hoisting himself slightly more upright with his elbow Holly turns and stares at me, big bold eyes through tortoise-shell rimmed glasses:

"What's your name then?"

It's impossible not to love Frankie Goes To Hollywood, and it's impossible not to hate them. So sudden, so strong, and so strange has been their rise to success that they have transgressed nearly every rule and anti-rule of pop music, for which they are both cheered and jeered. If you're the average Jamming! reader — slightly 'alternative' I suspect — then maybe the things you'll cheer are: the assault on taboos (sex, war), the use of anti-Reagan and anti-nuclear propaganda, the powerful antidote their music provides to the dishwater pop of Wham! and Duran Duran, and the use of art, artifice, and intellect in the marketing of pop. And the things you'll jeer: the wimp-out third single, the re-emergence of the hackneyed rock'n'roll stereotypes, the intellectual masturbation of their most excessive marketing ploys, the way they've sold you the same song again and again in a different shirt, the way they shy away from any definite political comment or commitment.

Jamming! 23

Easy to forget how different the world once was, back when celebrity was yet to become a cosy club, and when a pop group could be hugely successful yet still exist miles outside mainstream life; back when outsiderness was less a storyline stance than an honest description of where the world was choosing to place you.

I think of this Frankie Goes To Hollywood article as the first time I ever really began to work out how to do what I wanted to do. There's still plenty that makes me wince (pity that I couldn't spell "Buddha") but at least I seem to have noticed that I had landed right in the middle of a moment and had what I needed to tell its story. It's the part in

And if anyone thought Frankie were to be the great 80s *alternative*, the monumental destruction of all that went before, they've been disappointed. If they *are* the voice of a generation it's only of a generation that despairs at the very idea of having a voice of its own. If you go to Holly Johnson expecting the arrogant dismissal of the past as compared with the (artist's own) present which has become *de rigeur* for all budding pop messiahs all you get is talk of Bowie ("fabulous") and The Rolling Stones ("they're not 'just another pop group' — they're *The Rolling Stones*!")

But if (and I think this is a good idea) you instead look at Frankie as today's truly great exponent of the contradictions in music — between marketing and honesty, pleasure and paypackets, love and macho guitar posing — then you might understand why Frankie Goes To Hollywood are, if not a wonderful group, a truly wonderful phenomena.

Wham! may have "made it big" in terms of record sales, video shoots and suntans, but it's Frankie who have actually *made it*. It's Frankie who've actually rediscovered the *heights*, with all the excess, fantasy, mystique, naivety, charisma, calculatedness, legend, and unreality that makes pop music something which anyone intelligent must simultaneously love and loathe.

And Holly is, of course, the spearhead of all this. Some people see ZTT as the core and essence of Frankie, but these days they're wrong. ZTT may have been almost totally responsible for Frankie's genesis and early growth but nowadays, as Holly persuasively points out, "to the people in the street the five of our faces *are* Frankie Goes To Hollywood. It's got our faces stamped on it and they can't take that away from us. No-one's going to shout 'Frankie' at Paul Morley or Trevor Horn in the street."

Put like that it does sound a little ridiculous, doesn't it?

"I don't do many interviews or things like that," explains Holly, looking away as if a little embarrassed about trying to make me feel privileged. "I select them very carefully, because I don't really like doing them. Mainly because of the past results. It would enhance your reputation," he explains, angling his palm towards me, "a lot more if you said 'Oh, I met Holly Johnson and he was an absolute arsehole and talked a lot of drivel', and misquoted me. You'd be the boy of the week on the paper, have a good laugh, and it would be to your advantage. And that's what happens."

I reply silently with my beseeching 'well you can trust *me*, can't you?' look, and wonder if he believes me. Then we talk. I ask and he answers, confident, modest, intelligent, guarded. Sincere? I don't know — he may be too clever. Often he laughs : "ha ha ha, ha ha ha". It's a nice laugh, but then Holly's a disgustingly likeable person. I hate it when journalists go on about how nice people are — it smacks of a mixture of awe, sycophancy and self-congratulation — but Holly really is quite charming. Though I doubt he's an angel.

"It's felt like luck, incredible luck, the last twelve months. Though there were some people when it happened who stood up and said 'I created this, this is my baby, I'm responsible for this'. That was typical of certain people."

You mean Paul Morley?

"I'm not naming any names. Just saying that I find all that ridiculous. Not even *I* created Frankie Goes To Hollywood, nor Paul Rutherford, Mark

O'Toole, Brian Nash or Peter Gill. It was just the right people in the right place at the right time, and it *worked*. There was no central genius or 'very-clever-person' that invented the whole thing."

What of Paul Morley's role anyway? He seems to have disappeared into the background of late.

(*A long silence, then Holly answers hesitantly*) "That's alright by me. (*more silence*). Actually we're getting on quite well at the moment, better than we ever did. But I feel sorry for anyone who had to grow up in Manchester."

Do you meet him often?

"I meet him occasionally".

Does he have much say in what you do now?

"He just suggests interesting things. I rung him last week and said 'We've got to get Gilbert and George to do an album cover' and he said 'Yeah, yeah, definitely, I was going to ask them to do a video'. I thought 'brilliant, we're on the same wavelength at last'."

Aren't Paul Morley and Trevor Horn two of the

The Power Of Love is the only good song I've written. It may be the only good song I ever write

most unlikely people in the world for you to have ended up as friends with?

"Extremely unlikely. Trevor more so than Paul, but then I can have a much longer conversation with Trevor because you can discuss music with him. You can't discuss it with Paul. You can only discuss concepts with him, or a T. Rex single or two."

"I'd like to do three albums, then think 'can I cope with this?'."

And the next one is called "Warriors Of The Wasteland"?

"Yes it is."

That sounds like a Black Sabbath title.

"It does, but only if you look at it from a certain point of view. But if you look at it in terms of *The Wasteland* by T. S. Eliot, and the warriors from the film *The Warriors*, just street kids, then it gives a much more interesting slant."

So is that how you see yourselves — Warriors of the Wasteland?

"In so much as everyone has to be. A warrior is just a term for an angry man."

But it's particularly a word for those who rise up out of, and claim to represent others in their positions, isn't it?

"Yes, it has got that nuance to it. It's romantic. Self-glorification. Which is what pop music is all about to a degree.

"No, it will *not* be a double album. We want it to be an ordinary album at an ordinary price. I thought 'Pleasure Dome' was a bit expensive."

Are you proud of it?

"I think it's a good album. Note that I didn't say it's a good *double* album. The main weakness was that too much time was spent on the title track. It did need to be good, but it was dwelt on too much and some of the other tracks suffered. Like 'Black Night White Light' — that could have been *amazing*."

And now there's a fourth single, a remixed, re-edited (but *not* re-recorded) version of 'Welcome To The Pleasure Dome', backed by T. Rex's 'Get It On' (the Peel Session version) and a new song, 'Happy High'. Do you feel a great pressure to have a fourth number one?

"I don't. I reckon Island and ZTT do. Incidentally I originally envisaged 'Pleasure Dome' as our third single. My plan was 'Two Tribes', 'Relax', 'Pleasure Dome' then 'The Power Of Love'."

Is there any truth in the rumour that Island need a fourth single to repromote and help shift the remaining copies of the LP?

"I think that might have something to do with it. But I don't think there are many left."

So far the Frankie campaign has been beautifully orchestrated in the smooth way each single has been impregnated with a ridiculous significance — 'Relax' — the sex single, 'Two Tribes' — war, 'The Power Of Love' — religion/love.

"Ooooh, I know" (*as if confessing a guilty secret*).

Do you hate that?

"No, I think the symbols are awfully cute. I like the way it altered the whole thing and made it feel special. But I would have been happier if it had been done in a less obvious way. Because it put a pressure on the writing team to come up with a main life subject."

But weren't all the songs written before that campaign was thought up?

"Yes, but not with that in mind. They were just normal songs."

So what's the symbol for "Pleasure Dome"?

(*Evasively*) "I haven't seen the artwork."

Someone walks in and lobs a grey crumpled paper bag at Holly's feet. He feels inside and brings out two shirts. Gifts from a fan outside. "Are they for me?" he asks, as if they could be for anyone else. "I hope they fit," says the accompanying note. "Kenny from the fan club said you were a 24."

One is grey. "It's not a bad shirt, this," squeals Holly like a mother at the sales. "It's nice. I might wear this." The other is white, short-sleeved. He looks dubious. "This one's a summer shirt. Maybe I won't wear it. Though if I ever go to Barbados I will. It's the kind of shirt you should wear in Barbados."

Suddenly he discovers a small cheap pin-on brooch. "A little lizard! With green eyes!" he exclaims excitedly. "I'll wear this on a special occasion. It's sweet."

These things happen if you're a pop star.

As I mentioned earlier the accepted folklore is that 'Relax' and 'Two Tribes' are the masterpieces; 'The Power Of Love' is the embarrassingly flabby sequel that broke the spell, burst the bubble. I'd beg to disagree. Paul Morley (him again) used to annoy everyone when he went on about the magic of the perfect pop record, but he was on to something. And 'The Power Of Love' is a good example. The real *celebration*, the true *exuberance*, that pop can carry are here. Yes, that's right, it *does* revel in cliché, it *is* blatantly bold — but isn't that what the *power* of love is actually like? When it can, love screams and shouts, and does so in all the obvious ways because they're the only ways it knows how — its boldness (the way it's embarrassing, if you prefer) is perhaps the principle thing that convinces you that it's *real*. Love doesn't wait till dark and then tiptoe quietly into the room if it can help it. It promises the dual threats of a total freedom and a frightening acceptance of possession: "*I'll protect you from the hooded claw/keep the vampires from your door*". Wimp that I am, 'The Power Of Love' has made me cry more than once. Of course I don't tell Holly that, though I'm sure he'd understand:

"I think it's a classic, infinitely better than 'Relax'

24 Jamming!

the pub that I remember the best. It was intimidating, but exciting, too. To this day, I still like that split feeling where you know you don't belong somewhere yet feel like you're exactly where you're supposed to be. I was starting to learn how, if you could find yourself in just such a place, and then watch and listen and observe closely, and know when to talk but when to shut up and let the world happen around you, and then write it all down in the right kind of way — *be there, let it happen, write it down, repeat* — you might be able to say something that was exactly what it was, but was something else too. **Chris Heath**

or 'Two Tribes'. They were rock grooves. 'The Power Of Love' is a *song*. Anyone could sing 'The Power Of Love'. Frank Sinatra could – which I think is the mark of a good song. What do I think of those people that are cynical about it? They're the ones who've got C.S.E. English, aren't they? It's the sort of song old people can sing in a pub, which I think is fabulous."

So what reaction would he rather, I wonder, – two lovers swooning to it or a guy sitting alone in his bedroom aching to it?

"I'd much rather people sung it in a pub," he insists, "or at a football match. That's the mark of a popular song. Or walking past some building workers and seeing a painter up a ladder whistling it. That's writing a prole song.

"It's the only good song I've ever written. That's why I feel so protective about it. It may be the only good song I ever write."

Holly has plenty to say about other pop stars. Like Sade. Frankie gave her a rather over-the-top thumbs-up in the N.M.E. poll forms they handed in, and at first Holly tries to insist that "ooooh, we think she's fabulous, *so* stylish". But after a bit of goading he admits they hate "the vibe she's laying down. Very *Face* magazine – a cocktail bar with Humphrey Bogart in the background wearing a white tuxedo". Later he reveals that they all call her "The Marquis de Sade".

Bronski Beat next: "I must say I thought 'Ain't Necessarily So' was a fabulous thing to do, but I've heard on the grapevine that they hate us. And I don't like their extreme leftism. I find the whole thing about the Pink Triangle redundant. But they're sincere and they definitely have a place in the scheme of things, because there's that group in the Oxfam trenchcoats who like them and The Smiths."

Ah yes, The Smiths . . . "I liked the album cover with Joe Dallesandro. There's something I love about them and something I don't love. They're in danger of becoming a bit Howard Jones-y. Lyrically though, that album ('The Smiths') was a bit of a masterpiece. That is to say a masterpiece from living in a city that is perpetually under a grey sky. Morrissey's aware of his appeal and uses it to full advantage. There's a definite *cloak*

of alternativism there. There's the pretence of not being a pop idol, but he's far more a contender for pop idoldom than I am."

I refuse to believe this. Despite his protestations to the contrary the Holly Johnson before me, hair swept back ("I can't do anything else with it"), smartly preened, even to the extent of wearing a tie-pin ("because I always get dinner on my ties otherwise") is probably the ultimate candidate for pop idoldom. Still, he's right in suggesting that Morrissey isn't far behind.

Holly smiles. "I think we'd better go to the pub."

And we walk out into the evening breeze, past the fans sitting on a parked van outside the back exit. They say nothing, just stare as we pass.

"They're kind of part of the furniture," Holly explains, a little embarrassed that people actually spend their days waiting for a glimpse of him. "But one day they won't be there, and they weren't there last year." Will it be a better day for them when they're gone? "They won't be so cold," he answers with a wry smile.

"Even the President Of The United States sometimes has to stand naked", once rasped so-

meone called Bob Dylan. "Ooooh, I must have a wee," announces Holly on the walk to the pub. The effect isn't quite as strange, but the similarity is illuminating.

"It's a full moon," he observes, looking up, "maybe that's why I've got a sore throat." We go into the pub.

"It was just the right people in the right place at the right time and it *worked*

I take a stool between Nasher and Holly. Opposite me are Ped and Mark – Mark's arm encircles Zoe, an extra from their latest video. Paul sits detached from this circle, quietly chatting to Regine, their press officer. Changing to suit the mood of the new situation Holly grabs my notebook off me and sarcastically starts to recite my rough list of questions for the earlier interview. "What have the last 12 months meant to you! Ooooh!" I rise and wrestle to get it out of his hands until he releases it. Then the *Lads* – Ped Nasher and Mark – start. As they speak I copy down their words, to their chagrin, onto the pad on my knee. The Lads, as you will soon see, are the three rudest people I've ever met.

Mark: "Who are you?"
"Hi I'm Chris."
Ped: "Do you wear tart's nickers?"
I don't answer.
Ped: "My name's Jack The Lad and I'm dirty as fuck. I'll kick your fuckin' head in."
I scribble down his words.
Nasher: "You cut me out of the picture (*Nasher was missed off the last Frankie* Jamming! *cover, issue 19*). I'm not fuckin' talking to you."
Mark: "Paul Morley's got nothing to do with us."
Ped: "I'm going to get someone to show your arse off and show your balls to your chin."
Nasher: "I'm not talking to magazines anymore except when I'm sober. If you print anything *I* say I'll show your chin your balls."
Ped: "Write this down: 'Testicles!' 'Balls!' Write that down! If you're an iron hoof you're going to get decked. Do you know what an iron hoof is?"
I wait for elucidation.
Ped: "A poof! Are you a poof?"
Mind your own business.
Ped: "You are, aren't you? (*Pause*) You're just trying to be like Paul Morley, aren't you (*to the others*) He's a bit of a Morley, isn't he?"
Holly (*to the others*): "You all *hate* Morley!"
Mark: "No I don't!"
Nasher (*to Holly*): "We hate *you*. But we don't want that in the press."
Mark (*to Holly*, pretending to be servile – this is all a joke) "Would you like me to polish your shoes? (*to me*) Have you ever tried to tongue your own hoof?"
Not often, I answer sarcastically.
All: "So you have tried then?"

Nasher's food arrives. What's he having today? Yummy. A pastie, chips, baked beans, and one of those small bits of lettuce known as 'salad' in pubs. He literally smothers it all in HP sauce and, carefully disregarding everything his mother ever told him about etiquette and nutrition, gobbles it up. I venture a question.
Do you like being famous?
Nasher: "No, I like Cornish pasties."
Ped (*with ridicule*): "You've got cords on! Jumbo cords! He's got cords on! Ha ha ha ha ha ha."
Ped is wearing a black and white cloth shirt, old jeans and training shoes.

Mark (*about me*): "He's a Hersham boy."
Holly (*to me*): "Are you a Hersham boy? (*to Mark*) What's a Hersham boy?"
Ped (*about me*): "He's trying to get up us."
Nasher: "You've actually caught us at a bit of a weird moment after four pints. (*To Holly*, about his own messy haircut) I get it cut at *Smiles* in Knightsbridge – where David Bowie gets his done."
Ped (*to me*): "Why don't you ask us some questions?"
Nasher: "You're a bit of a Morley, aren't you?"
Mark (*to the others*): "He's *that* arty he doesn't even interview people."

We rise together to return to the Academy for photos. Holly is in a hurry – a dinner date. On the way out Nasher furiously feeds 10p pieces into the fruit machine. "Need the cash, eh?" I inquire. He doesn't answer. Suddenly, behind us, a fight erupts.

Apparently what has happened is that the locals at the bar, who'd obviously been unhappy about the invasion of their territory throughout our drink, had offered up an empty insult like "Frankie fuck off" as we left. Which on the face of it was no more of an invitation to respond than the offensive treatment I had just received from the Lads (which was *so* offensive that, in the context, it actually seemed totally inoffensive). But Frankie's new minder, eager to prove his credentials, moved up to the bar to challenge them. Fists pile on top of him and the place erupts. I thought this only happened in the movies. All of a sudden he's on the ground and I watch, as if in slow motion, as one of the aggressors raises a chair and deliberately brings it down on his head. Then Frankie's road crew pull him clear and we all walk briskly away. The minder is covered in blood running down from a wound on his head. Back at the Academy an ambulance is called, and he's taken to hospital.

"We don't need minders; this wouldn't have happened if he hadn't been there," says Paul softly. He seems the furthest removed from these antics, and the most troubled by them.

Later on an argument breaks out. Ped reckons they need *more* minders so that they can *win* the fights next time. The others, thankfully, insist he's wrong.

For once, Nasher looks depressed. "This is the price of fame," he scowls.

"I've never seen Spandau get fucked," retorts Ped, still trying to argue his case.

Nasher explodes: "They don't go to fuckin' ale houses, do they?"

... myth and reality ...

... the ad for Frankie's new single ('The Next Best Thing') parades 'THE BEST THING – listening to Mark O'Toole whisper words of wisdom in your ear while he strokes your inside thigh'...

... as my interviewees drift away I wander round the deserted Brixton Academy. Below me is the fully set-up stage with its backdrop of huge geometrical rises, all lit up with brilliant white-based lights. I turn round to see Mark O'Toole over in the darkness at the entrance of the foyer. He's with Zoe. Slowly he leans over her shoulder and with gentle confidence kisses her deeply again and again and again ...

These are the contradictions that make up Frankie. Holly, however, isn't one of The Lads. No, he talks about Picasso ("I know it sounds corny but I really like him"), Duncan Grant ("an English artist from the Bloomsbury Set – I'd love a carpet designed by him"), and The *Sun*. "I'm actually scared of them," he reveals, abandoning his earlier boast that Frankie can use them. "They constantly ask you about sex, drugs, and now Aids. I don't like that kind of interview I think it's bad." He chats about the 'banned' Frankie book (out soon) – "the others were stupid enough to get interviewed in the cupboard in ZTT; I got taken out to dinner" – how much he likes 'San José' ("I sung it lying on the couch with the words in front of me – the Lads don't like it though"), and about Prince: "He asked me to present that award to him. I've never met him. Would I like sex on the phone with him? Not in the least. I'd rather ask him questions like 'what synthesiser did you use on 'Erotic City' or where he gets his clothes from. He isn't my idea of sex on the phone."

And the final whispers. Any regrets?
"Je ne regrette rien. Ha ha ha. No, it's important not to regret anything, just to think 'oh, I've been there'."
Words for his disciples?
"I could only say something silly like the Bhuddah would say to his followers, 'whatever I say to you is ridiculous, you must find out for yourself'."
'Relax' in retrospect?
"It's one of those records. 'Relax' will sound great in ten years time, like 'I Can't Get No Satisfaction', or 'My Generation' or 'All You Need Is Love' do now. It's a monster. There's nothing we can do about that, I'm afraid. It was just an accident."
The most anybody could expect of you?
"To arrive on time. Ha ha ha, ha ha ha."
And now, world domination?
"It would be great. The total realisation of the arrogance of the name. It would be the total thing and I would enjoy it *loads*. Frankie Goes To Hollywood as the 1980's Beatles ..."

The 1980's Beatles? We'll see. I've no doubt they'll have further exuberant triumphs, but also tears and tragedy before the spectacle of Frankie Goes To Hollywood is finally ironed out and stuck in place in the history books. Maybe they'll end up fat and disgusting, or abandoned and bitter, or happy and accepted, or maybe worse, more unthinkable, disasters will grip them. Whatever, I know the image of Frankie Goes To Hollywood that will remain with me: Holly, centre stage, his right hand raised, pinching his forefinger and thumb delicately together as if catching an invisible butterfly. Then with his eyes to heaven, letting out a smile that is between a sigh and a gasp, releasing it. All of the passion, the control, the daring, the contrivance, and the indescribable magnetism of Frankie Goes To Hollywood is captured in that gesture. And I'll think of the stolen lies carried with 'The Power Of Love' ... *men are but bits of paper, whirled by the cold wind ... words, what are they? one tear will say more than all of them ... dreams are like angels, they keep bad at bay ...* and I'll know that for us, if not for them, it was all worthwhile. But I don't envy them.

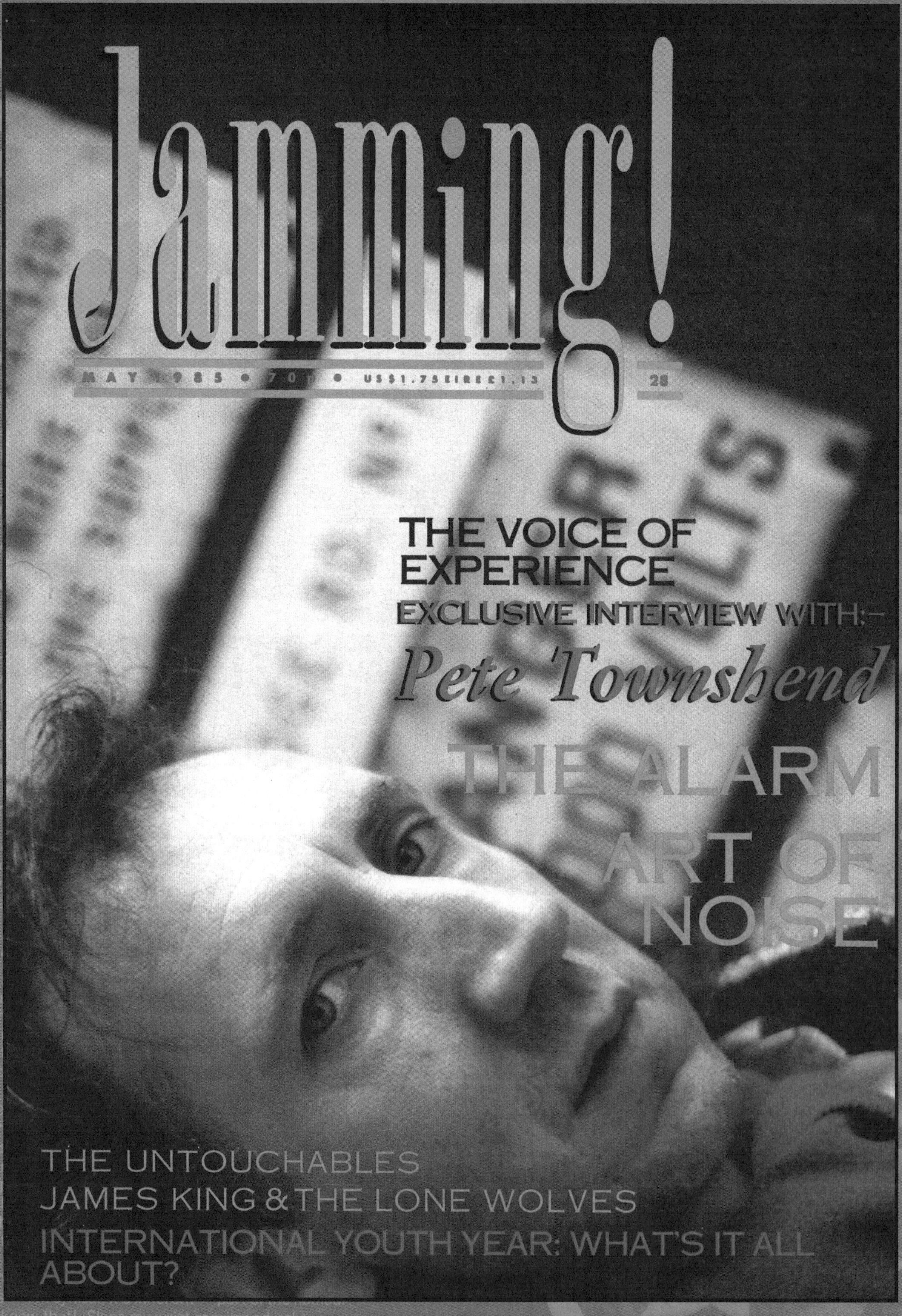

Jamming!

MAY 1985 ● 70p ● US$1.75 EIRE £1.13 — 28

THE VOICE OF
EXPERIENCE
EXCLUSIVE INTERVIEW WITH:–
Pete Townshend

THE ALARM
ART OF
NOISE

THE UNTOUCHABLES
JAMES KING & THE LONE WOLVES
INTERNATIONAL YOUTH YEAR: WHAT'S IT ALL
ABOUT?

16 Jamming!

SIMPLY RED

Spontaneous combustion in the form of eight-piece Simply Red, an unrelenting blend of funk and soul 'n' Roll. Singer Red and drummer Chris (ex-Wah!) sit and map out the meteoric rise to alternonsville from relative obscurity, having played their first gig in January 1984. Red had left The Frantic Elevators to team up with a band. So, how did all this come about?

"We were doing gigs", muses Red, "but we weren't going around asking for publicity. We didn't need it as at that time the band wasn't properly formed on the music scene whereas it. We preferred to let things evolve naturally, now it's reached the level whereby we can begin to show people what we're about.

"We got a lot of uming and aring from record companies. They were saying... (adopts swaggering A 'n' R approach). 'Well, we like the voice lads, but the material's a bit weak'. So why Elektra?

"They stuck with us and showed a lot of faith," adds Chris. "Instead of being arrogant and treating us like kids, they just seemed keen on the stuff. We went for the one we thought was best. Elektra wanted to buzz straight away, so we thought, why not?"

There's been some hearsay that you signed for a ridiculous amount of money. Care to set the record straight, chaps?

"You don't need terrific sums of money!" exclaims Red, incredulously. "We signed a reasonable, economical deal — it's only a loan and you've got to pay it back so what's the point? We've got a pretty tight organisation which we're running on a shoe string."

One of the reasons Simply Red chose to go with Elektra was because of a common agreement they had about recording demos, or rather not doing them, as Chris recounts.

"The only demos anybody has received from us were recorded on a Walkman during rehearsals — really dreadful quality. Spending hours on end doing a tape, you tend to lose all the energy which was there originally."

The day after this interview took place, Simply Red were due to record their debut single in Holland. Will they be able to recapture the potency of their live sound on vinyl?

"I used to DJ at Manchester Poly," says Red, "and the biggest test of a record is how hard it hits — which is what gets people dancing. We'll need to have attack in the studio but with the producer we've got, I don't see any problem."

Watching Simply Red play it's blatantly obvious how much they've been influenced by (predominantly American) black music. Red appears to absorb it — exuberance pours out of him.

"I love it," he enthuses, "I don't differentiate between playing live and singing for ourselves. I move around, even perform in a way, but I get lost in the music. Sometimes I'm completely ga-ga — gone! I don't know where I am. At the last gig we did in London (University) I nearly collapsed — ran out of breath! I could do with an oxygen tent at the side of the stage.

Being such a strong frontman, there's a danger of you being singled out from the rest of the band. Would you be tempted?

"If people think I'm using this as a vehicle to take off on a solo career then they don't understand why we've started this unit," states Red, emphatically. "The strength of the band as a whole has created the songs. I need them — they need me, it's the perfect partnership. We have the advantage that we all get on extremely well without any pretentions."

Manchester lads both, Chris and Red don't express any fervent desire to be a part of the northern music subculture. The idea of 'the local Manchester band makes good'.

"I don't think it is a 'following' kind of place," mulls Red. "It's full of cynics — I'm cynical, it's inherent — part of the humour, you should know that! (slaps my wrist reprimandingly).

There's one thing... people in Manchester don't hesitate to put you in your place, if you suddenly get too big for yer boots. We're just trying to get out of it!"

There you have it sincerely Simply Red, showing their true colours.

Some Scorching Hot Property Yells Ro NEWTON

Jamming! 9

What was it about cover sessions shot on the Soho streets? As with Jerry Dammers on the front of Issue 18, the chosen image of the venerable Pete Townshend, photographed by the otherwise innovative Coneyl Jay, came up severely short. So, for that matter, did the new logo, and the choice of colours, *and* to some extent the list of other cover names.

The Townshend interview was not necessarily a coup, but I'd long wanted to revisit my formulaic questioning of my idol as a 14-year-old, and granted a second opportunity in a post-Who environment, I held his feet reasonably close to the fire. A few months later, another journalist sitting at those same hallowed feet referenced this interview and Pete in turn noted that I had looked in need of a wank. Given that this came from the composer of 'Pictures Of Lily' and 'Mary Anne With The Shaky Hand', I like to think of that as a compliment.

Elsewhere within Issue 28, Paul Davies was considerably more combative with The Alarm's Mike Peters, while Chris Heath was much chummier with The Art of Noise than he had been with their ZTT label-mates Frankie Goes To Hollywood a month earlier. Interviews with Motown legends Eddie and Brian Holland, Bruce Cockburn, David Thomas of Pere Ubu, 1000 Mexicans, The Armoury Show, Immaculate Fools and Simply Red (*none* of them named on the cover) were joined by brisk pieces on James King and The Untouchables (who, oddly, were). Buried further within the increasingly black-and-white layout were pieces on International Youth Year (it was, apparently, a thing), the cabaret circuit, new movies and an earnest piece (by myself) on gigging. Looking back at the last sentence, perhaps the whole magazine was in need of a wank?

THROUGH THE YEARS

● **Tony Fletcher** on an eventful

passage through the past to

present with Pete Townshend.

● **Photos: Coneyl Jay.**

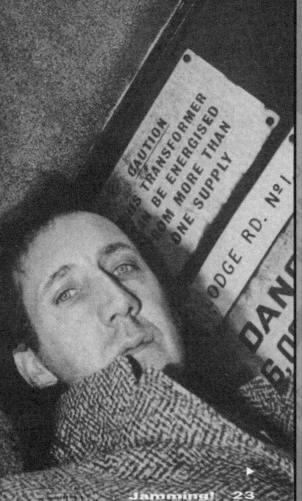

The man who meets me has a gentle handshake and a polite smile; he also looks desperately older than when we last met. Admittedly that was over six years ago, but then, in his mid-thirties and as leader of one of the world's biggest rock groups, he was coping well with it all, coming across as fit as any other contemporary. But the recent years of alcoholism, heroin addiction, break-up of marriage and band, and near-bankruptcy — all of which, apart of course from The Who's split, have since been rectified — have taken their toll. The eyes are hollowed out, the face thinner and the hair greyer: Pete Townshend is forty this May and looks it. As we wander round the back-streets of Soho for photographs, he remarks on agreeable dossing-places: "I could quite easily settle here for the night," he comments on a little cove off the back of his Broadwick Street studios — the last few years have regularly seen one of rock's more enigmatic characters sleeping in the London streets after a particularly heavy night. He can afford to smile now, for 1985 sees him almost a new man: clear of The Who, he can get on with his 'career' as a solo recording artist (not that, knowing Pete, we can expect records frequently) and his new part-time job as an associate editor at established publishing house Faber And Faber.

● The younger generation in Britain view Pete Townshend as yesterday's man, a forgotten hero. They can hardly be blames, as the last half-decent Who albums were the 'Kids Are Alright' and 'Quadrophenia' soundtracks of 1979, the year when The Who-financed film of a desperate sixties mod proved a box-office smash at the time of the mod revival. Even then, Townshend was talking about quitting The Who, yet for some reason Keith Moon's untimely death a year before had spurred them into a new line-up and new plans. The last Who albums — 'It's Hard'

and 'Face Dances' — hardly caused a ripple — in Britain, though Townshend's own "All The Best Cowboys Have Chinese Eyes' solo set was rather better received. In 1982 The Who went on a last massive jaunt around the States, and the recently-released 'Who's Last' double, culled from those dates, was rightly shunned by the British public.

● Yet despite those last years, most self-respecting music fans will never deny the enormous contribution The Who — and Townshend in particular — made to popular music. The original sixties punks, they went from classic singles band (the compilation of these early hits, 'Meaty Beaty Big And Bouncy' remains timeless) to classic rock band — 'Who's Next', 'Who Live At Leeds' and 'Quadrophenia' all maintaining power and emotion without slipping over into heavy metal. It was only when punk came along — Townshend rightly viewed as the Godfather, returning the compliment by welcoming the movement with open arms — that The Who lost their direction. That he didn't split The Who then was, of course, a betrayal to their image, but the financial carrots were such that it was never an easy move. Whatever, he remains 'Rock's Most Honest Man', a respected spokesman never lost for words.

● What follows is the spliced version of a two-hour conversation, almost totally dominated by Townshend's rambling voice. Left out are his sojourns about the political pop as orchestrated by Bob Dylan, and his distanced thoughts on today's music. Townshend never saw the Jam live bar their final TV appearance on the first ever Tube, searching through their back catalogue after the event: and he claims The Smiths to be the one band that scare him — 'I don't know what the fuck's going on, and I just find it all very interesting,' he says about them. As for other matters, read on . . .

Jamming! 23

Now that The Who have finally gone and you're doing this work with Faber and Faber, is it like starting afresh?

Well, no not really, because I'd been doing publishing with Eel Pie books for eight years already, so it's really just a continuation of that. But I do feel I'm starting afresh in a lot more sweeping ways. I think the emotional change that happened the day that I realised that the band was over . . . I started to take stock. I started to think about all the years that I'd been with the band. At first I thought 'Well okay, the last years were a bit unhappy, and I do feel that The Who began as such an idealistic band, and lost a lot of those ideals along the way'. But then I started to think that that didn't matter that much, that when taken on balance we were still a great band. We had a lot of good times, a lot of bad times. I had a lot of terrific friendships — I'd been playing with John Entwistle since I was 11 — and I started to feel very good about it. So in a sense what's been a new start for me, is that since I made that statement, which was in late '83, I've been feeling a lot happier.

Was it just like releasing a weight off your shoulders?

In a sense. I suppose it was just something that I felt good about, because I felt for the first time that I'd actually had the courage to do what it was that I wanted to do for quite some time. I wanted to leave the band before Keith died, around 1976, and I didn't really have the guts to do it then.

When I interviewed you in late '78, you were saying — to everyone — 'I don't want to play live again, we're never going to tour again. The band's reached *that* point'. It seems like it took five more years for you to call it a day. I don't know if it was the business pressures that meant you couldn't just stop . . .

No, it wasn't. In fact, at that point we could easily have stopped because we had no more contractual obligations. What happened was Keith died, that was the big thing.

You said at the time that Keith's death was the most positive thing that had happened to The Who in years . . .

It was, because we had to really think about what we were going to make of it, how we were going to respond. Whether we were just going to sit back and let it look like it was Keith's misadventure that meant the band had finished, or whether we were going to consciously say 'Alright, this is the end.' And we felt that in a sense it had given us the opportunity to try some experimenting, which we tried and it turned out that it was no experiment at all. Really it was between Roger and I: Roger resisted change and risk and danger, and felt that everything that was good about The Who was what we'd built up over the years, and I took the opposite stance. I said 'No, what was good about The Who was that in the early days they were dangerous and risky and we've got to take those risks.'

He had the showbusiness attitude didn't he? Always falling back on the hits?

We both agreed a lot more than is commonly known. But like politicians, one of us had to be on one side of the line, and one on the other. I would take the side where I was all for risk and danger and creative experiments, and he would be the traditionalist, the showbiz pro. But in actual fact, Roger has taken tremendous risks in his own career, doing acting and producing films. He's currently very interested in appearing in small musicals — he's very capable of taking risks.

As you say, it seemed at the time that you could try things. But it didn't happen, you didn't experiment . . .

Well, to a great extent we did experiment. We experimented a lot more than people knew. It didn't work because we realised it wasn't what people wanted from us. What people wanted was for The Who to be like Status Quo. They wanted us not to change.

You reckon? Because right back in the sixties when you did Tommy, no band could have made more of a change than that.

Oh, for Christ's sake! Tommy is still something which more people sneer at over anything else that we've ever done. It's been said that it was pretentious, that it was creatively immoral, that it was an abandonment of all the finer principles of rock'n'roll, all those things.

Surely enough people bought it to justify that it was a success?

It established us with a much wider, much more conservative audience. The kind of people who came to see The Who because of Tommy were much more of a Woodstock, White City-festival type of generation. And they to this day are still steeped with nostalgia. Whereas the people who are nostalgic for the early sixties, they're not nostalgic for The Beatles, The Who, The Stones, The Kinks and The Yardbirds, they're nostalgic for what happened then. And for the fact that it was a period of discovery. Well, that's a much more healthy thing isn't it?

Are you doing down Tommy yourself there?

No, not at all.

Do you still think it was a brave move?

I think it was dangerous, and I think it was quite pretentious, and there were parts of it that were quite daft and very tongue-in-cheek. But I'm not turning round now and saying it was meant to be a joke. There's always been parts of my work that were meant to be jokes. Anyway Anyhow Anywhere was a complete joke, Pictures of Lily was a complete joke. I just thought it was funny to have a record at no. 4 that was about wanking off. When Tommy came along, I wrote it with a strain of seriousness, not artistic pretentiousness. I did feel that there were a lot of deaf, dumb and blind people walking around, and that they needed waking up.

When it was on TV at Christmas, Tommy really looked dated . . .

Don't you think it looked that way at the time though? I think what's good about it is that the couple of times it's been on the TV, it's got funnier. Seeing Oliver Reed and Ann Margret and Jack Nicholson and Elton John, and even to some extent, Roger, with his Woodstock poses, it's nice and light, and it's funny. You can take it as an amusing piece of kitsch, it's like a bad taste kind of thing, and Ken Russell at his most gauche, but beneath the whole thing is this story of the way the British brutalise and stereotype their children.

Everybody talks about female stereotypes — we've just *started* to attend to the fact that since the Victorian times the worst thing that's happened in this country isn't female stereotyping, it's *male* stereotyping. Men who are incapable or unwilling to show their softer side, who are afraid to say that they're weak, who are afraid to cry in public, who are afraid to say they're afraid; who are afraid to say that they don't want to fight, who are afraid to say that they're afraid of dying . . . Those stereotypes, which date back to Victorian imperialist Britain, to the days when we were each expected to just do our duty, to go and die in some trench somewhere, leaving behind

our mothers and our lovers and our children, that's still deeply entrenched in the British mentality at a very very early age. I think a lot of the symptoms of what is wrong with British society, are rooted in the way we bring up our children.

I would say that you've done a lot in your time to try and break that down, but The Who were always quite macho . . .

My problem in the early days was that I was writing for a very macho voice. And that's why I laugh about Anyway Anyhow Anywhere, because it's the way Roger used to be. What's interesting is that twenty years later, I know that Roger is one of the most gentle men walking the face of the earth. And I do find it very difficult to reconcile it with the image that I had of him then.

The band as a whole had such a macho image anyway though: smashing up instruments, causing chaos everywhere — it was all very violent . . .

We weren't as macho or as tough as, say, The Jam were. We were much weaker; our shows would often break down in fits of petulence, we would often have public arguments. Our weaknesses were always seen as one of our strengths. Okay, we looked like a macho outfit, we rapidly learnt that that was how we felt we should look, but that wasn't how we were. So a lot of the guys who came to see us, because our audience was about 80% male, used to come because they felt the same sort of feelings towards us as perhaps football fans feel towards George Best: an element of real interest and admiration, but also an element of pity and identification with the childlike side.

Everybody in the rock business likes to think that above everything else we all share the belief that music has some kind of paliative, healing, uplifting effect. And that whatever we use it for, the fact is that it is a healing thing, and it is uplifting. That's universal, it's always been a quality of music. It's so easy in this world of people talking about music that carries messages, because of the power of lyrics, to forget that behind the lyrics is music, that has this tremendous healing effect.

You've always talked about the power of music and what it can do to people, but there's a lot of people in the mid-eighties questioning how relevant that is. Their attitude is — 'Rock music is nothing, it's just a background noise, people aren't worked up about it'. They're virtually saying that the whole idea of thinking of music as important has failed.

There's a debate there with two sides. One is that people are saying 'Listen, the likes of idealists like Townshend and all these other prats from the sixties saying that rock music is capable of changing the world, what has it actually done? Look at his life, he's made a lot of money, gone through a terrible marriage break-up, a personal breakdown, drug abuse . . . what kind of document for success is he? He's just like the rest. And in the end what have we got to show for it? Wham.' And on the other hand you've got people who still believe in something ornate which is carried in the frustrations and anger and desperation of young people — specifically young people, under 25 — that carries enough power, whatever the medium, whether it's music or art, or magazines, or whatever, to express itself.

I think that if you listen to something like Frankie Goes To Hollywood, particularly 'Two Tribes', what you're hearing in that music is the most unbelievably clever and most

sophisticatedly organised . . . There's all this energy and force brought together, and that music is unbelievably uplifting. I think when you put 'Two Tribes' on, the sound that comes out of the speakers is devastating. The words of the song though, have now been said a thousand fucking times.

The whole thing about Frankie is that they aren't bothered about war or anything. The idea of causing a big fuss to get their name in the papers is great but I'd say Frankie are a very dodgy example to use . . .

No, I don't think they are, I chose them very carefully. What I'm saying is that that is evidently true — they're mostly interested in success, and they'll use, as you say, whatever medium is necessary. But what is interesting, is despite that, their music is still uplifting. And what I'm saying is that music that is well-written and well-produced and has got the right elements, still stirs the blood in some way. I think we all carry round these music genes, and they respond first. Alright, two years later we can say "Oh God, I wish I hadn't gone out and bought 'Two Tribes', because Frankie are such a load of wallies", but it's too late now; we all have gone out and bought the fucking record.

I'm not alone when I want to know why you chose to address the Young Tories Conference about heroin. A lot of people felt you were declaring to be on their side.

Well they are in power, and they had the platform. Obviously most of my connections are socialist: I'm having dinner with Michael Foot on Sunday, I talk to Ken Livingstone on the phone. I'm a socialist. But I felt because the drug issue was being squandered by the press in the most dramatic way, what was needed was somebody to stand up and talk to the press at large about how parents might be able to recognise and help their kids. Okay, so they know how to look for dilated pupils, runny noses and the tin of small change going missing. Fine. How do they respond when one of their neighbours goes 'So-and-so's son is a junkie'? They hang their heads in shame. They shouldn't do, because the circumstances in society are so rife that any kid can become Christianne F.

So when I was invited, I said 'What is it about?' And they said 'It's a fringe meeting, and if you come and talk, we reckon there'll be about 200 press people there.' Now I happened to know that the room I would be talking in only holds 150 people. So I thought 'If there's 200 press people show up, there ain't gonna be any Young Tories there'. There were four. Four Young Tories. The rest of it was press.

But you still appeared under the banner of the Young Tories, and there was nothing that appeared in the press that showed that you had anything against them. Do you see that?

I do, but I don't particularly care, because I'm not a political animal. I've always resisted the pressure of my friends on the left to become active in socialist politics; I don't think it's right for me to do so.

Is that just a personal thing?

Yeah, it's my business. But I felt it was a pretty crafty move. Along comes a socialist who actually stands up and paints all of the policies that the Tory party had at the time as black as they could be painted. The kind of things that I was saying to the press under the Tory party banner were that we've got to show that we

care about the unemployment problem. That we've got to show that we care about young people, we've got to show that when somebody falls, we care about them. Well, Margaret Thatcher's reception of those kids from Liverpool the other day, goes to show that not only does she not care about them, but that she can't identify with them as her children. I think that's very sad, because I can identify with them as my children.

I don't really feel I have to make any defence. I think that anybody who hasn't now realised that it was the right platform to use is too cynical, and isn't really looking deeply enough into it. When I did the Brockwell Park Rock For Jobs thing, there were all these SWP representatives walking around giving people pamphlets for the revolution; it reminded me of 1967 when I had all these people telling me that what The Who should be doing is giving their money to Tariq Ali to buy guns with. I'm not part of that left and not part of that right. If you're a public figure you just have to use whatever platform you're given. I don't refuse to appear at The Royal Albert Hall on the basis that half the boxes there are owned by very, very rich families — I play there because it's a stage. Plus I don't refuse to give concerts for the Prince Charles Trust because I'm against the principle of royalty. I *am* against the principle of royalty, but I also think you have to make the best of a bad job. He happens to be a really good bloke. *He cares,* and he's lumbered with being Prince Charles just as much as you're lumbered with being who you are.

It's interesting you say that, because there is this idea that Prince Charles doesn't like having to do a lot of what he's expected to.

My feeling is not that there's anything about the way he lives that he would want to be able to change tomorrow, but what amazed me is that when we did this judging competition of bands at Tottenham Court Road, of which there were six, mainly reggae outfits, he not only knew the songs and had heard the tapes, but he'd seen them all play. He said 'Well my personal favourite is so-and-so' and I thought 'This is incredible. Here we have a guy who is going to be King sooner or later, and he's obviously spent a good bit of his time listening to reggae bands.' Well I've only ever seen two or three reggae bands. I just thought this guy has probably seen far more young bands than I have. If somebody's going to be lumbered with being King of this piss-pot country, then I'd much prefer it to be a man like that, rather than a man like, say, Norman Fowler.

You seem to be saying that if we can have gradual change then it's the best of a bad job.

'Won't Get Fooled Again' is a song about the futility of revolution. I've never been a revolutionary, I don't believe in bloodshed. Not for any cause. I'm an ardent supporter of the raising of black consciousness in South Africa, but I'm not an ardent supporter of supplying the militants over there with the machinery by which they can create an enormous bloodbath. I don't think bloodshed is ever justified. Politically I've always felt that rock music — and this is where I begin to sound again like my old idealistic self — is the healthiest kind of revolution, because it's the revolution of self-abandon, and of aspiration and transcendance. I don't think it's purely the domain of the young, because obviously rock is getting older all the time, but really the importance of that kind of thinking, the importance of being able to laugh at your difficulties is to the young.

Young people have to be able to feel optimism, they have to be able to feel that they have power, they have to be able to feel that

they don't need older people. The truth of the matter is that they don't; they don't need it. You don't need the help of the older people, you don't need their rules, you don't need their world, you don't need their regulations, you don't need their fucking hang-ups.

Going back to the heroin thing — was there any connection between what made you addicted and what would make a young kid on a council estate addicted? Because people could say you had everything, you had no need to dabble.

Well that wasn't actually true at the time, because when I dabbled, I had nothing. I had less than nothing.

Was this the point at which you were almost bankrupt?

Yeah. I was living away from my family, and I'd lost all sense of worth. I felt very undignified, I felt that I was too old to be doing the things that I was doing.

How long were you really addicted?

I'd started using heroin with cocaine — freebasing — in the early part of '81, and I was using it right up to the end. In November '81, I went for a recording session with Elton

John. I hadn't been playing, I'd forgotten really what it was like. So I went over, and while we were doing this song 'Ball And Chain', I was drinking the usual Remy Martin, about half a bottle or something, and we stopped, and I was absolutely flying. I looked at the bottle and thought 'Well it can't be the booze, I haven't taken any drugs, I'd slept right the night before' — it was the music that had done it.

It would seem that there's some similarity between, say, the unemployed kids that are getting hooked on drugs because they've got nothing to do with their time, and you, the big rock star with no tours coming up, no Who album . . . It was only when you found that you didn't actually need drugs to enjoy yourself . . .

It wasn't just enjoying myself, it was also burying myself. The unique thing about heroin in relation to other drugs, is that a lot of other drugs are quite nice to pass the time. Pot's quite nice to pass the time with, so's taking a few toots of speed; glue you can see some nice things on, and then if you're lucky enough to get a toot of decent coke, you might get the five-minute rush out of that. And then you think 'Oh I'll try heroin', and then *BANG!* It's com-

26   Jamming!

oletely different, it's not a time-passer — it's a life sentence, like it said on the T-shirt. It's "Ahh, this is where I wanted to be all the time.' It's 'Forget life, forget that I haven't got a job, that I've broken up with my girlfriend, that I've got a drink problem, they're nothing — now I realise what I was searching for all the time. *It was this.* It was the womb, it was going back to where I came from'.

So that's what happens: heroin comes along and it offers you something you never ever thought you were looking for. And so it's a terrible big cheat, and that's why the person who gives heroin to another potential user, is guilty of really the worst injustice to somebody else. Because you take it, and then suddenly find yourself on the other side of the room with a different head, a different body, a different heart, in a different time on a different planet. Everything is different, and it will never ever be the same again.

The worst thing about it is that apart from the initial novelty of finding yourself in a different place, practically immediately it becomes very boring. Being obsessed with getting your next fix is so much more boring than standing around doing nothing *(laughs)*.

Can you see any easy solution for the smack epidemic?

I can't see any rapid solution, but I can see ways of helping people that have gotten involved, and that is to get them out. You do have to be ready to get out, but when you are, you should be helped. And at the moment, there aren't enough beds, there aren't enough differing methods of treatment available. So where I'm concentrating my efforts now is on actually helping to persuade the government — the one in power, they happen to be the fucken Tories, I'm afraid to say — to provide more beds, and to help fund existing rehabilitation programmes, and to encourage people to do more. I think there's a lot of hope. Meg Patterson's treatment *(which cured Pete)* is still relatively unavailable. There's only two or three places — ten beds — where it's available in the whole of Britain. Most clinics are using maintenance programmes to get people off — in other words, they come out free of heroin, but they're probably going to be addicted to fucking methodone or something. If you could provide 200,000 beds next week, to the 400,000 people who are waiting for treatment, and give them the Meg Patterson treatment, the other 200,000 would be treated in the following two weeks, and that would be that lot over with. Meg

Patterson's treatment is absolutely unique, and uniquely effective. It's so on the verges of quackery and Chinese medicine, that it's difficult for the establishment to accept, but we're breaking that down slowly. I'm publishing her book later this year with Faber, so hopefully that will be another step.

Are you enjoying your solo career?

I've enjoyed making both my solo albums, despite the differing conditions; I'm immensely proud of both of them. And this record for me is unique, because it's the first one I'm making on my own, in that I haven't got The Who to fall back on if it's a flop.

That's more or less where you set Quadrophenia isn't it?

Yeah. It's actually a continuation, it's looking at the hero of Quadrophenia as a 25-26 year old, living in that area now, and what's happened to him. What I really liked about Quadrophenia was it was the first time I ever sat down and wrote songs about someone else. What I think has been great about the last couple of years is that I've risen above a lot of the personal problems that I've carried along for the last twenty years like a great big blubbering adolescent.

Looking back on the last few years of The Who, I don't mind saying that I found the last few albums embarrassing. (Pete laughs). Do you think I'm being really harsh?

I dunno . . . (pauses) . . . I find it very difficult to be as objective as you obviously are. It's strange isn't it — what's the difference between a record that really works and a record that really doesn't? It's such a fine line. 'Face Dances' and 'It's Hard' were made by a band who were very unsure about whether or not they wanted to be making a record. And I think that's a terrible doubt.

You could tell by listening that there was no bursting desire there to make a record. That's why I think they sound so bad. Also the live album, 'Who's Last', well I know you were playing to the biggest audiences of your life, but it *sounded* like a rock band that had been together for twenty years and lost the enthusiasm.

The terrible thing is we didn't want any of those albums to be as bad as they are. 'Who's Last' is not so bad it's embarrassing, it's embarrassing because it's competent. As a rule we would have said 'Stick it in the bin', but we put it out because it was all we had. And that's what starts to be a bit embarrassing, that the last years of The Who were so desperate.

But surely now that you've freed yourself of what was expected from you with The Who, you can get back into just doing what you want?

The funny thing really is the success of 'Scoop' in America, which sold 400,000 records there, which for a double album was incredible. It was just stuff I happened to do because I like playing music. It's no bigger or smaller than that. I do want what I write to inspire people. I don't feel like a leader or a spokesman, but I do recognise that some of the things that I've done have affected what people have come to expect from other bands, and from music and songwriting as a whole. And that's an amazing feeling. Once you've tasted that, you want to taste it again.

Am I right there was some acrimony after you left The Who? You'd just signed a new contract but had only delivered one or two albums, and having been paid all

these huge advances, it was a case of who was going to pay them back. I remember Roger saying in interviews 'I don't see why I have to pay them back because I'm prepared to carry on with The Who'. Was that all resolved?

Yeah, and I did actually bear the brunt of the payback to Warners. But Kenny, Roger and John all contributed as much as they could afford. We did have to buy our way out of the contract, and all I can say is Thank God we did, because I don't believe we would have made another record worth releasing. Warners wanted out anyway, because they'd signed the band up for too much money.

You were on one hell of a downward spiral by then . . .

Yeah, but both 'Face Dances' and 'It's Hard' were number one albums in America. We had a whole new generation of fans. Like I get 2-300 letters a week from 14-year old girls in America. If I get a letter from a 14-year old girl in Britain, I'll invite her down for the weekend.

Do you have to work again?

I would have to sell a lot of things I think, and unfortunately I would have to sell jobs with it. Because what I've bought is things that have created jobs, like studios, dubbing theatres, offices and publishing companies. But no, I don't think I'd have to work again, all I'd have to do is buy a much smaller house; just make do with one television and video, instead of eight! We don't live with works of art, we don't spend enormous amounts of money — my wife's got a silly fur coat that my daughters both hate, and I've got an old Merc that cost quite a bit of money. If I didn't work, I'd have to change my lifestyle, but I'd be happy. I'm happy doing my work at Faber, for which I get a small salary.

Is that salary relative to what other people at Faber get?

Yeah. It makes my feel I'm there because they want *me*, not my name. In America they'd buy you first, and then afterwards you'd learn the real terms and conditions. I'm only doing between eight and ten titles a year at Faber; I've edited a book of plays by Stephen Berkhoff, a book called 'Bikers' by a Hells Angel with a sociology degree, and then there's the book by Meg Patterson. My own book 'Horse's Neck' which has just come out is sort of autobiographical, but fiction. They're stories that are drawn from my life but not about my life.

All the companies that The Who owned — do they still exist?

The trucking company — ML Executives — still exists, the crew now totally own it themselves. We've sold off our sector of Shepperton Studios for a thumping great loss, and Who Films is just a dormant company now.

How did the films all do? Everyone knows they cost a fortune to make.

McVicar did okay, Quadrophenia did okay; The Kids Are Alright was very expensive and did not do okay. But you have to remember that when Tommy the film came out, The Who as a company probably earned six million pounds a year. With that money, we bought a load of PA gear, we bought a load of trucks, we bought a chunk of Shepperton Studios, and we started to invest in films. It was great while it lasted, until Keith died. When he died, his shares were wrapped up because he was an American resident; it was a shame, because Keith was having such a great time. At one time it looked like we were all set to become film moguls, and then he went and dropped dead. Most inconvenient; his timing was a bit off at the end. ●

Jamming!

JUNE 1985 ● 70p ● US $1.75 ● EIRE £1.13 ● 29

AFRIKA BAMBAATAA

SCRITTI POLITTI

ICICLE WORKS

THREE JOHNS

FAITH BROTHERS
Confronting the Myth

FREE

16 PAGE FOCUS ON LIVERPOOL

FLEXI: 10,000 MANIACS + SIMPLY RED

Paula Skidmore gives a guided tour through the sights — both cherished and despised — of a city on the Mersey. The map will give some idea of where to find them.

A stroll around Liverpool these days can be a real architectural education in how *not* to redevelop a city centre. Searching underneath the developer's rubble can be a fruitful exercise, however, if you choose to ignore the likes of Cavern Walks, Church Street, and Central Station.

Bold Street seems to be one of the more historically intact of the centre's attractions. If you take a stroll up its paved walkway, two-thirds up on the left you'll find the most interesting eating/meeting place of the moment. Called 'Berlin' it's a café/bar, done out in unassuming, but chic, pre-war German décor. Good music and obliging, friendly staff combine with an excellent variety of food at cheap-to-reasonable prices and a good selection of

The Berlin Café. Pic: Peter Henderson.

vegetarian meals as well. With a licence and evening opening, Berlin is gradually gaining the reputation it deserves. At the top of Bold Street there's the remarkable land-mark of St Michael's Church; obliterated inside by a World War II bomb, its outside walls and tower still stand. A No. 82 bus outside in Berry St, will take you to the trendy epicentre, Lark Lane, about ten minutes away. Full of *those* kind of shops/cafes/people, it's best in the good weather when you can stop off in the beautiful adjacent Sefton Park, where you can even go boating on the lake.

Alternatively, from Berry Street go up Leece St., Hardman St., and combine the tourist trappings of two Cathedrals at either end of a street called Hope, (best view of the city from the Anglican's Bell Tower), the Art College (Lennon's formative years), the Philharmonic Pub (tourists/students — good for jazz in the week) and the Everyman Bistro (avoid unless aspiring trendy/actor).

Turning left down Mount Pleasant at the bottom you'll find that monstrous relic, The Adelphi, grey and imposing it-does have nice pink tea rooms inside, if you can dodge the blue rinses in the foyer. And of course opposite, over Lewis' is *that* statue. Averting your gaze, and continuing down Ranelagh St., turn left into the cobbled Cases St. Full of creative design potential but looking set to be pulled down under Wimpy's redevelopment along with Clayton Square, thanks to Patrick Jenkin. Sober thoughts aside, past the Great White 'St. John's Precinct' Elephant,

to Williamson Square, where there's always a multitude of public speakers on a Saturday, and street sellers on any day. Cross over the Gyratory, avoiding the pedestrian-killer-motivated buses, to find the Open Eye Complex, on the corner of Whitechapel. This comprises a Photo Gallery, free and always of a high standard; a shop with a brilliant black & white postcard selection; a local film and video production upstairs, and Desperate Dan's cafe downstairs. The latter is cheap, cheerful, transport-cafe style, but still retaining credibility with it's ex-Eric's jukebox. Round the corner News From Nowhere radical bookshoop still provides it's comprehensive selection, despite fascist arson attacks repeatedly. Straight up if you want to find the bastion of Victorian architecture, in the shape of the Picton Library, Liverpool Museum, Walker Art Gallery, and St Georges Hall. The latter is worth visiting when there's a flea market on, to peek at its breath-taking grandeur (suitably the location of Crystal

Day Concert).

Back down Whitechapel to Church Street and off to the right past the revolting Top-Shop-Trash you'll find the comparative seclusion of the Bluecoat. Comprising concert rooms, Art Gallery, shop, cafe, craft centre, etc., it's always worth a visit for the latest exhibition, occasional record/book fair, or a quiet sit in the courtyard with a coffee and a cake. Back to Whitechapel and down Button Street to the legendary Probe, and then a nostalgic amble round the corner to Mathew Street. You'll probably find, though, whilst paying homage to Eric's, that you're trodden on by Day Trippers eager to spend their aristocratic millions in the tacky Cavern Walks erection; plastic pubs and plastic shops for plastic people. Even the Armadillo Tea Rooms, once the *only* place to eat in town, has succumbed to the big-money-mentality, now moved to snazzier premises.

Passing on swiftly (wipe that tear from your eye), head on into the business quarter of the city, all melodramatic mountains of solid Victoriana, with the occasional nod to '60's modernism. Wander around here at your leisure — as long as you walk downhill you'll never get lost. If you've time, take a look at India Buildings, Water St., with it's impressive genuine ornate arcade, but make a date along The Strand, and admire the Tax Offices, not for their ingenuity, but because they are known to most as the Liver Buildings (the ones with the funny looking concrete birds on).

Round about here you could walk to the Albert Dock redevelopment and admire the construction of those £40,000 a-piece flats none of us will be able to afford, but instead, why not round off the day with a Ferry Cross the Mersey. Traditions die hard, and anyway, we all need to blow the cobwebs out of our hair occasionally. Reflect on the changing skyline of Liverpool, see the now inactive dock, once the birthplace of the city, and watch the murky waters churning by.

Paula Skidmore

Faith Brothers may not have been *Jamming!*'s usual proven chart stars, and there may have been accusations of nepotism given my dual role, but they were riding the crest of a wave, had connected in a big way with *Jamming!* readers, and the visually arresting photograph, shot in front of the same Town House studios where I had spent much of the summer of '79 with The Jam, was certainly an improvement on the previous issue's shot of Pete Townshend (whom Faith Brothers were soon to be found supporting). Other names to make the cover list included established *Jamming!* favourites Scritti Politti and The Icicle Works, plus The Three Johns and Afrika Bambaataa. Hugh Morley's interview with Bambaataa, one of the three undisputed founders of hip-hop, was complemented by Jonh Wilde's profile of Morgan Khan, whose

ISSUE #29 5/85

Street Sounds compilations had helped synthesise that whole New York-driven electro-funk hip-hop revolution into album-sized samplers for an increasingly hungry British audience.

The American influence was additionally signified by coverage of the country's new rock bands, with The Long Ryders, Lone Justice and Jason & The Scorchers piled up in this issue. Add in an Ivor Cutler interview, a 'Group Therapy' article about getting a record deal and the fact that Russell Tate seemed to be doing more by way of design with less by way of colour, and this was a decent magazine. It was topped off by a flexi-disc produced in collaboration with Elektra Records featuring 10,000 Maniacs and Simply Red (not a bad scoop in hindsight), and another provincial bonus zine, this time a 16-page 'Focus on Liverpool'.

EXPLODES!

THE FAITH BROTHERS prepare to offer an alternative to the hollow chart promises, marrying hard-edged belief to a solid soul force. But are they any different to any other 'worthy' chart idealists? Paul Davies gets the faith!

In 1985 The Myth is still omnipotent. Nine years after Johnny Rotten and the boys had attempted to blowtorch and bazooka the wretched thing to the ground, The Myth of Rock 'n' Roll still flourishes, leering and breathing its rank and acrid fumes over all those who participate in its demented circus. The many headed manifestations of The Myth thrive and breed on the most iniquitous aspects of human nature — greed, egotism and the myopic pursuit of a specious and spurious type of glory. In submission to The Myth, musicians are elevated to god-like status and gingerly placed on gold lamé pedestals; the gulf between performer and audience widens and deepens; people are used and abused as objects and commodities, and as the money goes round the mug punters are fleeced and stitched up in order to keep the protagonists of this sordid masquerade in cocaine and caviar. What little resistance there is can usually be unceremoniously crushed, or else silenced with fistfuls of drugs and a lucrative recording contract.

Despite all this, there is hope. There is always hope. And, of course, *faith* . . .

The Faith Brothers are one formidable new group who won't be squashed or bought off so easily. One of their intentions is to erase The Myth and start anew, replacing the gorging lust for instant sensory gratification and ceaseless hedonistic excess with their own potent mix of honesty, morality, compassion and hard-edged politics.

But who are these Faith Brothers, where have they come from, and how have they created such an almighty commotion in the five months that they've been together as a band? Well, smug, smarmy bastards that we are here at Jamming!, it is my responsibility, nay duty, to remind you that you first read about The Faith Brothers within these very pages.

Billy Franks and Lee Hirons played together in numerous bands in and around the estate of Fulham Court in West London, before teaming up as a songwriting duo last summer. They recorded and released one of their collaborations, 'The Tradesmans' Entrance', in an extremely limited edition of five hundred copies. An enthusiastic review in Jamming! was followed up by a Faith Brothers feature in issue no. 21, and in the meantime, legions of record company A&R men had managed to extricate their heads out of their capacious arseholes long enough to offer the group a bewildering array of contracts. Franks and Hirons chose to go with Siren Records, an offshoot of Virgin, who acceded to their demands for TOTAL artistic control. Having acquired the necessary financial resources to recruit a band, the remaining four Faith Brothers were hand-picked from amongst a côterie of their closest friends within the community, the importance of which will become apparent later.

The dynamic duo of singer and guitarist Franks and bassist Hirons now became a six-piece group proper, the numbers swelled by Steve 'Gus' Howlett on drums, Henry Treise on piano, Mark Waterman on saxophone and 'Gripper' Will Tipper on trumpet.

Having assembled this redoubtable crew, The Faith Brothers recorded their debut single for Siren, 'The Country Of The Blind', by which time the up-to-the-minute and finger-on-the-pulse newshounds of the music press had emerged from

● **The first ever Faith Brothers photo, taken exclusively for Jamming! by Jason Pevovar**

their somnambulant midsummer sabbatical, and proceeded to greet the release with breathless praise and plaudits. A nationwide tour as support to The Boomtown Rats was hastily negotiated, and after its completion, with barely a pause for breath, The FBs were back on the road, this time supporting The Alarm.

The city of Bristol is as good a place as any to start a national tour and far from the whirring combine harvesters which clog up its main thoroughfares, I managed to pin down Billy Franks and Lee Hirons in a cluttered hotel room the morning after a highly successful opening night. Franks is clearly the lynchpin and keystone of the whole group, offstage his Faith Brethren cluster round him like protective grizzly bears.

Fundamental to the whole Faith Brothers ethos is the strength of their commitment to their own community of Fulham Court, a commitment which was galvanised when the council attempted to shunt out the residents and sell off the land to property developers. Despite fierce opposition, the land has now been sold, but the struggle continues, and the solidarity of the tenants' resistance is clearly a source of pride for Billy.

"It was far from successful but it drew up a sense of loyalty amongst the local people, which is something I really respected. And because I grew up with those people, that's where my loyalty stands, and I wanted to make that clear to people. And because we were writers and not a band from the off, it was important to make clear to people that we weren't just conjured up by the music industry, we actually did have roots, we wanted to make clear where we came from.

"If you're gonna have any kind of ideal society, then it will inevitably be based upon community life, people need an understanding of that. I have an understanding of that and the people around us have an understanding of that.

"Inextricably linked with the loyalty to the community is the solid, unifying spirit which anchors and binds the group. In the short time that I spent with them it became blindingly obvious that the bond of friendship within the group, and the empathy which exists between them is something that no earthly power could wrench apart. These are the ties that bind. Or, as Billy passionately puts it:

"It's everything, that is everything. As far as working, this aspect of it, coming out and playing, it's an intrinsic part of it. It would be difficult, if not impossible, without that."

The Faith Brothers have already been laboured and lumbered with a number of capricious comparisons which Billy regards as foolhardy and short-sighted.

"Most bands will say it, and it's invariably true, you don't invent your own labels. They're put upon you by people who are particularly narrow-minded and need that as a point of reference, to say 'this is a soul band' or 'this is a rock band'. We're not anything, there's no category that I'd go along with to describe The Faith Brothers.

"If people come and see The Faith Brothers I'd like them to leave having seen everything that they've ever loved about music, any music. And because we come from what is a multi-racial, multi-cultural community, the sort of music that we come into contact with reflects that, so it will obviously be apparent in what we do. And

Lee Hirons

Billy Franks

My association with *Jamming!* began in 1980. Tony, all of 16, was ten issues in with his fanzine already and caught a show in a London pub by The Shout, a three-piece band I'd formed with Tommy Mason and Steve Howlett that was stirring up interest with our fearless and dynamic performances. Tony's energy and drive matched ours, and we were delighted to find ourselves sharing the front cover of *Jamming!* 11 with some of our favourite bands.

Amusingly, some four years later, in the now glossy magazine, there is a fabulous interview with the Faith Brothers where Tony refers to Billy Franks and myself – aka the Brothers – as having previously played in various 'nowhere bands', even though Tony had briefly secured Tommy from The Shout as lead singer for his own (dare I say) nowhere band The Apocalypse.

By that point, though, Tony's glowing review of the self-pressed debut Faith Brothers single, 'The Tradesman's Entrance', in *Jamming!* in the spring of '84 had led to a series of thrilling events, culminating in the autumn with a major recording deal with Virgin off-shoot Siren Records.

It was about the only press we got, but it was all we needed. Interest grew from one record company (A&M) to just about every major at home and abroad. Publishers and producers soon followed and between them they funded the recording of another dozen songs, one of which, 'Newtown (The Promise Of Albion)', was issued by *Jamming!* on a flexi-disc.

After signing with Siren, we chose the producers, booked the studio and invited Tony to become our manager. It was the most exciting time of our lives. We gigged non-stop for our first year, including a memorable show at the Electric Cinema on Portobello Road for the re-launch of *Jamming!*, whose contributor Paul Davies came on the road with us a few months earlier for a cover story. We went on to release over twenty tracks in that first year – thanks, in no small part, to that one single review and the support from *Jamming!* that followed.

Billy Franks, my greatest friend, died suddenly in 2016. As the lyricist and frontman, he led the interviews, and his beautiful way with words inspired reporters and readers alike. I wish he could have been here to write these words, too. **Lee Hirons**

● **And at The Marquee**
Photo: Alan Reevell

I'd like people to appreciate that, we're only trying to put out everything we've ever loved about music, of all kinds.

"It's the performance that matters. We just go for 150% every night. We just give it as much as we can. For that one hour we're free to do or say what we want to, and you have access to people who are there to listen. So you're spurred by that, you're charged up . It's never a problem."

It certainly wasn't a problem at the Colston Hall, where The Faith Brothers played a set of bristling intensity and urgency. On stage, Billy Franks is the focal and pivotal point of the band. A manic bundle of energy, he leaps, spins, jerks and jumps as if his rocket-powered red patent leather shoes were wired up to the National Grid. the music draws on the disparate, multi-coloured threads of pop and soul's frayed and interlocking tapestry to create a dynamic, buoyant and thoroughly modern sound. In the live context, songs like 'Eventide', 'Whistling In The Dark', 'Newtown', 'Stranger On Home

Ground' (the next single) and 'Country Of The Blind' are performed with an abrasive vitality and reveal The Faith Brothers' ravishing and instinctive grasp of the importance and persuasive power of the rinky dink pop melody. The highlight for me, though, was the solo performance by Billy Franks of 'Easter Parade', a mournful ballad which fingers the rampant xenophobia, scabby jingoism and malevolent bloodlust of The Falklands War. They leave the stage to a fittingly rousing reaction.

Earlier on at the soundcheck I'd discovered a few Faith Brothers in what could only be described as close to a catatonic daze. On further investigation it transpired that this was due to the fact that they had just exchanged words with various members of The Alarm. According to the small print in The Myth, this is something that should definitely not go on — the distance between the two groups should be underlined and emphasised, support bands should remember their station as pieces of low life and tug forelocks and lick arse accordingly. It is one aspect of The Myth which The Boomtown Rats were quite content to surrender to, not one member of the band having uttered a single syllable to any of The Faith Brothers throughout the length of the entire tour! And that includes the venerable Saint Bob of Assissi, whose halo suddenly looks a trifle tarnished.

When Billy Franks speaks of The Myth he spits out the word with venomous contempt, as if he's just swallowed a mouthful of maggots. His thoughts on the record industry, from whence The Myth emerged, are equally bilious.

"I'd say it was generally overpopulated by hypocrites, morons, pimps and all kinds of disgusting people. But if you can come in and find some friends to work with, then you can go about communicating with people, amongst all that. I don't particularly enjoy it, but at the same time, we have met and we do work with some people that are, at least, encouraging. But they're very few and far between."

"I think it's very difficult for anybody in the music industry to understand what we're trying to do . . . but there's no reason why the music industry should shy away from putting their full weight behind bands that have an opposing view to a temporary government. There's no reason for that to be, it's never happened in the past. It just shows you the extent to which this Government has created a mood in which those sort of people are ridiculed and are kept down. But we can get through that.

"We live in a really critical age and if people have even an inkling as to what's really going on, then they should be saying something, and they should be saying so loud and clear. Because the young people are screaming for it, they need it badly. People with socialist convictions should never, never hold back, they should forever be talking and organising. They should do whatever they can, because it's all a contribution."

Billy Franks traces his socialism back to that fateful day in May 1979, when the British public, in all their infinite wisdom, chose to elect a mad, monetarist gorgon to the highest office in the land.

"I was never really politically aware, and like most people of my age, with the advent of Thatcher it became necessity to find out what the alternative was, because you were made aware of what capitalism really meant in its worst form. And that's when I started, and I read all the traditional socialists, your George Orwells, and then just started reading people I actually thought had a sense of vision, poets, writers and even playwrights. They were the sort of people that kept me going."

Despite the ongoing low-rent miserabilism of today's political climate, Billy feels that there is reason to be cautiously optimistic, confident that a radical type of socialism will win through in the end.

"It will take time for people to have a true understanding of what I consider to be the true socialist cause, and it will take a lot of people to make the effort, to just make it available. A lot of people are struggling and a lot of people are fighting, but there is still a lot of people that are unaware of what could be considered a *real* alternative, that's *REAL*, underlined with capital letters. It will take time for them to understand that. There are two philosophies: one that says that human beings are by nature capitalist, they are destructive, they will claw and tread over each other to get by; and then the real pure socialist belief says exactly the opposite, that you can care about people, you can work for common ends, you can contribute. 'From each according to his ability, to each according to his needs', that's a very fundamental statement, and people need to be made aware that this is possible, that there is that side of human nature as well. We've never really tried it before, and when change comes about, they're the things — to get people free from poverty, to get people free from drudgery, so that they can use their own potential and get their own rewards for it."

As far as The Faith Brothers are concerned, Billy is convinced that they can live up to their ideals and take up the massive challenge that they've given themselves, even if the outcome is uncertain.

"We know that as a band we're walking a tightrope from start to finish, and we're open to flak from both sides. But that's irrelevant. It's got nothing to do with what we're aiming at. We'll do it in our own time, by our own means, and regardless of what anybody inside the music industry thinks of it, and that is our objective. And you will find that in a few years time, we'll have stood by what we said more, and we'll have done more, than probably any other band in recent musical history. You'll find that. We'll have done more for change than any other band. It's because we want that so dearly that we will do it properly, and at our own pace, regardless of credibility . . . We'll just go until it doesn't seem worth going any more. You can't make any predictions about it, other than the fact that we will try like crazy.

"That's one of the exciting things about the whole affair, really, to set ourselves a big challenge and to see it through. And succeed or fail, it's the trying that matters, in anything, it's the trying."

Even at such an embryonic stage in the group's development, it is impossible not to take Billy Franks' bold assertions seriously. Because at this moment in time The Faith Brothers do have the potential, the inspiration and the motivation to go right ahead and pull off Franks' grand designs.

All they need to do is keep the hunger. And, of-course, the faith . . .

OTHER HEAVY CONCEPTS

Whatever happened to the Icicle Works . . .? Post-punk pop innovators turned retrogressive hippy has-beens? Tony Fletcher dons coloured beads and afghan coat for a 'whatever happened to . . .?' tip-toe trip through the tulips in search of Liverpool's forgotten sons

At the start of 1984, the future looked as bright for The Icicle Works as it did for virtually any* young group in the country. They had experienced a top 20 hit with only their second proper release, the classic 'Love Is A Wonderful Colour', and with an accomplished debut album just out and a healthy buzz in America beckoning them, they could afford to count their blessings.

A year and a bit later, and The Icicle Works admit that — in Britain at least — they're almost starting again, 1984 not quite going according to plan. When the re-issued debut '45 'Birds Fly' failed to make the grade, it caused the album to disappear unduly quickly; while the year ended miserably in the total failure of 'Hollow Horse', one of 1984s most obvious hits-that-weren't.

The reasons are all-too-clear and simple in hindsight, though a lesson for all bands who get success early on. Ian McNabb, the group's songwriter, vocalist and guitarist, explains. "We went to America at the start of the year, and while we were there 'Love Is A Wonderful Colour' started getting added to all the radio stations. We basically saw an American hit unfold before our eyes. We knew that if we didn't go home and push ourselves in England we'd let it slip away, but we didn't really think about it too much because we were so busy touring America. We just stayed there too long, and when we came back we'd been completely forgotten about."

Something that is hopefully going to change with the release of the new single "All The Daughters', a song recognisable instantly as The Icicle Works, but featuring brass for the first time and a more simplistic, though harder, approach. It is the start of a period of intense activity for the group who claim they won't be fooled again. "Last year we had a bit of a false start," admits Ian. The ideas and the intentions were there but suddenly we got a hit and we didn't really know what to do. Once we get another hit we won't let it slip away this time because we know what we're doing."

Certainly The Icicle Works have got an uphill struggle. If 'Love Is . . .' was recognised as a great, though slightly pretentious, pop single, the release of the album saw them roundly derided as closet hippies. With Ian's hair having developed from a closely cut mop to something resembling a jungle of spiders overhanging his face, these fears are hardly going to be allayed.

"I think Crass are hippies," he initially says in defence. "I think New Order are hippies, and I know the Bunnymen are definitely hippies. But I think hippy is an attitude, not the way you look. It's a state of mind — sitting down passing round the joints is to me, like a hippy attitude."

But is that something you're against?

"No, we're all for it!" he says as he bursts out into a fit of laughter. "People always call us hippies and it's very hard for me to deny it because we all have that attitude of having a good time and just lazing around getting wrecked. Nearly every band I know has that attitude, but they'd never admit to it."

Not that The Icicle Works are completely a band out of time. I can recall that at the period of their success with 'Love Is . . .' at the end of 1983, the group toured with only one tape blaring out of the van speakers — R.E.M.'s debut album 'Murmur'. As time has gone on, of course, R.E.M. have proved to be leaders of a new American invasion, but on their first visit over, Atlanta's finest were more than a little shocked to see The Icicle Works at The Venue play a steaming version of their anthem 'Radio Free Europe'.

But while The Icicle Works have been perfectly complementing the American bands who are causing such a fuss over here at the moment, they are more than a little miffed at being ignored and criticised in the midst of it all.

"We've always been a jangly-guitar Byrds-style band ever since we started. And all these American bands like R.E.M., The Long Ryders, Green On Red — who we all really like — we'd already seen them playing in America to twelve people or whatever. They're coming over here and suddenly everyone's saying "Isn't this fabulous?' The jangly guitar has come back, the Rickenbacker has come back . . . we've been using Rickenbackers since day one. So it heaves me a bit, yeah. But it's still healthy because these bands are about the best around."

> people always call us hippies and it's very hard for me to deny it because we all have that attitude of having a good time and just lazing around getting wrecked

Other criticisms levelled at The Icicle Works are unlikely to be conquered quite so easily. Tell us about the album, Ian (rock cliché no. 37) . . .

"We worked with a guy called Wally Brill who was very good but we didn't agree on anything. We argued all the way."

Does that bode well for the punters?

"Theoretically no, because if you've got a lot of people pulling in different directions, you're likely to get a piece of shit. But what actually happened is we went in with a very firm idea of what we wanted to sound like, and it went great for the first couple of tracks. But then the American record company knocked back the tracks and said they wouldn't get on American radio. so the producer then freaked out and said 'Well you'd better clean your sound up' and from then on we argued all the way. We got our way in the end though."

None of that's going to look good in print, Ian.

"Well, what do I say? I think lots of albums are done like that, with constant arguing. Think of The Byrds, think of The Who — always arguing and yet always making brilliant music. I don't believe that if you're arguing all the time it's necessarily going to be duff."

And the actual music?

"Well to me, side two of the album sounds like a compilation. There's one track that sounds like The Byrds — although a lot of ours do — there's one that sounds like The Eagles, there's one that's very like Neil Young, and there's one that's very Walkers Brothers-ish. It's very varied. It means that a lot of people like everything we've done, a lot like one thing, and a lot don't like anything."

I flinch at the comparisons Ian makes but there's worse to come.

"There's quite a few guitar solos on the new album, and one reason for that is that when Wah! played The Lyceum I got up, and was just mucking around. But everybody kept saying to me 'God, what a guitar player', and I just thought I should use it to my advantage rather than hiding it away.

"We are all really accomplished musicians, we're real musos — ha! — and it means we can play anybody else's material. Recently we've been doing 'You Ain't See Nothing Yet' by Bachman Turner Overdrive, purely because it's a great song."

By now, I feel it's a pretty safe comment to make that, instead of fighting off all the criticisms made of themselves, The Icicle Works are living up to those critics' worst fears.

"Well we've never specifically said 'We've been criticised for this so we'll go out and do it', we've made this kind of record simply because we wanted to make this kind of record."

But it sounds like it's going to be harder and harder for you to get real success.

"No, because I think we shit all over everybody in terms of songwriting, and if you've got a good tune, and a beat that people want to hear, you're going to get on the radio and have hits."

The album itself — titled 'The Small Price Of A Bicycle' — won't be out for a while for us to see whether it's really as, um, old-fashioned as it sounds. The group are going to make sure they get some hits first.

"We're not going to let this LP slip away like we did the last one. We're going to flog it to death. We're going to be on the road for a year, playing everywhere."

The title, intriguing to say the least, is in fact culled from the current single's line 'The small price of a bicycle isn't mine', a line furnanced by, as Ian subtly puts it, 'that cunt Tebbit who said get out on your bike and look for jobs'. And at least lyrically, there has now been some move away from the early, somewhat elaborate words.

"I was sick of fannying around with not being specific, beating about the bush instead of making my point. There's a line on a new song that goes *'I sing the song with my tongue in my cheek, but the jilted, the jaundiced, the angry young men, somehow believe that the status quo changes, with juvenile slogans and downmarket rags.'* Twelve months ago I would have found a much more poetic way of saying that."

Quite whether The Icicle Works manage to regain entry into the closed ranks of the Top 20 — and stay there — remains to be seen. Certainly, they've experienced a fair share of bad luck and operated with an equal portion of naivety, but their songs have been continually good and their aggression and optimism admirable. When Ian starts talking about hippies, Eagles comparisons, guitar solos and Bachman Turner Overdrive cover versions, however, I'm the first to admit I feel something rising in my throat. Maybe I should remember that it's only six months since I saw them in Switzerland end a gig with rabid cover versions of 'Substitute', 'Wild Thing' and 'Pretty Vacant'. At the heart of it all, The Icicle Works are essentially a rock'n'roll band with the same hopes and aspirations as the rest of us, but with an unwitting eagerness to display their weaknesses. Ian admits as much explaining why the album — which will be of course, the answer to any fears — has such a ridiculous title.

"It was just such a wacky line that we decided to use it. Flaunt The Imperfection . . . Who's got an album out called 'Flaunt the Imperfection'? China Crisis? We should have had that one, it's perfect."

LONG RYDERS ON THE STORM

• MARTIN WROE hails another band riding on the crest of the new American wave. But THE LONG RYDERS aren't just another band knee-deep in love with the American myth... Read on...

"If they call us a psychedelic band they're partially right; if they call us a country band they're partially right ... it just depends on the night that they've seen us."

Tom Stevens, bassist with Los Angeles' Long Ryders isn't overly bothered about the ways and words of journalists trying desperately to build some great tidal barrier of categorisation to explain the flow and capture the power of the huge wave of American traditional music currently roaring eastwards across the Atlantic. Not only roaring across the Atlantic but coarsing up the beaches of the British music scene and smashing destructively into its banks of synthesised, image-obsessed, techno-pap. Hopefully.

Surfing magnificently on the crest of this tidal wave are the Long Ryders themselves, just like drummer Greg Sowders used to do when he came home from his school in L.A. teens for a 'beach and beer Beach Boys style evening.' The Long Ryders on the Storm? At this particular second however, Sowders is sitting on his bedside in their London hotel having just crawled from his nocturnal pit, dressed only in shirt and Y-fronts, carefully considering the 'lesser-synthesized Americana phenomenon'.

"We like to think about it as a resurgence in original American rock bands playing with some passion and some feeling.

"It's like in the mid-seventies U.K. scene when all the punks got started — it was like a reaction because nothing interesting was going on.

"All these bands you talk about in the States and especially California — it's just a coincidence that we all formed bands round about the same time and all had such a friendship. Most of the time in the early days we'd do shows and the audience would be made up of the guys in the other bands!"

Without being in the least pretentious or arrogant about it Sowders sees the American contribution to the British music scene in 1985 (Green On Red; Los Lobos; The Bangles; The Blasters; Jason and The Scorchers; R.E.M.; Violent Femmes; The Rain Parade; Rank and File; and True West to name but ten) as a 'modern day' version and repayment-in-kind of the contribution of British punk rock to the mega-bore American music scene of the mid-seventies. He doesn't have too high an opinion of the state of the art of rock 'n roll in England in 1985. He's probably just realistic.

> **It's now like the pendulum has swung the other way and there's loads of bands in the States that are really hot. It would be really satisfying if we could have an influence on bands over here**

"I hope that all the American bands come over here and kick them in the arse and make them get back to basics the same as when The Clash and all those bands came to the States, kicked *us* in the arse and said, 'Let's get out of this seventies slump and start making music again!'

"It's now like the pendulum has swung the other away and there's loads of bands in the States that are really hot. It would be really satisfying if we could have an influence on bands over here."

The Long Ryders are fronted by Sid Griffin, most famous thus far for his lauded biography of Gram Parsons and for founding The Unclaimed, joined by Stephen McCarthy on guitar, Sowders on drums and Stevens on bass. Their live performance is an explosive blend of contagious melodies and searing guitar lines, a journey into the thus-far rarely charted realms of country-rock but injected and souped-up with the turbo-charged excitement of a Sex Pistols gig in '76. Described variously (those journalists again) as 'country-punk', 'acid-folk' and 'phoney-revivalism' Sowders says that for the Long Ryders "nothing is off limit".

"All we've done is said we don't have and don't want to have a set style of music, we don't want to follow trends, we just wanna be the Long Ryders, so whatever works out is cool."

Sowders doesn't even blink, let alone blush, on uttering those last six words — The Long Ryders are living B.C. — Before Cliché! They are also living before the pre-packaged, cellophane wrapped emptiness that T.O.T.P. describes weekly as 'The Charts'.

"It's real nice for an audience to hear real drums, real vocals, and real instruments rather than the plastic, pre-fab stuff making the rounds today," says Sowders.

But Greg, surely you can't be saying that if you didn't have a record deal (admittedly a minor one), that if the reverse-turning clock of music-fashion wasn't presently on "'sixties', that if the Long Ryders hadn't made it to the cover of N.M.E. — that the four of you would be locked in some L.A. garage covering 'Eight Miles High' and 'Masters of War' to your hearts content? Surely no. And those haircuts, those sideburns, Sid's confederate-flag stage jacket, the guitars — wouldn't you have swopped the mop-tops for a spike and dye, shaved off the burns, got some red and white stripey trousers and took out a mortgage from the Bank of Synths?

"No, we'd still be playing in that garage and for a whole lot longer than anybody else expected us to.

"If you decide you're going to 'go for it' with a special haircuit, special outfit, state of the art instruments and write very popular songs for the benefit of your 'big' manager ... then when you flop all you are is embarrassed.

"This way, doing what we wanna do in our own fashion, if we don't make it, it doesn't matter 'cus we can just go back home to our families and friends and say 'We did our best'. We got nothing to be embarrassed about."

The Long Ryders as individuals are far from naive politically, but as a band have wisely decided to avoid becoming a vehicle for party political sloganeering. Their sadness at what is happening to America under Reagan is apparent in their lyrics but, like Springsteen, through images, pictures and stories. Tom wrote 'Wreck Of The 809' about "a kids dad who dies in a train after working so hard for his family" as a reflection on life in his hometown of Allicott, Indiana where "buys on the factory line actually spend their life screwing in doors onto trailers..."

Tom: "We're just sharing our experiences."

Greg: "We don't really sing about if America is good or bad, we just sing about how it is."

Well, even is you don't write a song about it, perhaps you could explain to an ignorant young journalist why so many millions of young Americans voted in Ronald Reagan?

"It doesn't seem real to us" replies Greg, "Because it's so far removed from the way we feel. I can't make that equation and it's not like I haven't tried!"

Do you love America?

"Yeah, I couldn't live anywhere else. I love the country and I love what it stands for — but we just need to sort it out right now, sort out what we've done to our country — we're all guilty — like your government needs some sorting out too.

"America is about freedom and right now we need to get back to basics because certain people have more freedom than others."

JULY 1985 · 70P · US $1.75 · EIRE £1.13 · NO.30

Jamming!

FREE FLEXI DISC
PRECIOUS PROTÉGES
WET WET WET
THE FLOOR

WATERBOYS
HOOKED
ON THE BIG MUSIC

10,000 MANIACS · PREFAB SPROUT · LOOSE ENDS · TIM ROTH

WATERBOY
MIKE SCOTT
RE-EMERGES AT
LAST. CAN HE
EXPLAIN HOW
DEVOTION
STOPS HIM
TURNING INTO
TOM BAILEY?

• INTERVIEW ... CHRIS HEATH

• PHOTOGRAPHS ... CONEYL

On the Waterfront

Mike Scott returned to *Jamming!*, and this time as cover star, albeit in one of those typically oblique images we somehow thought was a good idea at the time. (There were much better photos by Coneyl Jay in the centre page spread.) Scott's band The Waterboys were joined by 10,000 Maniacs, as profiled (again) by Jonh Wilde and beautifully photographed (again) by Russell Young; The Fall's Brix Smith spin-off The Adult Net; the Kitchenware label's Prefab Sprout (Chris Heath); a profile of Glasgow's The Precious Organisation (appended by a flexi-disc featuring the label's flagship acts Wet Wet Wet and The Floor); a purposefully political profile of Midnight Oil's Peter Garrett; UK reggae star Maxi Priest; UK funk stars Loose Ends (apparently, Britain's biggest

selling black act at the time); actor Tim Roth; and a feature on 'How To Make Your Own Record' that made it sound none so much fun as when the subject had been explored back in *Jamming!*'s fanzine days. On the subject of the magazine's scrappy past, Tiny Fennimore profiled Robin Richards, without whom *Jamming!* might never have made its cultural leap in the first place. Robin could produce unreadable layouts alongside the most frustrating of designers, but as the contemporary *Jamming!* experimented with awkward typefaces and spacing, and dark and depressing covers despite the luxury of personal photo sessions, his visual energy and colourful vitality were sorely missed. Robin passed away too early in the 21st Century.

ISSUE #30
6/85

TREASURE
ON YOUR CHEST

● TINY GETS TO GRIPS WITH THE ROOTS AND RISKS OF T-SHIRT CULTURE IN INTERVIEW WITH DESIGNER, ROBIN RICHARDS.

Robin Richards is a T-shirt designer and it is a safe bet that even if you don't actually possess one of his 'objects d'art' yourself, you will have seen one adorning someone else's chest at some stage since 1977.

But for Robin, the path to success and recognition as a designer has not been an easy one. His career in design has been a constant battle against business sharks who, on the one hand, have inadvertently tried to squash his creative flair in the name of 'cost effectiveness' and on the other hand, have attempted to rip him off. Robin, characteristically, has vehemently resisted both endeavours.

But where does *he* come into the story?

The early seventies were not a particularly exciting era for the T-shirt or for T-shirt design. During the sixties, it has been a popular way of making a statement about who you were, and what you stood for without ever having to actually open your mouth. This was the time when the 'Che Guevera' and 'Legalise Marijuana' T-shirts were born and popularised. But effectively, the T-shirt as an art form died with the hippy and it was not until 1976 that it again emerged as a cheap and effective method of making a silent assertion.

At this time in the T-shirt's history, you could say that Robin and his mate Sodge played an important part in revitalising it as an element of style. The two were already working as sweat-shop boys in a printing factory which produced merchandise for big record labels. But at night, they would go to gigs in London and if they saw a band they particularly liked, Robin would design a T-shirt for them:

"We'd be working all day for this bloke but when he left to go home, we'd stay on with a bottle of Tequila and some orange juice and design our own T-shirts for people like X Ray Spex, Generation X and The Jam. Then, when we went to a gig, we'd meet them and get talking about maybe doing some more for them. In those days, T-shirts weren't a big money-spinning thing — now, when you go to design a T-shirt for a band, you have to talk to lawyers and distributors who use words like 'product' and 'percentages'. Sometimes you feel like the T-shirt's become more important than the bloody record."

● Many of Robin's T-shirt designs are silk screen printed — that is, printed by hand. This is the only form of printing which allowed you to cover the entire T-shirt as most machinery which is currently used for T-shirt printing cannot print over a larger area than 16 inches by 16. Without doubt, silk-screen printing produces the best results and the fact that the printing is all done by hand means that each one can be customised so that no two shirts are ever exactly the same. But it is not — to use the jargon — cost effective. This was to prove a serious problem for Robin and his mates when they eventually set up their own company under the name of 'Fifth Column'.

"We set up in a derelict storeroom above a motorbike shop in Kilburn. You could literally put your hand through the outside wall of this place and there was no water and no mains electricity. My dark-room was basically a converted toilet. And from this place — at one stage — we were hand printing as many as sixty shirts a day. It just got silly. The basic problem was that the process we were using was totally illogical in terms of production. The more T-shirts you printed, the more hours you worked or the more people you had to pay. Fortunately though, at the beginning, we'd get help from people who used to hang around the factory — truants mostly. Someone would be standing around watching you and you'd say 'don't just stand around doing nothing, hold this'. It'd end up that they'd be working a whole week for us and then we'd a phone call from the local Truant Officer saying did we know a certain Anthony Moriarty or whoever — It was crazy!"

Robin's style is unique (though it has been copied by many an aspiring designer or printer) and he gained much of his inspiration for his work from the great pop artists of the sixties who used comic type explosions to illustrate their work. Leichtenstein, for example, is a great personal favourite and some of his T-shirts produced for The Jam were based on this sort of illustrations.

Given the importance that Robin places on design and imagery in his work, I asked him for his opinion on the Katherine Hamnett and Frankie T-shirts which adorned most people's chests last summer: "Those T-shirts were the kiss of death for T-shirt design. Most people, who would ordinarily have looked at image, pattern or colour, looked at nothing but lettering. The actual political content of what was being said on those shirts was good but because of the mass consumerisation of the design, the message that was being put across became irrelevant. What was important was not the message but the fact that there was large lettering on the shirts."

▶

Nevertheless as Robin has become more successful, he too has had to compromise his ideals to a certain extent. It has become a physical impossibility to customise each T-shirt for example, as he used to in the early days.

"People often ask me how I can justify being a mass producer now when this is against all the ideals we originally held. The point is, you can't justify it. We reached a certain point when we thought 'Well we either give up now for our ideals or otherwise we go on and at least try and offer the market something that's better than what everybody else is producing.' But the T-shirt world has changed. It used to be that bands were happy to have T-shirts made for them regardless of whether they were 'official' or not. Now though, huge merchandising companies pay vast amounts of money to bands for exclusive rights on their 'merchandising' and then they sue all the little people who are designing their own stuff and put them out of business. It's a totally different world. It's big business and most big merchandising companies don't give a shit about whether the kids actually like the design of a shirt. The fact that a band is in the Top Ten is the only justification they need for turning out a 'Product'."

But whilst Robin's talent for design has developed considerably over the years, his business acumen has not; and this has led him onto dangerously thin ice on occasions. After Fifth Column, Robin left to set up a new company with an 'entrepreneur' who, intentionally or unintentionally, managed to fleece him of his money and exploit his art. This, coupled with other short sighted business dealings, has meant that whilst he may have designed a considerable numnber of T-shirts that have sold in their tens of thousands, he has received little in the way of remuneration. Designing the merchandise for the English or American tours of such big boys as Shalamar or Culture Club could have set him up for a good few years — but as things turned out, he has been left with scarcely enough money to keep himself, and his family, going. But his determination and his faith in his abilities are still as strong despite a heartfelt wish that he could be 'just a designer' and not 'a business man, accountant and manager as well'.

The trials and tribulations of trying not to compromise your art in the face of the demands of big business is something Robin knows all about. In many ways, his story is the story of punk — a story where the business sharks saw the chance of making a fast buck and, in the process, inadvertently trod on all those with any originality or creative flair. Despite the setbacks he has encountered with the business world, Robin is still designing T-shirts for bands and is also still producing them himself. Nowadays, however, he helps out in a factory which is in fact his family home, their front room having been partially converted into a printing plant for the purpose.

Old punks never die?

As a special offer to our readers, Robin Richards has designed a JAMMING! T-shirt which will be available from next month. Details in JAMMING! 31.

ADVERTISEMENT

54 Jamming!

WHAT

400 BLOWS

● photo, Coneyl Jay

I first became aware of 400 Blows in the summer of '84 with the release of their intriguingly, is a little misogynistic titled debut album, 'If I Kissed Her I'd Have To Kill Her First . . .' This disc seemed to be the closest anyone had come to a rapprochement between the experimental and the hardest of hard dance rhythms. The grail of Industrial Funk appeared in sight at last, Charles Manson's macabre ramblings could rest snugly beside the heaviest sounds this side of Maze, and, pardon my patriotism, 400 Blows were British. But could this kind of synthesis ever be commercially successful?

Now, twelve months later, the top spot has recently been occupied for the fourth week in succession by a London lad's combination of an obsessive D Train beat and the sombre tones of a Viet-vet talking about the horrors of daily exposure to death. These are strange days for 400 Blows, who have a new single out themselves this month, 'Moving', which takes the almost sacrosanct Brass Construction dance anthem and reassembles it for the eighties. Stranger still, there is a distinct similarity between '19' and 'Groove Jumping' from their album. Anthony Thorpe, bass player and general studio twiddler takes up the point. . . .

"Well, Paul Hardcastle has obviously heard our album, 'Groove Jumping' was the only other English record reviewed with his in Blues And Soul when it came out. It is quite flattering, but it would be nice if he gave us some credit for working out the groove!"

Like Mr Hardcastle, 400 Blows, essentially Anthony and Edward Beer, were content to work their material through in the studio, often utilising cut ups of old tapes, Nixon, Manson, etc., rather than featuring a real live flesh 'n' blood vocalist. Recently, however, they have been joined by elfin songstress, Lea, formerly with Island signings, Tomboy. As Edward modestly describes his partnership with Anthony, "We aren't really songwriters, we just come up with a groove and work out wacky ideas for it. Lea doesn't just sing, she can also write intelligent lyrics."

Some might say this expansion to a more conventional unit (racial/sexual similarities to the Thompson Twins are purely coincidental I'm sure) suggests a movement away from the more esoteric areas which gained the group its first notoriety, but Edward is quick to put me straight.

"There's no central dogma to the band, we just do what we like when we like. But since we are not a rock band, the only commercially viable music we can do is dance music, and this enables us to subsidise our more unusual projects I've just done a piece for the latest Abstract Magazine record where I crawled 200ft down a tunnel to record. Lea may not want to do that, but she can do something different herself. Critics always seem to wonder how we can be so different, but we listen to anything from Sheila E. to Buddhist Temple bells so our music will always go off in different directions."

Their own 'Ancestral Communications' acts as a form of information service on 400 Blows projects — contactable at PO Box 798, London W14 9NT.

It's a funny old world though, where chart success seems to go hand in hand with castration, each hit taking Wham! further from their dole boy origins, and as Morley himself pointed out, "Two Tribes was number one for nine weeks, but then George Michael was back". Pop changes nothing. But, maybe there is still hope, as a shiver of pleasure runs up my spine at the thought of 50,000 soul girls rushing out to buy '. . . If I Kissed Her . . .' when 'Moving' is a hit, only to hear the voice of Charles Manson coming from the speakers. Sorry girls, you can't do aerobics to this band all the time. . . .

Bruce Dessau

6 Jamming!

label: S. Rae, 45 Del... Kilbarchan, Renfrewshire PA10 2AT.

for sale, includes bargains, deletions, hits

Jamming!

AUGUST 1985 • 70p • US $1.75 • EIRE £1.13   No. 31

TALKING HEADS
STILL INVENTING THEMSELVES
PIRATE RADIO
WEATHERING THE STORM
WORKING WEEK · WOMACKS
GIL SCOTT HERON · BARRY NORMAN

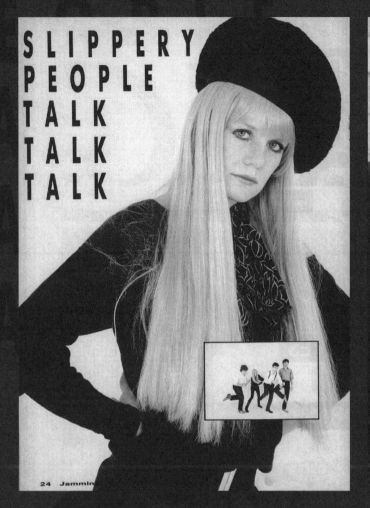

SLIPPERY
PEOPLE
TALK
TALK
TALK

24 Jammin

WORKING WEEK
and all that jazz!

LARRY STABBINS (top): Jazz veteran and silent partner, John McVicar impersonator.

SIMON BOOTH (left): "Morrissey's brilliant, what he stands for. But the music is shit. I don't think what they do is very skilful and I don't think it is going to last."

JULIE ROBERTS: (right): "I don't care. I got a big mouth. What I say goes."

Jamming! 17

ISSUE
#31
7/85

I recall a debate about Issue 31's Talking Heads cover. But what? Was it the momentous occasion of putting an American band on the front for the first time? Or that the photos were already familiar (if only to a handful of people) from their use in our American counterpart of sorts, *Spin*? Or was it in fact the cost of using those images? Regardless, the brightness of the group shot with its stark yellow background offered a welcome respite from the dark and gloomy recent designs, Chris Heath's feature on the group was a typically informative and comfortably breezy read and there was scant competition among the issue's other supposed prime draws: Working Week, the Womacks and Gil Scott-Heron. This increased focus on black music of all stripes was exemplified by Hugh Morley's excellent article on 'The Rise of the British M.C.'

There's an argument to be made that, had *Jamming!* been weekly, it could have taken more risks with its front cover allocations, but as things went, there was a firm need to play reasonably safe. Our sales had solidified in the mid-20,000s, which was not enough to make money, and as a result we remained far too dependent on ads from the likes of Wrangler jeans and Duracell batteries, along with typically crass governmental PSAs warning of the horrors of heroin.

THE RISE OF THE BRITISH M.C.

. . . so for all music-lyric lovers listen closely — these are the ten commandments of an . . .

WORDS AND PHOTOS: **HUGH MORLEY**

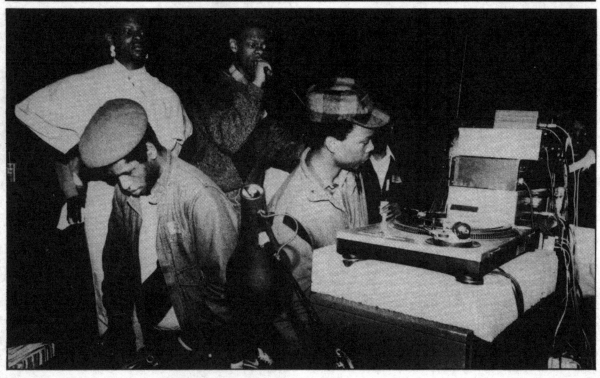

■ **"Shaka . . . he went through years ago what we're going through now" comments Trevor Ranking setting up the sound system.** The occasion is a benefit for Ethiopia, promoted under the auspices of Jah Shaka — veteran operator, one man army, and purveyor of 'roots' and 'warrior' style sounds — and Saxon Studio International; the hip young gunslingers.

Champion of the indigenous crop of rhythm and rhyme merchants currently in vogue, Saxon has furnished the world at one time or another with most of the names on the British MC map; from Smiley Culture, Asher Senator and Peter King (and singer Maxi Priest) to the current posse which includes the likes of Tippa Irie and Philip 'Papa' Levi. The 'sound' itself however, to their evident chagrin, is only now beginning to get recognition.

"If you go into competition with Shaka you have to come down to his level or you've got no say in the dance — Shaka's style is spiritual" explains Dennis Rowe, co-owner of Saxon, on the distinction between old and new. "I wouldn't say we were different but we're based in different forms. Shaka's sound is a one man operation whereas Saxon is a seven or ten man army.

"And the business has changed. Before when you went out you would just dance to the records you liked. Now people come along to get involved. They bring along whistles, foghorns, and beat anything they can to make a noise."

After nine years, first as a 'lovers rock sound' and then leading the transformation to MC style, Saxon's perseverance is beginning to pay off. With the reggae chart success of the 'Coughing Up Fire' live album at the turn of the year they are fresh back from New York and in demand; finally pulling away from their peers and attracting the kind of attention that those who passed through have received.

"The thing with Saxon" explains Dennis Rowe, "is that the sound has been pulled apart and built up, pulled apart and built up around the DJs rather than the DJs around the sound."

"I would have to say we're the top sound system in London" he continues immodestly. "Before Saxon came round people weren't getting treated properly and only pop tunes were getting played. Now reggae is getting more popular, with more play on the radio and the pirate stations . . . and I think Saxon has a lot to do with it."

Lloyd 'Musclehead' Francis, the second co-owner of Saxon, fingers a set of exclusive pre-dub 45s and eyes up the competition. The promoters are worried that the power won't hold up. Tippa Irie's worried that he won't get the tube back in time. Jah Shaka appears none too worried at all! . . . . *one, thou shalt not take licks off a MC/by that I mean is whip his style or his mel-o-deeee . . . .*

■ The roots of the DJ or MC style date back to Jamaica of the late fifties and early sixties when the likes of Count Machuki and King Stitt

▶

used to rap and scat spontaneously over R&B records. The words were meaningless, or unimportant, but were a means to whip up the dance hall.

The genre took a more recognisable form in the late sixties with the emergence of U Roy. Probably the most influential DJ to this day he brought forward a more ordered lyrical style, toasting over other people's records and eventually cutting his own versions.

Over the next decade names like Big Youth, Lone Star, Dillinger and General Echo took his lead, most of whose lyrics concerned the life of the poor urban black, with the exception of I Roy in the early seventies who for the first time displayed a wider, more political vision in his words.

But despite the popularity of the DJ, with few exceptions — Roy Ranking and Raymond Naptally, General Saint and Clint Eastwood, Ranking Dread; the last two of which were of Jamaican origin anyway — there were few notable British MCs. Those that were around at best imitated their Jamaican peers, unable to transcend the limitations of a snobbery that decreed 'if it was reggae it had to be Jamaican'.

. . . . five, thou shalt not chat without receiving money/because that's just another form of sla-v-ereeee . . . .

Sometime in the early part of the decade things started moving. Old sound systems swopped styles and new ones sprang up to accommodate the new MC style. Chris Lane co-founded Fashion Records with the idea of nurturing British reggae talent and found himself ideally placed to tap into the new contenders. Producing the records himself with the aid of the omnipotent 'Fairlight' he drew on a pool of musicians which included Tony Gad and Clifton Morrison of Aswad, Reg Graham and 'Spy' of The Investigators and Annie Whitehead.

"We started off with Papa Face's 'DJ Jamboree' which was about the fourth or fifth record we put out in '82 or '83, because Papa Face was the first MC from years ago. Then we got involved with Laurel and Hardy who in a way pre-dated the current style in that their lyrics had stories and they had catchy chorus. This was a very different style to Papa Face who was mostly drawing from the Jamaican style; they were very British in character."

Laurel & Hardy's first record, 'You're Nicked', caught the attention of CBS who signed them in a brief burst of enthusiasm. The relationship was shortlived however. Having signed, the duo recorded an album with Chris Lane producing and gave it to the record company who were either unsure, or uninterested, in what they should be doing. The two parted company leaving the album to emerge on Upright.

At the same time Saxon were gaining attention with a posse of MCs, homegrown and culled from the sound systems around the capital, and a play list of mainly Studio One sounds. Among them were Smiley Culture, Asher Senator, and Peter King who originated the 'fast-style' delivery. The style was seen as a 'crazy invention' at the time, recalls Dennis Rowe, but was quickly copied and became widespread.

"Peter King's style as performed on the sound system was the one that changed not so much the lyrical ideas but the phrasing that was used by the best MC's" explained Chris Lane. "He just happened to have this style on 'Me Neat Me Sweet' and went into fast style with it; but the record wasn't made until he'd been doing it for about two years."

Under the subsequent deluge of plagiarists Peter King dropped from the 'sound' circuit and returned only on the convictions of Smiley Culture and Asher Senator as to his importance as an originator. A return that has seen his latest record 'Step On The Gas' hit the top three in the reggae chart.

■ In 1983 'Mi God Mi King' by Philip Levi — a veteran of Saxon since 1976 — was released and became the proverbial 'massive' hit; sealing the reputation of the British MC both at home and in Jamaica where it hit the top of the charts, the first British reggae record to do so, and became the biggest selling single of 1984. Produced by Paul Robinson with Maxi Priest's 'Caution' band laying down the rhythm you can almost feel the changing of the genre when, in the middle of the song, the lyric shifts gear from a medium paced 'cultural' style Jamaican lyric to a double speed fast-style mash-up.

"After 'Mi God Mi King' came out it gave every English youth the chance to go into the studio" comments Dennis Rowe on the record. With its overwhelming success doors were opening fast and the records were coming out faster. Smiley Culture just missed the national chart with 'Cockney Translation' but scored with the follow up 'Police Officer', while Asher Senator snatched recognition with 'Abbreviation Qualification'.

From the Midlands came Pato Panton, who had earlier worked with Ranking Roger of the Beat, and Macka B. While Papa Face re-

● Dennis Rowe — owner of Saxon Studio International

● Asher Senator

● Tippa Irie

● Lorna Gee and
Ranking Anne

emerged with Bionic Rhona, one of the leading female MCs from
South London.

At the other end of town Greensleeves, led by Chris Cracknell and
fuelled by the Reggae Regulars, launched their UK Bubblers label by
signing the Saxon posse wholesale; pitching into the fray with twelve
inchers from Daddy Colonel, Sandy, Daddy Rusty and the hilarious
tale of 'Blind Date' by Leslie Lyrics from the Diamonds posse.

Most successful by far was the near hit of 'Good To Have The
Feeling You're the Best' from Tippa Irie; Greensleeves having
whipped him from under the nose of Chris Lane. Hailing from
Streatham in South London he recalls how he began MC-ing.

"I first started when I was fifteen. My father had a shop with a
basement where they used to hold dances and I'd listen to things like
U Roy and Prince Jazzbo, and then later General Echo and Ringo."

Chatting originally with King Tubby's sound in Brixton like a
number of MCs he gained attention on a series of three LPs — 'Live at
the Dick Shepherd Youth Centre' — put together by Sir Lloyd's sound
system, featuring among others Lorna Gee, Sister Candy, Leslie Lyrics
and members of the Saxon posse, who snapped him up for the Saxon
'sound'.

Similar to his contemporaries Tippa Irie found it incongruous to be
merely imitating Jamaican styles.

■"Since we're in England we talk about what's going on in England.
Like a 'yard' MC will talk about what's going on in Jamaica and he
has a natural 'yard' tone of voice. But since our parents are from
Jamaica and were born over here we try and relate the two."

With the shift in emphasis of subject matter came a more structured
song-like approach combined with the essential qualities of an MC,
defined by Chris Lane as "timing, a sense of wit and some sense of
what's going on — what people are interested in.

"I think the main difference is that British MCs now aren't afraid to
talk about their experience of being British. Obviously reggae is
drawn from Jamaican experiences but you used to go to a sound
system and listen to a DJ talking about Jamaica and you'd know the
bloke hadn't been there for five or six years."

"A lot of dancehall MCs realise there is an art to it now" explains
Ranking Anne, "Because they sit down and pen their lyrics — which
I've always done — whereas before it used to be very much 'off the
cuff' and you were laughed at if you did that."

As the first women's MC, pre-dating even Jamaica's now more
famous Sister Nancy, Ranking Anne came to the fore last year after
two albums, with the GLC sponsored 'Kill The Police Bill' and more
recently on Scritti Politti's 'The Word Girl'.

With on-one to look to, she evolved her own style around the
sounds of Brixton and Peckham and approached it from a different
direction to the likes of Saxon, seeing the dancehall trend as part of
the general drift of the early eighties away from more serious
subjects. A trend exemplified by the disinterest among MCs and the
MC audience in Rastafarianism.

"The difference between Saxon and me is that they've come up on
the dancehall scene where the main thing is to make people feel good
and dance around, and not to think too deeply about what's going
on. But I come from a long time before that when music used to be
about telling people what's going on; social and political things."
. . . . eight, nobody use long words without a dictionary/to fool the
people that you have to intell-igen-ceeee . . . .

■Undoubtedly the rise in 'MC-fever' has pushed reggae into a higher
profile than for a while (though it's tempting to believe that 'Police
Officer' was this years 'token reggae hit'). Inevitably perhaps,
though the records continue to flood forth — a new Tippa Irie single
on the way, a new Asher Senator single 'Match of the Day' out to
coincide with the football season, Pato's 'The Boss' not to mention the
current fave 'Horse Move' by Horseman — the phase is seen to have
peaked in terms of mass acceptance. Lorna Gee, one of the foremost
women's DJs whose first single 'Three Weeks Gone Mi Giro' was
released in January, could see no future in the dancehall scene: "I
don't know what they all want but I know what I want. It's all DJ this,
DJ that-dancehall style, dancehall style. But I don't know how it's
going to last."

"For the first time in Jamaican music, as a result of this fast style —
they call it 'speedrapping' — Jamaicans have actually imitated and
copied UK MCs "explained Capital Radio's reggae disc jockey
David Rodigan. "And Jamaican DJs that come to this country openly
admit that. I think that it's peaked but it will return. DJs come in waves
and this is just another wave. There was always a DJ and a dance
saying something and it may drop down soon but it will rise again
because it's a tradition in Jamaican music."
. . . .ten, thou shalt not chat slackness, cos chat slack is nasty/these
are the ten commandments of an MC ■

WAR GAMES

A PROPER GANDER AT NUCLEAR PROPAGANDA

In the wake of the fortieth anniversary of the first Atom Bombs being dropped on Hiroshima *and* Nagasaki, *a series of powerful TV programmes such as The War Game, Threads and Atomic Cafe have gone some way to reinforce a natural fear of and desire to avoid an horrific nuclear war. But how much nearer is that possibility becoming? And to what extent is Britain's economy being damaged in a mad race for all things nuclear?*

In this special five-page report, we look at the balance between nuclear weapons and nuclear power in this country, the costly burden of Trident, the facts behind the Molesworth Cruise Missile Air Base, and the Foreign Office-funded anti-CND pressure group Youth For Peace Through Nato.

Montage: Coneyl Jay

THE NUCLEAR STATE

Is nuclear power really a cheap, safe, viable means of fuel? And can it genuinely claim with a straight face that it does not work hand-in-hand with nuclear arms production? Tiny investigates further.

The question of nuclear power opens up a whole new horizon in understanding both the nuclear arms race itself and the society in which we live. Both nuclear power and nuclear arms are playing an increasingly important part in shaping our everyday lives and they are also helping to remove from our hands the power to control our environment at a national level.

The problem with the nuclear issue is that once you get past the general pro/anti arguments, the whole nuclear subject becomes prohibitively complex and very difficult for anyone without a degree in science to understand. As a result, we can only believe what we are told about safe and unsafe levels of radiation, about risky and risk free nuclear installations and about expensive and cheap sources of energy. This problem is made worse by a general reticence on the part of all those involved to reveal any real information about the work they are involved in. The need to protect 'national security' may be important but excessive resorts to silence about nuclear issues means that the public is unaware and therefore unable to make up its own mind about the subject. This has obvious implications in a democratic society. The 1976 report of the Royal Commission On Environmental Pollution alluded to this and other worrying developments: "What is most to be feared is an insiduous growth in surveillance in response to a growing threat as the amount of plutonium increases . . . the future might bring an increase in security measures and surveillance to a degree that would be regarded as wholly unacceptable."

Over the last 30 years the general public has been led to believe that the issue of nuclear power and the issue of nuclear weapons are entirely separate. Nuclear power has even been portrayed as a positive and peaceful alternative to the destructive and aggressive use of it in nuclear arms. In fact nothing could be further from the truth. Nuclear power stations and nuclear weapons are inextricably linked — and neither is able to survive without the other. Nuclear power plants produce as a bi-product the precise material needed for creating nuclear warheads, and though they are not a pre-requisite for nuclear arms — you can always import — it is much handier if you have your own supplies of technology and resources than if you have to rely on the goodwill of other countries to sell it to you. Neither can research be conveniently or easily separated into two individual camps, arms and power: In the Maud Report, one leading scientist points this out very frankly: "There will always be a very close relationship between the exploitation of nuclear energy for military explosive purposes and for power production."

Given this close link, it becomes much easier to understand the secrecy surrounding 'civilian' power installations such as those at Windscale.

Indeed the incestuous relationship between nuclear power and nuclear weapons production goes much deeper than simply shared facilities. Nuclear scientists and researchers form a very small elite in what has come to be known as the 'nuclear club'. As a result, it is they alone who ultimately control the direction of nuclear progress. When in February 1980 Mr Pym, Defence Secretary in the first Thatcher government announced the 'new' defence programme which was to include the introduction of Trident and the installation of 168 US Cruise missiles in British bases, he was in fact making public something that had been developing in private since the early 1970s. Preliminary design work on Trident missiles began over a decade previously and the decision to replace Polaris by a £5 billion (by '73 prices) Trident system had been taken by key ministers in 1975-77. So when Pym told the news to Parliament — our democratic decision making body — many of the major questions had already been decided. All that Parliament and the general public were left with to discuss were the details: dual keys etc. Meanwhile, for over ten years, the whole military machine had been thundering inexhorably towards Cruise and Trident.

This monoply of information held by the nuclear club also pervades safety regulations in nuclear power plants. The Atomic Energy Authority is the body which provides the government of the day (but rarely Parliament as much of its work is 'classified') with information upon which it can base its decision. It is c semi-independent arm of government which reports directly to a minister of senior rank in the Cabinet. At the time this body was set up (1954), Emelyn Hughes, then a Labour MP commented:

"If the government were intending to design a framework for the overall control of atomic energy, they could not possibly

Jamming! 21

have thought of a framework under which it would be more difficult to ensure public accountability and proper parliamentary control."

Yet it is this authority which makes many of the decisions regarding new installations. Meanwhile, the National Radiological Protection Board, which monitors safety measures for nuclear power plants, is permeated by ex- and future employees of this authority. Here again, it seems that there are few (if any) truly independent and objective bodies which can provide the government with information on the safety (or lack of it) in the power stations. The nuclear club rools OK.

But putting aside these issues for a moment, we should remember that the original reason for the adoption of the nuclear power programme was to provide a cheap and independent alternative to oil at a time when OPEC oil prices were soaring. Any economy needs energy to survive and Britain, at that time heavily dependant on imported oil, was taking a severe battering as a result. Put in this context, the benefits of possessing our own source of fuel are undeniable. Yet in 1963 and again in 1978, it seems that the electricity boards in Britain grossly miscalculated the amount of energy we would need for the 1980s and beyond and we are today left with a massive electrical over-capacity. Also the argument of the cost effectiveness of nuclear power as opposed to coal-fired electricity generation no longer seems to hold water. The USA, whose electricity boards must work to a strict profit and loss requirement, have made a major switch back to coal, away from nuclear energy. If you add this to the fact that Britain today is a net *exporter* of oil, there seems to be little justification for the plans of the present government to install 'one nuclear power station every two years from 1982 for 10 years'.

But hold on a minute! To have a nuclear weapons programme, you have got to have access to thermal reactors. And, by 1990, if we do not have a new generation of reactors working, we will be running out of plutonium. And we need plutonium for nuclear warheads, running out of it would be regarded as very serious in terms of defence and foreign policy. The need for power stations is not therefore necessary as an energy policy but as a *defence strategy*.

Greenpeace, and to a much lesser extent CND, are the only two organisations which seem to recognise the implications of the link between power plants and arms production. George Pritchard, who organises anti-nuclear strategy for Greenpeace, explains their strategy like this: "Greenpeace seeks to hinder the nuclear process at *all* points within the cycle, from the original mining of uranium which has serious effects on workers and local inhabitants, through to our opposition to nuclear power, nuclear weapon testing and the dumping of radioactive waste at sea. Through it all though we recognise that our resources are miniscule in comparison to the vast nuclear machine."

It seems amazing that among the political parties, no single group (whose access to information is much greater than my own) had yet been heard to consider a connection between things nuclear. It is evident of course that the Conservative Party supports both an increase in nuclear power plants and nuclear weapons. The now infamous Ridley report also shows that their liking for power plants is not based on economic reasons but on ideological and political ones. A leaked Tory Cabinet document of 1979's date recommended a nuclear power programme because "this would remove a substantial proportion of electricity from the danger of disruption due to industrial action by the NUM or transport workers."

As regards the SDP, their policy is pro Trident and pro Cruise — although they want a dual key system — but, as regards nuclear power, they see no need for any more power stations, other than those "which have been built or are currently being built."

The Labour party alone are the ones who seek to regain control of the atomic time bomb. As a unilateralist party, they are also seeking to return nuclear power and nuclear planning to the realms of public accountability. But if they come to power next time around, the 'nuclear club' cannot be depended on for too much help in putting Labour policy into practice. Meanwhile, greater people than ourselves are making the decisions for us on all things nuclear — Joe Public is considered much too uneducated to understand and make up his own mind. Surely, we should be able to do more than just sit back and hope that the clock keeps on ticking.

■ *Tiny*

22 Jamming!

YPTN
YOUTH FOR PEACE

Everyone is aware of CND; but who knows that its 'new' opponents, Youth For Peace Through Nato, are partly funded by the Foreign Office? Tiny meets their General Secretary James Holding to hear his arguments.

James Holding is the General Secretary of the youth branch of Peace Through Nato — an organisation committed to the nuclear deterrent, and the Nato alliance as a means of averting a major war.

Peace Through Nato was set up in 1981 in opposition to CND and though very small in number (3,000) its supporters are vociferous campaigners against the idea of unilateral disarmament. I spoke to their General Secretary For Youth about his firmly held convictions on defence:

"Our argument is that unilateral disarmament would lead to a less stable and less peaceful world. We also believe that if Britain was to leave Nato and kick out the Americans, the effect would be enormous in terms of the west/east balance and would be very dangerous because it would be misinterpreted by the Soviet Union. Stability is a key factor in maintaining peace. And for that reason we believe in the deterrent, and the Nato alliance.

"We from the outset, have been all-party — we have members of the Labour Party, the SDP and the Conservatives — but more independents really. There are a *lot* of members of the Labour Party who support us too.

"A lot of people don't like the Americans — and as it's well recognised that some Americans in the Pentagon have talked about a limited European war, we must convince them otherwise — but the Americans did rebuild Europe after WWII and that was probably the single greatest act of generosity in human history. We shouldn't forget that.

"If we rejected the Americans, the other choice would be to pay more for the cost of defence ourselves and that would be very expensive. But if you look at the figures, defence has actually fallen as a percentage of the British government's spending over the last 20 years. Nuclear weapons were first chosen by the West in fact because there was 'more bang for the buck', ie they got more firepower for the dollar. And we must remember that conventional weapons are very costly and conventional war is very nasty.

"In essence though our philosophy is based on a paradox — the paradox of deterrence — because if we ever have to use nuclear weapons then deterrence will have failed. But we believe that nuclear weapons are necessary because our peace and freedom are worth defending and defence of those values is the first duty of our government."

PTN is funded by the Foreign Office and shares the same staff and facilities as the British Atlantic Committee — an organisation seeking to provide public education about Nato. James Holding is also a prospective Tory candidate for Lambeth Council.

■ *Tiny*

Looking back on it, those *Jamming!* days now seem so innocent. It took my future co-worker at Go! Discs, Phill Jupitus (Porky the Poet during his time with *Jamming!*), to point out that I was living a Colin MacInnes lifestyle with my flatshare in Portobello Road, right by the Westway, and a job as a music journalist in Camden. It wasn't at all as glamorous as my kids say it sounds, but I was fighting the good fight and having a lot of fun. I can't fully remember how I started at *Jamming!* although Tony was going out with my flatmate Kelly, a publicist at A&M, so maybe that's how we connected.

Marek Kohn, who wrote about politics in *The Face*, was my hero and I set about trying to do something similar at *Jamming!* The first piece I had published was on Keith LeBlanc from Sugar Hill (see p.237). I met him in the cavernous Island Records offices in west London, and still remember his cool cowboy boots, his big smile and his American bad language! He had just released a collaboration with Kohn under the name The Enemy Within, sampling Arthur Scargill speeches about the miners' Strike. It was around that time I also met Norman Strike (real name!), the first real miner I had ever come across. He had gone on stage with The Redskins on *The Tube* to get the miners' views across, and somehow he ended up sleeping on my sofa for a while.

Working at *Jamming!*, I was able to plug myself into the world that as a teenager in the Home Counties I had only previously dared to imagine was out there. I was the only woman in the *Jamming!* office and about one of the only female contributors too, but it was a testament to my boss (Fletch) and my work colleagues that it never felt like that. Trying to get our political voices heard in the mainstream media was a hard task but I think we did a great job at *Jamming!* At a time when there were very few outlets for alternative music, ideas or political dissent, we wrote the kind of things we wanted to read about, and it was a labour of love for us all.

In the midst of it all, I met Billy Bragg at a benefit at the Wag Club. (He says this is ironic – for him maybe, but I was a soul girl from Watford!) Our conversation that night about the dark times we were living through in Thatcher's Britain and what we could do to try and fight back inspired me to try to help him with his work. And when *Jamming!* folded, that's exactly what I did. The friendships formed back then have remained to this day. **Tiny Fennimore** *(Excerpts above from Issue 32)*

MARK CORDERY MEETS HUGH

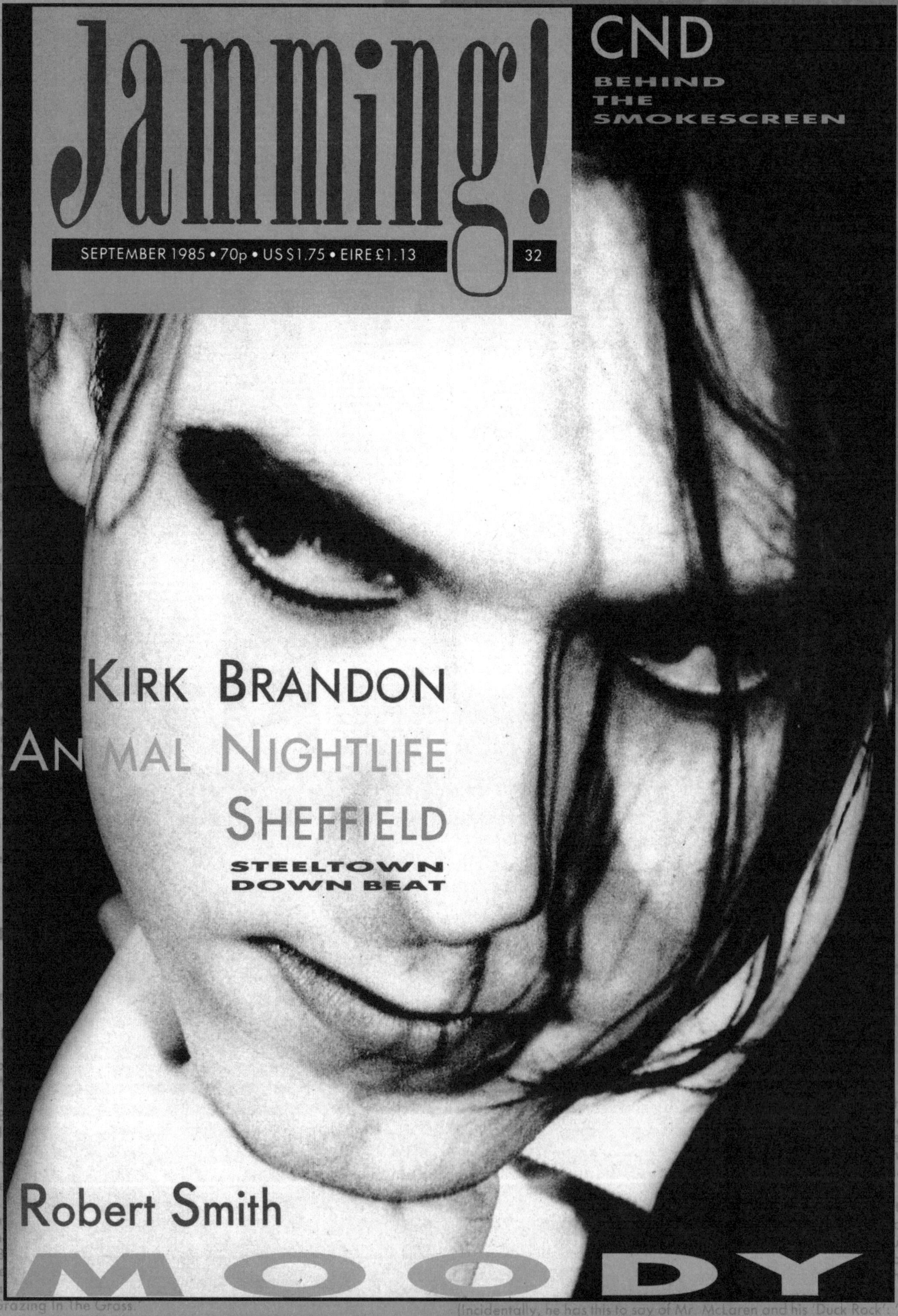
Jamming!
CND
BEHIND
THE
SMOKESCREEN
SEPTEMBER 1985 • 70p • US $1.75 • EIRE £1.13
32
KIRK BRANDON
ANIMAL NIGHTLIFE
SHEFFIELD
STEELTOWN
DOWN BEAT
Robert Smith
MOODY

iled 'Grazing In The Grass'.
Career opportunities knocked, but he didn't answer. "Unless your peo-
e are free, you're never free. You can have millions . . . I could live in a
astle and be Elton John's neighbour. I mean, I've had the opportunity to
e like that, but what's the point?" (Students of rock 'n' roll trivia may
are to note that it is Hugh Masekela's trumpet solo that is featured on The
yrds', currently in vogue again, 'So You Wanna Be A Rock 'N' Roll
ar').

(Incidentally, he has this to say of Mr. McLaren and his 'Duck Rock': "I enjoy Malcolm very much because he does things with an abandon, he doesn't take himself seriously. People expect me to knock him because of the South African things he did, but I think he did a lot to bring that mbaqanga sound out, otherwise a lot of people would never have listened to it. And I like what he did with the music as well, his adventurousness. I was able to see that I could do certain things with electronics. So there's a lot to be learned. Even from so-called hi-jackers!")

MARK CORDERY MEETS HUGH MASEKELA, GIANT OF THE JAZZ TRUMPET, AND FINDS OUT WHO'S REALLY BANGING THE SOUTH AFRICAN DRUM.

On my way to meet Hugh Masekela, I'm reading a newspaper report of a South African Army raid across the border into Gaborone, Botswana — where Masekela resides when not touring overseas. Twelve Africans were killed. At a press conference, a major in the security police displays captured weapons and African National Congress documents; proof that the ANC is engaged in "clandestine terrorist and subversive activities in Gaborone".

Hugh Masekela hands back the paper. "Oh no, I don't have to read it, I was there," he says, sounding deeply tired. "A commando invasion. Purportedly to raid ANC members who they say are terrorists. But they killed a lot of innocent people, people who were just in their homes, gunned people in their bedrooms. And they talk about finding arms. It's very easy to display guns when they spend so much time invading other countries. We're watching a very paranoid regime, which is trying to hang on."

"It's watered down by the media . . . what really happened was that they came in and murdered people in their homes at night. When you read it in the newspaper, it's almost as if they came in to raid an Army camp. If anyone was doing clandestine work why would they have weapons in their home? These are people we've known for a long time. Two of these people were very dear friends of mine. It was through them that, when I moved back to Botswana, I met the band. Now they've been murdered. The soldiers are so paranoid that when a child opened the door to them, they shot it."

What exactly, then, does one do? Another interview? Caught the show last night, Hugh, your new LP's big in our flat. . . .

If I don't know what to say, at least Hugh Masekela knows better by now. "To me it's very easy to understand — I grew up being called a monkey by boers, if I was in the wrong place at the time. And you're not usually in a position to fight back, because these are the sort of people that gang up on you, they always do things in fear. They live in fear because the setting of the sun is very obvious. One thing they may be doing now is trying to eliminate those elements that may ask for them to be brought to trial when the tables have turned."

Hugh Masekela left South Africa soon after the Sharpeville massacre of 1961. Gatherings of more than ten (black) people were prohibited; a measure which effectively ended The Jazz Epistles, featuring himself and Dollar Brand, who had been the first black group to record an LP in that country. His first trumpet had come to him from the Rev. Trevor Huddlestone, hoping to redirect the township youth's delinquent tendencies towards a more fruitful course. Not a hope in vain, since he proved no disgrace to the instrument's former owner, Louis Armstrong — if a somewhat less diplomatic ambassador.

His capability and enthusiasm endeared him to influential figures such as Yehudi Menuhin and Harry Belafonte. Thus, after a short stay at London's Guildhall he took up a scholarship to the Manhattan School of Music, and a job in Belafonte's publishing department. It was a good time for a bebop mad young trumpeter to arrive in New York. A determined night on the town could take in Coltrane, Miles Davis, Dizzy Gillespie, Charles Mingus, The Count Basie Orchestra.

Despite having planned on becoming a sideman for such as Art Blakey he found himself, encouraged by his peers to go his own way and play the kind of music that only he, being African, could play, fronting his own band and making several LPs — including 'The Americanisation Of Oooga-Booga' — before moving to California with his former Manhattan classmate, Herbie Hancock. Years of Afro-jazz-pop fusion followed, including a four million-selling US No 1 hit with a throwaway little number called 'Grazing In The Grass.'

Career opportunities knocked, but he didn't answer: "Unless your people are free, you're never free. You can have millions . . . I could live in a castle and be Elton John's neighbour. I mean, I've had the opportunity to live like that, but what's the point?" (Students of rock 'n' roll trivia may care to note that it is Hugh Masekela's trumpet solo that is featured on The Byrds', currently in vogue again, 'So You Wanna Be A Rock 'N' Roll Star').

● photo: J.A.K.KILBY

Masekela
AND THE FEAR OF FEAR!

★ ★

Being a prominent black African in 1960s America put him in the forefront of the (literally) burning issues of the time. Black Power spokesmen such as Stokely Carmichael and Eldridge Cleaver appeared at his concerts. Hugh himself appeared on TV chat-shows, informing astonished hosts that their inter-racial conversation would be an illegal activity in South Africa.

But by the time the 70s started to set in, he was in a musical rut. Unable to find like-minded musicians in the US or the UK, he toured central Africa with his friend Fela Kuti (still jailed in Nigeria), eventually taking up residence in Botswana where he has recorded two LPs for Jive-Afrika on the Battery Studio mobile; 'Techno—Bush' and now 'Waiting For The Rain', as well as recording other local talents.

(Incidentally, he has this to say of Mr. McLaren and his 'Duck Rock': "I enjoy Malcolm very much because he does things with an abandon, he doesn't take himself seriously. People expect me to knock him because of the South African things he did, but I think he did a lot to bring that mbaqanga sound out, otherwise a lot of people would never have listened to it. And I like what he did with the music as well, his adventurousness. I was able to see that I could do certain things with electronics. So there's a lot to be learned. Even from so-called hi-jackers!")

Amongst other things, the recent raids into Botswana (and Angola, Mozambique, Namibia . . .) furnish further evidence of a regime in decline. Unable to sustain its version of law and order at home — "Every day people die from police fire. Every day. On a slow day it's three people, on a serious weekend it's ten. From there it could be any number of people . . ." — and encouraged by the example set by the UK in the South Atlantic and the US in Central and South America, it attacks foreign subversives in an increasingly desperate attempt to reassure its supporters at home that they can still sleep peacefully in their beds at night. But that change will eventually come to South Africa, as it did in Zimbabwe, Hugh Masekela is in no doubt.

"There has never been a Government that has survived an oppressed people, and I don't think this Government is going to be the first. The whole African population is up in arms against them, people aren't afraid anymore. Every African child in South Africa under nineteen is less afraid of the Government than anyone, and a seven year old child wants to be strong enough when they're ten to carry their own rifle."

Hardly a thought to fill anyone full of unequivocal good cheer. "It will get worse before it gets better" is Hugh's assessment. For whites and blacks; collaborators and rebels alike. Not that armed insurrection is the

only way. Union action has already proven its capacity to damage the economy, although again, not without more suffering: "The South African Government legalised the unions so that they could arrest the leaders. And they kill a lot of them."

Of course, it all comes down to economics in the end, even after ignorance and bigotry, and Western interest in propping up South Africa is too great to expect any effective sanctions to be made. Nonetheless, a modified form of greed contains the germ of a solution, of sorts.

"In Zimbabwe the infrastructure was too well developed, there was too much money involved, so they did the Lancaster House thing — that was just to make sure that Smith and his boys didn't go to jail. Which I'm sure is in the back of the mind of South Africa. The leaders are saying to their partners now, 'Look guys, we'll hold this up for as long as we can, but in the end we've got to have an alternative — because we don't want to go to trial, we want to keep our money and our businesses'. What will happen is that apartheid will go and everything else will remain the same. Removal of apartheid doesn't automatically guarantee freedom for the African population."

And what of the cultural boycott? An irrelevance, and moreover one riddled with racism of its own. Witness — but you couldn't — Malopoets, a black South African group recently prevented from performing here by the Musicians' Union.

"They live under the gun in South Africa, and when they get a chance to go overseas they are told, 'We're boycotting you so we can help you'. But Shakin' Stevens can go to Sun City, Elton John can go, Queen can go, Elkie Brooks . . . and when they come back they don't get boycotted by the MU, and they are MU members. It's double standards. If that's not prejudiced, I don't know what is . . . The fact of the matter is that someone's saying they don't buy South African apples, so they're not going to buy South African music. How sick can you get?"

Hugh Masekela lives just over the border, which means that you're allowed to hear him. I can only recommend that you do so. Not because of any of the above, for goodness sake, but just because maybe you wish to hear something deeply human. With all that that involves.

40 Jamming!

Jamming! 41

How we had made it through thirty-two issues without interviewing Robert Smith is beyond me. Then again, Siouxsie Sioux never made it into our pages at all, nor John Lydon, and while I wish I could insist that such omissions were not for a lack of trying, it may well have been down to individual and collective editorial preferences. Regardless, in The Cure's case it was better late than never, and Paul Davies, another of the unsung *Jamming!* warriors who consistently delivered good copy on time for crap pay, turned in one of his typically direct interviews. That the front cover only further tagged Kirk Brandon (profiled by Chris Heath) and Animal Nightlife (by Mark Cordery) seems something of a slight against The Woodentops (Jonh Wilde), Hugh Masekela (Cordery) and Adrian Legg (Andy Kershaw). Elsewhere, Bruce Dessau's devotion to all things Creation ensured we featured Primal Scream at the start of a now illustrious career, and in a throwback to the fanzine days of the late 80s, a piece on Sheffield music attempted to bring together all the city's industrial funksters into one. Meantime, a multipronged investigation into various 'nuclear' issues affecting the UK at that dark time – meaning nuclear energy as well as weapons – reflected our continued attempts, whether they were realised or not, at solid journalism. And that was it for the A4 format. As sure as September rolled around once a year, *Jamming!* was about to reinvent itself.

ISSUE #32
8/85

WOULD
SMITH

t is indeed a rare occurre
when the blinkered, blocked
drains complacency of Top Of
Pops is shaken, stirred or in
way at all diverted from
homogenised manifesto
squeaky-clean, antiseptic
piffle, churned out by ludicr
lard-brained mannequins v
cerebral dysentery. But
when you thought it was saf
slip back into that weekly sta
glassy-eyed catatonia, al
come The Cure, kicking over
milk bottles and dustbin lids,
generally making a glori
transcendent din all over
place with their mega ch
busting smasheroo hit single
Between Days'.

Decked out in their best 'Esc
From The Batcave' Goth G
gladrags, The Cure were
through their paces by Ro
Smith, who twitched and jer
his way through three minute
delicious, subversive nonse
looking like he'd just been
humed for the Annual Transy
nian Derelicts' And Vagra
Convention. The juxtapositio
images, as the camera pan

24   Jamming!

his way through three minutes of
delicious, subversive nonsense,
looking like he'd just been ex-
humed for the Annual Transylva-
nian Derelicts' And Vagrants'
Convention. The juxtaposition of
images, as the camera panned

Byzanti
Punke

"When
things wer
And there'

THE UNREAL ROBERT
EASE STEP FORWARD

Paul Davies enters Robert Smith's black, black world of fantasy.

citing since punk happened. I still feel like when we first started, because we haven't been absorbed by the mainstream at all. We're more popular, I suppose, but I don't think we've really changed that much in our overall approach to what we do. Outside of that, there's always this thing that you're fighting against, which is this really tedious, grey mass of people making records because they think it's a race to get to number one.

"That's the only motivating thing, and it's reflected in their music, these people's attitudes. I detest 95% of contemporary music."

New York London Paris Munich. Everybody's talking 'bout Pop Music!

"People say the music's become more commercial. In the sense that it sells more, it is more commercial, but nothing we do is like formularised pop to me, it all still sounds odd. And I like the idea of us being odd. I'd hate to be someone like Nik Kershaw, that's my idea of eternal damnation, to walk about being Nik Kershaw.

"The only conscious decision I've ever made with regard to what we do was to do 'Let's Go To Bed' after 'Pornography', because I wanted to do something that sounded really horrible in my head before we did it. I thought of all the bits that I hated in all the records that I'd heard over the past year on the radio, and put them all into one song, and made it as banal as possible. Just to twist the whole thing round, so that people didn't know what we were gonna do next. And it worked really."

It's my art and I'll remain inscrutable if I want to. . . .

"I've never attempted to justify what I write. Some of the stuff I've written I think is really good, and some of it's absolutely garbage. But it doesn't really matter. . . .

"A lot of the lyrics are not coherent, in a sense that very few of the songs have a logic that you can follow. But again, that doesn't worry me. I've never sat and read through anyone else's lyrics, and tried to sort them out. It doesn't really bother me. I've no idea what 'The Killing Moon' is about. It's good for what it is. Were I presenting the words as poetry, it would be very different, I'd have to justify them far more. But a lot of the time, they're there in the context of the music of the song. Taken out of that, they lose probably half of their impact.

"I think that the words on the new album are probably the most straightforward that I've written for years. And that was on purpose. Because 'The Top' was so fucking deranged that I thought people would start to get the wrong idea about me, if I continued to write things like that."

I think I had too much to dream last night

"I'd list it as a hobby, dreaming, I know it sounds really coy saying that. I don't go to bed and have really wild dreams every night, but from time to time you'll wake up drenched in sweat, your heart's beating, your whole body's vibrating and you're actually still in the dream for a few seconds of waking. I love it. I can sometimes induce dreams, it's very easy, all you've got to do is suffer indigestion and you have the most violent dreams. And if you take that to an extreme you can induce all kinds of weird dreams. I still remember dreams I had when I was four or five years old, really strong dreams. If I wake up and I've had a really vivid dream, I sometimes feel exhausted, but it's really pleasurable. It's like going to a good concert or get-

I'D RATHER PEOPLE IN AFRICA GOT THE MONEY THAN WHAM! I THINK WHAM! SHOULD GIVE ALL THEIR MONEY. I THINK WHAM! SHOULD PAY TO RELOCATE ALL THE PEOPLE THAT ARE STARVING SOMEWHERE NICE, AND GO AND STARVE IN THE DESERT THEMSELVES

Here come the young men

"Songs can be misinterpreted, and there's always someone who will. People write to me occasionally, and say, 'did you write this song about me?', in all seriousness. There's a lot of really odd people who still write to me, people who want me to die for them. I shouldn't say it really, but it does amuse me. Because I've never had the intention of dying for my audience. But, again, people misinterpreted a lot of what we did a few years ago. They wanted me to be Ian Curtis. And someone like Ian Curtis, people think he died for them, and all that garbage, he didn't at all. . . .'"

ting drunk or doing anything that's good."

Angst and the memory

"Other people have been guilty of taking me too seriously, but I never have. I take what I *do* seriously to a certain point, because I know that, particularly when we started, in the first three or four years, a lot of people looked to us as some kind of inspiration to show that you could do things in a very, very different way and still maintain your integrity. I'm not sure if people worry about that so much with us now. I think that burden's been taken on by other people, I'm not really sure who, people like The Cocteau Twins, who are like the

to the fixed smiles and omies of Mikes Read and n, was truly awesome to ld. Clearly, an interview n order.

ostensibly painless task of nging an interview with the e Smith soon mutated into ghtmare of Kafkaesque ortions, as it rapidly became rent that it would have been inally easier organising a d of golf with The Pontiff. ver, after several days of ughs, cock-ups and false s, I was finally ushered into resence of the man who we ers of the tabloid press af-nately refer to as 'the y haired post-punk singer, rt Smith'.

se are his words, strange ue. . . .

one at the back ember the antine Age of k?

hen we started I thought s were very stale musically. here's been nothing as ex-

spiritual bearers of that 'angst' sort of thing.

"I enjoyed it at the time, but with 'Let's Go To Bed', that was the decision, when I thought 'I don't want this anymore'. I didn't want people to think that I was like that anymore. Because I wasn't, I'd changed. And I thought that if I want to carry on doing something, we've got to perceive our public image in a very, very different way.

"It is much easier now, because it's not as intense. I don't have to be as intense, I don't have to worry so much about what I'm doing in public, I don't really care anymore. Before, I couldn't really be violently sick in the middle of the dancefloor somewhere, because people would be horrified, their illusions would be shattered, their dreams would be broken. Whereas now I could do it and people probably wouldn't even notice."

Fame fame fame fame fame fame fame

"I don't get recognised enough for me to grasp hold of the idea of me being famous. When we do a concert we play to a lot of people, and I sing, and they look at me and listen to me, but then I'm doing something. I find that side of it's acceptable. Because I would do the same. I used to go and see Alex Harvey, and I used to just gawp at him, I used to think he was completely brilliant. But if I'd wandered out in the street and bumped into Alex Harvey, and he'd pushed me over and said, 'get out of the way you silly little bastard', I would have thought that's fine. Because there's no reason for him to be otherwise. That whole idea of building someone up into something that's larger than life I've never been interested in.

"I don't think we'll ever be in a position where I have to worry about being famous, which is good. It's something that other people derive pleasure from. Being around someone who's famous you get free drinks, you get into clubs for free, you experience the lifestyle, which is extraordinary. But actually be-

ing that person you have a fucking dreadful time, you really do, it's awful. The disadvantages are innumerable and enormous, but don't really affect me because I'm not at that level of fame where it starts to happen."

Live Aid — the greatest story ever told?

"As an idea it was really good, really laudable. If it physically did any good for anyone it was good. Part of me screams that it doesn't really matter anyway, if people die now or die later, die in pain or die comfortably, the fatalist in me would say that. But I'd rather people in Africa got the money than Wham! I think Wham! should give all their money. I think Wham! should pay to relocate all the people that are starving somewhere nice, and go and starve in the desert themselves. But that's just me being vicious.

"We didn't do anything like that as a group because we never publically front anything as a group, because individually we don't have the same politics, we don't agree about the same things . . . If you align yourself to anything, it demeans both parties if you're a pop group. A pop group standing up and saying 'the Government's awful' means absolutely nothing. It's like the Government saying 'you make awful records'. It makes absolutely no difference either way."

Keeping politics out of politics — how I learned to stop worrying and embrace the SDP

"To be honest, I think the SDP is the best party, I have done since it formed. Because I hate any kind of stupidity, and both the Labour and Conservative Parties are guilty of the most inane policies, that are just very unrealistic, very naïve and very patronising. The thing that puts me off Labour is the work ethic, the dignity of labour, I've always found that really ludicrous and

laughable ever since I can remember . . . You've got the one side saying that they're going to get everyone back to work. I was unemployed for eight months and I loved it, I thought it was really good. I didn't have any money but I used to go and sit in the library. Obviously I couldn't spend my whole life doing that. . . .

"On a scale of ten, the Conservatives are a ten in the idiot stakes. And Labour, it's very unfashionable to say so, but I don't think they're that far behind. The other thing is the class ethic, which I find is a most ugly thing, it's almost as ugly as racism. It's so outdated and yet it's reinforced continually by an image the Labour Party doesn't seem that willing to shake, the cloth cap image.

"I find it all very, very frustrating, I don't think there's an answer. It'll just continue, it gets worse, sometimes it gets better. It's always pretty awful, real life, that's probably why I never wanted to be involved in it. . . ."

Robert Smith — the artist as full time escapist?

"Yeah that's my profession, escape artist, the new Houdini. . . ."

Robert Smith is evidently posing no Rad Prole Art Threat. And whilst he possesses the streetwise savvy and political knowhow of a seriously underdeveloped , ideologically rightoff dung beetle, The Cure have managed to record one of the best LPs of the year so far. A million miles away from the swirling maelstrom of 'Pornography' and the cloying whimsicality of 'The Love Cats,' 'The Head On The Door' is a fine LP, bunged up with real tunes of epic, bold and memorable dimensions. An essential purchase if you like your pop stars cocooned in a hermetically sealed, baco foil vacuum of their own creation. But whatever you do, don't expect to be confronted by any of that nasty real world shit. This one's strictly for the dreamers.

While America gasps under a welter of Reaganism, Rambo, jingoism and attempts to escalate intervention in South America, it comes as some surprise that the initiative for a new anti-apartheid record should originate in the 'land of the free' itself.

Strange, but true. Entitled '**Sun City**', after the luxurious white South African leisure complex set on the edge of the black 'homelands', the record is the brainchild of Little Steven, aka Stevie Van Zant, who last year spent a month in South Africa checking out the situation for himself. Shocked and horrified, he returned and set about recording an album, a testament to the area, and found recent events overtaking. He ditched the album (temporarily) and went for a single. Aided and abetted by a mouthwatering selection of the more 'socially or politically aware' artists around—amongst them Jackson Browne, Jimmy Cliff, Lou Reed, George Clinton, Bono, RUN DMC, Linton Kwesi Johnson, Miles Davis, Arthur Baker—the record attempts to mix the range of musical styles found therein.

"**Sun City** represents the whole relocation policy," explained Van Zant, holed up in The Mayfair hotel on a recent brief visit. "Every time someone plays there, it endorses the policies."

This fact however does nothing to prevent the vast sums of money offered by South Africa—eager for Western acceptance—attracting numerous white (and black) artists. Frank Sinatra, Elton John and Queen are but a few to have sold their souls to apartheid.

"In the end, it's a statement *from the* musical community *to the* musical community," says Van Zant, aiming to raise consciousness rather than cash, though any money raised will go to anti-apartheid groups. But what chance of any impact on ultra conservtive Uncle Sam?

"I think it's a matter of the times. Last year people didn't want to hear me being critical of the American government (the 'Voice of America' tour) but this year the colleges are starting to demonstrate again, not only about South Africa but about Nicaragua as well. Maybe the cycle of apathy and escapism is turning."

Maybe. Or maybe not. An interesting aspect of the recent Band Aid extravaganza is the way the likes of Elton John and Queen lined up to raise money for one African nation, safe in the knowledge that they had endorsed the brutal oppression of another. The Lord giveth . . . and the Lord taketh away!' HUGH MORLEY

Housemartins: Hosanna! Preaching the Left-Wing Gospel.

REVELATION! I have heard, seen, written about and vomited over a lot of bands in my extremely long and distinguished career. I have only just discovered the truth and seen the light. The wrath of The Housemartins is about to be released upon ye, the unbelievers.

The Housemartins are a soulful, yet abrasive, pop band with roots in gospel and branches in the late seventies, that have hoisted themselves head and shoulders above the melée of a vibrant music-scene that constitutes the East Yorkshire region. They grew from a nucleus of Paul Heaton (vocals/sermons) and Stan Cullimore (guitar/satirical wit-head) who, as a duo, served their apprenticeship as buskers in the devil-ridden streets of Western Europe. A year ago they expanded to their present format with the baptism of Ted Key (bass) and Hugh Whittaker (drums). Since then the city of Hull has been thoroughly exorcised, the following fanatical and suitably devout.

Every Housemartins gig is now an exuberant, emotional, dance-filled evening with the forefathers of the 'Left-Wing Gospel' as your hosts. Their optimism and belief in collective strength is overwhelming. Their message is equality; their sermon "Question everything that the Devil attempts to condition you with, be it through the general media of through the hypocritical morals of society."

There will never be any doubt about the growth of The Housemartins, for their enthusiasm for playing anywhere and ability to spread the left-wing gospel, is relentless. Don't worry my children, don't make the obvious mistake of equating them with any religious jelly-fish of the Cliff Richard ilk. As they explain, this isn't religion in the accepted sense.

"The rich and powerful are evil and yet they are part of the conventional church. This is in fact the Devil working from within. We want everyone to realise that. This is the religion of the people."

Paul takes the pulpit. "The amount of miners' benefits we've been involved in over the last year is phenomenal. We and thousands of others rallied around the solidarity of those excellent people and yet they were starved back to work by the Devil. People's heads have dropped since then. The Housemartins want to help pick them up, we want to spread the word of optimism, hope and spiritual belief in ourselves. That's the basis of our Left-Wing Gospel Music."

After an apparently stirring live show up in Edinburgh, hopes are high for the debut single on Go! Discs. 'Flag Day' pursues typical Housemartin concerns with an assured hop, skip and a jump, the 12" polishing things off with 'Stand At Ease', 'You' and the seminal 'Coal Train to Hatfield Main!'. Should you pant for more, 70 Grafton St., Hull is the place to confess your capitalist sins.

Their message is profound, Jesus the Revolutionary died on the cross for you bastards, so wake up and kick out the Devil. People of the world join hands, form a love train. SWIFT NICK

PHOTOGRAPH : NIKKI RODGERSON

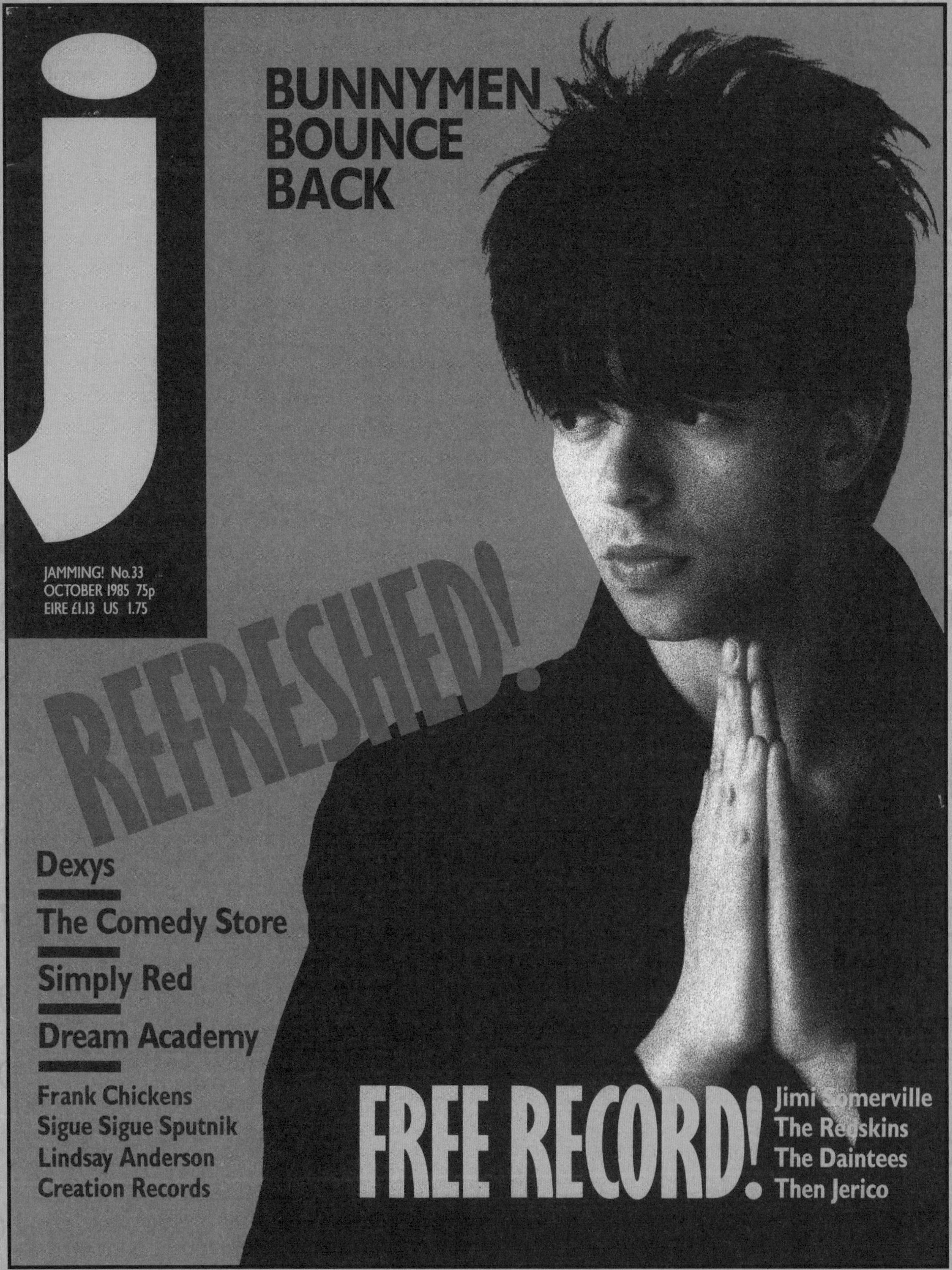

j

BUNNYMEN BOUNCE BACK

JAMMING! No.33
OCTOBER 1985 75p
EIRE £1.13 US 1.75

REFRESHED!

Dexys

The Comedy Store

Simply Red

Dream Academy

Frank Chickens
Sigue Sigue Sputnik
Lindsay Anderson
Creation Records

FREE RECORD!

Jimi Somerville
The Redskins
The Daintees
Then Jerico

jREFRESHED! That's us. It won't take a genius to spot the changes in **jamming!** After all these years, what better than a new look and a new feel? Welcome if you will, a new logo, a new page size and design, more pages (yes!), a higher cover price (slight), a new assistant editor, and, please!, a free EP! Yes, on this very page should be your own **jamming!** Record. Produced in conjunction with London Records, we give you the very first Jimi Somerville release, a totally re-mixed Redskins song, and new and unheard music by The Daintees and Then Jerico. Unavailable in the shops, we are talking great value! Ringing in the changes we may be, but **jamming!** will remain **jamming!**, and you can continue to expect only the best from us. The best for big names, new bands, opinions, enthusiasm, verve and all those other out-dated words. From this moment, **jamming!** broadens its options. It's a long way from being a six-page fanzine, but the attitude is still there. And **jamming!** is still ready and willing to hear your comments and feedback. Keep with us, and we won't let you down.

THE WILD-HEARTED OUTSIDER
A PROFILE OF KEVIN ROWLAND

Kevin Rowland and Dexys Midnight Runners, one of the most inspirational and provocative groups of recent times, are back after two-and-a-half years in the wilderness. Following the release of their third LP 'Don't Stand Me Down', Tony Fletcher looks back on their six-year history.

● Dexys Mk I, 1980. Mean and moody

SEARCHING FOR THE YOUNG SOUL REBELS

With Issue 33, *Jamming!* underwent more than just a redesign: it embarked on something of a transformation. On the visual front, Russell Tate departed as designer after two valiant years pulling deadline-induced all-nighters with a cheerful demeanour, and more than a few politically/sexually incorrect anecdotes, some of which unfortunately made it into print. He was replaced by the solicitous duo of Dunmore & Brown, who worked out of their own studio, from where they produced a new logo – a simple j – that indicated confidence in *Jamming!*'s identity. The physical page size increased to compete with similar large-format monthlies, allowing for more white space (or off-white, the thin paper stock having a certain fashionable graininess to it), which in turn confirmed our final capitulation to the influential designs of Neville Brody, as instigated at *The Face* over five years earlier. Then again, the type size itself appeared to change little, the articles were often as difficult to discern as ever and the blank space merely provoked said articles to run longer!

These significant visual changes were part of a larger reshuffle, in which yours truly, having been MIA while managing Faith Brothers, returned to the fold to find Jonh Wilde eager to continue editing without me. In consultation with our backers, I agreed to an upstairs role as editor-in-chief, and immediately embarked on two special projects. One was a 4-track EP attached to the cover of Issue 33, produced in collaboration with London Records and featuring The Communards, The Redskins, The Daintees and Then Jerico. The other was a trio of late, late-night shows at the Electric Screen in Notting Hill, held during relaunch week, each featuring two bands (including The Icicle Works, Wet Wet Wet, Virginia Astley with The Daintees and Faith Brothers),

a compère (among them our own Porky The Poet) and a classic movie (*Saturday Night, Sunday Morning, Raging Bull* and *The Devils*). This was a notable line-up by any standards, let alone that of what was still, in the overall scheme of things, a relatively small magazine evidently still seeking to punch above its weight.

Afforded what he took to be his editorial independence, Jonh Wilde hired his friend Paul Mathur full-time as assistant editor. Mathur turned in the cover feature on Echo & The Bunnymen, for which Ian McCulloch was unusually restrained, and the roundabout nature of that article was reflected in the wider absence of Q&As, long our fanzine-based fallback. Still, the editorial content was generally solid, and if some of the larger features leaned heavily towards the commercial (Simply Red, Dream Academy, Sigue Sigue Sputnik), then Anthony Blampied's interview with Lindsay Anderson, Jonh Wilde's article on the Comedy Store, my reflective essay on Dexys Midnight Runners, Kevin Samson's first-hand account of the horrific scenes in Brussels with his fellow Liverpool fans, separate articles on Charly Records and Creation Records and a Group Therapy article on management (penned by myself under a pseudonym) proved that *Jamming!* maintained a broad remit.

Overall, the redesign, reformatting and editorial changes were well received. There were those, however, who bemoaned the final eradication of any lingering fanzine elements – including one of the contributors… I commissioned a short piece on a new band from Hull called The Housemartins, written by their home city's own ranting poet, Swift Nick, and after I cleaned up his story grammatically, he sent me a virulent letter promising never to write for us again!

j

JAMMING! No 34
NOVEMBER 1985 75p
EIRE £1.20 US $1.75

LLOYD COLE
BURNING BLUE

FREE!
LP's FOR 3 YEARS
COMPETITION INSIDE

Fine Young Cannibals
Kenneth Williams
Jesus and Mary Chain
Dammers and Wyatt

Hüsker Dü / Derek Jarman / Eighth Wonder

THE CELLULOID TERRORIST

As contemporary cinema blands out into the palest of shadows, only folk like director Derek Jarman seem capable of investing the medium with a modicum of vitality. Through everything from pop promos and work with Psychic TV to his latest project – the life story of 16th century painter Carravagio – Jarman maintains an admirable jagged edge. Anthony Blampied dons surgical garb at the bedside and asks Derek: "Is cinema dead?"

The power of the moving image is immense. Lenin claimed cinema as the most useful of the arts, whilst Kenneth Anger spoke of its creation as the blackest day in mankind's history.

For most people nowadays Cinema equals the dubious attractions of the local Odeon. Coarse American macho violence or Bill Forsyth's homegrown coyness. No thanks.

It is fair to say that the cinema's success has also been its hindrance. Film is expected to fall into the Hollywood entertainment mould, audiences bringing with them a demand for linear narrative, and conventions that are broken at the risk of the box-office. The time element seen as 'difficult' or 'pretentious' in the films of Nic Roeg would, as he has pointed out, be perfectly acceptable in a novel.

"The cinema", wrote Louis Lumière, "is an invention without a future." People reading that today laugh, how amusing! how ironic! But I can't help wondering . . . is it true? Is the cinema dead!

Among current film-makers, Derek Jarman is maybe not unique but certainly rare in not regarding the move to features ('real films') as a progression. Instead, he uses his experience in the maligned medium of Super-8 to capture that magical quality seen so infrequently on the big screen. In his four to date — 'Sebastiane', 'Jubilee', 'The Tempest' and 'The Angelic Conversation' — he has managed, like the contemporaries he mentions with admiration (Roeg, Lindsay Anderson, Mike Leigh), to bridge the supposedly impassable divide between Art and Entertainment.

Incorporating the immediate, dangerous thrill of Super-8 he has struggled for an unashamedly personal cinema, however unacceptable that may be to the British — as a reminder of his link with the notorious Ken Russell (he designed 'The Devils' and 'Savage Messiah'). He is dismissive of the frequent accusations, towards both himself and Russell, of self-indulgence.

"Whenever I hear something called self-indulgent I realise that the cinema is there. I mean, it has to be. Unless one pulls one's own self into the cinema . . . this sort of myth that one's working for other people is ridiculous. It's something that everyone pulls the wool over their own eyes about.

"As for those people who are not self-indulgent, God alone knows what films they're making. I suppose they're making things like 'Revolution', but they're wasting millions and millions of dollars on their nonself-indulgent films for everyone.

"I'm not certain that the cinema

should be always aiming for these vast, popular audiences. It seems to me that area is dying. It should really diversify, more specialist films for more specialist audiences is really the answer."

While dollar-eating blockbusters are spewed from the major studios at an alarming rate, Jarman has struggled for years to find backing for his film on the life of the 16th century Italian painter Carravagio. In Germany and Spain, such projects are encouraged but here, lacking a tradition of a cinema of ideas, they are considered subject-matter for television documentaries and ignored.

Jarman began his artistic career in the 1960s as a painter with no thought of becoming involved in film. Designs for Frederick Ashton's ballets led to work with Ken Russell and, shortly after that, the discovery of Super-8 and its revolutionary potential . . .

What is seen as most threatening about Jarman is his ability to view, like Lenin and Anger, film in its most basic form as an unsettling agent, a perfect device for stirring the emotions. In his autobiography, 'Dancing Ledge', he continually comes back to those cinematic experiences which have meant so much to him throughout his life – Cocteau, 'The Wizard of Oz', Pasolini (the closest thing to a reincarnation of Carravagio, he feels).

His collaborations with Psychic TV reveal an instinctive knowledge of the true power of film.

"It's seen as potentially really dangerous because visual images are the main method of communication in our culture. Therefore it's incredibly carefully controlled by economics in the West, by the Party in the East, and it's made as difficult as possible to make film.

Photos: Coneyl Jay.

Russell Young had been *Jamming!*'s go-to photographer for two long years already, and it was a thrill to watch his craftmanship improve along the way. With Issues 34 (Lloyd Cole) and 35 (The Cocteau Twins) he developed portrait shots far and above our usual standard, far and above those of most music magazines to be honest, and it came as no surprise that within the next year he was hired to shoot the cover for George Michael's album *Faith*, after which he went on to further portrait fame, the lucrative music video realm and, eventually, his own fine art. The highly professional look of the Cole cover was matched inside, with Chris Heath profiling not just Cole but also Creations Records' frontrunners The Jesus & Mary Chain and Felt, plus wide-ranging features on Fine Young Cannibals (Dessau), Hüsker Dü (Andy Darling), Anne Pigalle (Paul Mathur), Sydney's Hot Records (Wilde) and Henry Jackson's look at 'Namibian political oppression' via the Robert Wyatt/Jerry Dammers collaboration with the SWAPO Singers for 'The Winds of Change', which probably inspired some lively conversation with our South African backers. Eighth Wonder were trailed on the cover but absent from the interior, though I don't believe we received any complaints

ISSUE #34
10/85

about that latter aspect.

The rest of the magazine was even more of a hodgepodge: Derek Jarman (interviewed by Anthony Blampied, with inspired photography by Coneyl Jay) and Clive Barker (Jackson/Young) were joined by Paul Mathur's profile of *Carry On* star Kenneth Williams and Chris Heath's evening in the company of James Last, seemingly the unlikeliest of profile contenders. We had clearly moved into a phase of hipster irony that was perhaps lost on our more long-standing readers.

Meanwhile, I was none too subtly frozen out of contributing to the magazine I had started; there was an especially heated debate about whether the top-drawer concerts that had promoted the relaunch should even receive coverage, with their pictorial celebration ultimately confined to less than a page up front. Additionally, where we had once been taking writers almost literally off the streets, new commissions were now being handed out to already established freelancers. The masthead was becoming increasingly difficult to discern from other conventional music magazines, and was, consciously or otherwise, and with Tiny's role editing the letters page and writing political stories a notable exception, back to being almost exclusively male.

Ever since the first thrashings of punk there has been a place in Pop's scheme for the overtly political platter. Of course a rich history of political songwriting flourished well before that time but this drew mainly on folk or blues traditions; the distance between 'Strange Fruit' and 'Anarchy In The U.K.' cannot simply be measured in years. The range and quality of political pop since '76 has improved concurrently with its wider acceptance, as if a new vocabulary had been discovered that would articulate the emotions of the dispossessed but still maintain enough music to avoid sounding like a musical broadsheet.

The latest example 'Wind Of Change', is the superb new Rough Trade single from Robert Wyatt and The SWAPO Singers. At his London home a few weeks ago, he discussed the background to the song.

"Richard Muzira phoned us up on behalf of The Namibia Support Committee who in turn were trying to help SWAPO (South West African People's Organisation) get together a particular campaign because it would help them if more people knew about what the South African Government is doing in Namibia. Richard used to do a radio programme in Zimbabwe and played songs from outsiders who were sympathetic. Funnily enough he included a song of mine, 'Born Again Cretin', which was about The New Right and how it affected people like Nelson Mandela. So when he came to England he contacted musicians who were sympathetic to making a record to publicize the Campaign.

"I couldn't think of any tunes. Jerry Demmers phoned us up and said, 'Look what are we going to do about this? Shall we try something'. So I got hold of this Namibian record I'd had for a long time made by SWAPO called 'Namibia One Nation' and I lent that to Jerry. Namibia Support gave him a more recent recording of SWAPO Singers and he chose some songs from that album. He then took over completely and decided on two songs; one which was a simple dance number that used slogans known in Africa and the other a specifically

Frank Spooner Pictures

Police break up a SWAPO rally in Windhoek

THE WIND OF CHANGE

Behind Robert Wyatt's infectiously sharp-set new single, 'Wind Of Change' lies the sinister backdrop of Namibian political oppression. Henry Jackson digs deep to find out how the brutal jack-boot of colonialism and apartheid made Wyatt, Jerry Dammers and The SWAPO Singers respond with this polemic song and dance.

Namibian song interspersed with a poem written by a Namibian working in London at the moment. So the way Jerry worked it out was the B-side would be the Namibians themselves and on the A-side I sing the song. It's a sort of Special AKA revisited in some ways."

Joined for the rest of the interview by Richard Muzira, a former member of the Zimbabwian army, we take the time to backtrack on Namibia's tragic history.

A vast territory on the South Western part of Africa, it has been under colonial rule for over a century; first by the Germans and then, from 1919 by the South Africans. Originally South Africa was supposed to administer Namibia for Britain; however the country was soon all but included in the Republic and became an integral part of that economy. The repression of opposition, begun in 1919, has continued to the present day with up to 125,000 South African troops at the moment stationed in Namibia, making sure the forces of resistance in the shape of SWAPO (South West African People's Organization) and its military wing PLAN (People's Liberation Army of Namibia) never achieve the political power their popularity among the indigenous population merits.

of money funding terrorism? They were aware that Radio One might attempt to ban the record although 'Free Nelson Mandela' managed to slip the censors. Maybe that's because Mandela seems a far more acceptable kind of rebel . . .

Robert: "SWAPO and The African National Congress are allies and, if you respect ANC and its representatives, such as Mandela, you should really respect SWAPO. Of course newspapers like to talk about military operations in such a way as to suggest that liberation struggles have only a military dimension to them but I should point out that the people singing on this record are agriculture and law students who are studying to become responsible Africans in a country of their own. Anyway there isn't a country in the world that hasn't got a military back-up to it and any organization that has to respond to a terrorist government has to respond in kind."

Richard: "There has to be consistency in the policy. The UN of which this country is a member state recognises SWAPO as the sole and authentic representative of the Namibian people. So this country is bound by what the UN agree. Moreover, if Radio One can be made to understand that SWAPO are

Right: A South African ranger in Namibia being showered by his black aide

Robert Wyatt with the SWAPO Singers

ABC Press, Amsterdam

What's behind this new campaign?

Richard: "Well, apart from popularizing the whole concept of the Namibian situation, there are two main issues being picked up; that all political prisoners should be released and also that Koevoet be disbanded. This is a counter-insurgency unit, an assassination squad which was formed in 1979 after the UN resolution 435 was decided. That ruling included Koevoet in any transitional plan for Namibia. We are saying that on no account should Koevoet be considered as any part of a settlement for Namibia."

Were they worried that when people discover that all proceeds from the single are going directly to SWAPO, there would be accusations

freedom fighters in the same way as The Resistance were in The Second World War, then I see no problem."

Were the lyrics chosen deliberately to be uncontroversial?

Robert: "The lyrics came from the record we already had. Jerry thought about this issue. He knows the world of Radio One and one of the reasons for asking Jerry to do it was precisely because he would understand that field of operations. He's been braver than most in what he's been able to say in that context. We're hoping that Jerry's got it right." ●

For more details, contact NAMIBIA SUPPORT COMMITTEE, PO Box 16, London NW5 2LW.

THE BOY
WHO WOULD BE
KING

Swaggering testily through Pop Miseryland, Lloyd Cole has spent the last couple of years resurrecting the delightful combination of clever word and couldn't care less jangle.
As The Commotions prepare to unleash their long-awaited second album, Crazy Chris Heath corners Lloyd and digs deep for That Essential Truth.
Sombre snaps by Russell Young.

"I was at the launderette yesterday. I suppose it's quite good that I still go. I don't like it but the laundry service would be, frankly, too expensive. I go to the launderette at home in Glasgow too, I haven't got a washing machine."

Do you get stopped in there for autographs and stuff?

"Occasionally, yes. It's the worst place in the world to be stopped."

Because people can see your dirty underwear?

"Yes."

Who'd have thought it? Lloyd Cole, famous singing star and bookworm, goes to the launderette. Poor bloke – it must be very hard being the serious artiste, frowning professionally, jotting down notes on avant garde literary Americans and thinking great thoughts while surrounded by huge unstable piles of soiled undergarments, dirty bedlinin and putrid socks. But then the dull "I'm-so-serious" intellectual pose he's been lumbered with doesn't really fit Lloyd that well at all. For one thing he likes bananas.

I find this out when a bleary-eyed and slightly confused Lloyd ("you're from *No 1*, aren't you?") greets me in his hotel foyer and then wanders off to satisfy his mid-morning craving for a banana sandwich. Sadly the cafe is right out of bananas so he has to settle for a banana-milk from the newsagent. Out of tiredness, rudeness or shyness – perhaps all three – Lloyd doesn't encourage conversation as we walk back to the hotel and I wonder what I'm doing here at all. Then I remember.

It was in the summer of '84 that I decided Lloyd Cole was important. 'Perfect Skin' had impressed me with all the right references – breathy Lou Reed vocals, jangly guitars, clever lyrics – but didn't especially move me. 'Forest Fire' was different. I'd put it on when everyone was out and sing along to those ridiculously tragic words – "*it's just a simple metaphor/for a burning love/don't it make you smile/like a forest fire*" – and, like Lloyd, was amazed when it flopped.

'Rattlesnakes' the album, followed. I dismissed it at first as nice but too dull, American and old-fashioned – thankfully the friend on whose floor I was sleeping at the time insisted on playing it in strict rotation with Sade's 'Diamond Life' and Hall & Oates 'Rock'n'Soul Pt 1' until I succumbed. It was the self-pitying couplet in 'Patience' that finally did it – *"she says the one thing that she needs is happiness/I don't believe that she's happy till she sees that I'm in distress"* – maybe it struck a chord somewhere.

Then earlier this year I saw the Commotions in Brighton and was completely won over. I thought that these even-textured wordy songs would fall flat live but instead they sounded better than ever, especially an incredible chaotic version of Jim Webb's 'Wichita Lineman' and a new song, 'James', which Lloyd sung the words to off a scrap of paper in his hand, "a portrait of a particular character – ugly child, pale complexion, hides himself away, to live in bed-and-breakfast places, walk in the shadows. The very sad type of characters who never actually move into the social world in their whole lives." And a sensitive enough song to make me want to find out more about this man in black, centre stage, head hung low, who looked up shyly, trying desperately to appear cocky, and sing these songs . . .

"There's nowhere I really think of as home," says Lloyd, explaining how he now lives in Glasgow, hopes to soon buy a flat and move down to London and was born in Chapel-En-Le-Frith in Derbyshire, "a reasonable-sized town, not too rural, though the area is." By which he means that, though it's nothing more than a medium-sized collection of houses

snugly fitted between the bare hills of the peak district, Manchester is less than an hour away and casts a powerful influence over the place. "The kids in the town," he explains, "were Manchester United supporters and went to see them each weekend." Lloyd, we can safely assume, did not. "They used to take great pleasure in beating the hell out of me whenever they could which I think must have had a profound effect on me at a certain age. Between the ages of nine and thirteen, there were certain places I was afraid to go to."

The trouble was, reveals Lloyd, "they thought I was a snobby poof. I used to have these velvet trousers – Marc Bolan had a pair so I got a pair like them. I think that might have started it off." Very likely by the sound of it, especially as he denies all charges of being snobby.

Still at school, where he showed an early talent not for English but for Maths, things were fine to start with. "Until ten or eleven, I was one of the 'boys' at school," he remembers, "I was even in the football team. Well," he says bitterly, "I was substitute." He still sounds resentful.

'I used to go to this very promiscuous school and everyone was intent on doing as many things that they weren't supposed to do as possible. I was still regarded as a bit of a poof then. I find it difficult to appreciate in retrospect, but I was probably more effeminate than most other boys.'

Then he took 11 plus and while most of his friends went to the local Chapel comprehensive – "quite frankly one of the worst schools in the world, a *dreadful* school" – he went a few miles up the road to New Mills. Before now he has claimed that he should have gone onto Stockport Grammar but was refused because of his father's lowly occupation. "That's true, I really believe it is," he insists. "I took the exam and I know through hearsay that I did very well. They *told* me that I was passed. And the two sons of the local doctor," he mutters "they both went. Still, in retrospect, I'm very pleased because my school was very good and at Stockport I think that they're all boys. That would have been *dreadful*."

Whereas at New Mills he discovered girls? "I certainly did," he grins with uncharacteristic enthusiasm. "It was very exciting." Presumably there was lots of kissing behind the bikesheds?

"It was *far* more sordid than that," he laughs, "though it was much in that vein. It was a very promiscuous school and everybody was intent on doing as many things that they weren't supposed to do as possible." Then he frowns with puzzlement as a stray memory strikes him. "Though I was still regarded as a bit of a poof then."

Perhaps he was still wearing the velvet trousers?

"No, no. I don't know why. I find it difficult to appreciate in retrospect but I probably was more effeminate than most other boys. If you see pictures of me, then I do look a bit effeminate which I never realised at the time."

He indicates how his hair used to be – a straight fringe which dropped down at right angles to run below his ears. "A real early '70s haircut," he laughs. "If I was really lucky I used to let the fringe grow really long over my eyes like The Byrds."

He smiles when he thinks of those adolescent experiences. "They were very funny in retrospect and they were very much an adventure. The way one was trying to get girls all the time!"

I suppose he too used to invent ludicrous excuses to continuously cross the path of whoever he had a crush on that week. He nods his head knowledgeably.

"I even fought a boy once over a girl. He was my friend and I remember not wanting to but I did." He thinks he won – "I can usually remember all the fights that I lost" – but it didn't matter much anyway. "I don't think she was very interested in either of us."

'These days, I'm definitely coming to thinking I should punch people more often. There's a few journalists who, if I met, I think a good sock on the jaw would be far better than an argument.'

Presumably it's a long time since he's used his fists on anybody? "These days," he answers "I'm definitely coming to thinking I should punch people more often. There's a few journalists who, if I met, I think a good sock on the jaw would be far better than an argument. There are some very pretty and nasty things said just to keep people amused – listing me as a prick because I play golf, calling me 'an excuse for a pop star' – which is a very unpleasant way to make a living. What is the point in talking to these people? A sock on the jaw is what is needed."

Like all healthy adolescents Lloyd tripped from infatuation to infatuation. "I never really had a love affair properly," he says, "until the one I'm in." But he used to lose lots of weight – "the whole business, the whole business", he laughs. And yes, he recalls, it didn't really matter who you were starving yourself over.

"I think it's a physical thing," he says. "You're in a position to be infatuated and so you find somebody to be infatuated with. I was very infatuated by a girl four years ago when I was quite old. It was dreadful, really awful. We had a brief fling and it wasn't working out and we both knew it but she was more willing to cut it off than I was. I was clinging."

But now such escapades are behind him. He's in love with Elaine who works in "the newspaper business". Their love is obviously a great joy to him, but is it also a relief to be properly in love at last?

"It's nice to know there's someone you can fall back on and rely upon. In some ways though it's quite bad. The two of us used to have quite a lot of friends but we don't any longer. We tend to rather be with each other most of the time." But he says he has no fears about what might happen if it ends – "I don't think it will," he insists.

The more we talk the more it becomes clear that Lloyd has little time for the popular myths of how artists should create. He reckons that all that tortured artist stuff about people's best work coming out of their suffering and pain is rubbish. Being happy has enhanced his creativity, not stifled it. "I do the same things as I used to do but a bit better. I'd only written two decent songs ('Are You Ready To Be Heartbroken' and 'Patience') before I met Elaine. Afterwards I wrote about six in six months."

He's got no time either for all those soul music myths about how the best, most natural music comes out when you're at your most spontaneous and emotional, not considered and thoughtful. Live, he says that the songs do not come from the heart, they are purely recitals, and he totally rejects the idea that the 'muse' can inspire a whole song inside someone as it is supposed to in the 'I-wrote-this-song-in-15-minutes' tradition of pop music.

"That's a lovely idea, isn't it," he smiles scornfully. "I think in the name of that idea, in the name of spontaneity a lot of garbage has been written. I think the muse often does come through and provide two or ▶

three good lines and the idea for a song but after that you've just got to work on it. I'm very plodding, very slow. It usually takes me weeks and weeks to get a song finished. Other people just get ideas quickly and rush off songs and it strikes me listening to most pop records that not much thought is being put into them. There's a school of thought that says that spontaneity is a very good thing and it's more emotional to write just what comes into your head but I can't think of many successful examples."

So, instead, Lloyd ekes songs out of his imagination bit by bit. He carries a notebook round the whole time so he can capture every precious little spasm of inspiration. "I'm a dreadful worrier. I'm always pessimistic about things and I imagine that if I didn't carry it around I'd probably come up with all my good ideas when I didn't have a pen or paper." I point out that he uses exactly the same technique as Gary Numan. "Yeah?" he smirks. "Most great arists do."

> **'Musically, I can write tunes but I need help to make them into good records, and living a normal life I'm fairly useless on my own. I need people to check me into hotels, to hold my hand.'**

The new LP – out soon but as yet untitled – will be the result of Lloyd's toil over the last year. It has, he says, one love song ('Why I Love Country Music') and quite a few songs about "attention and needing someone to talk to." These loner figures – are they him, I wonder?

"Not really," he insists. "As an adolescent one tends to see loners as very romantic figures because maybe you find it an appealing situation to be in yourself. But quite a lot of the songs deal with the ridiculous loner situation like Jack Kerouac who did *everything* spontaneously and on his own and who, in the name of spontaneity, wrote some of the worst books *ever*. Myself I've learnt that on my own I'm not very capable of producing anything. I need help in most departments of life.

"Musically I can write tunes but I need help to make them into good records, and living a normal life I'm fairly useless on my own. I need people to check me into hotels, to hold my hand."

And, he says, for him at least, sitting on hillside in the country waiting for inspiration is utterly useless – "I need people to talk to or

books to read." One of the new songs, 'The Lost Weekend', deals with this discovery.

"It's a happy song," he explains, "but it's relating a really pathetic situation which is exposing all the faults in the main character. He goes on a little excursion to Amsterdam for the weekend because he feels he can get some work done there – he's a writer. When he gets there the snow starts to thaw and the weather is really horrible, so he gets double pneumonia and ends up spending all of his romantically envisaged holiday trying to find a doctor, paying huge medical bills and having a really miserable time."

And this is a *happy* song?

"Yeah. Because it basically says: it took a lost weekend in a hotel in Amsterdam to make him realise how he's pretty useless doing things on his own. I like the idea of there being lots of gory images and it still being happy – it's quite grotesque."

The whole thing's just dreamt up, is it?

"No," he confesses. "It was originally conceived as my first excursion into autobiography though it's not going to end up like that. I did go to Amsterdam to write and I got absolutely nothing done at all, I went to one exhibition and that was it. I really was ill and the sickest joke of all was the price of the medicine – I got a really bad cold. But double pneumonia sounds much better."

How things *sound* in songs, is, he says, crucial. "If the words don't sound good then nobody's going to want to listen to what they mean anyway. That's one thing Paul Weller's never learnt, that the sound of words is actually very important. Like 'Walls Come Tumbling Down' – they just sound clumsy, don't they?"

What other pop stars *does* Lloyd Cole like these days? After objecting to the terms of the question – "I still don't really adhere to being called a pop star, I don't think that's fair" – he names a few.

"Simon Le Bon, he chuckles, "I quite like him with his new haircut, he looks *much* better. I like Green a bit. Not a lot. Musically we're about as far in opposition as you can get and I think he does his best to disguise the fact that he's got a brain. Jesus wept, he puts so much thought into his lyrics and you can't hear a single one of them, which seems really stupid. Still, he's got a weight problem too which is good."

And what about Morrissey? Lloyd always refers to them as mutual admirers, but when confronted, Morrissey always seems to shy away

from endorsing the Commotion's actual songs.

"Well," says Lloyd in retaliation, "when people confront me with the Smiths I have to admit that I didn't really like 'Shakespeare's Sister' or all of 'Meat Is Murder'. But Morrissey seems to accept that easily. I said to him that I think 'Barbarism Begins At Home' is one of the most horrible songs I've ever heard, I think it's *rotten*. And he said 'it's not very good, is it?'"

> **'I think that a lot of people see The Velvet Underground as some kind of icon and if they see something like it they tend to be grossly offended. I know for a fact that we've got very little in common with them – we've got more in common with a group like The Beatles. We're more obviously a part of the pop world.'**

I start to tell Lloyd a story. David Thomas, I begin . . .

"I really like him!" butts in Lloyd. "He's one of my favourite singers . . ."

Oh! Well as I was saying, he said to me the other day that 'on *Top Of The Pops* the other night was this absolute straight rip-off of The Velvet Underground just made more acceptable by being in tune. If I want to listen to The Velvet Underground I'll listen to The Velvet Underground, not a couple of kids from Scotland'.

Lloyd is momentarily lost for words. "That's quite sad," he finally murmurs, trying to find a reason for this put-down. "I think that a lot of people see The Velvet Underground as some kind of icon and if they see something like it they tend to be grossly offended. I don't think 'Brand New Friend' is like them – lyrically it's as far opposed as you can be. I know for a fact that we've got very little in common with them – we've got more in common with a group like The Beatles. We're more obviously a part of the pop world." He shakes his head. "That's sad what David Thomas said – I like him and Pere Ubu." He laughs. "I hate him now!"

When it finally arrives the new LP will have ten songs – two, 'The Lost Weekend' and 'Cut Me Down' are as yet unfinished, but some of you may have heard the other eight ('Brand New Friend', 'Rich', 'Pretty Gone', 'Grace', 'Why I Like Country Music', 'Minor Character', 'James' and 'Perfect Blue') on their recent tour. Live, Lloyd clowns about playfully,

disrespectfully reinventing his songs. Some of the changes are for good reasons – the last line of 'Perfect Skin' often becomes *"the moral of this song is/we need a new government"* and 'Forest Fire' includes the lines *"if you don't slow down/I swear that I'll come round/and beat up your kids"*.

"That was the original line," he explains. "The whole idea was that there's this real tension and I always wanted to get it into the song that the woman had kids."

Mostly though the changes just involve giving characters new names or throwing in lines like 'Frankie says' and 'Feed The World'.

"I don't like people holding the songs in such reverence, singing along with them," he explains, "so I try to stop them by changing the lyrics. 'Feed The World'! Yeah, that was this year's line."

Surely though he must realise that some people are going to take such flippancy as a sign that Lloyd Cole just doesn't care, that he's prepared to crack jokes while babies are dying in the desert?

"Yeah," he answers unperturbed, "but I think that you can, just by basic nonsensical irreverence, make people think more – that's why Morrissey works quite well. The new Smiths LP is apparently to be called 'The Queen Is Dead' and I think that through making statements like that you can jolt people." He shrugs his shoulders once more. "To be honest, I don't mind if people of limited imagination think I'm a fascist." ●

Happy Mondays sound like they use a lot of guitars and look as if they're satanists . . . or postmen.

"Look we don't want any of this printed about postmen, but there does tend to be a huge postal connection anyway. Everyone's either been a postman, and been sacked from the job, is a postman, or works for Royal Mail or Royal Parcels. There's only one who hasn't really and that's Gaz the drummer although he did nick a mail sack once."

Happy Mondays remember Sunday evening.

"Right, about 1979, Shaun the lead singer and a guy who did artwork on the cover . . . all right this is just giving you some background, they hardly possessed one guitar with two strings on it between them and they used to put up posters saying that they were appearing at such and such a place, you know, the following week, but they didn't really exist. Whether anyone actually turned up to these . . .

"So at this time there's three members of the band plus one other who leaves to become a designer, and no drummer, one on guitar, two bass players and Shaun singing. Something like that. But the designer is playing different tunes to the rest of the band basically because he's such a tripped out sort of a bloke. Dead nice though, he does all the covers and comes to the gigs so it's not a Pete Best sort of a situation."

Happy Mondays have got someone called Paul Davies in them.

"Knew him for years, Paul that is, and he used to do things like follow them round pinching everybody's cigarettes and draw and that, he's a

bit like that isn't he? 'Got a fag Phil?' That's what he says. He's the one Tony Wilson's afraid of."

A Happy Monday spokesman pulls back the curtains and peeks at the mess on the lounge carpet.

"As to what the band actually are is a different matter altogether. I thought they were different musically and different because of who they are. I mean there's nothing happening now apart from the theory that you must be daft if you're not bummed every night. Also you've got a lot of weirdness happening. Now I happen to believe that the majority of weirdos come from middle-class backgrounds and it's all false. Now whether I'm right or wrong is beside the point because it's what I happen to believe and it's what conditioned my response to Happy Mondays. They're real lads, we're actually it. The noun or whatever.

"We're the numbers that everyone's arguing about as to whether we should be voting left or right wing or something."

Happy Mondays furrow their brows and talk wittily and perceptively about their musical impetus.

"One thing to remember is that the minute you start getting lots of equipment you've moved away from who you were when you started. I mean the majority of facilities on the average keyboard are obsolete as far as we're concerned, because we just don't use them. We just stick to an extension of what's real."

Happy Mondays have a single called 'Delightful' on Factory Records. PAUL MATHUR

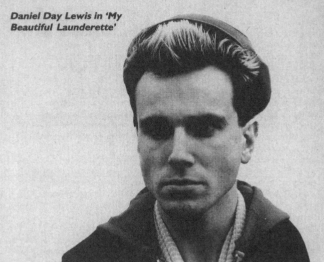

Daniel Day Lewis in 'My Beautiful Launderette'

The word is out. There's a new young male star in our midst. He's 28, amazingly attractive, intelligent . . . and he can act. Oh yes, people are predicting that the name **Daniel Day Lewis** will soon be inscribed on our hearts in indelible neon.

Last night, in the latest in successful media hypes, it was 'Wogan' and the dubious charms of Selina Scott. Together, along with half the nation, they chortled over his designer stubble, and agonized about 'effete' stereotyping. Today it's a small Polish cafe in Kensington, a lot of flirting on my behalf, and some frantic coffee drinking. His background is perhaps rather daunting. The grandson of Sir Michael Balcon, son of poet laureate Cecil Day Lewis and actress Jill Balcon, I had

wondered whether plums might be rolling round curiously horse shaped mouths. But no, he's remarkably unpretentious and genuinely modest. In 'My Beautiful Launderette', a film much lauded by the critics, he plays Johnny, a gay working class London lad with National Front sympathies. So Daniel, do you know people like Johnny?

Yes, although less well than I used to. I grew up in south east London. My parents were comfortably off, but not by any means rich, and my lifestyle was quite different to my contemporaries and friends. But most of them came from that world, and a lot went on to have National Front sympathies and encounter the same sort of problems that Johnny had. Most of my heroes, and I had a great capacity for hero worship at that age, were pretty nasty characters in retrospect.''

After seeing 'My Beautiful Launderette' a lot of gay people out there are probably sighing 'At last!'. It's a lot of things, but one of the film's most worthy aspects is its positive handling of the romance between Johnny and his friend Omar. Yes, there's kissing and cuddling, and it's all signposted as quite normal and healthy. Not a child molester or neurotic queen in sight. Do you think that new images of men are becoming more acceptable?

"I think Derek Jarman has done an awful lot for the male physique. He's a unique director and a wonderfully imaginative man. He's broken down so many barriers, but sadly has a small audience. But other people are beginning to take risks, and I think they'll find out that they're not really risks at all in the end.''

So what's next? Any immediate plans for risk taking in the future? He shakes his head, explaining that he's a bit tied up right now with interviews and film festivals. The rest of today however is free, and after a hearty handshake, our budding superstar wanders off to a nearby park to quietly watch the ducks. JANE BARTLETT

PHOTOGRAPH: KEVIN CUMMINS

j

COCTEAU TWINS
the greatest story ever told

JAMMING! No. 35
DECEMBER 1985 75p
EIRE £1.20 US $1.75

REM

Derek Hatton

Peter Murphy

Men They Couldn't Hang

Cameo
Aswad
Angela Carter
Angus McBean

AFTER THE HUSH

Jonh Wilde side-steps the secrecy and finds the Cocteau Twins in the mood to muse. Flashes and snaps by Russell Young.

INTO THE RED

2 Following the success of Billy Bragg's Jobs For Industry tour earlier this year, various left-wing entertainers have grouped together to forget petty differences, and lend their whole-hearted support to the Labour Party. While not towing the party line, the 'Red Wedge' organisation is committed to working towards a Labour Government. *Tiny* investigates further.

What have Lenny Henry, Paul Weller, Robert Elms and Katherine Hamnett got in common? Apart from being young, talented and often on the telly, they are all signatories to a new campaign, launched this month under the banner of 'Red Wedge', whose aim is to provide a focus of support for the Labour Party in the build-up to the next election.

Traditionally, the Labour Party has always had support among the arts from individuals sympathetic to their ideas. But this is the very first time that the young and talented have got together to pool their knowledge and flair with the intention of giving Socialist views an airing via the world of entertainment.

Red Wedge, which now includes comedians, poets, actors, and writers as well as musicians, has been set up as an independent movement, so whilst it is supported by the Labour Party, it is not subordinate to it. The aim is to draw people from the arts and the youth of Britain together and to encourage people to take control of the things that affect them by getting actively involved in politics and making the Labour Party do what's important for them. Red Wedge also intends to use its influence on the party to get an arts policy together that makes real British culture a priority; live venues as opposed to opera, for example.

"It's very important that we convince working class people about the Labour Party because the Tories and the SDP aren't going to do anything to help." Jimi Somerville

The first concrete action to emerge from this still embryonic organisation is a tour to be headed by The Communards, Billy Bragg and Paul Weller which will take place in January 1986 in order to get the Labour Party and its ideas 'out of their smoke filled rooms and through to the people who can make a difference'. The tour, which will go on the road under the title 'Don't Get Mad, Get Organised' will start in Manchester and cover seven different venues across Britain, none of which, incidentally, are in London. The boys in red will be joined by other luminaries along the way who will be making guest appearances on various dates. Jimi Somerville explained what he hoped to see emerge from his involvement in Red Wedge:

"It's very important that we convince working class people about the Labour Party because the Tories and the SDP aren't going to do anything to help. As entertainers, this tour is a very positive way that we can get Socialist ideas across."

Jimi's involvement in Red Wedge has come as part of a conscious decision to get more active in politics; an option that was not really open to him in Bronski Beat where other members of the band were unwilling to stand up and be counted. Billy Bragg, as a one man band, doesn't have that problem and is certainly not all mouth and no trousers:

"What we're doing on this tour is using the medium of popular entertainment to get ideas across that aren't given an airing through any other popular medium." Bragg comments. We don't think music will change the world and we're not even saying vote Labour. We're saying 'Here are the arguments, what do you think of them?'

Red Wedge see themselves as continuing the tradition of the Left Book Club and the Arts and Crafts movement of the '30s who sought to campaign for Socialist ideas through the popular arts. With two years to go before the next scheduled general election, they already have plans for books, videos and exhibitions across the country. And the number of Red Wedge supporters is growing by the day. So if you've got the talent and your heart is in the right place, don't get mad, get involved! And let's get something organised . . .

Red Wedge is contactable on 01-708 1400.

Elizabeth Fraser offers a wistful, impenetrable gaze from the front cover, slightly askew from Russell Young's camera lens. Her two bandmates linger behind, in soft focus. It's a perfect visual companion to Cocteau Twins' beautifully elegiac music; along with the Billy Bragg cover from Issue 22, it's my favourite *Jamming!*-commissioned front page and it's also, I hate to admit, the only time in the magazine's thirty-five issues that said cover was given over exclusively to a female-fronted band. Inside, Jonh Wilde waxed lyrical about the Twins across five pages, an increasingly standard cover story length pursuant to the redesign and all that white space.

It was Cocteau Twins' second in-depth interview (both with Wilde), and elsewhere, there was a similar sense of repetition: REM (as spelled on the cover) returned for a third interview, The Men They Couldn't Hang and Aswad for a second. Making their debut appearances were Suicide, The Flowerpot Men (both profiled by Wilde), Peter Murphy

ISSUE #35
11/85

(Chris Heath), Happy Mondays (Paul Mathur) and, courtesy of Mark Cordery, who always worked hard to push our musical envelope as far as we would take it, Cameo. I went to Liverpool to interview the Labour Party's bad boy Derek Hatton, a feature that was followed over the page, with perfect timing, by Tiny's article on a new music-and-politics movement called Red Wedge. A two-page piece on the legal trial faced by bookshop Gay's The Word further solidified the magazine's unapologetic leftist stance; it also represented a long overdue correction of *Jamming!*'s embarrassing history of poorly chosen, gay-related puns. Alongside Jane Bartlett's piece on author and poet Angela Carter, a profile of photographer Angus McBean and two pages of poetry edited by Pete May, *Jamming!* 35 was unquestionably an excellent arts magazine. But was it still *Jamming!*? That was open to frequent debate, both within and outside of the office.

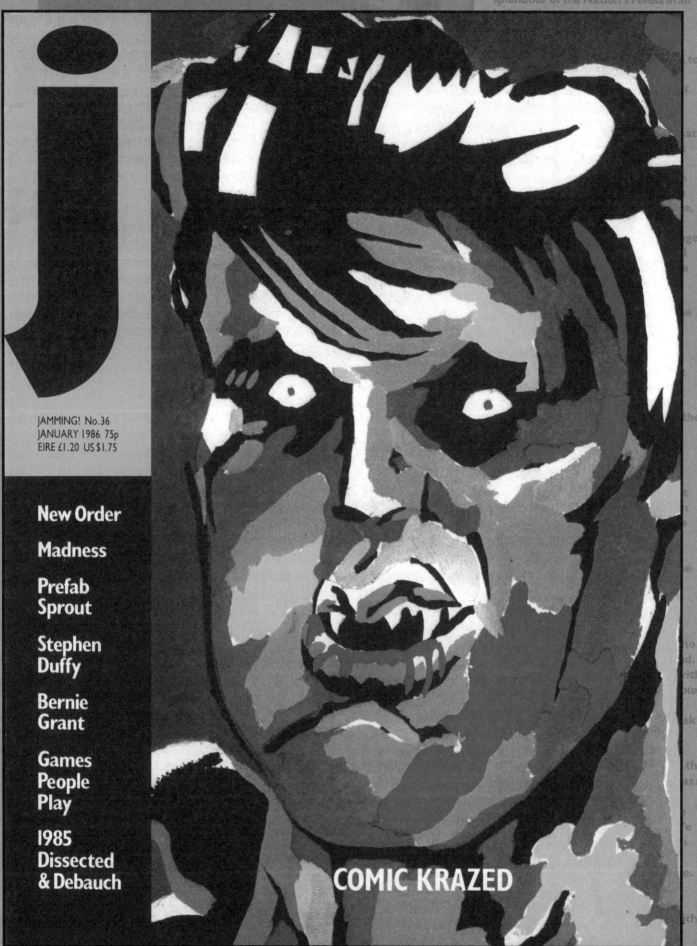

j

JAMMING! No.36
JANUARY 1986 75p
EIRE £1.20 US $1.75

COMIC KRAZED

I t is ironically and unintentionally apt that the final cover of *Jamming!* should feature neither a musician nor a band, not even a collage of the previous year's major moments but, as with Issue 1, an illustration. It was ever more sweetly suitable that *this* illustration was promoting a six-page special on independent publishing, in the form of 'Comic Culture'. (*Fumeos! Tebeos! Manga!*) The article was written by Paul Gravett, editor of Britain's own comics magazine, *Escape*, which rather threw our own purpose into question, and the ongoing full-page ads for *NME* (no longer, it would seem, the Enemy) further suggested we had joined a friendly, supportive mainstream media world in which we all scratched each other's backs and hired each other's writers.

The rest of *Jamming!* 36 further contributed to this feeling of familiarity. It was, in fact, something of a Greatest Hits of our most beloved artists, with New Order (Mick Middles), Madness and Prefab Sprout (both Chris Heath) all returning to the magazine, in Madness' case for the fourth time, making them the most interviewed band in *Jamming!* history. A challenging interview with the latest red-flagged left-wing politician, Bernie Grant (by Henry Jackson), and another with American short story icon Raymond Carver (Wilde) helped offset gushing profiles of Tin Tin and Raymonde (cited as 'best group in the entire universe' in the subheader of a Paul Mathur interview). But, and especially with the pages full of personal year-end round-ups (in which The Jesus & Mary Chain's debut LP, *Psychocandy*, appeared to be our critics' choice of '85), there was a distinct sense of 'Haven't we been here before?'

And then it ended.

Here is how. (Other accounts may differ.) I knew I'd been frozen out of the magazine I'd started by the very people I'd entrusted it to. I knew that things were being said behind my back and that some of those who were writing for *Jamming!* – only a minority of them mind, and they will go nameless – were responsible for saying them. The atmosphere in the office when I walked in would tense up, people would cease conversations and, as likely as not, launch into suitably provocative fresh ones. Not to say I didn't contribute to the tension at times, nor to say that I couldn't be a dick – at 21, my brain was apparently not yet fully formed! – but still, it was an unpleasant place to be. At one point, Jonh and I got in a fully fledged fight and had to be physically pulled apart by Alan McLaughlin. Over the Christmas holidays, I reached the conclusion that I didn't want to be part of it any more. I was going to live up to the ideals of every band member who'd ever told me, 'When it stops being fun, I'll stop doing it.' It had stopped being fun; I was going to stop doing it.

I came back to the office two days after New Year (taking the first day off to reassure myself of my convictions), immediately requested a meeting with our backers, and promptly told them I was out. They then made their own decision. *Jamming!* had been losing money all along, and though there had been occasional glimmers of light, the paucity of advertising in this current issue – we had been forced by our ad department to run a 'Gaming' section to secure quarter-page ads for Dungeons & Dragons-related retail shops – confirmed the magazine's current cultural drift. Our backers cut their losses, effective immediately. It was all over in the space of a single morning. There were tears, there was some shouting, the office emptied out, and then there came the slow shock of realisation. *Jamming!* had had a classic band break-up. Our editorial equivalent of 'musical differences' were translated in tactfully and tersely worded statements, such as always serve merely to mask the underlying causes: feuds, animosities, a break-down in trust, financial uncertainty, you name it. Very few bands ever walk away with a handshake and a smile. *Jamming!*, a fanzine-turned-magazine that had come to feel more like an unruly orchestra than a compact band, was no different.

The epilogue, or the coda, came over the next couple of weeks, as the established music press afforded *Jamming!* a series of obituaries such as I'd never anticipated or expected. Our former competitors seemed genuinely sad to see us go. I was sad, too. But *Jamming!* had served its purpose. It had served its time. And it was time for us all to move on. *Jamming!* had only been around for eight years, only been publicly available for seven of them, and twenty-two of its thirty-six issues had been published in just the last twenty-eight months. As noted back at the beginning of this book, there had been no great plan, no grand scheme, and that had been both *Jamming!*'s editorial strength and its financial weakness. Whether as a scrappy zine bouncing from printer to printer and laid out on my bedroom desk and floor with cowgum and spray glue, collated over the course of weeks by a gaggle of corralled neighbourhood school friends; or as a slick monthly designed by professional companies and distributed in newsagents nationally, *Jamming!* never made money, and I carried the debts from the earlier incarnation all the way to the new life I started in the USA barely a year later.

But what the hell? Regardless of its inconsistencies, irregularities and occasional comical errors in design and print, *Jamming!* had an impact on some people's lives, somewhere along the line. I'll take that. So, to every single person who ever contributed in any way shape or form, be it writing, taking photos, drawing illustrations, working on layout, transcribing interviews or staking claims to poetry; to every struggling musician who begged us in person to listen to their demo, through to the pop and rock stars and their record labels who granted us interviews, sometimes on foreign soil; to everyone who bought a copy, and especially to the friends in the early days who sold copies for us; to every independent, DIY record label and shop that offered support in the early days; to every band that put us on a guest list, or hosted us on their couches; and to everyone who made opening the mail so much fun for so long, including those who called bullshit on us and no doubt righteously so, thanks for being a part of the journey.

Looking back, writing for *Jamming!* was an even bigger deal than it seemed at the time. Personally, it opened doors, ushered me out of a small and cozy life of gush pieces and fanzines and into a brute new world of rock'n'roll glamour and big, proper journalism. That was the river, this is the sea. Although I cringe at some of the stuff I wrote back then, *Jamming!* was an opportunity and a proving ground.

For a while, young-gun music-mag mogul Tony Fletcher had it going on. Eventually, however, as it is wont to do, the biz part of the equation consumed the music part. Bold and idealistic don't pay the bills. After Tony lost control, things began to slide. But, while *Jamming!* lived by its own rules, when it was innocent, when it was all about the music... that was something rare and exciting. I'm proud to have been involved. Of course, it was always going to be short lived. I later learned nobody knows what they're doing. Only when you recognise that does it all make sense. **Ross Fortune**

ISSUE #36
12/85

BARNEY RUMBLES AND SCENIC RAMBLES

New Order main man Bernard 'Barney' Albrecht scrapes the sleepy dust from his eyelids and spins a long yarn.
Mick Middles takes another swig of the magic potion, leans back and falls over.
Photos by Steve Wright.

Preamble.

"I wanna tell you about maa two dogs, 'cos, 'cos they are luvlee."

Beer breath exploded in my face. I step away from the bar in careful avoidance of the unsteady arm which I know is about to extend round my shoulders. If there is one thing I detest more than a violent drunken slob, it's a friendly drunken slob.

Unfortunately, this latter category are the only humans stupid enough to brave the terrifying frost on this most unromantic of Stockport evenings. On nights like this, all the cloth cap clichés you may wish to throw at the life of a northern town . . . will be gratefully accepted.

They are all true, tonight. Like our football team, we have no defence. I'm not in here for drunken conversation. Merely for a modest measure of Dutch courage.

I've interviewed New Order before.

The enveloping sadness of the pub diverts my thoughts away from the list of questions in my pocket. The drunk next to me is the eccentric embodiment of a dour lifestyle. Too real. Far too real. I feel pretentious and stupid. Grabbing my foaming smelly prize, I retreat to my cohorts and dive back into the safe world of unadulterated sycophancy.

Amble on.

So we spill out of the smokey pocket of comfort and tread an icey pathway towards the welcoming lights of Yellow Two Studios. From the outside it looks for all the world like a branch of McDonalds. From the inside, it looks like a Habitat showroom. Copies of The Face on the coffee table, a copy of The Mary Chain album on the record deck and bottles of Champers in the fridge. The day's exploits are scattered across the rest room in the form of a collection of personal objects. Empty beer cans, half eaten chocolate biscuits, synthesizer operation manuals, one extremely famous red Gibson and a number of suspicious Rizla packets. Unfortunately, though hardly surprisingly, the owners of these objects are not in evidence. Further investigation reveals that they have whisked their American producer John Robie away and across the sprawling metropolis of Stockport in search of a Thanksgiving celebration.

The interview was to begin at 10pm. It is now 10.30pm. One senses a lengthy evening ahead. With this possibility in mind, one feels no guilt in removing the inner contents of the beercans and placing the liquid, with the greatest of ease, in one's stomach.

By the summer of 1985, Manchester music was a scene reborn. A schizophrenic rebirth perhaps, with extremes of house and indie tugging in opposite directions, but a rebirth nonetheless. A flood of venues – The Boardwalk, The International, Haçienda, Gallery, and so on – had galvanised a mess of bands, DJs, poets, comedians and sundry lunatics into unlikely action.

It dawned on me that this new action wasn't represented fully by the national music press, which was hanging by a thread above parody. The once great *NME* had twisted into a seriously dull organ while *Sounds*, who I still freelanced for, remained in the unsteady balance by regularly drifting towards metal and punk.

Largely due to the perception and unpretentious intelligence of its editor, the London based *Jamming!* filled a Manchester void. Well, for me it did. At one point, following an interview on Camden High Street between me and *Jamming!*'s Tony Fletcher and Jonh Wilde, I almost moved to the smoke. I am glad I didn't, because Manchester exploded into Madchester. It was a place to be, once more. *Jamming!* allowed me the freedom to add my gruff northern tone. And so I did, whether bashing ineffectively against the talented though egotistical Mick Hucknall at an Indian eatery or absorbing a nonplussed New Order as they pieced together 'Shellshock' in a Stockport studio, fuelled on a raft of electronic gizmos and champagne. *Jamming!* allowed me to breathe. It was the greatest fun to write for and, I strongly sense, to read.

Mick Middles

Ramble on.

I hate the way the trendier areas of the music press portray New Order. That is, the image of obnoxious and aloof pillars of arrogance. Drunken yobs, the antithesis of Joy Division pretension. The recent NME double page did little but further the image. The band, it seems, cannot win. The irony being that yours truly must take a certain amount of the blame for this after penning a fairly bawdy little New Order travelogue in the heady 'Blue Monday' days of 1983. I admit to being over-exposed to the band's violent sense of humour. It was a rather patchy and unconfident piece of writing. However, it did help pull the band free from a suffocating stigma of arty-farty nonsense. So let us wipe the slate clean, once and for all. New Order are not obnoxious people. To the best of my knowledge, they have never been deliberately obstructive. The music press, on the other hand, have strived to continue the most intense of love/hate relationships. Significantly, one month after the NME had heaped bucketfulls of essential importance on the band's shoulders, they failed to place them within their truly banal '100 Best Albums' chart. A strange omission but, then again, New Order's hugely successful flirtations with dance music hardly makes them fashionable amongst the raincoats.

11.15pm. Three quarters of the way through 'The New Avengers' and half way through the second can of Boddingtons . . . a stirring in the reception. A look of anticipation (well, it is a little like a dentist waiting room. Thinks, "who is drilling who?") is met by the beaming smile of manager Rob Gretton. I'd know that sarcasm anywhere.

"The thing is," he states, in genuine apologetic terms . . .

"That Barney has yet to finish his vocals. It could take some time, in fact it could take a great deal of time. Like eight o'clock tomorrow morning. I'm not kidding."

He isn't kidding. For reasons best known to myself, I'd singled out Barney for the interview proper. Just my luck.

"I'll wait."

"Good. Then we might as well enjoy ourselves. You'd better settle in."

Hookey offers a welcoming hand. Polite, affable and typically sardonic. Steve Morris and Gillian Gilbert are, as always, the most approachable of people . . . and many a journalist tremors at the thought of this interview. Downstairs, the studio kicks into action. The beat (which slides so close to electro) punches through the floorboards. The vocals take the scenic route and drift up from the staircase.

"I've been good and I've been bad but common sense I've never had. No matter how I try and try I hide the truth behind our lies."

That's Barney. Inflicting the, by now, accepted dosage of pathos into the song. Interesting how New Order's lyrics often lower into submission before attacking with a vengeance in a climatic flurry. That's the formula and it is, without any shadow of a doubt, the most effective lyrical usage this side of Morrissey.

"I've never forgiven you for some of the things you've written in the past," spits forth a relaxed Gretton.

"You called me a fat man."

"I did not."

"You did."

And so on. I didn't, as it happens but Hookey seizes an opportunity he cannot resist.

"Way back. I remember you calling us a bunch of fascists."

"I never did. I didn't say that either."

"You implied it though. You can't deny that you implied that we were fascist by quoting our lyrics."

"Well . . they weren't my lyrics, were they?"

The quality of conversation improves into mundanity. They are only baiting me. The trouble is that there is no hint of malice. C'mon lads, play the game. Being nice is extremely boring.

The interview

Barney shuffles in.

"Okay, okay I'm ready. We might as well do the interview now. We might not get another chance."

> **'Getting that sound, getting it just how we want it. Getting a song to a perfect conclusion. That's the one important thing. That's success. Much more than how many records you sell . . . it's just about getting that feeling of satisfaction.'**

I glance at my watch, 3.35am Jeezus. Too much Champers blurs my aggressive potential. Jolly trendy, what.

Downstairs. Alone aside from the infernal whirring of the camera device, Barney patiently casts his longing for sleep aside and utters the immortal words.

"Right, go on then. Switch that damn tape recorder on."

Into the first elongated probe.

Do you feel that you are presently undergoing a period of audience transition? There seems to be an identification problem at your most recent gigs, an unhealthy mixture of casuals and raincoats?

"Yes. I've wondered about this recently. I think it depends on where we play. The more regional the venue, the younger the audience. At Preston recently, there were two hundred people all involved in a giant fight. This was because of the odd mixture we attracted. I can't put my finger on why."

Maybe because those who followed you through Joy Division are now being equalled by those picking up on you from the dancefloors?

"Er . . . I don't know. Last year, in America we played 'Love Will Tear Us Apart' and nobody could understand why we were playing it. They knew the song but they didn't know it was by us."

Which is good, in a way. It means that you are not resting on old laurels?

"Yeah, maybe but I don't think that we get anything like the recognition we deserve. We are much better than people give us credit for. We are very underrated."

And unfashionable? Your drift away from rock and into disco has torn you apart from what is, perhaps stupidly, considered hip. Are you conscious of this?

"We are not like that all the time, though. Sometimes we make pure dance music and if some people have decided to ignore dance music then that's their problem, not ours. We can't be blamed for people's narrowmindedness. But a lot of our music isn't what you would consider to be dancefloor anyway."

True enough, but your most successful singles seem to have been born in the discos. This creates a different audience. One which doesn't really care about the personalities of the band or their lifestyles or their background. It's a good way to move away from stardom . . . to become faceless.

"Not sure about that. 'Blue Monday' brought us back in there, didn't it."

Yep but . . . never mind . . . *slurp*. Change tack.

Do you enjoy fame?

"I don't enjoy it when you go into a pub and people start nudging each other. I don't enjoy being recognised at all but . . . well . . . it's a small price to pay. We are very, very lucky to be living this lifestyle. I couldn't ever work to routine. I never have been able to."

But there must be some routine in being in a band. Today, for example, you have been tied to the studio.

"No, not to any specific thing. If I felt like laying in bed all day I would have. If I want to write, I will. I don't have to do anything unless I want to and I enjoy this . . . so much. It's the most satisfying thing I know."

What, being in the studio?

"Yes, getting that sound. Getting it just how we want it. Getting a song to a perfect conclusion. That's the one important thing. That's success. Much more than how many records you sell . . . it's just about getting that feeling of satisfaction."

Are you fascinated by the way people attach their own individual importance to your music. Where, once you have released a record it is out of your hands and it takes on a thousand different facets?

"Oh yes I still am. We have always played on that anyway. That's why we never deal in specifics. If you deal in specific situational lyrics, you freeze the music."

But your lyrics are specific to you?

"Yeah, they always mean something special . . . something personal to me."

When playing live, you often seem to twist the meaning to suit the evening. You often ad-lib. It can sound quite spiteful.

"It's meant to. That's the whole point of playing live. To take your music into different situations and see how it copes."

But this can verge on flippancy?

"Maybe . . . that's another aspect."

And flippancy can verge on rip off (and sometimes, at a number of gigs I could mention, it has).

"Depends on how we feel."

You had a set of original ethics, it always seemed to me, which prevented you from, say, miming on TV. Often this was at the expense of the music. 'Blue Monday' on Top Of The Pops being the classic example. Don't you think that these ethics dilute into silliness as time goes by?

"It is difficult to stick to original ethics but no, they don't really change."

But how do you square this with your now extensive use of synths and tapes?

"We never, ever use tapes live."

You do.

"We don't. We use sequencers, not tapes."

Sequencers then. I've seen them carried on after you've left the stage?

"You can't ignore technology and, more importantly, you've still got to play these things. It doesn't matter if you play a Fairlight or a saw. It's the tune that matters. A strong melody was always the most important thing and always will be. However easy it is to play, you have still got to produce that melody. That's the art."

You have always had a certain naivety in the way in which you produce your music. That's not a put down. In fact, I believe that to be your most endearing quality. Rather than sitting back and becoming boringly competent on one set of instruments, you move on and remain forever fresh.

"I'm not sure about that, y'know. We are very polished in some ways. 'Blue Monday' for instance, was a result of us reaching a certain perfection. We knew it was good. That wasn't a naive song."

> **'I'm still excited about what we are doing, yes. When we first began we were excited by punk and The Stooges. Now, maybe it's a different music but it's still the same basic thing.'**

You are creeping towards being thirty. Are you still excited by popular music or are you more interested in retiring and building boats . . or something?

"I'm still excited about what we are doing, yes. When we first began we were excited by punk and The Stooges. Now, maybe it's a different music but it's still the same basic thing."

Other people? The Jesus And Mary Chain?

"Well yes, it's all just as important to me. I, for example, really like The Smiths. I think that what they are doing is wonderful."

Do you think that some of your fans have taken you far too seriously in the past?

"I don't know. I've taken our stuff very seriously so I can't really comment on how other people take it."

What are you doing in this studio?

"This is music for a film. What's it called? *(Scratches head)*. I don't know but I must say that I don't think the film is any good. It's one of those American teenage things, very dodgy but we thought it would be interesting to do. Might make a good single y'see, we don't have to pay recording costs for this. Plus John Robie is a genius. He's very like us which is, misunderstood. I think that what we do is genius."

Why have you not attached this genius to the form of video? You've always had an uneasy relationship with video and yet it would seem to be a perfect vehicle for your experimentation.

"Well, I've always believed that the recording studio comes first, touring comes second and, maybe video third. So, simply, we have not had time to involve ourselves in video. We have spent six months touring this year so . . . where is all the time?

And for a home life? "My wife hasn't seen me for four days. Not at all because I've been working fifteen hours a day . . . and she's still managed to fall out with me."

So I let him go now. As his eyelids creep slowly downwards and my ability to communicate veers towards irritable fatigue. Back in the control room, Robie plays the mixing desk like a theatre organ and the band survey the finished result of the past four days. Only Hookey fails to make this final judgement as he is probably dreaming about riding motorbikes through muddy fields. Even in sleep, the drumstick clasped in his left hand taps a steady rhythm. The three awake band members listen intently, desperately seeking to be objective about the product of their obsession. Robie dances with ecstacy, spinning round, sliding the faders in perfect time with his movement. He looks like Ken Russell's idea of a modern pop producer . . . the whole room swirls with his madness.

"Well, I think that is a wonderful piece of music," he splutters forth at the track's beaty conclusion.

New Order look unsure. Bite their lips and decide to sleep on it. Upstairs the rest room has suffered from the blitz. A Philip Glass movie careers to a halt on the video. More madness.

So we leave the building which contains such intense escapism. A shivering Stockport awaits. The blackness of reality has never seemed so unfriendly. A stark, crumbling town with a sick hospital and a mass of old people who can't afford to stretch to two bars on the electric fire. On a night like this, escapism *is* important. Looking back, the studio seems like a Tardis.

It *is* a Tardis. ●

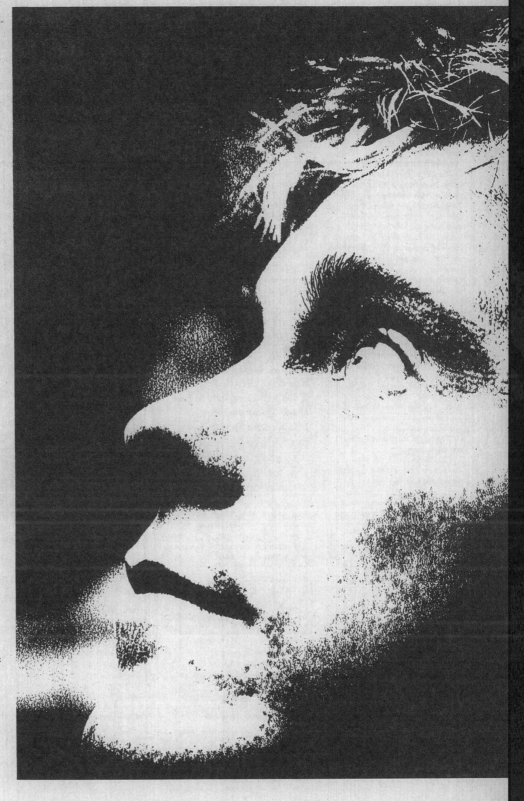